BUDDHISMS

BUDDHISMS

An Introduction

JOHN S. STRONG

ONEWORLD

A Oneworld Book

First published by Oneworld Publications, 2015
Reprinted in 2015

A CIP record for this title is available from the British Library

ISBN 978-1-78074-505-3
ISBN 978-1-78074-506-0 (eBook)

Typeset by Tetragon, London
Printed and bound in Great Britain by
Clays Ltd, St Ives plc

Oneworld Publications
10 Bloomsbury Street
London WC1B 3SR
England

For Sarah

and for friends and teachers along my way, who formally or informally have taught me lessons about Buddhism/s: Don Swearer (Oberlin), K. N. Jayatilleke (Peradeniya), Nyanaponika Thera (Kandy), Jeffrey Hopkins (Dharamsala), Geshe Ngawang Dhargyey (Dharamsala), Zhao Puchu (Beijing), Holmes Welch (Kyoto), Aramaki Noritoshi (Kyoto), Frank Reynolds (Chicago), Joe Kitagawa (Chicago), Michel Strickmann (Sammitsu Gakudōin), Kobori Roshi (Daitokuji), Hubert Durt (Hōbōgirin), Anna Seidel (Matsugasaki), Lily De Silva (Peradeniya), Mahinda Deegalle (Kandy), Daw Mae Kyi Wynn (Yangon), Louis Gabaude (Chiang Mai), Geoff DeGraff (Mettā Forest Monastery), Steve Kemper (Bates), Trian Nguyen (Bates), and John Holt (Bowdoin).

Contents

List of Tables

List of Figures

Preface

In 2005, the fifth edition of a much-used college textbook on Buddhism was published under a new title. Originally authored in 1970 by Richard Robinson, and then repeatedly expanded and significantly revised by Willard Johnson and Thanissaro Bhikkhu (Geoffrey DeGraff), it had long been called *The Buddhist Religion: A Historical Introduction.* But with the new edition it was given a new name: *Buddhist Religions: A Historical Introduction.* The move from the singular to the plural in the title raises and reflects a question of primary importance in the writing of a book such as this one: is there one or are there many Buddhisms? Is the Buddhism found today in Sri Lanka (for example) similar enough to the Buddhism found in Japan, or Western Europe, or Tibet, or any other place, for them all to be said to be somehow part of the same religion?

The question is a real one. General courses on Buddhism typically start with the life of "the" Buddha and try to set him in his ancient Indian context. Then they talk about his teachings and the foundation of his monastic order. Then, at some point, they explain how, from Northern India, the religion that the Buddha founded gradually spread through the Indian subcontinent, to Sri Lanka, to Southeast Asia, and to Gandhāra in the Northwest (in present day Pakistan and Afghanistan), and thence, via ancient trade routes, to Central Asia and China, and the rest of East Asia. However, at least in my experience, by the time the course gets to the Pure Land tradition in Japan – with its stress on faithful dependence on the grace of the Buddha Amida and salvation by rebirth in his Western Paradise, and with its tradition of married priests inheriting their temples from their fathers – some student inevitably asks: "How is this still Buddhism? Isn't this a drastic departure from everything we learned about the religion in India at the start of the semester?" It is and it isn't. And by the time the class visits Vajrayāna Buddhism in Tibet – with its immense pantheon of buddhas and bodhisattvas, wrathful and benign; with its kinetic visualizations of mind-made realities; with its emphases on ritual and on scholarship, and a plethora of lineages of incarnate lamas – again, the question is posed: "Is this still the same Buddhism?" It is and it isn't. In this book, I will try to do justice to *both* the multiplicity and the unity of the tradition.

I wanted to try to signal this double intent by entitling my work "Buddhism/s: an Introduction." Alas, in this I failed, and had to settle for the plural "Buddhisms"; it turns out that a "slash-s" runs the risk of confusing the computers that need to list this book online. (An "s" in parentheses is no better.) Nevertheless, although our electronics may be antipathetic to ambiguity, safe within the pages that follow I will attempt to restore that ambiguity by using the double form.

It is sometimes said that one of the things that holds Buddhism/s together is the fact that, either explicitly or implicitly, Buddhists all turn to the "three refuges" or "triple gem" of the tradition: the Buddha, his Teaching (called the Dharma), and his community (called the Saṃgha). At the same time, however, it must be recognized that the Buddha, Dharma, and Saṃgha can mean different things to different Buddhists, so that while the three refuges may unite Buddhists everywhere, they also divide them. Some, for example, see the Buddha as a singular historical personage, the human teacher who lived in India over two millennia ago and founded the religion called Buddhism. Others see him as but the most recent of a long line of masters who have periodically appeared to renew the teaching (Dharma) and reestablish the community (Saṃgha). Still others espouse the notion that there are an almost infinite number of buddhas spread out through space, all expedient manifestations of a transcendent truth. Or they find the Buddha (or at least the Buddha-nature) in themselves, or in things of this world such as rivers, rocks, and trees. In other words, who (or what) the Buddha was (or is) has varied radically from place to place, school to school, tradition to tradition, and time to time in Buddhist history. As we shall see, much the same sorts of things can be said about the Dharma and the Saṃgha. Accordingly, I will occasionally extend the ambiguity embodied in the notion of Buddhism/s and speak of "Buddha/s," "Dharma/s," and "Saṃgha/s."

SCHEMES AND THEMES

With these points in mind, let me say a bit more about my approach in this book and some of its recurrent themes. Like many other authors of works such as this, I will use the three refuges mentioned above as a basic organizational scheme, but make two "passes" through them. After an introductory chapter (see below), I will start with some chapters on the Buddha: I will first examine, in chapter 2, not only what little we know about the Buddha historically and the world he lived in, but also varying legends about him; and in chapter 3, I will present different ways Buddhists have continued to venerate the Buddha after his passing – something I call "overcoming the Buddha's absence" – by means of relics, pilgrimages, Buddha images, and by honoring the future Buddha, Maitreya, who is yet to come. Then I will turn to look at the Dharma, examining in some detail the contexts and contents of the Buddha's very first sermon, focusing on the notion of the Middle Way (chapter 4), and on the Four (Noble) Truths (chapter 5). In chapter 6, I will start a section on the Saṃgha, talking about the role of laypersons and the establishment and basic structure of the monastic community, and then, in chapter 7, various kinds of divisions in that community. Following this, in part II of the book, I will begin my second "pass" through the three refuges, first cycling back to the Buddha, in chapter 8, to look at various ways Mahāyāna Buddhists have sought to find the Buddha/s not only in India, but in East Asia and Tibet as well. Then, in the next two chapters, I will pick up the story of the Dharma/s, with a look at Mahāyāna developments, again in India, East Asia, and Tibet (chapter 9), and with an examination of the bodhisattva path (in chapter 10). Finally, I will return to the theme of the saṃgha/s, by presenting a series of vignettes – what I call "saṃgha situations" – illustrative of the practice of three Buddhism/s: the Thai, Japanese, and Tibetan traditions (in chapters 11, 12, and 13). In each of these final chapters, I will end with an example of the presence of these traditions in the West – Europe and the United States – as a reminder that, in the twenty-first century, Buddhism is no longer just an Asian phenomenon.

Before undertaking this twofold triple journey, however, it will be necessary to give the reader some preliminary notion about "Buddhism/s" more generally. To do this, I propose, in an introductory chapter, to visit the pilgrimage site of Lumbinī, Nepal, where the Buddha Śākyamuni is said to have been born, and where, in recent years, a bewildering variety of temples, monasteries, stūpas, pagodas, etc. have sprung up representing Buddhist groups from all over the world in all their multiplicities, but somehow united by their being in Lumbinī. I think of it as a sort of Buddhist world's fair. Thus, after visiting the Buddha's birth site, we will look at centers reflecting South Asian, Southeast Asian, East Asian, and Tibetan traditions and become initially acquainted with them.

This book is intended as an introduction to the whole of Buddhism/s for seriously interested students. It is based on over thirty years of reading and teaching and travel and research in (and away from) Buddhist lands. It does not assume any previous knowledge of the topic, but it does presume readers will learn as they go along. I have endeavored to be clear and direct in my presentation of material, and have occasionally included summarizing tables in the text, but I have also tried not to cut corners in my explanations, preferring, within the given constraints of length, to cover a limited number of subjects with some degree of thoroughness than a vast number superficially.

This has meant, I fear, that certain topics have been left out altogether. Thus, there is nothing in this book about Buddhism in Indonesia or Laos or Mongolia, and precious little about it in Cambodia or Korea or Nepal. I hope readers will accept these and other lacunae. Even within the traditions I do examine, there are gaps. I have made no attempt, for instance, to narrate systematically the history of Buddhism/s in the various countries where it has been important. In part, this is because I find the too-easy and too-quick narration of historical "facts" to be problematical, carving regions up into countries, and time up into eras, in ways that generally privilege hegemonic powers. Nevertheless, history can be important, and I do, on occasion, sketch partial histories of Buddhism/s in some places for contextual purposes. For students who want more, I have included, in the appendices, chronologies of Buddhism/s in various countries, with bibliographic suggestions for further study.

I also hope that scholars of Buddhism will find some of what I have to say fresh and interesting. Over the last twenty-five years or so, dozens of general works on Buddhism have been published. When I first agreed to write this book, I started reading some of them more or less systematically. Part of me, I am sure, was looking for their shortcomings, hoping to justify the need for yet another introduction to the field. But actually I found most of them to be really quite good. It was at that point that I decided that if I were to go ahead and write this book it would have to try to contribute some new perspectives to our knowledge of the field, and not just a summary of what we already know. At the same time, I realized that too much originality can make a textbook unusable, frustrating to teachers, and potentially confusing to students. So a balance of sorts must be sought between new perspectives and established topics. I hope to have achieved such a balance.

Among the "new perspectives," readers will find, I think, a number of themes occasionally surfacing in the chapters that follow, but it may be worth pointing out some of them here. First is the theme of the "middle way." Buddhism is often called a "middle way teaching," but this important notion is generally not fully explored. In this book, I have tried to make a distinction between two types of middle way: one going between the extremes and rejecting them, and one going around the extremes and embracing them. I call these the "neither/nor" and the "both/and" middle ways. This distinction is spelled out most explicitly in chapter 4, where I use it to analyse Buddhist doctrines vis-à-vis other ancient Indian schools of thought, but it is more widely applicable in other areas as well. It is, in fact, caught up in the very notion of "Buddhism/s" being both singular and plural. Historically, for instance, some Buddhist monastics may be seen as finding a single middle path between the "extremes" of social engagement and world renunciation; others, however, may be seen as espousing one and/or the other of those two poles. Whether singular or plural, both of these ways, I would contend, are part of Buddhism/s.

A second theme, not unrelated to this, is an emphasis on multiple ways of overcoming the absence of the Buddha. It is sometimes said that, following his death, the Buddha completely transcended this world of rebirth and so (unlike, for example, Jesus Christ or Christian saints or Hindu gods) was no longer available to respond to the petitions or prayers of devotees. Images of the Buddha, for example, are proclaimed as honoring the memory of the Buddha, not embodying him or making him present. This view was especially popular with an earlier generation of Western buddhologists and those who were influenced by them. In this book, however, especially in chapters 3 and 8 but elsewhere as well, we shall draw attention to the many ways Buddhists sought to "meet" the Buddha/s either in this world, or in another world, or in a future world, or in various objects or places of veneration.

Finally, a third theme underlines the importance of "place" in Buddhism/s, in addition to biographies, doctrines, rituals, or social structures. Much can be learned by visiting (virtually or actually) locales that, for one reason or another, have become important to Buddhists.[1] This approach is featured in the introductory chapter that looks at modern-day Lumbinī to present an overview of Buddhism/s everywhere. It surfaces again in chapter 2, which traces the lifestory of the Buddha according to an established set of pilgrimage places, and it is also featured in chapters 11, 12, and 13, which use various "places" to explore "saṃgha situations." In these instances, I have not hesitated to include perspectives that have come from my own personal visits to these locales.

TECHNICALITIES

In closing this preface, let me make a few technical points. The footnotes are intended not only to cite sources for the information and views I present, but also to act as prompts for further research, such as student term papers. When I quote something directly, I give the source immediately following in parentheses. Otherwise, so as not to pepper the text with references, I generally give a single summary footnote, at the bottom of a paragraph or section. Since this is an introductory text in English, I have generally sought to limit my references to English sources, even when more standard ones in other languages are available. On occasion, however, for want of English alternatives, I have had to refer to sources in French or German, indicating when I do, in brackets, which language they are in. There are, however, no citations of editions of texts in any original Buddhist language (for instance, Sanskrit, Pali, Chinese, or Tibetan), but only references to translations of the same. Buddhist terms and titles of works are translated or explained on first occurrence, but they may later be referred to in their original language. Except where inappropriate, I have chosen to give most Buddhist names and terms in their Sanskrit forms. When the context really calls out for it, however, I have sometimes used Pali forms. Chinese and Japanese terms and names are written in the Pinyin and Revised Hepburn transcription systems respectively. I have not included Chinese characters. Tibetan terms and names present a special dilemma for students unfamiliar with that language as, in the Wylie system of transliteration, they often contain many prefixed and superscripted consonants that are not pronounced, at least in the standard Lhasa dialect. Accordingly, I will write Tibetan words and names more or

1 For a discussion of the importance of this kind of approach, see Robson (2009). For an interesting example, see Pratt (1928).

less as they might be pronounced by an English speaker (following to some extent the model adopted in Powers, 2007), with their full Tibetan Wylie-spellings in parentheses at the first occurrence.

Finally, in closing I would like to acknowledge the input and help of the following persons: the students in my Buddhist Traditions class at Bates College, upon whom I inflicted drafts of some of the chapters that follow, and my colleagues in Buddhist Studies at Bates, Steven Kemper and Trian Nguyen; Hugh Curran who welcomed me to the Morgan Bay Zendō, and Myra Woodruff and Gaylon Ferguson who did likewise at Karmê Chöling; Stephen Berkwitz and Kate Crosby who read an earlier version of the manuscript and each offered excellent advice, caught numerous errors, and made multiple suggestions; Will Ash at Bates, for helping with the illustrations; Kathleen McCully for catching many errors in the manuscript; Novin Doostdar of Oneworld Publications, who was patient and adaptable as this project evolved; and James Magniac and Paul Nash, also of Oneworld, for seeing it through to completion. Finally, I would like to thank Sarah Strong for her assistance and advice, and for putting up with ever-changing visions and revisions of the text as a whole.

Whitman Spring, Auburn, Maine
October 2014

NOTE ON ABBREVIATIONS

Where a word is noted in more than one language, the following abbreviations have been used:

Ch.	Chinese
Jpn.	Japanese
Kor.	Korean
Skt.	Sanskrit
Tib.	Tibetan
Vtn.	Vietnamese

Chapter 1

Introduction: Lumbinī, a Buddhist World Exposition

Nowadays, the birthplace of the Buddha, Lumbinī, in Southern Nepal, not far from the Indian border, is fairly easy to get to. After all, it has been a UNESCO World Heritage Site since 1997, and pilgrims and tourists flock to it from all over the world. They go there for many reasons, but one of them is surely to see the Māyādevī Temple, named after the Buddha's mother, Queen Māyā. This shelters what is claimed to be "the spot" where the Buddha Śākyamuni was born, around 2,500 years ago. At the center of the building, pilgrims can gaze down on a piece of rock proclaimed by some to be "the marker stone" of the birthplace, although this has been disputed by others. At a deeper level, archaeologists have recently uncovered traces of an earlier wooden structure that has been carbon-dated to between the eighth and the sixth centuries BCE. On a wall above the marker stone has been set a life-size sandstone bas-relief sculpture of Queen Māyā holding on to the limb of a tree at the time of her giving birth to the Buddha. She is flanked by images of a woman supporting her and of the gods Indra and Brahma receiving the child born from her side. The sculpture, which was found at the site, has been dated to the Gupta period (fourth to sixth centuries). Some claim it may possibly be the same image of Māyā that the Chinese pilgrim Xuanzang reported seeing when he visited the place in the seventh century.[1]

1 Some of the contemporary descriptions of Lumbinī in this chapter are based on my visit there in 2010. See also Weise (2013). On the most recent excavations at Lumbinī, see Coningham et al. (2013). In general, on the history and archaeology of the site, see Uesaka (2001) and Deeg (2003). On the marker stone, see Bidari (2009), pp. 66–74. On the question of its identity, see Deeg (2003), p. 21n. For Xuanzang's account of the image, see Li (1995), p. 82.

1.1 *The Māyā Devī Temple, Lumbinī: Site of the Buddha's Birth*

Outside the building there is a pool of water where, according to legend, the Buddha's mother bathed prior to giving birth. The pool itself is a recent reconstruction, carried out by an archaeologist in 1939 and restored since then, but it is fed by two ancient artesian springs, and Xuanzang, as well as an earlier Chinese pilgrim, Faxian (early fifth century), both report having seen it, just twenty paces from the birth site (see figure 1.1).[2]

Nearby, there stands a famous polished stone pillar, erected in the third century BCE by the Indian emperor Aśoka. It bears an inscription in ancient Brahmi script, recording the sovereign's visit to the place in the twentieth year of his reign (*c.*250 BCE), and his proclamation that "here the Buddha Śākyamuni was born." Over the centuries following Aśoka's reign, countless other pilgrims must have visited Lumbinī and the various other sites in the region. Only a few of these ancient pilgrims (such as the already mentioned Chinese travelers, Faxian and Xuanzang) wrote accounts of their visits and so are known to us by name. Perhaps the last of the ancient nameable visitors to the site was Ripu Malla, the king of Karnali in Western Nepal who, in 1312 CE, recorded his presence by having the top of the Aśoka pillar engraved

2 For Xuanzang and Faxian's accounts of the pool, see Deeg (2003), pp. 47, 54.

with the Tibetan mantra "Oṃ Maṇi Padme Hūṃ," under which he signed his name – a piece of royal graffiti that can still be read today. Soon thereafter, however, as Buddhism declined in India, the identity and fame of Lumbinī were forgotten, and the place went to ruins as it was overtaken by the forest. For the next five hundred years, we hear nothing more about Lumbinī until the 1890s when a joint British–Nepali archaeological expedition to what was then a jungle area rediscovered the Aśoka pillar and, on the basis of its inscription, re-identified the site as the Buddha's birthplace.[3]

Today, the Māyādevī temple and the Aśoka pillar stand at the center of what is called "the Sacred Garden." It is both an archaeological site and a pleasant park for pilgrims who can rest and reflect there amidst the great trees festooned with prayer flags. But the Sacred Garden and the birthplace are but the apex of a huge complex – a vast enclosed park about three miles long and a mile wide – whose layout was set forth in the so-called Lumbinī "Master Plan," first drafted in the early 1970s by the renowned Japanese architect, Kenzō Tange. The project was the result of an initiative of U Thant, then general-secretary of the United Nations and himself a devout Buddhist from Myanmar (then Burma). Tange's plan was for a landscaped complex of buildings that would be "an expression of the Buddha's universal message of peace and compassion ... accessible to all of humanity" (Bidari, 2009, p. 35). In 1978, the overall project was approved by the Government of Nepal, and supervision of it devolved, a few years later, to the Lumbinī Development Trust. Over the many years since then, there have been various financial, political, and administrative difficulties and delays, and the pace of planning and construction has been slow, to say the least. Originally, plans called for the project, conceived in 1978, to be finished within seven years but, by the year 2000, only twenty percent had been completed. More recently, however, progress has been made and development has picked up.[4]

Part of the Master Plan includes provision for two "monastic zones" on either side of a mile-long navigable canal which forms a north–south axis to

3 On King Aśoka, see 6.1.6 below. The reference to Ripu Malla comes from Bidari (2009), p. 23. See also Weise (2013), p. 54. The mantra "Oṃ Maṇi Padme Hūṃ," an invocation of the bodhisattva Avalokiteśvara, is the most commonly inscribed and recited mantra in Tibetan Buddhism (see 1.4.1). For a lively account of the saga of the modern discovery of Lumbinī, see Allen (2002), pp. 256–279.

4 For the last version of the Master Plan, see Tange (1978). Tange's design originally called for development of a twenty-five-square-mile area of restored jungle and nature preserve, but that was abandoned (see Molesworth and Müller-Böker, 2005). On the timetable for the plan, see Nyaupane (2009), p. 164.

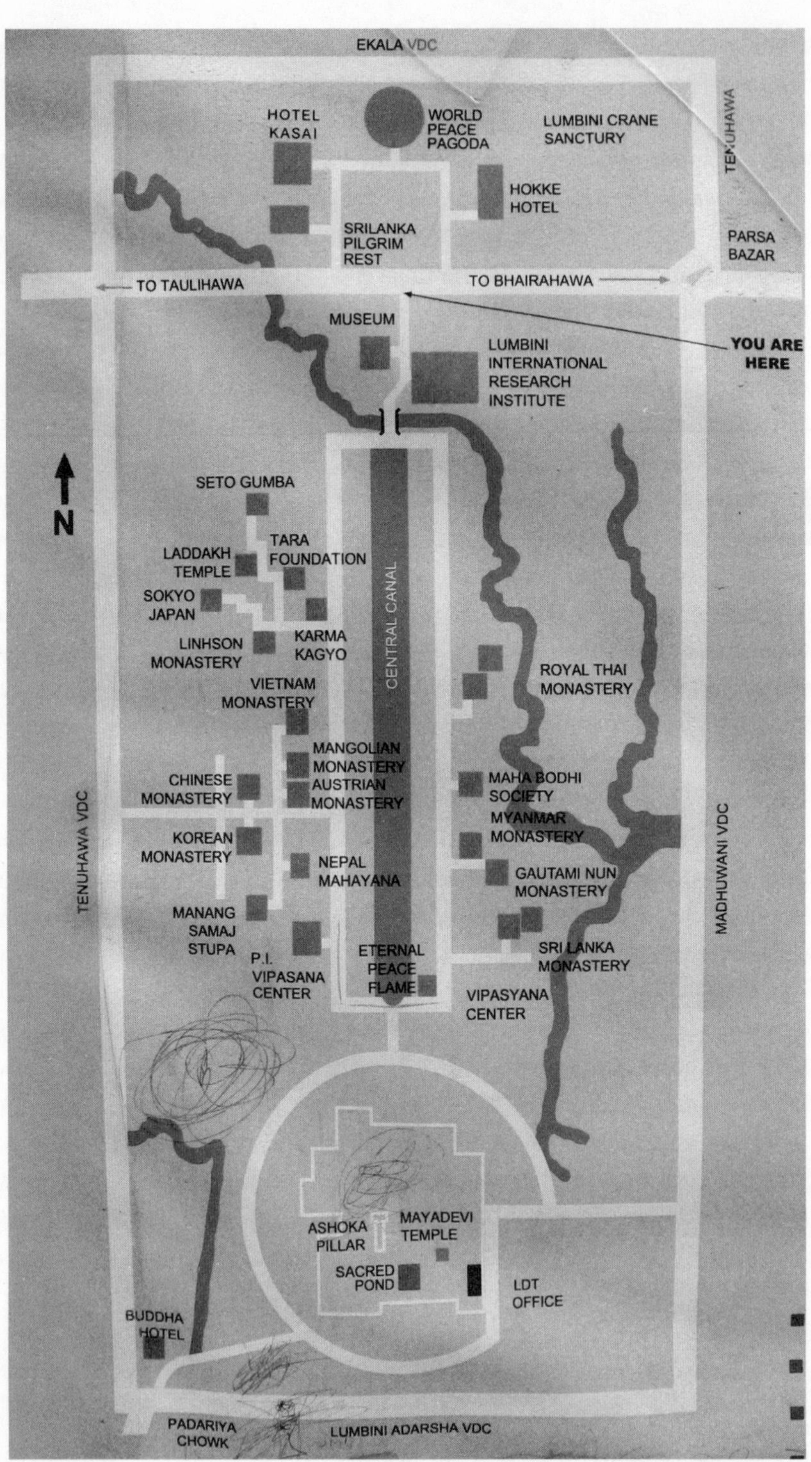

1.2 *Lumbinī Master Plan*

the park, joining the Sacred Garden at one end to a "New Lumbini Village" at the other, where there are to be facilities (some are realized, but many are still in the planning stage) for tourists, pilgrims, and research scholars (see figure 1.2). In these two monastic zones, Buddhist nations and Buddhist organizations from various countries have been invited to build temples or monasteries or other structures, which they have erected sometimes, but not always, in architectural styles reminiscent of their homelands. The overall effect is not unlike that of a world's fair with various national and corporate pavilions, each trying to epitomize its own traditions, and, to some extent, to outdo those of others. (This is not altogether surprising since one of the Kenzō Tange's other great projects was the design of Expo '70 – the Osaka (Japan) World's Fair.) Taken all together, then, this serves to make the Lumbinī monastic zones into a sort of Buddhist World Exposition, a good place to get a snapshot glimpse of Buddhist traditions from all over Asia and the globe, in their present-day complexity and relation to their past history. Before looking at some of the specific places in the monastic zones, however, I would first like to reflect on a major assumption of the overall structure of the Lumbinī Master Plan.

1.1 THERAVĀDA AND MAHĀYĀNA

Somewhat ironically for a pilgrimage center that seems intended to unite all Buddhists, the two distinct monastic zones, located to the east and west of the median canal respectively, are specified as places for Theravāda institutions on the one hand, and Mahāyāna ones on the other. It should be said that this traditional division of the religion into two types of Buddhism is riddled with all kinds of problems. Had Kenzō Tange and the other formulators of the "Master Plan" been advised by scholars today, they probably would have been warned against so clear-cut a distinction (or at least been advised to provide a bridge across the canal separating the two zones!). But the structure is in place, and it does provide an entry point to a discussion of how Buddhism as a whole has been conceived.

Theravāda (the "Tradition of the Elders") is the name generally used to designate the Buddhism/s predominantly found today in Sri Lanka, Myanmar (= Burma), Thailand, Laos, and Cambodia, although there are also Theravāda communities in Nepal, India, Bangladesh, Vietnam, and Yunnan (in Southwestern China), as well as in the West. This label, however, quickly becomes problematic when we look at the Buddhism/s in these countries in a broader context.[5]

First, it should be said that Theravāda is often wrongly equated with Hīnayāna (the "Lesser" or "Small Vehicle") which, in turn, is distinguished from Mahāyāna (the "Great Vehicle"). Because "Hīnayāna" ("Lesser Vehicle") is a derogatory term invented by Mahāyānists and intended to demean and belittle, some modern-day scholars use the term "Mainstream Buddhism" as a non-pejorative alternative for "Hīnayāna," and, in this book, I shall follow them in this practice.[6] In any case, historically speaking, the Theravāda was but one of many Mainstream schools (the traditional number of them being eighteen). Besides the Theravāda, these Mainstream schools included important movements such as the Sarvāstivādins ("Pan-realists"), the Pudgalavādins ("Personalists"), and the Mahāsaṃghikas ("Great Community-ites") that had their own ordination lineages and particular doctrines, distinct from the Theravādins. We shall look at all of these in due course in chapter 7. 2. Today, it is true, the Theravāda is the only Mainstream school that is still institutionally extant, but this should not hide from us the fact that some of these non-Theravāda Mainstream schools, as well as various Mahāyāna and Tantric traditions, have been and continue to be influential in the so-called Theravāda countries of South and Southeast Asia. These influences have varied from country to country, region to region, and historical period to historical period.[7]

Second, the label "Theravāda" masks the fact that, in all of these countries, Buddhism has always existed in the context of other religious traditions (such as Hinduism) and in complex syncretic admixtures with indigenous animistic beliefs and practices (sometimes called "spirit cults"). These also differ from country to country and region to region. Thus, contextually and historically at least, "Theravāda-Buddhism-in-Sri Lanka"

---

5 For a recent anthology of articles on the problematic of how to define Theravāda, see Skilling et al. (2012). See also Crosby (2014).

6 The term "Mainstream Buddhism" was first featured, as far as I know, in Cheetham (1994), and then given an imprimatur by Paul Harrison. It was intended to replace not only "Hīnayāna" but also the occasionally used substitute term "Nikāya Buddhism." For a discussion of these nomenclature problems, see Williams (2000), pp. 255–256n.

7 For a quick introduction to the major features of Theravāda, see Crosby (2004). For an authoritative work that deals with the whole scope of Theravāda, see Crosby (2014). See also Gombrich (1988). For examples of the influence of non-Theravāda schools in nominally Theravāda countries, see Ray (1936), Strong (1992), Crosby (2000), and Harvey (2013), pp. 201–202.

is different from "Theravāda-Buddhism-in-Thailand" or in Myanmar, Laos, or Cambodia.[8]

Third, even within individual national traditions, there are significant divisions. Some of these are regional (e.g. Theravāda-Buddhism-in-Central-Thailand is not the same as Theravāda-Buddhism-in-Northern-Thailand), and some are sectarian (e.g. in Sri Lanka there are, at present, three Theravāda sects [nikāyas]). We shall examine all these divisions and others in chapter 7.3.

Finally, within both the monastic and lay communities today, it is also possible to distinguish more broadly between "traditional" Theravāda practitioners and those whose views reflect what some have called "Protestant Buddhism" (i.e. a form of Buddhism influenced by Western culture during the colonial period). More generally, the impact of Western culture and colonialism has been felt everywhere in the Theravāda tradition. The presence of the British in Sri Lanka and Myanmar and of the French in Indochina stimulated among Buddhists various movements of reform, revival, and reactionary response, and substantially changed the attitudes of a group of intellectuals towards their own tradition. Space does not permit presenting the social, cultural and political developments of all these places over the past two centuries or so, but Peter Harvey has helpfully listed some of the factors: colonization, Christian influences, Communism, Marxist-nationalism, war and ethnic conflicts, modern capitalism, consumerism, modernity, democracy, egalitarianism, secularization, globalism, to which one might add genocide, military dictatorship, and so on.[9]

This is not to say that there are not contacts and commonalities and continuities between, across, and within all of these boundaries, and we shall examine these in due time. For now, let it simply be said that one of the things that is brought home by a visit to the Lumbinī Theravāda zone, if only architecturally, is the sheer *variety* of traditions within it.

* * *

8 Some works that look at Theravāda in the context of spirit cults and other religions in various countries include Holt (2004) (Sri Lanka), Holt (2009) (Laos), Hayashi (2003) and Tambiah (1970) (Thailand), Tannenbaum (1995) (the Shan), and Spiro (1967) (Myanmar).

9 On Protestant Buddhism, see Gombrich and Obeyesekere (1988), pp. 202–240 (and the review by Holt, 1991), and Bond (1988), pp. 45–74. On Buddhism in the colonial and modern periods in various Theravāda lands, see Blackburn (2010) (on Sri Lanka), Hansen (2007) and Marston and Guthrie (2004) (on Cambodia), and Charney (2006) and Schober (2011) (on Myanmar). The list of factors affecting modern-day Theravāda is from Harvey (2013), pp. 376–377.

Mahāyāna (the "Great Vehicle") is the name generally used to designate the Buddhism/s predominantly found today in China, Korea, Japan, Vietnam, Mongolia, Tibet, and parts of the Himalayas (Ladakh, Bhutan, Sikkim, and Nepal), although in the case of Tibet, Mongolia, and the Himalayas, the term "Vajrayāna" ("Diamond" or "Thunderbolt" Vehicle) is sometimes also used to distinguish the Buddhism/s there from other Mahāyāna traditions. Once again, it should immediately be cautioned that there are several problems with this kind of labeling.

First, as we shall see in 7.4, historically speaking we are not at all certain how or when the Mahāyāna began or indeed whether it was a single movement. It is generally thought that it had its origins in India sometime around the beginning of the common era (year 0 CE), but why it started there and how long its gestation period lasted are matters of great scholarly dispute.[10]

Second, as in the case of the Theravāda, the application of the single label "Mahāyāna" to the Buddhism/s of different East Asian countries tends to obscure the significant historical, cultural, and religious contextual differences between them, and within them. In China, for example, the influences of Daoism and Confucianism and "popular religion" (for want of a better word) were significant factors in the shaping of Chinese Mahāyāna that in turn influenced them. In Japan, a rather different additional set of characteristics emerged with the mixing of Shintō and the Mahāyāna, which, for large portions of Japanese history, might better be thought of as a single syncretic whole rather than as two different religious systems. In Tibet as well, indigenous beliefs and practices, loosely and problematically labeled "Bön," strongly colored (and were colored by) the Vajrayāna/Mahāyāna traditions imported from India as well as from China.

Finally, at the same time, in all these countries, the Mahāyāna itself comprised and comprises a bewildering variety of schools, religious preoccupations, and practices, which could be quite different from each other. In China, for example (as we shall see in 7.5.2), Chan (= Zen) and Pure Land practices, Tiantai and Huayan doctrines, esoteric and exoteric traditions all existed side by side, while in Japan Mahāyāna sectarianism (to which can be added, in the modern period, the emergence of a host of Buddhist-inclined "new religions") proliferated greatly, at least at the institutional level (see 7.5.3). In Tibet, a series of different schools (e.g. Nyingma, Sakya, Kagyu, Géluk) came into being along with their subdivisions, all with their distinct emphases on certain practices, doctrines, and lineages (7.5.4).

10 For a review of some of the issues, see Drewes (2010; 2010a).

We shall have to unpack all of this in the course of this book, but once again, perhaps nowhere can this variety and complexity (at least in its modern iteration) be encountered better, in the scope of a short mile, than on a visit to present-day Lumbinī. In the rest of this chapter, therefore, I propose to lead a "guided tour" of sorts to some of Lumbinī's monasteries and centers. This is not intended as a comprehensive survey of all the Buddhist traditions represented there; it should be viewed, rather, as an incomplete and somewhat idiosyncratic introduction to the histories and practices of Buddhism/s in a number of different places.

1.2 LUMBINĪ'S EASTERN MONASTIC ZONE: SOUTH AND SOUTHEAST ASIAN TRADITIONS

Let me begin with the so-called Eastern Monastic Zone that comprised, when I visited it in 2010, about a dozen temples, monastic institutions, and meditation centers, some in a more advanced state of construction than others. As mentioned, these include temples representing various Theravāda nations, as well as centers connected to specific Buddhist organizations. All of these places merit some comment, but in what follows, I will limit myself to the following: the Indian Mahā Bodhi Society Temple, the Sri Lankan Monastery, the Nepalese-founded center for Buddhist nuns, a Burmese pagoda, and a couple of Theravāda meditation centers.[11]

1.2.1 *The Mahā Bodhi Society*

More or less in the middle of the Eastern Monastic Zone, one comes across a relatively small building called the Mahāmāyā Vishwa Shanthi Buddha Vihara ("Mahāmāyā World Peace Buddhist Monastery"), established by the Mahā Bodhi ("Great Awakening") Society of India in 2000. I begin our tour here to make two simple points: first, despite the fact that the Buddha was born in what is today Nepalese territory, he spent all of his career as a wandering preacher in different parts of the Ganges river basin in Northern India, and it was there that Buddhism first became established as a religion; and, second,

11 In addition to these, mention might be made of the following establishments in the Eastern Monastic Zone: the Royal Thai Monastery, the Myanmar Golden Temple, and the Cambodian Monastery (still a construction site in 2010).

despite the fact that it flourished there for over a millennium, eventually, around the twelfth or thirteenth century, Buddhism pretty much died out in India (although it continued for a while in isolated pockets, and survived in Himalayan regions such as Sikkim and Ladakh). The reasons for its eclipse are much debated: competition from various Hindu devotional movements resulting in a transformation of its social base, lack of support from various North Indian rulers, the destruction of its great monasteries by Muslim armies, increasing irrelevance at the popular level, etc. Today, the only significant groups of Buddhists in India are relatively late comers: Tibetan exiles who fled their homeland and settled in India after 1959; followers of Dr. Bimrao Ambedkar (1891–1956), the leader of the Mahar caste of untouchables who, together with his people, converted en masse to Buddhism in the 1950s; and members of the Mahā Bodhi Society.[12] (See appendix A for a chronology of Buddhism in India.)

The Mahā Bodhi Society was founded in the late nineteenth century by a Buddhist activist from Sri Lanka, Anagārika Dharmapāla (1864–1933), with the general purpose of once again spreading the Buddha's teaching. More specifically it sought to restore and regain control over traditional Buddhist sites in India, especially Bodhgaya, the place of the Buddha's enlightenment. When Dharmapāla first visited Bodhgaya in 1891, he was appalled at the dilapidated condition of the place, and upset by the fact that it was owned and controlled by a Hindu priest who was a worshipper of Śiva. He immediately resolved to take action to "restore Bodhgaya to the Buddhists" (as though over five centuries of absence could be erased). This involved a political, legal, and public relations campaign that dragged on for more than half a century and is not entirely over yet. But the Mahā Bodhi Society was also a Buddhist educational institution that eventually established branches in many countries, dedicated to working for the physical and spiritual well-being of persons, regardless of race, creed, or gender. Today, in many locations in India, there are Mahā Bodhi Society monasteries and meditation centers as well as clinics and schools, all carrying out its mission.[13]

The Mahā Bodhi Monastery in Lumbinī is one of these centers. Established in 2000, with the financial support of a devotee philanthropist from Japan,

12 On the decline of Buddhism in India, see Joshi (1977), pp. 298–327, and Omvedt (2003), pp. 149–185. On its decline and later revival, see Ling (1980). On Ambedkar, see Sangharakshita (1986), Zelliot (1996), Queen (1996), and Beltz (2005).

13 On Anagārika Dharmapāla and the Mahā Bodhi Society, see Trevithick (2006), and Kemper (2015).

and under the supervision of the Venerable Dodangoda Rewatha Thera, the somewhat controversial Sri Lankan general secretary of the Indian Mahā Bodhi Society, it is an unusual octagonal structure (symbolic of the eightfold noble path) with an outlying building housing a school. In the main shrine room, the central image is of the Buddha's mother, Mahāmāyā, after whom the temple is named. She is portrayed as holding on to the tree with, at her feet, the just-born baby Buddha taking seven steps, his right hand uplifted, in the act of declaring that this will be his last birth.

1.2.2 The Sri Lanka Monastery

A short distance from the Mahā Bodhi Society may be found the Sri Lanka Monastery. Buddhism was brought to Sri Lanka from the Indian mainland sometime in the third century BCE. Archaeological evidence suggests that it was first established there as a movement of cave-dwelling forest monks. The legendary literary tradition embodied in the Sri Lankan chronicles, however, tells a somewhat different story. It claims that the island was first "prepared" for Buddhism by the Buddha himself who made three different visits to it (flying through the air from Northern India) during which he subdued or chased away indigenous demons. Then Buddhism was formally introduced in the third century BCE by Mahinda, an enlightened monk who was none other than the Indian emperor Aśoka's son. Mahinda arrived as a missionary and quickly converted the Sri Lankan king, and, with his help, established an order of monks there on the island. On Mahinda's advice, the king built a great monastery in the capital city of Anurādhapura called the Mahāvihāra. He also constructed a major stūpa, the Thūpārāma, to house some relics of the Buddha. Shortly thereafter, Mahinda's sister (i.e. Aśoka's daughter), Sanghamittā, arrived from India in order to found an order of Buddhist nuns on the island. She brought with her a cutting from the Bodhi tree at Bodhgaya – the "Tree of Awakening" – under which the Buddha had attained enlightenment. This cutting was transplanted in the grounds of the Mahāvihāra monastery, where it quickly took root and became an important symbol of the Buddha's presence on the island and of the legitimacy of the king's rule. In the centuries that followed, the Mahāvihāra went through a roller-coaster history of competition for patronage with other monasteries and with Mahāyāna influences, but it eventually emerged as the dominant sect in the twelfth century. Today, both Mahinda's and Sanghamittā's arrivals are commemorated by annual festivals in Sri Lanka, and the Bodhi tree (more realistically, a descendant of the tree) still stands in Anurādhapura, where it remains an important focal point for devotion, pilgrimage, and Sinhalese Buddhist pride.[14] (See appendix B for a fuller chronology of Buddhism in Sri Lanka.)

The Sri Lankan Monastery at Lumbinī is, not uncoincidentally, also named the "Mahāvihāra" ("Great Monastery"), and to that extent it may be intended to recall the early glory days of Sri Lankan Buddhism. Construction on it started in 1998 but petered out eight years later due to a lack of funds. Eventually, however, the resident Sri Lankan monk and a group of influential Sri Lankan laypersons (who happened to be in Lumbinī on pilgrimage and were disturbed by the eyesore of the idle construction site) appealed to the Sri Lankan government for help and sponsorship. It was not long before they prevailed upon some of their powerful friends and acquaintances to enlist the backing of the President of Sri Lanka, Mahinda Rajapaksha, who promptly promised that the monastery would be built, and agreed to personally chair a new "Sri Lanka Lumbinī Development Trust." Soon, things began to happen: construction picked up; a sapling from the sacred Bodhi tree in Anurādhapura was brought to Lumbinī and planted in a specially constructed enclosure at the new Mahāvihāra there; a number of Buddha images were consecrated and installed; some Buddha relics were brought from Sri Lanka to be ceremonially enshrined; and not long thereafter, some young boys were ordained as novices into the new community. Finally, in October 2009, President Rajapaksha himself traveled to Lumbinī to officially declare the Mahāvihāra there open.

Virtually all Sri Lankan monasteries are marked by the presence of monks, relics (stūpas), Buddha images, and a bodhi tree, so in this sense there is nothing unusual about the new establishment at Lumbinī. On the other hand, the name of the place – Mahāvihāra – is intended to reflect a particular image of Sri Lankan Buddhism and its history on the island. Not only does it look back to the early greatness of Buddhism in Sri Lanka, but also to the close connection of Buddhism and the state. The involvement of the Sri Lankan President in its establishment underlines the continuity of what Holt has called a close "symbiotic relationship entailing mutual

14 For the archaeological evidence of early monks in Sri Lanka, see Coningham (1995). The legendary accounts are from the two chief Sri Lankan chronicles (written in the fifth century CE), the *Mahāvaṃsa* and the *Dīpavaṃsa*. For translations, see Geiger (1912) and Oldenberg (1982). For an analysis of these legends and a discussion of their putative value as history, see Walters (2000).

support and legitimation between the Lankan kings and the Buddhist Saṃgha (Community) [that has been] sustained either as an ideal or in actual practice [ever since the arrival of Buddhism in Sri Lanka over two millennia ago]" (2004, p. 795). This symbiotic relationship of sponsorship and support further reflects the pattern of what has been called "the two wheels of Dharma," found to some degree across Buddhist Asia throughout history. On the one hand, there is the wheel of Buddhist kingship, and on the other, the wheel of the Buddhist monastic order, the saṃgha, and together they drive the chariot of Buddhism forward. As one scholar put it in a different context, "We must treat Buddhist notions of polity and kingship not as mere appendages or compromises necessary for the survival of the faith in the world, but as integral parts of Buddhism" (Orzech, 1998, p. 4). This is a pattern we shall encounter again.[15]

1.2.3 *The Gautamī Center for Nuns*

Not far from the Mahāvihāra Monastery is a very different sort of place: an international temple for nuns called the Gautamī Vihāra (see figure 1.3). As mentioned, when Aśoka's daughter, the Eldress Sanghamittā, brought the Bodhi tree to Sri Lanka, she also established a Buddhist order of nuns on the island. Eventually, that female monastic lineage was eclipsed in Sri Lanka (and indeed in all of South and Southeast Asia). The reasons for this are complex, but basically the argument was that once an ordination lineage is broken, it cannot easily be restored, since the ordination of new nuns requires the presence of at least five already ordained nuns (as well as the presence and participation of five fully ordained monks). Thus many female monastics in Theravāda countries, today, may technically not be "nuns" but rather "renunciant laywomen" who are celibate and vow to follow a limited number of precepts and who may or may not live in monastic communities.[16]

There are, however, fully ordained nuns in East Asia, where the lineage

15 On the two wheels of Dharma, see Reynolds (1972), Smith (1978), and Tambiah (1976).

16 The nuns' order disappeared in Sri Lanka around the tenth century. See Falk (1979) and Skilling (1993–1994). On movements of non-ordained renunciant laywomen (sometimes called "precept nuns"), see Bartholomeusz (1994) (for Sri Lanka), Kawanami (2010) (for Myanmar), and Kabilsingh (1991) and Falk (2007) (for Thailand). More generally, see Crosby (2014), pp. 230–235.

1.3 The Gautamī Center for Nuns, Lumbinī

was not broken, after its introduction by some Sri Lankan nuns in the fifth century CE. In recent times, there have been various moves by concerned Buddhist women (and monks) all over the world to use the East Asian lineage to restore the full ordination for nuns in Theravāda countries. Progress was slow at first, and initially encountered resistance from conservative male forces. But since 1996, great advances have been made, and a large number of nuns have been fully ordained.[17]

The Gautamī Vihāra provides a home in Lumbinī for female renunciants (both nuns and non-ordained laywomen) from all Buddhist traditions. It is named after Mahāprajāpatī Gautamī, the stepmother of the Buddha who was instrumental in the founding of the order of nuns in the first place. We shall examine her story in chapter 6.3. Though international in its outlook

17 On the transmission of the ordination lineage of nuns to China in the fifth century, see Tsai (1994), pp. 53–54, and Heirman (2001). On a possible loophole in one of the Vinayas that might allow for the resumption of ordination, see Clarke (2010). On the recent reinstitution of the nuns' order in Sri Lanka and other Theravāda countries, see Crosby (2014), pp. 225–229, Bodhi (2009), and De Silva (2004).

and outreach, the Gautamī Vihāra is actually a Nepalese Theravāda establishment that was founded by a charismatic Nepalese nun named Dhammavatī, who originally trained in Myanmar, but became one of the leaders of the Theravāda reform movement in Nepal that started in the 1920s and has kept growing up to the present.[18]

Dhammavatī's tale is an extraordinary one. Frustrated by the lack of opportunity for women to get an education or study Buddhism in Nepal in the late 1940s, she ran away from home at the age of fifteen and, as she later put it, "walked to Burma" where she was arrested for illegally entering the country. In time, she was released and, becoming a renunciant laywoman (anagārikā or, in Burmese, thilashin), she entered a "nunnery" in Moulmein where she studied for fourteen years, attaining an advanced degree of mastery in Theravāda doctrine and practice. She then returned to Nepal with the intention of spreading the Theravāda teaching, especially to women. In Kathmandu, she established the Dharmakīrti Vihāra, a residential place of practice for women, independent of any male monastic institution. In 1987, she attended (and spoke at) the First International Conference on Buddhist Nuns in Bodhgaya, India, which marked the beginning of a new movement of Buddhist women from all over the world called "Sakyadhītā" ("Daughters of the Buddha") and dedicated to the cause of promoting Buddhist spirituality among women and resolving gender issues in Buddhism (including the question of full female ordination). Moved by her experience at the conference, Dhammavatī actually became fully ordained as a nun (bhikṣuṇī) the following year at a Chinese monastery where the ordination lineage for nuns had been preserved. She then returned to Nepal, and, in the 1990s, as the Lumbinī Master Plan began to take off, she undertook the establishment of the Gautamī Vihāra as a place to house pilgrims, but also as a center for training women in the practice of meditation. It also was intended to be a conference center, and, in the year 2000, it hosted the Sixth International Sakyadhītā Conference.[19]

18 The Theravāda tradition was reintroduced into Nepal in the 1920s by devotees who, dissatisfied by the prevailing state of Nepalese Buddhism, went to India where they were strongly influenced by Theravāda missionary monks from Sri Lanka and Burma affiliated with the Mahā Bodhi society (see above). Women such as Dhammavatī played an important role in this. See LeVine and Gellner (2005).

19 On Dhammavatī's life, see Levine and Gellner (2005), pp. 76–79. See also Levine (2001), pp. 227–236. For her founding of the Gautamī Vihāra, see Levine and Gellner (2005), p. 215. On her participation at the 1987 Sakyadhītā conference in Bodhgaya, see Tsomo (1988), pp. 138–139. For more on Sakyadhītā, see www.sakyadhita.org.

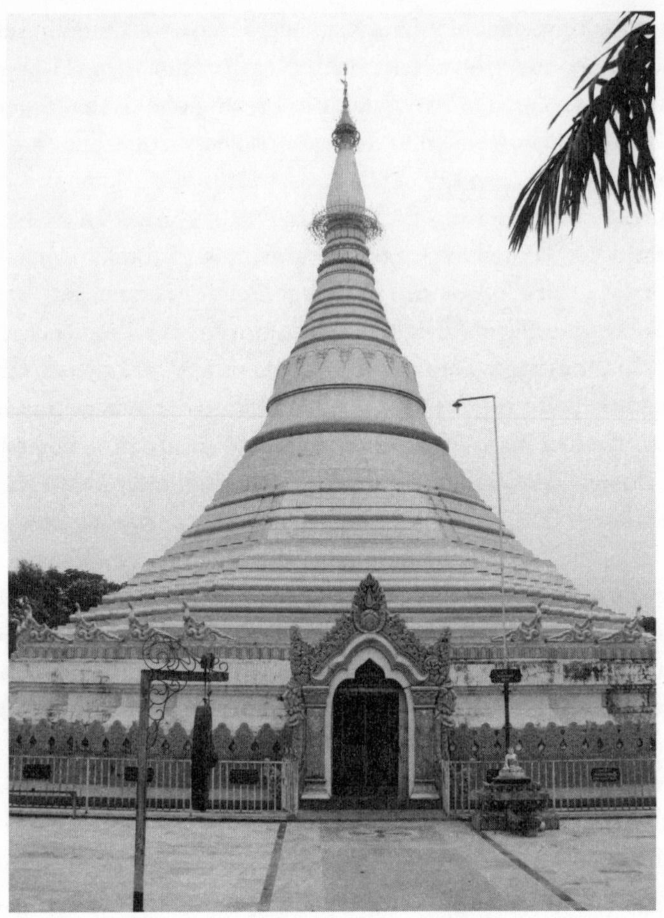

1.4 The Lokamani Cula Pagoda, Lumbinī

1.2.4 Myanmar (Burma)

Next to the Gautamī Vihāra in Lumbinī can be found the Burmese compound which features several structures. One of these is the Lokamani Cula Pagoda, a golden spire modeled (on a reduced scale) on the great Shwedagon Pagoda in present-day Yangon (= Rangoon), the capital of Myanmar (see figure 1.4).[20]

20 Next door to the Lokamani Cula Pagoda at Lumbinī may be found another Burmese monument: the Myanmar Golden Temple, which is topped with a tower that reproduces on a smaller scale the tower of the Ananda Temple, one of the most famous of the almost three thousand ancient monuments that dot the central Burmese plain around the ancient city of Pagan. See Strachan (2004), and Stadtner (2005), pp. 96–115.

According to epigraphic and archaeological evidence, Buddhism was first introduced into the region in the fourth century CE, and, over the next several centuries, we can find there the presence of various Mainstream schools and Mahāyāna traditions, in conjunction with several types of Hinduism (Śaivism, Vaiṣṇavism, and Brahmanical court rituals), all mixing with local indigenous animist cults. Burmese legendary tradition, however, tells a different story, or, rather, several different stories. The Pali chronicles claim that Theravāda Buddhism was first introduced into the region by missionaries sent by King Aśoka at the same time that Mahinda was sent to Sri Lanka. These included most notably the monks Soṇa and Uttara who are said to have been dispatched to the land of Suvaṇṇabhūmi ("the Golden Land") which the Burmese identify with the region of Thaton in Lower Burma (the land of the Mon people).[21]

A separate Mon tradition, however, claims that Buddhism was introduced to Lower Burma some centuries earlier, by the Buddha's disciple, Gavāṃpati, who brought with him a tooth relic of the Buddha immediately after the Blessed One's passing. Yet another Mon tradition goes one step further, and claims that the first relics of the Buddha were brought to the region by the merchants Trapuṣa and Bhallika during the lifetime of the Buddha himself (see 2.7.7). They had obtained some hairs from the Buddha right after his enlightenment at Bodhgaya, and, returning home to Suvaṇṇabhūmi, had them enshrined in what is now the Shwedagon pagoda in Yangon. The same monument is said also to contain relics of the three past buddhas of this aeon, and so, in its extraordinary grandeur, it remains today one of the great monuments of the world and epitomizes the history and glory of Burmese Buddhism. It is no accident, then, that Burmese Buddhists should have chosen this monument as the model for the Lokamani Cula Pagoda in Lumbinī; it legendarily spans the whole of Burmese Buddhist history from start to the present.[22] (For a fuller chronology of Buddhism in Myanmar, see appendix C.)

Part of the worship at the Shwedagon in Yangon and at its smaller-scale replica at the Lokamani Cula Pagoda in Lumbinī involves devotees making offerings to and bathing Buddha images appropriate to the day of the week on

21 For a short introduction to Buddhism in Myanmar, see Pranke (2004). For a longer introduction, see Bischoff (1995). On the early mix of religions in the region, see De Casparis and Mabbett (1999), pp. 286–303. More broadly, see also Assavavirulhakarn (2010), and Guy (2014). On the Soṇa and Uttara legend, see the claims made in the chronicle *Sāsanavaṃsa* (Law, 1952); for a historical assessment, see Aung-Thwin (2005), pp. 68–77.

22 On the story of Gavāṃpati, see Shorto (1970), and Strong (1992), pp. 179–181. On the story of the hair relics, see Strong (2004), pp. 76–80. For a reassessment of the role of the "Mon paradigm," see Aung-Thwin (2005).

which they were born. In Burmese tradition, for ritual purposes, the week is divided into eight days (Wednesday A.M. and Wednesday P.M. are counted as separate days) that are each associated astrologically with a particular heavenly body (the five visible planets (Mercury, Saturn, Jupiter, Venus, and Mars) + the sun and the moon + the mythical planet Rahu), and represented by a particular animal sign. The eight cardinal points of the pagoda (which, at its base, is octagonal) are each marked with a Buddha image and a corresponding planetary figure. Depending on which day of the week they were born (or depending on which planetary power their astrologer has told them to placate or propitiate), devotees will approach the appropriate Buddha image and make their offerings and devotions at that place.[23]

1.2.5 Meditation Centers

Lumbinī is not all about national monasteries, however. There are also a number of meditation centers where practitioners of all sorts of origins can train and practice for varying amounts of time. Two that represent Theravāda meditation traditions are: (1) the Dhamma Janani Vipassana Center (near the Burmese Lokamani Cula Pagoda); and (2) the Panditarama Lumbinī International Vipassana Meditation Center (which is actually in the Western Monastic Zone). Both emphasize the practice of Vipassanā (Insight) meditation which stresses the development of mindfulness and the purification of the mind so as to come to a perception of reality as it truly is (i.e. as characterized by the three marks of existence: impermanence, non self, and stress) (see 4.3 and 5.1).

(1) The Dhamma Janani Vipassana Center in Lumbinī is but one of many centers established by the lay teacher, Satya Narayan Goenka (b. 1924), a Burmese of Indian origin who trained under the lay teacher U Ba Khin (1899–1971) in the lineage of masters started by the monk Ledi Sayadaw (1846–1923). After training with Ba Khin, Goenka moved to India where he propagated Vipassanā practice by holding intensive ten-day meditation courses open to anyone. Eventually, he started traveling widely and established centers all over the world. Today, there are Vipassanā centers in the Goenka tradition in over eighty different countries. At the center in Lumbinī, a full schedule of over a dozen ten-day retreats are held every year, in addition to other events.

23 On the Shwedagon and worship there, see Stadtner (2011), pp. 72–105.

(2) The Panditarama International Vipassana Meditation Center traces its practice to a different line of Burmese teachers. It was established (in 1999) by the Venerable Sayadaw U Panditabhivamsa (b. 1921), a disciple of the famed monastic teacher, Mahasi Sayadaw (1904–82). He too was the fountainhead for meditation centers all over the world. In the United States, the Insight Meditation Center in Barre, Massachusetts, founded by Jack Kornfield, Sharon Salzberg, and Joseph Goldstein, is rooted in this tradition. At the center in Lumbinī, retreats can begin and end at any time. They involve maintaining the eight precepts (no killing, no stealing, no sex, no lying, no intoxicants, no eating after noon, no enjoyment of secular entertainment, no personal adornments), and following an intensive daily meditation schedule as follows:

04.00	Wake up
04.30–05.00	Walking meditation
05.00–06.00	Sitting meditation
06.00–07.00	Breakfast
07.00–08.00	Sitting meditation
08.00–09.00	Walking meditation
09.00–10.00	Sitting meditation
10.00–11.00	Walking meditation
11.00–12.00	Lunch
12.00–12.30	Rest
12.30–13.00	Walking meditation
13.00–14.00	Sitting meditation
14.00–15.00	Walking meditation
15.00–16.30	Sitting meditation
16.30–17.30	Walking meditation
17.30–19.00	Dhamma talk
19.00–20.00	Juice and walking
20.00–21.00	Sitting meditation
21.00–22.00	Walking meditation[24]

The place of meditation in the Theravāda tradition (as in other forms of Buddhism) has not always been so central as this schedule might lead us to believe. Many students of Buddhism, especially in the West, assume that meditation is part of what all Buddhists do – that it is a centerpiece and

24 For information on the center, see http://www.panditarama-lumbini.info/.

hallmark of the religion. While it is true that there has been in the twentieth and twenty-first centuries a renewed emphasis, of sorts, on meditation, in fact most Buddhists in Asia did not and do not practice meditation, or, if they do, they do not do so regularly. This is true not just of laypersons, but also of monks.[25]

It should also be said that Vipassanā ("Insight") – the form of meditation practiced at the Panditarama Center in Lumbinī – is but one type of meditation in the Theravāda world. Classic works on the Buddhist path, such as Buddhaghosa's *Visuddhimagga* (The Path of Purity – fifth century CE), distinguish between "insight" and the cultivation of "calmness" (samatha; Skt., śamatha), which is said to lead to one-pointed concentration and trance. Today, in Theravāda lands, further distinctions need to be made. Kate Crosby, for instance, describes a variety of contemporary methods that may be found more or less throughout the region and some of which have spread worldwide. These include, in addition to (1) Burmese Vipassanā, (2) the "weikza" ("wizard") tradition aimed at achieving supernatural powers and prolonging one's life until the time of the future Buddha Maitreya, by means of meditative trances and alchemical practices; (3) what Crosby calls "borān kammaṭṭhāna" ("traditional meditation"), also known as Yogāvacara or as "the unreformed Mahānikai" – a complex esoteric practice reflecting many influences including those of Tantra, which used to be widespread in Southeast Asia and Sri Lanka, but now, except for a few pockets, has disappeared; (4) a simplified form of Insight meditation, founded by the Thai teacher and activist, Buddhadāsa (1906–1993), which has some resemblances to the Zen-connected methods of the Vietnamese master, Thich Nhat Hanh; (5) the Thai forest-monk tradition associated with a lineage of teachers, such as Ajan Sao and Ajan Mun (see 11.3.1); (6) the modern and controversial Dhammakāya movement which was developed in Thailand by Luang Pho Sot (b. 1884), and has since spread internationally, and may be thought of as a simplification and popularization of aspects of the borān kammaṭṭhāna (number 3 above). When it comes to meditation, there are, in other words, a plethora of practices, even within just the Theravāda tradition.[26]

---

25 On the question "Who meditates?" see Crosby (2014), p. 147.

26 On all of these, see Crosby (2014), pp. 157–166, and the extensive bibliography therein. For a translation of Buddhaghosa's *Visuddhimagga*, see Ñāṇamoli (1976).

1.3 LUMBINĪ'S WESTERN MONASTIC ZONE: EAST ASIAN TRADITIONS

The so-called Western Monastic Zone at Lumbinī comprises monasteries, temples, and stūpas (some quite large and lavish), belonging to several different Mahāyāna and Vajrayāna traditions. Here, over a stretch of about one mile, set back somewhat from the western bank of the Central Canal (see figure 1.2), may be found not only edifices built by Buddhists from various East Asian countries, but also constructions sponsored by Western European Buddhist organizations with Mahāyāna affiliations. In this way, a truly international picture of modern Buddhism emerges. In what follows, rather than treat all of the places in this zone, I propose to visit selected sites associated with Chinese, Korean, Japanese, Vietnamese, and Tibetan traditions. In each case, I will take the opportunity to make a few introductory remarks about some of the features of these Buddhism/s. More specifically, however, I propose to focus on particular themes: in the case of China, the theme of Buddhism and the state; in the case of Korea, the theme of pilgrimage; in the case of Japan, the theme of Buddhism and World Peace; in the case of Vietnam, the theme of Engaged Buddhism; and in the case of Tibet, the theme of lineage-based sectarianism.

1.3.1 China

Perhaps the most traditional-looking of the Mahāyāna monasteries in Lumbinī, in terms of its embodiment of a classical building style, is the Zhonghua si – the Chinese Monastery (see figure 1.5). Completed in 2006, it reflects an architectural pattern that goes back over a thousand years. The whole consists of a set of buildings centered symmetrically along a north–south axis and all arranged within a circumferential wall. The gateway entrance hall, in a layout found in many traditional Chinese monasteries, contains, facing outwards, an image of the future Buddha Mile (Skt., Maitreya). Sometimes known as the fat or laughing Buddha, he is welcoming, smiling, a promiser of prosperity and good fortune. Back to back with Mile, on the other side of a screen wall and facing inwards toward the temple courtyard, is an image of Weituo (Skt., Skanda), protector of the Dharma; dressed in armor, stern and solemn, carrying a club but with his hands raised in salutation towards the Buddha in the main hall towards whom he looks, he ensures the purity of the monastery, its residents, and its visitors. To the sides are images of the four guardian kings

1.5 The Chinese Monastery (Zhonghua si), Lumbinī

of the four quarters; they are rather more ferocious-looking and have the function of keeping external malignant forces out of the monastery (and more generally out of the nation as a whole).[27]

Leaving this entranceway, one crosses a pleasantly green courtyard to reach the well-proportioned main Buddha hall, with its double row of yellow-tiled roofs. Its principal image is that of Śākyamuni Buddha. Further back are other courtyards leading to other halls and quarters for monks and for the abbot. Even though the number of permanent residents is quite small, the monastery has a traditional-style refectory, at the center of which sits a small image of Maitreya. On the wall are posted the "Five Contemplations" (wuguan) to be chanted before the meal and thought about while eating: "Consider that each grain of rice is precious, and the fruit of the work of others; consider your own behavior and what you have done to deserve this food; consider your own attitudes in eating – do not get greedy for good-tasting food, do not get upset over bad-tasting food; consider the food to be

27 The four heavenly guardian kings and their directions are: to the North, Vaiśravaṇa (Ch., Duowen); to the East, Dhṛtarāṣṭra (Ch., Chiguo); to the North, Virūḍhaka (Ch., Zengzhang); to the West, Vīrūpākṣa (Ch., Guangmu). For descriptions of various Chinese Buddhist monasteries, see Prip-Moller (1967), pp. 20–33.

medicine to stave off thirst and starvation; consider that you should eat food only so that you can continue practicing the Buddhist way."[28]

Returning to the main building, we can observe that the inscription plate over the entrance hall, bearing the name of the monastery in Chinese characters, 中華寺 (Zhonghua si), was done by the late Zhao Puchu (1907–2000). Famed for his calligraphy, Zhao was the longtime head of the Chinese Buddhist Association (CBA), an organization founded, sponsored, and funded by the Chinese Communist state, and presently under the supervision of its Administration for Religious Affairs. It may come as a surprise that a Marxist, nominally atheist, government should have disbursed significant sums for the building and maintenance of a Buddhist monastery in a faraway land, but the action makes sense when it is seen it its proper context. For most of the twentieth century, but especially since the Communist victory in 1949, Buddhism in China (along with other religious traditions) has been on a sort of roller-coaster ride, variously affected by the forces of secularization, revival, reform, repression, and modernization. A low point perhaps was reached during the Cultural Revolution (1966–1976), which saw the destruction of many temples and the oppression of practitioners in an attempt to do away with the practice of the faith as one of the "olds" of traditional society. Since that time, however, a revival of sorts has been occurring.[29]

Throughout much of the Communist period, whatever its attitude towards the domestic practice of Buddhism, the Chinese government also sought to use the nation's Buddhist heritage as part of its diplomacy towards other Buddhist countries, especially in South and Southeast Asia. Starting in the 1950s, the CBA, under the leadership of Zhao Puchu, helped sponsor cooperative scholarly endeavors, participated in international Buddhist meetings, and sent relics of the Buddha (in particular a famous tooth relic housed in a new pagoda built for it in 1966 in the Western Hills, outside Beijing) on international tours so that they could be venerated in places such as Sri Lanka and Burma.[30]

---

28 I would like to thank my colleague Fan Xing for help with this translation. On such verses, see also Batchelor (2006), p. 33.

29 On developments in Buddhism on the mainland, since the Cultural Revolution, see Birnbaum (2003).

30 For a brief introduction to Buddhism in China in the last hundred years, see Fisher (2012). For a more thorough study of Buddhism during the Communist period up until the Cultural Revolution, see Welch (1972). On Zhao Puchu and the CBA, see Aviv (2011), pp. 53–56. On Buddhism during the Cultural Revolution, see Strong and Strong (1973). On the Chinese relic tours of South and Southeast Asia, see Strong (2004), pp. 205–209. The relic tours resumed in the 1990s; see Schober (1997).

The Chinese Monastery in Lumbinī may be seen as a new iteration and extension of this same diplomatic outreach. This was made clear at the ritual held for the installation of the monastery's new abbot in late March 2011. At that ceremony, the new president of the CBA, who had come from Beijing for the event, proclaimed the monastery to be "an everlasting symbol for the traditional friendship between the peoples of Nepal and China, [and] a platform for friendly exchanges among Buddhists [everywhere]." Significantly, the ceremony was also attended by high-ranking dignitaries from both China and Nepal who echoed the sentiments that the monastery would contribute to cultural exchange.[31] This does not mean, however, that the Chinese Monastery in Lumbinī is not a place of religious practice. It is; if it were not, it would be less effective as a tool of Chinese diplomacy.

From a long-range perspective, there is, in fact, nothing new about the Chinese state's interest in Buddhism, and its use of it (or suppression of it) for political purposes. The pattern itself goes far back in Chinese history, though its specific iterations and contexts have varied. Almost since its introduction into China from India and Central Asia in the first century CE, Buddhism has been used, controlled, upheld, or suppressed by various Chinese dynasties, and by various emperors within dynasties. Occasional periods of persecution have alternated with periods of government support and devout patronage, as well as periods of general indifference. In response, through the ages, Chinese Buddhist practitioners have repeatedly repositioned themselves vis-à-vis the state, according to its attitudes towards them.

Buddhism initially gained a foothold in China in the latter Han dynasty (25–220 CE) as a somewhat exotic faith with foreign affiliations. If we read through the legends of its first introduction (such as the story of the dream of the emperor Ming), it appears that it was received by the state with a combination of guarded interest and mistrust. But it put down roots and grew, sometimes in harmony and sometimes in tension with the dominant Confucian ideology of the empire, and with the nascent traditions of religious Daoism. After the six dynasties period (311–589 CE), during which China was divided between the North and the South, Buddhism (which had continued to exist in both regions in different ways) was used by the devoutly pro-Buddhist founder of the Sui dynasty (589–618 CE) to help reunite the empire. During the subsequent Tang dynasty, with the patronage of several emperors (including China's only empress, Wu Zetian [r. 624–705]),

31 For an account of the occasion, see http://english.cri.cn/6909/2011/03/29/2821s629348.htm.

Buddhism "reached great heights of intellectual creativity, religious vitality, institutional vigor, and monastic prosperity" (Poceski, 2004, p. 141). At the same time, despite occasional claims "to secure a semblance of independence for the monastic community," Buddhist leaders sometimes became enmeshed in the affairs of the state, serving to legitimate particular rulers and offering merit and supernatural protection to them and the empire as a whole through their rituals and magical powers.[32]

Prosperity, however, sometimes gave way to (and was partly responsible for) occasional anti-Buddhist reactions from the state. Probably the most important of these occurred towards the end of the Tang, in 845 CE, when the emperor Wuzong ordered a great persecution of the saṃgha (unrivalled again, perhaps, until the suppressions of the Cultural Revolution over a thousand years later). Monasteries were destroyed, monastic properties were confiscated, statues were melted down for their precious metal, and monks and nuns were laicized and put back on the tax rolls. The suppression did not last long, however, and the subsequent Song dynasty (960–1279) saw a time of renewed vitality for Chinese Buddhism, especially for the Chan and Tiantai schools. During the Song, some of the developments of the Tang period were given definitive form.[33] (See appendix E for a fuller chronology of Chinese Buddhist history.)

Such focus on rulers and Buddhist leaders should not detract from the fact that, starting in the Tang and continuing in the Song and subsequent dynasties, Buddhism also appealed at the popular level to members of all social classes. Gradually, over the centuries, the process of sinicization and popularization was completed, and "Buddhism in China" truly came to be "Chinese Buddhism." In making this move, Buddhism also tended towards syncretism with "folk" traditions, as well as Daoist practices and neo-Confucian beliefs.[34]

At the same time, the cult of local divinities, and of various figures in the Mahāyāna pantheon of buddhas and bodhisattvas, became widespread. Among the latter, the following were especially important: the bodhisattva

32 On the dream of the emperor Ming, see Tsukamoto (1985), 1: pp. 41–50. On different aspects of the history of the relation of saṃgha and state in China, see Ch'en (1973), pp. 65–124, Orzech (1998), Chen (2002; 2002a), and Yu (2005), pp. 90–134. For a brief, overall introduction to Buddhism in China, see Zürcher (1984).

33 For two collections of studies of Buddhism in this period, see Ebrey and Gregory (1993), and Gregory and Getz (1999).

34 See Davis (2001), Strickmann (2002), and Hansen (1990). More generally, on the popularization and sinicization of Buddhism, see Ch'en (1973), Overmyer (1976), Davis (2001), Sharf (2002), Halperin (2006), Mollier (2008), and Robson (2009).

of compassion Guanyin (Skt., Avalokiteśvara) (originally a male figure, but feminized in China from the tenth century on); the bodhisattva due to become the next Buddha, Maitreya (Ch., Mile), especially in his manifestation as Budai (lit., "cloth sack" after the bag that he carries), a fat, short, smiling Buddha, thought to bring prosperity and good fortune; the bodhisattva Dizang (Skt., Kṣitigarbha) who liberates beings from hell; the bodhisattva of wisdom, Wenju (Skt., Mañjuśrī), famed for his association with the sacred mountain of Wutaishan; and many others as well. Images of most of these figures may be found in the various halls of the Chinese temple at Lumbinī, along with representations of the Buddha Śākyamuni.[35]

1.3.2 *Korea*

The Korean monastery (Dae Sung Suk Ga Sa) is just across the road from the Chinese monastery. Its huge main hall, still under construction in 2010, is destined to be the largest building in the whole of Lumbinī. In the meantime the monastery functions (1) as a place of practice and meditation for Sŏn (Zen) monks; and (2) as a place with guest accommodation for pilgrims and tourists. Since I shall be looking at Zen meditative practices in 10.6 below, I will here focus on this second function.

Westerners tend to think of Buddhist monasteries as places of retreat and isolation, withdrawn from the world. To some extent this may be true in certain circumstances, but, historically, monasteries were also, in the words of one prominent scholar, "public places" in constant interaction with the world (Gernet, 1995, p. 223). Indeed, in Korea, in addition to monks devoted to meditation and scholarship, monasteries also typically have a "support division" – monks appointed to various offices to deal with the day-to-day running of the monastery's operations as well as contacts of various sorts with the laity.[36]

In Korea (as well as in China and Japan), one of the roles of Buddhist monasteries was to serve as hostels, providing simple lodgings and meals

35 On the cult of Guanyin, see Yü (2001) and Idema (2008). On Mile (Maitreya), see Sponberg and Hardacre (1988), pp. 91–170. On Budai, see Chapin (1933). On Dizang, see De Visser (1914) and Zhiru (2007). On Wenju (Mañjuśrī), see Stevenson (1996), Harrison (2000), and Tribe (1997).

36 The term "support division" comes from Buswell (1992), p. 107, who devotes a chapter to describing its functions. Much the same structure may be found in monasteries throughout the Buddhist world, but especially in China and Tibet.

for travelers. Almost all monasteries had an obligation to welcome guests if they could, and the larger ones, in fact, had a "guest prefect" (Kor., chigaek; Ch., zhike), who handled visitors to the monastery, regardless of whether they stayed overnight or not. Guests included itinerant monks, lay patrons, ordinary pilgrims, government officials, or just plain travelers.

In Korea, the annual monastic calendar was divided into four periods of three months each: "retreat seasons" in the winter and summer, and "free seasons" in the spring and fall. During the retreat seasons, monks were expected to stay put in their monasteries and practice; during the free seasons, however, they were at liberty to travel if they so chose. When they did, they had the security of knowing that wherever they went they could be put up, free of charge, in any monastery or hermitage in the country, for up to three days. The same applied to laypersons, although they were generally expected to make a donation to the monastery in return for their room and board. In time, at least in China, such expected "donations" became set fees, and the monasteries functioned as inns – indeed, they served the important role of making travel about the empire practicable, and so caught the attention of secular governmental authorities who occasionally sought to regulate them. Virtually all monasteries had a few rooms for guests, but these could be quite numerous at establishments near or at major centers of pilgrimage, where travelers naturally gathered in considerable numbers. In China, for instance, there was a whole network of monastic hostels for pilgrims, strung out every half-day's march, all along the roads to Mount Wutai, an important Buddhist holy mountain. Anyone and everyone was welcome in these "common cloisters" that could house up to a hundred persons.[37]

Even those monasteries not associated with pilgrimage sites could become very busy places at times of major festivals that tended to draw monastics and laypersons alike. They could also be popular places for day trips or longer excursions by members of the elite. Important lay visitors would be invited to meet with the abbot; common folk could as well, but only if they requested to do so. Guests were expected to abide by the monastic rules of decorum and dietary restrictions, although there was no obligation to participate in any of the monastery's rituals or meditative practices.

37 On travel in the free season, see Buswell (1992), pp. 39–40, and Batchelor (2006). On the Korean practice of hospitality in monasteries, see Buswell (1992), pp. 102–104. For China, see Gernet (1995), pp. 223–228. On Buddhist monasteries and monastic life in East Asia in general, see Benn, Meeks, and Robson (2010). On the establishment of Mount Wutai as a magnet for pilgrims, see Lin (2014), pp. 51–87.

The Korean Monastery in Lumbinī, in many ways, can be seen as perpetuating these public accommodating functions of traditional East Asian monasteries. Tourists/pilgrims come and go. Bicycles are made available for those who wish to tour Lumbinī. Overnight visitors are put up in simple rooms and are fed plain vegetarian meals in exchange for a "donation" fee of $3.50 per night. The old rule of a maximum stay of three days is still maintained, during which guests can attend (or not) the daily devotional rituals of the monastics. Smoking, drinking, music, dancing, etc. are not allowed. In this way, the Korean monastery in Lumbinī, like so many temples traditionally throughout East Asia, provides a service to pilgrims and a way for them to make merit by getting a taste of monastic life.

1.3.3 Japan

There are two Japanese Buddhist establishments in Lumbinī and they are each quite different in character from the Chinese and Korean monasteries we just looked at: (1) the not-yet-completed Nippondera (Japan Temple) which is situated in a central spot in the Mahāyāna zone, and is the project of the Sōkyō ("Whole Teaching") Foundation, a Japanese religious corporation that was established in 1986; and (2) the World Peace Buddha Relic Stūpa (Seikai Heiwa Busshari Tō), better known as the World Peace Pagoda, a forty-meter-high white dome set in a landscaped park. It is not located in either monastic zone but at the far northern end of the whole Master Plan area, over three miles from, but in a direct line with, the Māyādevī Temple (see figure 1.2).[38]

Since I will have more to say about the first of these places – the Nippondera and the Sōkyō Foundation – in 12.5, I will here focus on the World Peace Pagoda. (For a brief chronology of Buddhism in Japan, see appendix G.) Construction on the World Peace Pagoda started in 1993 and was completed in 2001 by the Nipponzan Myōhōji, a Japanese Nichirenist organization founded by the Venerable Nichidatsu Fujii (1885–1985). Nichiren Buddhism as a school was founded in Japan during the Kamakura period (1192–1333) by the fervent Buddhist monk Nichiren (1222–82), who stressed devotion to and reliance on the salvific powers of the *Lotus Sūtra*. This was epitomized

---

38 In addition to the two Japanese temples mentioned, there are a number of hotels in Lumbinī sponsored by Japanese Buddhist groups, and also the Lumbinī International Research Institute, sponsored by the Buḍdhist "new religion" Reiyukai.

in the practice of chanting the "daimoku" – the praise of the title of the *Lotus Sūtra* in the formula "Namu Myōhō renge kyō" ("Praise to the Lotus Scripture of the Wonderful Law"). The *Lotus Sūtra*, which was originally composed in India in Sanskrit, became in East Asia one of the chief scriptures of the Mahāyāna tradition. There are many aspects to its teachings and we shall look at several of them in due course (see chapters 8 and 9). For now, suffice it to say that one of the sūtra's features is its own self-proclamation as containing – or more literally embodying – the teaching and truth of the Buddha. In this way the text itself – somewhat like the Bible or the Torah or the Qur'an for some Christians, Jews, or Muslims – came to be seen by some Buddhists (e.g. Nichirenists) as having salvific power and being worthy of veneration, recitation, and invocation.[39]

As a young man in early twentieth-century Japan, Nishidatsu Fujii, the founder of the organization that built the World Peace Pagoda at Lumbinī, was inspired by his reading of Nichiren's writings, in particular by a prediction that the name of the *Lotus Sūtra* would eventually resound again in the land of its origin, India. Realizing that this was not yet the case, Nishidatsu Fujii took it upon himself to go to India to spread the veneration of the sūtra. He arrived in Calcutta in 1931 and immediately proceeded to chant the daimoku ("Namu Myōhō renge kyō") through the streets of the city, beating a drum, and attracting followers, or at least attention. Eventually, in 1933, he made his way to Maharashtra, where he met Mohandas K. Gandhi at his ashram there, and stayed with him for some time. Gandhi seems to have been the one who inspired and reinforced in Fujii a commitment to nonviolence, disarmament, and peace walks. Indeed, back in Japan, in the late 1930s, Fujii tried (unsuccessfully) to convince the Japanese government to abandon its militarism. It was after the devastation of the nuclear bombs at Hiroshima and Nagasaki, however, that he resolved to build peace pagodas all over the world. Today, the pagoda at Lumbinī is just one of over eighty peace pagodas constructed by Nipponzan Myōhōji in five continents. The motivation to build these pagodas (stūpas) ultimately stems from the *Lotus Sūtra* itself which famously asserts that stūpas will appear wherever the *Lotus* is preached.

Enclosed in a stone set in the top of the stūpa in Lumbinī are some relics of the Buddha, a potent symbol of his post-mortem presence (see 3.3). The stūpa itself is much visited by tourists and pilgrims from all over the

39 For a translation of the *Lotus Sūtra*, see Watson (1993). For studies of various aspects of the text, see Teiser and Stone (2009).

world who circumambulate it, always in the auspicious clockwise direction. As they go around, they can stop at niches in the four sides of the dome, containing golden images depicting the birth, enlightenment, First Sermon, and passing away of the Buddha. On the aureole behind the image of the just-born Buddha (facing south towards the Māyādevī Temple) is a reproduction of the daimoku in Nichiren's own distinct calligraphy: Namu myōhō renge kyō.[40]

1.3.4 Vietnam

Just as in the case with Japan, there are two religious establishments in Lumbinī reflecting Vietnamese traditions: (1) the quite new and magnificent Linh Son Buddhist temple, financed by French Buddhists belonging to the worldwide Linh Son Buddhist Congregation founded by Thích Huyền Vi (b. 1926), who now lives at his organization's headquarter temple in Joinville-le-Pont, outside Paris;[41] and (2) the Vietnam Buddhist Monastery (Việt Nam Phật Quốc Tự Temple), one of the first temples to have been built in the Mahāyāna monastic zone (see figure 1.2). In what follows I will limit myself to some comments about the latter. (For a brief chronology of Buddhism in Vietnam, see appendix H.)

In 1993, with backing from the then King of Nepal, land was allotted for the Vietnam Monastery to the Venerable Thích Huyền Diệu, a monk from Vietnam who had been involved in the building of a similar temple in Bodhgaya. Huyền Diệu originally left Vietnam because of the war there, and, after getting a graduate degree from the Sorbonne in Paris, traveled to India. When he first visited Lumbinī in 1969, he was distressed to find the place dilapidated and forlorn. Making a vow to try to help develop it in some way, he welcomed the opportunity given him in 1993. Camping out for the first six months in a small tent on the site, he began clearing the land and laying out the foundations of what was to become a charming monastic complex in the Vietnamese style. At the same time, his Buddhist compassion led him to want to help the poor villagers in the region, some of whom had been displaced by the Lumbinī Master Plan project's eviction of local farmers. Thus, for example, he organized the building of a much-needed

40 On Fujii's career, see Green (2000). For a list of Nipponzan Myōhōji Peace Pagodas, see http://en.wikipedia.org/wiki/Peace_Pagoda.

41 On the Linh Son movement, see http://www.linhson.org.au/en/aboutus. On its temple in Lumbinī, see Molesworth and Müller-Böker (2005), pp. 201–202.

bridge (now called the Vietnam Bridge) across a river given to flooding in a nearby village.[42]

Thích Huyền Diệu stayed on in Lumbinī, and eventually became the head of the International Buddhist Society of Lumbinī, which was originally founded with several intents: to establish health centers for villagers in the area; to start projects aimed at making available pure drinking water, sanitation, and drainage; and to promote literacy and non-formal education aimed at skill training and income generating. He has also issued a number of calls for peace between all factions in the civil war that started wracking Nepal in 2002. Here we can see some of the practical sides of the Mahāyāna bodhisattva ethic of compassion. In Huyền Diệu's own words: "whenever we are lucky enough to come across an opportunity to do good, we must do it right away since we might never have that opportunity again, and one good thing will always breed another good thing."[43]

Huyền Diệu's efforts and actions reflect what has been called "engaged Buddhism," a movement found in both Theravāda and Mahāyāna that emphasizes not only traditional practices such as meditation and monasticism but also altruistic programs of social work, community concerns, political involvement, and peace activism. In the Vietnamese tradition, such engagement is generally associated with the life and work of the Zen (Vtn., Thien) monk, Thich Nhat Hanh, whose peace activism started during the war in Vietnam and continues to this day in exile, in France.[44]

1.4 LUMBINĪ'S WESTERN MONASTIC ZONE: TIBETAN VAJRAYĀNA TRADITIONS

The sites we have looked at so far in the Western Monastic Zone are all connected with various Mahāyāna groups. There also exist in this part of Lumbinī, however, quite a few establishments associated with the Vajrayāna Buddhism of Tibet. Vajrayāna ("Thunderbolt vehicle") as a term appears

42 See http://www.vietnamphatquoctu.net/E-NepalPeaceIsAtHand.php. On the eviction of farmers by the Master Plan, see Molesworth and Müller-Böker (2005). The extent of the flood plain can be seen clearly in Tange (1978).

43 On the International Buddhist Society of Lumbinī, founded by the Venerable Maitri Mahathero, a Nepalese Theravādin ordained in Sri Lanka, see http://theravadanepal.net/information/vihar/66-international-buddhist-society.html. For Thích Huyền Diệu's calls for peace, see http://www.quangminh.org.au/index.php?option=com_content&view=article&id=662:venerable-thich-huyen-dieu.

44 On Engaged Buddhism, see Queen and King (1996), and Queen (2000).

around the eighth century in India to denote a type of Tantric Buddhism that had formed there and was soon exported to different countries, including Tibet. We shall consider some of its features in 8.6 and 10.5 below. There are at least two ways of viewing its relationship to Mahāyāna: as a distinct practice and "vehicle" in its own right, or as a logical extension of or a capstone to Mahāyāna doctrine and practice. Both views may be found in the Tibetan Buddhist tradition.[45]

Buddhism came relatively late (*c.* seventh century CE) to the Tibetan plateau. In chapter 13, we shall consider some of its histories, legends, and practices, and a chronology of the tradition may be found in appendix I. Here, I would like to introduce four major schools of Tibetan Buddhism which are commonly enumerated in descriptions of the tradition and which all have representative establishments at Lumbinī.[46]

(1) The first of these is the Nyingma (written Rnying ma), the "Old school" which claims to follow the "old Tantras" introduced during the first advent of Buddhism into Tibet in the seventh century and then hidden away by the saint Padmasambhava for discovery in a later age by Nyingma teachers called "treasure-finders" (Tib., tertön [gter ston]). Its most distinctive teaching is the "Great Perfection" (Tib., Dzokchen [Rdzogs chen]), which we will look at in 10.5.3.[47] The only Nyingma establishment in Lumbinī is the Dilgo Khyentse Memorial stūpa. It was inaugurated in December 2010 by the royal grandmother of Bhutan, in honor of the late internationally known Nyingma teacher, Dilgo Khyentse Rimpoche (1910–1991), and financed by some of his French Buddhist disciples. It is the residence of a number of Nyingma monks and is intended to give Nyingma Buddhists a place to stay and to worship in Lumbinī.[48]

(2) The Sakya (Sa skya) school, so named because of the "grey earth" (Tib., sakya) in the area of Western Tibet where it originated. From its start, in the eleventh century, it emphasized scholarly achievement, and by the thirteenth century came to be the dominant sect, politically, with the support

45 For a brief introduction to Vajrayāna, see Davidson (2004). For more substantial studies, see Davidson (2002; 2005). See also Snellgrove (1987).

46 For presentation of Tibetan schools, see Powers (2007). For a rather different approach, see Samuel (1993).

47 For brief introductions to the Nyingma school, see the article by Jacob Dalton in Buswell (2004), pp. 729–731, and Powers (2007), pp. 367–397. For a thorough presentation, see Dudjom (1991).

48 On the stūpas built by Dilgo Rimpoché, see http://shechen.org/cultural-preservation/stupas-for-peace/. On the life of Dilgo Khyentse, see his autobiography in Dilgo (2008). For his writings, see Dilgo (2010).

of the Mongol rulers, Kublai Khan and his successors. Its most distinctive practice is the "Path and Fruit" (Tib., lamdré [lam 'bras]).[49] The only Sakya monastery in Lumbinī is Tashi Rabten Ling, built in 2004 at the initiative of Chogye Trichen Rimpoche, the head of the Tsarpa (Tshar pa) subsect of the Sakya school.

(3) The Kagyü (Bka' brgyud), or "Oral Lineage school," which is associated with a long lineage of accomplished Tantric masters such as the Indian Tantric adepts Tilopa (988–1069), Nāropa (1016–1100), and Marpa (1012–97), and his disciple, the Tibetan hermit Milarépa (Mi la ras pa) (1028–1111) (perhaps Tibet's most popular yogin), and *his* disciple Gampopa (Sgam po pa) (1079–1153), who managed to unite both Tantric and monastic practice. The most distinctive Kagyü practices are the "Great Seal" (Mahāmūdra) which we shall look at in 10.5.3, and the Six Yogas of Nāropa.[50] There are a number of Kagyü establishments in Lumbinī, two of which we shall look at in more detail below.

(4) Finally, there is the Géluk (Dge lugs) or the "Virtuous" school. Sometimes known in the West as the Yellow Hats, the Géluk is the youngest of the Tibetan schools and was established by the great scholar and reformer Tsongkhapa (1357–1419).[51] It was in the Géluk school (with help from the Mongol Khans) that the tradition of Dalai Lamas developed – successive reincarnations of teachers said to be manifestations of the bodhisattva of compassion, Avalokiteśvara (Tib., Chenrézik [Spyan ras gzigs]) (see 8.5.1). This was a system of succession that the Géluk tradition borrowed from the Kagyü, who first instituted it, but the Dalai Lamas came to rule with political authority and religious prestige in the capital city of Lhasa. The present Dalai Lama is the fourteenth incarnation in this line, and has lived and ruled in exile in Dharamsala, India, since fleeing Chinese-ruled Tibet in 1959. The Dalai Lama, however, was by no means the only high-ranking Tibetan Buddhist leader to go into exile. As we shall see below, there were many others – both incarnate lamas and non – from all of the different schools listed above. Interestingly, the only Géluk center in Lumbinī – the rather grandiose Mother Temple of the Graduated Path to Enlightenment (Jangchup Lamrim Temple) belongs to what might be called a Géluk splinter organization, the Geden (Ganden) Foundation of Austria, that has set itself

49 On the Sakya tradition, see Cyrus Stearns's article in Buswell (2004), pp. 751–752, Powers (2007), pp. 433–466, and Stearns (2001).

50 On the Kagyü school, see Quintman (2004), Powers (2007), pp. 399–432, and Gyaltsen (1990).

51 On the Geluk tradition, see Dreyfus (2004), and Powers (2007), pp. 467–496.

in opposition (sometimes rather vehement opposition) to the present Dalai Lama's ban on the veneration of the Dharma Protector Dorjé Shukden. I will say more about this controversy in 7.5.4.

It is not possible here to visit all of these Vajrayāna sites in Lumbinī. Suffice it to look briefly at two Kagyü temples.[52]

1.4.1 The Great Lotus Stūpa

The first of these is the so-called Great Lotus Stūpa. This is an extraordinary building – a huge assembly/meditation hall, square on the outside but round on the inside – topped with a massive Tibetan-style stūpa (chörten [mchod rten]), rising to a height of forty meters. It was built by the Tara Foundation of Germany, under the leadership of a German Kagyu monk, Ferdinand Rinchen Phuntsok, who now lives in Kathmandu.[53]

One of the features of the Great Lotus Stūpa is a depiction of the Wheel of Life (Skt., bhavacakra; Tib., srid pa'i khor lo). This is a classic representation of the six realms of rebirth in saṃsāra, typically found in the entranceways of many Tibetan monasteries. The tradition is traced back to the Buddha himself who, according to legend, instructed his monks to paint the wheel so as to be able to explain graphically to visiting laypersons the painful and pleasurable results of positive and negative karmic deeds. The six realms of rebirth depicted at the Great Lotus Stūpa are: the heavens, the human world, the realm of angry spirits (asuras), the animal world, the realm of hungry ghosts, and the hells. At the hub of the wheel are painted symbols for the three forces that keep the process of rebirth going: a cock (= desire), a snake (= hatred), and a pig (= delusion). Around the rim of the wheel are images representing the twelve links of interdependent origination (see 5.2).[54]

Also at the Great Lotus Stūpa may be found another common feature of Tibetan monasteries: a giant prayer wheel which pilgrims and tourists alike will cause to spin, always in a deemed-to-be-auspicious clockwise direction. The cylindrical drum of the prayer wheel, about twelve feet in height and five

52 In addition, there is a third Kagyü temple in Lumbinī, the relatively small Drubgyud Chöling Gompa built in the classic Tibetan style by Buddhists from Singapore and Nepal and opened in 2001, with the blessing of the Seventeenth Karmapa.

53 For a video on the construction of the stūpa, see http://www.youtube.com/watch?v=dvU9NY_DKGo. For a list of the different branches of the Kagyū school, see Powers (2007), p. 402.

54 On the Wheel of Existence, see Teiser (2006).

feet in diameter, is filled with thousands of slips of paper on which is written the Tibetan mantra par excellence – Oṃ Maṇi Padme Hūṃ – an invocation of the bodhisattva of compassion, Avalokiteśvara (Tib., Chenrézik), who is without a doubt the most popular and important figure in the Tibetan Buddhist pantheon. A single rotation of the wheel is thought to be equivalent to the repetition of the total number of mantras contained within it. There are many interpretations of the meaning of this mantra. One that is relevant here is that each of the six syllables of the mantra – Oṃ Ma Ṇi Pad (in Tibetan pronounced Pé) Me Hūṃ – represents one of the above-mentioned realms of rebirth. Reciting the mantra or spinning the wheel is thus not just a matter of invoking the aid of Avalokiteśvara for oneself, it is also asking him to extend his compassion throughout the realms of the cosmos.[55]

1.4.2 The Lumbinī Udyana Mahachaitya

The Drigung branch of the Kagyü school, which sponsored the Great Lotus Stūpa, was started in the thirteenth century. A different branch, the Karma Kagyü, is a bit older. It is traditionally said to have been established in the twelfth century by the first Karmapa lama, who established a famous lineage of incarnations that has continued to the present day, and has its headquarters in exile at Rumtek in Sikkim (now a province of India). The Karma Kagyü branch is represented by two temples at Lumbinī: the largest of these (and the only one to be discussed here) is the Lumbinī Udyana Mahachaitya, now also called the World Center for Peace and Unity. It was inaugurated in April 2011, and built by the United Trungram Buddhist Foundation (UTBF) which has offices in Nepal, the United States, Hong Kong, Taiwan, and Malaysia. The UTBF was founded by Dr. Trungram Gyaltrul Rinpoché, the fourth in a distinct line of reincarnations within the Kagyü Karma sect. Born in 1968 in a Sherpa family in Nepal, Trungram Gyaltrul studied at Rumtek in Sikkim and with different teachers from all four Tibetan sects. He then pursued a Western education, earning a Ph.D. in Indo-Tibetan studies from Harvard University. Though he belongs to the Kagyü school, he intended the Lumbinī Udyana Mahachaitya to be a non-sectarian center of World Peace and Unity, open to any Buddhist or non-Buddhist, regardless of religious affiliation or lineage. Even more specifically, he intended it to be a place for pilgrims

55 For a study of the origins and significance of the mantra, see Studholme (2002). On its interpretation by Westerners, see Lopez (1998), pp. 114–134.

whose own traditions are *not* represented at Lumbinī. Architecturally, this has meant a main hall, which, by Trungram Gyaltrul's own admission, is "very unique and quite huge,"[56] and is topped by a full-scale stūpa dome (the whole being inspired by the so-called Śāriputra stūpa in Nālanda in India). In the spirit of inclusivity, the hall, which has a special indoor circumambulation path, also enshrines a broad array of Buddhist images representing all traditions. The main image is Śākyamuni, flanked by the buddhas of the past (Dīpaṃkara) and of the future (Maitreya). Also present, however, are various other forms of the Buddha (Amitābha, Vajrasattva, Vairocana, Akṣobhya, Bhaiṣajyaguru), many bodhisattvas (e.g. Avalokiteśvara, Tāra), famous disciples of the Buddha (e.g. Śāriputra, Mahāmaudgalyāyana), the four heavenly guardians, great teachers, the Buddha's mother, etc. The purpose seems to be to appeal to everyone within the Buddhist world. As the temple's website puts it, all of these figures "standing or sitting, in peaceful or wrathful mode, are models and inspirations of great love and compassion. They are all our spiritual friends, protecting, encouraging, and motivating us along our way to Buddhahood."[57]

Enough has been said about Lumbinī to make it clear that the Buddhism/s of the world present a bewildering variety of aspects and traditions. If there is any place that brings them altogether in their diversity, it is the Mahāmāyā Temple in the Sacred Garden, thought to be the place where the Buddha was born. All Buddhist traditions, even those that focus on other buddhas, honor Śākyamuni, though they may differ as to their estimate of his nature and role. It is to the figure of the Buddha, then, that we must now turn.

---

56 Speech to disciples in Hong Kong, 10 April 2010: http://lumbiniworld.org/news1a.html.

57 http://www.lumbiniworld.org/events_detail.php?id=5. For floor plans and descriptions of the great shrine, see http://www.utbf.org/en/projects/dharmaprj/lumbini/floorplan.php. For a video on the center, see http://www.youtube.com/watch?v=kL1NIXt9iOs. For a book of photographs, see United Trungram Buddhist Foundation (2013).

Part I

Foundations of the Triple Gem: Buddha/s, Dharma/s, and Saṃgha/s

Chapter 2

Śākyamuni, Lives and Legends

The word "buddha" is not a personal name but an epithet (see table 2.1) that literally means an "awakened one," or "one who has awoken [to the true nature of reality-as-it-is]." A buddha is thus one who has experienced bodhi ("awakening" – sometimes called "enlightenment" or nirvāṇa), and who, as a result of this experience, will never again be subject to suffering in the cycle of death and rebirth known as saṃsāra.

Not everyone who experiences awakening, however, is a buddha. Buddhas, more specifically, are persons who have attained awakening on their own, without the immediate help of a teacher, and who, moreover, go on to teach the way to awakening to others. To use a common Indic metaphor, a buddha is like one who discovers for himself the ford – the shallows – across the river of saṃsāra, and who then shows others where to cross. Persons who attain bodhi on their own but then fail to go on to teach the way to others are not called buddhas, but pratyekabuddhas ("ones awakened-for-themselves-alone"), while persons who attain bodhi by following the teachings pointed out to them by a buddha (e.g. disciples of the Buddha) are not called buddhas either but arhats ("worthy ones") or śravakas ("listeners"). Though they too, by virtue of their enlightenment, get across the "river" of saṃsāra, their route to that attainment is much easier since the way across (the ford) has already been shown to them.[1]

Theoretically, there can be many buddhas, and we shall, in chapter 8, consider a number of them. When, however, people talk about "*the* Buddha," without further specification, they generally are referring to the historical Buddha, Siddhārtha Gautama, a.k.a. Śākyamuni ("the sage of the Śākya [tribe]"), who is credited with having founded the religion that the world

1 On Buddha/s, generally, see Nattier (2004).

has come to call Buddhism, but that Buddhists traditionally referred to as "the Order" (śāsana), or "the Teaching" (Dharma).

Historically speaking, we know very little for certain about the life of "*the* Buddha" Śākyamuni. As one scholar has put it: "it is fair to say that he was born, he lived, and he died. The rest remains lost in the mists of myth and legend" (Faure, 2009, p. 12). Later in this chapter, I shall examine some of these myths and legends, for they are important to any understanding of the Buddhist conception of the Buddha. For now, let me make a few comments about what we may know about the historical Buddha, and the context in which he lived.

SANSKRIT	ENGLISH	PALI	TIBETAN	CHINESE	JAPANESE
Śākyamuni	"sage of the Śākyas"	Sakkamuni	Shākya thub pa	Shijiamouni	Shakamuni
Siddhārtha	Personal name: "one whose aim is achieved"	Siddhattha	Don grub	Xidaduo	Shiddatta
Gautama	Clan name ("best cow")	Gotama	Go ta ma	Jutan	Kudon
Buddha	"Awakened one"	Buddha	Sangs rgyas	Fo	Butsu/ hotoke
Samyak-saṃbuddha	"Altogether completely awakened one"	Sammāsaṃ-buddha	Yang dar par rdzogs pa'i sangs rgyas	Zhengbianzhi	Shōhenchi
Tathāgata	"Thus gone (or come) one"	Tathāgata	De bzhin gshegs pa	Rulai	Nyorai
Bhagavat	"Blessed one"	Bhagavan	Bcom ldan 'das	Shizun	Seson
Sugata	"Well gone one"	Sugata	Bde bar gshegs pa	Shanshi	Zenzei
Jina	"Victorious one"	Jina	Rgyal ba	Zuisheng	Saishō
Śāstṛ	"Teacher"	Satthar	Ston pa	Shi	Sa
Mahāśramaṇa	"Great renunciant"	Mahāsamaṇa	Dge sbyong chen po	Dashamen	Daishamon

Table 2.1 Some Epithets and Names of the Buddha

2.1 THE HISTORICAL BUDDHA

Although we know next to nothing *for certain* about the historical Buddha, there are at least a few things about him that there is "no good reason to doubt," given the lack of any contradictory evidence.[2]

The first of these is that there was such a person, i.e. that he existed. This seems uncontroversial to us now, but this was not always the case; prior to the nineteenth century, Westerners tended to view the Buddha as a god, or as the incarnation of a god, or as a figment of "pagan" imagination. Even well into the nineteenth century, there were those who saw the Buddha's life as "pure fiction," and portrayed him as a solar hero, or the personification of some other natural phenomenon. We now feel assured that he was a human being, although, as we shall see, the tradition came to exalt him in a variety of ways.[3]

Second, we know more or less *where* he lived; there seems to be no good reason to doubt that he was born at or near the site of Lumbinī (see chapter 1), or in the nearby town of Kapilavastu, the chief seat of the Śākya tribe. Although Indian and Nepalese archaeologists dispute the precise location of Kapilavastu, for our purposes this makes no difference. More generally, we can say that the Buddha spent all or most of the rest of his life in the North Central part of the Indian subcontinent, in various places in the Middle Ganges River basin.[4]

Third, we know more or less *when* he lived, at least within a century or so. It used to be common for scholars to date the death of the Buddha at 486 or 483 BCE. Then, starting around 1990, the evidence for this was reassessed, and most prominent authorities came to be inclined to put it rather later, at *c.*400 BCE +/– 20 years, and to place his birth some eighty years earlier than that (*c.*480 BCE). Recently, however, some scholars have begun reassessing

2 For examples of different types of scholarly biographies of the Buddha, see Carrithers (1983a), Foucher (1963), Nakamura (1977), Penner (2009), Strong (2001), and Thomas (1927).

3 On the assumption of the Buddha's existence, see Gombrich (2009), p. 17. On eighteenth- and nineteenth-century Western views of the Buddha, see Almond (1988), pp. 54–79, and Lopez (2005), pp. 13–36. Kern (1901) [in French], p. 239, calls the life "pure fiction," while Senart (1882) [in French] emphasizes mythological connections. In English, on Kern and Senart, see De Jong (1997), pp. 28–32. More generally, see Strong (forthcoming b).

4 The Nepalese tend to locate Kapilavastu on their side of the India–Nepal border at the town of Tilaurakot. The Indians claim it was on their side of the border at a place now known as Ganwāria. On the controversy, see Deeg (2003), pp. 24–36.

the reassessment, and pushing his dates back to about where they were. Thus, although we cannot be precise about the Buddha's dates, it is safe to say that he was alive in some portion of the fifth century BCE. His death-date, usually referred to as the date of his final extinction (parinirvāṇa), is what is focused on because, in many parts of the Buddhist world, it is taken to mark the start of the Buddhist calendar, just as the birth of Jesus Christ is taken as the start of the Christian (or Common) era, and Muhammad's departure from Mecca to Medina marks the beginning of the Muslim era.[5]

Lastly, we know that a religious community subsequently grew up in India that looked back to the Buddha as its teacher and founder. From the traditions preserved by this community, as well as from other non-Buddhist sources, we can begin to form some idea of the social, economic, and religious environment that probably existed in North India in the fifth to fourth century BCE – what might, for our purposes, be called "the Buddha's world." This knowledge, in turn, can provide a useful context for evaluating many of the traditions that subsequently developed around the Buddha's lifestory.

2.2 THE BUDDHA'S WORLD

North India, in the fifth to fourth centuries BCE, was marked by the coexistence of declining tribal oligarchies (sometimes called tribal republics), and nascent, expanding monarchies. The Śākya tribe, to which the Buddha belonged, was an example of the former, and the Buddha's family was presumably one of its ruling clans. Subsequent tradition, probably under the influence of ascendant royal models, was to proclaim the Buddha's father to have been a king, and the family to be the scions of a long royal solar line traceable all the way back to the paradigmatic first ruler, Mahāsammata, but there is no firm evidence of this. Whatever its claims to pedigree, the Śākya tribe as a political unit was "on its way out," and was not long to survive the Buddha himself. What effect all this had on the Buddha and on the formulation of his lifestory is still being debated.[6]

Buddhist texts constantly portray the Buddha as interacting with various kinds of persons. Among these, there is frequent mention of "brāhmaṇas" and "śramaṇas" ("renunciants"). The brāhmaṇas (brahmins) may, first of

5 For a collection of articles on the topic of the Buddha's dates, see Bechert (1995), to which should be added Gombrich (1992). Recently Verardi (2010) and Coningham et al. (2013) have begun reassessing the reassessment of the dating.

6 On the royal lineage of the Buddha, see Reynolds (1997), and Strong (2011).

all, be thought of as householders who are representative of the mainline brahmanical tradition (that eventually informs what comes to be known as Hinduism). They were oriented towards the practice of Vedic sacrifice, with its emphasis on the correct performance of ritual, on purity, on the importance of the domestic household, and on the expertise and prestige of a class of priests, the brahmins. The renunciants (śramaṇas) are those who, in a variety of ways, presented an alternative to brahmanical life, rejecting the householder's status in favor of a life of wandering, mendicancy, celibacy, asceticism, and questing for spiritual liberation.

The relationship between brāhmaṇas and śramaṇas has been a topic of much discussion. Some have suggested that the renunciant movement may be seen as a reaction against an increasingly rigid and essentially rural brahmanical tradition that was failing to respond to significant socio-economic change, such as the growth of trade and of cities, and political unification. Others have portrayed the two groups as reflective of the clash of two distinct cultures – the one centered in the upper Gangetic plain and connected to the Indo-Europeans who entered the Indian peninsula in the previous millennium, and the other centered in the lower Gangetic plain and perhaps associated with more indigenous peoples. According to some, the influence of the latter cultural group on Buddhism was primary, while that of the former came later.[7]

Either way, this too simple bi-polarity between brāhmaṇas and śramaṇas needs to be problematized. For one thing, it does not do justice to the history and complexity of the two traditions, nor does it comprise all the social groups that were present in the Buddha's world. Indeed, the śramaṇas were not a single movement, but included a whole conglomeration of disparate groups that varied significantly in terms of their degree of renunciation and the doctrines and practices they espoused. Not only were there, among the śramaṇas, other organized religious movements such as Jainism and the Ājīvikas, but also a shambolic host of other wanderers, naked monks, heretics, matted-haired ones, ascetics, avoiders, hermits, etc. Of special importance, however, were the Jains, whose community most likely predates that of the Buddhists and who owed their allegiance to an older contemporary of the Buddha, Mahāvira.[8]

Similarly, the brahmanical tradition was not a single movement. For one

7 For various views of the context of early Buddhism, see Bailey and Mabbett (2003), Bronkhorst (2007; 2011), Chakravarti (1987), and Sarao (2010).

8 On the variety of types of ascetics, see Freiberger (2006), pp. 237–238. For two views of the relationship of early Buddhism and Jainism, see Gombrich (1994), and Bronkhorst (1995).

thing, by the time of the Buddha, it no longer comprised only householders and priests devoted to the performance of sometimes elaborate sacrifices, but sages such as those featured in the Āraṇyakas (forest books) and early Upaniṣads, who lived and taught and practiced yoga in hermitages in the forest. They are important not only for their practice, but also because, within the brahmanical tradition, they too began to raise questions about the deeper significance of the sacrifice and the more abstract inner meaning and purpose of the ritual.

Finally, it should also be pointed out that, in addition to brahmins, other groups of householders were coming to the fore in the fifth to fourth centuries BCE. Buddhist texts commonly mention brahmins in a list that also includes kṣatriyas (warriors/rulers/kings) and gṛhapati (literally, house-masters) – squires, who were sometimes landowners but could also be merchants, or guild-leaders. The Buddha is often shown in interaction with members of these groups, in addition to tradesmen, courtesans, barbers, hunters, etc. It is not clear how much the ramifications of the caste system that eventually became a major and well-formulated feature of Hinduism were developed in the Buddha's day, but questions of social class were clearly more than incipient. All in all, then, the Buddha's world was a complex, dynamic, diverse place, marked by a multiplicity of religious views and practices, and by the interaction of an array of different types of persons and the communities to which they belonged.[9]

Within this world, the Buddha may be classified as a renunciant – a śramaṇa – and, in the texts, he is commonly addressed as such by non-Buddhists. Nonetheless, as we shall see, he was a renunciant of a rather special type, and it may be better to think of him as falling ideologically somewhere between śramaṇas and brāhmaṇas. He neither completely rejects nor completely accepts the views of either group, but often may be seen trying to reinterpret them.

2.3 THE BUDDHA OF STORY

Although we do not know much about the "Buddha of history," and only a bit about the world in which he lived, we know a great deal about the "Buddha of story." Buddhists, traditionally, have narrated many tales about the founder of their tradition which they have remembered and reformulated

9 On the question of caste at the time of the Buddha, see Chakravarti (1987), pp. 65–93.

over the centuries. It may well be that some of these legends are ultimately grounded in history, but clearly they also contain much fiction. Yet these "fictions" about the Buddha may in some ways be "truer" than any "facts," for they reflect the ongoing concerns and feelings of Buddhists. The following stories, therefore, should be read and studied not just for what they tell us about the Buddha, but for what they tell us about the views of early Buddhist communities.

More specifically, as we shall see, stories about the Buddha are marked by two perhaps contradictory things. On the one hand, there is a desire in them to magnify the greatness of the Buddha and his accomplishments; hence stress is laid on his extraordinary qualities, on the miracles that mark his career, on his supernatural abilities, on his divine, kingly capacities. On the other hand, there is a desire in them to make the Buddha into an emulatable model, a master whose path ordinary people can follow; hence stress is laid on his human down-to-earth qualities, on his efforts and strivings and uncertainties. There is, perhaps, a natural tendency for us, as twenty-first-century persons, to want to consider the latter as somehow more "historical." It is probably safer, however, to think of both the unbelievable and the believable – the "fictions" and the "facts" – as stories told with certain purposes in mind. As one great student of early Buddhist literature pointed out long ago, rational plausibility is not necessarily a sign of antiquity or historicity because "even inventions can look quite credible" (Frauwallner, 1956, p. 164). There are many traditional biographies of the Buddha, written from a variety of perspectives over many centuries (see table 2.2), and all of them exhibit, to one degree or another, this combination of the ordinary and extraordinary.

2.4 PAST BUDDHAS AND THE BIOGRAPHICAL BLUEPRINT

One of the earliest "biographies" is found in a canonical text known as the *Discourse on the Great Legend* (*Mahāvadāna Sūtra*). It tells the story of a man's glorious birth, of his upbringing in the palace, of his seeing the four signs, of his great departure, of his attaining enlightenment, of his preaching his First Sermon, etc., i.e. all the things we shall be examining in greater detail below. However, it turns out that this is the story not of Śākyamuni but of a buddha named Vipaśyin who lived ninety-one aeons ago. An aeon (kalpa), according to one calculation, is 4.32×10^8 years long, so this is a long time ago indeed!

I. SOME BIOGRAPHICAL FRAGMENTS IN CANONICAL SOURCES	ENGLISH TRANSLATIONS
1. *Acchariyabbhutadhamma-sutta* (*Discourse on Wonderful and Marvelous Things*) – account of the Buddha's conception and birth	Ñāṇamoli and Bodhi (1995), pp. 979–984; Anālayo (2011a), pp. 702–711
2. *Ariyapariyesana-sutta* (*Discourse on the Noble Quest*) – account of the Buddha's great departure from home	Ñāṇamoli and Bodhi (1995), pp. 253–268; Anālayo (2011a), pp. 170–189
3. *Mahāsaccaka-sutta* (*Discourse to Mahāsaccaka*) – account of the Buddha's austerities	Ñāṇamoli and Bodhi (1995), pp. 332–343; Anālayo (2011a), pp. 232–246
4. *Padhāna-sutta* (*Discourse on Striving*) – account of the Buddha's overcoming Māra	Norman (1996), pp. 71–73
5. *Mahāvagga* (*Great Division*) of the Pali *Vinaya* (*Book of the Discipline*) – account of the events following the Buddha's awakening	Horner (1938–1952), vol. 4, pp. 1ff.
6. *Catuṣpariṣat-sūtra* (*Discourse on the Fourfold Assembly*) – account of the Buddha's life from awakening to the conversion of his two chief disciples	Kloppenborg (1973)
7. *Mahāparinibbāna-sutta* (*Discourse on the Great Extinction*) – account of the final events of the Buddha's life	Walshe (1987), pp. 231–277
II. AUTONOMOUS TRADITIONAL LIVES OF THE BUDDHA	
Abhiniṣkramaṇa Sūtra (*Discourse on Going Forth*) – incomplete life ending with the Buddha's return to Kapilavastu. Chinese	Beal (1875)
Buddhacarita (*Acts of the Buddha*) – complete life attributed to the poet Aśvaghoṣa. Sanskrit (partial), Tibetan, Chinese	Cowell (1894); Johnston (1936; 1937); Willemen (2009)
Lalitavistara (*Playing out of the Game*) – incomplete life ending with the First Sermon. Sanskrit, Tibetan	Bays (1983)
Madhuratthavilāsinī (*The Clarifier of Sweet Meaning*) – contains in its last chapter an incomplete life ending with the First Sermon. Pali	Horner (1978), pp. 387–425
Mahāvadāna Sūtra (*Discourse on the Great Legend*) – incomplete life of the past Buddha Vipaśyi ending with his enlightenment. Sanskrit, Pali, Chinese	Walshe (1987), pp. 199–222
Mahāvastu (*The Great Story*) – incomplete life ending with the conversion of the three Kāśyapas. Sanskrit	Jones (1949–1956)
Nidāna-kathā (*Narration of Causes*) – "Introduction" to the Pali *Jātaka Commentary (Jātakaṭṭhakathā)*. Incomplete life ending with the dedication of the Jetavana monastery. Pali	Jayawickrama (1990)
Vinaya (*Book of the Discipline*) *of the Mūlasarvāstivādins* – complete life of the Buddha contained within the "historical sections" of the Vinaya. Sanskrit, Tibetan, Chinese	Rockhill (1907) (partial trans. from Tibetan)

Table 2.2 Some Buddhist Sources on the Life of the Buddha Available in Translation

NAME OF BUDDHA (CASTE)	WHEN HE LIVED	TYPE OF TREE UNDER WHICH AWAKENED	NAMES OF CHIEF DISCIPLES / AND ATTENDANT	NAMES OF PARENTS	SON'S NAME
Vipaśyi (kṣatriya)	91 aeons ago	Pāṭalī (trumpet-flower tree)	Khaṇḍa + Tiṣya / Aśoka	Bandhumat Bandhuvatī	Susaṃvṛtta-skandha
Śikhi (kṣatriya)	31 aeons ago	Puṇḍarīka (artemisia)	Abhibhū + Śaṃbhava / Kṣemakāra	Aruṇa Prabhāvatī	Atula
Viśvabhuj (kṣatriya)	31 aeons ago	Śāla (sal tree)	Śroṇa + Uttara / Upaśānta	Supradīpa Uttarā	Supra-buddha
Krakucchanda (brahmin)	Present aeon	Śirīṣa (acacia)	Sañjīva + Vīdura / Bhadrika	Agnidatta Dhavavatī	Pratāpana
Kanakamuni (brahmin)	Present aeon	Uḍumbara (cluster fig)	Bhujiṣya + Uttara / Svastika	Yajñadatta Yaśovatī	Sārthavāha
Kāśyapa (brahmin)	Present aeon	Nyagrodha (banyan)	Tiṣya + Bharadvāja / Sarvamitra	Brahmadatta Viśākhā	Vijitasena
Śākyamuni (kṣatriya)	Present aeon	Aśvattha (ficus religiosa or pipal tree)	Śāriputra + Maudgalyāyana / Ānanda	Śuddhodana Māyā	Rāhula

Table 2.3 List of Seven Buddhas[10]

In addition to Vipaśyin, the *Discourse on the Great Legend* lists six other buddhas: Śikhin (who lived thirty-one aeons ago), Viśvabhuj (who also lived thirty-one aeons ago), and Krakucchanda, Kanakamuni, and Kāśyapa who, like our own Śākyamuni, all lived in the present aeon. Their lifestories are more or less identical, although the names of their family members and other details vary (see table 2.3). Thus, many of the episodes in the account of Vipaśyin's life are introduced with the phrase: "it is the norm." For example: "It is the norm that whereas other women give birth sitting or lying down, it is not so with a [buddha's] mother who gives birth standing up," or "it is the norm that as soon as he is born, a [buddha] ... takes seven strides... scans the four quarters and then declares with a bull-like voice: 'I am chief in the world ...'" etc. The implication of such statements is that these things "are the norm" not just for Vipaśyin but for the six other buddhas as well. The effect of this is to create the impression that all these buddhas have certain things they are expected to do in order to

10 See Davids (1899–1924), vol. 2, pp. 6–7, and Waldschmidt (1953–1956), pp. 169–175 [in German].

be buddhas, that their lifestories are governed by what I call a buddha-biography blueprint.[11]

In time, the particulars of this bio-blueprint became quite detailed and specific. One Sanskrit text, for example, enumerates ten "indispensable actions" which every buddha must necessarily accomplish. The Tibetan tradition favored instead a list of the "Twelve Great Acts" of all buddhas, while the Theravāda commentarial tradition expanded the number of obligatory deeds and events to thirty.[12] The notion of such blueprints is important, for we are accustomed to thinking of individuals as making their own lifestories by virtue of their decisions and actions. In the case of Śākyamuni, however, it appears that, in some instances, the reverse is true and that his decisions and actions are being made "by his lifestory," i.e. that he is following the pre-established buddha-life pattern. Thus, for example, when the Buddha arrives at the Bodhi tree in Bodhgaya, under which he is to attain awakening, at first he does not know on which side of the tree he should sit, until he realizes that "the seat of meditation of all buddhas is on the eastern side" (Jayawickrama, 1990, p. 94). Similarly, when the Buddha is loath to give full ordination to women, one of the things that finally convinces him to do so is the realization that all the past buddhas instituted orders of nuns.[13]

Scholars generally ascribe no historicity whatsoever to any of the past buddhas, but it should be said that the tradition they represent is clearly an old one. Mention was made in the introduction of the inscribed pillar that Aśoka (third century BCE) left at Lumbinī. This was not the only Aśoka column in the region. Two others have been found at two sites about thirty kilometers away. One of these, at Nigalisagar (near the village of Nigliva), bears an inscription in which Aśoka records his visit to the site fourteen years into his reign, and declares having enlarged there the already existing stūpa (memorial mound) of the past buddha Kanakamuni to twice its original size; the other, in the village of Gotihawa, is not inscribed but is thought to mark the site of the stūpa of another past buddha, Krakucchanda. Taken together, these Aśoka pillars bear witness to the fact that, already in the third century BCE, the Buddha Śākyamuni was thought not to have been the first person to have reached buddhahood and taught the Dharma

11 The "it is the norm" quotations (slightly altered) are from Walshe (1987), p. 204. For a description of the buddha-biographical blueprint, see Strong (2001), pp. 15–16.
12 The list of ten indispensable actions may be found in Rotman (2008), pp. 163–164; for a discussion of the Twelve Great Acts, see Powers (2007), p. 37; for the Pali list of thirty obligatory deeds, see Horner (1978), pp. 429–430.
13 On the institution of orders of nuns by past buddhas, see Strong (2008), p. 66.

(doctrine), but was rather seen as only the most recent buddha in a whole series of "awakened ones."[14]

The names of several of the past buddhas in this series also appear in inscriptions on a bas-relief at Bharhut (*c.* second century BCE) where each is represented by the particular type of tree under which he attained enlightenment; and all seven of the buddhas mentioned in the *Discourse on the Great Legend* (the six plus Śākyamuni) are featured together in sculptures at the great stūpa of Sanchi (first century BCE).[15]

The buddhas of the past were, moreover, not irrelevant to cultic practices. In the group of the seven buddhas, special attention was paid to the last four – Śākyamuni and his three predecessors – who were all thought to be buddhas in our own present "fortunate" era (bhadrakalpa). By the time the Chinese pilgrims started coming to India in the fourth century CE, it was common for sites to be marked with monuments commemorating all four of these buddhas. The same is often true today; many pilgrimage sites in South and Southeast Asia are said to have been visited and marked by all four of these buddhas (and will be visited by Maitreya in the future). The great Shwe Dagon Pagoda in Yangon, Myanmar, for instance, which (as we saw in 1.2.4) is famous for enshrining some hair relics of Śākyamuni, is also said to contain the waterpot of Krakucchanda, the staff of Kanakamuni, and the bathing cloth of Kāśyapa, and has separate shrines for each of these past buddhas. Similarly, not just Śākyamuni but his three predecessors as well are each said (apocryphally) to have visited Sri Lanka in their lifetimes and to have left relics there. One legend, especially popular in Southeast Asia, even posits that all the buddhas of the present aeon were once, in a distant previous existence, brothers, the offspring of a single mother crow who got separated from each other, and that when one lights an oil lamp in honor of the Buddha Śākyamuni, one is actually also honoring his predecessors and their mother of long ago.[16]

---

14 On the pillars of the past buddhas, and the reports of the Chinese pilgrims, see Deeg (2003), pp. 36–56. Most of Aśoka's pillar inscriptions (including those at Lumbinī and Nigalisagar) may be found in Thapar (1961), pp. 250–266.

15 On the representations of the buddhas at Bharhut and Sanchi, see Nattier (2004), p. 72.

16 On the monuments to past buddhas at Indian sites, see Lamotte (1988), p. 338. On the past buddhas at the Shwe Dagon, see Stadtner (2011), pp. 98–99. The Ānanda temple in Pagan also has images of the four buddhas of the present era, set in the cardinal directions (see Stadtner, 2005, p. 97). On the visit of the past buddhas to Sri Lanka, see Oldenberg (1982), pp. 196–201. For a discussion of the Southeast Asian legend of the mother crow, see Strong (1992), pp. 203–204; for a translation of a text pertaining to it, see Strong (1995), pp. 220–221.

The tradition of an enlightened master having precursors or predecessors who set patterns for him was not exclusively a Buddhist one in ancient India. The Jains, for example, compiled a list of twenty-four tīrthaṃkaras ("ford-makers"), leading up to and including their "founder" Mahāvira, an older contemporary of the Buddha. Similarly, the Ājīvikas had a tradition of twenty-four such departed masters, leading up to and including their "founder" Maskarin Gośālīputra. It is perhaps not surprising, then, to find that, at least in the Theravāda tradition, the list of past buddhas got expanded to total twenty-five.[17] This list of twenty-five ends with the seven past buddhas noted above, but adds eighteen more prior to that, beginning with Dīpaṃkara who is said to have lived an unimaginable "four incalculable ages and one hundred thousand aeons ago." An aeon (kalpa), as mentioned, may be described as lasting 4.32×10^{8} years, but an incalculable (asaṃkhyeya) age is much longer; as its name implies, it is impossible to fathom, but it is sometimes defined as 10^{140} years. From the point of view of Western cosmology (modern or traditional), this would mean that the Buddha Dīpaṃkara lived long before the creation of the earth or even of the universe (the "big bang" is said by some to have occurred 13.75×10^{9} years ago). This is possible because in Buddhism (as in most Indian religions) there is a cyclical notion of time, which knows no ultimate first creation, and in which the universe repeatedly evolves and returns to dissolution before evolving again. Many such world-cycles have passed since Dīpaṃkara's lifetime. Even so, life in his time, apart for certain details, does not seem to have been significantly different from life in Śākyamuni's; it is marked by the same classes of humans, the same topography of the land, the same religious concerns for devotion and liberation.[18]

2.5 THE START OF ŚĀKYAMUNI'S CAREER

In the context of the Buddha's lifestory, Dīpaṃkara is chiefly important for the fact that he was the buddha in the world when Śākyamuni first embarked

17 On the Jain tradition of ford-makers, see Dundas (1992), pp. 11–39. On the Ājīvika tradition, see Basham (1951), p. 27. See also Gombrich (1980). In some lists, the number is expanded to twenty-eight.

18 The estimate of the length of an incalculable age at 10^{140} years is from Childers (1909), pp. 59, 185–186. Another tradition (see La Vallée Poussin, 1988–1990, vol. 2, pp. 188–189) has the Buddha's career starting three incalculables ago, and defines one incalculable as 10^{59} years. For a lifestory of Dīpaṃkara, see Jones (1949–1956), vol. 1, pp. 158–187.

on the path that eventually resulted in his buddhahood. Four incalculable ages and one hundred thousand aeons ago, we are told, in a previous life, Śākyamuni was a brahmin ascetic named Sumedha. One day he encountered the previous Buddha Dīpaṃkara. Inspired by the sight and reputation of this enlightened being, Sumedha prostrates himself on the muddy ground at his feet, and utters a vow that he too, someday, will become a buddha, just like Dīpaṃkara. In one version of the story, he states: "I would ... attain the highest Enlightenment, and taking humankind aboard the ship of the Dharma, ford them across the ocean of saṃsāra" (Jayawickrama, 1990, pp. 17–18). Recognizing the firmness of his resolve, Dīpaṃkara responds by predicting that, indeed, in the distant future, Sumedha will become the buddha known as Śākyamuni.[19]

This succession of events – encounter with a buddha, act of merit, resolve to attain buddhahood, and prediction of the same – is a pattern of some significance that we will encounter again. In the case of Sumedha, it monumentally marks the start of his bodhisattva-career – his path to buddhahood – and begins what, in the Theravāda tradition, is sometimes called the "distant epoch" of his lifestory which will last up until the time of his final birth in Lumbinī. During the ages and aeons covered by this distant epoch, the bodhisattva, i.e. the future Śākyamuni, will meet the twenty-three other previous buddhas on the list of twenty-five after Dīpaṃkara, and under each of them, he will renew his own vow for buddhahood and receive from them an assurance that he is still on the right track (see table 2.4). These stories provide a model of sorts for how to behave when one meets a buddha, but they also drive home the importance of meeting a buddha in the first place, of being inspired by him in person to undertake the long arduous journey to buddhahood. This is also a theme to which we shall return.

2.6 PREVIOUS LIVES (JĀTAKAS)

It is important to note, however, that not all of the stories of Śākyamuni's previous lives – known as jātakas ("births") – were tales of encounters with past buddhas. Indeed, the vast majority of them deal with situations in which there is no buddha alive and so they may serve as models for action in buddhaless

19 I am here presenting the Sumedha story as it is found in Jayawickrama (1990), pp. 17–18. In some sources, Sumedha is called Sumati or Megha. On the issue of when Śākyamuni's career begins, see Strong (2001), pp. 24–36.

	PERIOD	BODHISATTVA BORN AS	PAST BUDDHA	DEED DONE FOR PAST BUDDHA
1	4 incalculable ages + 100,000 aeons ago	Sumedha, a brahmin ascetic	Dīpaṃkara	Lies in mud so buddha can pass on the road
2	3 ages ago	Kṣatriya	Kauṇḍinya	Gives food
3	2 ages ago	Brahmin	Mangala	Gives perfumes, garlands, and food
4	"	Serpent king	Sumana	Gives music, food and robes
5	"	Brahmin	Revata	Takes refuge, gives a robe
6	"	Brahmin	Śobhita	Gives food and drink
7	1 age ago	Yakṣa	Anomadasrśi	Gives food and drink
8	"	Lion	Padma	Bows down, roars three times, stands guard
9	"	Matted-haired ascetic	Nārada	Gives food and drink and sandalwood
10	100,000 aeons ago	District governor	Padmottara	Gives food and cloth
11	70,000 aeons ago	Brahmin youth	Sumedha	Gives wealth
12	"	Cakravartin king	Sujāta	Gives his kingdom and seven treasures
13	1,800 aeons ago	Brahmin	Priyadarśi	Gives monastic park
14	"	Matted-haired ascetic	Arthadarśi	Gives heavenly flowers
15	"	The god Indra	Dharmadarśi	Gives heavenly music, perfumes, and garlands
16	94 aeons ago	Ascetic	Siddhārtha	Gives fruit of jambu tree
17	92 aeons ago	Kṣatriya renunciant	Tiṣya	Holds three heavenly flowers over buddha
18	"	Kṣatriya	Puṣya	Renounces kingdom to become a monk
19	91 aeons ago	Serpent king	Vipaśyin	Gives music and golden set
20	31 aeons ago	Kṣatriya	Śikhin	Gives food, drink, cloth and elephant
21	"	Kṣatriya	Viśvabhij	Gives great gift
22	In the present aeon	Kṣatriya	Krakucchanda	Gives bowls, robes, and medicines
23	In the present aeon	Kṣatriya	Kanakamuni	Gives cloth and sandals
24	In the present aeon	Brahmin youth	Kāśyapa	Becomes monk
25	In the present aeon	Gautama		Becomes our Buddha Śākyamuni

Table 2.4 The Future Śākyamuni Under Twenty-Four Past Buddhas

times. In other words, there are two basic types of jātakas: stories like those we have just presented in table 2.4, in which the bodhisattva, inspired by a past buddha, reiterates his determination to become a buddha himself, while making a fairly ordinary gift to the past buddha and his community; and stories like those we shall look at presently, in which the bodhisattva is reborn in a setting in which there is no living buddha present, in which, in fact, there usually is no Buddh*ism*. In these settings, he will not generally undertake devotional actions directed towards some venerable object or person, but will endeavor to practice one or more of the ten perfections of giving, moral conduct, renunciation, wisdom, effort, patience, truth-telling, resoluteness, loving-kindness, and equanimity.[20]

Typically, these jātaka stories are narrated according to a set format. Something happens in the "present" that demands a karmic explanation. The Buddha responds by declaring that "this is not the first time" that such a situation has arisen, and he proceeds to recount a "story of the past" – the jātaka proper – in which similar relationships or events manifested themselves. When that is done, he concludes by identifying various characters in the story of the past with various persons in the present such as himself, members of his family, particular disciples, or others. Usually, but not always, the bodhisattva is the main protagonist of the story of the past, and so the jātakas serve the function of telling many stories about him, featuring his great (and sometimes not so great) karmic deeds.

The Pali *Jātaka Commentary* recounts no fewer than 547 past lives of the Buddha. In eighty-five of these, the bodhisattva appears as a king; in eighty-three as an ascetic; in forty-three as a tree god; in twenty-four as a brahmin; in twenty-four as a prince; in twenty-three as a nobleman; in twenty as the god Sakka (Indra); in eighteen as a monkey; in thirteen as a merchant; in eleven as a deer; in ten as a lion; and fewer than ten times as a variety of other beings. The last ten of the Pali jātaka stories, consisting of the longest tales, became especially popular and are sometimes anthologized together or depicted in temple murals. Elsewhere, all 547 jātakas may be represented in single-scene representations. For instance, at the Wewurukannala monastery in Dikwella, Sri Lanka, which features a colossal (fifty-meter) seated image of the Buddha, one can mount a staircase inside the building at the back of the statue, and pass in review cartouches summarizing all 547 jātakas. Once one reaches the top, one has, through art, relived all the lives of the Buddha. Similarly, but less vertically, at the Shwe

20 On the place of the perfections in the jātakas, see Appleton (2010), pp. 25–28, 66–68.

Dagon Pagoda in Yangon, all 547 jātakas are depicted on tiles embedded into a low wall surrounding the spire.[21]

2.6.1 *The Donkey in the Lion's Skin*

It is obviously impossible to do justice to the hundreds of jātakas that exist in the Pali and other Buddhist traditions. I shall limit myself below to comments on two of the more famous ones. But first, I want to start by presenting a rather simple and pretty typical jātaka that may be said to be an adaptation of a story that belongs to world folklore. Readers familiar with the *Pancatantra*, or Aesop's Fables, or even the works of Jean de La Fontaine, will recognize it as the tale of "The Ass in the Lion's Skin," but here it is given a Buddhist spin.

Once upon a time, some disciples of the Buddha who were very learned knowers of scripture, recited whole texts for the community with such loud and confident voices that they were likened to roaring lions. At this, the Venerable Kokālika, an ignorant but ambitious monk, became envious. He then went about complaining that no one ever asked him to recite any texts out loud. Finally his fellow monks agreed to give him a chance, and invited him to recite the following day. In his vanity, he decided to get dressed up for the occasion: over his yellow monk's robe, he put on a fancy blue and white garment, and, carrying an elegant fan, he mounted the speaker's chair. But, as soon as he began to recite his chosen verses, he completely forgot the text, and could only spout nonsense. Embarrassed, he had to flee the assembly, and everyone realized how ignorant he was.

Sometime later, the Buddha overheard some monks talking about this incident, and he said to them: "This is not the first time that Kokālika has betrayed himself by his voice," and he proceeded to recount the following story of the past: once, long ago, when King Brahmadatta was reigning in Benares, the bodhisattva was born as a farmer in a certain village. In those days, there was a hawker of goods who traveled about leading a donkey

21 For translations of all 547 Pāli jātakas, see Cowell (1895–1907). For a modern translation of a selection of them, see S. Shaw (2006). The statistics about the Buddha's past lives are from Davids (1880), p. ci. On the depiction of the last ten jātakas in Thai murals, see Wray, Rosenfeld, and Bailey (1972). On the jātaka tiles at the Shwe Dagon, see Stadtner (2011), p. 99. All the jātakas are also famously depicted on roof level plaques at the Ānanda temple in Pagan, on which, see Stadtner (2005), pp. 101–103, and Duroiselle (1920–1921). For an important study of the jātakas, see Appleton (2010). For a translation of a Sanskrit collection of jātakas, see Khoroche (1989).

which carried all his merchandise for him. Wherever he went, the hawker was in the habit of taking the bundle of goods off his donkey and throwing a lion's skin over it; he would then turn it loose to graze in the farmers' fields confident that no one would go near it, thinking it to be a lion. One day, the hawker came to the bodhisattva's village and, as was his custom, set his donkey free to browse in a farmer's barley field with the lion's skin on. The field watchmen were afraid and ran back to give the alarm. Hearing the news, the bodhisattva and the other farmers rushed to the scene and decided to try to scare off the "lion" by blowing on conches and making a racket. The donkey, frightened, brayed loudly, and the bodhisattva then pronounced the following verse (in W. H. D. Rouse's quaint translation): "Nor lion nor tiger I see, / Not even a leopard is he; / But a donkey – the wretched old hack! / With a lionskin over his back!" The villagers then chased the donkey and it fled away, while the bodhisattva declared: "The donkey, if he had been wise, / Might long the green barley have eaten; / A lionskin was his disguise: / But he gave a hee-haw, and got beaten" (Cowell, 1895–1907, vol. 2, p. 76). After finishing this story of the past, the Buddha then made the identifications: "At that time, Kokālika was the donkey, and the wise farmer was I myself."[22]

2.6.2 *Vessantara Jātaka*

A much more famous and developed jātaka is the tale of Prince Vessantara (Skt., Viśvantara), versions of which are known throughout the Buddhist world, but are especially popular in Southeast Asia. It is commonly recited on ritual occasions and forms the basis for sermons delivered by monks. I will limit myself here to the "story of the past": this is the tale of a prince (the bodhisattva) who perfects generosity and selflessness by giving away everything that is asked of him. He first gives away the state elephant to a neighboring kingdom; as a result, he is sent into exile with his immediate family by his disgruntled subjects. En route, he gives away his horses and chariot when they are asked of him; then he gives away his children to a passing brahmin who needs servants; finally he gives away his wife to another passing brahmin who wants her. Each relinquishing, each abandonment, is portrayed in a very poignant way, and the reader/listener is in awe of the magnitude of Vessantara's determination to perfect the art of giving in

22 Adapted from Cowell (1895–1907), vol. 2, pp. 45–46, 76–77. For a discussion, see Davids (1880), pp. v–vii.

his quest for buddhahood. Ultimately, it is true, there is a happy ending for Vessantara and his family; all the demands made on him turn out to be tests of his dedication orchestrated by the gods, and he recovers kingdom, wife, and children, but this does not detract from the greatness of his deed.[23]

The Vessantara story is important for many reasons. Among these is the fact that Vessantara is a layperson. He is not a brahmanical ascetic like Sumedha, nor is he a Buddhist monk, but a prince, a householder who is in the position of being able to be generous. Giving (dāna) is one of the fundamental moral injunctions incumbent upon lay Buddhists today. To be sure, Vessantara gives to the extreme, and the Buddhist tradition was not without raising questions about the appropriateness of giving away one's wife and children, but he nonetheless presents an awesome model of generosity and selflessness.[24]

Secondly, though Vessantara remains a layperson, he nonetheless abandons some of the same things (i.e. personal possessions, wife, and children) that Buddhist monks abandon when they become monks, and that the Buddha abandoned when he left the palace on his Great Departure (see 2.7.4). The Vessantara story can thus make Buddhists think about the intersection between "giving away" (generosity) and "giving up" (renunciation).

Finally, Vessantara is living at a time when there is no buddha alive in the world. Unlike Sumedha and the others listed in table 2.4, he does not encounter a past buddha – a Dīpaṃkara – who can serve as a model of inspiration. This serves to make him especially appropriate for our contemporary situation, in which there is similarly no buddha alive in the world. In this, we can see one of the important features of the Vessantara story and of the jātakas more generally: in these accounts of his past lives, the Buddha can show us how a bodhisattva acts when there is no buddha.

2.6.3 The Tigress Jātaka

Another popular jātaka emphasizing yet another awesome paradigm of behavior is the tale of the bodhisattva's gift of his body to a hungry tigress.

23 For a translation of the Pali Vessantara jātaka, see Cone and Gombrich (1977). For other versions, see Khoroche (1989), pp. 58–73, and Lenz (2003), pp. 157–166, 228–237. For a discussion, see Collins (1998), pp. 497–554. See also Lefferts, Cate, and Tossa (2013), and Collins (forthcoming).

24 King Milinda raises questions about Vessantara's ethics in giving away his wife and children; see Davids (1890–1894), vol. 2, pp. 114–132. See also discussions in Collins (forthcoming).

Though not found among the 547 stories of the Pali *Jātaka Commentary*, it is featured in other traditions: once upon a time, the bodhisattva, together with a companion, came across a starving tigress. Weak with hunger, she was unable to feed her two cubs, and was contemplating eating them herself. The bodhisattva promptly sent his companion off to search for food, but then, fearing that would take too long, he resolved to assuage the tigress's hunger more immediately. Reasoning "why should I look elsewhere for meat when the whole of my body is available?" he sacrifices his own life by throwing himself off a cliff to land at the tigress's feet, thus giving her his own corpse to eat.[25]

Like the Vessantara story, this jātaka raises the question of whether this is a model to be emulated or a perfection to be marveled at, but it does several other things as well: it recognizes the impermanence and non-self nature of the body, two doctrines which we shall examine in 4.3; and it also stresses the urgency and immediacy of practicing the path, and being ever set on the goal of enlightenment. Indeed, later Buddhist traditions were to cite the jātaka of the tigress to show how the Buddha, by his immediate self-sacrifice, moved ahead of his companion in the story on the path to buddhahood. In this reading we are told that the bodhisattva and his companion were, at the start of the story, neck and neck on the path to buddhahood, but that, by the urgency of his self-sacrifice, the bodhisattva moved ahead in the "race," and so has already become the Buddha Śākyamuni, while his companion, who went to search for food rather than throw himself off the cliff, is still on the path as the future buddha, Maitreya.[26]

Not all jātakas, of course, are so dramatic. As seen above, some of them are simply adaptations of popular non-Buddhist tales, so that the jātakas were a way for Buddhism to incorporate into its own tradition elements from the more general reservoir of folk-stories. Taken together, however, the jātakas may be said to serve several purposes. As already suggested, they can provide different models and contexts of behavior than those found in the final lifestory of the Buddha as Śākyamuni. These paradigms may inspire emulation or devout admiration among devotees. Secondly, they stress the length and difficulties and extraordinariness of the path to buddhahood and the greatness and awesomeness of the deeds the bodhisattva had to accomplish in order to reach his goal. Thirdly, they add karmic depth to the Buddha's

25 Translations of versions of the tigress jātaka may be found in Khoroche (1989), pp. 5–9, Frye (1981), pp. 13–16, and Emmerick (1970), pp. 85–97.

26 On the sacrifice of the body in jātaka and other literature, see Ohnuma (2007). On the competition between Maitreya and Śākyamuni in this and other stories, see La Vallée Poussin (1928) [in French].

life, by showing how his present deeds and relationships with many of his disciples are reiterations of situations they faced together in a previous existence; they thus are not only stories about the Buddha's individual karma but about the communal karma of his community. In this, sometimes jātakas are like déjà-vu accounts that make it clear that the present is but a repeat of the past – that, for example, good guys have always been good guys and villains have always been villains, or that mothers have always been mothers and children have always been children. I call this pattern karmic repetition or karmic parallelism; as the French saying has it: "plus ça change, plus c'est la même chose" ("the more things change, the more they stay the same"). Other times, however, roles are reversed as the story moves through time: victimizers in the past become victims in the present and vice versa. I call this pattern criss-cross karma. Especially interesting in this regard are those few jātakas that explain minor sufferings of the Buddha in his last life as due to a negative karmic act in a previous life. In this way, a bad headache suffered by the Buddha in his last life is explained by the fact that, long ago, in a past existence, he was a little boy who delighted in seeing some fishermen knock the heads of their fish against a rock in order to kill them. A backache is explained by the fact that, in a past life as a wrestler, he broke the back of his opponent in the ring.[27] But these stories also serve to send a message of hope: if the bodhisattva could overcome such bad karma and attain enlightenment, surely we may be able to do so as well.

2.7 A LIFESTORY OF ŚĀKYAMUNI

We come now to the legend of Śākyamuni's final life, in which he puts an end to the quest that began so long ago under Dipaṃkara, and that took him through so many previous existences. In what follows, I want to use a rather short account of his life as a framework for our discussion. It is imbedded in the *Legend of King Aśoka* (*Aśokāvadāna*), a Buddhist work in Sanskrit dating perhaps from the second century CE. One of the features of this narrative is that it links episodes in the Buddha's life to the places where they happened. The influence of pilgrimage traditions on sacred biography (and vice versa) is something that is still being studied by scholars. Suffice it to say that it can be a "chicken-and-egg" relationship where it is not always clear what came

27 On jātakas in general, see Appleton (2010). On the Buddha's negative karma, see Walters (1990), Cutler (1997), and Strong (2012).

first: the story or the place where it happened. On the one hand, sites became established as the places where certain stories occurred and were visited by pilgrims. On the other, new stories came to be told to explain the existence (or bolster the popularity) of certain sites that were already being noticed (perhaps for their unusual physical features or topography).[28]

Real pilgrims (such as the Chinese monks Faxian and Xuanzang, for instance), did not always visit all of the extant sites connected to the life of the Buddha, and did not usually go to them in bio-chronological order, for practical reasons. The account in the *Legend of King Aśoka* is not a real pilgrimage, but an imagined one made by the Indian emperor Aśoka (who historically lived in the third century BCE), under the guidance of a Buddhist elder named Upagupta. Together they do visit, in bio-chronological order, over thirty sites associated with the Buddha. These can serve to provide us with a glimpse – a sort of shorthand synopsis – of what places and what events in the life of Śākyamuni were deemed to be important at the time of the text's composition.

Together, Aśoka and Upagupta go (1) to the Lumbinī grove in which Śākyamuni was born. Then they visit a series of sites in and around nearby Kapilavastu, where the bodhisattva grew up: (2) the place where his father was first shown his son and saw that he possessed on his body the thirty-two marks of a great man, (3) the temple of the Śākya clan where the young bodhisattva was presented to the gods, (4) the place where he was shown to the fortunetellers, (5) the place where the sage Asita predicted he would become a buddha, (6) the place where he was reared by his stepmother Mahāprajāpatī, (7) the place where he learned the art of writing, (8) the place where he mastered various martial arts, (9) the place where he trained in the same, (10) his harem, (11) the place where he saw an old man, a sick man, and a dead man, (12) the rose-apple tree under which he first meditated, and (13) the gate through which he left Kapilavastu on his Great Departure. Following this, Aśoka and Upagupta visit a set of sites associated with the bodhisattva's quest for enlightenment: (14) the place where he sent back his servant and his horse, (15) the place where he exchanged his clothes for the robe of a hunter, (16) the place where King Bimbisāra offered him half of his kingdom (Rājagṛha), (17) the hermitage of the potter,[29] (18) the place where he met his teachers, Ārāḍa and Udraka, (19) the place where he

28 On the relationship of pilgrimage and lifestory, see Strong (2001), pp. 7–10.

29 For convenience's sake and on the basis of other sources, I have reversed the order of 16 and 17.

practiced austerities for six years, (20) the place where he accepted a meal of milk-rice, (21) the place where he met the nāga king Kālika, and (22) the tree of Awakening at Bodhgaya. The pilgrims then proceed to go to a number of places associated with events immediately following his enlightenment: (23) the place where the Buddha received four stone begging bowls from the gods of the four quarters, (24) the place where he received alms from the merchants Trapuṣa and Bhallika, (25) the place on the way to Benares where he was praised by the Ājīvika Upaga, ending up at (26) the Deer Park in Sarnath near Benares where he preached his First Sermon. Following this, they visit different places where the Buddha converted various types of beings, and performed notable miracles: (27) the place where a thousand long-haired ascetics were converted (in Uruvilvā), (28) the place where he preached to King Bimbisāra (in Rājagṛha), (29) the place where he taught the Dharma to Indra, king of the gods (Indra's cave), (30) the place where he put on a great display of miracles (Śrāvastī), and (31) the place where he came down from heaven after spending a rains-retreat there preaching to his mother (Saṃkāśya). Finally, they end up at (32) Kuśinagarī, the place where the Buddha died and passed into final nirvāṇa. In the rest of this chapter, I would like to comment on these various sites and the events that, legend tells us, occurred at them.

2.7.1 *Birth and Childhood*

(1) Appropriately, Aśoka and Upagupta begin at Lumbinī. Acting as a guide, Upagupta points out the very tree whose branch the Buddha's mother, Queen Mahāmāyā, held on to while giving birth to him standing up. Then he adds a brief description of the event: "This is the first of the shrines of the Buddha whose eye is supreme. Here, as soon as he was born, he took seven steps on the earth, looked down at the four directions, and spoke these words: 'This is my last birth; I'll not dwell in a womb again'" (Strong, 1983, pp. 244–245).[30]

Already here, several features of Śākyamuni's birth story become evident. Although no mention is made of some of the extraordinary phenomena emphasized in other sources – his descent into his mother's womb from Tuṣita Heaven (the place of his last birth) in the form of a great six-tusked white elephant, his residence and activities inside his mother in a wondrous

30 On different aspects of the Buddha's birth, see Cueppers, Deeg, and Durt (2010).

translucent uterine palace (what one scholar has called a "womb with a view"; Sasson, 2009), the fact that he is born not vaginally but from his mother's side (hence escaping the impurities of the birth canal, and the trauma of parturition that wipes out memories of previous lives), or his reception by the gods and his being washed by them with streams of heavenly water – it is clear, nonetheless, that his birth is extraordinary, not to mention miraculous. From the start, he can walk and talk. His declaration that he will "not dwell in a womb again" indicates an awareness and assurance that this will be his last life in which he will, finally, attain buddhahood. The seven steps he takes (in artistic representations, each step is typically marked by a lotus blossom, or by a footprint) and his gazing down in the four directions, are assertions of his superiority and sovereignty over the world.[31] They are reinforced in other texts by his additional declaration: "I am chief in the world, supreme in the world, eldest in the world" (Walshe, 1987, p. 205).

Despite all these supernatural phenomena, I would contend, the text wants to make clear that this event is not happening on some supernatural plane, but that it is something that serves to make the Buddha present in this world, in a specific place. In the very next passage of our text, Upagupta, having described the birth itself, then summons the goddess of the tree under which the Buddha was born (in ancient India all significant trees were inhabited by divinities) and asks her to bear witness to the fact that this marks the spot where the Buddha entered the world. The same assertion of presence, perhaps, may be found in art and ritual. Typically, iconic Buddha images that represent him at the time of his birth show him as a young boy, wearing a simple cloth dhoti, with his right hand raised straight in the air above his head. This is the case in many of the temples in Lumbinī, and in modern-day East Asia (especially Korea and Japan) such images figure prominently in ritual bathings of Buddha statues, usually performed annually by devotees on the Buddha's birthday (see 12.4). They thereby seek to reenact the legendary bathing of the Buddha done by the gods (or alternatively by two nāga kings). One of the thrusts of this ritual (and of the legend) is to assert the supernatural extraordinariness of the Buddha, but another is to affirm his humanity. Bathing newborns is, of course, a common human postnatal rite, but it also assumes the need to wipe away impurities (which technically

31 For elaborations on the narrative of the Buddha's descent from Tuṣita, see Luczanits (2010). For an analysis of the significance of the elephant in the conception scenario, see Deeg (2010). On the Buddha's birth and memories of previous lives, see Hara (1980; 1989/1994). On his reception by the gods and the seven steps, see Sasson (2007), pp. 141–148.

the superhuman Buddha should not have).[32] In the traditions surrounding the Buddha's birth, we can, therefore, see both elements that emphasize his superior, otherworldly status, and others that stress his humanity, his being in this world.

(2) From Lumbinī, Aśoka and Upagupta proceed on to nearby Kapilavastu, the chief seat of the Śākyas, and the Buddha's hometown. Upagupta continues to act as guide: "Great king," he declares, "in this place here, the bodhisattva was brought before his father, King Śuddhodana. Seeing that his son's perfect body was adorned with the thirty-two marks of the Great Man, he prostrated himself full length at his feet" (Strong, 1983, p. 246).

It was apparently the custom, in the Buddha's time, to examine a newborn infant's physiognomy for bodily marks portending its future, auspicious or otherwise. The thirty-two physical marks of the Great Man (mahāpuruṣa) are not listed in the text, but the tradition was well known, and they are fully spelled out in other sources. The marks include such things as a turban-shaped protuberance (uṣṇīṣa) on the top of the head, a tuft of hair (ūrṇā) between the eyebrows, wheel marks on the soles of the feet, hair curling to the right, etc. (see table 2.5). At least some of these characteristics are probably simply due to the iconographic tradition that dictated how the Buddha should be represented, once images of him came to be made. Apparently, Śuddhodana does not, at first, know what these marks mean specifically (they will later be interpreted for him), but he recognizes them as signs of greatness and bows down in front of his child, an extraordinary gesture for a father, not to mention a king.

(3) Upagupta and Aśoka then proceed on their way to the ancestral temple of the Śākya clan, where the bodhisattva was brought soon after his birth so that he could be presented to his ancestral deities. Instead, we are told, "all the divinities fell at the bodhisattva's feet and King Śuddhodana declared that his son was a god even for the gods, and so gave him the name "Lord of lords" ("Devātideva").

The greatness of the child is further reinforced by these events. It may be that the Śākya clan into which the Buddha was born had a tribal republican form of government, but Buddhist tradition has emphasized its kingly connections and traced the Buddha's ancestry (both on his father's and his mother's side) through thousands of generations of royalty back to the first mythical paradigmatic king, Mahāsammata. This visit to the

32 On the bathing of the Buddha, see Sasson (2007), pp. 142–145. On the ritual in East Asia, see Rhi (2010).

1. He has feet with level tread
2. The soles of his feet (and his palms) are marked with thousand-spoked wheel-signs
3. He has projecting heels
4. He has long toes and fingers
5. He has soft and tender hands and feet
6. He has hands and feet that are net-like
7. He has well-rounded ankles
8. He has legs like an antelope's
9. His hands come down to his knees when he stands up straight
10. His penis is enclosed in a sheath
11. His skin is the color of gold
12. His skin is soft and smooth
13. He has but one body hair to each follicle
14. His body hairs grow straight up, are black, and curl to the right
15. His body is perfectly straight
16. His body has seven convex surfaces (backs of his arms, legs, shoulders, and chest)
17. His bust is like a lion's
18. He has broad shoulders
19. His body is perfectly proportioned like a banyan tree
20. His bust is well-rounded
21. He has an excellent sense of taste
22. He has a jaw like a lion's
23. He has forty teeth
24. His teeth are even
25. There are no gaps between his teeth
26. His canine teeth are white
27. His tongue is long and broad
28. He has a voice like Brahmā's
29. He has blue eyes
30. He has eyelashes like those of a bull
31. He has a tuft of hair (ūrṇā) between his eyebrows
32. The top of his head has a turban-shaped protuberance (uṣṇīṣa)

Table 2.5 The Thirty-Two Marks of the Great Man on the Body of the Buddha[33]

33 See Buswell and Lopez (2014), pp. 1094–1095, and Burnouf (1852), pp. 553–583 [in French].

clan shrine serves, therefore, to make clear the newborn Śākyamuni's ancient glorious royal lineage, and to assert that he will be its culmination and continuation. This is emphasized not only by the fact that the clan's divinities (or, perhaps, just their statues?) bow down at the young child's feet (instead of the bodhisattva acknowledging and venerating them), but also by his father, Śuddhodana, proclaiming him to be "Devātideva" ("Lord of lords"). The word "deva" (generally translated as divinity but rendered ambiguously here as "lord"), means both "god" and "king," so it is possible to interpret this scene as reflecting not only Śuddhodana's hope for his son to be (or become) some sort of superior divinity, but for him to be (or become) a "king of kings" – a great world-ruling emperor (cakravartin) who will continue the Śākya lineage and restore the glory of Mahāsammata's rule.[34]

(4) This hope is somewhat undermined, however, in the very next episode: "In this place, great king," Upagupta goes on, "the bodhisattva was shown to the learned brahmin fortunetellers" (Strong, 1983, p. 247). Here, ambiguity is introduced into the picture; though our text does not elaborate on this, it is well known that the brahmin fortunetellers, seeing the thirty-two marks of the "great man" on the bodhisattva's body, give them a twofold reading: they tell Śuddhodana that the marks mean that his son will become a great world-ruling emperor, a cakravartin king, but only if he stays at home. If, on the other hand, he should wander forth and undertake a religious life of renunciation (i.e. become a śramaṇa), he will become a fully enlightened buddha, an Awakened One. It is clear from what follows that Śuddhodana (like any father perhaps) would prefer the former option, if only for his clan's sake. After all, the conceit of the text is that, in his day, the glories of buddhahood were unknown (the past buddhas having been forgotten), so that Śuddhodana, understandably, would prefer his son to become a great world-ruling monarch than to have him drop out of society and become some sort of as yet undefined śramaṇa. In any case, he soon will take steps to try to ensure that his son stays at home.[35]

(5) This dual prediction of the fortunetellers, however, can only make for a pretense of ambiguity, since any Buddhist reader or listener to the story already knows that, in fact, Śākyamuni will *not* stay at home and *will* become a buddha. This is made clear in the very next episode of

34 On the Mahāsammata lineage, see Strong (2011), pp. 172–178.

35 For an account of the soothsayers' predictions, see Jayawickrama (1990), pp. 74–75. For a discussion of early sources, see Bareau (1974), pp. 209–218 [in French].

our story in which Upagupta takes Aśoka to the site where the sage Asita definitively predicted that the bodhisattva *would* become a buddha in this world. In Buddhist tradition, Asita is usually presented as a more knowledgeable prognosticator than the anonymous brahmin fortunetellers. Asita is able to read not only the thirty-two major marks of the Great Man on the bodhisattva's body, but also the additional eighty minor marks, and from these he is able to say with certainty that the young Śākyamuni will become a buddha.[36]

What are we to make of this series of not altogether consistent predictions and anticipations about the life of the infant bodhisattva? It could be argued, perhaps, that the ambiguous twofold qualified prognostication of the brahmin fortunetellers serves a plot function within the confines of the narrative, by introducing an element of uncertainty. But why then counter this immediately with Asita's more definitive prediction?

It seems to me that we should view these two predictions together with the episode in the clan temple of the Śākyas that immediately precedes them. Read as a whole, they can be seen not so much as instances of fortunetelling (i.e. predictions that will or will not come true), but as expositions of character traits that will inform the portrait of the Buddha and the rest of his lifestory. As we have seen, the episode in the Śākya temple serves to emphasize his royal (and divine) connections, two factors that will periodically reappear throughout his life. To be sure, the Buddha will not be an actual this-worldly king, but his biography as Buddha will constantly be informed by a parallelism between his career and that of a wheel-turning cakravartin monarch. And throughout his life, he will deal commandingly with both kings and gods, showing himself to be truly a "lord of lords." But the Buddha is not just a "lord"; he is also an ordinary human being, and this is where the double prediction of the brahmin soothsayers comes in. It introduces the theme of human uncertainty, and shows that the bodhisattva's decision to quest for buddhahood was a real and genuine and difficult one. Like all of us, he will struggle; he will make fallible decisions; he will choose teachers who cannot ultimately help him, and he will undertake practices that bear no fruit, before finding the right way.

Yet throughout it all, the Buddha is also, paradoxically perhaps, a buddha – an omniscient awakened one, absolutely certain about what he says, what

36 In the Pali tradition, Asita is called Kāḷadevala, or Kondañña (see Jayawickrama, 1990, pp. 72, 75). See also Malalasekera (1966), vol. 2, pp. 175–176. For a list of the eighty minor marks, see Buswell and Lopez (2014), pp. 1096–1098.

he does, where he has been, where he is going. He is a figure about whom there can be no doubts, and this is reflected and foretold in the certainty of Asita's prediction. As we look at the rest of the Buddha's lifestory, then, and consider other traditions about multiple buddhas, it may be good to keep in mind these three aspects of Śākyamuni: his royal sovereignty, his human limitations, and his buddhaic certainty.

2.7.2 *Life in the Palace*

(6–10) The Buddha's magnificence and specifically his royal connections come to the fore in the very next places visited by Aśoka and Upagupta. "In this place," Upagupta declares, "the bodhisattva was reared by Mahāprajāpatī; here he was taught how to write; and here he became a master of the arts appropriate to his lineage such as riding an elephant, a horse, or a chariot, handling a bow, grasping a javelin, and using an elephant hook. And this was the place where the bodhisattva trained. And over here, great king, surrounded by a hundred thousand deities, he pursued pleasure with sixty thousand women" (Strong, 1983, p. 247).

These sites/episodes can quickly be explicated. The Buddha's father, Śuddhodana, had (at least) two wives, the sisters Mahāmāyā and Mahāprajāpatī. Śākyamuni is brought up by his foster mother (who is also his aunt) Mahāprajāpatī, because his birth mother, Mahāmāyā, is said to have passed away seven days after his birth. This is part of the buddha-biographical blueprint which dictates that, by definition, the mothers of all buddhas pass away seven days after giving birth. The reasons for this are much debated, even within the tradition. He is said, for instance, in other traditions, to have been assigned as an infant multiple nurses to feed him, wash him, hold him, and play with him. As a youth, he enjoys three palaces built for him by his father, one for the hot season, one for the rainy season, and one for the cold season. In these he is surrounded by maids and slaves who meet his every need. His clothes are of the best Benares silk, and his meals are sumptuous. Within this perfect world, the bodhisattva is, moreover, the perfect prince. Thus, in some biographies, his accomplishments in the classroom as well as his training in the arts of the warrior appropriate to his lineage (in ancient India, kings were warriors) are magnified as being particularly glorious and superlative. For instance, in one text, when the still young bodhisattva arrives at his school on the first day of class, he asks his teacher which of the sixty-four scripts he is going to teach, and then proceeds to list them all. Rather than call him a "smarty-pants," the teacher is astounded at this display of erudition and declares that the bodhisattva knows more than he does! Likewise, in the same text, when the bodhisattva competes in an archery contest with his cousins, he not only beats them all, but he shoots an arrow that passes through all the targets they hit, and then buries itself in the ground with such force that it causes water to gush forth. This spring, later known as the "Well of the Arrow," remained a minor pilgrimage place in Kapilavastu.[37]

Another aspect of the householder's princely life in the palace is his enjoyment of the harem (of sixty thousand women!) that his father provides for him. Though able to resist their seductive ways, in one text he is also said to be able to fully satisfy them all; in other words, to use the title of a recent book about this aspect of his character, he is a "bull of a man" (Powers, 2009). The clothes, the food, the palaces, the women are all part of Śuddhodana's attempt to surround his son with worldly things so that he will remain willingly in the palace, inherit the throne, and become a great Śākyan cakravartin king. Curiously not mentioned in our text, but elsewhere part of this same scheme, is Śuddhodana's arranging for the bodhisattva to get married to the most beautiful woman in the realm, Yaśodharā, who eventually gives birth to a son, Rāhula. In this way Śuddhodana seeks to tie the bodhisattva down to family life, to fetter him in the household (indeed, one of the meanings of the name Rāhula is "fetter").[38]

It is sometimes stated that all these luxuries of courtly life, all these princely accomplishments are emphasized so as to show the magnitude of the bodhisattva's sacrifice – the greatness of what he gives up when he wanders forth from the palace. This may well be true but it should not blind us to the positive valuation of these things in the Buddhist tradition. The pleasures of royalty (and of divinity) are upheld as meritorious goals to be

---

37 On the reasons for the Buddha's mother's death, see Sasson (2007), pp. 148–151, and Ohnuma (2012), pp. 79–82. Mahāprajāpatī later plays an important role in the Buddhist tradition as the foundress of the order of nuns (see 6.3), which the Buddha agrees to in part out of a desire to repay the debt he owes her because of her nursing him (see Ohnuma, 2006). On the Buddha's childhood, see Sasson (2013). On his schooling, see Strong (2001), p. 59. The episode of the archery contest is from Bays (1983), p. 233. Xuanzang's account of the Well of the Arrow may be found in Li (1996), p. 179.

38 On the Buddha's wife, see Obeyesekere (2009), Ohnuma (2012), pp. 139–46, Strong (1997). Alternatively, in some traditions it is said that the Buddha has three wives. On Rāhula, see Crosby (2013).

sought after, if not in this life, then in the next. Riches and luxury may not be ultimately fulfilling, but they are rarely maligned (though attachment to them may be).

2.7.3 *The Beginnings of Discontent*

The bodhisattva's perfectly sheltered courtly life cannot last forever, however: after visiting the palace at Kapilavastu, Aśoka and Upagupta move on to see the places in the region where the bodhisattva first experiences an existential restlessness. This marks the start of a period of questioning that will last right up until his buddhahood.

(11–12) "In this place," declares Upagupta, "upset over the sight of an old man, a sick man and a corpse, the bodhisattva went out to the woods; and over here he sat down in the shade of a rose-apple (jambu) tree ... and attained the first level of meditative trance, a joyful and blissful state ... And when it was afternoon and ... the lengthening shadows of the trees slanted towards the east, the shadow of the jambu tree did not leave the body of the bodhisattva" (Strong, 1983, p. 247).

Our text has here fused together and abbreviated two episodes that are often kept distinct and made more elaborate. When they are, they are usually (but not always) presented in the reverse order, with the tale of the bodhisattva's first meditation under the rose-apple tree coming first, and the story of the three (or four) encounters with the old man, sick man, etc. coming later. In this more developed form, the first meditation under the rose-apple tree occurs when he is still an infant or a young boy, and it is occasioned by a different realization of suffering; the bodhisattva is taken along with his family to attend a festival marking the first ploughing of the fields in springtime. Sitting in the shade, he watches from a distance and observes the laboring oxen, the sweating men, and the insects and worms that are turned up by the ploughs and quickly eaten by the birds. In a later text, a whole chain of suffering is narrated: the worms exposed by the plough are snapped up by a frog, which is swallowed by a snake, which is eaten by a peacock, which is killed by a hawk, and so on. From this, the young bodhisattva realizes not only that life and death are interconnected, but that this festival which is supposed to be a pleasant, joyous occasion is actually filled with suffering. This causes him to fall (apparently involuntarily) into a reflective trance that is said to occasion a minor miracle: for the meditating bodhisattva, time stands still, as marked by the shadow of the rose-apple tree under which he is sitting that does not leave his body, while the shadows of all the other trees turn with the passing afternoon. This causes the bodhisattva's father to bow down in front of his son a second time, in recognition of his extraordinary nature.[39]

The episode under the rose-apple tree is a biographically significant one in that it will be referred to later in the Buddha's lifestory, at the time of his enlightenment. More specifically, it marks a double experience for the young bodhisattva: a first realization that there is suffering in the world, and a first realization that meditation may be a way of escaping from it. In this sense, it is an inkling of things yet to come.[40]

Much the same double-realization may be found in the full version of the story of the four encounters. It should be said that this well-known episode is generally thought to have been a relatively late addition to the Buddha's lifestory. According to this, while on a chariot ride to a pleasure park outside the city, the bodhisattva has his first realization of suffering; he meets (either on separate occasions or all at once) the three things referred to in our text: an old man, a sick man, and a corpse.[41] The story wants us to believe that the bodhisattva-prince's life has been so sheltered that this is the first time he has actually seen such things, for he asks his chariot driver: "What kind of man is this with white hair, supporting himself on a staff, his eyes veiled by his brows, his limbs drooped and bent?" (Johnston, 1936, p. 37). He is moved to learn that this is an "old man" and that all persons, himself included, will one day become like this. Much the same dialogue and realization are then repeated at the sight of the sick man and the dead man, and all this distresses the bodhisattva very much. He has come to realize the inevitability and universality of three things – old age, sickness, and death – which will later be encapsulated into his definition of the first Noble Truth of "suffering" (duḥkha). All is not lost, however, because the bodhisattva then encounters (though not in every version of the story) a fourth sign – the sight of a wandering holy man, a mendicant who seems to be at ease with the world and himself, a sight which gives the bodhisattva hope and inspires him to believe

39 On this episode in general, see Strong (2001), pp. 61–62; for a discussion, see Durt (1982) [in French].

40 For retrospective references to the meditation under the Jambu tree, see Anālayo (2011a), vol. 1, pp. 240–241.

41 In some versions of the story, these visions are placed there by the gods who thereby thwart Śuddhodana's order to have the road to the park cleared ahead of time of all such sights, as part of his efforts to shelter his son.

that there is a way out of suffering, or at least a way towards understanding its nature.[42]

2.7.4 *The Great Departure*

(13) Either separately or together, episodes 11 and 12 serve to inspire the bodhisattva to leave home and quest for enlightenment. Accordingly, the very next pilgrimage site visited by Aśoka and Upagupta is the following: "through this gateway over here, great king, the bodhisattva left Kapilavastu at midnight, surrounded by a hundred thousand deities" (Strong, 1983, p. 247).

This "Great Departure," as it is sometimes called, marks the crucial moment in the bodhisattva's life when he "wanders forth" – when he abandons the life of a householder for one of homelessness. Interestingly, no mention is made in our text of an experience often featured in other sources as the immediate reason for the bodhisattva's leaving: his disgust at the sight of the dancing girls of his harem who, having failed to distract him, have fallen asleep and lie, disheveled, drooling, and denuded, snoring with limbs akimbo. The sight reminds him of a vision of a cremation ground and revolts him very much.[43] Nor is any mention made of his final visit to his wife Yaśodharā and his son Rāhula, who are asleep together in an inner chamber, and whom he decides not to wake, lest they deter him from his determination to leave. Nor is any mention made of his visit to his father Śuddhodana, thinking that it would be unfilial for him not to say goodbye. In one text, Śuddhodana urges him to change his mind, but the bodhisattva tells him he will do so only if his father can guarantee him a life without old age, sickness, misfortune, and death, which, of course, his father cannot do. In another text, his father is sleeping soundly, and rather than wake him, the bodhisattva circumambulates his bed and says: "Father, I am not leaving out of lack of respect ... but for no other reason than that I wish to liberate the world ... from the fear of suffering that comes with old age and death" (Strong, 2001, p. 72).

Instead, here, the bodhisattva merely asks his servant, Chandaka (a.k.a. Chanda), to saddle his horse, and, together with him, he leaves by the city gate in the middle of the night. To be sure, in other versions of the tale, he is

42 On the relative lateness of this episode, see Anālayo (2011a), vol. 1, p. 172. For other versions of this episode, see Jones (1949–1956), vol. 2, pp. 145–151, and Beal (1875), pp. 115–123. See also Strong (2001), pp. 62–63.

43 This episode, it is generally agreed, was a relatively late addition to the Buddha's biography.

surrounded by thousands of divinities, and, in some cases, he flies through the air over the city walls, but from now on the royal splendor of the palace will be left behind, and the very human aspect of striving for enlightenment will commence.[44]

(14) This is perhaps highlighted in the very next episode: "over here," Upagupta declares, apparently when they have gone some distance from the city, "he sent his horse and his ornaments back with [his attendant] Chandaka ... and all by himself, without an attendant, heroic, he entered the forest of asceticism." In order to signal his new status, he further gives up his expensive clothes: (15) "in this place over here," Upagupta goes on, "he gave his clothes of Benares silk to a hunter in exchange for a yellow robe, and began his ascetic practice" (Strong, 1983, pp. 247–248).

No mention is made here of another episode that is usually said to occur near this point: using his own sword, the bodhisattva cuts off his hair (or at least his topknot). It may be that our text has boxed itself into a corner by sending Chandaka and the horse and ornaments home early before the acquisition of the robes, since the bodhisattva's sword would have gone back to Kapilavastu with the rest of his lay royal accoutrements, leaving him nothing with which to cut his hair. The painful alternative (pulling out his hair by hand) would not be possible for the Buddha since that is identified as a practice of Jain monks – one of the reasons, perhaps, that one of the allowed possessions for Buddhist monks is a razor.

These two acts – putting on a yellow robe and cutting one's hair – coupled with the act of leaving home are, of course, major features of the Buddhist ritual of ordination. It is by doing these things that one becomes a monk (or a nun). To this day, at least in South and Southeast Asia, Buddhists interested in the monastic life consciously imitate the events of the bodhisattva's Great Departure (see 11.2.2). They dress up in princely garb, bedeck themselves with ornaments, and proceed (often on horseback) from their home to the monastery, only to divest themselves of their finery and have their heads shaved prior to donning the yellow robes.[45]

In some versions of the story of the Great Departure, the bodhisattva's monastic robes are provided not by a hunter, but by a deity who comes down in disguise and who then takes his old robes back up to heaven where they

44 For these and other embellishments of the story of the Great Departure, see also Jones (1949–1956), vol. 2, pp. 141–144, Bays (1983), pp. 303–334, and Jayawickrama (1990), pp. 82–87. For a full presentation of early sources, see Bareau (1974), pp. 245–260 [in French].

45 For the connection to the ordination ritual, see Strong (2001), p. 13.

are enshrined in a stūpa as relics. Similarly, in these sources, the Buddha's hair (his topknot) is taken up to Indra's heaven where it is preserved to be worshiped by the gods.[46] No mention of any of this at all is made by Upagupta in our text. Instead, we seem to have reached the point in the lifestory that Alfred Foucher calls "the dismissal of the gods." "Siddhārtha," he proclaims, "was no more; he had been replaced by Gautama the Ascetic. And as such he found himself in an indifferent world, without guidance or support, confronted with both the noble task of seeking mankind's salvation and the lowly but pressing one of securing his daily bread; for before philosophy comes living" (Foucher, 1963, p. 90).

(16) The gods, moreover, are not the only ones whose help is dispensed with. Soon, the bodhisattva also rejects royal help, in the form of his refusal of King Bimbisāra's offer to share his sovereignty. The event is alluded to by Upagupta in his next declaration that "here King Bimbisāra offered him half of his kingdom" (Strong, 1983, p. 248). The episode is elsewhere said to have taken place in Rājagṛha, the capital of Magadha. King Bimbisāra, seeing him from a distance, is tremendously impressed by his demeanor and invites him to receive untold wealth and power. But the bodhisattva is not tempted. Having abandoned his family and possible career as a cakravartin monarch, he is not interested, and having dismissed the gods, he now dismisses the king, though he promises to come back once he has attained enlightenment.

2.7.5 *Paths Not Taken*

(17–18) The bodhisattva does not immediately reject, however, the help of various spiritual teachers. It was customary for renunciants leaving home in ancient India to seek out, at least at first, a spiritual master – a guru – who could help them with their quest. Therefore, according to our text, the bodhisattva was next received "at the hermitage of Bhārgava," or alternatively, of a potter ("bhārgava" means "potter"). This is a very obscure reference. A few texts indicate that the bodhisattva sought out other teachers before studying under Ārāḍa, and Bhārgava may have been one of them.[47]

Far better known are the next two teachers: "Here," states Upagupta, "he met the sages Ārāḍa and Udraka ... and in the forest ... studied and practiced

46 Strong (2004), pp. 66–67.

47 See Anālayo (2011a), vol. 1, p. 175, and Pruitt (1998), p. 4, where it is stated that, at this point, the bodhisattva "went to Bhaggava's [= Bhārgava's] park and grasped his doctrine."

austerities under them" (Strong, 1983, p. 248). In other sources, Śākyamuni commonly meets these two sages one after another (in the town of Vaiśālī), but here they are lumped together. In fact, his studies under them follow a very similar pattern: he masters everything they have to teach him, but that is not enough to fulfill his quest to comprehend and put an end to suffering; he still feels he has not reached enlightenment. Ārāḍa is said by some to have been a teacher of Sāṃkhya dualism, and Udraka a master of yoga. What the bodhisattva learns from them, however, is not a doctrine but a meditation technique that enables him to achieve high levels of trance: the trance of no-thingness, under Ārāḍa, and the even higher trance of neither-perception-nor-non-perception under Udraka. In such states of mind, the meditator has quite removed him- or herself not only from the sensory world but from the ordinary mental world as well. But neither of these trances, though they will be incorporated into some Buddhist meditational practices, is equivalent to nirvāṇa. Neither of them resolves definitively the fundamental questions of old age, sickness, and death, and so the bodhisattva, dissatisfied with these practices, leaves Ārāḍa and Udraka and moves on.[48]

(19) Having pursued one (or two) wrong path(s) (the teachings of Ārāḍa and Udraka), the bodhisattva then embarks on another: the practice of extreme asceticism. Upagupta leads Aśoka to their next stop, the place "where for six long years, the bodhisattva undertook fierce austerities, and then gave them up realizing that this too was not the way to highest knowledge" (Strong, 1983, p. 248).

In canonical texts, these practices are described as comprising two things: extreme breath-retention (a practice in some forms of yoga), and extreme fasting (a practice associated with Jainism). The bodhisattva undertakes both of them, to the point of pain and utter emaciation. In one famous account, he describes his limbs as being "like the joints of withered creepers, his buttock as being like a bullock's hoof, his backbone like a string of balls, his ribs like the crazy rafters of a tumble-down shed, his scalp shriveled and shrunk like a bitter white gourd" (Horner, 1954–1959, vol. 1, p. 300, slightly altered). Nothing but skin and bones, at the end of six years of striving he is left so weak he can no longer even think, let alone meditate. He collapses in a faint and a rumor spreads that he is dead. Hearing the rumor, his mother Queen Māyā (according to one later tradition) comes down from the heaven where

48 For reference to sources on this episode and on the trances, see Anālayo (2011a), vol. 1, pp. 174–177. Wynne (2007), pp. 9–26, has argued for the historical reality of Ārāḍa and Udraka, as has Zafiropoulo (1993), pp. 22–23.

she has been reborn, and, seeing the prone body of her son on the ground, begins to lament:

> When you were born in the garden called Lumbinī, O my son, like a lion you took seven steps forward all by yourself, and after gazing in the four directions, you pronounced these beautiful words: "This is my last birth." Now these words will go unfulfilled. When Asita declared: "He will be a Buddha in this world," his prophecy proved false ... Nor have you tasted the splendor which delights the heart of cakravartin kings. O my son, without obtaining supreme Enlightenment, you have gone to your death in the forest!
>
> (Bays, 1983, p. 385)[49]

(20) This is enough to rouse the bodhisattva from his stupor and to renew his determination. Realizing that the way of extreme asceticism is the wrong path, he decides to resume eating: "In this place," Upagupta tells Aśoka, "Nandā and Nandabalā, the daughters of a village headman, offered the bodhisattva sweetened milk-rice ... and after enjoying it, he set out for the seat of enlightenment" (Strong, 1983, p. 248).

In the Pali tradition, Nandā and Nandabalā are replaced by a woman named Sujātā. In any case, this decision to start eating again is traditionally said to mark the final turning point in the bodhisattva's quest: it signals the start of the middle path, between the extremes of indulgence (life in the palace) and intense asceticism. In some texts, this decision is coupled with an account of the bodhisattva recollecting the meditative state he achieved as a boy, while sitting under the rose-apple tree watching his father's ploughing ceremony (see above). "That," he recalls, "was a state that was free from sensual desires, free from sinful and demeritorious things, thoughtful, reflective, arising from discrimination and blissful. That must be the way, that must be the path that will lead to knowledge, seeing, and unsurpassed total enlightenment" (Strong, 1995, p. 16).[50]

With this in mind, he sets out for another tree – the Bodhi tree or tree of Awakening at Bodhgaya – under which he will renew his meditative

49 The Buddha's extreme austerities became a famous theme in art (see Bautze-Picron, 2008). For a canonical account of the near-death of the bodhisattva, see Ñāṇamoli and Bodhi (1995), pp. 332–343.

50 For one account of the offering of milk-rice, see Jones (1949–1956), vol. 2, pp. 195–197. For a discussion, see Strong (2001), pp. 88–92. For a much later different elaboration, see Lewis and Tuladhar (2010), pp. 173–176.

endeavors. Various signs immediately indicate that this time he is on the right path and will be successful. According to one tradition, having finished eating the milk-rice, he takes the bowl in which it was brought to him, and sets it in the river, resolving that it should float upstream if he is to succeed in becoming a buddha. Miraculously, it does. It goes upriver for a bit and then sinks down to the bottom where it comes to rest on the bowls of the three previous buddhas of this aeon, who had all consumed milk-rice at exactly the same spot. Hearing the sound the bowl makes as it lands on the others, the nāga king, Kāla, who has dwelt in this river for a whole aeon, realizes that the time has come for another buddha to appear in the world.[51]

(21) In our text, this affirming episode seems to be replaced by another. Upagupta takes Aśoka to a place on the road to Bodhgaya where "the bodhisattva, on his way to the Bodhi tree, was praised by the nāga king Kālika" (Strong, 1983, p. 249). Upagupta then summons the nāga in person and asks him to describe the splendor of the Tathāgata as he processed towards the place of his enlightenment, which Kālika proceeds to do:

> Beneath his feet, the whole earth
> and its mountain ranges trembled
> in six different ways.
> The Sugata [= Buddha] shone on the world of men
> like a beautiful never-waning moon
> surpassing the sun in splendor.
>
> (Strong, 1983, pp. 247–248)

2.7.6 *Awakening*

(22) With this assurance in mind, our pilgrims finally reach Bodhgaya. "Then the elder Upagupta led King Aśoka to the foot of the Bodhi tree, stretched out his right hand and said: 'In this place, great king, the bodhisattva first defeated the forces of Māra with the power of his loving kindness, and then completely realized total unsurpassed enlightenment'" (Strong, 1983, p. 250).

Bodhgaya (in Bihar province in Northern India) remains to this day a most important site of pilgrimage and is visited by Buddhists from all over the world. In our text it is not called Bodhgaya, which is a later appellation, probably intended to distinguish it from the Hindu pilgrimage site of Gaya

51 Jayawickrama (1990), p. 93.

nearby. The place, however, is very ancient in Buddhist history and mythology. In fact, it is said to mark the spot not only of Śākyamuni's enlightenment, but of that of all past buddhas as well.[52]

It is possible to divide the Buddha's experience there into two parts: his defeat of Māra, and his actual attainment of nirvāṇa, referred to in our text as "total unsurpassed complete awakening" (anuttara samyaksaṃbodhi). Māra is often thought of as a demonic figure, the Buddhist equivalent of Satan, but this is misleading. He is actually a high-ranking god, one of the chief divinities of the realm of desire and so a lord of death and rebirth. He is, by nature, opposed to any attempt by anyone to escape from his realm; hence he tries to block the bodhisattva from attaining buddhahood. In a variety of texts, he is portrayed as trying to do this in several ways. First, there is armed attack: Māra gathers his minions, his legions of demons and beasts and monsters, and tries to scare off the Buddha, but the latter counters all this vehemence by directing towards it overpowering waves of loving kindness. Second, Māra uses his daughters, named Pleasure, Restlessness, and Desire, to try to sexually seduce the bodhisattva as he meditates, but the bodhisattva remains unmoved. Third, Māra tries to assert that the seat of enlightenment rightfully belongs to him, that his merit as a high god is superior to that of the bodhisattva, but the latter reaches down and touches the earth, calling it to bear witness to his own countless merits. The Earth, portrayed as a goddess, responds by causing a great flood that washes away all the forces of Māra (see figure 2.1). It is from this story that the defeat of Māra came to be epitomized in art by images depicting the buddha in the "earth-touching gesture." In all of these episodes, Śākyamuni's epithet "lord of lords," given to the bodhisattva by his father at birth, clearly comes to the fore. But the moment is also crucial soteriologically for the bodhisattva: in Māra, death and desire have been defeated, and the way is cleared for definitive, total enlightenment – nirvāṇa, buddhahood.[53]

Following such a cosmic scenario, the actual attainment of buddhahood seems a bit sedate. Generally speaking, it is divided into a succession of three "knowledges" (triveda) attained in the three watches of the night. The first is the Buddha's knowledge of all of his previous births, of the whole of his karmic history, which he passes in review; the second is his knowledge of the transmigrations of all other beings as they die in one life and are reborn

52 On the importance of Bodhgaya, see Leoshko (1988).

53 On the figure of Māra and his other forms in South and East Asia, see Strong (2005a), and the sources referred to there. The iconography of the Earth Goddess became especially important in Southeast Asia (see Likhitpreechakul, 2011; Guthrie, 2004).

2.1 *The Defeat of Māra (Mural at Wat Doi Suthep, Northern Thailand)*

in another; the third is the knowledge of the āśravas, the negative inclinations that attach a person to this world. More specifically, these are defined as sensual desire (kāma), clinging to existence (bhāva), speculative views (dṛṣṭi), and ignorance (avidyā). Definitively liberated from all of these, the bodhisattva has at last become an awakened one, a buddha. He has put an end to suffering and escaped from the round of rebirth and redeath. In other versions, in the third watch, the Buddha attains knowledge of the Four Truths (see chapter 5) and/or of dependent origination (pratītyasamutpāda) (see 5.2).[54]

2.7.7 *After Enlightenment*

In most traditional accounts, the newly awakened Buddha stays in the vicinity of Bodhgaya for the next seven weeks. At the end of this time, a crucially important event takes place: the Buddha decides to remain in this world and preach the Dharma, convinced by the god Brahmā that there are some who will understand his message. In other words, he decides not to be a pratyekabuddha who, it will be remembered, enjoys awakening for himself alone and refrains from preaching to anyone. Śākyamuni contemplates the

54 For a fuller presentation of the Buddha's Awakening at Bodhgaya, see Strong (2001), pp. 92–100.

question of whom he should preach to first. He initially thinks of his former teachers, Ārāḍa and Udraka, but realizes that they have both passed away. He then decides to preach to his former five companions with whom he had practiced extreme austerities and who are now living in the Deer Park of Sarnath, outside Benares. Accordingly, he sets out to find them.[55]

(23–24) On the way, several events occur and the sites where they take place are duly noted by Upagupta. The first two go together: "In this place, great king, the Blessed One received from the celestial guardians of the four quarters four stone begging bowls which he joined into a single bowl. And over here, the merchants Trapuṣa and Bhallika made him an offering of alms food" (Strong, 1983, p. 250).

It is worth noting that this is the first time that our text refers to Śākyamuni as "the Blessed One" (Bhagavan). This is because that epithet is generally reserved for a buddha and this is the first episode that takes place after his enlightenment, after his attainment of buddhahood. It is as the Buddha, then, that he encounters the two merchants, Trapuṣa and Bhallika, and they, perceiving him to be someone special, resolve to make him an offering (of food). They thereby become established as the very first lay disciples of Śākyamuni.[56]

Before they can make their food offering, however, the Buddha needs a bowl, in part because buddhas (and by extension, Buddhist monastics), by definition, do not beg or receive offerings with their bare hands. This is another of the things that distinguishes them from Jains who do. The need for a bowl, then, is what occasions the first episode mentioned above. The Buddha is now a buddha and the time of the "dismissal of the gods" has passed. Responding to his wants, the guardian gods of the four quarters draw near and each offers him a bowl. Not wanting to offend any of them, the Buddha accepts them all and fuses them into a single bowl, using his supernatural powers to squeeze them together. This little story is cited to account for a traditional feature of Buddhist begging bowls: they have incised, just below their rims, three more concentric rings – traces of the original four bowls. At the same time, the story has a greater cosmic significance. At the end of each Buddha-age, it is said, the Buddha's bowl will divide into its original four bowls and return into the possession of the four guardian deities of the four quarters, where they will remain until it is time for those gods to present them, once more, to the next buddha who

55 Strong (2001), pp. 101–107.

56 For one version of the story of the two merchants, see Strong (2008), pp. 56–58.

will again squeeze them together to make a single bowl. Thus, just as all buddhas are enlightened at the same spot in Bodhgaya, all buddhas may be said to use the same bowl.[57]

(25) There is another event that occurs as the Buddha is traveling in this first post-enlightenment journey. It is referred to by Upagupta when he points out "the place where the Blessed One, on his way to Benares, was praised by the ājīvika Upaga" (Strong, 1983, p. 250). The story of Upaga (a.k.a. Upaka), in brief, is this: seeing the Buddha coming along the road, he asks him who his teacher is – a normal inquiry for one renunciant to make to another. The Buddha answers that he has no master, that he attained enlightenment on his own, and that he is, moreover, a Jina, a Victorious One. This is said to disturb Upaga who says "if you say so ..." or something to that effect and departs by another way. This story is sometimes read (by me!) as the Buddha's failure to convert the first person he meets, by means of his sheer charisma, but it should be realized that Upaga is an Ājīvika – a member of a fatalist school of renunciants who were in competition, so to speak, with the early Buddhists (see 4.2.2). It may be that, having just distinguished himself from the Jains by insisting on having a begging bowl, the Buddha is here distinguishing himself from the Ājīvikas by showing them to be intransigents refusing a wonderful opportunity to become Buddhists. In this regard, the Buddha's calling himself a Jina is interesting; it has been pointed out that this was a title used more often in Jainism than in Buddhism, but it was also prominently used by the Ājīvikas for their own teacher, Makkhali Gosala, hence perhaps further contributing to Upaga's confusion.[58]

2.7.8 The First Sermon

(26) At last, the Buddha arrives at the Deer Park in Sarnath, near Benares. Upagupta describes the site as follows: "In this place, great king, the Blessed One set in motion the holy Wheel of the Dharma which ... teaches the Four Noble Truths" (Strong, 1983, p. 250). The Deer Park, today, is an important pilgrimage site. In the Buddha's time, it was a gathering ground for ascetics and sages – indeed, it is known as Ṛṣipatana, the place "where the seers alight." There the Buddha seeks out his five companions, with whom he had

57 On the legend of the Buddha's recycled bowl, see Strong (2004), pp. 211–226.

58 On Upaga, see Anālayo (2011a), vol. 1, pp. 183–184. On the Ājīvikas' use of the title Jina, see Basham (1951), p. 79.

2.2 *The First Sermon (Mural at Wat Doi Suthep, Northern Thailand)*

formerly practiced austerities, and it is to them that he proclaims the good news that he has achieved nirvāṇa and it is to them that he preaches his First Sermon (see figure 2.2).[59]

This is the famous *Discourse on the Setting in Motion of the Wheel of the Dharma* (*Dharmacakrapravatana Sūtra*), in which the Buddha first clarifies that his teaching is that of the middle way between hedonistic attachment to the things of this world and ascetic renunciation of them. Then he proceeds to describe the Four Truths. The first of these is that life, in all realms of rebirth, is ultimately unsatisfactory or stressful (duḥkha), in part because it involves sufferings such as old age, sickness, and death, and in part because it is characterized by impermanence, so any lasting satisfaction is impossible. The second is that there is a reason for this suffering, an origin (samudaya) that is bound up with desire, with the "thirst" (tṛṣṇa) that stems from ignorance of impermanence, and leads us to cling to possessions, to persons, to life itself. Third, there is nonetheless such a thing as freedom from or cessation (nirodha) of this unsatisfactory situation that will come with the rooting out of its causes, the eradication of ignorance and desire. Finally, there is a way to do this – the middle way mentioned above – which is also

59 For one story of the prehistory of Ṛṣipatana and the reason for its name, see Lessing and Wayman (1978), p. 41.

specified as the Noble Eightfold Path combining wisdom, ethical conduct, and meditation.[60]

We shall return to the middle way and the Four Truths in chapters 4 and 5 below, and analyse them thoroughly there. For now, suffice it to say that their exposition is successful; at the conclusion of his sermon, it is said that the eldest of the five disciples of the Buddha, Kauṇḍinya, perceives the truth of the Buddha's words, and the Buddha immediately ordains him as a monk, by uttering the simple formula, "Come, monk, the Dharma is well proclaimed. Follow the chaste course to complete termination of suffering" (Robinson, Johnson, and Thanissaro, 2005, p. 26). Eventually, the four other members of the group of five also come to understand and to be ordained as monks. The First Sermon thus leads directly to the first formation of the Buddhist community, the samgha.

2.7.9 *Various Conversions and Miracles*

The First Sermon is followed by countless others. Over the course of the next forty-five years, up until his death, the Buddha was to continue preaching and spreading his Dharma, and the community of his followers was to continue to grow and become gradually more institutionally organized (see chapter 6).

Upagupta, acting as guide, leads Aśoka in rapid succession to a series of other sites where, at various points in his career, the Buddha converted various beings, either by means of miracle-displays and/or by preaching to them.

(27–29) The first stops are back in Magadha, the region where the Buddha attained awakening. There, he points out three places: "Over here, great king, the Blessed One initiated a thousand matted-haired ascetics into the religious life. And in this place, he taught the Dharma to King Bimbisāra, and the king along with ... several thousand Magadhan brahmin householders perceived the Noble Truths. And in this place, he taught the Dharma to Śakra, king of the gods, and Śakra, along with eighty-four thousand other deities, perceived the Truths" (Strong, 1983, p. 251).

The matted-haired ascetics (jaṭila) are brahmins who, though they lead ascetic lives in a hermitage, still maintain the sacrificial fires, and so are colloquially known as "fire-worshipers." These particular ones are the disciples of Uruvilvā Kāśyapa, who is elsewhere described as being 120 years old, and

60 For translations of two versions of the First Sermon in the context of his lifestory, see Jones (1949–1956), vol. 3, pp. 322–327, and Horner (1938–1952), vol. 4, pp. 15–17.

a venerable teacher who was "honored, esteemed, revered, respected and celebrated ... by the people of Magadha" (Kloppenborg, 1973, p. 50). Rather than start by preaching to him, the Buddha decides first to demonstrate his superior mastery of supernatural powers so as to overcome his arrogance. Especially emphasized is the Buddha's mastery over the element of fire, which is so crucial to his opponent's brahmanical practices. Uruvilvā Kāśyapa is no pushover; it is said to take the Buddha three and a half thousand miracles before he finally wins him over, but, at long last, he and his followers give up their dedication to the performance of fire sacrifices and, requesting ordination, they cut off their matted locks which they throw into the river. Only then does the Buddha preach to them. Appropriately, he chooses to talk to them about "fire." "Everything," he says, "is burning ... The eye is burning ... the ear, the nose, the tongue, the body, and the mind are burning ... With what are they burning? With the fire of passion, with the fire of hatred, with the fire of delusion. They are burning because of birth, old age, disease, death ... They are burning because of suffering" (Strong, 2001, p. 118). At the conclusion of the sermon, all the former fire-worshipers are enlightened.

News quickly spreads throughout Magadha that the Buddha and Uruvilvā Kāśyapa have joined forces; there is still some confusion, however, about who has become the disciple of whom. To resolve the issue, Bimbisāra, the king of Magadha, invites everyone – Buddhists and Kāśyapa-followers, and all the people of his kingdom – to come to the royal court, and there Uruvilvā Kāśyapa makes it clear, in no uncertain terms, that he has become a Buddhist, that the Buddha is his master. The people of Magadha are duly impressed and the Buddha is not slow in taking advantage of his newfound prestige. He uses the occasion to preach the Dharma to Bimbisāra and the assembled Magadhan brahmin householders. They quickly take refuge and become lay disciples of the Buddha, and Bimbisāra publicly signals his conversion by offering to the Buddha his own pleasure park, the Veṇuvana or "bamboo-grove," which becomes the first permanent monastic park (ārāma) of the Buddha (see 6.2.2).

Thus far, in Magadha, Upagupta has shown Aśoka places where the Buddha has converted brahmanical ascetics (the jaṭilas), a king (Bimbisāra), and brahmin householders. The next site concerns divinities. Śakra is the common Buddhist name for Indra, one of the chief gods of the Vedic pantheon. His appearance as a kind of *deus ex machina* in support of Buddhism is quite common in Buddhist texts. Here, however, we have reference to the story of his conversion. The place where this occurs is a cavern called "Indra's rock-cave" (Indraśailagūha) in the hills east of Rājagṛha.[61] The place was still inhabited when Faxian visited it in the early fifth century. According to tradition, it was here that Indra came down from heaven to visit Śākyamuni and asked him a series of questions about the Dharma. Impressed and convinced by his answers, Indra was awakened to the truth of the Dharma, along with eighty thousand other deities.[62]

(30–31) From Magadha, where these various conversions take place, Upagupta leads Aśoka back west to Śrāvastī and Saṃkāśya, two sites associated with a well-known sequence of stories: "In this place, great king, the Blessed One performed a great miracle. And over here, surrounded by a host of gods, he descended from the Trayastriṃśa Heaven after spending a rains retreat there teaching the Dharma to his mother" (Strong, 1983, p. 251).

The "Great Miracle" (mahāprātihārya) refers to the "Great Miracle at Śrāvastī," in which the Buddha puts on various displays of supernatural powers, in order to win over King Prasenajit of Kosala, to impress the crowd of thousands who have assembled from all over India for the occasion, and to defeat six non-Buddhist heretical masters. The net effect of the event seems to be to emphasize the greatness and superiority of the Buddha over ordinary human beings, over non-Buddhists, and over his disciples. Textual descriptions and artistic depictions of the Śrāvastī miracles vary, but they include such things as the Buddha's ability (while levitating) to emit streams of water and jets of flame from his body simultaneously; his ability to illuminate and adorn the entire universe and make everyone in it connected to himself and to each other; and/or his ability to project multiple images of himself (indeed to fill the sky with them) that are capable of operating independently. The latter miracle is important for understanding the development of conceptions of the Buddha since it shows that images of the Buddha (see 3.4) are just as "alive" and capable of action as the original.[63]

After performing the Great Miracle at Śrāvastī, the Buddha travels up to the Heaven of the Thirty-Three Gods (Trayastriṃśa) where his mother,

---

61 In Pali the place is "Indra's sal tree cave" (Indasālaguhā) after the sal tree planted at its entrance.

62 Davids (1899–1924), vol. 2, pp. 299–321. For Faxian's visit to the site, see Legge (1886), pp. 80–81.

63 For two accounts of the Great Miracle at Śrāvastī, see Rotman (2008), pp. 253–288, and Burlingame (1921), vol. 3, pp. 35–47. On the art historical record, see Rhi (1991), Foucher (1917a), and Brown (1984). On miracles in Buddhism in general, see Fiordalis (2008).

Māyā, has been reborn as a god (it will be remembered that Māyā passed away seven days after the Buddha's birth). The episode is, in part, motivated by questions of filial piety: the Buddha repays the debt that he owes to the one who gave birth to him, by preaching the Dharma to her in her new life in heaven and bringing her (and other gods in that heaven) to the first stage of enlightenment.[64]

Upagupta and Aśoka do not visit the site (in heaven) where this took place (theirs is purely a pilgrimage to "this-worldly" places), but they do go to the city of Saṃkāśya where the Buddha came back down from Trayastriṃśa Heaven when he was done preaching to his mother. According to a tradition much represented in Buddhist art, this "descent" occurred on a great "triple ladder," with the Buddha coming down the central flight of steps flanked on either side by the gods Indra and Brahmā, and hosts of other deities. It is said to be a great moment when the links between heaven and earth are opened up, and the people gathered in Saṃkāśya to welcome back the Buddha are able to see the gods, and the gods are able to see the people, face to face. The event also has important ritual connections; to this day, it is reenacted in great festivals at the end of the three-month "rains-retreat" during which monks are supposed to stop their wanderings and be cloistered in their monasteries. It marks thus not only a change of season, but a welcoming back of the Buddha, and reassertion of his presence (or that of his monks) in this world.[65]

2.7.10 *Death and Parinirvāṇa*

Finally, from Saṃkāśya, Upagupta leads Aśoka back east to Kuśinagarī (a.k.a. Kusinara), the last stop on their tour. "In this place," he declares, "the Blessed One, having finished doing the work of a Buddha, entered the state of complete nirvāṇa without any remaining attributes ... The great, wise, most compassionate Sage converted everyone to the eternal Dharma and Vinaya – gods, men, asuras, yakṣas, and nāgas. Then he went to rest, his mind at ease, because there was no one left for him to convert" (Strong, 1983, p. 251) (see figure 2.3).

The full tale of the Buddha's death and final nirvāṇa, including his funeral

64 On the Buddha's sermon in heaven, see Anālayo (2012). For a discussion of the contents of the Buddha's sermon to his mother, see Skilling (2008).

65 On the descent from Trayastriṃśa, see Strong (2010; 2012a).

2.3 *The Parinirvāṇa (Mural at Wat Doi Suthep, Northern Thailand)*

rites, is recounted in the *Discourse on the Great Extinction* (*Mahāparinirvāṇa Sūtra*) and cannot be gone into here.[66] Basically, it tells the story of the final journey the Buddha (now aged eighty) makes, together with his disciple Ānanda, as they gradually make their way to Kuśinagarī. Along the way, the Buddha stops to deliver sermons to various communities, gives last-minute instructions on various topics, and has a number of encounters with Māra. As he proceeds, it is clear that the Buddha is getting physically weaker. As he puts it, he has reached the term of his life and feels like a broken-down cart, held together with straps. At one point, he gets very ill with dysentery, but overcomes his illness by sheer willpower. Even so, he is still the Buddha. In an episode that exists in only one version of the story, even in his feeble condition, when he comes across a huge boulder blocking the road, he is able to use his superpowers to pick it up and set it aside. In time, he arrives at the house of Cuṇḍa, the blacksmith, and there he is served a meal featuring "pig's delight" (sūkaramaddava), the nature of which has plagued Buddhist and non-Buddhist scholars through the ages.

66 For a fuller summary of the *Mahāparinirvāṇa Sūtra*, see Strong (2001), pp. 163–193. For translation of one version, see Walshe (1987), pp. 231–277. For translations and discussions of other versions, see Bareau (1970–1971) [in French]. This sūtra should not be confused with the *[Mahāyāna] Mahāparinirvāṇa Sūtra* which is quite a different text.

In any case, after the meal, he suffers a recurrence of the bloody diarrhea that had plagued him earlier.[67]

Still, he struggles on, and finally lays down on his right side at Kuśinagarī, between the two śala trees, and there, surrounded by his disciples, he utters his last words: "all conditioned things are of a nature to decay – strive on untiringly" (Walshe, 1987, p. 270).[68] He then passes away into parinirvāṇa.

Suffice it to say that the event marks a key moment in the lifestory of the Buddha and in the development of Buddhist religious sentiments. The Buddha's parinirvāṇa is called "nirvāṇa without any attributes remaining," or, more technically, "nirvāṇa without any mind-body substratum remaining." This is to distinguish it from the Buddha's earlier awakening at Bodhgaya, which is called his "nirvāṇa with a mind-body substratum remaining." What this means is that, with his parinirvāṇa, the Buddha's karmic stream which led him to be reborn again and again in different mind-bodies throughout the aeons has now come to an end. Realizing this, we are told, Aśoka faints with emotion and has to be revived by his ministers.[69]

Aśoka's reaction is noteworthy, for it shows the intensity of feeling at the loss – at the present absence – of the Buddha. Simply put, Buddhists today are living in a Buddha-less age; having been present in the world first as a bodhisattva, and then as a buddha – an enlightened one – Śākyamuni will now no longer be present, at least not in the same way. This, I would suggest, caused some major problems for the Buddhist religion, which it sought to overcome in a variety of ways that we will examine in chapter 3.

67 On the episode of his removing the rock, see Zin (2006), pp. 340–358. On "pig's delight," see the discussion in Strong (2001), pp. 175–177. Various theories may be found in Waley (1931–1932) and Wasson (1982). More generally on the Buddha's final illness, see Strong (2012). For one theory of the actual nature of the Buddha's illness by a monk who is also an M.D., see Mettanando and Von Hinüber (2000).

68 For alternative versions of his last words, see Strong (2001), p. 183.

69 On the Buddha's funeral and death, see Strong (2007).

Chapter 3

Overcoming the Buddha's Absence

One possible interpretation of the Buddha's death and parinirvāṇa is that the Buddha is no more. He has totally put an end to death and rebirth in saṃsāra, and so is not available to respond to the queries, petitions, and praise of devotees. It is not that he has gone elsewhere; he is everywhere absent, existing neither on earth nor in some kind of heaven nor in some kind of transcendent state. Logically, this is sometimes expressed in terms of a quadruple negation. As the Buddhist philosopher Nāgārjuna was to put it: after his parinirvāṇa, the Buddha can "neither be said to be existent, nor be said to be nonexistent, nor both [existent and nonexistent], nor neither [existent nor nonexistent]" (Garfield, 1995, p. 75). Be this as it may, Buddhism is a religion, and, as we shall see in this chapter, Buddhists found a number of ways to affirm the ongoing presence of the Buddha in their lives, despite his parinirvāṇa.

Some of these ways are said to have been prepared by the Buddha himself who, on his deathbed, is portrayed as having had a series of conversations with his disciple Ānanda about what should be done after he passed away. In three of these, he touched on ways that his disciples can still encounter him after his death: (1) by following his teachings, his Dharma; (2) by going on pilgrimage to places associated with his life; and (3) by honoring his physical remains, i.e. his relics. In the next three sections of this chapter, I shall examine these three factors. Then I want to turn to some other ways Buddhists have sought to solve the issue of the Śākyamuni's absence after his parinirvāṇa: (4) by making and venerating images of him; by honoring or revering members of his saṃgha as his successor-substitutes, such as (5) the Masters of the Dharma or (6) the Arhat Dharma-protectors. Finally (7), I want to look at the cult of the next Buddha, Maitreya, which initially developed as a way for

Buddhist devotees to meet *a* buddha if they were so unfortunate as not to have had a chance to meet *the* Buddha.

3.1 SEEING THE BUDDHA IN THE DHARMA

Virtually all discourses (sūtras) attributed to the Buddha begin with the sentence "Thus have I heard" – which supposedly are the words spoken by the Buddha's disciple Ānanda when, with his prodigious memory, he recalled all the sermons of the Buddha verbatim at the First Council, held shortly after the Buddha's death (see 7.1.1). Some years ago, Andy Rotman published a noteworthy book entitled *Thus Have I Seen*, in which he stresses the importance of the visual, instead of (or in addition to) the aural and the mental dimensions of Buddhist religious experience. Indeed, in the Indic context, the *sight* (darśana) of a teacher, a master, or a deity could and can be a liberating religious experience, sometimes sufficient in itself for enlightenment or salvation. The same is true of the Buddha's teaching, his Dharma, which, as we shall see, can be both heard and "seen."[1]

At one point in the deathbed conversations that Ānanda has with the Buddha, the question is raised of who should take the place of the Buddha as teacher after he is gone? The Buddha famously replies that his Dharma, or his Dharma and his Vinaya (his teaching and the disciplinary rules that he has established), should replace him after his passing.[2]

This statement is probably as much about substitution as it is about succession. The Buddha himself, it was thought, might be encountered – by being "seen" or "met," or "heard" – after his death, in his Dharma. Texts – especially sūtras thought to be the word of the Buddha – were considered to be embodiments of the Buddha himself. This was reflected in such statements as "One who sees the Dharma sees the Buddha." The same point could be made in the auditory dimension. Indeed, in one of the accounts of the First Council held right after the Buddha's death, Ānanda begins to recite all of the Buddha's discourses. As he does, some elders who are seated where they cannot see him exclaim: "What! How is this possible? The Buddha has come back on earth, and is still speaking! It is the Buddha whom we hear preaching

1 Rotman (2009). Another work that emphasizes the visual, in a very different way, is Eckel (1992). On the importance of "seeing" in Hinduism, see Eck (1981).

2 Walshe (1987), p. 270.

thus!" (Przyluski, 1926, vol. 1, p. 84).[3] Thus it might also be said that "one who hears the Dharma hears the Buddha."

Of course, this kind of seeing and this kind of hearing are not exactly like ordinary seeing and hearing, in that they have a different object of perception. In this regard, it should be pointed out that the Buddha is sometimes thought to have had two bodies: a physical body, also identified as his "birth-body" or the "body he got from his parents," which, after his parinirvāṇa, came to be thought of as connected to his relics or depicted in his images; and the corpus of his teaching – his Dharma-body. The latter is sometimes associated literally with the embodiment of the Dharma in texts – in sūtras, or single verses, or anything recording the Buddha's teachings. But it also took on a more abstract, deeper meaning, as the embodiment of the truth of the Buddha's Dharma, a notion which, as we shall see (in 8.2), became much developed in the Mahāyāna.

Significantly, both the physical body and the Dharma-body were thought to be in some way "visible"; the physical body could be seen with the eye of the flesh, the Dharma-body could be seen with the "eye of Dharma" or "eye of wisdom" that opened up when one first realized the truth of the Buddha's teaching. Seeing the Dharma-body was thus, in this sense, equivalent to understanding the Dharma, to having an awakening experience, to having "right view," or to entering what the Mahāyāna tradition would call "the path of seeing" (darśana mārga – see 10.3.2).[4]

It was also, however, a way of more literally "seeing" the Buddha when he was physically absent, i.e. after his parinirvāṇa. A brief anecdote may serve to illustrate this: when the Buddha descends from Trayastriṃśa Heaven after spending a rainy season there preaching to his mother, a great crowd of people assembles in Saṃkāśya to welcome him (see 2.7.9). Prominent among them is the nun Utpalavarṇā, who so desperately wishes to *see* the Buddha, face to face, that she uses her supernatural powers to take on the form of a great cakravartin king in order to push her way through the crowd to the first ranks. Rather different is the attitude of the elder Subhūti who, upon hearing that the Buddha is descending from heaven, resolves *not* to go and meet him, because he has *already seen him* with his eye of wisdom. What

3 On sūtras being embodiments of the Dharma, see Gummer (2005), p. 1261. See also Tsiang (2005). For several versions of the equation "seeing the Dharma = seeing the Buddha," see Strong (2004), pp. 8–9.

4 On the two body theory of the Buddha, see Gummer (2005). See also Lancaster (1974). For complications and caveats about this theory, see Radich (2010), and also Collins (2014).

Subhūti means, of course, is that, by virtue of his own enlightenment, he has seen the Buddha in his Dharma-body, and so, satisfied with that vision, he stays in the cave where he has been meditating.[5]

The text in which this story is told is a Mahāyāna text on the "perfection of wisdom" (see 9.1), and, true to its heritage, it extols Subhūti as the one who has "truly" seen the Buddha, and denigrates Utpalavarṇā's vision as being inferior. In this, it reflects the fact that there were groups of Buddhists who critiqued bodily relics and images as means of recapturing the presence of the absent buddha, and for whom the vision of the Dharma-body that came with enlightenment was the only true way of seeing the Buddha after he was gone.[6]

More generally, as substitutes for the Buddha, Buddhist sūtras – sometimes individual texts, sometimes whole canons – came to be venerated and worshiped. Copying, publishing, or distributing texts were (and remain) acts of merit, regardless of whether or not one reads (or can read) them. In East Asia, revolving bookcases were sometimes built so that volumes of sūtras could be spun by devotees, each rotation being equivalent to a recitation. Among Tibetans, the same thing can be accomplished by the spinning of a prayer wheel that is stuffed with copies of a mantra (see 1.4.1). Listening to the recitation of a text might not provide edification (since few people understand the classical language in which it is written, including often the reciter), but it does make merit. It also can provide magical protection. Some of the most popular and most commonly preserved Pali works, for instance, are collections of "paritta" – "protective" texts whose recitation was felt to be particularly effective in guarding persons, houses, and villages against malignant forces.[7]

We should not leap to the conclusion, therefore, that the only (or even the primary) purpose of canonical texts was to be read or recited or listened to for their actual lexical meaning. Even without being seen, texts could stand as guardians of sorts, intended to preserve the Dharma until the coming of the next Buddha Maitreya. In a sealed cave at a monastery not far from Beijing, archaeologists excavated in 1957 over 4,000 stone slabs that had been carved with the entirety of the Chinese Canon and buried in the ground where they had remained intact since the eleventh century. In

5 This story is recounted in Lamotte (1949–1980), pp. 634–636 [in French].

6 See Gummer (2005).

7 On the non-scholastic use of texts in Buddhism, see Gummer (2005). On paritta, see De Silva (1981). On the related rakṣa literature, see Skilling (1992). On revolving bookcases, see Goodrich (1942).

1999, after scholars were done recording them, the monastery decided to bury the slabs again.[8]

Another aspect of the devotional dimension of texts may be seen in what has been called "the cult of the book." According to this, copies of a sūtra – or perhaps more precisely, shrines (caitya) where sūtras are copied or kept or first recited – are treated very much as though they are relics and become places of pilgrimage and worship in their own right. It is thus meritorious and conducive to enlightenment to make offerings (of lamps, incense, flowers, etc.) to the sūtra which should be treated in every way as though it were the Buddha himself.[9]

This understanding of texts – of the Dharma – as instruments of salvation and objects of worship came to be especially prominent in the Mahāyāna, as we shall see in the case of the *Lotus Sūtra* (see 8.1). In some instances, particular texts were thought to be even more efficacious than the Buddha himself, given the fact that he was in parinirvāṇa while they were still present in this world. Thus, the *Discourse on Unbounded Life* (*Aparimitāyuḥ Sūtra*) states that venerating a copy of itself is *more* meritorious than worshiping all the buddhas of the past.[10]

3.1.1 *Excursus on the Buddhist Canon/s*

In light of this discussion, it may be appropriate at this point to pause and make a few remarks about the structure and nature of the Buddhist "canon," or rather "canons," as there are several of them. What are these texts that were deemed "authentic" and that came to stand in for the Buddha in his absence?

Today, there exist three major canonical collections of Buddhist teachings – one in Pali, one in Chinese, and one in Tibetan. In addition, there are fragments and individual texts extant in other languages, such as Sanskrit, Gandharī, and Khotanese, not to mention original works in and translations into a host of vernacular languages.[11]

8 Ledderose (2004). On similar practices in Japan, see Moerman (2010).
9 On the cult of the book, see Schopen (1975).
10 See Strong (2008), p. 197.
11 For a helpful survey of all of Buddhist canonical literature, see Lancaster (2005), and Harrison (2004). On the history and concept of the Pali Buddhist Canon, see Collins (1990). On the canon in Tibet, see Koros (1982), Schoening (1996), and J. B. Wilson (1996).

Although, as we shall see in 7.1, the tradition asserts that texts in the canon were codified by being recited at the First Council immediately after the Buddha's death, and then periodically reaffirmed at later councils, scholars today readily accept the fact that the Buddhist canons as we have them contain many things that are in no way the "word of the Buddha." In fact, Buddhists themselves made the same point, centuries ago. They countered it, however, by invoking a principle according to which "whatever is well-spoken is the word of the Buddha." In other words, whatever accords with the Dharma and is conducive to nirvāṇa is canonical. This long kept the door open for the addition of new texts.[12]

The corpus of Buddhist canonical texts that have thus been preserved and passed on is immense. For individuals brought up in Western monotheisms, it is important to realize its scope. The copies of the Bible and of the Qur'an I have on my shelf are 981 and 464 pages long respectively. The texts of the Pali canon come to about 10,000 pages in forty-nine volumes. The Chinese Tripiṭaka (or Great Storehouse of Scriptures [Dazangjing]), in its so-called Taishō era edition, consists of 2,184 texts in fifty-five large volumes of about one thousand pages each (plus a supplement of forty-five more volumes containing Japanese Buddhist writings, iconographies, etc.). The Tibetan Canon comprises the Kangyur (written bka' 'gyur ["Translation of the Word"]) which, in one edition at least, contains 108 volumes of texts; plus the Tengyur (written bstan 'gyur ["Translation of the Treatises"]) which has 224 volumes of commentaries and independent works. All this, moreover, represents only a portion of what once existed. As we shall see, many of the Mainstream sects besides the Theravāda once had their own versions of the canon, only parts of some of which have been preserved, mostly in Chinese translations.[13]

It is obviously not possible to describe here the contents of all these collections but some mention should be made of one important structure found in them. As we have seen, Buddhist canons are often called "Tripiṭaka" because they are divided into three (tri-) baskets (piṭaka) or collections of texts:

12 On this principle, found in both Theravāda and Mahāyāna texts, see McDermott (1984a), p. 29, and MacQueen (1981).

13 For lists of contents of the Pali, Chinese, and Tibetan canons, see Harvey (2013), pp. 459–462. For a list of translations into Western languages of texts from the Chinese canon, see http://mbingenheimer.net/tools/bibls/transbibl.html.

A. The Basket of Discipline (vinaya-piṭaka) (see table 3.1). In one recension, this contains three major sections: (1) rules and regulations for the behavior of monks and nuns with explanations of how they came about; (2) procedures to be carried out for various monastic rituals; and (3) an appendix summarizing various matters. The Theravāda Vinaya is extant in Pali and comes to six volumes in English translation. In Chinese, there are several different Vinaya texts (all translated from the Sanskrit) representing different Mainstream schools (see 7.2) which both parallel and sometimes vary significantly from the Pali Vinaya. In Tibetan, there is a translation of the Vinaya of the Mūlasarvāstivāda school.[14]

PALI	SANSKRIT (EXTANT IN CHINESE AND SOME SANSKRIT FRAGMENTS)	TIBETAN
(Theravāda) Vinaya		
	Mahīśāsaka Vinaya	
	Mahāsaṃghika Vinaya	
	Dharmaguptaka Vinaya	
	Sarvāstivāda Vinaya	
	Mūlasarvāstivāda Vinaya	Mūlasarvāstivāda Vinaya

Table 3.1 The Vinaya Piṭaka/s (Basket of (Monastic) Discipline)[15]

B. The Basket of Discourses (sūtra-piṭaka). This consists of sermons, the vast majority of which are attributed to the Buddha. These are arranged in five "collections" (Pali, nikāyas; Skt., āgamas), extant fully in Pali and, largely, in Chinese translations of now lost Sanskrit originals (see table 3.2). In addition, there are many Mahāyāna sūtras extant in the Chinese and Tibetan canons (as well as in some surviving Sanskrit manuscripts). These are, generally speaking, later works, but they lay claim to have been authored by the Buddha; for the most part, they start with the "Thus have I heard" formula, and sometimes invoke the principle mentioned above that "whatever is well-spoken is the word of the Buddha"; in other words, whatever accords with the Dharma and is conducive to awakening is canonical.

14 For a survey of Vinaya literature, see Prebish (1994).

15 Complete or partial English translations of these texts may be found in: Horner (1938–52) (=Theravāda Vinaya); Jones (1949–56) and Hirakawa (1982) (=Mahāsaṃghika Vinaya); Heirman (2002) (=Dharmaguptaka Vinaya); Schopen (2000) (=Mūlasarvāstivāda Vinaya). For a description of the latter text as a whole, see Schopen (2004a).

ENGLISH NAME	PALI NAME (+ NUMBER OF SŪTRAS)	SANSKRIT NAME (FULLY EXTANT ONLY IN CHINESE TRANSLATION)
Collection of Long Discourses	Dīgha nikāya (34)	Dīrgha āgama
Collection of Medium Discourses	Majjhima nikāya (152)	Madhyama āgama
Collection of Grouped Discourses	Saṃyutta nikāya (7,762 sūtras grouped in 56 topics)	Samyukta āgama
Collection of Numerical Discourses	Anguttara nikāya (9,557 sūtras arranged into 11 groupings)	Ekotta[ri]ka āgama
Collection of Minor Texts	Khuddaka nikāya (15 separate works, some quite old, some comparatively young)	No collected āgama but various separate works corresponding to some of those in the Khuddaka nikāya

Table 3.2 The Sūtra Piṭaka/s (Basket of Discourses)[16]

C. Finally, the Basket of Further Teaching (abhidharma-piṭaka) includes seven books of various lengths, most of which consist of analytic scholastic schemes for enumerating and classifying elements of reality (dharmas) (see 4.3.2). The Pali Abhidharma texts are quite different from those of the Sarvāstivāda school (the only other extant ones, which were originally in Sanskrit and now are, for the most part, extant in Chinese) (see table 3.3.).

PALI (THERAVĀDA)	SANSKRIT (SARVĀSTIVĀDA) (FULLY EXTANT ONLY IN CHINESE)
Vibhanga (Analysis)	Sangītiparyāya (Discourse on the Recitation of the Doctrine)
Puggalapaññatti (Designation of Persons)	Dharmaskandha (Aggregation of Factors)
Dhātukathā (Discussion of Elements)	Prajñaptiśāstra (Treatise on Designations)
Dhammasangaṇi (Enumeration of Factors)	Dhātukāya (Collection on the Elements)
Yamaka (Pairs)	Vijñānakāya (Collection on Perceptual Consciousness)
Paṭṭhāna (Foundational Conditions)	Prakaraṇapāda (Exposition)
Kathāvatthu (Points of Discussion)	Jñānaprasthāna (Foundations of Knowledge)

Table 3.3 The Abhidharma Piṭaka/s (Basket of Further Teaching)[17]

16 Complete or partial English translations of these texts may be found in: Walshe (1987) (=Dīgha nikāya); Ñāṇamoli and Bodhi (1995) (=Majjhima nikāya); Bingenheimer, Anālayo, and Bucknell (2013) (=Madhyama āgama); Bodhi (2000) (=Samyutta nikāya); Bodhi (2012) (=Anguttara nikāya).

17 The order of these texts and the translation of their titles are based on Cox (2004). Complete or partial English translations may be found in: Thittila (1969) (=Vibhanga); Law (1924) (=Puggalapaññatti); Narada (1962) (=Dhātukathā); Davids (1900) (=Dhammasangaṇi); Ganguly (1994) (=Dhātukāya); Narada (1969–81) (=Paṭṭhāna); Aung and Davids (1915) (=Kathāvatthu).

3.2 PLACES OF PILGRIMAGE

The Dharma was not the only way of seeing the Buddha after his demise. At another point in his conversations with the dying Buddha, Ānanda expresses his sorrow that, in times past, after they had spent the rains-retreat in various places, monks used to come for the sake of seeing (Pali, dassanāya) the Buddha (i.e. of having darśan with him), but that, after the Blessed One's passing, they will no longer be able to do so. What, Ānanda wants to know, should they do now? The question is actually posed only in one Chinese translation of the text, but is implied in the others. The Buddha's answer is that, after his death, they should visit (in other words, they should go on pilgrimage to) four sites – the places of his birth, of his awakening, of his First Sermon, and of his parinirvāṇa, i.e. Lumbinī, Bodhgaya, Sarnath, and Kuśinagarī. There, it is implied, they will still be able to "see" the Buddha, even while recognizing that he is no more.[18]

The devotional importance of these four sites can be seen in the legend of the pilgrimage made by King Aśoka and the elder Upagupta that we used in the account of the Buddha's life in chapter 2. Of all the places associated with the lifestory of the Buddha that Aśoka visits, it is only at the four listed above that he builds commemorative shrines (caityas) and is said to make offerings of 100,000 pieces of gold. At two of these four sites – Lumbinī and Bodhgaya (or more precisely, the road to Bodhgaya) – Upagupta summons minor divinities (a tree spirit, and a nāga king) who had been present in those places when the Buddha was there. They appear bodily before Aśoka and testify as to what they saw. In their recalling the glories of the Buddha, the language of darśan (of seeing) is fully in play, and Aśoka responds ecstatically, as though their testimony gave him a direct vision of the Blessed One. The same point is made even more explicitly later on when Aśoka returns to visit the Bodhi tree at Bodhgaya: "When I look at the king of trees," he declares, "I know that, even now, I am looking at the Master" (Strong, 1983, p. 257).

In a sense, taken together, these four sites came to epitomize the whole lifestory of the Buddha – his coming into this world, and his departure from it. In fact they do it twice: Lumbinī makes clear his physical coming into the world; Bodhgaya features his dharmic transcendence of it; Sarnath and the First Sermon emphasize his dharmic re-entry into the world; and Kuśinagarī stresses his physical final departure. Thus, even when not visited individually,

18 See Strong (forthcoming). The four sites recommended by the Buddha were, in time, expanded to include four others: the cities of Śrāvastī, Saṃkāśya, Rājaṛgha, and Vaiśālī – each the site of a significant miracle (see Strong, 2008, p. 3).

the four sites could be recalled collectively. For instance, they are remembered to this day as far away as Japan where, at the start of every meal, Zen monks (who have never been to India) commonly chant: "The Buddha's birth was in [the kingdom of] Kapilavastu / his attaining of the way in [the kingdom of] Magadha / his preaching the Dharma in [the Deer Park near] Benares / his entering nirvāṇa in Kuśinagarī" ("Busshō Kabira / jōdō Makada / Seppō Harana / Nyūmetsu Kuchira").[19]

3.3 RELICS

Another question Ānanda asks the Buddha on his deathbed is how they should carry out his funeral. The Buddha replies that they should treat his body in the same way as they would the body of a cakravartin king. He then clarifies just what this involves by specifying a whole set of things that need to be done, ending with the injunction that, after his cremation, his relics should be collected, and they should be enshrined in a single stūpa (memorial mound) that should be built for him at a crossroads. In the actual event, all of the Buddha's instructions (except, as we shall see, for the very last) are followed scrupulously: the funeral ceremonies are carried out, his body is cremated, and his followers gather his relics from the ashes of his funeral pyre, and they are handed over to the Mallas, the people in whose city the Buddha passed away.[20]

According to a later commentary, these relics came in three sizes, and looked like small nuggets of gold, washed pearls, and jasmine buds. In other words, they appeared not to be ashes and bits of charred bone so much as transmogrified somatic substances, jewel-like beads much like the relics that are still found today in the funeral pyres of great Buddhist teachers. In time, however, it was also thought that among the Buddha's relics were certain bones, such as his teeth, his collarbones, etc.[21]

The Mallas are all set to enshrine the relics, presumably in a single stūpa at a crossroads, when a dispute arises; seven other kings or rulers in the North Indian region learn that the Buddha has passed away and has been cremated, and set out to Kuśinagarī to lay claim to the relics for themselves. From the

19 The Japanese verses may be found in Yakai (n.d.). See also Foulk (2008), p. 65.
20 On the funeral of the Buddha, see Strong (2005), and Snellgrove (1973).
21 The description of the relics as nuggets of gold, etc., may be found in An (2003), p. 206.

start, then, the Buddha's relics are recognized as a valuable and much desired commodity. Just when a violent dispute seems about to erupt, a compromise is reached, and the relics are divided into eight equal shares, one for each of the rulers who promptly carries his portion off and has it enshrined in his home country. The Buddha's remains, then, are not kept in a "single stūpa at a crossroads"; rather they end up being spread far and wide and enshrined in eight distinct stūpas.[22]

This is the first division of the Buddha's body (or rather of what remains of that body – his relics), but it will be followed by others in due time. Most notably, according to Buddhist tradition, King Aśoka, a hundred or so years later, is responsible for further dividing the eight original shares of relics into 84,000 portions which he will have enshrined throughout his realm.[23] In this way, the body of the Buddha which had been "one" in life becomes "many" in death. Division results in multiplication, for each relic comes to symbolize not just a portion of the Buddha, but the totality of the Buddha himself. For relics, religiously speaking, are synecdochical. In other words, they follow the law of "pars pro toto" (a part for a whole), in which a piece or portion of something effectively stands for the whole. Thus, just as certain Christians, when they venerate bodily remains of certain saints – a tooth of St. Peter, the head of St. Catherine, a finger of St. Thomas – do not venerate those relics as the body parts they are but as the saint whom they represent, so too Buddhists, when they venerate a bone of the Buddha, or a tooth, or some other relic, do not worship those parts, but the whole Buddha.

Relics today are found in great profusion throughout the Buddhist world. In Sri Lanka, for instance, virtually every Buddhist monastery possesses a Buddha-relic (or what is believed to be one).[24] In addition to these more or less "generic relics," of course, there are also famous, important relics that attract pilgrims and devotees from far and wide. One such relic is the Buddha's tooth relic housed in the Temple of the Tooth in Kandy, one of Sri Lanka's former capital cities. There, every day, in a ritual that dates back to the fourteenth century, the tooth is awakened and offered water with which to wash its hands, a toothstick, water for a bath, a towel to dry itself, fresh clothes, a seat, a fan, a fly-whisk, the sound of a bell, sweet-smelling camphor, lights, perfumes, flowers, and then a full meal consisting of gruel, rice, curry, and

22 Strong (2004), pp. 116–121.
23 Strong (2004), pp. 136–142.
24 Gombrich (1971), p. 106.

sweetmeats. Then, after a pause during which the relic is left alone to eat, the meal is cleared away and a chew of betel is offered. Finally, the sanctum is censed, swept, and then closed. In this way, the "Buddha," in his relic, is treated very much as though he were alive.[25]

In recent years, scholars have presented many theories in attempts to understand the importance of relics of the Buddha. For purposes of this discussion, it may be useful to think of them as special kinds of Buddha-bodies that extend Śākyamuni's life after his death. This may sound paradoxical, but it helps capture the sense of the physicality of these things and how the Buddha may continue to be "present" in them even after his final nirvāṇa. Just as Śākyamuni had many different "prenatal" bodies (as a king, an ascetic, an animal, a divinity, etc.) in his former lives (jātakas), so too in the relics, he has many different "postmortem bodies," in which his ongoing presence can be found. The only difference is that whereas the jātaka-bodies succeeded one another in time, the relic-bodies are spread out simultaneously in space. As we shall see, this change – from a temporal to a spatial emphasis – is one of the things that marks the transition from Mainstream to Mahāyāna Buddhism.[26]

As postmortem bodies, relics are imbued with "the same spiritual forces and faculties that characterize ... constitute and animate the living Buddha" (Schopen, 1997, p. 132), and as such, they may be seen as continuators of the Buddha's mission. In this regard, it is worth considering the fact that not all buddhas of the past (see 2.4) had relics, or, more precisely, they did not all have their relics spread far and wide. For some (Dipaṃkara and Kāśyapa, for example), their skeletons were simply kept intact and buried under a single stūpa. The reason for this is that, at their deaths, their mission, their ministry, was essentially complete. Those buddhas, however, whose lifespans or circumstances were such that, at their passing, their ministries were not finished, had their relics spread in order to continue and complete the job. Just as the Buddha, in his lifetime, is said to have sent out his disciples to spread the Dharma, so too he seems to be doing that with his relics, after his demise.[27]

---

25 On the rituals of the tooth relic, see Seneviratne (1978), pp. 38–60, and Herath (1994), pp. 136–161.

26 The argument that relics are Buddha-bodies is made convincingly in Radich (2007), pp. 447–588. Major studies of Buddhist relics include Trainor (1997), Schopen (1997), Sharf (1999), Ruppert (2000), Germano and Trainor (2004), Strong (2004), Skilling (2005), Bronkhorst (2005), Ritzinger and Bingenheimer (2006), and Flügel (2010).

27 On the different kinds of relics, see Strong (2004), pp. 29, 44–47.

3.4 BUDDHA IMAGES

It is said that one day, when the Buddha was off on a journey, the people of Śrāvastī, wishing to see him, came to the Jetavana monastery where he was usually residing. Wanting to have darśan with him, they were very upset to find him out of town on a journey. In order to remedy this situation, the Buddha, upon his return, asked Ānanda to take a seed from the original Bodhi tree at Bodhgaya and to plant it in front of the Jetavana. The idea was that the tree (which grew miraculously quickly into a full-size specimen) could act as a substitute focus for people's devotions whenever the Buddha was not in residence.[28] This story of the first (or rather the second) Bodhi tree – itself a kind of relic – is very similar to a number of stories about first Buddha images: both are seen as viable substitutes for the Buddha even during his own lifetime.

Images of the Buddha are found today throughout the Buddhist world on countless altars in countless Buddhist temples or monasteries, and in countless Buddhist homes. As one authority has put it, "image worship is central to Buddhist praxis," and everywhere Buddhism spread (e.g. China, Tibet, Japan) it arrived "on the coattails of its images" (Sharf and Sharf, 2001, p. 3). Art historians and other scholars have much debated the question of the origin of the Buddha image: were the first images of Śākyamuni made in Gandhāra (present-day Pakistan and Afghanistan) under the influence of Greco-Roman classical art, or were they made in Mathurā (one hundred kilometers south of New Delhi), following local Indian styles? Were they made in the first century CE or the first century BCE? Either way, it is clear that in the earliest surviving phases of Buddhist art, as seen in the sculptures from Bharhut (second century BCE) and Sanchi (first century BCE), the Buddha himself was not represented anthropomorphically in scenes depicting his lifestory or his worship. This did not come from some reticence to depict the human form; other human beings, and divinities, and the Buddha himself as a bodhisattva in his past lives (jātakas) are amply and beautifully represented in the same bas-reliefs. Nor did it have anything to do with his supposed transcendence in enlightenment; the lack of anthropomorphic figuration starts with his birth at Lumbinī and not with his awakening at

28 The story of the Ānanda Bodhi tree is taken from Cowell (1895–1907), vol. 4, pp. 142–143. The tree (or more likely one of its descendants) may still be seen in the park in Śrāvastī today, where it remains an object of much devotion by pilgrims. On Bodhi tree relics, see Strong (2004), pp. 152–157.

Bodhgaya. Thus, in all scenes from his final life as Śākyamuni, where one would expect to see the Buddha, one sees instead an empty throne, a set of footprints, a Bodhi tree, a wheel of the Dharma, or some other symbol. The reasons for this Buddhist "aniconism" as it is called have been hotly debated.[29]

There exists no such debate in the Buddhist legendary tradition in which the first image is said to have been made during the lifetime of the Buddha himself, in order to stand in for him during his absence (much like the Ānanda Bodhi tree at the Jetavana). Perhaps the most famous of these early legendary images is the so-called sandalwood image of King Udayana, about which there are dozens of stories. One of the early versions recounts how, when the Buddha was spending a rains-retreat in the Trayastriṃśa Heaven preaching to his mother (see 2.7.9), King Udayana of Vatsa longed to see him. Accordingly, he asked the Buddha's disciple, Mahāmaudgalyāyana, to take thirty-two artists up to the heaven to craft a statue of the Buddha out of sandalwood. (Each artist was supposedly responsible for one of the thirty-two marks on the Buddha's body.) They did so and returned with the first image ever made of the Buddha and had it installed in the Jetavana monastery in Śrāvastī. When, at the end of the rains-retreat, the Buddha came down from the heaven on the triple ladder, the sandalwood image got up from its seat and went to welcome him by bowing to him. The Buddha then told it to sit back down, predicting, however, that it would have a great role to play later on in the propagation of Buddhism, after he himself was gone.[30]

There are many variants to this story, but in all of them, several points are clear: (1) the image serves as a replacement for the Buddha while he is away in heaven; (2) the image will serve as a successor to the Buddha after his death, and (3) the image is, in some way, alive. In the story above, it moves, it talks, it interacts. This is typical of such "living images" which, in the words of Sharf and Sharf, were "known to walk, to fly through the air, to sweat and weep, to appear in dreams, and to perform a host of miracles on behalf of the faithful." Lest we think that this is merely a matter of popular superstition, the Sharfs add that such tales were not "associated with, or intended for, the gullible masses alone; learned monks regularly communed with Buddhist deities through supernatural encounters with miraculous images" (Sharf and Sharf, 2001, pp. 2–3).

29 On the origin of the Buddha image, two classic articles are Foucher (1917), and Coomaraswamy (1926–1927). On the issue of Buddhist "aniconism," see Huntington (1990; 1992; 2012), Dehejia (1991), and Karlsson (1999).

30 For this story of Udayana image, see Carter (1990), p. 7, and Soper (1959), p. 261.

Part of the power and appeal of the sandalwood image of Udayana was the notion that it had been copied directly from the body of the Buddha. There are similar stories about the making of an image by King Prasenajit, about King Bimbisāra's tracing of an image on cloth from a shadow the Buddha projected on a screen, and about a number of famous images in Southeast Asia, such as the Mahāmuni image, presently enshrined in Mandalay, but originally modeled on the body of the Buddha when he, according to an apocryphal legend, was visiting Rakhine (Arakan, in Western Myanmar).[31] Sometimes, a further intermediate step is said to intervene: thus the famous "Sinhala image" (Phra Sihing), presently in Chiangmai, in Northern Thailand, was said to have been cast in Sri Lanka, seven hundred years after the death of the Buddha. At that time, there were no humans left alive who had seen the Buddha in person, but there was an old nāga king (serpent deity) who had. He was duly summoned by some arhats and asked to use his magical powers of transformation to take on the form of the Blessed One. He promptly did so, and it was on the basis of seeing that guise of the Buddha magically fashioned by the nāga, that the Sinhalese kings then had the Phra Sihing image made. Then, after many further adventures, the image eventually made its way to Thailand.[32] As we shall see in 11.5, similar stories were told about the Emerald Buddha now in Bangkok.

The key role of kings in all these stories should not go without notice. Buddha images were, in fact, a way not only for monks and ordinary laypersons to assert the presence of the Buddha, but for royalty to do so on a grander scale. In fact, Buddha images figure prominently in the myths of the introduction of Buddhism into many countries such as China, Japan, and Tibet, and it comes as no surprise to find that, in time, the famous golden image first brought to China as a result of the dream of the emperor Ming was said to be none other than the Udayana image.[33]

Not all Buddha images, of course, are "great" Buddha images; most are ordinary, plain, routine. But even these may be thought of as sharing in some of the Blessed One's charisma. In this regard, it should be noted that images that are manufactured today to represent the Buddha need to be consecrated in order to *become* or *be* the Buddha. In this there is another difference from

31 On the story of the image of King Prasenajit, see Strong (2008), pp. 50–52. On the story of King Bimbisāra's image, see Strong (1995), pp. 39–41; on the Mahāmuni image, see Schober (1997b), and Kyaw and Crosby (2013).

32 On the Phra Sihing image, see Notton (1933), and Tambiah (1970), pp. 230–242.

33 On the golden image, see Tsukamoto (1985), vol. 1, pp. 412–450. On the importance of images in the advent of Buddhism to Japan and Tibet, see Deal (1995) and 13.1 below.

bodily relics, which do not need to be consecrated, but fulfill their function by virtue of their pedigrees. Consecration rituals serve to bring about this transformation: they feature "opening the eyes" of the statue by painting them in, thereby awakening (i.e. enlightening) the piece of metal, wood, or clay. They may also feature instructing the statue in what it means to be a buddha by infusing it with its own lifestory, something that is done by the recitation of the Buddha's biography in the presence of the image, or they may involve the installation of bodily relics of the Buddha into the image. All these are means of making an image come "alive": "Once consecrated, the physical image is no longer a mere *representation* of the deity, any more than my own physical body is a mere *representation* of me" (Sharf and Sharf, 2001, p. 11).[34]

Moreover, ritually speaking, one image can serve to enliven another. Although today most Buddha images are made in a shop, they can sometimes be cast on the grounds of a monastery. In such cases, "life and miraculous powers are transfused into new images from an older one – the chief cult image of a monastery which in turn has received them from a still older one, and so on back to one of the original likenesses." To "power" this transmission, a "sacred cord" is passed from the original image through a line of monks to the molds in which the new images are to be cast, and back to the original image. "One or more of the monks go into meditative trance, producing an invisible charge in the circuit which transmits the life and supernatural qualities of the cult image to the new ones as the metal is poured" (Griswold, 1957, p. 47).

The same transmission, of course, can be accomplished by making a replica of a sacred image. Thus, as the cult of the Udayana buddha became established in East Asia, it was spread by the tradition that many copies of the first image were made, copies which, however, retained the powers and features of the original. The only extant copy today is the famous sandalwood image kept at the Seiryō-ji temple in Kyoto, which, when it was examined closely in 1954, was found to have been "enlivened" by the insertion into its hollow core of internal organs made of padded cloth.[35]

34 For a description of an opening of the eyes ceremony in Sri Lanka, see Gombrich (1966). More generally, and on the infusion of statues with the Buddha's lifestory, see Swearer (2004). On the insertion of bodily relics into images, see Brinker, Kanazawa, and Leisinger (1996), pp. 87–97.

35 On the Seiryōji image, see Henderson and Hurvitz (1956), McCallum (1998), and Horton (2007), pp. 22–48.

3.5 THE MASTERS OF THE DHARMA

We have seen so far that, in a variety of ways, relics and images, and, in a certain way, the Dharma itself, may all be viewed as post-mortem buddha-bodies who can make the Blessed One present once again despite his absence. But they can also be seen as successors of the Buddha who stand in for him in so far as they continue and further extend his mission.

It is sometimes claimed that the Buddha's pronouncement to Ānanda that the Dharma and Vinaya would be his successor signified his refusal to establish a clerical hierarchy – a "church" headed by a patriarch or "pope," who would be seen as carrying on the authority of the founder. Protestant scholars, in particular, were enthusiastic about this scenario, for it echoed their own notions of the authority of scripture and their distaste for ecclesiocracies. Be this as it may, certain Buddhist traditions did establish lineages of patriarchs who were deemed to be the Buddha's successors and the transmitters of his Dharma.

The Theravāda school focused on the series of Chiefs of the Vinaya, starting from the elder Upāli (who recited the Vinaya at the First Council – see 7.1.1), and ending with Moggaliputta Tissa (who presided over the Third Council – see 7.1.3) and Mahinda who was responsible for spreading the tradition to Sri Lanka. Other Mainstream schools, however, featured the series of Masters of the Dharma (dharmācārya), which I shall focus on here. According to this tradition, just prior to his parinirvāṇa, the Buddha transmitted the Dharma to Mahākāśyapa. For this reason, in one text at least, Mahākāśyapa is actually called "a second Buddha" (Li, 1993, p. 112). In another text, he is praised as one to whom the Buddha gave his own robe (see below), and as the disciple who "held the community together" (Strong, 1983, pp. 253–254) after the Buddha's death.[36] It is worth pausing here, therefore, to consider some parts of his lifestory in more detail.

Mahākāśyapa's lay name was Pipphali. He was a brahmin, born some years before the Buddha. His family was rich, but he, from a very young age, felt a desire to renounce the world. When he came of age, however, his parents started planning for him to marry. In order to thwart them, he commissioned some artists to make a gorgeous statue out of pure gold of a beautiful woman, and declared he would only consent to marry someone as beautiful as that image, thinking that would not be possible, for

36 On the Chiefs of the Vinaya and the Masters of the Dharma, see Lamotte (1988), pp. 203–212, and Strong (1992), pp. 60–67.

no person could be so glorious. His parents, however, found just such a woman in Bhadrā, the daughter of a brahmin family from a neighboring kingdom. It turned out, however, that Bhadrā was as intent on renunciation as Mahākāśyapa. By their separate inclinations, then, the couple were dead set against marriage, but they were given no choice in the matter and were soon wed. By mutual agreement, however, they did not consummate their union and slept in bed with a garland of fresh flowers between them.

Eventually, Mahākāśyapa's parents died, and he took over responsibility for their large estate. One day, supervising some of his farmhands ploughing a field, he noticed (like the Buddha, see 2.7.3) that the birds eagerly followed the plough, devouring the worms that were turned up, and he came to a double realization: the householder's life he now led inevitably brought suffering upon living beings, and he himself would have to bear the karmic consequences of such actions as a householder. He resolved then and there to renounce the world.

Meanwhile, back home, Bhadrā had a similar experience, and when she learned of her husband's decision, she resolved to renounce the world with him. Fashioning some robes out of yellow cloth, they shaved one another's heads, and, after granting freedom to all of their slaves, they wandered forth, begging bowls in hand. Soon, however, they felt it was unseemly for them to be seen together, and so, coming to a crossroads, by mutual consent, Bhadrā went one way and Mahākāśyapa went the other.[37]

Mahākāśyapa's road leads him to Rājagṛha where he meets the Buddha and immediately realizes he has found his true master. Likewise the Buddha realizes that Mahākāśyapa is destined to become his chief disciple and ordains him on the spot. Soon thereafter, the Buddha gives Mahākāśyapa his own rough hempen rag robe, and Mahākāśyapa, putting it on, resolves thenceforth to practice the thirteen ascetic practices (dhutānga), the first of which is the wearing of rag robes. Eight days later, after diligent practice, he becomes an arhat.

I shall, in 7.3.4, return to Mahākāśyapa's practice of asceticism. For the present, I want to focus on his role as a master of the Dharma, and his concern for the well-being of the community. This comes to the fore at the end of the Buddha's life when Mahākāśyapa emerges as a leader of the saṃgha. Indeed,

37 On the story of Mahākāśyapa and Bhadrā, see Nyanaponika and Hecker (1997), pp. 109–119, and Ray (1994), pp. 105–117. Bhadrā eventually makes her way to Śrāvastī where she is converted by the Buddha; she is ordained as a nun and becomes enlightened. See Murcott (1991), pp. 101–104.

we are told, the Buddha's cremation cannot begin until Mahākāśyapa arrives to light the pyre, a task often undertaken, in the lay context, by the eldest son, and, in the monastic one, by a chief disciple. Immediately following the Buddha's funeral, it is Mahākāśyapa who puts an end to an imminent crisis: many enlightened disciples of the Buddha, despondent at the news of their master's death, begin "following him into extinction" by entering parinirvāṇa themselves. Worried that the world will soon be empty of enlightened monks, Mahākāśyapa sounds a gong that can be heard throughout the universe; then, with his stentorian voice, he issues an interdiction forbidding enlightened disciples of the Buddha from extinguishing themselves in nirvāṇa, and summoning them all to the First Council.[38]

Not long after the conclusion of the First Council, Mahākāśyapa, feeling that his mission is complete, decides to enter parinirvāṇa. In fact, the tradition is not altogether consistent about whether or not he passes away into parinirvāṇa immediately or just enters a long-term "trance of cessation" before attaining parinirvāṇa much later. One thing that is clear is that his body is not cremated but preserved (either dead or in a trance), dressed in the Buddha's old hempen robe, in a sealed cave under a mountaintop where it is to remain until the arrival of the future Buddha Maitreya. When Maitreya comes, the mountain will open and he will receive (or take) from him Śākyamuni's robe. In this way, Mahākāśyapa (or at least his body) will act as a sort of link between two buddhas – the last one and the next one – and so as a kind of guarantee of the continuity and ongoing presence of the Dharma, in the absence of the Buddha.[39]

There is another way in which Mahākāśyapa acts as a "link" to the future. Before entering his mountaintop, he formally goes to Ānanda and declares: "the Buddha transmitted to me the baskets of the Law. Now I wish to enter parinirvāṇa; therefore, in turn, I am committing the Dharma to your good keeping" (Strong, 1992, p. 62). In this way, Ānanda becomes the second Master of the Dharma.

Ānanda, it should be said, was the Buddha's cousin, and so was a member of the Śākya tribe. There are differing accounts as to when he actually joined the Buddhist order, but, in due time, he was appointed as the Buddha's personal attendant. From then on, he rarely left the Buddha's side; he not only

38 The story of Mahākāśyapa forbidding monks from entering parinirvāṇa and summoning them to the First Council is from Przyluski (1926), vol. 1, pp. 3, 37, 58–59 [in French]. See also Wilson (2003), pp. 38–40.

39 On this story, see Strong (1992), p. 63, and Silk (2003). On the transmission between the first and second patriarch, see Faure (1995), pp. 338–340.

waited on him personally, anticipating and meeting his various needs, but he also acted as a kind of chief of protocol, ushering in visitors, arranging meetings, and handling communications. The Buddha is said to have named him as foremost among his monks in five categories: best of those of wide knowledge, of retentive memory, of good behavior, of those who are resolute, and of personal attendants.[40]

Ānanda was known not only for his devotion to the Buddha, but also for his remarkable memory which, according to tradition, enabled him to remember all of the Buddha's sermons. We have already seen how, when he starts to recite these at the First Buddhist Council, some of the elders present confuse him with the figure of the departed master himself.

We shall, in 6.3, examine Ānanda's important role in helping to establish the order of nuns. For now, I would like to focus on the story of his parinirvāṇa, which differs rather markedly from that of Mahākāśyapa. If the latter's legend emphasizes preservation, unity, and continuity, Ānanda's picks up on the notions of impermanence and division.

Again, there are several versions of this story but, in gist, it may be recounted as follows: at a very advanced age, Ānanda decides that he, in turn, is ready to pass into parinirvāṇa. So he approaches a monk whom he had previously ordained named Śāṇakavāsin who, like Mahākāśyapa, was known for his vow always to wear a hempen robe, a sign of his asceticism. Addressing him, Ānanda declares: "The Blessed One entered nirvāṇa after transmitting the Dharma to Mahākāśyapa, and Mahākāśyapa entered nirvāṇa after transmitting the Dharma to me. Now I wish to enter nirvāṇa; you should accept and guard this Dharma of the Buddha" (Li, 1993, p. 118). He then enjoins him, in turn, to pass the Dharma on to the elder Upagupta, who, he predicts, will come to be born in the town of Mathurā, and who is also destined to "perform the functions of a Buddha," and who will be known a "Buddha without the [thirty-two] marks [of a buddha]" (alakṣaṇakabuddha) (Strong, 1992, pp. 39–40).

Ānanda then goes on his way. Realizing that, after his death, his relics might become objects of contention, he heads for that part of the Ganges river which marks the boundary between two rival kingdoms and resolves to pass into parinirvāṇa there, so that no one group can claim he passed away in their territory. Before doing so, however, he encounters a renunciant named Madhyāntika, whom he ordains and brings to enlightenment. Then, using

40 Woodward and Hare (1932–1936), vol. 1, pp. 19–20. On Ānanda, see Witaṇachchi (1966), and Nyanaponika and Hecker (1997), pp. 137–182.

exactly the same formula he used with Śāṇakavāsin, he transmits the Dharma on to Madhyāntika and tells him to go and spread the Buddha's teaching to the land of Kashmir in the Northwest. Finally, having done all that he needed to do, Ānanda flies up into the sky over the river and passes into parinirvāṇa, autocremating in mid-air. As planned by him, his relics fall into four shares: one for the people of Rājagṛha on the southern bank of the river, one for the people of Vaiśālī to the north, one for the gods in Indra's heaven, and one for the nāgas under the water.[41]

What we see here is the beginnings of bifurcation. Not only are Ānanda's relics (like the Buddha's) divided, but so too is the lineage of the Masters of the Dharma, although the later pretense is that it is not, for Śāṇakavāsin, Madhyāntika, and Upagupta come to be counted as the third, fourth, and fifth patriarchs, succeeding Mahākāśyapa and Ānanda. In time, they all come to stand at the head of a family tree that spread out to all subsequent teachers, especially in East Asian Buddhism. Thus today, every Mahāyāna monk, especially in the Zen schools, can trace his ordination lineage from master to disciple back through the generations of patriarchs – of Masters of the Dharma – all the way to the Buddha. Indeed, upon ordination, Chinese monks typically receive a new surname, "Shi" (Jpn., Shaku; Vtn., Thich) – short for "Shi-jia-mou-ni" (Śākyamuni) – signifying that they are now a "son of the Buddha" (fozi) (Welch, 1967, p. 279). The term, in fact, goes back to India, where monks were also called "sons of Śākyamuni" (Śākyaputra). To this extent, becoming a monk was thought to be entering into a kinship relationship with the Buddha, in which the adage "like father, like son" may be thought to have been taken literally. In other words, the Masters of the Dharma were not just successors and inheritors of the Buddha; they were also, in some sense, buddhas themselves. As Paul Mus has pointed out, in India, "one does not inherit *from* one's father, one *inherits one's father*" (1998, p. 7, emphasis added).

3.6 THE ARHAT DHARMA-PROTECTORS

The lineage of the Masters of the Dharma assumes a scenario of transmission in which each patriarch passes the teaching on to the next generation, just prior to entering parinirvāṇa (although, as we have seen in the case of Mahākāśyapa,

41 On this story of the final days of Ānanda, see Lamotte (1988), pp. 206–208, and Strong (1992), pp. 62–66.

there is some ambiguity as to whether he attains parinirvāṇa or merely goes into a lengthy trance to await the coming of the next Buddha Maitreya). In a somewhat different tradition that represents yet another way that Buddhists dealt with the absence of the Buddha, the Blessed One, just prior to his death, asks Mahākāśyapa (along with three other arhats – Piṇḍola, Pūrṇa, and the Buddha's own son Rāhula) *not* to enter parinirvāṇa but to extend their lives and remain in this world as protectors of the Dharma, until the coming of the next Buddha Maitreya. Here then, we do not have a lineage of successive masters preserving the Dharma, but a set of arhats who are contemporaries of the Buddha who will extend their own lifespans and so ensure the ongoing preservation and protection of the Dharma in the world. In this way they are the living functional equivalents to the Buddha relics and Buddha images discussed above.[42]

The full development of this tradition may be seen in the tradition of the sixteen arhats, who became especially popular in East Asia. Indeed, images of the sometimes eccentric-looking sixteen (or eighteen or even 500) arhats (Ch., luohan; Jpn., rakan) are commonly found in Chinese Buddhist temples, and they were a popular theme in painting as well. Textual accounts make clear that their function is to stand in for the Buddha Śākyamuni until the coming of the next Buddha Maitreya, at which point they will all, at long last, pass into parinirvāṇa. Generally speaking, their leader is said to be the arhat Piṇḍola who, in Indian Buddhism, is portrayed as being 120 years old at the time of King Aśoka. He is reputed to have himself been in the Buddha's presence on several occasions, and so provides a direct link to the departed master. When Aśoka meets him, for example, he is thrilled and declares: "By looking at you, I can, even today, see the Buddha" (Strong, 1983, p. 261).[43]

3.7 MEETING MAITREYA

We have, so far, looked at various ways of encountering the Buddha Śākyamuni, after his parinirvāṇa – in his Dharma, in pilgrimage traditions, in relics, in images. And we have also looked at ways his dharmic presence was preserved or passed on by the patriarchs and by some of his arhat disciples. But as we

42 This tradition is found in several Chinese canonical texts. See Strong (1992), p. 237. On Piṇḍola, see Strong (1979/1980; 2013).

43 For a list of the sixteen arhats, see Buswell and Lopez (2014), p. 1089. For studies, see Lévi and Chavannes (1916) [in French], Kent (1994), and De Visser (1923). For an English translation of a basic text on the arhats, see Li (1961).

know, Śākyamuni was not the only Buddha, and the lineage of past buddhas that led up to him (see 2.4) did not stop with him but will continue into the future.

Mention has been made several times of the very next Buddha Maitreya who will be coming most immediately (relatively speaking). Indeed, it is thought that Maitreya (who, like all buddhas, follows the same Buddha-biography blueprint) has presently reached his penultimate existence – rebirth as a god in Tuṣita Heaven – from where he will descend to take his "final birth" as a buddha. Estimates vary widely as to when that will be, from 5,000 years after the parinirvāṇa of Śākyamuni to over five and a half billion years, but he *will* come and will preach the same dharma as Śākyamuni. There is, therefore, another way for devotees in this day and age to overcome the absence of the Buddha: that is to look to the future and take steps to ensure that they are reborn at the right time and place in order to "catch" Maitreya when he appears on earth.[44]

Typically, when Buddhists in South and Southeast Asia today undertake merit making activities, they end them with a wish or aspiration (patthanā or paṇidhi), which can take several forms but often involves a determination to be reborn at the time of Maitreya and to attain nirvāṇa under him. Sometimes, it is explained that such persons find the quest for nirvāṇa too difficult to undertake at present, and so "postpone" it to the distant future, content for now to make merit to ensure better rebirths. It is perhaps more fruitful, however, to think of such "vows" as merely recognizing the importance of meeting a buddha face to face (having darśan with him), and wishing to take advantage of that. Merit making is not just meant to insure a happier, better future life; it is also a mechanism for getting to meet a future buddha, under whom attaining enlightenment will be easier than it is now. In many ways, then, Buddhists today (at least in South and Southeast Asia) are caught in between the eras of two buddhas, and so may be as much focused on Maitreya as they are devotees of Śākyamuni.[45]

Because of his relative proximity to us, Maitreya is the most important (or at least the most relevant) of all the future buddhas. In this sense, he is "our" future buddha, in the same way that Śākyamuni is "our" immediately past buddha. But he is not the only future buddha, and, in time, various traditions developed about other buddhas yet to come after him. A late

44 For a handy list of estimates as to when Maitreya will come, see Soothill and Hodous (1937), p. 456b. For studies of various traditions about Maitreya, see Sponberg and Hardacre (1988).

45 On this ceremony of patthanā, see Gombrich (1971), p. 224.

Pali text, for instance, recounts the stories of ten future buddhas, beginning with Maitreya. Significantly, each of these stories ends with a statement, the gist of which is to declare that anyone who did not reach enlightenment under *this* buddha (the one whose story has just been completed) will have a chance of doing so under *the next* buddha (whose story is to follow). In this scenario, then, hope is never quashed; there will always be another buddha to meet. Even more future buddhas are listed in a late Mahāyāna text known as the *Discourse on the Fortunate Aeon* (*Bhadrakalpika Sūtra*). It recounts the lives of no fewer than a thousand buddhas, four of whom have already appeared and 996 of whom are yet to come, starting with Maitreya.[46]

As the Maitreyan ideology developed, various ways of meeting him were envisaged. Nattier has usefully summed these up under four simple rubrics: (1) Maitreya can be met "here/later," that is to say, in a future lifetime when Maitreya comes down to earth from Tuṣita Heaven and attains buddhahood. This is the scenario invoked by the merit making Buddhists just described who "postpone" their quest for nirvāṇa until his arrival. (2) Maitreya can be met "there/later." According to this scenario, devotees, unwilling to await Maitreya's advent here on earth, can aspire (through good deeds and determination) to be reborn "later," i.e. in their next life, "there," i.e. in Tuṣita Heaven where Maitreya is presently residing. In this context, Tuṣita Heaven may be viewed as a sort of "Pure Land" of Maitreya (see 8.3), attainable only after death, and Maitreya himself may be thought of more as if he were already a buddha than still a bodhisattva. In fact, in many ways, Maitreya came to be thought of as if he were both a buddha and a bodhisattva (a confusion which, we shall see, was quite common in the Mahāyāna). Examples of this kind of "there/later" Maitreya cult may be found in early Chinese Buddhist groups such as that formed by the monk Dao'an (312–385), who organized a sort of Maitreya society, all the members of which vowed to be reborn in Tuṣita.[47] (3) Maitreya can be met "there/now." This is for those serious Maitreya-devotees who cannot even wait to be reborn in Tuṣita Heaven, and so seek to "visit" with Maitreya there in this life, either through meditative visualization, or through magical flight ascensions to Tuṣita itself. Often such devotees were already enlightened monks who had the abilities to make the journey, and who did so in order to consult with Maitreya about certain doctrinal questions.

46 On the Pali tradition of future buddhas beyond Maitreya, see Saddhatissa (1975). On the thousand buddhas of the fortunate aeon, see Yeshe De Project (1986).
47 See Tsukamoto (1985), pp. 753–756.

It is in this context that certain scholarly works, especially in the Yogacāra school, came to be identified as inspired (or even authored) by Maitreya.[48] (4) Finally, Maitreya can be met "here/now." According to this scenario, espoused by various Buddhist messianic/apocalyptic sects, the time until Maitreya's advent on earth is radically foreshortened, and the expectation is that he will be arriving very soon, and, in some cases, that he is already here, now. Many of these movements were millenarian cults, venerating a charismatic leader who proclaimed himself or was proclaimed to be Maitreya, and seeking to overthrow the government, often through violent insurrection.[49]

The ways of overcoming the Buddha's absence dealt with in this chapter are not the only solutions Buddhists found to the dilemma presented by the Buddha's parinirvāṇa. Mention could also be made of different other ways of "meeting the Buddha" – by visualizing him in meditation, by being reborn in his pure land, by ritually encountering him in a maṇḍala, by merging with him in certain Vajrayāṇa rites, by meeting him in the intermediate state between rebirths (bardo), by encountering him in an incarnate lama. All these are features of the Buddhist devotional tradition that we shall return to in chapter 8 below.

48 On devotees who go to Tuṣita Heaven to meet Maitreya, see Demiéville (1954), pp. 376–381 [in French].

49 For examples of East Asian belief in the advent of Maitreya, see Overmyer (1988), and Zürcher (1982). For beliefs in Myanmar, see Mendelson (1961), and Sarkisyanz (1965), pp. 43–67.

Chapter 4

Some Permutations of the Middle Way

Most reviews of Buddhist doctrine begin with an account of the Buddha's First Sermon. Known as the *Discourse Setting in Motion the Wheel of the Dharma* (*Dharmacakrapravartana Sūtra*), this was supposedly preached by the Buddha at the Deer Park in Sarnath to the five ascetics who had formerly been his companions and who became his first disciples (see 2.7.8). Most accounts of the First Sermon feature its presentation of the "Four Truths," often called the Four "Noble Truths" (ārya satya), or sometimes the "Four Truths for the Noble Ones," i.e. realities that are true for those who have attained enlightenment.[1]

The Four Truths are an important and useful way of presenting early Buddhist doctrines. However, if we look at the various versions of the Buddha's First Sermon, it will be noticed that in almost all of them, the Buddha does not start with the Four Truths, but with a declaration that he has discovered a new path – a middle way – that "leads to peace, to direct knowledge, to enlightenment, to Nirvāṇa" (Bodhi, 2000, p. 1844). In some texts, the Buddha even stops with this proclamation and makes no mention of the Four Truths at all, or delays teaching them until the next day. This led the French scholar Bareau to speculate that the scheme of the "Four Noble Truths" was a relatively late addition to the Buddha's First Sermon, and so not "the very basis of Buddhist thought" that we commonly think it to be

1 For translations of Pali versions of the First Sermon, see Bodhi (2000), pp. 1843–1847, and Harvey (2009); for a Sanskrit version, see Strong (2008), pp. 42–45. For a comparative study of all versions, see Anālayo (2012/2013). In dropping the epithet "noble" and referring simply to the "Four Truths," I am following Anālayo (2006). On the truths being "true" from the perspective of enlightened beings ("noble ones"), see Harvey (2009), who calls them the "Four True Realities for the Spiritually Ennobled." For a book-length discussion of the Four Truths, see Anderson (1999).

(1963, p. 180). Accordingly, I shall start with the middle way in this chapter and leave off consideration of the Four Truths until chapter 5.[2]

4.1 THE MIDDLE WAY

The Buddha initially describes his Middle Way as the path that avoids two extremes which he specifies as the pursuit of pleasures, on the one hand (this is deemed to be "low, vulgar, the way of worldlings, ignoble, and unbeneficial"), and the ascetic pursuit of self-mortification, on the other (which is deemed to be "painful, ignoble, and unbeneficial"; Bodhi, 2000, p. 1844). He goes on immediately to further identify this Middle Way with the noble eightfold path, which is also the fourth of the truths, with which we shall deal later.

The way between hedonism and asceticism, we have seen, is reflective of (or, more likely, constructive of) the Buddha's lifestory which features his double abandonment of his life in the palace (= the extreme of hedonism) (see 2.7.4) and then of the practice of extreme austerities exemplified most notably by śramaṇa groups such as the Jains (see 2.7.5). This particular middle way obviously had repercussions for monastic life. As we know, Indian Buddhist monks practiced a middle way of eating – they did not fast, but neither did they take a meal after noon; a middle way of dressing – they did not go naked but neither did they wear adornments; a middle way of living – they combined both residing in one place (during the rainy season) and wandering about (at other times of the year – see 6.2); and, when in residence, a middle way of location – in monasteries neither too close to nor too far from towns.[3]

The Middle Way, however, was also important for its broader doctrinal repercussions. Rather than being just a specific lifestyle path between hedonism and severe austerities, between the life of a non-Buddhist householder and the life of a non-Buddhist ascetic, it may be seen as a general blueprint for a way of thinking that had a significant influence on the formulation of the Dharma. Early Buddhists lived in a world that was marked with many varieties of views on topics of fundamental philosophical and religious importance. From a Buddhist perspective, many of these were seen as "extremes" to be avoided (or at least radically reinterpreted), and Buddhist doctrines

2 On the First Sermon stopping with the declaration of the Middle Way, see Dessein (2007), pp. 20–21, and Bareau (1963), p. 173 [in French]. See also Anderson (1999), p. 5. For the Buddha's teaching the truths the next day, see Kloppenborg (1973), pp. 21–24.

3 On the Buddha's biography being formulated with the Middle Way in mind, see Bareau (1963), p. 49 [in French].

consistently expressed middle way positions on various spectrums of ancient Indian thought.

As we shall see, there are two basic ways in which they did this. I shall nickname these the "neither/nor" and the "both/and" approaches. Imagine for a bit, if you will, two students trying to achieve a "C" average in a course. (In the world of this exercise, "C" is the desired grade.) The first student achieves this goal by only getting Cs on all of her tests. The other one does it by getting As and getting Fs in equal proportion. Both end up with a C average; both are middle way students, but one is a neither/nor student who avoids the extremes, receiving neither As nor Fs, while the other is a both/and student who bounces off them, receiving only As and Fs. Similarly, "neither/nor" doctrines find a single stable middle way position that follows a straight line down the center between two extremes, or that falls within a band of possible lines directly on either side of that center. Both/and doctrines, however, are found when there is no viable in-between position and the only way to express a middle way is to zigzag back and forth between the two extremes, or to embrace them both simultaneously in a paradoxical dialectic tension.

With this in mind, in what follows, I want to explore a number of basic Mainstream Buddhist doctrines: karma and saṃsāra (in 4.2), and non-self (anātman) and impermanence (in 4.3). Then, in chapter 5, I will examine the Four Truths and doctrines related to them, which shall be presented as another expression of a Buddhist middle way mentality. In chapter 8, I will go on to see further repercussions of this while looking at Mahāyāna doctrines.

4.2 KARMA AND SAṂSĀRA

It is often said that karma was a doctrine – or perhaps better, a world view – that Buddhism acquired and accepted from its Indic context. This is true but it should not cause us to ignore significant differences between Buddhist and other understandings of karma. Moreover, as we shall see, not everyone in ancient India believed in karma. From the Buddhist perspective, then, there were both particular views of karma to be avoided, and particular views denying the existence of karma, that were also to be avoided.

Karma literally means "action" (and not "fate" as is sometimes assumed in the West). Originally in India, karma referred to ritual action (specifically, in performing a Vedic sacrifice), which, if carried out properly, was thought to have positive results (i.e. the gods would respond to the sacrifice). Eventually, however, the concept of karma took on broader implications as it was ethicized and linked to developing notions of rebirth. Simply put, karmic actions came to be defined morally – as positive meritorious deeds and as negative demeritorious ones – that were thought to result not just in fruits in this life but in determining what kind of future life – good or bad – one might enjoy or suffer. The metaphor was primarily an agricultural one (you "reap what you sow"), but it may reflect also the growth of trade and investment in ancient India at the time (you "profit or lose from what you invest").[4]

Merit (or demerit) is not allotted by some judge or divine arbiter; rather it follows positive (or negative) karmic action as a matter of course. It may help to think of karma as a law of nature somewhat like gravity: just as an object released falls to the ground, meritorious deeds lead to positive results, and demeritorious deeds lead to negative results. When they are mixed together, they may lead to mixed results.

As was mentioned (in 1.4.1), Buddhists distinguished various realms of rebirth into which individuals could be reborn. Three of these were thought to be "lower" or "unfortunate," accessed by demeritorious deeds: the various hells, the hungry-ghost states, and the animal realms. Two were thought to be "higher" or "fortunate," accessed by good, meritorious deeds: the human states, and the various heavens. Whether fortunate or unfortunate, all these realms are called "passageways" (gati) because existence in any of them is not permanent. In particular, it should be noted that, for Buddhists, neither the hells nor the heavens are eternal. One may stay in them for a very long time but one will eventually "pass on" and be reborn out of them, according to one's karma.

Buddhists in general were much preoccupied with the workings of karma. Whole texts were devoted to spelling out which kinds of actions led to which kinds of rebirths. The different realms of rebirth (gati) were subdivided into different kinds of hell, different kinds of heaven, different kinds of animals, of hungry ghosts, of humans, to accommodate different kinds of karmic results for different kinds of meritorious or demeritorious actions (see table 4.1). For example (on the negative side): "People who slay living beings, out of greed, delusion, fear or anger ... are surely going to the Sañjiva hell ... People who have angered their mother or father or relations or friends ... are destined for the Kālasūtra hell ..." Or again: "By passionate attachment to sensual pleasures, people are reborn as geese, pigeons, donkeys and other passionate animals;

4 For general discussions of Buddhist karma, see McDermott (1984), Bronkhorst (1998), Egge (2002), and Gombrich (2009), pp. 19–59.

PATHWAYS	DIVISIONS	DISTANCE ABOVE OR BELOW THE EARTH IN YOJANAS (1 yojana = *c.*10 kilometers)	LIFESPAN OF BEINGS IN YEARS
HEAVENS	Para-nirmita-vaśavartin	$+1.28 \times 10^6$	9.216×10^9
	Nirmāṇa-rati	$+6.4 \times 10^5$	2.304×10^9
	Tuṣita	$+3.2 \times 10^5$	5.76×10^8
	Yāma	$+1.6 \times 10^5$	1.44×10^8
	Trayastriṃśa (heaven of the 33 gods)	$+8 \times 10^4$ (top of Mount Meru)	3.6×10^7
	Caturmahārājakāyika (heaven of the four great kings)	$+4 \times 10^4$ (slopes of Mount Meru)	9×10^6
	FOUR CONTINENTS:		
HUMANS	Uttarakuru in the North	0	1,000
	Aparagodānīya in the West	0	500
	Pūrvavideha in the East	0	250
	Jambudvīpa in the South	0	Variable
ANIMALS	Various kinds	0	Up to one eon
PRETAS (HUNGRY GHOSTS)	Various kinds	−500 (realm of Yama)	1.5×10^4
HELLS	Saṃjīva ("reviving")	−5,000	
	Kālasūtra ("black string")	−10,000	
	Saṃghāta ("dashed together")	−15,000	
	Raurava ("weeping")	−20,000	
	Mahāraurava ("great weeping)	−25,000	
	Tāpana ("heat")	−30,000	
	Pratāpana ("extreme heat")	−35,000	
	Avīci ("uninterrupted")	−40,000	

Table 4.1 Pathways of Rebirth in the Realm of Desire[5]

those who erred through stupidity are reborn as worms." Or again: "The man who does not restrain his thoughts and unites with the wives of others, or who finds delight in illicit parts of the body, will be reborn as a woman."

5 See Kloetzli (1983), pp. 33–39, Sadakata (1997), pp. 41–68, and McGovern (1923), pp. 60–72.

Alternatively, on the positive side: "People who revere their mother, father, and family elders, who are generous, patient, and do not delight in strife, will be reborn among the gods of the Trayastriṃśa heaven ... People who are inclined toward morality, giving, and discipline and who make strenuous efforts are certainly on their way to the Nirmāṇarati heaven." Or again: "One who, in this world, makes donations of alms food will be reborn ever-happy, endowed with long life, good complexion, strength, good fortune, and good health." Or again: "The woman who is of good morals and little passion, who abhors her femaleness and constantly aspires to masculinity, will be reborn as a man." Or, a mixed example: "One who takes goods that were not given but who also gives gifts will, after death, first become wealthy but then exceedingly poor."[6]

The flow of rebirths and redeaths in the various realms – whether pleasant or unpleasant – is commonly called saṃsāra – a beginningless cycle of existence, in which we are trapped by karma. The historical origins of this concept are much debated, but, in time, the question of how to escape from or put an end to the cycle of saṃsāra came to be established as one of the primary ultimate preoccupations of most Indic religious systems (including Buddhism). Many answers to this question were given, including, as we shall see, the Buddhist answer of nirvāṇa.

4.2.1 Why Do Good Deeds?

Often, when I present to my students the workings of karma and the ways in which both meritorious and demeritorious deeds can keep one in saṃsāra, an important question comes up: why bother doing "good" karmic deeds if they help perpetuate one's cycle of rebirth, and so seem to be part of the problem and not the solution?

Three possible answers may be given. First, not all Buddhists are necessarily looking to put an end to rebirth immediately. Many seem willing to postpone that quest until a later rebirth, and engage in what might be called "karmatic" Buddhism. Since the higher realms of rebirth (human and heavenly) involve much less pain than the lower ones, it makes sense to make merit in order

6 The examples are taken from a text known as the *Verses on the Six Pathways of Rebirth* (*Saḍgatikārikā*); see Strong (2008), pp. 38–42. For a canonical text similarly "spelling out" the workings of karma, see Anālayo's (2011, pp. 767–68) discussion of the *Discourse on the Analysis of Karma* (*Karmavibhanga Sūtra*). The popularity of that work is attested to by the fact that it is extant in fourteen different versions: one in Pali, two in Sanskrit, six in Chinese, two in Tibetan, and one each in Khotanese, Sogdian, and Tocharian.

to be reborn in them and avoid intense suffering, even though this is not a permanent solution.[7]

Second, this focus on merit making also makes sense for eventual seekers of nirvāṇa, since it was and is widely thought that escape from saṃsāra is possible only from the fortunate human and divine realms of rebirth. (It is sometimes said that one cannot attain enlightenment from a heavenly realm, but only from the human. This, however, is belied by many stories in Buddhist literature in which gods, after hearing the Buddha's preaching, are enlightened.) We shall, in due time, see the reasons for this. Suffice it to say now that it can be argued that it is wise to do good deeds in order to be reborn in a good realm so as to be in a position in which the quest for nirvāṇa will be possible in the future. Indeed, as we saw in 3.7, merit makers even today commonly express the wish that, by their act of merit, they may, after many births in the heavenly and human realms, be reborn at a later time (often the time of the future Buddha Maitreya) and attain nirvāṇa then.[8]

Finally, it is important to point out that Buddhists distinguish between two kinds of good deeds. There are good deeds that are the product of a desire to achieve a better rebirth. These, as we have just seen, make merit and may put one in a position to eventually reach enlightenment. As one scholar has put it, they are "directly karmatic" and "indirectly nirvāṇic." But there are also good deeds – the product of non-greed, non-hate, and non-delusion – that are linked to meditation and produced by and productive of wisdom. These aim at liberation while also making merit as a by-product. They are "directly nirvāṇic" but "indirectly karmatic." Sometimes (although the parameters of the two words are manifold) these two genres of good deeds are distinguished by the terms "puṇya," often translated as "merit," but more precisely explained as "an action bringing good fortune," and "kuśala," meaning "good" or "skillful," or "produced by and productive of wisdom." In this way a kuśala karma (a skillful, wise act) is sometimes paradoxically said to be "a karma (act) that leads to the cessation of karma" (Bodhi, 2012, p. 344).[9] We are, then, left with a paradox with regard to good karma which, however, we may think of as a first example of a both/and middle way doctrine: it both keeps one in saṃsāra and it liberates one from it.

---

7 Karmatic is a Sanskritization of the Pali-based term "kammatic" whose character is spelled out in Spiro (1982). See also Ames (1964), p. 40.

8 See Strong (2005).

9 For the distinction between "directly" and "indirectly" karmatic or nirvāṇic, see Harvey (2010), p. 205, which is in part inspired by Velez de Cea (2004). The definitions of kuśala and puṇya come from Cousins (1996).

4.2.2 *Contexts of Karma I: Neither Free Will nor Determinism*

At the time of the establishment of Buddhism, there were, among brahmins and various groups of renunciant śramaṇas, many different attitudes towards karma and rebirth, and various theories about how to escape from saṃsāra. We cannot deal with all of them here, so, in what follows, I would like to describe two relevant ideological spectrums – the one among groups who did not believe in karma, the other among groups who did. I will then try to locate the Buddhist view on each of these spectrums.

At one end of our first spectrum were those who simply denied that there was any such thing as karma, and who drew from that the conclusion that nothing one does – good or bad – has any consequences for oneself. As a result, one has complete freedom to do as one wills. This stance is well-illustrated by the naked wanderer, Pūraṇa Kāśyapa, a supposed contemporary of the Buddha, who is famously said to have proclaimed that he could proceed along the south bank of the Ganges, killing and raping and plundering, and suffer no demerit as a result, or he could go along the north bank, handing out gifts and performing sacrifices, and reap no merit therefrom. A common corollary to this kind of metaphysical libertarianism was a denial of rebirth, most notably proclaimed at the time of the establishment of Buddhism by various materialists whose view was that when we die, we are not reborn but are annihilated and dissolve back into the four elements of earth, air, fire, and water, whence we came. How we act thus does not matter; the four elements of which we are made may recombine to form another individual but that person will have no connection whatsoever to the person who just died.[10]

At the other end of this spectrum of karma-deniers, we find determinists who proclaim that there is no such thing as free will because all of our actions and indeed our ultimate end are preset. This was the view of the Ājīvikas who were followers of a teacher named Maskari Gośāla, another of the Buddha's supposed contemporaries. They essentially replaced the notion of karma with something that they called Fate (Niyati), which controlled all of an individual's actions, good or bad. Unlike the materialists, the Ājīvikas believed in rebirth and accepted the ideal of escaping from saṃsāra, but asserted that both the patterns of one's rebirths and the timing of one's liberation were not subject

10 Pūraṇa Kāśyapa's views as well as those of the materialists may be found in Walshe (1987), pp. 93–94, 82. In general, on these and other non-Buddhist thinkers, see Jayatilleke (1963), pp. 69–168.

to alteration. Strictly speaking, there was no choosing of actions – no striving for enlightenment. Some individuals, when their time came, would be liberated from saṃsāra; others would have to wait a bit longer, depending on their Fate over which they had no control. The analogy that is commonly cited is that we are each like a different sized ball of string which will unwind itself over our lifetimes until it – the course of our rebirths – comes to an end. There is no way we can alter this or speed it up.[11]

Both of these views presented real challenges to the Buddhists who sought to counter them by establishing a middle-way position between the extremes of complete free will and absolute determinism. Philosophically speaking, the Buddhist view on this matter can be described as a form of compatibilism, sometimes called "soft determinism." This asserts that, within a given situation which has to some extent been set by our actions in previous lives, we have a certain amount of free will.

This, of course, immediately becomes more complicated when one realizes that those actions in a previous life were similarly freely decided upon, within the parameters set by one's situation at that time, which was the result of actions from an even earlier life, and so on and so forth, ad infinitum, to beginningless time ... For simplicity's sake, however, we can say that, in any given lifetime, the things that define one's life-setting (realm of rebirth, family status, gender, lifespan, health, beauty, wealth, intelligence, etc.) are generally determined karmically by one's own past volitional actions, but what one does in that karmically determined situation – how one acts – is not set; it may be influenced by previous karmic patterns, but it does reflect a modicum of free moral intentional choice. It is up to the individual to decide whether to do good or not to do good, within the parameters of his or her situation. As one scholar put it succinctly, "although the present is conditioned by the past, it does not dictate the future" (Gutschow, 2004, p. 135).

This sets the context for the Buddhist understanding of karma as *intentional actions of a moral nature* – good or bad deeds that have been consciously decided upon and carried out. For Buddhists, these are the only acts that count karmically, i.e. the only deeds that will bear some kind of fruit – positive or negative – either in this life or a future existence.[12] This understanding has one obvious important immediate consequence. It means that unintentional (i.e. accidental) deeds do not count karmically. Let us

11 For more on the Ājīvikas, see Basham (1951).

12 On karma as intention, see P. Williams (2000), pp. 72–74.

consider the following situation: there is an ant crawling on my kitchen floor, but I fail to see it. From a Buddhist perspective, if I inadvertently step on it and kill it, that is not karma; it is an accident. My killing the ant will not result in my future suffering for that deed, because the act was not intentional. If, however, I see the ant and take a can of bug spray and kill it, that is karma, for it was intended and will have (negative) future consequences. I may myself, for instance, be reborn as an ant and get sprayed again and again.

This, of course, is to greatly oversimplify things; it totally ignores, for instance, the ant's karma. It also fails to take into consideration the multitude of my other actions – good or bad – which may serve to mitigate or worsen the negative results of killing the ant. Moreover, it could be argued that I should have taken precautionary measures to avoid "inadvertently" killing the ant, by increasing my awareness and being on the lookout for ants, or by sweeping my kitchen floor more often so as not to attract ants in the first place. Karma, in other words, rapidly becomes very complex.[13]

Complications aside, however, we can see that the Buddhist view represents a neither/nor middle-way position, falling somewhere between that of the Ājīvikas (whose decision whether or not to step on an ant will ultimately have been predetermined by Fate), and anything-goes free-will advocates such as Pūraṇa Kāśyapa (who would deny that his stepping or not stepping on an ant would have any consequence whatsoever).

4.2.3 Contexts of Karma II: Both Jain and Upaniṣadic Views

There was a second spectrum of opinions about karma in ancient India that helped define the Buddhist position. This was one that was marked by the views of the Jains on the one hand and of certain Upaniṣadic sages on the other.

The Jain view of karma is rather complex – there were different kinds of karma, some more negative and powerful than others – but one of its most distinctive features was that the results of karmic action were conceived of in material terms, as particles of dirt or dust called "atoms" (pudgala) that adhere to one's jīva (one's soul or life-monad). The jīva is eternal and may be identified as pure consciousness and will. All living beings – gods, humans, animals, hellbeings, insects, plants, and miniscule "microbes" (nigoda – somewhat

13 On good actions mitigating bad actions, see Anālayo (2011), pp. 770–771. On the complexities that karma can take on, see Harvey (2007).

akin to bacteria) – have jīvas. Indeed, the world is thought to be full of them, for their number is infinite.[14]

Just how karmic "dirt" sticks onto and entraps each jīva is not precisely described, but the net result is that karma is what is responsible for our different bodily forms. Liberation can be seen as realizing one's true self, one's jīva, by freeing it from the body, from this accumulated karmic dirt that occludes it. This logically entails not only reducing one's actions so as not to accumulate more "dirt," but also purification so as to get rid of the "dirt" one has already acquired.

Bronkhorst has argued that the logic of the Jain view points to an ideal of total abstention from all actions. Be this as it may, certain actions were seen as being particularly "agglutinative" – particularly negative, karmically speaking, and so to be avoided at all costs. These included first and foremost the taking of life. Jains were early proponents of the doctrine of non-injury or non-violence (ahiṃsa). For the Jains, non-injury was, in fact, no easy feat because, as we have seen, life was literally everywhere. A famous Jain analogy declares that no place on earth is devoid of living souls (jīva), just as no place in a goat pen is without goat excrement. With such a view, one has to be extremely careful and extremely disciplined not only about where one steps, but about everything one does: any action is likely to be harmful and to have negative karmic results, so one needs to take precautions. In terms of the example given above, Jains would say that if I paid close attention to where I was going, I could avoid "inadvertently" stepping on an ant. Thus Jain monks are famous to this day for sweeping the path in front of them so as not to potentially harm insect life, and for filtering their drinking water so as not to swallow the same.[15]

If non-violence, restraint, vegetarianism, and meditative trances (in which one cuts down on the activities of both the body and the brain) are all endeavors connected to the first goal of reducing karmic accumulation, asceticism and fasting and getting rid of any possessions are part of the second, purificatory process. Fasting in this context makes good sense: one literally (and symbolically) reduces one's accumulated karmic "fat." Indeed,

---

14 On Jain views of karma and of the jīva, see Dundas (1992), pp. 80–83, 83 ff. For two contrasting views of the relationship of Jain and Buddhist views, see Gombrich (1994) (or Gombrich, 2009, pp. 45–59) and Bronkhorst (1995). On karma as a reaction to Brahmanism, see Gombrich (1996), pp. 27–64.

15 Bronkhorst's argument about the Jains and total abstention from action is found in his 1998 and 2004. See also Bronkhorst (2000), p. 37. The reference to the souls being as omnipresent as goat excrement in a goat pen can be found in Dundas (1992), p. 81.

the founder of the Jains, Mahāvīra, is reputed to have starved to death in old age, having stopped eating altogether. The same can be said for not having any material possessions (e.g. clothing): they too are a kind of "fat," or "baggage." Thus, part of asceticism, at least for some Jains, involves going naked, i.e. not owning anything.

Over against this Jain view, as Bronkhorst points out, we may place the "solution" of various Upaniṣadic sages who proposed a radically different way of dealing with the problem of karma. Rather than try to cut down on or eliminate karmic actions, they sought to cut through them and transcend them by means of meditative wisdom. Simply put, "if acts lead to undesired consequences [i.e. further birth in saṃsāra] it is sufficient to realize that one has never committed those acts to begin with ... Because that which one really is, one's true self (Ātman [which is transcendent]) does not act by its very nature" (Bronkhorst, 2004, p. 416). We shall deal further with the Upaniṣadic notion of Ātman below. For now, suffice it to say, in terms of our example, that whether I inadvertently or intentionally stepped on an ant, "I" (i.e. my Ātman) would not ultimately have killed "it" (i.e. its Ātman) since ultimately Ātman does not participate in action. In the final analysis, karma is illusory, a product of ignorance.

The polarity we are dealing with here, then, on this Jain-Upaniṣads spectrum is between those who, on the one hand, view karma – both mental and physical – as creating a real *material* trap which has to be dealt with through discipline and self-purification, and those who, on the other hand, view karma – both mental and physical – as creating an *illusory* trap, which can be dealt with through knowledge and awakening.

How did the Buddhist view fit onto this spectrum? Here, I would suggest, we come to another example of a middle way that is "both/and" rather than "neither/nor." As we shall see, instead of forging a single path to liberation, Buddhism proposes a double-sided one, incorporating elements akin to parts of both the Jain and Upaniṣadic point of views. On the one hand, Buddhist enlightenment means awakening ("bodhi") to reality as it is, a breakthrough realization that eliminates ignorance. On the other hand, Buddhism saw the trap or saṃsāra as something very real. Moreover, it developed elaborate lists of defilements or outflows – āśravas (also a Jain word) – that kept one from realization and that gradually needed to be systematically eliminated. This is a topic to which we shall return. For now, let me simply cite the words of one scholar who pointed out that in Buddhism, we can find both the "path of knowledge which nullifies error" and also "the path of purification which burns up defilements" and whittles away attachments (Buswell and Gimello, 1992, p. 14). It has been suggested that these two paths lie at the basis of all subsequent Buddhist expression of Buddhist practice, with one sometimes more prominent than the other. In any case, together they may be thought of as creative reinterpretations of what we might label Jain and Upaniṣadic methods of dealing with karma, and are another expression of the Buddhist middle way.[16]

4.3 THE DOCTRINE OF NON-SELF (ANĀTMAN)

One of the other hallmarks of Buddhist thought has been its distinctive doctrine of non-self (anātman). Like karma, I would argue, it is best understood as a middle way doctrine to be placed on a spectrum of different Indic views of the self. This spectrum runs between the ideological extremes that were known as "eternalism" and "annihilationism."[17]

A discourse from the Pali canon illustrates this stance well: "One day," we are told, "Vacchagotta, the wandering ascetic, approached the Blessed One, greeted him courteously ... and said: 'Well, now, good Gotama, is there a Self?' The Blessed One remained silent. 'Well, then, good Gotama, is there not a Self?' Once again, the Blessed One remained silent, and the wandering ascetic Vacchagotta got up and went away" (Strong, 2008, p. 105). The Buddha then explains to his disciple Ānanda that if he had said to Vacchagotta that there is a self, that would have meant associating himself with those śramaṇas and brāhmaṇas who are eternalists. But if he had asserted that there is no Self, that would have meant associating himself with those śramaṇas and brāhmaṇas who are annihilationists.

Who were these eternalists and annihilationists? Mention is made of such thinkers in a number of different Buddhists texts, and distinctions are even made between different kinds of eternalists and different kinds of annihilationists.[18] Most scholars would identify the eternalists with the early Upaniṣadic sages who, as we have seen, asserted that there exists, within beings, an absolute, unchanging, unborn, undying, indivisible Ātman – a

16 On the importance of the āśravas (defilements), see Hosaka (1966). See also Cox (1992).

17 On eternalism and annihilationism, see Anderson (1999), pp. 34–35. On anātman doctrine in general, see Collins (1982), and Harvey (1995).

18 For lists of several types of eternalist and annihilationist views, see Bodhi (1978), and Ñāṇamoli and Bodhi (1995), p. 842.

Self with a capital "S," something that, in a different context, might be called a Soul. The Ātman is free from the vagaries and sufferings of this world, and can leave the body in dreams and at death and move from life to life. The Ātman, moreover, is identified with Brahman, which at the time of early Buddhism probably did not mean the absolute, monistic principle underlying the universe that later philosophers were to attribute to it, but simply the world, the totality of existence. According to this view, at death, someone who has realized Ātman rejoins, merges with Brahman, and does not then return to this world. Importantly, such an Ātman is to be realized by the mind, by knowledge, by awakening to the realization that this is what we have always been.

There existed, however, at the time of the Buddha, other eternalist notions of the unchanging Self, ones that were rooted in śramaṇa circles. We have already seen that the Jains, too, had a notion of unchanging permanent indivisible selves, each individual's jīva (which, in fact, they sometimes called ātman). Moreover, recently, one scholar has suggested that at least one version of the Buddhist argument against a permanent self was directed against the Ājīvikas. It may be, therefore, that in opposing the eternalists' doctrine, the Buddhists had several specific targets in mind.[19]

At the other end of the spectrum were the annihilationists who did not accept any notion of personal continuity. A specific example of their views may be found, perhaps, in the opinions of the so-called "Chance-Originists" (Adhiccasamuppanna-vādins), who are also mentioned as contemporaries of the Buddha. The individual, they maintained, comes about purely by happenstance: at one moment we do not exist; at the very next we do; then at the next we do not; and there is no necessary relation between the beings in these moments. This view was most notably applied to discussions of rebirth, but it can be extended to discussions of life as a whole. At each moment, the self (or the world) is annihilated, and at each moment it is created anew, but not in any connection to the self or world just gone (although we may create illusions of connection). There is, in other words, no such thing as an ongoing person.[20]

Another way of viewing the difference between these two poles is to think of the former (the eternalists) as those who see constancy and continuity – the ongoing existence of an unchanging Self from life to life and moment to

19 For the argument that the Buddhist was addressing the Ājīvikas, see Kuan Tse-fu (2009).
20 On the chance originists, see Walshe (1987), pp. 81–82, and Jayatilleke (1963), pp. 261–262.

moment – and of the latter (the annihilationists) as those who see inconstancy and discontinuity – the existence of no such thing. The two positions can be illustrated with a very simple example: to the question, "Am I the same self now as I was in a previous life?" the eternalists would answer "yes," and the annihilationists would answer "no." Their positions get a bit trickier but remain essentially the same when we change the question to: "Am I the same self now as I was when I was three years old?" Again, the eternalists would say "yes" and the annihilationists would say "no."

Because the word "Ātman," in the context of early Buddhism, denoted something "unchanging" and "eternal," there has been an inclination among scholars to view the Buddhist notion of an-ātman (no-ātman) solely in terms of its rejection of the eternalist extreme. In addition to this, however, we need also to see how the notion of anātman is a rejection of the annihilationist notion that there is no such thing as personal continuity. In fact, Buddhists went to some length to argue their position both ways – against one extreme as well as the other, and to come up with a view of what Collins (1982) has felicitously called "selfless persons."[21]

In what follows, we shall first investigate further the anti-eternalist (anti-continuity) side of the anātman doctrine. This will lead us to look at the Buddhist analytical breakdown of the selfless person into component parts – into the aggregates (skandhas) and elements (dharmas). Then we shall investigate the anti-annihilationist (anti-discontinuity) side of the anātman doctrine. This will lead us to consider various Buddhist attempts to attribute to these aggregates some sort of ongoingness. As we shall see, the Buddhist doctrine of anātman, although it is phrased negatively, actually depends on holding these two trajectories in tension. It is, in other words, essentially a both/and middle way, paradoxically affirming "yes and no."

4.3.1 Breaking Down the False Sense of Self: the Five Aggregates and Impermanence

One of the ways in which Buddhists sought to counter the eternalist notion of an ongoing, indivisible Self was to break down our experience of the world – our sense of ourselves and of others – into its component parts, and to apply to them the notion of impermanence (anitya).

21 For an example of focusing on the eternalist extreme, see Gombrich (2009), p. 9.

The Hindu Upaniṣads contain a famous dialogue in which a disciple asks his master to tell him about the Self (the Ātman). The master tells his pupil to bring him the fruit of a banyan tree. He does. The master then asks him to cut it up and to describe what he finds. He does and he says, "I find some small seeds." The master then asks him to cut one of the seeds up and to describe what he finds. He does, and he says he finds nothing. The master then exclaims: "that nothing that you can't see; that, my son ... is the truth; that is the Ātman" (Olivelle, 1996, p. 154).

In a sense, the early Buddhists proceeded in an analogous way, by "chopping up" the person and analysing its contents. However, when they got to the end of the process, and found no "core," rather than declaring, mystically, that here was the unseen Self, they concluded, rather practically, that the parts were all that there was and none of them constituted a Self.

They did, however, name the parts and subparts that they found as a result of their analytical breakdown. These they called the "aggregates" (skandhas), each of which, in turn, comprises various component elements (see table 4.2). The five aggregates may be described as follows: (1) we have a body or form (rūpa) which comprises our sense organs (eye, ear, nose, skin, tongue, and mind), which help us perceive and experience various forms, sounds, smells, touches, tastes, and ideas. (It will be noted that Buddhism, like other Indian schools of thought, includes the mind as one of six sense organs, a not unproblematic move).[22] Rūpa is also said to result from various combinations of the different elements earth, water, fire, and wind. (2) We have feelings, which may be positive, negative, or neutral and are related to experiences of the five senses and the mind. (3) We have perceptions (saṃjñā) which enable us to recognize and name our experiences – to give labels to the visibles, sounds, smells, tastes, tangibles, and thoughts ("thinkables") we encounter (what I see – that oblong shape in the grass – becomes a different kind of reality, and engenders different sorts of feelings, when I perceive it to be "a snake"). (4) We have volitions or karmic constituents (saṃskāra), i.e. both karmic acts and their results.[23] And (5) we have consciousnesses (vijñāna), which are of various types defined by the senses and the mind and enable contact between the eye, ear, nose, etc., and visibles, sounds, smells, etc.

22 On the inclusion of the mind among the six senses, see Hamilton (1996), pp. 14ff.
23 On saṃskāra, see Gombrich (2009), p. 141.

AGGREGATE: SKANDHA (PALI, KHANDHA)	ENGLISH EQUIVALENTS
Rūpa (rūpa)	Body, form, materiality
Vedanā (vedanā)	Feeling, sensation
Saṃjñā (saññā)	Perception, discrimination, conceptual identification
Saṃskāra (saṅkhāra)	Volition, karmic constituent, conditioning factor
Vijñāna (viññāṇa)	Consciousness

Table 4.2 The Five Skandhas (Aggregates)

The skandhas are commonly invoked in arguments for non-self (anātman), not just because they break down the integrity of the individual but also because they are constantly changing. By definition, it will be remembered, the Self – the Ātman – must be permanent, unchanging. None of the skandhas can be the Self because each is characterized by impermanence. As the Buddha is said to have put it in one of his similes: "form (rūpa) is like a lump of foam, feelings like a water bubble, perception is like a mirage, volitions like a plantain trunk, and consciousness like an illusion" (Bodhi, 2000, pp. 252–253). Each of the skandhas is constantly changing: corporeal forms are in constant flux; this is most evident with bodies (we grow taller or fatter, our bowels move, our heart beats, we shed dead cells), but it is also true of physical objects (the color of the corner of my desk on which the sun shines has faded a bit, the springs of my chair have gotten weaker). Change and impermanence are even more evident in the other skandhas – feelings, perceptions, and volitions – and are perhaps most pronounced in our consciousness which is likened to a monkey, constantly swinging from branch to branch, from one thing to the next. The attribute of impermanence is important because it means that none of the skandhas can be an Ātman, an unchanging self. Nor can their combination be an unchanging self, for that combination itself is constantly changing.

4.3.2 The Elements (Dharmas)

The Buddhist analytical breakdown of the world as we experience it did not stop with the five aggregates (skandhas), however. In time, the Mainstream schools elaborated upon the contents of these skandhas and came up with expanded lists of component parts. Early schemes included the lists of the twelve sense-spheres (āyatanas), i.e. the six senses and their six corresponding sense-objects; and the lists of the eighteen elements (dhātus), i.e. the twelve āyatanas and the six consciousnesses linking them together (see table 4.3). Eventually, these schemes were reorganized and expounded upon in Abhidharma texts of various schools to form lists of what were called "dharmas" – "elements of reality" (not to be confused with the word Dharma meaning Doctrine).[24] Typically they include material dharmas (such as the first five sense organs and their corresponding sense-objects), mental dharmas (which include the mind and the consciousnesses corresponding to the various sense organs), non-material dharmas that are present in any moment of perception (such as feeling, notion, attention, contact, etc.), and non-material dharmas that are concomitant to various positive or negative moments (such as faith, diligence, equanimity; or anger, envy, deceit). All of these are said to be conditioned or "constructed" (saṃskṛta) elements, although there are, in addition, some unconditioned dharmas, such as nirvāṇa, and empty space. What there is not is anything besides dharmas. The abhidharmic analysis covers the whole of "reality." Any "person," any "object," any "experience" can be described in terms of the co-existence of various impermanent elements. This could be thought of as a kind of atomism, as long as it is recognized that the "atoms" are not just material, but also mental, and emotional, and volitional.

ORGAN	CONSCIOUSNESS	SENSE-FIELD
Eye	Eye-consciousness	Forms
Ear	Ear-consciousness	Sounds
Nose	Nose-consciousness	Smells
Tongue	Tongue-consciousness	Tastes
Touch	Touch-consciousness	Tangibles
Mind	Mental-consciousness	Thoughts

Table 4.3 The Eighteen Dhātus (Senses, Sense-Fields, and Consciousnesses)

In Mainstream Buddhism, the dharmas are generally thought to last only a moment (arising from a cause and ceasing to exist in the twinkling of an eye). According to one view, the duration of a moment is 1/64th of a fingersnap, but that is usually taken as a metaphor for saying that a moment effectively

24 For an introduction to the notion of dharmas, see Willemen (2004), Stcherbatsky (1970), and Takakusu (1947).

has no duration.[25] Nonetheless, the dharmas are thought to be ultimately real, because they are endowed with "svabhāva" (inherent self-existence). Thus the Self of a person (or of any compounded thing) has no ultimate reality, but is made up of components (the dharmas) that do. (This was true at least in Mainstream Buddhism; we shall see that the Mahāyāna was to disagree with this.) In such a view, there is no glue, no underlying notion of "self," to keep all these self-contained dharmas together: they are like beads on a string, but without there being any string.

At this point, we have at least a provisional answer to our first question. Why is the selfless person not an ongoing indivisible Ātman? Why am I completely different now than I was at the age of three? Because what appears to be "me" is, in fact, explainable as a conjunction of impermanent parts, in which, and underlying which, and besides which no unchanging "Me" can be found. We can see here that this abhidharmic view of things comes very close to the annihilationist view of no-continuity of the person.

4.3.3 *Countering the Breakdown of Self: Personal Continuity*

And yet, it stays shy of it, for just at the point at which the annihilationist extreme is approached, the tradition bounces off it, and considers the other side of our dialectic and looks at our second question, namely, what holds all of these component parts together? What makes for continuity from one set of disconnected inherently self-existent but momentary dharmas to the next? How is that I *am* the *same* person now that I was at the age three?

This side of the argument – this question of the continuity and contiguity of the dharmas – is crucial; for one thing, the very doctrine of karma and the very quest for nirvāṇa depend on it. Simply put, if a "person" at moment A (or in life A) is not somehow connected to the same "person" at moment B (or in life B), how can that "person" be thought to be reaping the fruit of his/her own actions? If there is no continuity, either karma cannot exist, or, absurdly, the fruits of person A's action would be reaped by person B. Similarly, how could – why should – anyone quest for the attainment of a nirvāṇa that, apparently, would be reached by someone else?

Some Buddhists answered this question by invoking the notion of a kind of

25 On the momentariness of dharmas, see Collins (1982), p. 234. More generally, see Silburn (1955) [in French].

practical or provisional reality: even though, ultimately, there is no unchanging Self, we give names ("Mary" or "John") to certain constantly changing combinations of skandhas, or, to use a frequently invoked Buddhist metaphor, we call an assemblage of particular parts a "chariot," and that "chariot" is able to take us places. Specifically, it is able to take us to a realization that it does not exist as a "thing" – that it has no Self.[26]

When this provisional and paradoxical "non-self thing" is a person and is on the path to enlightenment, it is, in fact, sometimes said to be a "great self" (mahātma), or "self-like," or a "developed self," or, to use Harvey's term, a "self without boundaries" (Harvey, 1995, pp. 54–63). Canonical Buddhist texts are, in fact, filled with references to enlightened selves who have realized non-self, a paradoxical theme which, as we shall see, was to be taken up by various Mahāyāna schools (see 9.7.1).

Other Buddhists, facing the question of continuity, were to invoke the scheme of interdependent origination (pratītyasamutpāda) which helped explain the intercausality of the various skandhas – how they both come into existence and are annihilated. This became a standard response to our question, and we shall examine it below, in a different context (see 5.2).

For now, mention will only be made of various ingenious other answers to this question that were developed by various Mainstream Buddhist schools, reflecting what Conze called a "hankering after a permanent personality" (1967, p. 132). All of these solutions try to explain what it is that makes for the continuity of the person, sometimes coming dangerously close (at least in the opinion of other Buddhists) to the notion of an Ātman. These theories are generally not very well known to students of Buddhism or to Buddhists themselves, but they are important because, taken together, they reflect a realization of the need to keep annihilationist tendencies in check.

4.3.4 Explications of Continuity: Pseudo-Selves and Ersatz Ātmans

First and foremost of these, perhaps, was the doctrine of the "Person" (pudgala) espoused by a couple of Mainstream sects (see 7.2). These Personalists

26 A canonical reference to the simile of the "chariot" may be found in Bodhi (2000), p. 230. For the fuller development in the *Questions of King Milinda*, see Strong (2008), pp. 101–104.

(Pudgalavādins), as they were known, posited an ineffable entity called a "Person" that was "neither the same as nor different from the aggregates," but that ensured that the individual who committed a karmic act was the same as the one who reaped its reward, or that the one who quested for nirvāṇa was the same as the one who attained it. Despite the Personalists' insistence that this was not equivalent to a Self, and so did not contradict the anātman doctrine, other Buddhist sects vociferously condemned them for being too close to the Ātman extreme. Even so, according to the Chinese pilgrim Xuanzang, as many as twenty-five percent of the monks in India in the seventh century CE were Personalists.[27]

The Pudgalavādins were by no means alone in looking for ways to explain the continuity of the individual. Among the Mainstream sects, the Mahīśāsakas became known for distinguishing between three types of aggregates (skandhas): aggregates that lasted for one instant (kṣaṇa-skandha), aggregates that lasted for one lifetime (ekajanmāvadhi-skandha), and aggregates that lasted until the end of saṃsāra (āsaṃsārika-skandha). This ingenious solution obviously had certain advantages: it gave several ongoing identities to "persons" for various lengths of time, but without absolutizing any of them. The "aggregate that lasts until the end of saṃsāra," it could be argued, was not an Ātman because it was not eternal. Rather than being realized at the moment of liberation from rebirth (like the Upaniṣadic Ātman), it was discarded.[28]

Another Mainstream school, the Sautrāntikas, similarly maintained that there was what they variously called an "aggregate with a unique flavor" (ekarasa-skandha) or an "ultimate person" (paramārtha-pudgala). Other schools sought continuity in modified forms of consciousness. Thus the Mahāsaṃghikas developed the notion of a "root consciousness" (mūla-vijñāna) – a kind of ongoing subconsciousness whence the other consciousnesses arise. And the Theravādins eventually posited an unconscious mental continuum called "bhavanga-citta" which acted as a kind of stopgap or glue that held the distinct moments together, and so ensured "the identity and continuity of one karmic unit – of one 'person' or 'individuality' within a lifetime, and of a single series of them, across a number of rebirths" (Collins, 1982, p. 247). Even so, they insisted that this was not some sort of Ātman,

27 The principal espousers of the Personalist view were the Vātsīputrīyas and the Sammatīyas. On the Pudgalavādins, see Conze (1967), pp. 125–131, Bareau (2013), pp. 145–146, Thiên Châu (1999), and Priestley (1999).

28 On the different kinds of skandhas for the Mahīśāsakas, see Bareau (2013), p. 250, Lamotte (1935–1936), p. 250 [in French], and Silburn (1955), p. 251 [in French].

because they paradoxically asserted that the bhavanga-mind moments themselves were instantaneous.[29]

It should be said that these attempts at explaining continuity were not to stop with Mainstream Buddhism. For instance, both the mūla-vijñāna as well as the bhavanga-citta are cited by Vasubandhu as precursors of the Mahāyāna Consciousness-Only school's notion of a storehouse consciousness (ālayavijñāna) (on which see 9.5.2). Within Mainstream Buddhism, however, one final, rather different, approach to this question should be mentioned. That is the view of the Sarvāstivāda school. Their "solution," much criticized by other Mainstream Buddhist schools and subsequently by the Mahāyāna, was to find continuity in the dharmas themselves, declaring that "all dharmas" "exist" whether they are past, present, or future. The only difference between them (according to one explanation – there were several others) is that past and future dharmas (unlike present ones) lack "activity" or "function." In this way the dharmas themselves could be thought to be ontologically eternal (and so able to be perceived whether in the past present or future), but functionally annihilated from moment to moment.[30]

4.4 SUMMARY

We have, in this chapter, sought to explore various iterations of the Middle Way, a notion which the Buddha sets forth at the start of his First Sermon. In order to unravel the many implications of this principle and its applicability to other Buddhist doctrines (something the Buddha did not do in his sermon), I have presented several of its expressions and sought to set them within the context of various philosophical and religious movements that may have been around at the time of the Buddha. Thus, early Buddhists can be seen as finding their way between karma-deniers and karmic absolutists; and as combining views of saṃsāra both as a real material trap and as an illusory trap; and as shying away from the extremes of affirmation of an Absolute Self and denial of personal continuity. The Middle Way, however, is not the only thing set forth in the First Sermon as we have it, a text which is mostly devoted to the doctrine of the Four Truths, to which we shall now turn.

29 On the Sautrantika view, see Silburn (1955), p. 252 [in French]. On the Mahāsaṃghika notion of a mūlavijñāna, see Silburn (1955), p. 237, and Bareau (2013), p. 80. On the Theravāda view of bhavanga, see also Harvey (1995), pp. 155–179, and Gethin (1994).

30 For studies of Sarvāstivāda views, including those on time, see Willemen, Dessein, and Cox (1998), Cox (1995), and Prasad (1991), pp. 113–432.

Chapter 5

The Four Truths

The Four Truths, a.k.a. the "Four Noble Truths" or "Truths for the Noble Ones," are perhaps the most famous comprehensive summation of Buddhist teaching. They are generally said to have been preached by the Buddha in his First Sermon, right after his proclamation of the Middle Way. Elsewhere they are presented as a kind of specialty of the Buddha's disciple Śāriputra who is said to have had an inordinate ability for making them clear. Knowledge of the Four Truths is presented as the equivalent of having "right view," which itself is defined as a middle way that avoids the extremes of "wrong views."[1]

The Four Truths (see table 5.1) may be described as follows: (1) Life as we live it is characterized by stress (duḥkha; Pali, dukkha). "Stress" is increasingly being used by some scholars as a modern but more or less apt translation of the word "duḥkha" which is more generally rendered either as "suffering" or "unsatisfactoriness," or "ill," or "pain."[2] None of these (including "stress") is without its problems, but "stress" has the advantage of having a cognate adjectival form. The truth of stress means not only that life is occasionally "stressful" in that it involves suffering and disappointment, but that our very way of being in this world is stressful. (2) There is a reason for this stress: desire or craving (or more literally, "thirst" [tṛṣṇā]). This leads us to long for and to cling to things that bring passing enjoyment here and there but that cannot finally be clung to – things such as sensual passions, possessions, persons, continued existence. This "thirst" (coupled, as we shall see, with ignorance) is called the truth about the arising (samudaya) of stress. (3)

1 Śāriputra preaches the Four Truths in the Buddha's stead in the *Discourse on the Exposition of the Truths* (*Saccavibhanga Sutta*). See Ñāṇamoli and Bodhi (1995), pp. 1097–1101, and Anālayo (2006).

2 I borrow the translation "stress" from Thanissaro (1996), p. 278. Although Harvey (2009) has nice things to say about it, he does not adopt it.

Nonetheless, by eliminating our inherent craving ("thirst") and all its subtle and not-so-subtle manifestations and connections, it is possible to bring an end to stress, to be free from it. This is the truth of the cessation (nirodha) of stress, which is commonly identified with nirvāṇa. (4) Finally, the way to do this is to practice the path (mārga), which is seen as the way to the cessation of stress. There are many understandings of this path; in the context of the Buddha's First Sermon, it is identified as consisting of eight practices, and so is called "the noble eightfold path" (or "the eightfold path of the noble ones"). This is also, as we have seen, said to be equivalent to the Middle Way. But the Buddhist tradition as a whole was to go on and give a variety of understandings of the path, so, in 5.4 and 5.5, I will not only consider the limbs of the path, but other schemas for describing it.[3]

TRUTH	SANSKRIT: SATYA	PALI: SACCA
Stress	Duḥkha	Dukkha
Arising (of stress)	Samudaya	Samudaya
Cessation/extinction (of stress)	Nirodha/Nirvāṇa	Nirodha/Nibbāna
Way (to the cessation of stress) (see 5.3)	Mārga	Magga

Table 5.1 The Four Truths

5.1 THE FIRST TRUTH: STRESS

In one early presentation of the Four Truths, the truth about stress is defined as follows: "Birth is stressful, old age is stressful, disease is stressful, death is stressful; dejection, sorrow and vexation are stressful; association with what is disliked is stressful; being dissociated from what is liked is stressful; not obtaining what is searched for is stressful; in short, the five aggregates of clinging [upādāna-skandhas] are stressful – this is called the truth of stress."[4]

Some of these examples of stress are perhaps more readily apparent than others. Few people would deny that times of transition, such as birth, aging, sickness, and death, getting into college, finding a job, and raising children, whether actually painful or not, are stressful. So are negative emotions

3 For a presentation and concise discussion of the Four Truths, see Gethin (1998), pp. 59–84.

4 I follow the translation in Anālayo (2006), p. 148, inserting "stress" or "stressful" for "suffering." For a discussion of the text's wording, see Vetter (1998), on which, however, see also Anālayo (2011a), p. 805 n239.

involving sadness and frustration, and bad circumstances such as being unsatisfied with one's situation. All this we can agree with. The Buddha, however, goes on to state that the five aggregates – the five skandhas which, as we have seen, define the entirety of our experience in this world – are stressful. This appears to amount to the Buddha declaring that life, anywhere and everywhere in saṃsāra, is inherently stressful – duḥkha.[5]

When students in my classes get to this point – especially if they are reading a version of the First Sermon in which "duḥkha" is translated as "suffering" or "pain" – they often protest that they do not see life in this way, and ask, "Why was the Buddha so pessimistic?" In this they are echoing generations of Western scholars who drew similar conclusions. The common answer given by some Buddhist scholars – that Buddhism is not pessimistic but "realistic" (Rahula, 1959, p. 17) – has never struck me as very reassuring. It is a bit more helpful to point out that the notion of "stress" (duḥkha) goes hand in glove with the notion of "impermanence" (anitya). Therefore stress comes with the realization that good times will not last but always give way to bad times. But then some of my students point out that yes, this is true, but it is also the case that bad times do not last, but give way to good times, even if only in one's next life. So why dwell on the negative?

What my students have realized in their own way may be used to highlight a point made by Hamilton. She says that we should view the truth of stress *not* as an ontological statement concerned with the nature of things – about their state of *being* – but rather as a description of an experience of things. As she puts it, the First Truth (and Buddhist doctrine more generally) has nothing to do with "what things are" but rather with "how things are" (Hamilton, 1996, p. 195). Things are stressful not in and of themselves by their very nature but because they are involved with "clinging" (upādāna).

Hamilton's distinction is important because it allows for the possibility of change. By getting rid of "clinging" (and the craving that causes it), we can alter "how we are" in the world. Before we can do so, however, we have to come to at least an initial realization of the extent of our clinging, the stressfulness of our situation. Buddhism is optimistic, but it is not naively so. Stress is somewhat like an addiction; it will not do simply to deny it. If we are alcoholics, we cannot really start to do anything about our alcoholism until we realize for ourselves the extent of our dependency and desire – of our "clinging." So too we cannot do anything about duḥkha until we realize its nature. But this realization is a gradual process. Just as there are stages to

5 On the five skandhas being stressful, see Hamilton (2000), pp. 29–30.

our realization of the full dimensions of our dependency if we are addicts, so too there are stages in the realization of the truth of stress (as well as the other truths). According to at least some versions of the First Sermon, one first grasps the First Truth intellectually: "this is stress." Then one endeavors to know it thoroughly. Finally, with right wisdom, one comes to realize that one does indeed know it thoroughly. The same process is applied to the other truths. Only then can it be said that one has attained "unsurpassed complete enlightenment."[6]

This leads me to a final point. It is important not to take the First Truth in isolation from the other truths. For the First Truth (stress) and the Second Truth (craving) are truths that are ultimately to be contradicted by the Third Truth (cessation) and the Fourth Truth (the path). In this sense, the Four Truths as a whole denote a kind of spectrum with two extremes: at one end is the true understanding of the problem (stress and its origin – craving); at the other end is the true fulfillment of the solution (stresslessness and its origin – the path). The middle way aims at realizing *both* stress *and* stresslessness.

5.2 THE SECOND TRUTH: THE CONTINUAL ARISING OF STRESS AND INTERDEPENDENT ORIGINATION

If the First Truth defines the scope and nature of stress (duḥkha), the second describes its continual arising (samudaya), not in terms of its absolute beginning or origin, but rather in terms of the conditions in which and by which it perpetuates itself. The Buddha's First Sermon defines this truth as craving, which it calls "thirst" (tṛṣṇā): "[It is] the craving for further existence that is associated with greed and satisfaction, that takes pleasure in this and that, namely, craving for the objects of the senses, craving for existence, craving for non-existence" (Gethin, 2008, p. 244).

The connection of craving to stress is spelled out in terms of the doctrine of interdependent origination (pratītyasamutpāda; Pali, paṭiccasamuppāda), which is another hallmark of Buddhist thought. Indeed, it has been called "the radical insight at the heart of the Buddha's teaching, the insight from which everything else unfolds" (Bodhi, 1995, p. 1). The Buddha himself is said to have declared that one who sees interdependent origination sees the Buddha, and the Mahāyāna philosopher Nāgārjuna was later to equate interdependent

6 On the gradual realization of the Four Truths, see Strong (2008), p. 44.

origination with the doctrine of emptiness, one of the fundamental building blocks of the Mahāyāna (see 9.1).

The basic principle of interdependent origination is summed up in the statement: "When this is, that is; this arising, that arises. When this is not, that is not; this ceasing, that ceases" (Yamada, 1980, p. 373). This, in turn, reflects what elsewhere has been called the "import" or "gist" of the Buddha's teachings – namely that what the Buddha did was to "explain the cause of those elements of reality (dharmas) that arise from a cause, and also to explain their cessation" (Strong, 2008, p. 62). This alone, as we shall see in 6.7.1, was enough to bring the Buddha's two chief disciples, Śāriputra and Maudgalyāyana, to enlightenment. In a simpler form it also occasioned the awakening of the Buddha's very first disciple, Kaundinya, who, as a result of the First Sermon, realized that "whatever dharma is subject to origination, is also subject to cessation" (Collins, 1982, p. 227).[7]

It will immediately be seen that these statements imply a double process of explaining how something comes about, and also how something ceases to be. In this light, interdependent origination is akin to the doctrine of the Four Truths which, as we have just seen, explain both the nature and origin of suffering, and of its cessation. Indeed, the formula of interdependent origination is usually repeated twice in the texts – once to explain how the presence of each conditioning cause results in the arising and existence of the succeeding element, and the second time to explain how the eradication of the conditioning cause results in the cessation (non-existence) of the preceding element.

The formula of interdependent origination – the spelling out of the actual specific causal links – varies somewhat from one text to another. In what follows, I will first present a common scheme that defines twelve links, spread out over three lifetimes (see table 5.2). Each factor "conditions" the one below it, i.e. it colors or affects its nature. To that extent it may be said to "cause" it, but not always. It is important to specify that a "conditioning" relationship is not necessarily the same as a "causal" one and the nature of the connection between the various links in the chain of interdependent origination may vary. For instance, though birth (no. 11) may be said to lead inevitably to aging and dying (no. 12), and so, in this sense, to cause it, the same is not true of the relationship between feelings (no. 7) and craving (no. 8): feelings can condition craving, but they do not necessarily cause it. This is important; as Bhikkhu Bodhi puts it, it "has the profoundest implications

7 For further discussion of this verse, see Boucher (1993).

for a teaching of deliverance. For if [interdependent origination] described a series in which each factor *necessitated* the next, the series could never be broken. All human effort directed to liberation would be futile and the round would have to turn forever. But a relationship of conditionality, unlike a [causally] necessitarian one, allows for a margin of freedom in responding to the condition" (Bodhi, 1995, pp. 9–10). The conditioning links thus are where the chain can be broken.

PREVIOUS EXISTENCE	1. Ignorance (avidyā)	Process of activity
	2. Karmic constructions (saṃskāra)	
PRESENT EXISTENCE	3. Consciousness (vijñāna)	Process of maturation
	4. Mind and body (nāmarūpa)	
	5. Sense bases (āyatana)	
	6. Contact (sparśa)	
	7. Feelings (vedanā)	
	8. Craving (tṛṣṇā)	Process of activity
	9. Clinging (upādāna)	
	10. Becoming (bhava) ("a karmic action which gives rise to re-existence")	
FUTURE EXISTENCE	11. Birth (jāti)	Process of maturation
	12. Aging and death (jāramaraṇa)	

Table 5.2 Interdependent Origination[8]

It is easiest, perhaps, to explicate the links of the chain of interdependent origination in the reverse direction. Let me begin, therefore, with aging and death (no. 12). Few would deny that this is a fact of life, and few would deny that this is characterized by suffering, by stress (duḥkha). In his sermons on interdependent origination, the Buddha asks the question: in the presence of what factor does aging-and-dying come about? and his answer is "birth" (no. 11). Birth, old age, illness, and death, it will be remembered, were described in the First Truth as the most evident causes of suffering, of stress (duḥkha). Thus together, links nos. 11 and 12, though sometimes associated with a future life, are really denotative of duḥkha, and the rest of the links will thus address the broader question of how duḥkha arises.

Pursuing his inquiry, the Buddha asks how birth comes about, and his answer is "bhava" (no. 10). Bhava literally means "existence" but here, as Lamotte points out, it actually signifies "a karmic action which gives rise to re-existence" (1988, p. 38). Sometimes it is translated as "becoming." In the

8 Based on Lamotte (1988), p. 39.

context of karma and reincarnation, birth (in a future life), or becoming, may be seen as the ripening of the fruits of actions in this life. These actions are, in turn, conditioned by "upādāna" (no. 9), a word which is usually translated as "clinging" or "grasping" but which, as Thanissaro Bhikkhu points out, can also mean sustenance, as in the fuel needed for a fire, or soil needed for a tree. Like a fire that clings to its fuel and grasps for more fuel, or a tree that clings to its soil by its roots and seeks to grow them further, a person clings to existence and wants to extend it. More specifically, several types of upādāna are distinguished according to what is the object of clinging: clinging to sensuous pleasures, clinging to wrong views, clinging to habitual rules and rituals, and clinging to the notion of a Self.[9]

All this clinging – this attachment – is, in turn, conditioned by craving (tṛṣṇā, no. 8), a word that literally means "thirst," and which, as we shall see, is one of the key links in the whole chain of interdependent origination, and the one that, as we have seen, is most emphasized in the First Sermon's description of the cause of stress (the Second Truth). Craving, it should be pointed out, is not the same as desire or just "wanting" something – otherwise one could not "want" to put an end to stress. Craving involves attachment and is obviously not possible without "feelings" (vedanā, no. 7), which are conditioned, in turn, by "contact" (sparśa, no. 6) between one's "sense organs and the fields of the senses" (the twelve āyatanas, no. 5). Sense organs are dependent on one's having a "mind and body" (nāmarūpa, no. 4), and this is inseparable from "consciousness" (vijñāna, no. 3). Consciousness is here distinguished from the other constituents of the person, because it is seen as playing a crucial role in the conception of a new being. According to Buddhist notions of conception, without consciousness, an embryo would not form. This does not mean that consciousness should be viewed as some sort of soul that implants itself in the generative physical mix of the embryo, for it is not permanent and unchanging; it does, however, play a special role in ensuring the link from a past existence to a present one.

We have at this point arrived at link no. 3 (consciousness) in table 5.2. One of the major canonical discussions of interdependent origination – that found in the *Mahānidāna Sutta* (*Great Discourse on Causation*) – ends its list of links right there. Mind and body, it declares, are dependent on consciousness and consciousness is dependent on mind and body; one cannot

---

9 On upādāna as fuel or soil, see Thanissaro (1993), pp. 38–39. See also Gombrich (2009), pp. 113–114. On the several types of upādāna, see Ñāṇamoli and Bodhi (1995), p. 161.

tell which comes first (see Bodhi, 1995, pp. 18–20). This chicken-and-egg solution makes good sense in view of Buddhism's eschewing a doctrine of absolute beginning in favor of a circular notion of the universe and time. Other accounts of interdependent origination, however, go on to speak of two more links which are characterized as occurring in a previous existence: consciousness, as the first factor of a new life, is seen as the result of karmic constructions (saṃskāra, no. 2) done in a previous life or lives. These are intentional actions, good or bad, which through the law of karma, necessarily entail results. In a sense, this link of karmic constructions is akin to that of bhava – "a karmic action which gives rise to re-existence" (no. 10), except that it is here viewed from a different perspective. Rather than being seen as conditioned by craving and clinging, it is seen as conditioned by ignorance (avidyā, no. 1). Ignorance means ignorance of the Four Truths, of the three marks of existence (impermanence, stress, and non-self). As one discourse puts it, it means not just not knowing, but wrong-knowing – "taking for eternal what is transitory, for pleasant what is unpleasant, for pure what is impure, for a Self what has no self" (Lamotte, 1988, p. 36). In other words, ignorance of the true nature of things and of the self leads us to believe in their desirability and so reinforces the factors of craving and clinging.

5.2.1 The Double Bind of Saṃsāra

In the Second Truth as presented in his First Sermon, the Buddha traces the origin of stress (duḥkha) not to ignorance, but only to craving (tṛṣṇā). The full picture of interdependent origination, however, shows us that, in the end, we are kept in saṃsāra – in the stressful cycle of life and death – not by a single chain but by a double bind which originates in craving and clinging (tṛṣṇā/upādāna, no. 8) on the one hand, and in ignorance (avidyā, no. 1) on the other.[10]

Importantly, ignorance and craving/clinging are also the "weak links" in the chain that are breakable by our efforts. This in turn suggests once again that the path to stresslessness – the path to nirvāṇa – contains basically two approaches for breaking the chains that bind us. One is to eradicate ignorance through the attainment of knowledge or insight; the other is to eradicate craving through the establishment of discipline and the elimination of the defilements.

10 See the helpful introduction to pratītyasamutpāda in Bodhi (2000), pp. 516–526.

These two paths complement one another, of course, but are nonetheless distinct, stemming perhaps, as I suggested in 4.2.3, from different ideological contexts. As we have seen, the notion that knowledge (Skt., jñāna) can be salvific has its earliest full expression in India in the Upaniṣads where it is declared that the person who *knows* Ātman/Brahman (absolute reality) *is* Ātman/Brahman, i.e. is liberated from saṃsāra. The notion of freeing oneself from attachments and desires and defilements by means of purification may, on the other hand, be seen as rooted in śramaṇic traditions of discipline and renunciation (e.g. the Jains). Once again, here, we can see how Buddhism forges a middle way between (or perhaps rather around) the two general ideologies in which it grew up.

5.3 THE THIRD TRUTH: THE CESSATION OF STRESS – NIRVĀṆA

Many years ago when I was studying at the University of Peradeniya in Sri Lanka, I came across a faded piece of notepaper that had been randomly left between the pages of a book that had belonged to T. W. Rhys Davids (1843–1922), a great scholar and one of the founders of Pali studies. He had left many of his books to the university. The paper was covered with notes written in what I had come to recognize as Rhys Davids's hand. Half way down, in a scrawl in brownish ink, he had written: "vāta – wind" and then just below that: "nirvāṇo – where there is no storm." I have always remembered that suggested etymology, even though it is not the one that Rhys Davids propounded in his own *Pali–English Dictionary* (Davids and Stede, 1921–1925, p. 362).

One often reads that nirvāṇa means "blowing out," or "extinction," as in the extinction of the fires of desire, hatred, and delusion – a sort of a "petering out" of a flame when there is no more fuel to burn. And indeed, one can find much support for this view in canonical texts.

Etymologically, it can be argued that the prefix "nir" means "the absence of something," and the verbal root "vā" means "to blow," so one of the meanings of nirvāṇa could simply be "devoid of blowing." To my mind this suggests not so much a petering out of the "flames of passion" due to lack of fuel, but due to their no longer being fanned. As any Boy Scout knows, to keep a fire burning, you need to blow on it. When you stop blowing, the fire goes out. But Rhys Davids's note also brings to mind a different metaphor: nirvāṇa as a refuge, a shelter, a place where the wind does not blow anymore. This too is an image that can be found in canonical texts.[11]

The two metaphors – suggestive of extinction and of shelter – have marked Western discussions of the term nirvāṇa. For good parts of the nineteenth and twentieth centuries, scholars engaged in a lively debate along just these lines. The notion of "extinction" was quickly extended to mean "annihilation"; since extinction means the elimination of the craving and ignorance that fuels (or fans the flames of) karma and rebirth, it was thought that one who attains nirvāṇa is not reborn, and for many Westerners, no more birth meant non-existence. On the other hand, the notion of refuge was extended to mean some kind of transcendent indescribable state of bliss.[12]

The same two metaphors – of extinction and shelter – can also be seen in some of the Buddha's disciples' poems about their attainment of enlightenment, but without the just-mentioned extensions. Two examples of these will suffice here. In the *Verses of the Eldresses* (*Therīgāthā*), the nun Pāṭacāra (whom we shall encounter again in 6.7.2) recalls her enlightenment experience in the following terms suggestive of extinction:

> Ploughing their fields, sowing seeds in the earth, men look after their wives and children, and prosper.
>
> Why can't I, who keep the precepts and follow the teachings of the Master, attain nirvāṇa? I am neither lazy nor conceited.
>
> After washing my feet, I note the water, and watch it going down the drain; that makes me collect and control my mind ...
>
> Then taking a lamp, I enter my cell; thinking of going to sleep, I sit down on my bed;
>
> With a pin, I pull out the wick. The lamp goes out: nirvāṇa. My mind is freed.
>
> (Strong, 2008, p. 119)[13]

The enlightenment poem of the monk Girimānanda, from the *Verses of the Elders* (*Theragāthā*), is rather different. He recalls sitting in his thatched hut, when it begins to rain hard. But he stays dry and comfortable, sheltered from

11 There are other possible interpretations of the etymologies of nirvāṇa. For a full discussion, see Collins (1998), pp. 191–201. There are also other metaphors for nirvāṇa (see ibid., pp. 213–233).

12 On Western views of nirvāṇa, see Welbon (1968).

13 For a translation of the full text of the *Verses of the Eldresses*, see Norman (1995). For the commentary on the text, see Pruitt (1998).

the storm. In a series of verses, he exults in his state of quiet appeasement, and tells the gods to send as much rain as they wish, for out of the wind, his mind at ease, he dwells free from desire, free from hatred, and free from delusion.[14]

In neither of these poems is there any suggestion of transcendent bliss, and certainly not of annihilation. Here the metaphors of extinction and shelter suggest something less extreme: nirvāṇa as letting go, and nirvāṇa as being untouched by the world. In both cases, a state of stresslessness has been reached.

Less personal, more theoretical Buddhist texts, however, make it clear that language cannot adequately describe this state of stresslessness which is deemed immeasurable, ineffable, incomparable. The Buddha felt that "what is nirvāṇa?" was one of those questions that could not profitably be answered, and so, by implication, should not be asked! Positives cannot describe it, but neither can negatives. Even statements such as "stresslessness" are inadequate. The Mahāyāna philosopher Nāgārjuna was to take this kind of ineffability to its logical heights (or depths): the Buddha in nirvāṇa, he asserted, cannot be said to exist, cannot be said to not exist, cannot be said to both exist and not exist, and cannot be said to neither exist nor not exist. Or, as Beyer translated the passage: "After his final cessation / the Blessed One isnt is / isnt isnt / isnt is & isnt / isnt isnt is & isnt" (1974, p. 214).[15]

At this point, it might seem that there would be nothing left to say (or not say) about Nirvāṇa. However, to do justice to the tradition as a whole, a few more points need to be made.

First, one line of thought did maintain that, whether describable or not, nirvāṇa has to exist if there is to be any escape from saṃsāra (a possibility which lay, unquestioned, at the base of most Indic religious systems). An often-cited early Pali text makes this clear: "There is, monks, that in which there is no birth, where nothing has come into existence, where nothing has been made, where there is nothing conditioned (asaṃskṛta; Pali, asankhāta) ... [If there were not, no way out from the] born, become, made, conditioned [could be found]" (Collins, 1998, p. 167). In contrast to this realm of stress (duḥkha), nirvāṇa is viewed as "the highest happiness" (paramam sukham), the "summum bonum" which "structures and

14 See Strong (2008), p. 119. For a full translation of the *Verses of the Elders*, see Norman (1969).

15 On the ineffability and unmeasurability of nirvāṇa, see Norman (1996), pp. 171–172, Collins (1998), p. 162, and Strong (2008), p. 117. On the "undetermined questions" that cannot profitably be answered, see Harvey (1995), pp. 83ff. See also Warren (1896), pp. 117–128.

systematizes the [whole Buddhist] cosmology of imagined felicities" (Collins, 1998, pp. 116–117).[16]

Second, in line with the affirmation of its necessary existence, nirvāṇa is consistently asserted by Abhidharma scholastics to be what is technically called "an unconstructed (or unconditioned) element of reality (asaṃskṛta dharma)." This means it is real – it is a dharma – but it is different from all the "constructed" elements of reality (saṃskṛta dharma), such as the five aggregates, etc. Interestingly, in the abhidharmic lists of dharmas, nirvāṇa is not the only such "unconditioned dharma." The Theravādins also included empty space in this category, and other schools added various kinds of cessation (nirodha).[17]

As an unconstructed element, nirvāṇa is not characterized by stress (duḥkha) or by impermanence (anitya). It is, however, characterized by non-self (anātman). Thus, as a refuge, it is a place where persons who experienced stress and constant change can find ongoing stresslessness. It should not be thought, however, that in so doing, they suddenly find "their true selves." As Buddhaghosa puts it, "nirvāṇa exists but there is no nirvanized person" (Ñāṇamoli, 1976, vol. 2, p. 587).[18]

Finally, it should be said that Buddhist texts commonly distinguish between two types of nirvāṇa. There is the nirvāṇa that comes with awakening (bodhi). This amounts to the destruction of desire and the end of ignorance – the seeing of reality-as-it-is. This is what the Buddha discovered at Bodhgaya, and what disciples of the Buddha discover when they reach arhatship. This makes for the extinction of the defilements, but not for the extinction of the aggregates. The awakened person is still alive and still has a body and a mind, with all its feelings, perceptions, and consciousness. This is commonly called nirvāṇa-with-a-psycho-physical substratum remaining.

It is only at the death of an enlightened person that the second type of nirvāṇa comes in – that which is called "without-a-psycho-physical substratum remaining." When a buddha's (or an arhat's) body dies, we are told, he can no longer be seen, and there are no words for speaking of him, or ways of conceiving of him. This is parinirvāṇa (complete extinction/refuge), sometimes called the nirvāṇa of the aggregates (skandhas).[19]

16 On nirvāṇa as the highest happiness, see also the discussion in Anālayo (2011a), pp. 410–411. See also Ñāṇamoli and Bodhi (1995), p. 613.

17 On the varying lists of unconstructed dharmas, see Willemen (2004).

18 See, however, 9.7.1. for some rather different Mahāyāna takes on this question.

19 On the two types of nirvāṇa, see Collins (1998), pp. 147–151, and Lamotte (1988), p. 41. On the ineffable nature of the nirvāṇa without substratum, see Norman (1996), p. 170. Confusingly, the term "parinirvāṇa" is sometimes used for the first kind of nirvāṇa, and vice versa.

Bronkhorst connected the first type of nirvāṇa (that with remainder) with the mokṣa (liberation) by knowledge described in the Upaniṣads. He connected the second type (the nirvāṇa without remainder) with the final liberation (sallekhana) of the Jains, the final divestment of all remaining karmic agglutinations. In Buddhism's assertion of two kinds of nirvāṇa, he thus saw another example of its synthesis of elements from two other Indic traditions, and we can see another instance of a both/and middle way.[20]

With parinirvāṇa (the nirvāṇa without remainder), the metaphor of extinction appears to have won out. Yet this is not entirely the case; as we have seen in chapter 3, even after the breakup of his skandhas, the Buddha was thought to be present and ongoing in various other bodies: his Dharma, his relics, his images, etc. And the Mahāyāna, as we shall see in chapter 8, was to make similar assertions at the doctrinal level, claiming that the "extinction" of the Buddha in parinirvāṇa was not finally real but an expedient means of teaching the Dharma.

5.4 THE FOURTH TRUTH: THE PATH TO THE CESSATION OF STRESS

The Fourth Truth is generally said to be the "noble eightfold path to the cessation of stress." However, as mentioned above, Buddhists developed many different ways of describing a salvific path, and it is worth introducing some of those here as well. Accordingly, in this section, I will look first at the noble eightfold path, and then turn to some other models for presenting Buddhist practice.

As mentioned in 4.1 above, the eightfold path is described twice in the Buddha's First Sermon: once, at the very beginning, as an illustration of the Middle Way, and a second time, at the very end, as the definition of the Fourth Truth which leads to the cessation of stress, i.e. to nirvāṇa. Accordingly, we have now come full circle; having started with the path, we are ending up with the path. What this may reflect is that there is a certain chicken-and-egg quality about the Four Truths; you have to practice the path before you know that it is the right path to practice. You have to realize the truths before you know that they are the true reality.[21]

The eightfold path consists of a number of practices called "limbs" (anga)

20 Bronkhorst (2000), p. 57.

21 Dessein (2007), p. 21, has argued that the Fourth Truth was actually taught first.

that are labeled as being "right" or "correct" (samyak): (1) right view; (2) right application of the mind; (3) right speech; (4) right action; (5) right livelihood; (6) right effort; (7) right mindfulness; and (8) right concentration. Implicit in the notion of something being "right" (samyak) is an opposition to something being "wrong" (mithyā; Pali, micchā). Thus to the list of eight "rights" in the noble eightfold path, there corresponds a list of eight "wrongs." In this way, the path is as much about what one stops doing as about what one does.[22]

These eight limbs of the path are regularly grouped into what are known as the three "trainings" of wisdom (comprising limb nos. 1–2), moral discipline (comprising limb nos. 3–5), and meditation (comprising limb nos. 6–8) (see table 5.3). When they are thus grouped, however, they are usually discussed in the altered order of moral discipline, meditation, and wisdom, and accordingly, I shall consider them in that way.[23]

WISDOM (PRAJÑĀ)	1. Right view (samyag-dṛṣṭi)
	2. Right intention (samyak-saṃkalpa)
MORAL DISCIPLINE (ŚĪLĀ)	3. Right speech (samyag-vācā)
	4. Right action (samyak-karmānta)
	5. Right livelihood (samyak-ājīva)
MEDITATION (SAMĀDHI)	6. Right effort (samyak-ājīva)
	7. Right mindfulness (samyak-smṛti)
	8. Right concentration (samyak-samādhi)

Table 5.3 The Three Trainings and the Eightfold Path

5.4.1 Moral Discipline

Moral discipline comprises right action, speech, and livelihood, which together involve three dimensions of human activity: body, speech, and mind (or more specifically in this context, what might be called "habitual mind-set"). Right action is usually described as refraining from three bodily misdeeds: killing, theft, and sexual misconduct. As we shall see in 6.4, these injunctions also form the first of the ten moral precepts for novices, and the first of four cardinal rules for monks, the violation of which supposedly

22 For a presentation of the eightfold path, see Williams (2000), pp. 52–55, and Harvey (2013), pp. 81–88. For a listing of the eight wrongs, see Walshe (1987), p. 503. See also Anālayo (2011a), p. 662.

23 For a presentation of the three trainings, see Cantwell (2010), pp. 58–91.

entails expulsion from the community. As such, great energy was spent on describing the specific parameters of each of them, and defining what exactly counts as "killing" or "theft" or "sexual misconduct" and how much. As part of the path, however, these can be seen less as "rules" not to be violated and more as general moral guidelines to be followed. Thus, for example, one well-known text describes abstaining from killing as follows: "having laid down his stick and his sword, he lives in modesty, showing kindness, compassion, and concern for the welfare of all living beings" (Strong, 2008, p. 123). Similarly, abstaining from theft also implies being generous and acting magnanimously towards others, while abstaining from sexual misconduct will depend on the situation of the person; for monastics it generally means no sex; for laypersons, however, it means following whatever sexual norms are dominant in the culture.[24]

Right speech is described as refraining from four things: lies, slander, harsh talk and frivolous talk. These too may be found in the ten precepts of novices, but, again, here, they are not just rules but meant as attitudes. Not lying thus also means "being reliable, open and trustworthy." Abstaining from slander means not only that, but "reconciling persons who are at odds, promoting concord, and rejoicing, delighting and taking pleasure at it." Forsaking harsh speech means being "kind, heart-warming, polite, delightful and charming to many people," while abstaining from frivolous talk means not just refraining from gossip, but speaking words that are "worth treasuring, reasonable, well defined, and purposeful" (Strong, 2008, p. 122).

Right livelihood fits into this same general notion of moral stances, although it is directed almost exclusively at laypersons. It means, essentially, opting for an occupation that does not involve one in wrong actions, i.e. not being a butcher, or an arms merchant, or a prostitute, or a gambler, etc. Buddhists were aware that part of moral discipline involves avoiding situations in which the habitual mind-set (or perhaps more accurately mindless-set) calls for routine performance of wrong actions.

5.4.2 Meditation

Meditation is often thought to be the core and crux of Buddhist practice. Westerners, in particular, are inclined to emphasize it, sometimes exclusively so. The eightfold path, however (as well as other descriptions of the path),

24 On this, see Crosby (2014), p. 116.

makes it clear that, while important, meditation is only one aspect of practice. Moreover, as we have seen (1.2.5), only a small minority of Buddhists, lay or monastic, regularly practice meditation. Nevertheless, ideologically, meditation is presented as fundamental.[25]

Right mindfulness (smṛti; Pali, sati) and right concentration (samādhi) are two limbs of the eightfold path that are traditionally considered to be part of the training in meditation. They are to be pursued with a third limb – right effort – which is usually described as persistence in preventing unwholesome states of mind from arising and diligence in cultivating wholesome states. Right effort, it should be stated, is not always paired with the practice of meditation and may be thought to apply more generally to all the other practices of the path as well. Interestingly, in one early version of a discourse describing the eightfold path, it is called "right expedient means" (upāya; Ch., Fang-bian), a topic to which we shall return in 9.3.[26]

Mental training, which is a prerequisite for both mindfulness and concentration, can be developed by practicing sustained focused attention on a particular object of meditation, such as a flat colored disk or any one of nine other constructed "visual objects" (Pali, kasiṇa), or such as one's breath.[27]

Generally speaking, it is possible to distinguish two sorts of mindfulness: (1) awareness of the different postures and activities of the body and of the world around us, i.e. being conscious of when one is going, or standing, or sitting, or lying down, being conscious of when one is looking forward, or backward, of when one is bending one's limbs or stretching them out, of when one is carrying one's bowl or setting it down, of when one is breathing in, and when one is exhaling, as well as how one is doing all these things (e.g. "I am breathing in a long breath," or "I am breathing in a shallow breath"); (2) applications of mindfulness (smṛtyupasthāna; Pali satipaṭṭhāna), in which the mind is made to focus sustainedly on a variety of more abstracted notions such as the impurities of the body, feelings, the mind, and the dharmas (elements of existence). Sometimes these more abstract notions are concretized by particular objects of meditation; thus the impure aspects of the body and its impermanence and non-self are made vivid by the so-called "cemetery

25 For a bibliographic essay on Buddhist meditation, see McMahan (2013). For an anthology of Pali texts on meditation, see Shaw (2006a).

26 On right effort in general, see Bodhi (2000), p. 1529. On right effort as right expedient means, see Anālayo (2006), p. 148.

27 For a list of the objects of meditation and a description of their use, see Crosby (2014), pp. 150–152.

meditations" in which one focuses on ten different stages in the decomposition of a corpse.[28]

More generally, mindfulness is described as a precursor to knowledge or insight (vipaśyanā) into the nature of phenomena as impermanent, stressful, and devoid of self. Vipaśyanā (Pali, Vipassanā) is not listed as part of the eightfold path, but later Pali systematizers such as Buddhaghosa (fifth century CE) presented it, along with śamatha (see below), as one of two key practices. Starting in nineteenth- and twentieth-century Myanmar (see 1.2.5), and spreading from there throughout the world, it later came to be propagated as "Insight meditation," and presented as a self-sufficient meditation technique in its own right.[29]

Mindfulness, however, is also a precursor to the practice of "calm-abiding" (śamatha). This leads to the attainment of various levels of trance (dhyāna) which are a feature of samādhi (concentration), which *is* listed as a limb of the path. The trance states are traditionally said to be eight (or nine) in number. The first four are described as belonging to the realm of form, and the second four (or five) to the formless realm (see table 5.4). These trances represent a gradual shutting down of thought and the sensory experiences to attain states that are increasingly abstracted from the world without. One author has summarized them as follows:

> In the first dhyāna there is deliberation, thought, joy and bliss; in the second dhyāna deliberation and thought come to rest. Inner tranquillization, unification of the mind, concentration, joy and bliss are present; in the third dhyāna one is no longer attached to joy. Equanimity, mindfulness, circumspection and bliss are present; in the fourth dhyāna bliss and misery are abandoned, as well as cheerfulness and dejectedness. Equanimity and mindfulness remain.
>
> (Bronkhorst, 2000, p. 88)

Beyond the fourth dhyāna are the four formless attainments (samāpatti) in which the meditator is focused on the infinity of space, the infinity of

28 See Crosby (2014), pp. 150–51. On cemetery meditations, see also L. Wilson (1996), pp. 41–76, and Boisvert (1996).

29 On the two forms of mindfulness, see Bronkhorst (1985), p. 311. For an introduction to and translation of an important discourse on the fourfold establishments of mindfulness, see Gethin (2008), pp. 141–151. On the development of Burmese Vipassanā, see Crosby (2014), pp. 161–164; on particular masters of this tradition, see Kornfield (1977), pp. 51–256.

perception, nothingness, and neither ideation nor non-ideation. And beyond this, there is still the stage of "cessation."[30]

REALM	TRANCE	FEATURES
FORMLESS REALM	9. Cessation (nirodha)	Foretaste of nirvāṇa
	8. Attainment of the sphere of neither perception nor non-perception	
	7. Attainment of the sphere of nothingness	
	6. Attainment of the sphere of unlimited consciousness	
	5. Attainment of the sphere of unlimited space	
REALM OF FORM	4. Fourth trance (dhyāna)	One-pointedness, equanimity. Six higher knowledges (abhijñā) including supernatural powers. Gateway to nirvāṇa
	3. Third trance (dhyāna)	One-pointedness, happiness, equanimity
	2. Second trance (dhyāna)	One-pointedness, happiness, joy
	1. First trance (dhyāna)	One-pointedness, happiness, joy, discursive thought

Table 5.4 Meditative Trance States

The fourth trance is often emphasized in Buddhist texts as critical. Coming as it does at the conjunction of the realm of form and the formless realm, it is itself a sort of middle-way state in which the meditator may be thought to be both in this world of forms and yet not confined to them. It comes as no surprise, then, to find that this is the stage at which meditators are said to develop supernatural powers such as the ability to multiply one's body and make it one again, to disappear and reappear, to walk on water, to pass through the earth, to fly through the air. Some of these we saw the Buddha performing at Śrāvastī in 2.7.9. It is also the stage from which awakening (bodhi) is attained, at least by the Buddha.[31]

30 On meditation on the trance states, see Cousins (1973). For a thorough discussion of the trance of cessation and its implications, see Griffiths (1986).

31 For a bibliographic essay and discussion of the supernatural powers, see Fiordalis (2013).

It is sometimes suggested that these trance states, and the practice of calm-abiding that leads to them, were not originally part of Buddhism. They are variously associated with classical yoga, or with the Buddha's first two teachers (Udraka and Ārāḍa) whose views he surpassed and rejected. In contrast, vipaśyana is presented as the Buddha's original contribution to meditation.[32]

In my view, however, whatever the origins and particularities of the trance states, they represent an important mode of meditation in Buddhism which, when paired with vipaśyana, form another both/and iteration of the Buddhist middle way. Simply put, in the trance states of calm-abiding (śamatha) and samādhi, we see a shedding of attachment to the world, a transcendence coming from detachment, the reaching of what Conze called "an objectless inwardness." With mindfulness (smṛti) and insight (vipaśyanā), we see an emphasis on awareness of the world and on one's connections to it, leading to a transcendence coming from understanding of what Conze termed "an unsubstantial emptiness" (1956, p. 16). Long ago, the great Belgian buddhologist Louis de La Vallée Poussin similarly distinguished between two ways to nirvāṇa when he paired śamatha and samādhi with gradual (ascetic) purification, a gradual suppression of thought, leading to a transcendent reality of nirvāṇa, while he associated vipaśyanā with "the discernment of dharmas," the understanding of the Four Truths, and the wisdom that comes with knowing reality "just as it is" (yathābhūtam) (1936–1937, pp. 190–191).

Once again, here, we can see that the Buddhist middle way is effectively combining two paths taken from the ideological context in which it was formed: in a sense, samādhi is a meditational or mental equivalent to Jain bodily asceticism and discipline: a gradual whittling away of the contents of the mind through the various trance states, a removal of the self from the world. Vipaśyana, on the other hand, is a way of remaining in the world by understanding its true nature by wisdom.

5.4.3 Wisdom

Wisdom also comes into play in the third "training" of the noble eightfold path which comprises two limbs: right view and right intention. Right view we have essentially dealt with already. It means acceptance and then cultivation

32 Bronkhorst (1985), p. 308, suggests that the four formless trances are not part of the original Buddhist scheme, but an importation from Jain practice. On the primacy of vipaśyana, see Rahula (1959), pp. 68–69.

of the doctrines covered in this and the previous chapter: karma, non-self, impermanence, the Four Truths, etc. It is also intimately linked to the middle way. For instance, in one Pali canonical discourse, the monk Kaccāna asks the Buddha: "We always hear talk of 'right view, right view.' What *is* 'right view?'" And the Buddha answers that most people view the world either in terms of existence or non-existence. "Everything exists: – this is one extreme. Nothing exists: – this is the other extreme. Not approaching either extreme the Tathāgata teaches you a doctrine of the middle way" (Davids and Woodward, 1917–1930, vol. 2, pp. 12–13). This is right view.

Right intention, sometimes called right application of the mind, is perhaps the least discussed of the limbs of the eightfold path. It is thought to be part of wisdom, and implies doing the rest of the practices for the right reasons, i.e. not practicing morality so that one will be admired; not meditating in order to achieve super powers, etc. One Pali discourse describes it as follows: "What is right intention? Intention of renunciation, intention of non-ill will, and intention of non-cruelty – this is called right intention" (Ñāṇamoli and Bodhi, 1995, p. 1100).

5.5 OTHER SYSTEMATIZATIONS OF THE PATH

The noble eightfold path is not the only description of the way to put an end to stress. Buddhist texts often mention various other schemes, some of which are comprehensive and some of which are partial. In what follows, I want to present a few of these briefly: the seven factors conducive to enlightenment (5.5.1); the path known as "the graduated training" (5.5.2); the four divine abidings (5.5.3); and finally the four stages of attainment or fruits of the path (5.5.4).

5.5.1 The Seven Factors Conducive to Enlightenment

We have seen that meditation forms one of the trainings of the noble eightfold path. One systematization of the path that highlights even more the importance of meditation and goes into it in greater detail is the scheme of the so-called "seven factors conducive to enlightenment" (sapta bodhyangāni), often mentioned in canonical texts (see table 5.5). The practice is described by Bhikkhu Bodhi as follows:

SEVEN FACTORS CONDUCIVE TO ENLIGHTENMENT	GRADUATED TRAINING	FOUR FRUITS OF THE PATH	FOUR DIVINE ABIDINGS	THIRTY-SEVEN FACTORS CONDUCIVE TO ENLIGHTENMENT
1. Mindfulness (smṛti)	1. Fear of wrongdoing	1. Stream-winner (śrotāpanna)	1. Loving-kindness (maitrī)	1–4. The four establishments of mindfulness (smṛtyupasthāna)
2. Discrimination (pravicaya)	2. Cultivating pure conduct in body,	2. Once-returner (sakṛdāgāmin)	2. Compassion (karuṇā)	5–8. The four correct efforts (samyakpradhāna)
3. Energy (vīrya)	3. in speech,	3. Non-returner (anāgāmin)	3. Sympathetic joy (muditā)	9–12. The four foundations of supernatural power (ṛddhipāda)
4. Rapture (prīti)	4. in mind	4. Arhatship	4. Equanimity (upekṣā)	13–17. The five spiritual faculties (indriya) – faith, vigor, mindfulness, concentration, wisdom
5. Tranquility (praśrabdhi)	5. Purifying livelihood			18–22. The five powers (bala)
6. Concentration (samādhi)	6. Guarding doors of senses			23–29. The seven factors conducive to enlightenment (see column 1)
7. Equanimity (upekṣā)	7. Moderation in eating			30–37. The eight limbs of the noble path (see table 5.3)
	8. Training in being awake and alert			
	9. Mindfulness			
	10. Abandon five hindrances			
	11. First trance			
	12. Second trance			
	13. Third trance			
	14. Fourth trance			
	15. Remembering past lives			
	16. Divine eye			
	17. Destroying defilement and knowing Four Truths			

Table 5.5 Other Schematizations of the Path

> First one attends mindfully to an object of meditation, generally selected from among the four objective bases of mindfulness (body, feelings, mind, phenomena): this is the enlightenment factor of mindfulness [no. 1, smṛti]. As mindfulness becomes steady, one learns to discern the object's features more clearly, and can also distinguish between the wholesome and unwholesome states of mind that arise within the process of contemplation: [this is] the enlightenment factor of discrimination [no. 2, dharma pravicaya]. This fires one's efforts: [this is] the enlightenment factor of energy [no. 3, vīrya]. From energy applied to the work of mental purification joy arises and escalates: [this is] the enlightenment factor of rapture [no. 4, prīti]. With the refinement of rapture the body and mind calm down: [this is] the enlightenment factor of tranquility [no. 5, praśrabdhi]. The tranquil mind is easily unified: [this is] the enlightenment factor of concentration [no. 6, samādhi]. One looks on evenly at the concentrated mind: [this is] the enlightenment factor of equanimity [no. 7, upekṣā]. As each subsequent factor arises, those already arisen do not disappear but remain alongside it as its adjuncts (though rapture inevitably subsides as concentration deepens). Thus, at the mature stage of development, all seven factors are present simultaneously, each making its own distinctive contribution.
>
> (Bodhi, 2000, pp. 1499–1500)[33]

Here it will be seen that the path is presented entirely as the cultivation of certain mental states through meditation. The assumption of the commentaries, however, is that this will be accompanied by the development of wisdom and moral discipline.

5.5.2 *The Graduated Training*

A fuller sequential description of the way to enlightenment may be found in a number of different discourses of the Buddha which describe the path as a gradual sequence of stages from the start up to arhatship. This scheme, which

33 The seven limbs as well as the eightfold path are both incorporated in a still more comprehensive scheme called the thirty-seven factors conducive to Awakening (saptatriṃśad bodhipakṣyā dharmāḥ), found in both Pali and Sanskrit texts (see table 5.5). See Gethin (1992).

is called "the graduated training" (anupubbasikkhā; Skt., anupūrvaśikṣā), is not usually mentioned in discussions of the path and yet it is found in a good number of Pali and Sanskrit texts (see table 5.5). One of the fullest descriptions is in the sermon that the Buddha is said to have given at Assapura ("Horse-Town"). "People call you renunciants (śramaṇas)," he says to his monks, "but do you know what that really means?" And, proceeding to tell them, he gives a complete outline of the path that all "true renunciants" should follow to arhatship. The path has seventeen steps: (1) developing a sense of shame and fear of wrongdoing; (2) cultivating pure conduct in body, (3) in speech, and (4) in mind; (5) purifying one's livelihood; (6) guarding the doors of the senses so as to cut down on grasping things that one sees, hears, smells, tastes, touches, or thinks; (7) training oneself to be moderate in eating; (8) training oneself to be wakeful and alert (lying down only during the middle watch of the night); (9) achieving mindfulness and full awareness (of when one is walking, where one is looking, when one is moving, when one is eating, drinking, defecating, urinating, speaking, remaining silent, falling asleep, waking up, etc.); (10) moving out to a hermitage to achieve complete abandonment of the five hindrances (nīvaraṇa), which are (a) sensual desires (kāmacchanda), (b) ill-will (vyāpāda), (c) laziness and lethargy (styānamiddha), (d) restlessness and regret (auddhatya-kaukṛtya), and (e) doubts (vicikitsā); (11–14) successively attaining the first four trance states; (15) recollecting one's past lives; (16) surveying the whole world with one's divine eye; (17) destroying all the defilements (āśravas) and achieving direct knowledge of the Four Truths. Such a person is called "a recluse, a Brahmin, one who has been washed, one who has attained to knowledge, a holy scholar, a noble one, an arhat."[34] The last three stages, it should be noted, exactly replicate the experience of the Buddha during the three watches of the night of his enlightenment at Bodhgaya.

5.5.3 *The Four Divine Abidings*

A somewhat different conception of the path describes attitudes one should cultivate towards the world. These are the so-called four "divine abidings"

34 Ñāṇamoli and Bodhi (1995), pp. 362–371. See also pp. 34–38 for a general discussion of the gradual training. For a discussion of Sanskrit and Chinese parallels to the *Discourse at Assapura*, see Anālayo (2011a), vol. 1, pp. 256–261. On the five hindrances, see Harvey (2013), pp. 249–250, and La Vallée Poussin (1988–1990), vol. 3, p. 851.

(Brahma-vihāra) (see table 5.5). This is a practice in which one extends to all four quarters – to all beings everywhere – thoughts of loving-kindness (no. 1, maitrī). In Mainstream Buddhism, one starts by focusing on one's own character and comes to accept and appreciate it for what it is – good and/or bad – before projecting the same sentiment on to all others. Then one extends to all beings who are suffering or in any kind of trouble, thoughts of compassion (no. 2, karuṇā). Then one extends similarly thoughts of sympathetic joy (no. 3, muditā), rejoicing in the success and pleasure of others. Finally, one extends to all quarters an attitude of equanimity (no. 4, upekṣā), a state of "even-mindedness towards all beings, regarding them with neither attachment nor aversion" (Buswell and Lopez, 2014, p. 943).[35]

The practice of the divine abidings is also said to have immediate effects on others. By extending one's loving-kindness, for instance, one is supposedly able to stop threatening wild animals (not to mention humans) in their tracks. Thus the Buddha himself is said to have used loving-kindness to stop a charging great elephant (see 7.3.4). Buddhist texts more commonly portray the meditation as being effective in dealing with poisonous snakes. The meditation's effectiveness is often thought to be enhanced when it is accompanied by an oral recitation – a kind of spell. For example, in one text a monk is told to recite (in part): "Love from me for the footless / Love for the two-footed from me / Love from me for the four-footed / Love for the many-footed from me" (De Silva, 1981, p. 24, quoting Horner, 1938–1952, vol. 5, p. 148).

We can find in the divine abidings the same kind of combination of concern for the world and detachment from it that we have seen before: involvement coming through compassion, sympathetic joy, and loving-kindness, and withdrawal coming through the practice of equanimity.

5.5.4 *The Four Fruits of the Path*

However one practices the path, in Mainstream Buddhism it was assumed (if one is not a future buddha) that, at the end of it, there were four stages of attainment, or four "fruits" of the path. The first attainment was that of (1) stream-winner (śrotāpanna), after which one would no longer be reborn in a lower realm of rebirth, and full enlightenment was assured in no fewer than

35 On maitrī starting with self-love, see Harvey (2013), p. 327. For studies of the four abidings, see Conze (1967), pp. 80–91, and Aronson (1980).

seven more lifetimes. Then came the attainment of the stage of (2) once-returner (sakṛdāgāmin), which meant that one could expect one more rebirth as a human before full enlightenment. This was followed by (3) non-returner (anāgāmin), which meant one would not be reborn in this world, although one could experience a final birth in one of the pure abodes. Finally there was (4) the achievement of becoming a liberated saint, an arhat, i.e. one who has completely put an end to death and rebirth.[36]

Each of these stages was marked by the abandonment of a certain number of "fetters" (saṃyojana). Stream-winners and once-returners have given up the first three fetters which are: (1) wrong views of the self (satkāyadṛṣṭi), (2) doubt (vicikitsā), and (3) attachment to rules and rites (śīlavrataparāmarḍa); non-returners have, in addition, abandoned two more fetters: (4) sensual desire (kāmacchanda) and (5) ill will (vyāpāda). These five so-called "lower fetters" bind a person to the realm of desire. The next five "higher fetters" bind one to the realms of form and formlessness. They are: (6) desire for forms (rūparāga), (7) desire for formlessness (ārūpyarāga), (8) restlessness (auddhatya), (9) conceit (māna), and (10) ignorance (avidyā). These are all abandoned by arhats.[37]

5.6 SUMMARY

We have, in this chapter, looked at the Four Truths that are featured in most versions of the Buddha's First Sermon. Together these form, in a way, a summation of early Buddhist doctrine, setting forth an understanding of the human situation, of the reasons for it, of the possibility of ameliorating it, and of ways of going about doing that. We have seen that awakening (enlightenment) comes through realizing both the way *out* of saṃsāra, and the way *of* saṃsāra; thus the Four Truths are themselves another expression of a both/and middle way. We shall return to further elaborations of Buddhist doctrines in chapters 8 and 9, but more immediately, I would now like to turn to the third "refuge" of Buddhism: the community that received and propagated the Dharma just described.

---

36 On the four fruits of the path, see Horner (1936), pp. 205–256, and Katz (1982), pp. 83–95.

37 On the ten fetters, see Bodhi (2000), pp. 1565–1566, and La Vallée Poussin (1988–1990), vol. 3, pp. 835–841.

Chapter 6

The Establishment and Character of the Early Buddhist Community

Buddhism was, from the start, a missionary religion. One of the functions of the Buddha (as well as of his disciples) was to preach the Dharma so as to attract new followers or reinforce the faith of existing ones. It was not long before these early Buddhists organized themselves into a community – a saṃgha. In common usage, the word "saṃgha" is often taken to refer only to the celibate monastic order. In early sources, however, mention is also made of the "fourfold" assembly consisting of monks (bhikṣu), nuns (bhikṣuṇī), laymen (upāsaka) and laywomen (upāsikā).[1]

The importance of the laity cannot be overstated. The Buddha's first converts, the merchants Trapuṣa and Bhallika (see 2.7.7), were laymen, and indeed, the monastic saṃgha of monks and nuns would not have survived without the subsequent support of others like them. It is appropriate therefore to start this chapter with a look at the roles of laymen and laywomen in the foundation and formation of the Buddhist community (6.1). I will then examine the establishment and growth of monasticism (6.2), the foundation of the order of nuns (6.3), the recognition of common moral commitments (6.4), and the growth of monastic rituals of ordination (6.6). Then I will illustrate all these subjects with stories about exemplary disciples of the Buddha (6.7).

6.1 MONASTIC–LAY INTERACTIONS

The relationship of lay supporters to monastics is often said to be one of symbiotic exchange: the laity provide for the monastics' material needs

1 For a list of references to the fourfold community, see Lamotte (1988), p. 54.

with offerings of food, clothing, shelter, etc., and, in return, the monastics support the laity spiritually by giving them instruction in the Dharma, and by giving them an opportunity to make merit. This, however, implies a tit-for-tat relationship that is somewhat misleading and simplistic. In fact, as we shall see, laypersons interact with monastics for a number of reasons: aspiration for the Dharma, a wish to make merit (or perhaps simply to "feel meritorious"), the apotropaic concern to keep evil forces at bay, a desire to enhance their own social prestige, family custom, or just because it gives them spiritual satisfaction.[2]

6.1.1 Dāna (Giving) and Other Forms of Making Merit

A prime expression of the relationship of laypersons and monastics is the practice of "giving" (dāna) which usually carries with it the thought of making merit. This expectation of possible karmic rewards is reinforced by the view that the monastic community is a most effective "field of merit," much more productive of good karma than, for instance, giving to a secular charity. The monastics, on the other hand, have a duty to make sure, through their behavior and discipline, that they are indeed effective fields of merit, and that, as such, they make themselves available as recipients of lay generosity. One of the ways in which they did this in ancient India (and continue to do today, but only in certain Theravāda countries such as Thailand and Myanmar) was to visit the houses of laypersons, begging bowl in hand, on their daily almsrounds (the Sanskrit word for monk, "bhikṣu," literally means "beggar"). Thereby they would regularly give the laity a chance to make merit by placing some food in their bowls. Alternatively, on special occasions, monastics might accept invitations from laypersons to come to their house for a meal, after which they might preach a sermon to them or chant some Dharma texts. Or, in still other ways, certain laypersons might make even more substantial offerings to the saṃgha as a whole, such as contributing financially to the repair or construction of monastic buildings, to the endowment of certain rites and rituals, or the sponsorship of other saṃgha projects. They would thereby enhance their own reputation, as well as that of their community, as pious Buddhist devotees.[3]

---

2 On the symbiotic relationship of monastics and laypersons, see Gombrich (1988), p. 115.

3 On these various types of occasions, see Bailey and Mabbett (2003), pp. 232–256. On merit making in general, see Brekke (1998), Findly (2003), and Heim (2004).

(The saṃgha, it should be said parenthetically, is not the only recipient of lay generosity. It was common to distinguish, in ancient India and still in certain Theravāda countries today, between offerings made to the Buddha (i.e. his images, his stūpas, his relics) and offerings made to the saṃgha. Though both types of offerings are handled and used by monastics, the former technically belong to the Buddha and should be used for him, e.g. for the upkeep and veneration of his images.)[4]

In any of these practices of giving, laypersons might not only make merit for themselves, but also share their merit with others, especially with deceased members of their family. Indeed, on ritual merit-making occasions in South and Southeast Asia today, it is common to see laypersons solemnly pouring water from one vessel into another, or onto the ground, while reciting certain verses. They are thereby signaling their intention to share the merit they have made with others, usually their deceased parents or other kin. Being an act of giving, this transference of merit (which has roots in early Buddhism and Brahmanism) is itself an act of merit. Hence, it does not result in a depletion of one's own merit supply but rather in an increase of it. Similarly, one can "cash in" on the merit of others simply by rejoicing at their merit making, for such rejoicing is seen as a meritorious deed in its own right.

Crucially important in the efficacy of all this is the monastic community. It is not thought to be possible to make offerings directly to one's dead relatives. Rather it is by making gifts to the monks that one can assure oneself of helping others, for the saṃgha acts as a sort of merit-transfer station between the living and the dead. In the case of relatives who have been reborn in the hells or in the realms of the hungry ghosts, the merit that is transferred, moreover, gets translated into actual relief of suffering or hunger and thirst. As one relatively early Pali verse puts it:

> Without the walls they [the hungry ghosts] stand and wait
> and at the junctions and road-forks;
> returning to their erstwhile homes,
> they wait besides the jambs of gates.
> But when a rich feast is set out,
> with food and drink of every kind ...
> they who are compassionate at heart
> do give for relatives [for] ...

4 On offerings to the Buddha, see Schopen (1997), pp. 258–289.

the ghosts of [one's] departed kin
live there on giving given here.

(Ñāṇamoli, 1960, pp. 7–8)[5]

Giving, of course, is not the only way for lay Buddhists to make merit. A well-known catalogue of "ten meritorious actions" (daśakuśalakarma), for instance, gives it pride of place at the top of the list, but then goes on to mention nine other practices: observing the moral precepts; meditating; showing respect to one's superiors; attending to their needs; transferring merit; rejoicing at the merit of others; listening to the Dharma; preaching or propagating the Dharma; and having right views.[6] It is noteworthy that some of these actions (e.g. meditating and teaching the Dharma) are typically associated with monastics. What this list implies, therefore, is twofold: first, monks and nuns are also interested in merit-making activities, and, second, laypersons are not uninvolved in such things as meditating and teaching.

6.1.2 *Lay Ethics*

A somewhat different listing of lay practices may be found in the instructions that the Buddha is said to give to the son of a rich householder named Sigāla. The text, which is sometimes called the "Vinaya of the Householder," was quite popular and exists in multiple versions. One day, we are told, the Buddha, on his almsround, comes across a young non-Buddhist householder – the son and heir of a recently deceased rich merchant. He is engaged in the brahmanical practice of paying ritual homage to the six directions (the four cardinal points and the zenith and nadir). The Buddha interrupts him and tells him he is not doing the practice correctly – would he like to know how to do it in the right manner? The young man, of course, says yes. The Buddha then launches into a sermon that basically has two parts.

First, preliminarily, the young man should commit to abandoning four kinds of negative actions (taking life, theft, lying, and adultery), and four kinds of negative attitudes (attachment, ill-will, delusion, and fear). Then he should give up six specific things that are described as bad for his family business,

5 On the theory and practice of the transfer of merit, see Gombrich (1971a), Holt (1981a), Keyes (1983), Schopen (1997), pp. 23–55, and Bechert (1992).

6 On the ten meritorious actions, see Strong (2005); for a canonical source, see Walshe (1987), p. 509; for Abhidharma sources on it, see Trafford (2010). For a discussion of its importance in the Mahāyāna, see Hirakawa (1963), pp. 73–79.

because they will cause him to lose his inherited wealth: addiction to drink, wandering the streets at the wrong time, attending fairs, gambling, keeping bad company, and idleness. In some versions of the story, the Buddha adds to this some financial advice, recommending that Sigāla divide his income into six portions: for food, for business, for savings, for repaying loans, for family marriages, and for building a new house. All these practices are said to be ways to "guard" the six directions – to protect the self.

Second, the Buddha then turns to ways in which the young man should "cultivate" the six directions. The six directions, he explains, actually represent relationships with six kinds of people. The east denotes one's mother and father; the south denotes one's teachers; the west denotes one's spouse and children; the north denotes one's friends and companions; the nadir denotes one's servants and employees; the zenith denotes renunciants (śramaṇas) and brahmins. One should worship the "east" by being dutiful to one's parents, by serving them, by maintaining the family line, being worthy of one's inheritance, and transferring merit to them after they have passed. Similarly, one should "worship" the south, west, north, nadir, and zenith, by honoring and respecting and treating properly one's teachers, wife and children, friends, servants, and renunciant religious figures. All of these actions are to be reciprocated in appropriate ways.[7]

The sermon to Sīgala is interesting because, in it, the Buddha appears to be advocating a way to worldly success and prosperity which is, at the same time, moral and disciplined. Riches do not have to be achieved by cut-throat competition, by cheating, lying, exploiting others. Instead honesty and morality are shown to breed success. This, of course, is a standard message about how karma works, but it is here applied not to the rewards one reaps in a future existence, but in this very life.

6.1.3 Magical Protection

The saṃgha, however, is not just a field of merit, but also an engine of magical protection. Simply put, it is good to have monks around, and for them to recite texts, because these are seen as efficacious in guarding against malignant forces. In a practice with a long history in Indian Buddhism, monks

7 For a translation of the Pali version of the sūtra, see Gethin (2008), pp. 129–138. For translations of four other canonical versions from the Chinese, see Pannasiri (1950). For a study, see Strong (forthcoming a).

in South and Southeast Asia today are commonly invited by laypersons to chant protection texts (called paritta or rakṣā) as magical safeguards, at times of passage such as births, weddings, illnesses, and death, or on other family occasions. The same is true at festivals and national holidays. Indeed, Sri Lankan radio starts its broadcast service each morning with paritta texts chanted by monks.[8]

In Thailand, perhaps the most popular protective text is the one called "Verses on the Victor's Armor" (Jinapañjara gāthā). It is especially noteworthy for our purposes because it describes how a devotee can visualize the Buddha (= the "Victor") and several of his prominent disciples and "station" them as guards on different parts of one's body. Thus the Buddha Śākyamuni (and all the buddhas of the past) are imagined to be "posted" above one's head. The Buddha's disciples Śāriputra and Maudgalyāyana are visualized as guarding one's right and left side. Ānanda and Rāhula are at one's right ear, while Kāśyapa and Mahānāma are at one's left ear, etc. In this way the Buddha and his disciples – that is to say, the early saṃgha – together with the Dharma, are made to form a protective cage around one's body. As the text puts it: "I am completely well sheltered, well protected. Whatever [misfortune] arises is conquered by the power of the [Buddha]. The horde of unworthy ones is conquered by the power of the Dharma. Danger is conquered by the power of the saṃgha" (McDaniel, 2011, pp. 77–78).[9]

6.1.4 *Laypersons and the Monastic Rules*

Another aspect of lay–monastic interaction was the interest of the laity in the uprightness and purity of the saṃgha. If one reads the Vinaya (the Buddhist monastic disciplinary code), it will be noted that many of its rules and regulations are occasioned by the complaints and distress of the laity. Time after time, a situation arises in which a monk does something that is deemed improper or unseemly by laypeople who observe it; they then go to the Buddha and complain: "Your monks are doing such and such: we don't think it's right!" And time after time, the Buddha institutes a new rule, thereafter forbidding that practice. To give a banal example: at one point, the Buddha is said to have allowed a monk named Soṇa, who had been a

8 On paritta in Sri Lanka, see De Silva (1981); more generally, see Skilling (1992).

9 For a discussion of the "Verses on the Victor's Armor," see McDaniel (2011), pp. 77–120.

very rich layman and had delicate feet, to wear sandals. But the local laity criticized Soṇa for being granted this special privilege and keeping this degree of attachment to bodily comfort. So Soṇa went to the Buddha and said he would not use sandals unless all monks were allowed to do so. The Buddha, worried about Soṇa's foot problem, agreed to let all his disciples wear sandals. Some monks, however, then started wearing sandals of different bright colors, sandals that had straps that came up to their knees, embroidered sandals, well-heeled sandals, boot-like sandals with pointed tips, sandals decorated with peacock feathers, with owl feathers, with ram's horn, with scorpions' tails, sandals made out of tiger-skin, etc. On each occasion, the laity complained, thinking the particular "sandal" unsuitable for "their" renunciants whom they were in the habit of supporting. And so, on each occasion, the Buddha, acknowledging their concerns, banned the use of that particular footwear.[10]

We shall examine, later on, the role that the Vinaya plays as part of the monastics' program of spiritual development and practice, but the examples just given (which could easily be multiplied) also raise the question: whose are the rules of the saṃgha? Who sets them and who enforces them? In some cases, the answer is obvious: they are rules for monastics and govern their lives in the monastery. In other cases, however, things are not so clear.

Some years ago, on a crowded bus in Sri Lanka, I observed something that made me reflect on this issue. As the bus neared a stop, a woman who was planning to get off found her way blocked by a monk standing in the aisle, leaning over and talking to some of his fellow monks in the front seats reserved for "clergy." As the bhikṣu swayed back and forth, oblivious to the woman behind him, I could see her carefully gauge the widening and narrowing gap between his back and the driver's seat, somewhat like a child timing her entry into a game of jump rope. One of the rules of the Vinaya is that monks are not supposed to come into bodily contact with women, and this woman clearly wanted that rule maintained. As she hesitated, however, I thought to myself, "There is no way she will make it off the bus without touching that monk!" But just then the (male) driver, seeing the woman's plight, tapped the monk on the shoulder and indicated to him that he needed to leave more room, and the woman scampered off the bus without coming into contact with him. The point here, of course, is that though we think of the purity of the saṃgha as something that is maintained (or violated) by monastics,

10 The sandals' case is recounted in Horner (1938–1952), vol. 4, pp. 245–247.

in this case, the person worrying about it was the laywoman (and perhaps also the driver). The situation, in fact, is even more ironic than this, because even if the woman had come into physical contact with the monk, the latter would not have been guilty of a Vinaya violation; as the Theravāda Vinaya puts it in its explication of the rule against monks having physical contact with females: "there is no offence if it is not on purpose, not intentional, not knowing, not agreeing" (Horner, 1938–1952, vol. 1, p. 211). Thus the laywoman on the bus was taking the rules of the Vinaya more strictly even than the Vinaya itself, and was concerned about maintaining a rule which, in any case, would not have been broken. Though she was a layperson, she had, in fact, internalized this "monastic" rule.

6.1.5 Royal Supporters

Dāna, merit, magical protection, and the purity of the saṃgha were not, of course, only of interest to ordinary laypersons; they were also concerns of the state, specifically of kings who became major supporters of the saṃgha. The monastic relationship to kingship was not without ambiguity. As we have seen, according to legend, becoming a great cakravartin king was something that Śākyamuni gave up when he opted to leave his home. Nonetheless, kings were important and influential in the affairs of the early saṃgha. Canonical texts often mention the role of Bimbisāra, king of Magadha, a contemporary and patron of the Buddha. It was Bimbisāra, for instance, who convinced the Buddha to establish the rule that soldiers (i.e. deserters) and slaves could not be ordained, when he found that some of his military forces were becoming monks in order to escape fighting in a border war.[11]

More generally, Bimbisāra was in a position to be influential by his generosity and support. As we shall see in 6.2.2, he was the first to give the saṃgha a monastery when the Buddha visited him in Rājagṛha shortly after his awakening. He also convinced the Buddha to let him give monastery attendants (ārāmika) to the saṃgha, lay individuals or sometimes whole villages of individuals attached to particular monasteries whose main function was to take care of the buildings and serve the monks. In this way, the practice of kings attaching serfs to monastic institutions began. Such generosity, as has been pointed out, was a double-edged sword: on the one hand, it insured

11 For this and many other Bimbisāra stories, see van Zeyst (1966).

the prosperity of the community and the practice of its monastics; on the other hand, it could lead to contentedness and corruption.[12]

In this light, another role of kings becomes more understandable: they are the ones who are said to periodically "purify" the saṃgha. There are, of course, sociological explanations for this: the monastic saṃgha, in India, had no institutional hierarchy above the local level, no overarching centralized authority by which it could regulate and systematically propagate itself. Such authority had to be provided by an "outside" layperson, the king. But the king (like all laity) had vested interest in maintaining the purity of the saṃgha, on its keeping its own rules so that it would be a potent and viable field of merit.

6.1.6 King Aśoka

The most important royal supporter and purifier of the saṃgha, at least according to Buddhist legend, was King Aśoka. Historically, Aśoka (third century BCE) was the third monarch of the Mauryan Empire, which extended over most of the Indian subcontinent. He is best known, perhaps, for his rock and pillar edicts and inscriptions which he erected all over his kingdom, from present-day Afghanistan to the South of India, from the Arabian Gulf to the Bay of Bengal. In these, he sets forth his dedication to "Dharma" (= "righteousness"), which he desires to propagate throughout his realm. Aśoka's "Dharma" in the edicts does not correspond exactly to the Buddha's Dharma as we know it; rather it seems to imply an active polity of social concern, religious tolerance, the observance of common ethical precepts, and the renunciation of warfare. Some of his edicts, however, deal more specifically with the Buddhist saṃgha. We already saw one example, in the introduction, in his pillar inscription recording his pilgrimage to Lumbinī, the site of the Buddha's birthplace. Other Buddhist-specific inscriptions include his declaration of having visited Bodhgaya; his so-called "schism edict" which appears to state his attempt to unify local monastic communities that have become fractious; and his Bhabra edict, in which he recommends certain Buddhist texts to monks, nuns, and laypersons.[13]

12 The story of Bimbisāra gifting a whole village of monastery attendants may be found in Horner (1938–1952), vol. 4, pp. 281–283. On monasteries owning servants or slaves, see Silk (2004), and Schopen (2004b), pp. 193–218. On the dangers of corruption brought on by lay generosity, see Gombrich (1988), pp. 95–96, 115–117.

13 On the schism edict, see Bechert (1982), Sasaki (1992), and Tieken (2000); for translations of all of Aśoka's edicts, including those more particularly concerned with Buddhism, see Nikam and McKeon (1959), pp. 66–68, and Thapar (1961), pp. 250–266.

In Buddhist legends, however (as opposed to the edicts and rock inscriptions), it is clear that Aśoka is completely committed to the welfare of the saṃgha. He is said to undergo a dramatic conversion experience, and to undertake to collect all the scattered relics of the Buddha and enshrine them in 84,000 stūpas which he builds all over India. Because of this, scholars have occasionally credited him with spreading Buddhism widely and making it into the Mauryan state religion, and subsequent Buddhist monarchs in places as far away as China and Japan took Aśoka as a model, and sought to emulate him in their actions.[14]

In their praise, the legends generally emphasize two features of Aśoka's rule. First, his generosity to the Buddhist Order knows no bounds; on several occasions, he is said to empty the coffers of the state and to give the entire kingdom, including his own sovereignty, to the saṃgha.[15] Second, as mentioned, he is a purifier of the saṃgha. According to legend, in Aśoka's time, the Buddhist order, in part because royal largesse had made it so prosperous, was infiltrated by "heretics" who became ordained, but "proclaimed their own doctrines as the doctrine of the Buddha and carried out their own practices even as they wished" (Geiger, 1912, p. 46). So great were their numbers that the "orthodox" monks could do nothing to expel them, and could only refuse to carry out monastic rituals with them. Thus, it fell to Aśoka to do something about it. In the Theravāda tradition, we find that his solution is to hold a great council of elders, to consult a particularly venerable monk about the doctrine, and then to purify the saṃgha by ejecting from it monks disagreeing with his views (see 7.1.3). He then sends out missionaries to spread this "orthodoxy" to far-flung lands such as Sri Lanka and Southeast Asia.[16]

6.2 THE MONASTICS: WANDERING AND SETTLING

The laity, of course, formed only one part of the Buddhist community. In the rest of this chapter, I want to focus on the monks and nuns. The foundation of the monastic saṃgha is attributed to the Buddha himself, but its structure and character may be thought to have considerably evolved during and after his lifetime. Scholars interested in the growth of the saṃgha generally paint

14 On Aśoka's building of the stūpas as a paradigm for Buddhist rulers all over Asia, see Strong (2004), pp. 124–125, and the references cited there.

15 On the great quinquennial festival of giving by Aśoka and other monarchs, see Strong (1990), and Deeg (1995/1997).

16 On all these actions of the legendary Aśoka, see Strong (1983).

a picture somewhat like the following: the Buddha, through his preaching and charisma, attracted a good many disciples, who responded to his call to join his order. Somewhat like Jesus who is said to have enlisted his first disciples simply by saying "Follow me!", the Buddha first "ordained" his disciples by saying, "Come, O monk." In this way, the community gradually grew. When he had gathered around him a significant number of disciples (about sixty), the Buddha decided they should all spread out and preach the Dharma on their own. In a famous declaration, he is said to have told them to wander by themselves for the benefit of many people, no two of them going the same way.[17]

The image that is thus projected is of an early diffuse community of individual mendicants who were given to "wander solitary as a rhinoceros's horn." Soon, however, it is said that Buddhist laypersons complained that their monks, unlike other renunciants (śramaṇas), were wandering all year round and rarely available to them, so it was decided that, in common with other peripatetic mendicant orders of the time, Buddhist monks should not be allowed to wander during the three or four months of the annual monsoon rains, when travel in any case was difficult and likely to harm insect life and do damage to fields. Instead, they were to spend the rainy season in one place, generally with the support of local laypersons.[18]

What did this actually mean? Although the basic rule for residence during the rains is that monks are not allowed to be out of the "monastic dwelling" even for one night, the Vinaya is quick to allow for all sorts of exceptions. A look at some of these may give us a bit more sense of some of the life-circumstances of monks, if not at the very start of the community, at least at some point in its early history. Absence from residence during the rainy season is allowed – for up to seven days – if a monk has some urgent personal matter to take care of. This can relate to another member of the saṃgha, or to a layperson, or if his parent or brother or sister or other relative is ill; or if he needs to carry out some saṃgha business, such as accepting a donation of a new monastic building; or if there is a marriage at the home of a layperson, and he is invited to receive dāna or to chant sūtras. Moreover, monks may abandon the rains-residence altogether if unavoidable circumstances arise

17 For an account of these early conversions, see Strong (2001), pp. 113–115; see also Kloppenborg (1973), p. 43.

18 The expression "wander lonely as a rhinoceros's horn" comes from the early Pali Buddhist text known as the *Sūtra Collection* (*Suttanipāta*) (see Norman, 1996, pp. 7–10). On the complaint of the laity about their monks' constant wandering, see Wijayaratna (1990), pp. 19–20.

such as danger from wild animals or snakes or thieves or ghosts or floods, or the nearby village on whom they depend for their sustenance is pillaged by brigands, or if there are no suitable attendants, etc.[19]

A number of noteworthy things about the early saṃgha emerge from this list of exceptions. First, even though monks have supposedly renounced their families and wandered into homelessness, in fact, they maintain a special connection with close kin (parents, siblings, etc.). They are allowed to go home if someone in their family is sick, or dies, etc. This is a theme to which I shall return below. Second, we can also see here the importance of maintaining good relations with laypersons in general, especially if they are well-endowed and influential. Monks are allowed to travel to take care of "saṃgha business," such as fund raising or the ritual needs of the community. Finally, a basic common-sense practicality about the Buddhist attitude towards monastic rules is evident here; exceptions are allowed if the circumstances are such that the rule becomes absurd (e.g. staying in a place overrun by wild animals).

These exceptions aside, the basic default expectation was that monastics would stay put during the rainy season. For this reason, the "rains-residence," as it came to be known, was a crucial building block for community life. Even though it is often called a rains-"*retreat*" and some monks did use it as an opportunity for sustained meditative practice, it was also a time when individual monastics, of necessity, had to live together; rules had to be established, procedures agreed upon, decisions made about what rituals to observe, etc. Moreover, it was also a period of increased interaction with lay supporters, given the fact that the monastics were staying put in one place for a goodly amount of time, and that laypersons in nearby communities, who often took it upon themselves to make provisions for the rains-residence of monastics near them, had time to visit with them. No one disputes the importance of the rains-residence in the formation of the early saṃgha and it has remained to this day a key time in Buddhist monasticism, and in the overall Buddhist calendar. Major festivals and rituals occur on either side of the rains-residence, at its start and at its conclusion. Monastics, moreover, count the length of time since their ordination (and hence figure their seniority vis-à-vis other monastics) according to the number of rains-residences they have spent in the saṃgha.[20]

19 On these rules about absence during the rains-residence, see Upasak (1975), pp. 198–199.

20 Jean Przyluski (1926, p. 281) [in French] has emphasized lay presence in the rains-residence. For a modern example, see Crosby and Khur-Yearn (2010). On rituals framing the rains-retreat, see Holt (1981), pp. 132–137. For a classic presentation of the growth of monasteries around the rains-retreat, see Dutt (1924), pp. 90–112.

6.2.1 Monastic Lifestyles

Focus on the rains-residence and its importance in the formation of community life has meant that comparatively less attention has been paid to the question of what the monastics did for the rest of the year. One answer, of course, is that they "wandered"; but this was not necessarily always the case. Part of the complexity of the situation, perhaps, may be seen in the following story about the Venerable Dhaniya, a man who had been a potter before he joined the order. Along with several other monastic friends, he is said to have built for himself – for the rains-residence – a hut out of grass and sticks on the slopes of a mountain outside Rājagṛha. At the end of the rains, his fellow monks all abandoned their huts and left, but Dhaniya stayed on, and spent the cold season there, and then the hot season, i.e. the whole year. Unfortunately for him, one morning when he had gone to town on his begging round, some women, gathering grass and firewood on the mountain, demolished his hut and made off with its grass and sticks. Presumably they thought it was unoccupied. This, it is said, happened to Dhaniya three times, until finally, in frustration, he gave up rebuilding his grass hut and used his former skill as a potter to make himself a dwelling out of mud which he then baked hard by building a fire in it. It turned out to be a nice place; red in color (perhaps from the clay or the glaze), it was said to look like a ladybug. One day, however, the Buddha happened to be in the area. Seeing the hut, he asked his entourage: "What is this ladybug house?" Finding out that it had been built by a monk, he roundly condemned Dhaniya for it, stating that the building process of baking mud entailed the killing of many bugs and small creatures. Such a hut was not to be allowed, and he ordered his monks to destroy it. Having now lost both his straw hut and his mud hut, Dhaniya was somewhat at a loose end. But rather than resume a peripatetic lifestyle, he got some planks from the king's woodyard in order to build himself a solid and acceptable hermitage.[21]

This tale can be used to suggest a number of answers to our question of what monastics did for the rest of the year. None of the following options is mutually exclusive; monastics might do combinations of some or all of them. (1) First, like Dhaniya's erstwhile companions, they could abandon their

21 The story of Dhaniya may be found in Horner (1938–1952), vol. 1, pp. 64–67. Actually, the tale is more complicated than this: Dhaniya appropriates the planks under false pretenses, claiming that they had been given to him by the king. His deed occasions the Buddha's monastic rule against "taking what is not given."

rains-residence. Where would they go? Several possibilities come to mind: they might resume their "traveling," spread the Dharma, go on pilgrimage, seek out teachers, etc. We know, for example, from the Pali Vinaya that it was the custom for monks, at the end of the rains, to go and see the Buddha wherever he was, out of devotional longing or a desire to make merit, or to report to him on their spiritual progress and get new instruction, etc. After the Buddha's death, they might similarly go to "see" him at places of pilgrimage (see 3.2). Such wandering, of course, was not non-stop. As one scholar has put it, "When [a monk or] a group of monks arrived in a town or a village they might stay for several days or weeks, for as long as there were people to listen to the Buddha's teaching. Sometimes monks would come to the town where the Master was staying to visit him ... Sometimes [they] would stay for a few days in an ascetic's hermitage or in a public place in town ..." (Wijayaratna, 1990, pp. 21–22).[22]

(2) Second, another possibility is that, in the midst of these "travels," or instead of them, these monks might go home. It used to be thought that this was not an option. Home, after all, is what monastics abandon when they "wander forth" and become ordained. But studies of the Vinaya have increasingly shown that some monastics, after their ordinations, maintained considerable contact with the families they supposedly left behind. Simply put, the dividing line between monastic and home life was and probably is much more permeable than has been realized. Monks or nuns (free from families of their own) might look after elderly parents, or attend family rites of passage, or go back home for a while to visit or help out with the harvest, or other chores.[23]

(3) Finally, like Dhaniya, they might stay put, and extend their residence in the place where they spent the rains. In this regard, it should be noted that when the Buddha sees the baked mud hut, he does not object to it on the grounds that Dhaniya should not be living in one place outside the rainy season, but because it was made with a material and by a process that took life. In other words, the rule supposedly established by the Buddha about *not* traveling during the rainy season said nothing about *being obliged to travel* the rest of the time. Staying put appears to have always been an option. Dhaniya stays on alone, but he could have done so with some fellow

22 On the custom of monks visiting the Buddha, see Horner (1938–1952), vol. 4, p. 209 and vol. 1, p. 153. See also An (2003), p. 151.

23 Clarke (2014), pp. 37–77. This is a pattern often encountered today among certain types of Tibetan monastics. For a good example concerning contemporary nuns, see Gutschow (2004).

monks. Indeed, one theory about the origins of year-round monasticism was that it was precisely a result of such monks gradually extending their rains-residences.[24] Moreover, it might be noted that Dhaniya's hut, for a number of reasons, gradually evolves from something rather flimsy to a more solid and permanent building.

6.2.2 Monasteries

It would seem, then, that from early on, monks enjoyed a variety of lifestyles as members of the saṃgha. Gradually, however, a settled existence in a community became the norm. The monks, of course, were not the only ones involved in bringing about this trend. In addition, laypersons, eager to make merit, were happy to build better and better places for "their" monks, and to invite monastics to reside in their vicinities for longer and longer periods of time. This is reflected in the lifestory of the Buddha himself. According to tradition, no later than one year after his enlightenment, when the Buddha was in Rājagṛha, King Bimbisāra, eager to offer the Blessed One and his monks a "middle way" place to stay ("neither too far from town nor too near"), gifted him the magnificent wood known as the Bamboo Grove (Veṇuvana). It may be that at first this was not an actual monastery, but just a "pleasance" (ārāma), a quiet park where the community could camp out, but it obviously quickly developed into something more established and built up. Indeed, it is not long before we hear of the Venerable Dabba Mallaputra being given the monastic post of "assigner of lodgings" (and "issuer of meals") at the Veṇuvana. His duties were to tell monks arriving for the rains-residence (as well as those wanting to stay on after the rains) where they should stay, a task at which he was very adept.[25]

The story of Dabba in the Theravāda Vinaya is interesting because it gives us an inkling of some of the structures and divisions and preoccupations of monastic life. Dabba assigns lodgings in the same place for monks of the same inclinations; thus, he has monks who recite the sūtras room together so they can rehearse the texts with one another; monks who specialize in the

24 For this theory, see Dutt (1962), pp. 45–57.

25 On Dabba, see Horner (1938–1952), vol. 5, p. 167. The Vinaya specifies that there are three times for assigning lodgings: at the start of first rains, at the start of second rains (one month later), and between the end of the rains and the start of next one. Once monks decide where they want to spend the rains, they may reserve places ahead of time, but are forbidden to do so in more than one place. See ibid., pp. 235–236.

Vinaya, so they can discuss matters of discipline; monks who like to preach the Dharma, so they can discuss sermons; monks who are meditators, so they will have a quiet place together where they will not be disturbed. To each of these groups, Dabba would assign lodgings, saying: "this is your bed, this is your chair, this is your cushion, this is your pillow, this is the latrine, this is the urinal, this is the drinking water, this is the water for washing ..." All this seems to fit with what we can readily imagine about the lives of serious monastics. But then we are also told that Dabba would assign common lodgings to "monks who like to talk about trivial matters" and to monks "who are devoted to bodily strength, so they can do what they like"; and that there was a category of "monks who arrive late at night" whom Dabba would escort to their rooms by the light of his upheld finger, which he would make glow brightly, by means of his supernatural powers. Indeed, this, the Vinaya hints, became a problem because monks, desiring to see Dabba perform this feat, began deliberately coming in late at night![26] The image one gets from all this is that large monasteries such as the Veṇuvana, somewhat like modern university campuses, had theme-houses or fraternities for monks who had common interests or inclinations. Such a picture is not significantly different from the image one gets of great Tibetan monasteries today.[27]

The Veṇuvana was by no means the only monastery gifted to the Buddha and the community. Another place of great significance was the Jetavana monastery which was given to the Buddha by the rich layman, Anāthapiṇḍada. Located just outside of Śrāvastī, the Jetavana became a sort of "headquarters" for the Buddha during the second half of his preaching career. The Buddha is said to have spent twenty-four of his last twenty-five rains-retreats either at the Jetavana or the nearby Purvārāma in Śrāvastī; in contrast, he was much less "settled" earlier in his career, having spent his first twenty rains-retreats in sixteen different places.[28]

The story of the Jetavana is quickly told: Anāthapiṇḍada (meaning "giver of alms to the destitute") was a fabulously wealthy merchant. He first met the Buddha at the house of his brother-in-law on a business trip to Rājagṛha. Impressed by the Master's charisma as well as by his teaching, he quickly converted to Buddhism; he then asked the Buddha to come and visit him in Śrāvastī, and the Buddha accepted. Delighted, Anāthapiṇḍada returned home and began to make preparations for the Buddha's visit. He looked for a quiet

26 Ibid., pp. 98–99.

27 See Goldstein (1998), pp. 20–22, and Gyatso (1998), pp. 85–118.

28 On the rains spent by the Buddha at the Jetavana, see Strong (2001), p. 133.

place near Śrāvastī where the Buddha and his monks might stay, and decided on a park owned by one Prince Jeta. Unfortunately, Prince Jeta was reluctant to sell his property. After some haggling and trickery, however (and a court case decided in his favor), Anāthapiṇḍada convinced Jeta to sell it to him for as many gold pieces as it would take to cover the whole surface area of the land. In this way, it is said, Anāthapiṇḍada spent 180 million buying the park, and then another 180 million on building the monastery itself. Mention is made of monastic dwellings, porches, cells, assembly halls, meditation walkways, kitchens, bathrooms, latrines, wells, storerooms, etc., and in the center, the so-called "perfumed chamber" for the Buddha himself.[29]

In many ways, the Jetavana represents the full monasticization of the Buddhist movement, and it is not surprising that it became a model of an ideal monastery, much invoked in later centuries by Buddhists in many countries. One of the major monasteries in Anuradhapura, the capital of ancient Sri Lanka, for instance, was named the Jetavana. The Chinese Vinaya Master Daoxuan (596–667 CE) even wrote an illustrated book on the Jetavana as a paradigmatic monastery, and his descriptions went on to inspire others; in Japan, a district in Kyoto was named after the Jetavana (Jpn., Gion), a number of classical gardens were modeled on it, and the sounds of its bells (which supposedly rang whenever a monk passed away) became a famous trope for impermanence in Japanese literature.[30]

6.3 MAHĀPRAJĀPATĪ AND THE ESTABLISHMENT OF THE ORDER OF NUNS

We have, so far, been dealing primarily with the establishment of the community of monks. The Buddhist monastic saṃgha, however, also included a female branch, the order of nuns (bhikṣuṇīs), the foundation of which by the Buddha merits separate attention.

As mentioned in 1.2.3, the Buddhist order of nuns today looks back to the Buddha's aunt and foster-mother Mahāprajāpatī as its foundress. Mahāprajāpatī, it will be remembered, took over responsibility for rearing

29 For a translation of the Sanskrit version of the *Mūlasarvāstivāda Vinaya*'s story of the construction of the Jetavana, see Schopen (2000), pp. 109–131. For a translation of various Chinese accounts, see Tan (2002), pp. 88–122.

30 On Daoxuan's view of the Jetavana, see McRae (2005), and Tan (2002). On its influence on Japanese gardens, see Takei and Keane (2001), pp. 94–101. For a classic Japanese literary reference to it (in the *Heike monogatari*), see McCullough (1988), p. 23.

the Buddha when his birth-mother (Māyā) died, seven days after he was born. Here we need to focus on her role in convincing the Buddha to institute an order of nuns.

One common version of the story goes like this: after her husband, Śuddhodana, died, Mahāprajāpatī began to think about renouncing the world. So too, we are told, did five hundred other Śākyan women (said to be her companions) whose husbands had all become monks, or had been killed in battle. Unfortunately, there was no way for them to become nuns at the time, since a Buddhist order of bhikṣuṇīs had not been established. So Mahāprajāpatī decided to take action; during one of the Buddha's trips back home to Kapilavastu, she went to him to request that he instate a bhikṣuṇī order so that she and her five hundred companions might be able to wander forth and become ordained. But the Buddha refused to do so and soon went on his way. The women, however, shaved their heads anyway and donned yellow robes and followed the Buddha on foot, thinking they would thus show their determination, and if the Buddha relented, they would become nuns, and if he did not, they would lead a chaste life in his presence. Then Mahāprajāpatī repeated her request for permission to ordain a second time, but the Buddha refused a second, and again a third, time. Despondent, Mahāprajāpatī enlisted the help of the Venerable Ānanda, asking him to intervene on her behalf. But Ānanda's request that the Buddha allow for the ordination of women was also turned down repeatedly by the Buddha, who, this time, predicted that the ordination of women would devastate the community of monks in much the same way that a rust fungus could lay waste a field of rice or sugarcane. It would, moreover, cut the duration of the Dharma in half.

Ānanda, however, persisting with his request, gets the Buddha to admit that previous buddhas had all established orders of nuns, that women are capable of attaining enlightenment, and that Mahāprajāpatī herself was not just anyone but had suckled and nourished and raised the Blessed One in his infancy and childhood, thereby implying that the Buddha owed her special consideration.[31] In the face of these arguments, the Buddha finally, reluctantly agreed to establish an order of nuns, but only on condition that they submit to eight special weighty rules (gurudharma): (1) even the most senior of nuns must respectfully salute the most junior of monks; (2) nuns have to be ordained twice – once by the order of nuns but also by the order of monks. Moreover, before being ordained, they have to complete a two-year probationary period; (3) nuns may never criticize monks for real or imagined

31 On the importance of this last reason, see Ohnuma (2006).

offenses; (4) nuns may not receive offerings ahead of monks; (5) nuns who have violated disciplinary rules must seek restitution from both the order of nuns and the order of monks; (6) every fortnight on festival days, nuns should ask monks for instruction; (7) nuns may not observe the rains-retreat in a place where there are no monks; (8) at the end of their rains-retreat, nuns must request the pravāraṇā ceremony (judgment of one's conduct – see 6.6.2) from the order of nuns and the order of monks. Mahāprajāpatī accepted these rules, was ordained, and then went on to be the leader of the order of nuns.[32] Indeed, she became revered by nuns not only as the foundress of their community but, as Walters has argued, as a sort of female counterpart to the Blessed One – a "Buddha for women," a mother figure, from whom all nuns could trace their spiritual descent. As he puts it: [In the Pali text, "Gotamī's Story," Mahāprajāpatī's] own achievement, like a buddha's, is realized only by assuring the salvation of others ... Another oddity is that she is always called "Gotamī," which is ... grammatically speaking the exact female equivalent of the name [the] Buddha was known by, "Gotama." [There is thus an] apposition between Gotama and Gotamī, the Buddha and the Buddhī" (Walters, 1995, p. 117).[33]

Be this as it may, it is clear from the special weighty rules that the order of nuns was to be subordinate to and dependent on the community of monks. Moreover, these rules were only the beginning; throughout the years and centuries that followed, women ordained into the saṃgha found themselves facing a far greater number of Vinaya regulations than their male counterparts, and partly because of this, the lineage and order of nuns eventually died out in many countries.[34]

The story of the institution of the Buddhist bhikṣuṇī order has received considerable scholarly attention. One of the more interesting recent interpretations (and the only one I will present here) is that of Bhikkhu Anālayo who has highlighted the importance of the Chinese *Madhyamāgama* version of the tale. In the story as given above, it should be noted that, even after (apparently)

32 On the eight weighty rules, see Strong (2008), p. 67, Murcott (1991), pp. 196–199, and Hirakawa (1982), pp. 47–98. Hüsken (2000) has suggested that the eight special rules were not part of the original layer of tradition. On the blaming of women for the decline of the Dharma, see Williams (2002). For a different critique of the eight rules, see Kusuma (2000).

33 See also Walters (1994), and M. Shaw (2006), pp. 150–151. On the importance of mother imagery in Buddhism, see Ohnuma (2012).

34 On the subordination of the order of nuns, see Schopen (2004b), pp. 329–359, and Falk (1979). On its demise and revival in modern times, and the possibilities of reviving it, see 1.2.3, above, and Clarke (2010). On differing attitudes towards nuns, see Anālayo (2010a).

being refused ordination, Mahāprajāpatī and her companions shaved their heads and put on yellow robes. This, according to Bhikkhu Anālayo, would have been an unthinkably defiant act, had this not already been acceptable for them. Moreover, at no point does the Buddha reprimand them for this. It is noteworthy therefore that, in the *Madhyamāgama* version of the story, the Buddha does give Mahāprajāpatī permission to shave her head, don yellow robes, and practice the pure life, but on condition that she do so at home. What he refuses is the request to let women become homeless wanderers. This was unacceptable because walking the highways and byways of India was considered to be far too dangerous and hard for Śākyan ladies, not to mention too ethically problematical and unseemly. What would laypeople say? However, once Mahāprajāpati and her companions showed the Buddha that they were capable of enduring such hardship (by trailing along after him on his travels), he reluctantly relented. Anālayo further suggests, on textual grounds, that this feature of the narrative was dropped from other versions of the story and concludes that "for the Buddha to tell Mahāpajāpatī Gotamī that she can live a semi-monastic life at home ... is rather significant."[35]

6.4 COMMON MORAL COMMITMENTS

At the start of this chapter, a distinction was made between monks and nuns and laymen and laywomen as constituting the so-called fourfold assembly. A later classification (the sevenfold assembly) distinguishes three more categories of monastics in addition to fully ordained monks and nuns: male novices (śrāmaṇera), female novices (śrāmaṇerikā), and (female) probationers (śikṣamāṇā), i.e. women who are spending a two-year probationary period imposed on them prior to full ordination, by the second of the eight weighty rules.[36]

35 See Anālayo (2011). The final quotation is from p. 293. This view of things also fits in with Williams's (2000) argument that there were nuns before Mahāprajāpatī. Among the many fine other studies of the story of the institution of the order of nuns, see Paul (1979), pp. 77–94, Gross (1993), pp. 29–54, and Heirman (2001).

36 On female probationers, see Hüsken (2000a). Men converting to Buddhism from certain other renunciant groups were also asked to undergo a four-month probation period (parivāsa) prior to full ordination (see Upasak, 1975, pp. 144–145), while monks and nuns who had been found guilty of violating a rule meriting expulsion but had *not* been expelled were given a special "penitent" status (called śikṣādattaka) and put into the hierarchy between the level of novices and fully ordained monastics (see Clarke, 2000; 2009).

All members of this sevenfold saṃgha have formally taken refuge in the Triple Gem. This consists of ritually repeating three times the simple utterance: "I go for refuge to the Buddha" (Buddham śaraṇam gacchāmi), "I go for refuge to the Dharma" (Dharmam śaraṇam gacchāmi), and "I go for refuge to the Saṃgha" (Saṃgham śaraṇam gacchāmi). Beyond this basic statement of faith and commitment, there is also a list of ten moral "precepts" which comprise the determinations to refrain from: (1) taking life; (2) stealing; (3) sex (or, for the laity, illicit sex); (4) lying; (5) intoxication; (6) eating after noon; (7) going to dance, music, or other shows; (8) wearing garlands, perfumes, jewelry, or cosmetics; (9) luxurious beds; and (10) handling gold and silver.[37]

Differentiations can be made between laypersons and novices and female probationers on the basis of the number of these precepts that they undertake. Laymen and laywomen routinely ritually assert their intentions to follow the first five of them, although a number of Buddhist schools affirmed the possibility of their being "partial upāsakas" (Agostini, 2008) who were recognized as bona fide laypersons but who did not observe all five of the precepts. On special occasions, however (e.g. when attending ceremonies at the local monastery), they may commit to observing, in addition, precepts 6–9 (actually these are counted as only three additional ones because, in this figuring, precepts 7 and 8 are combined). Female probationers, if they are not novices, are expected to undertake to observe constantly the first six precepts only. Novices permanently undertake not only precepts 1–9 but also the tenth precept – to refrain from accepting gold and silver, i.e. money. Although, historically and at present, various practical ways around this limitation have been devised, it is this tenth precept – this symbolic withdrawal from the moneyed economy – that theoretically (if not practically) marks the dividing line between laypersons and monastics. Fully ordained monks and nuns, as we have seen, are subject to their own, far more extensive set of rules, although they too will follow the ten precepts listed above in that they undergo the novitiate ordination prior to their full ordination as monastics.[38]

37 See Strong (2008), p. 121.

38 On the female probationers maintaining six precepts, see Lamotte (1988), p. 57, and Wijayaratna (1991), pp. 52–53. In modern times, certain lay renunciant women, like novices, may also undertake this tenth precept. On the issue of taking money, see Juo-Hsüeh (2008).

6.5 INITIATION RITUALS: WANDERING FORTH AND ORDINATION

Novices commit to following the ten precepts at a formal rite of passage called their "wandering forth [into homelessness]" (pravrajyā); their heads are shaven, they don monastic robes, and then generally live at the monastery under the twin guidance of two older and fully ordained monastics, a preceptor (upādhyāya) and a teacher (ācārya). A candidate for "wandering forth" must be at least seven years old. Candidates for full ordination as a monk or a nun (bhikṣu or bhikṣuṇī) must be at least twenty. Their new monastic status is conferred upon them in a ceremony called upasaṃpadā (ordination). In what follows, I will describe the ceremony for a man. The ceremony for women is basically the same, with the addition of a few extra provisos.

Equipped with his robes and bowl, a male candidate for upasaṃpadā stands before the community and is asked to affirm that he is not afflicted with certain contagious diseases; that he is a free (not slave), male, human being, without debt or obligation to the state; that he has his parents' permission to be ordained and is twenty years old; and that he has a full set of robes and a bowl. Having satisfactorily passed these qualification tests, the candidate then proceeds to express, three times, his desire to obtain ordination as a monk. The ordination of the candidate is then formally moved, and the community chapter is given three chances to object. Silence is taken to be assent, and failing any objection, the candidate is thenceforth considered to be a full monk (bhikṣu).[39]

The new monk is then informed of the four recourses of monastic life (niśraya). These initially paint a picture of the life awaiting him as something rigorous, strict, and hard. The homeless life he is about to embark upon, he is told, is characterized (1) by wearing robes made of rags from the rubbish heap; (2) by subsisting on morsels of food gathered on almsrounds; (3) by lodging in the open at the foot of trees; and (4) by using only decomposed cow's urine for medicine.[40] Will he be able to abide by all of these? As soon as he says "yes," however, he is immediately informed that there are certain allowable "exceptions" to these standards. (1) Exceptions to the first rule regarding robes made of rags include: robes made of linen, cotton, flax, goat's

39 One full listing of the questions asked to a candidate may be found in Banerjee (1957), pp. 119–122. For another, see Vajirañāṇavarorasa (1973).

40 This is the order found in the Vinaya of the Mūlasarvāstivādins. The order varies in other texts. Nuns are only told of three recourses since living under a tree is against their rules.

hair, silk, fine linen, fine wool, fine muslin, wool, hemp, etc., or any other suitable material. (2) Exceptions to the second rule regarding food include: boiled rice, gruel, soup, meals offered on various special days of the lunar fortnight, regularly offered meals, meals offered on the spur of the moment, condiments, etc., or any other suitable meals. (3) Exceptions for the third rule regarding dwellings are: a monastery, an apartment on the top of a house, an attic, a thatch hut, a turret, a terraced building, a portico, a storehouse, a dirt cave, a rock cave, a mountain cave, a straw hut, a leaf hut, etc., or any other suitable dwelling. (4) Exceptions for the fourth rule regarding medicine are: ghee, oil, honey, molasses, medicines stored for a day, for up to seven days, for life, medicinal roots, medicinal stalks, medicinal leaves, medicinal fruits, etc., or any other suitable medicines.[41] It is sometimes said that these "exceptions" reflect a softening of an originally ascetic wandering monastic lifestyle, which is thereby proclaimed as a paradigmatic ideal. This, however, may be to paint a misleading "scenario of decline" from some hypothesized ideal of original homelessness. It may be better to view the "standards" and the "exceptions" as coexisting options.

6.6 MONASTIC RULES

After being made aware of the four recourses, the candidate is informed of the four cardinal precepts he will be expected to observe. These are: (1) to refrain from all sexual intercourse; (2) to refrain from taking anything not given to him; (3) to refrain from intentionally killing someone or encouraging someone to kill themselves; and (4) to refrain from falsely claiming to have superhuman qualities.[42]

In a different context, these four cardinal precepts are said to be the first of several hundred rules of the Vinaya which are enumerated in a list called the prātimokṣa (the "regulation" – Pali, pāṭimokkha). The precise number of rules in the prātimokṣa varies from one Mainstream school to another and is different for monks and nuns (the latter having far more than the former) (see table 6.1). By and large, however, these rules are categorized into different classes, according to the type of punishment that their violation theoretically entails.

41 These lists taken from Banerjee (1957), pp. 128–132. The Theravādin list is much less extensive (see Strong, 2008, pp. 77–78).

42 For a step-by-step description of the Theravāda ordination ceremony from Thailand, see Vajirañāṇavarorasa (1973), pp. 20–45; for Sri Lanka, see Warren (1896), pp. 393–401.

MAINSTREAM SCHOOL	NO. OF PRECEPTS FOR MONKS	NO. OF PRECEPTS FOR NUNS	COUNTRIES CURRENTLY USED IN
Theravāda	227	311	Cambodia, Laos, Myanmar, Thailand, Sri Lanka (for monks only)
Dharmaguptaka	250	348	China, Japan, Korea, Vietnam (for monks and nuns)
Mūlasarvāstivāda	258	354	Himalayas, Mongolia, Nepal, Tibet (for monks only)

Table 6.1 Prātimokṣa Rules According to Different Mainstream Schools[43]

The four cardinal precepts listed above – against sex, stealing, murder, and lying about one's attainments – are called pārājikas and violation of any them is said to result in expulsion from the community, even though, in practice, various loopholes were found and exceptions were made. In all of the various Vinayas (except the Pali), a monk, if truly remorseful, may be allowed to stay on in a "special penitential status known as a śikṣādattaka" (Clarke, 2014, p. 103).[44]

Of lesser severity are thirteen rules called saṃghāvaśeṣa (Pali, sanghādisesa), which entail suspension from the community for a period of time. These include five rules concerning various endeavors of a sexual nature short of actual intercourse, two rules concerning building overly luxurious dwellings, two rules concerning falsely accusing a fellow monk of having committed a pārājika offence; and four rules concerning acts liable to cause schism in the community or to bring disrepute to the saṃgha in the eyes of the laity.[45] In addition, there are six more categories of rules (see table 6.2).

---

43 For translations of the Theravāda prātimokṣa for monks, see Davids and Oldenberg (1882), vol. 1, pp. 1–70; for nuns, see Thanissaro (2007–2012). For translations of the Dharmaguptaka prātimokṣa for monks, see Beal (1871), pp. 204–239; for nuns, see Tsomo (1996). For translations of the Mūlasarvāstivāda prātimokṣa for monks, see Prebish (1996), pp. 34–40; for nuns, see Tsomo (1996). On prātimokṣa in general, see Tsomo (2004). For the various bhikṣuṇī prātimokṣas, see Kabilsingh (1984), and Chung (1999).

44 For more on this, see Clarke (2009). The same status was available to nuns (even though some have claimed otherwise). See Clarke (2000).

45 See Davids and Oldenberg (1882), pp. 7–15.

CATEGORY	POSSIBLE PUNISHMENT	NO. FOR MONKS	NO. FOR NUNS
Pārājika	Expulsion	4	8
Sanghādisesa	Suspension	13	17
Aniyata (not determined)	Varied	2	0
Nissagiya pācittiya	Confession and forfeiture of object misappropriated	30	30
Pācittiya	Confession	92	166
Pāṭidesanīya (lesser offenses)	Confession	4	8
Sekhiyā (rules of etiquette)	N/A	75	75
Adhikaraṇa samatha (procedural rules)	N/A	7	7
TOTAL		227	311

Table 6.2 Categories of Prātimokṣa Precepts (Theravāda Tradition)[46]

It should be pointed out that for nuns there are an additional four pārājikas. Not only can nuns be expelled for sexual intercourse, stealing, etc., but they can also be expelled for the following causes: if a nun, moved by desire, "touches, strokes, takes hold of, or presses up against a man, anywhere between his neck and his knees"; if a nun fails to denounce another nun whom she knows is guilty of a pārājika offence; if a nun refuses to stop supporting a monk who has had some of his privileges suspended by the community; and if a nun engages in any kind of non-Dharmic (i.e. sensual) behavior with a man.[47]

6.6.1 The Elaboration of the Disciplinary Code

The prātimokṣa list of rules, however, does not represent the entire regulatory thrust of the Vinaya. As time went on, attempts were made to spell out all possible circumstances in which a rule applied. New situations arose requiring new refinements of the rules and new questions about their application. For example, although "sexual intercourse" with all types or persons and with animals is forbidden in Pārājika no. 1, and masturbation is forbidden in saṃghāvaśeṣa no. 1, what about sex with spirits? with

46 For full explanation of the Theravāda Prātimokṣa rules, see Thanissaro (2007).
47 On extra rules for nuns, see Strong (2008), p. 81.

dolls? with corpses? What about cases of being raped? What about cases when the monk or nun has passed out? What about instances in which a monk changes into lay clothes before having sex, and so, in a sense, is not a monk during the act? All these questions and many other even harder-to-imagine ones are raised in the Vinaya and answered, supposedly by the Buddha himself.[48]

The same kind of elaborations are developed with regard to the other rules involving expulsion (stealing, killing, and making false claims of superhuman achievements), as well as for all the other prātimokṣa rules involving lesser punishments. In all these cases, the question of intentionality is a key one. Did the offender mean to kill, lie, steal, have sex, etc.? If not, there is generally no offense, or a lesser offense. Thus, for example, although deliberately killing an animal is a violation "requiring confession," inadvertently killing an animal is not.[49]

Obviously, in such situations, complications can readily arise. To deal with them, the Vinaya writers developed additional classifications of offenses, beyond those listed in the prātimokṣa. Two categories, in particular, became common: offenses that were deemed "serious transgressions" (Pali, thullaccaya), and less grave "wrong-doings" (dukkaṭa). Thus, for example, when some monks, in fun, rolled down a rock from a mountain top, and it accidentally killed a cowherd, the Buddha declared: "This, monks, is not an offense meriting expulsion [because it was unintentional], but you should not throw down rocks in fun. Whosoever does so [from now on] commits an offense of wrong-doing." Several cases involving abortion (which in South Asia was generally considered to be intentionally killing a human) are particularly interesting in this regard: once a woman who got pregnant when her husband was away asked a monk who was a relative of hers to find her something that would cause her to miscarry. The monk gave her an abortive concoction, and the fetus died. The Buddha deemed it to be murder and thus an offense meriting expulsion. In another case, a woman asked a monk to give her rival, who was pregnant by her husband, an abortive concoction. He did, but the mother died; the unborn fetus survived. The Buddha deemed this not to be murder meriting expulsion, but only a "serious transgression," because the intent had not been to kill the mother but the child. In another case, a woman asked a monk to get her a fertility drug so she could get pregnant.

48 On the elaboration of rules about sex, see Faure (1998), pp. 64–97, and Gyatso (2005).

49 For discussion of these types of rules, see Thanissaro (2007a).

The monk did, but the drug killed her. The Buddha deemed it not to be an offense meriting expulsion, but merely a "wrong-doing."[50]

6.6.2 Enforcement of the Rules: Prātimokṣa Recitation and Pravāraṇa

The rules of the monastic code were not just left for the monks themselves to learn once and follow. Every lunar fortnight, on the day of the full moon and the new moon, the entirety of the prātimokṣa is recited in an assembly that is mandatory for all monks in a given monastery. Monks not in good standing, novices, nuns, laymen, and laywomen are not allowed to participate. At the end of the recitation of each category of rule (see table 6.2), the monks are asked to disclose whether or not they are "pure" with regard to any infractions they may have committed of those particular rules. Usually, they will remain silent. This means either that they have not committed any violation, or that they have already cleansed themselves of it by acknowledging it to fellow monks ahead of time. If not, though, this is time to do so. Either way, appropriate steps may then be taken to punish or purge the monk in question.[51]

Once a year, a somewhat different kind of ritual, called the "invitation" (pravāraṇa) takes place. On the full moon day marking the end of the rains-retreat, all the monks in a given monastery assemble, and each one, in a squatting posture, formally "invites" all the members of the community to point out any wrong-doing he has committed. A monk who accuses another of a violation must specify which rule he thinks has been transgressed and explain his reasons for so thinking. False accusations are themselves considered to be violations. This method, then, does not depend on a monk voluntarily confessing his own faults but leaves the policing up to other monks.[52]

Finally, mention should be made of another set of disciplinary texts. The prātimokṣa list of rules, though it did guide behavior, was to some extent primarily a ritual text, to be recited, as we have seen, every fortnight and reinforced at the pravāraṇa. But monastics, for the most part, did not study

50 On the evolution of the Vinaya, see Gombrich (1988), pp. 87–117, and also Blackburn (1999). For discussions of Buddhist views of abortion, see Keown (1999), and Harvey (2000), pp. 311–352. See also Agostini (2004).

51 For the ritual, see Strong (2008), pp. 79–81; see also Thanissaro (2007), pp. 20–28.

52 Upasak (1975), pp. 147–149. For a discussion, see also Holt (1981), pp. 131–134.

the prātimokṣa list, nor did they read the Basket of Discipline (Vinayapiṭaka) as a whole. Instead, in Theravāda countries, they used and use a number of Pali and vernacular condensations of and commentaries on the rules, which are more contextually relevant and form part of what Blackburn (1999) calls a "practical canon." Similarly, in East Asia, monks employed various summary monastic codes called "Rules of Purity" (Ch., Qinggui; Jpn., Shingi) while in Tibet most monks came to use the so-called *Vinayasūtra* of Guṇaprabha, a synopsis of Mūlasarvāstivāda rules.[53]

6.7 SOME EXEMPLARY DISCIPLES OF THE BUDDHA

The saṃgha, of course, was not all about community structures and rules and regulations. It was also about individuals in all their diversity and interactions. One of the ways to see this dimension of things is to look at the lifestories of various disciples of the Buddha. This will give us an idea – not necessarily of what life was like in the saṃgha at the time of the Buddha – but of the ways in which Buddhists within a few centuries of the Buddha retrospectively conceived of the saṃgha in his time. In other words, these lifestories should not be read as historical documents; they most likely represent a mixture of oral traditions about the biographical particularities of various monks and nuns, with an attempt to emphasize the role these individuals played as exemplars of specific monastic qualities.

One important canonical source designates the principal disciples of the Buddha (monks, nuns, laymen, and laywomen) as being "foremost" in a particular quality or ability (see table 6.3 for a partial list). For instance, Śāriputra is "foremost among those monks of great wisdom," Maudgalyāyana is "foremost among those endowed with supernormal powers," etc. Sometimes, certain figures (e.g. Ānanda) are said to be "foremost" in several categories.[54]

These designations had hagiographic implications, as they both reflected and gave rise to stories about these disciples. But they also had ritual cultic

53 On "Rules of Purity," see Foulk (2004; 2006). On the *Vinayasūtra* of Guṇaprabha, see Nietupski (2009). On "practical canon," see Blackburn (1999). On the related notion of a "ritual canon," i.e. the books actually used by monastics and actually found in monastic library collections, see Collins (1990), pp. 103–104.

54 This list may be found in Bodhi (2012), pp. 109–113. For another much shorter group of prominent disciples, see Anālayo (2011a), vol. 1, pp. 209–216. Another popular scheme lists eighty disciples of the Buddha.

DISCIPLE	CATEGORY IN WHICH RANKED FOREMOST
MALE MONASTICS (SANSKRIT/PALI)	
Kauṇḍinya/Koṇḍañña	Seniority
Śāriputra/Sāriputta	Wisdom
Mahāmaudgalyāyana/Mahāmoggallāna	Supernormal powers
Mahākāśyapa/Mahākassapa	Ascetic practices
Ānanda/Ānanda	Learning, memory, quick to grasp, resoluteness, personal attendants
Mahākātyāyana/Mahākaccāna	Explaining in detail what has been stated in brief
Aniruddha/Anuruddha	Divine eye
Darba/Dabba	Assigning lodgings
Batkula/Bakkula	Good health
FEMALE MONASTICS (SANSKRIT/PALI)	
Mahāprajāpatī/Mahāpajāpatī	Seniority
Kṣemā/Khemā	Wisdom
Utpalavarṇā/Uppalavaṇṇā	Supernormal powers
Paṭācārā/Paṭācārā	Mastery of the Vinaya
Nandā/Nandā	Meditative trance
Bhadrā/Bhaddā	Recollection of past lives
Kṛśā Gautamī/Kisā Gotamī	Wearing coarse robes
LAYMEN (SANSKRIT/PALI)	
Trapuṣa/Tapussa and Bhallika/Bhallika	Going for refuge
Anāthapiṇḍada/Anāthapiṇḍika	Donors
Citra/Citta	Preachers of the Dharma
Śūra Āmraṣṭha/Sūra Ambaṭṭha	Unwavering trust
Jīvaka/Jīvaka	Trusted by people
Nakulapitṛ/Nakulapitā and Nakulamātṛ/Nakulamātā	Intimate companionship
LAYWOMEN (SANSKRIT/PALI)	
Sujātā/Sujātā	Going for refuge
Viśākhā/Visākhā	Donors
Supriyā/Suppiyā	Comforting the sick
Kātiyānī/Kātiyānī	Unwavering trust
Uttarā/Uttarā	Meditative trance

Table 6.3 Partial List of Disciples Eminent in Various Categories[55]

55 See Bodhi (2012), pp. 109–13, for full list.

implication; in time, in some places, shrines were built honoring some of these disciples where they could be venerated by monastics and laypeople particularly interested in their prominent qualities. Thus, in one legend, we read that, at the Jetavana monastery, there were stūpas erected in honor of no less than five of the Buddha's male disciples – Śāriputra, Maudgalyāyana, Mahākāśyapa, Ānanda, and the lesser known Batkula – each of whose "prominence" is described and recognized. Much the same thing may be seen in the accounts of the Chinese pilgrims Faxian and Xuanzang who visited India in the fifth and seventh century CE. Xuanzang, for instance, states that, at one monastery he visited, on feast days, brethren dedicated to Abhidharma study would offer worship at the stūpa of Śāriputra; those engaged in śamatha meditation would venerate that of Maudgalyāyana; Vinaya specialists would go to the shrine of Upāli (reciter of the Vinaya at the First Council); the nuns would venerate Ānanda (instrumental in getting the Buddha to establish a bhikṣuṇī order), the novices would honor Rāhula (the Buddha's son who was the first to become a novice), while the Mahāyānists would venerate various bodhisattvas.[56]

It is not possible here to examine the lives of all of these figures. Some (e.g. Mahākāśyapa, Ānanda, and Mahāprajāpatī) we have already encountered; others (e.g. Batkula) we will meet in a different context (see 7.3.4). For the present, by way of examples, I want to look briefly at the preeminence of Śāriputra and Maudgalyāyana, and then at an exemplary nun, Paṭācārā. Finally, I will close this chapter with two examples of lay devotees.

6.7.1 Śāriputra and Maudgalyāyana

Śāriputra and Maudgalyāyana are often called the Buddha's two chief disciples. The two were friends from childhood, each brought up in brahmin families in villages near Rājagṛha. One day, as young men, they went to see a theatrical performance at a local festival, featuring a play about a beautiful young dancer who was transformed into an old hag.[57] This caused them to reflect on the impermanence of life, and together they resolved to renounce the world. They became disciples of the non-Buddhist teacher Sañjayin,

56 An account of the disciples' shrines at the Jetavana may be found in Strong (1983), pp. 252–256. For Faxian's account of the veneration of the disciples, see Legge (1886), pp. 41–46. For Xuanzang's, see Li (1995), p. 68.
57 For an account of the festival called the girivalgusamāgama, see Feer (1891), pp. 280–284 [in French].

who was a famous sceptic and agnostic. Early in their practice, they made an agreement with each other that whoever attained what they called "the deathless state" (i.e. enlightenment) would tell the other. One day, in Rājagṛha, Śāriputra happened to meet one of the Buddha's first disciples, Aśvajit, one of the "fortunate five" monks who had been present at the First Sermon in Sarnath. Impressed by Aśvajit's demeanor, he asked him who his master was and what was his teaching. Aśvajit replied that he was a follower of the Buddha and repeated to him the verse that he said summed up the whole of his teaching: "The Tathāgata has explained the origin of all those elements of existence that have an origin and he has also explained their cessation." Upon hearing this verse, Śāriputra's Dharma-eye was opened, i.e. he reached the first stage of enlightenment. A bit later, Śāriputra met Maudgalyāyana who immediately realized that something momentous had happened to his friend: "Your senses are serene," he exclaimed, "your face is at peace, and the complexion of your skin is utterly pure. Did you reach the deathless state?" "I did," replied Śāriputra, and he told Maudgalyāyana what had happened. Upon hearing the same verse, Maudgalyāyana too was enlightened. Together, the friends went to see the Buddha, and were promptly ordained by him. Maudgalyāyana attained arhatship seven days later, and Śāriputra a week after him. Shortly after their ordination, the Buddha announced to the assembly of monks that he was making Śāriputra and Maudgalyāyana his chief disciples (agraśravaka). The monks who were already members of the saṃgha were annoyed that these relative newcomers should be given such an honor, until the Buddha explained how the pair had been striving to attain this position through good deeds for countless past lives, some of which he then recounted.[58]

Though paired in their conversion story, and similar in that they both predeceased the Buddha, Śāriputra and Maudgalyāyana represent two rather different but complementary inclinations within the Buddhist saṃgha, which embody polarities that we will become more familiar with in subsequent chapters. Śāriputra was renowned for his wisdom which came from his scholarly intellectual understanding of the Buddha's teachings. He was a "paradigmatic textual scholar and master of doctrine" and a "champion of settled monasticism" (Ray, 1994, pp. 131–132). In time, he came to be particularly associated with Abhidharma studies. Maudgalyāyana, on the other

58 The account of the pair's conversion is based on Kloppenborg (1973), pp. 92–95. Other versions of the story may be found in Horner (1938–1952), vol. 4, pp. 52–57, and Jones (1949–1956), vol. 3, pp. 56–70. More generally on Śāriputra and Maudgalyāyana, see Ray (1994), p. 132, and Nyanaponika and Hecker (1997), pp. 1–106.

hand, became known for his mastery of supernatural powers, resulting from his command of trances achieved through śamatha meditation. He is often depicted as utilizing his superpowers on behalf of the Buddha. He used them, for instance, to shake the palace of the god Indra (who was suffering from too much pride in his own splendor), and to subdue and convert the nāga kings Nanda and Upananda. He used them also regularly to fly through the air and visit various parts of the cosmos, in order to report on beings who had been reborn there. In one story, he searches far and wide for his mother, who has been reborn in a different world system, and, when he finds her, manages, with the Buddha's help, to convert her to Buddhism and bring her to a state of realizing the truth of the Dharma. This story is much developed in East Asia where Maudgalyāyana, known as Mulian in Chinese (Jpn., Mokuren), becomes a paradigm of Buddhist filial piety.[59]

Interestingly, Śāriputra appears to have shared Maudgalyāyana's attitude of filiality. When Śāriputra realized he had but a week more to live, he resolved to convert one more person – his mother – and then to pass into parinirvāṇa in his natal home. Indeed, even though Śāriputra's mother was the parent of seven children, all of whom became arhats, she herself remained an unbeliever. In fact, it is said that she rued the days when each of her children had become ordained. Out of filial concern for her, Śāriputra decided to do something about this. Taking his final leave of the Buddha, he went back to his home village. Upon arriving there, he was received by his mother and moved into the room in which he had been born. There he immediately became gravely ill with dysentery. During the night, he was visited by a number of deities who came to attend on him in his final hours: the four divine guardians of the quarters, and also Indra, and Brahmā. Seeing these figures coming and going, his mother inquired who they were; finding out their identity, she asked her son if he was really greater than the gods, one of whom (Brahmā) she in fact worshipped. He told her they were like lay supporters of his. Impressed, and finally understanding that her son's faith was remarkable, she was filled with pride and joy. Realizing that the moment was ripe for her conversion, Śāriputra preached to her, and she finally saw the truth of the Dharma and became a stream-winner. Śāriputra then passed away at dawn.[60]

---

59 On Maudgalyāyana's use of supernatural powers, see Malalasekera (1960), vol. 2, pp. 543–544. For the Indian version of his search for his mother, see Rotman (2008), pp. 111–114. On Maudgalyāyana in East Asia, see Mair (1983), pp. 87–121, Teiser (1988), pp. 113–124, Cole (1998), pp. 80–115, and Glassman (1999).

60 On Śāriputra's passing, see Nyanaponika and Hecker (1997), pp. 47–57; on his relics, see Schopen (2004b), pp. 285–329.

6.7.2 Paṭācārā

In 6.3 above, we looked at the important figure of Mahāprajāpatī and her role in founding and then heading the order of nuns. In what follows, I want to introduce another important early leader of the bhikṣuṇī saṃgha: Paṭācārā.

Among the many stories of women joining the Buddhist order, Paṭācārā's is surely one of the most poignant. She was born into the house of a guild master in Śrāvastī. As a young woman, rather than marry the man her parents had chosen for her, she ran away with her true love, one of the servants in her household. In time, she became pregnant. As her due date approached, she decided to go back to her parents' home to have the child, but before she got there, she went into labor, and gave birth by the side of the road. That being the case, she decided there was no reason any more for her to go home, and so she and her husband returned to their village. Before long, she got pregnant again, and once more she set off to have the child at her parents' home, and once more she went into labor on the road before getting there. This time, however, a thunderstorm was threatening to burst out, so she asked her husband to build her a shelter from the rain. He went off to cut some branches and some grass for the roof, but as he was gathering these materials, a poisonous snake bit him and he died. Paṭācārā gave birth alone in the rain and discovered his corpse the next day. Distraught, she picked up her newborn and took her older child by the hand and continued on the way to her family home. She soon came to a river that was swollen from the rain. Unable to carry both children across at once, she left the older one on the near bank and forded the stream with her baby, whom she laid on a cloth on the far bank. She then set out back across the river to get her first child, but, when she was in midstream, a hawk flew down and started pecking at her infant. She waved her arms and yelled at the bird; seeing her gesture, her little boy, on the near bank, thought she was calling him and so he went down into the river. He fell in and was carried away by the stream and drowned. Meanwhile, the hawk carried off the infant and disappeared. More grief-stricken than ever, she still decided to proceed onwards to her home. When she got there, however, she found that her parents' house had collapsed in the storm and all the members of her family had been killed; they were just then being cremated on a funeral pyre.

Now out of her mind with grief, Paṭācārā went insane. Unable to bear even the clothes on her body, she stripped them off and wandered aimlessly, lamenting, "Both my sons are gone / and my husband is dead upon the road!

/ And my mother and father and brother / burn on a single pyre!" Roaming about, completely crazed, in time she came to a place where the Buddha was preaching to a great crowd. Seeing her there, the Blessed One interrupted his sermon and said to her: "Sister, regain awareness, acquire mindfulness." As soon as she heard those words, she sat down. The Master then recited for her a verse from the *Dhammapada*:

> Neither sons, nor parents, nor kinfolk are a refuge.
> Relatives offer no shelter for one seized by Death.
> Knowing this situation, the wise, exercising moral restraint,
> Can quickly clear the way that leads to nirvāṇa.

Hearing this, Paṭācārā reached the first stage of enlightenment. She went to the Buddha and asked to be ordained. The Buddha agreed to her request.[61] As a nun, Paṭācārā became famous for her strict observance of the discipline (vinaya), and her determination to attain nirvāṇa, something that occurred to her one day (as we saw in 6.3) when, after taking a bath, and preparing for bed, she put out the oil lamp in her cell (nirvāṇa literally means extinction).

Pāṭacārā went on to become a renowned eldress and teacher of the Dharma who became the inspiration and guide for numerous other nuns. The *Verses of the Eldresses (Therīgāthā)* is a Pali canonical text that recounts the stories and "songs" of over seventy nuns. Among these are several who recount their debt of gratitude to Pāṭacārā. For instance, here are some of the verses of a nun named Caṇḍā:

> I was in a bad way,
> a widow,
> no children, no friends ...
> I was a beggar with a bowl and a stick
> and wandered house to house ...
> for seven years.
> But I met a nun
> who [gave me] food and drink ...
> She was Pāṭacārā.

61 The story of Pāṭacārā is told in Bode (1893), pp. 556–60, Pruitt (1998), pp. 143–154, and Nyanaponika and Hecker (1997), pp. 293–300. For an analysis of another story with a similar plot, see Durt (2001).

Out of pity, she guided me,
in leaving home,
encouraged me,
and urged me to the highest goal

(Murcott, 1991, p. 37)

6.7.3 The Laypersons Nakulapitṛ and Nakulamātṛ

I began this chapter with a discussion of the importance of the laity to the Buddhist monastic community; it is now time to come full circle and end it with some instances of exemplary laypersons. In 2.7.7 above, we saw that the Buddha's very first converts after his enlightenment were laymen, the merchants Trapuṣa and Bhallika, who came to be known as the "first of those who took refuge"; and in 6.2.2, we touched on the story of the rich merchant Anāthapiṇḍada whose gift of the Jetavana monastery to the Buddha earned him the recognition of being "first among donors." In what follows, I want to look at a rather different example: a lay couple, Nakulapitṛ (Father Nakula) and his wife Nakulamātṛ (Mother Nakula), who were deemed to be foremost not for their gifts to the Buddha, but for their faithfulness, by which is meant not just their loyalty to Buddhism, but also their loyal support of each other.

According to a Pali tradition, the first time Father and Mother Nakula met the Buddha, they addressed him as "son," and reproached him for not having visited them in a long time. Asked by his monks for an explanation of this somewhat bizarre encounter, the Buddha recalls that the couple had actually been his parents in five hundred of his previous births. The story is cited not just to make a point about the close relationship of Father and Mother Nakula to the Blessed One, but about their intimate fidelity to each other that kept them together through so many lifetimes. Indeed it is this relationship that the Buddha underscores in declaring them to be the foremost of his disciples in faithfulness.

The power of these bonds is illustrated in another story, which is interesting as another example of lay values: towards the end of his life, Father Nakula becomes deathly ill, and is worried about the fate of his wife should he pass away before her. How will she cope when he is gone? Mother Nakula seeks to allay his fears (for it is not good to die with an anxious mind): she tells him he need not worry about her and the children, for she is skilled "at weaving cotton and knitting wool [and so] will be able to maintain the household";

and he need not worry that she will want to take another husband, since for the past sixteen years she has lived chastely with him and has no desire to remarry; and he need not worry that she will fall from the faith, since she will continue visiting the Buddha, and in fact will see him probably more often than before. So powerful are these assurances that they act as a tonic for her husband who, rather than pass away, revives to live on with his wise and loyal spouse.

Simply put, then, Father and Mother Nakula love and respect and support each other, and this is seen as worthy of praise, reflective, perhaps of the kind of marital relationship advocated by the Buddha in his sermon to Sigāla which we touched on in 6.1.2. But there is something else that holds them together: their common faith. This, in fact, is what is said to cement their bond, and the Buddha predicts that their mutual faith, virtuous behavior, generosity, and wisdom will keep them together not only in the present but in future lives to come as well.[62]

6.7.4 Viśākhā, Preeminent Laywoman

Finally, for another example of a preeminent disciple, I shall turn to Viśākhā, whom the Buddha named as the best among laywomen supporters of the saṃgha. Viśākhā was born in a very wealthy family that had earned its fortune through their past meritorious actions. At the age of seven, when the Buddha came to her hometown, she went to listen to him preach and was immediately converted, along with her companions and servants. In due time, a marriage for her was arranged with the son of a rich Jain merchant named Mṛgāra who lived far off in the town of Śrāvastī. Viśākhā was in every way a loyal devoted wife, pandering to her in-laws' every need except in one area: as a steadfast Buddhist, she refused to join her husband's family in their support of the local community of Jains. She was, in fact, repulsed by the nudity of the Jain monks who came begging at their door, and rather than make offerings to them, would snub them by retiring to her chamber. They responded by maligning her and encouraging her father-in-law, Mṛgāra, to send her away. Viśākhā, however, was not to be gotten rid of so easily. By clever means, she convinced her father-in-law to let her invite the Buddha to

62 On Father and Mother Nakula's relationship to each other and to the Buddha, see Bodhi (2012), pp. 445–446, 871–873. More generally, see Nyanaponika and Hecker (1997), pp. 375–378.

come to their house for a meal. He reluctantly agreed, but when he heard the Buddha's sermon after the meal, he immediately became convinced of the truth of his words and realized the first level of enlightenment. Thereafter he expressed his eternal gratitude to Viśākhā for having introduced him to the Dharma, and, declaring that henceforth he would respect her as he would his own mother, he began calling her Mṛgāramātṛ ("Mother Mṛgāra").

Eventually, Viśākhā became a kind of matriarch of the family. She had ten sons and ten daughters, each of whom had twenty children of their own. And she led her family in tending every day to the needs of the Buddhist monks, and in listening to the Buddha preach the Dharma. On one occasion, she decided to sell a very precious piece of her own jewelry to give further alms to the saṃgha. Not finding anyone in the whole of Śrāvastī who could afford to purchase it, she decided to "buy it from herself" (with the rest of her wealth) and to use the proceeds to build a new monastery for the Order in Śrāvastī. Called the "Eastern Park" (Pūrvārāma), it was also known as Mother Mṛgāra's Mansion, and it came to rival the better-known Jetavana monastery founded earlier in Śrāvastī by the great male donor, Anāthapiṇḍada (see 6.2.2). Indeed, while in Śrāvastī, the Buddha came to split his time more or less equally between the two monastic establishments.

Viśākhā's renown as a paradigmatic lay supporter was due, however, not just to her generosity, but also for her spiritual endeavors. That these were directly related to her practice of dāna is emphasized in the following episode: once, Viśākhā asked the Buddha to grant her eight boons. The Buddha replied that he never made such promises without knowing what the requests were. So Viśākhā then specified that she wanted permission to make the following gifts to the saṃgha: (1) rain cloths for the monks (for she had noticed that some monks, during the monsoon, went about naked to preserve their robes and so were mistaken for naked ascetics); (2) food for monks who had just arrived in Śrāvastī (for they were tired from the journey and were unfamiliar with the town so did not yet know where to go on their begging rounds); (3) food for monks going off on a journey (since they might have difficulty begging in unfamiliar places); a constant supply of (4) medicine, and (5) food for sick monks, and (6) for those taking care of sick monks who could not beg for the same; (7) a constant supply of rice gruel (conjee) (since it would help keep monks in good health); and (8) bathing cloths for the community of nuns since it was unsuitable for them to bathe naked in the river.

Having heard these requests, the Buddha then asked Viśākhā what merit she intended to receive from such gifts. Her reply is significant: recalling the fact that the monks (or nuns) have benefited from her various gifts will give rise in her to delight and joy in her mind, and this will result in her feeling calm and at ease in her body, which will make for contemplativeness and lead to growth in spiritual powers and the factors conducive to enlightenment. Hearing this, the Buddha then praises her and approves her request for the boons.[63] In the case of Viśākhā, then, we can see once again how laypersons are interested in more than just reaping merits in a future life, but also how their merit making is part and parcel of a greater spiritual endeavor to lead wiser, calmer, more serene, and enlightened lives.

6.8 SUMMARY

In this chapter, we have looked at the establishment of the monastic community during the lifetime of the Buddha, at least as it was recalled by subsequent generations of monks. We have examined lay–monastic interactions, and the importance of merit making, of magical protection, and the role of laypersons and kings in the formulations of certain monastic structures. We have seen that monastics had various lifestyles, both peripatetic and settled, both solitary and in community, and that monasteries, as they developed, were structured places filled with persons of varied inclinations, and held together by common observance of certain rituals and rules that governed both morality and community. Finally, we have illustrated some of the realia and ideals of the saṃgha by looking at the lifestories of some exemplary monks, nuns, and laypersons. In the next chapter we will look at some developments in the institutional history of the Buddhist community.

63 The story of the eight boons is taken from Horner (1938–1952), vol. 4, pp. 416–419. More generally on Viśākhā, see Nyanaponika and Hecker (1997), pp. 247–255; for a discussion, see Falk (1990), pp. 131–139, and Lewis (2014a). On the life of another prominent laywoman disciple of the Buddha, see Scheible (2014).

Chapter 7

Visions and Divisions of the Saṃgha

We have, so far, been looking at the saṃgha as though it were a single community, whatever the diversity of its individual members. In this chapter, I would like to present some of the history (or, perhaps better, some of the stories about the history) of the gradual division of the saṃgha into various sorts of factions. I shall start with stories of the early Buddhist councils (7.1), and the emergence of different Mainstream Buddhist schools (7.2), as well as other sorts of divisions that cut across these various groups (7.3). Then, I will examine the split between Mainstream and Mahāyāna (7.4), as well as the proliferation of Mahāyāna schools in China (7.5), Japan (7.6), and Tibet (7.7).

7.1 COUNCIL STORIES

Reference has already been made several times to the so-called First Council that was reputedly held immediately after the Buddha's death. We saw in chapter 3 how Mahākāśyapa summoned all of the arhats together in Rājagṛha for the occasion, arhats who were threatening individually to follow the Buddha into extinction. The Council at Rājagṛha was just the first in a series of councils that, according to various traditions, periodically met to reaffirm the unity of the community and the canonicity of the teachings. In fact, in their reaffirmations, they also exposed a number of divisional issues and factional splits which are well worth examining.[1]

1 For a summary of information on the various councils, see Buswell and Lopez (2014), pp. 198–200, and Prebish (2004).

7.1.1 The Council at Rājagṛha

Scholars today seriously question the historicity of the First Council, so what follows should only be taken as story. Nonetheless, much can be learned from legend. A major purpose of the First Council seems to have been to establish the unity of the Dharma and the saṃgha. A number of stories about the council, however, seem to highlight potential divisions in the community. One of these in particular will concern us here: the so-called "trial" of Ānanda.[2]

According to most versions of the events, at some point during the proceedings of the council, Mahākāśyapa accuses Ānanda of having committed a number of wrong-doings to which he must confess. These include: (1) Ānanda should never have asked the Buddha to allow the ordination of women; (2) when the Buddha told him that buddhas, if asked, could remain in this world until the end of the aeon, he neglected to ask him to do so; (3) he stepped on the Buddha's robe (when he was mending it); (4) he once neglected to get the Buddha some water when he asked for it; granted, the river had been muddied by some ox-carts passing through it, but why did he not ask the gods for some water?; (5) when the Buddha declared that the monks could change certain minor rules of the discipline, he failed to ask him which ones; (6) when the Buddha's body lay in state, he ushered some women mourners in to see the Buddha's body up close and let them stain his feet with their tears; (7) and, for some women, he disrobed the body of the Buddha to allow them to see his sheath-encased penis (one of the signs of the Great Man), thinking this would inspire them to make merit so as to become disgusted with their female bodies and achieve rebirth as males (sic).[3]

These accusations are perhaps best understood if we view them as occurring in a ritual context. The tradition makes it clear that the First Council is taking place at the end of the rainy season, i.e. the beginning of a new year. With this in mind, Przyluski has argued that we consider this part of its proceedings as reflective of the ceremony called the "invitation" (pravāraṇa) which anciently and still today marks the end of the rains-residence. As we have seen (6.6.2), the pravāraṇa is a special annual "purification" of the saṃgha in which monastics do not merely confess to a fellow monastic any transgressions they might have made (as they do fortnightly at the recitation

2 On the "trial" of Ānanda at the First Council, see Witanachchi (1966), p. 532, Lévy (1968), pp. 61–81, and Przyluski (1926), pp. 257–306 [in French].

3 This list is based on the various accounts found in Przyluski (1926), pp. 3–20 [in French].

of the prāṭimokṣa), but in which members of the assembly as a whole are asked to speak up and denounce any individual whom they suspect of having committed a wrong-doing. Przyluski has argued that this is a kind of annual ritual cleansing of the whole community in which all grievances are aired and settled. He even goes so far as to suggest that, as in a number of other cultures, Ānanda is here playing the role of a scapegoat on whom all sins are loaded and who is then chased from the community.[4]

In any case none of Ānanda's "slip-ups" listed here seems very grave. They are all deemed to be "wrong-doings" (see 6.6.1) which can be annulled simply by being confessed, and Ānanda readily admits to them. If we look at them more closely, however, we can detect a clear polarity between two lifestyles and world outlooks. As we shall see, Mahākāśyapa represents those monks who are sticklers for strict discipline, for the "qualities of the purified"; Ānanda, on the other hand, is more down-to-earth and relaxed, more concerned with encouraging the laity (especially women) in their devotions, and more used to dealing with the Buddha on a human-to-human level.

This same polarity is reflected perhaps in one more "fault" mentioned by Mahākāśyapa: (8) Ānanda has failed to become enlightened – he is not an arhat and so, according to Mahākāśyapa, cannot participate in the First Council, which, he declares, is open only to fully enlightened monastics. He must leave the council (or, like a scapegoat, be expelled) since this is not a "fault" that can be repaired simply by confession.

In the accounts of the council, this presents a problem. As another prominent monk, the Venerable Anuruddha, points out, Ānanda is the only one who knows all of the Buddha's sermons by heart. They cannot exclude him; they need him to recite the Dharma! Nonetheless, at least in some versions of the story, Mahākāśyapa is adamant. He insists that, until he becomes enlightened, Ānanda cannot participate; the council is a kind of "arhats-only club" and its work would be rendered invalid and impure by the presence of a still-worldly being. The problem, of course, is soon remedied; that very night, Ānanda attains arhatship (when he is neither sitting nor lying down, just before his head touches his pillow), and he is allowed into the assembly the following day.[5]

Some have argued that we should see in Mahākāśyapa's actions here an expedient means – a clever way of pushing Ānanda to enlightenment. Mahākāśyapa knows that Ānanda knows that the recitation of the Dharma depends on him, and so that he will make every effort to strive for arhatship,

4 Ibid., pp. 257–279 [in French]. See, however, Lévy (1968), p. 77.

5 Witanachchi (1966), p. 532.

which he does. But it is more likely that Mahākāśyapa's intransigence reflects an issue that was a matter of some debate and contention within the early saṃgha. This was the question of elitism: did the arhats form a kind of super-saṃgha, an elite of male monastics who claimed the right to determine and govern the affairs and direction of the community?

As we shall see, some Mahāyānists were later to be critical of arhats from a doctrinal perspective as concerned primarily with their own salvation and not following the bodhisattva path. It is interesting, therefore, to note that a number of Mahāyāna texts modified the account of the First Council to say that, after it was over, a large number of monks who had not been admitted to its ranks because they were as yet unenlightened gathered under the leadership of the elder Bāṣpa (one of the five disciples converted at the Buddha's First Sermon) and compiled their own version of the Tripiṭaka. Because they were more numerous than the arhats convened by Mahākāśyapa, they called themselves the Mahāsaṃghikas (Great Community-ites).[6]

This, it should be noted, is a totally apocryphal story. As we shall see, the Mahāsaṃghikas were not formed until well over a century later, and this anecdote seems intended merely to give them an older pedigree. But it reflects retrospectively the controversy perhaps incipient from early on. Bareau has spoken, with regard to the First Council, of a "latent opposition between a largely democratic spirit, according to which the community in its totality retains supreme authority, and an aristocratic spirit, according to which the influence of a small elite of elders must be preponderant" (Bareau, 1955, p. 146).

The council of Rājagrha did not put an end to this polarity. It may be seen again, a little over a century later, in the so-called "Five Theses" of an elder named Mahādeva. His claims, which caused much debate at the time, were a direct attack on the perceived elitism of arhats. He maintained that (1) arhats could have "wet dreams," i.e. involuntary ejaculations of semen while they were asleep; they thus were not completely pure; (2) arhats were not omniscient but still subject to ignorance of some things (e.g. they might not know the name of a certain stranger, or plant); they thus were not completely knowledgeable; (3) arhats were subject to doubts; they thus were not completely certain; (4) arhats could still learn from others; and (5) arhats cry out when they attain the path.[7]

6 On this tradition, see Lamotte (1988), p. 286.

7 On the five theses, Mahādeva, and this schism, see Silk (2009), Nattier and Prebish (1977), and Lamotte (1988), pp. 274–275.

7.1.2 Vinaya Disputes: the Council of Vaiśālī

The status of arhats was not the only thing to be contested in the early saṃgha; so too were the rules of the discipline, the Vinaya. According to a tradition which might just be historical, about one hundred years after the parinirvāṇa of the Buddha, a second council was held in Vaiśālī. Its purpose was to deal with a group of local bhikṣus known as the Vṛjiputrakas who were supposedly proclaiming ten contested practices as being legitimate. Most of these practices may be seen as a softening of the rules and regulations of the order. For instance, they declared that it was acceptable for monks to eat their main meal "somewhat after noon"; or to go on a second begging round in the morning, if they were dissatisfied with the first; or to make communal decisions in the absence of a quorum of monks; or to drink "new palm-wine" (toddy that had not quite fermented); or to handle gold and silver. Indeed, it is said that the Vṛjiputraka monks were in the habit of using a collection bowl on the fortnightly uposatha observance and asking the laity who had come to put gold and silver coins in it.[8]

It is important to realize that the Vṛjiputrakas were not only *doing* these things; they were proclaiming them to be legal, and that was unacceptable to a number of monks who opposed them. Foremost among these monks was an elder named Yaśas, who, on a visit to Vaiśālī, condemned the Vṛjiputrakas' views. They responded by trying to expel him for trying to instruct them without authority. He, however, simply went elsewhere and gradually amassed support for his cause. He sought out the help of Śānakavāsin who had become Master of the Dharma after Ānanda (see 3.5). The Vṛjiputrakas, on the other hand, went to an elder named Revata and tried to bribe him into supporting them. But he instead called for a council to settle the dispute. Seven hundred elders then assembled in Vaiśālī and the practices were condemned. It is not clear, however, how much effect this condemnation had on the actual behavior of the Vṛjiputrakas.

7.1.3 The Councils of Pāṭaliputra

The council of Vaiśālī was called to deal with some disciplinary issues when the normal community methods for doing so broke down. According to

8 For a listing of all ten Vṛjiputraka theses, and on the council of Vaiśālī, see Lamotte (1988), pp. 126–127. Bareau (1955), p. 67 [in French], thinks that point 10 is the main one and that points 1–9 were later additions by the Theravādins. See also on this Juo-Hsüeh (2008).

some sources, it resulted in the first major institutional division of the saṃgha – the schism between the school of the Sthaviras (the Elders) and the Mahāsāṃghika (the Great Community-ites). According to other sources, however, this schism did not occur until somewhat later, about 116 years after the parinirvāṇa, when a council was convened in the Mauryan capital of Pāṭaliputra. Various theories have been advanced to explain this split. Some say that it emerged out of the controversies that started at Vaiśālī, others that it was prompted by a desire to deal with the Five Theses of Mahādeva about the nature of an arhat discussed above. Some scholars claim that Mahādeva's schism came later as an internal split within the Mahāsāṃghika branch. The most convincing theory, perhaps, is that it was not instigated by the future Mahāsāṃghika monks, but by the future Sthaviras who sought to expand the number of rules in their Vinaya. To this the Mahāsāṃghikas objected, and opted for retention of the original, unexpanded rules. This is interesting because the Mahāsāṃghikas are usually presented as the more liberal and innovative of the two early branches of Buddhism; according to this scenario, they would be the more conservative.[9]

Traditions about this council of Pāṭaliputra that gave rise to the Mahāsāṃghika/Sthavira split should not be confused with those about a different council said to have been held in the same city somewhat later, under the sponsorship of King Aśoka and the presidency of the elder Moggaliputta Tissa. This council is known only to Pali sources and seems to have been called to settle a division within the Sthavira branch of Buddhism between the Vibhajyavāda and the Sarvāstivāda. Supposedly, King Aśoka himself ruled in favor of the former (who eventually gave rise to the Theravāda tradition on Sri Lanka), and Moggaliputta Tissa wrote a book (the fifth book of the Pali Abhidhamma, *Points of Controversy* [*Kathāvatthu*]) refuting the doctrines of the other side.[10] As we have seen in 1.2.2, it was at the end of this council, according to Theravāda tradition, that missionaries were sent out to Sri Lanka, Southeast Asia, and various parts of India to establish the Buddhist saṃgha in those regions.

---

9 On the dating of the Sthavira/Mahāsāṃghika schism, see Nattier and Prebish (1977). For various theories on the nature of the schism, see ibid., p. 238, and Prebish and Keown (2006), p. 80.

10 The book which contains interesting discussions of doctrinal issues is translated in Aung and Davids (1915).

7.1.4 *Other Council Traditions*

The tradition of periodic councils was made necessary, perhaps, by the diffuse institutional structure of the saṃgha. In the absence of a centralized hierarchy after the death of the Buddha, pan-Buddhist principles and authority were hard to enforce. In any case, once established, the "custom" of having a council (or council-like event) occasionally resurfaced. According to the Theravāda tradition, a subsequent council was held in the first century BCE in Sri Lanka, where, following a period of famine and decline, the king brought the monks together to commit the teachings to writing for the first time. Up until then, Buddhist doctrines had been preserved orally. Not to be outdone by the Theravādins, the Sarvāstivādins then reportedly held a council of their own in Northwest India under the auspices of the great Kushan ruler, King Kaniṣka. According to tradition, it was then and there that the vast compendium of Sarvāstivādin doctrine, the *Great Exegesis* (*Mahāvibhāṣā*), was composed. Finally, the custom has extended into modern times: in 1871, the Burmese king Mindon convened what the Theravādins reckoned as their fifth council, at which the Pali canon was recited. This followed upon the heels of another of Mindon's Dharma-preservation undertakings: from 1860 to 1868, in a project that took almost eight years, he had fifty stone carvers inscribe the entire Pali Buddhist canon on 729 marble steles which were then enshrined at the Kuthodaw (Royal Merit) pagoda in Mandalay. Finally, in the following century, in 1956, the then prime minister of Burma, U Nu, convened a sixth Theravāda council, at an eschatologically significant time: the celebration of the 2,500th anniversary of the Buddha's parinirvāṇa, traditionally thought to mark the half-life of the Dharma.[11]

7.2 THE FLOWERING OF MAINSTREAM FACTIONALISM

It is said that out of the early Buddhist councils and the debates surrounding them, as well as for other reasons, there emerged a wide range of Mainstream schools. The traditional number of these schools is eighteen, but there is mention of several more than that. It is not possible to review here the history and development of each of these schools which, in any

11 For a brief account of these councils, see Berkwitz (2010), p. 45; see also Buswell and Lopez (2014), pp. 199–200, Prebish (2004), and Frasch (2012). On King Mindon's sūtra copying project, see Stadtner (2011), pp. 296–297.

case, are often confused and obscured by conflicting sources.[12] Suffice it to distinguish between two major branches: (A) the Mahāsāṃghikas (the Great Community-ites) and (B) the Sthaviras (the Elders). Each branch, in turn, may be said to have several divisions and subdivisions, whose identity and relationships are much debated. Here I will follow the lead of one scholar who sees each branch as comprising three major subgroups (see table 7.1). (A) The Mahāsāṃghikas may be said to have been divided into: (1) the Kaukkuṭikas (whose name perhaps reflected their affiliation with an eponymous monastery in Pāṭaliputra in Northern India, and whose affiliates, the Bahuśrutīyas and the Prajñaptivādins, had differing views on the nature of the Buddha's speech); (2) the Lokottaravādas, whose name reflects their view that the Buddha and his teachings are supramundane (lokottara); and (3) the Caityas, who were centered in southern India and who were associated with the five points of Mahādeva discussed above. (B) The Sthaviras may be said to have been divided into (1) those schools who maintained variations on the view of the Personalists (Pudgalavāda); (2) those schools who maintained the existence of dharmas in the three times (Sarvāstivāda); and (3) the remainder of the Mainstream schools.[13]

It is sometimes thought that the causes for divisions among the various Mainstream schools were exclusively doctrinal. If, however, their various names are anything to go by, it would appear that there were all sorts of reasons for their splits and identities. As Cox has noted, many of their names point to a variety of origins:

> a geographical locale (e.g. Haimavata, "those of the snowy mountains"), a specific teacher (e.g. Vātsīputrīya, "those affiliated with Vātsīputra," or Dharmaguptaka, "those affiliated with Dharmagupta"), a simple descriptive qualification (e.g. Mahāsāṃghika, "those of the great community," or Bahuśrutīya, "those who have heard much"), or a distinctive doctrinal position (e.g. Sarvāstivāda, "those who claim that everything exists," or Vibhajyavāda, "those who make distinction," or Sautrāntika, "those who rely upon the sūtras").
>
> (Cox, 2004a, p. 503)

12 For a quick introduction to some of the major ones, see Berkwitz (2010), pp 51–67. A standard source, now available in English, is Bareau (2013).
13 Cox (2004a).

BRANCH	SCHOOL	AFFILIATES OR CRITICS
Mahāsāṃghika ("those of the great community"	Kaukkuṭika ("those from the Kukkuṭārāma monastery"[?])	Bahuśrutīya ("those who have heard much") Prajñaptivāda ("those who offer provisional designations")
	Lokottaravāda ("those who claim [the Buddha is] transcendent")	Ekavyavahārika ("those who make a single utterance")
	Caitya ("those who worship at shrines")	
Sthavira ("the Elders")	Pudgalavāda ("those who claim that persons exist")	Vātsīputrīya ("those affiliated with Vātsīputra") Saṃmatīya ("those who are in agreement")
	Sarvāstivāda ("those who assert everything exists")	Mūlasarvāstivāda ("the original Sarvāstivāda") Vaibhāṣika ("those who follow the vibhāṣa (treatises)") Sautrāntika ("those who rely on the sūtras")
	Vibhajyavāda ("those who make distinctions")	Mahīśāsaka ("those affiliated with he who governed the land") Dharmaguptaka ("those affiliated with Dharmagupta") Kāśyapīya ("those affiliated with Kāśyapa") Theravāda ("The Way of the Elders" (Sri Lanka))

Table 7.1 Mainstream Schools – One View of Their Affiliations[14]

In addition, it is thought that many of these schools developed their own versions of the Buddhist canon. Most of these were in forms of Sanskrit, except for the Theravāda canon, which is in Pali. Many of the Sanskrit works, however, are no longer extant and exist only fragmentarily in Chinese and sometimes Tibetan translations. Still, comparisons between texts belonging to various

14 Based on Cox (2004a). For a different scheme, see Buswell and Lopez (2014), pp. 1091–1092.

canons can be made. Generally speaking, different schools' versions of the oldest texts (e.g. doctrinal discourses) can be quite similar, with variations and bifurcations becoming more apparent as the schools developed independently. Thus, the different schools' Vinaya lists of prātimokṣa precepts, while similar in structure and content, do contain variants as to the number of accepted rules (see table 6.1). By the time we get to Abhidharma texts (see table 3.3), the texts themselves are entirely dissimilar.

7.3 OTHER DIVISIONAL ISSUES

We will return to a discussion of the Mainstream schools later in this chapter when we look at the origins of Mahāyāna Buddhism. First, however, it is important to introduce several other divisional fault lines in the history of the saṃgha.

7.3.1 *Practice vs. Study*

The first of these, which traces a distinction between monastics who practice meditation and those who devote themselves to textual study, originates in India, but it has been most important, perhaps, in South and Southeast Asia, and, as we shall see, is not irrelevant to East Asia and Tibet.

In a relatively late Pali text, the Buddha is asked to describe the various vocations open to monks. He declares that these are two: "the vocation of books and the vocation of meditation." In the former, the Buddha declares, "a monk memorizes one section of the canon, two sections of the canon, or all the texts of the entire canon," but in the latter, "a monk cultivates insight into the perishable nature of existence until he reaches enlightenment" (Strong, 2008, p. 228).

It might be thought from this that the vocation of meditation was valued more highly than the vocation of books. But another Pali text, reflecting a different tradition, takes just the opposite point of view, claiming that practice (paṭipatti) depends on textual knowledge (pariyatti), and that "even if ... a thousand monks were to undertake the practice of meditation, without learning there would be no realization of the Noble Path" (Strong, 2008, p. 230).

All told, then, the relative stress placed on one or the other of these vocations will depend on who is doing the evaluation. It will also depend on the aptitudes and situations of the various monks. For example, the vocation of books tended to be followed, at least initially, by those monastics who joined the order as novices, while still young. Those, however, who became ordained late in life might declare themselves to be too old for the memorization of great numbers of texts, and interested principally in practicing meditation.[15]

This does not mean, of course, that the two career paths were mutually exclusive. In India, there are reports of a systematized scheme (which to some extent has continued in Tibet) according to which scriptures were first "heard" (and recited and memorized), then critically reflected on for their meaning, and then made into an object of meditation. In this way, the vocation of books could become the basis for the vocation of practice. On the other hand, in both India and Tibet, there were some practice-oriented hermits who were opposed to what Samuel has called "clerical Buddhism," and who disdained books and scholarship altogether for a life devoted exclusively to meditation.[16] Similarly, in East Asia, one can find monks, especially in the Chan/Zen tradition, who maligned scholarly preoccupations in favor of practice (see 10.6).

Neither the vocation of books nor that of meditation was a single-track affair. Early texts focusing on the vocation of books make mention of some monks who were "versed in the sūtras" (sūtradhara) or in the Vinaya (vinayadhara), or in scholastic summaries (mātṛkādhara), or even in legends such as avadānas, and inscriptions and post-canonical texts have reference to monks who were masters of one or several "baskets" of the canon (e.g. tipiṭakadhara).[17] Similarly, as we saw in 1.2.5, within the vocation of practice, there were (and are) many different forms of meditation.

7.3.2 Meditators and Merit Makers

It might be thought from the preceding paragraphs that most, if not all, monks are either meditators or scholars, or both. The two vocations of practice and study, however, do not really describe a division of the entire saṃgha, but only of a small portion of it. Many students of Buddhism, especially in

15 Strong (2008), p. 228.
16 On the progression from hearing texts to meditating on them, see Cabezon (2004). Samuel (1993), pp. 24–38, makes an interesting comparison between Tibetan and Theravāda Buddhism with regard to meditating hermits and "clerical Buddhism."
17 On the masters of portions of the canon, see Lamotte (1988), pp. 149–150. On avadānikas, see Strong (1985). More generally, see Cabezon (2004).

the West, assume that meditation is part of what all Buddhists do – that it is a centerpiece and hallmark of the religion. While it is true that there has been in the twentieth and twenty-first centuries a renewed emphasis, of sorts, on meditation, in fact most Buddhists in Asia did not, and today do not, practice meditation, or, if they do, they do not do so regularly. Nor are very many of them "scholars" of the sort described above. This is true not just of laypersons, but also of monks. This is true not just in the Theravāda tradition, but in the Mahāyāna and Vajrayāna as well. As one scholar put it: "Meditation is found only infrequently in Burma, and even less frequently in other Buddhist societies ... Typically, [it] is practiced by monks living in meditation monasteries ... by laymen who seek meditation instruction from them; and by monks living in forest hermitages" (Spiro, 1982, p. 54).

More generally, Spiro, the author who was just cited, has distinguished between two soteriological "norms" in Buddhism – an "ordinary norm intended for the religious majority" (which he called "kammatic" because it aimed principally at making merit so as to improve one's karma [Pali, kamma]), and an "extraordinary norm confined to a much smaller group" (which he called "nibbanic" because it aimed at achieving nirvāṇa [Pali, nibbāna]) (Spiro, 1982, p. 11). While there are problems with this too easy bifurcation of Buddhism, for our purposes it can be said that meditation and scholarship represent minority vocations – part of an "extraordinary norm" – and so are pathways for only a small minority of the monastics, and not for the saṃgha as a whole.

7.3.3 Forest Monks and Town Monks

A second, more comprehensive division that is sometimes said to run parallel to the one between practice and study is that between "forest-dwelling" (araṇyavāsin) monks and "town-dwelling" (grāmavāsin) monks. Today these two designations may be more a matter of institutional affiliation and lineage than actual lifestyle. Thus, in Sri Lanka, for example, the Malwatte Monastery and the Asgiriya Monastery are said, respectively, to head the town and forest "branches" of the Siyam Sect (see 7.3.6), but both places are located within the city of Kandy and are not readily distinguishable by their practice. Traditionally, however, forest monks (who are sometimes called "wilderness monks") are thought to be inclined towards a life of meditation (and sometimes also study) in relative isolation from laypeople and from other monks, dwelling in a hermitage removed from all settlements, or leading a wandering life, while town monks are thought to be more inclined toward interaction with laypersons, chanting sūtras for them on ritual occasions, conducting ceremonies, offering advice, teaching the Dharma, and dwelling in a monastery in town. In fact, these two lifestyles may overlap; forest monks do not completely shun rituals and interactions with laypersons, and town monks do not entirely forsake meditation and study, but the distinction between the two is something that still structures monasticism in South and Southeast Asia, and, less formally, in East Asia and Tibet as well.[18]

Today, in Theravāda lands, forest hermitages and the forest monks who dwell in them occupy an important position not only in the lives of monks who are serious about meditation, but also as symbols of that seriousness in the eyes of laypeople (and hence as significant fields of merit). Tambiah has proposed that, for Thailand at least, forest-dwelling monks play a key symbolic and practical role in a tripartite relationship between the "periphery" where they live, and the town-dwelling saṃgha-establishment and the ruler, who are both located in the "capital."[19]

Historically, it is clear that forest monks also played important roles in the development of divisions in the saṃgha, as advocates of a stricter lifestyle. Thus the two monks who were principally responsible for resisting the erosion of the rules at the Council of Vaiśālī, Śāṇakavāsin and Revata, were known as forest monks (see 7.1.2). And one theory of the origins of the Mahāyāna movement is that, far from being a movement of liberalization and popularization, it was a movement of an elite of ascetically inclined forest monks. On the other hand, in time, some Mahāyāna texts began to praise city monks, while in some Mainstream texts, those "who take refuge in forests ... or in the shrines of sacred trees" are associated with heretics.[20] We are thus left with a record of ambiguity concerning forest monks.

Some of the ambiguity with which forest monks were viewed can be seen in the following story about Mahākāśyapa, whom Ray (1994, p. 106) has presented as a paradigm of the forest renunciant. One day, we are told, the

18 For some studies of forest monks, see Yalman (1962), Tambiah (1984), Tiyavanich (1997), Carrithers (1983), and Taylor (1993). For a general short introduction, see Thanissaro (2004). For a list of forest-monasteries in Sri Lanka, see http://www.buddhanet.net/pdf_file/Monasteries-Meditation-Sri-Lanka2013.pdf.

19 Tambiah (1984), p. 72.

20 On forest monks and the Mahāyāna, see Ray (1994), Boucher (2008), and Nattier (2003), pp. 89–96. On the praise of city monks in Mahāyāna texts, see Thanissaro in Buswell (2004), p. 897. On the criticism of those who take refuge in forests, see Rotman (2008), p. 282.

Buddha, along with all of his monks (including Mahākāśyapa), was invited to dine at the house of his wealthy patron, Anāthapiṇḍada. Because he had been off meditating in the forest, Mahākāśyapa was late arriving. When he got there, however, he was refused entry by Anāthapiṇḍada's gatekeeper. The reason was that Mahākāśyapa had been meditating so long in the forest that his hair and beard had grown long, his robes were in rags, and the gatekeeper did not recognize him for the prominent elder that he was, but mistook him for a non-Buddhist renunciant – a heretical ascetic. Being roughly told to go away, the Venerable Mahākāśyapa accepted his situation with equanimity, and decided to go to beg for his food amongst the poor in the town. He came across a destitute disfigured woman who was suffering from an advanced stage of leprosy but who agreed to offer him some rice-water (all she had) from her own bowl. As she was ladling some of it into Mahākāśyapa's bowl, however, one of her leprous fingers fell off into the gruel. Much to her astonishment, Mahākāśyapa was not disgusted by this; instead, he sat down by the side of the road and began to eat, telling the leper that he was really happy for he could last the whole day and night on the meal she had provided him. Then and there, the leprous woman's faith was awakened, and when she died she went to heaven from the merit of her offering.[21]

The story is interesting not only for showing Mahākāśyapa's indifference, in his total renunciation, to distinctions between pure and impure, but also, sociologically, in its reflection of the fact that forest monks might not look like Buddhists but, indeed, approached non-Buddhist renunciants in their demeanor, a worry that we already encountered above in the story of Viśākhā (see 6.7.4).

7.3.4 *The Question of Asceticism*

The story of Mahākāśyapa makes it clear that another division that parallels the forest/town polarity is the distinction between those monks who are ascetically inclined, and those who are not. It will be remembered that extreme asceticism (to the point of self-starvation) is one of the things that the Buddha, during his quest for enlightenment, tried and abandoned in favor of a middle way (see 2.7.5). That does not mean that asceticism in a lesser degree had no place in Buddhism. Such asceticism came to be defined

21 The story of Mahākāśyapa and the beggar woman may be found in Rotman (2008), pp. 162–164.

as the practice of the "qualities of the scrupulous" (dhūtaguṇa or dhūtānga), for which Mahākāśyapa was a paradigm. According to one tradition, these austerities are thirteen in number and comprise such things as wearing only cast-off rags for robes, refusing invitations to people's homes but depending solely on one's begging round, opting not to beg only at rich or generous people's houses, not dwelling in a village, not dwelling in a building, never lying down to sleep, meditating in cemeteries, etc. Such practices are said *not* to have been outlawed by the Buddha but made optional; individual monks could choose to follow them if they wished, or refrain from doing so. In Thailand, many forest monks are practitioners of one or more of the thirteen ascetic practices and so are known as "Thudong" (dhūtānga) monks. We shall, in 11.3, look at two examples of such monks in modern times.[22]

Historically speaking, however, some of those who were inclined towards asceticism felt that the "qualities of the scrupulous" should define a community-wide standard and be imposed on all members of the saṃgha. The classic example of such a monk was Devadatta. Reportedly the Buddha's cousin, Devadatta was a monk who became renowned in legend for his rivalry and antagonism towards the Buddha. Even as a boy, as well as in his previous lives, he is said to have been constantly jealous of his cousin. (Some have argued that such jealousies are actually typical of cross-cousin relations in ancient India.) Later, he tried to split the community and convince the Buddha's disciples to follow him instead. When that failed, he hatched various murderous plots against the Buddha: he rolled a boulder down from a mountain top in an attempt to kill him, but missed; he sent archers to assassinate him, but they were converted by the very sight of the Buddha; he maddened an elephant with toddy and goaded it into charging the Buddha, but he subdued it with his loving-kindness.[23]

Most scholars who have studied the traditions about Devadatta, however, feel that the sources recounting these tales have generally painted an unflattering picture. The real problem, they theorize, was that Devadatta was threatening the unity of the saṃgha by advocating that the strict practices of asceticism (dhūtaguṇa) be mandatory for all monks. Such a schism may in fact reflect some historical reality, for it is likely that Devadatta's movement was more successful than is commonly acknowledged in canonical texts. We

22 For a fuller list and discussion of the dhūtaguṇa, see Ray (1994), pp. 293–323. On thudong monks, see Crosby (2014), pp. 160–162.

23 For a study of Devadatta, see Ray (1994), pp. 162–173. On the possible cross-cousin rivalry between Devadatta and the Buddha, see Hocart (1923), and Mitra (1924). See also Hayes (2000).

know from the Chinese pilgrim Faxian that, in the early fifth century CE, there existed a number of groups of followers of Devadatta who made offerings to the past buddhas, but not to Śākyamuni. Two centuries later, the pilgrim Xuanzang mentions three monasteries in which there were monks who, following the teaching of Devadatta, did not drink milk. And subsequently, the pilgrim Yijing comes across some sectarians whom he associates with Devadatta.[24]

A somewhat different angle on the practice of asceticism may be found in the story of another disciple of the Buddha – Batkula. Not a particularly well-known elder, Batkula nevertheless made the hall of fame list of prominent disciples as one who was renowned for his good health, his long life, and, more generally, for his lack of desires. This quality is highlighted in the *Batkula Sūtra* which tells the following story about him. One day, in very old age, Batkula meets a former friend of his, a non-Buddhist naked ascetic, who asks him, rather abruptly, how many times, in the eighty years he has been ordained, he has had sex. Batkula replies that not only has he not had sex in all that time, he has not even conceived of a single sensual thought, nor, for that matter, has he had any thoughts of ill-will or cruelty toward anyone. Instead, he has remained aloof. He then goes on to describe his lifestyle of non-dependence which marks him as an ascetic monk: in eighty years, he has never accepted a robe from a layperson (instead he has worn rags, gathered by himself from the dustheap); he has never sewn or dyed a robe, nor made one for any fellow monk; he has never accepted an invitation to a meal (instead, he has always begged for his food); in fact, he has never entered a layperson's house, nor ever preached the Dharma to the laity; nor has he ever taught it to a nun, or a female novice or probationer; indeed, he has never had any contact whatsoever with women; he has never had a novice wait on him; he has never bathed in a bathhouse; he has never used bathpowder; he has never taken medicine; he has never lain down (to sleep); he has never used a back support while sitting in meditation; he has never spent a rains-retreat in a village.[25]

It is clear that the Buddhist tradition had some ambivalence towards monks like Batkula. On the one hand, the sūtra just cited goes out of its way to praise Batkula, commenting parenthetically that each of his actions is "wonderful

24 For a discussion of all these references, see Deeg (1999).

25 The details of Batkula's life are from Ñāṇamoli and Bodhi (1995), pp. 985–988, and Bingenheimer et al. (2013), pp. 271–275. On Batkula, see also Anālayo (2007; 2010) and (2011a), pp. 711–716, and Legittimo (2009).

and marvelous," the Pali equivalent of "awesome" (Ñāṇamoli and Bodhi, 1995, pp. 986–987). On the other hand, another source portrays Batkula negatively for failing to do anything for anyone. Though he was an arhat, he remained aloof: "he had so few desires that he did not act as the other elders did for the benefit of humankind" (Strong, 1983, p. 255).

Here, perhaps, we can see the flipside of the life of those renunciants who are inclined to asceticism. Unlike Mahākāśyapa who was also an ascetic but who cared deeply about preserving the saṃgha and the Dharma (for instance, in his actions at the First Council), Batkula is a loner who wishes to have as little to do with the community as possible. He is uninterested in preaching the Dharma, uninterested in mentoring novices; he has little contact with the laity, no contact with any nuns, and minimal interaction with his fellow monks.

Much the same kind of ambivalence that is directed towards Batkula may be seen, perhaps, in attitudes towards the class of ascetics known in Buddhism as pratyekabuddhas (solitary buddhas). Pratyekabuddhas were ascetic figures who "embodied the old ideal of a solitary and silent life" (La Vallée Poussin, 1908, p. 155). Unlike Batkula and other arhats, they are not immediate disciples of the Buddha since they find their own ways to enlightenment without the aid of the Buddha. For this reason, some scholars have thought that they should not be considered to be Buddhist renunciants at all. Ray, however, has explicitly related them to the Buddhist "saints of the forest," and highlighted their importance in Buddhist mythology and as exemplars for monks inclined to a particular lifestyle. Indeed, pratyekabuddhas are thought to attain the same enlightenment as other awakened Buddhists (e.g. the Buddha himself). The only difference, in their case, is that (like Batkula) they choose not to preach the Dharma to others, and are not interested in founding a community.[26]

7.3.5 The Question of Bon-Vivant Monks

At the other end of the spectrum from Batkula and the ascetically inclined may be found those monks who had a reputation for their laxity, and yet here, too, in my opinion, we shall find a certain amount of ambivalence in attitudes towards them. I will take as my primary examples of such bon-vivant monks

26 Ray's view of pratyekabuddhas as saints of the forests is found in his book *Buddhist Saints in India* (1994), pp. 232–3. More generally on pratyekabuddhas, see Kloppenborg (1974), and Wiltshire (1990). On the etymology of the word pratekabuddha, see Norman (1983).

(as they may be called) the elders Aśvaka (Pali, Assaji) and Punarvasuka (Pali, Punabbasu). Somewhat like Devadatta (with whom they are sometimes associated) Aśvaka and Punarvasuka are routinely condemned in Buddhist texts as miscreants. They are said to be leaders of the "gang of six" (ṣaḍvārgika), monks who were troublemakers and constant violators of the Vinaya rules. If, however, we read through their condemnations, we can perhaps see examples of a monastic lifestyle that may have been fairly common in an early saṃgha and that was oriented towards involvement with the local lay community. Aśvaka and Punarvasuka lived in a monastery in the town of Kiṭāgiri, halfway between Benares and Śrāvastī. In the Pali Vinaya, we are told, disapprovingly, of their many misdeeds: they plant flowering bushes and use the blossoms to make garlands for local women and girls; they eat from the same dish as these women, drink from the same jar, and sit on the same seat with them; they partake of an evening meal (in violation of the rule that says monks are not to eat after noon); they wear garlands of flowers themselves and dance, sing, and play musical instruments. Moreover, they engage in all sorts of games: dice, checkers, pick-up-sticks, tipcat, ball, tumbling; they blow on trumpets made of leaves; they make toy windmills, toy carts, and toy bows and arrows for the children; they guess at letters that others trace on their backs; they play a game of mimicking deformities; they train in various sports; they whistle, they snap their fingers, they wrestle, they spread out their upper robes on the ground and invite girls to dance on them.[27] All of these things are presented, in the Vinaya, as unbecoming of monks, if not specifically against the rules. And yet, it is apparent in the same text that the people of Kiṭāgiri (who are also condemned for this) view these acts as positive things, as evidence of their bhikṣus' whole-hearted involvement and down-to-earth participation in community affairs. Indeed, Aśvaka and Punarvasuka are, locally, very popular figures, and when a wandering monk of more strict demeanor comes to town on his begging round, the people refuse to give him alms because they find him haughty, arrogant, uncommunicative, disdainful. "Our masters ... Aśvaka and Punarvasuka," they declare, "are polite, genial, pleasant of speech, beaming with smiles, saying 'Come, you are welcome.' They are not supercilious, they are easily accessible, they are the first to speak" (Horner, 1938–1952, vol. 1, p. 318). Aśvaka and Punarvasuka's behavior was by no means unique. We find much the same thing recognized (and condemned) in other texts, and we can only

27 For this list of activities, see Horner (1938–1952), vol. 1, pp. 314–318, and vol. 5, pp. 14–15.

conclude that these condemnations are reflective of common practices among monks at the time of these texts' compilations. Such monks are not murderers, fornicators, or thieves; simply put, they like to have a good time and are involved in the community life around them, but whether they are so to an excessive degree or not will depend on one's point of view.[28]

7.3.6 Sect vs. Sect

In addition to groups of ascetically inclined forest monks and pastorally involved town monks, mention should be made of yet another fault line in Mainstream Buddhist communities. In most Theravāda countries, today, the saṃgha is subdivided into various sects (sometimes called nikāyas) which represent different ordination lineages. In Sri Lanka, for instance, historically, the community was divided between three major sectarian groups, each of which was affiliated with a major monastery in the ancient capital city: the Mahāvihāra (see 1.2.2), the Abhayagiri, and the Jetavana. All of these sects were Theravādin by definition. Their views and doctrinal alignments, however, differed. Like political parties, they often changed their stances, depending on whether or not they had the favor of the king. Generally, the Abhayagiri seems to have been more liberally receptive to changes in Buddhist doctrine (Mahāyāna, Tantra, etc.) coming from India, whereas the Mahāvihāra presented its own history as a struggle against three things it tended to lump together: fragmentation of the saṃgha, laxity in discipline, and the corrupting influences of South Indian imports. Eventually, the Mahāvihāra had considerable influence on the development of Buddhist sectarianism in Southeast Asia where it came to define a type of Theravāda orthodoxy.[29]

Today, in Sri Lanka, these sects are gone and instead we find a different set of divisions between the Siyam Nikāya, the Amarapura Nikāya, and the Ramañña Nikāya. The first was, as its name implies, imported from Thailand (Siam) in the eighteenth century and is headquartered in Kandy in the center of the island. The second and the third were both imported from Burma in the nineteenth century and are predominant in the lowland coastal areas. One of the differences between the first and the other two is that the Siyam Nikāya will only ordain members of Sri Lanka's upper caste, while the Amarapura

28 For another example of such "lax monks," see those monastics who are condemned in the *Questions of Rāṣṭrapāla* (Ensink, 1952, pp. 134–135; Boucher, 2008, pp. 137–145).
29 On the Abhayagiri, see Cousins (2012).

and Ramañña are open to everyone, though caste may still influence who can hold high office in them as well.[30]

In Thailand, today, distinctions are made between monks belonging to two sects: the Mahanikai ("Great group") and the Thammayut ("Dharma followers"). The Mahanikai traces its origins to Sri Lanka whence it was imported in the fifteenth century, but, actually, the present Mahanikai is a grouping of all those monks of various lineages who did not join the Thammayut sect that was established by royal decree in 1833 by King Mongkut, who thereby sought to reform Thai Buddhism and purge it of what were thought to be various lax and superstitious practices. The Thammayut/Mahanikai distinction was established in Cambodia and Laos as well. In general the Thammayut monks, who are in a minority but are powerfully connected to royalty, tend to be stricter in their observances of the Vinaya, refusing, for instance, to handle money. On the other hand, they reach out by preaching sermons in the vernacular language rather than in Pali.[31]

In Myanmar, there are today officially nine nikāyas called "gaing" (Pali gaṇa) ("groups"). The vast majority of monks belong to the two largest of these – the Thudhamma, which traces its roots to the late eighteenth century, and a reformist movement, the Shwegyin, that broke away from it in the nineteenth century under the leadership of an elder who was especially strict in his observance of the Vinaya.[32]

The issues that divided these various sects in these various Theravāda saṃghas varied tremendously, both historically and at present. They were rarely doctrinal, and often caught up in particular social, economic, and political contexts. They usually involved considerations of lineage and affiliation with certain influential charismatic leaders. Sometimes they involved matters of practice and questions of lifestyle.

As an example of the complexities of this kind of sectarianism, let me present here one instance of a controversy that divided the Burmese saṃgha for much of the eighteenth century. This was the dispute between the "covered" monks who covered both shoulders with their robes while out on their begging rounds, and the "one-shouldered" monks who maintained that the proper mode of dress while outside the monastery was to put the robe over one shoulder and to leave the other bare. This controversy cut across other divisions such as that between forest monks and town monks, meditators and

30 On the origins of these sects, see Blackburn (2012; 2001).

31 See Crosby (2014), pp. 270–272.

32 See ibid., p. 214.

scholars. Nor was it limited to Myanmar; even today, in Sri Lanka, monks who belong to one of the sects (the Siyam Nikāya) still bare one shoulder when out of the monastery while the members of the other two sects do not.

It is hard for us sometimes to comprehend fully the intensity this issue took on, and scholars are still debating some of its ramifications. Part of the problem was the interference of various Burmese kings, who, under the influence of different monastic advisors, tended to favor one party or the other and to make decrees that all monks in their kingdom should dress in a particular way. When one king, however, in a spirit of conciliation (apparently) proposed allowing monks to do whatever they wished in this matter, he was not listened to. Underlying this controversy, perhaps, was a more fundamental disagreement between monks who felt they should follow the "Word of the Buddha," and those who felt they should follow the tradition of their lineage. Thus the two-shoulderites, led by a charismatic elder named Munindaghosa, tended to support their position on the grounds of a Vinaya passage that said they should "go out covered," while the one-shoulderites claimed they were merely observing the practice that their teachers and their teachers' teachers had passed on to them. Both sides, however, were willing to use the debate tactics of the other: when the two-shoulderites were asked who their teacher was, they pointed to a statue of the Buddha, while the one-shoulderites invoked an obscure (and perhaps forged) subcommentary that they claimed gave their position scriptural authority. In the end, the two-shoulderites won out, but only after a series of acrimonious debates.[33]

7.4 THE ORIGINS OF THE MAHĀYĀNA

All of the visions and divisions of the saṃgha we have looked at so far in this chapter have, in a sense, really been "subdivisions" of what we have been calling Mainstream Buddhism. It is now time to look at the other major branch of the Buddhist tradition – the Mahāyāna or "Great Vehicle," and the visions and divisions therein.

The question of the origins of the Mahāyāna is a matter of some complexity and confusion. In trying to address it, I am well aware of Barthe's caveat, early in the twentieth century, that "The best way of explaining the Mahāyāna

33 On the great robes controversy, see Law (1952), pp. 129–131, and Mendelson (1975), pp. 58–61.

is still not to try too hard to define it."[34] As we shall see, the Mahāyāna is a slippery thing and any attempt to pin it down too definitively may see it escaping from our grasp. Nonetheless, some attempt to clarify issues is necessary and possible.

Let me start with the matter of how some of the Mainstream Buddhist schools we looked at above (table 7.1) are related to the formation of the Mahāyāna. It used to be that scholars generally affirmed that the Mahāyāna arose out of the Mahāsāṃghika school(s), in part because the latter's view of the Buddha as being supramundane appeared to resemble certain Mahāyāna doctrines. Today, scholars are much less sanguine about what the lines of filiation were. To put it bluntly, historically speaking, we are not at all certain how or when (or even whether) the Mahāyāna began or indeed if it was a single movement. It is generally thought that it had its origins in India sometime around the beginning of the common era (year 0 CE), but why it got started there and how long its gestation period lasted remain matters of great scholarly dispute.[35]

One of the problems is that there are chronological disconnects between at least four things: the first appearance of texts that self-identify as Mahāyāna scriptures, the first mentions of Mahāyāna in archaeologically discovered inscriptions, the first clearly Mahāyānist art, and the first developments of Mahāyāna philosophy. For example, early textual evidence comes from a collection of clearly Mahāyāna sūtras translated into Chinese by the Kushan monk Lokakṣema *c.*180 CE, whose Indian originals are usually assigned to the first century CE, but when we look for inscriptional or art historical evidence for the Mahāyāna at this time in Northern India, and indeed for several centuries thereafter, we find almost nothing.[36]

A second problem is that scholars have proposed such a bewildering variety of characterizations of the Mahāyāna that we are not quite sure what to apply the label to. Was it originally a popular movement aimed at appealing to the religious needs of the laity, and reacting against scholastic monasticism? Or did it start from groups of monks interested in the "cult of the book" and the propagation of particular texts? Or did it originate among monks undertaking ascetically inclined lives of rigorous practice in forest-hermitages? Or among others inclined to view themselves as a new

34 See Auguste Barth (1918), p. 450, quoted in Silk (2002), p. 361.

35 For good surveys of the different views of the origin of the Mahāyāna, see Drewes (2010) and Harrison (1987; 1995). Silk (2002), p. 392, is critical of the tendency to see Mahāyāna as emerging out of or reacting to Hīnayāna.

36 Harrison (2003); Schopen (2004).

elite devoted to the demanding vocation of being a bodhisattva? Or among still others inspired by the model of the Buddha's previous lives? Or did it have its roots in communities of specialists in the recitation and preservation and study of certain Mahāyāna texts? All of these viewpoints have been suggested; none is unproblematic, and none has, thus far, carried the day.[37]

One thing appears to be clear: there is a basic lack of symmetry between the Mahāyāna and Mainstream Buddhism (a.k.a. Hīnayāna). Though both are called "vehicles" (yāna), the two really have different sorts of identities. As we have seen, the Mainstream schools (or at least those we know most about) basically represented different ordination lineages, defined by their vinayas. The Mahāyānists, however, had no vinayas or ordination rituals of their own in India, nor, for a long time, in East Asia or Tibet either. In other words, though certain monastics may have been interested in Mahāyāna ideas and practices, there were, ordination-wise, no "Mahāyāna monastics" (although, in time, a Mahāyāna bodhisattva ordination ceremony was developed and is still used in East Asia, along with Mainstream ordination).

We know from the Chinese pilgrims Faxian and Xuanzang that Mahāyāna and Mainstream monks happily lived side by side in the same monasteries; the two movements also happily co-existed in the same individual. The relationship between Mahāyāna and Hīnayāna was thus not an either/or relationship. There could be Mahāyānist-Sarvāstivādins, Mahāyānist-Mahāsaṃghikas, even Mahāyānist-Theravādins, in much the same way that we might find, for instance, vegetarian Baptists, vegetarian Presbyterians, and vegetarian Episcopalians, without suggesting that vegetarianism was categorically akin to or that it emerged from Protestantism. In time, however, primary identities could shift, and, even though Mahāyānist-inclined monks might still be, ordination-wise, affiliated with one of the Mainstream sects, they might on other bases come to identify themselves as *Mahāyānists*, first and foremost.[38]

By the time Buddhism established itself in East Asia and Tibet, this kind of shift had already taken place. Though Mainstream Buddhist texts continued to be studied and Mainstream ordination rituals continued to be followed, for the most part, those monks who introduced Buddhism to China, and then Korea, and Japan, and Tibet, and those who further propagated the teachings in those regions, did self-identify as Mahāyānists.

37 For statements and criticism of each of these positions, see Hirakawa (1963), Lamotte (1954), Vetter (1994), Schopen (1975), Durt (1991), Ray (1994), Boucher (2008), Harrison (2003), Nattier (2003), and Drewes (2010a).
38 On the crucial role of ordination lineages, see also Bechert (1973).

7.5 PROLIFERATION OF MAHĀYĀNA SCHOOLS

We shall, in the next several chapters, be making reference to a variety of Indian, Chinese, Japanese, and Tibetan Mahāyāna schools, but it may be useful, by way of introduction, to survey the field here, and look also at the nature of these divides, for just as Mainstream schools differed along all sorts of lines (doctrinal, geographical, lineal, etc.), so too did the Mahāyāna.

7.5.1 Mahāyāna Schools in India

Discussions of Mahāyāna schools in India usually focus on "schools of thought" which may or may not have had any institutional identity, but which focused on certain doctrines as propounded in certain texts or by certain teachers. These included the Middle Way (Madhyamaka) school of thought, famous for its doctrine of Emptiness (śūnyatā) systematized by Nāgārjuna and Āryadeva; the Embryonic Buddha (Tathāgata-garbha) school of thought, with its doctrine that we all have the actuality or the potential for buddhahood within us; the Garland (Avataṃsaka) school of thought which propounded the interpenetration of all elements of reality; and the Practice of Yoga (Yogācāra) school of thought developed by Asanga and Vasubandhu, with its doctrine of the primacy of consciousness. We shall examine the doctrines of all of these schools, and some of their subdivisions, in chapter 9.

7.5.2 Mahāyāna Schools in China

In East Asia in general, the situation is somewhat more complex, since the bases for sectarian differentiation are more varied. For China (see table 7.2), McRae has usefully distinguished between (1) "exegetical lineages" oriented towards the study and interpretation of various Buddhist texts, most of which had been imported from India (and then translated); (2) "systematic schools" which endeavored to present total schemas for a comprehensive understanding of all aspects of the Buddhist doctrine; and (3) "modal traditions" which were primarily oriented towards specific religious practices.[39]

39 McRae (2005b).

SCHOOL	ENGLISH/SANSKRIT	SOME MAJOR FIGURES (INCLUDING KOREANS)
Sanlun	"Three Treatises" (Madhyamaka)	Kumārajīva (334–413), Sengzhao (384–414), Jizang (549–623)
Lü	"Vinaya"	Daoxuan (596–667), Huaisu (634–707)
Tiantai	Named after Mt. Tiantai in China	Huisi (515–577), Zhiyi (538–597)
Huayan	"Flower Garland" (Avataṃsaka)	Dushun (557–640), Fazang (643–712), Zongmi (780–841), Wŏnhyo (617–686), Ŭisang (625–702)
Faxiang	"Dharma Characteristic" (a.k.a. "Consciousness-Only school")	Paramārtha (499–569), Xuanzang (600–664), Kuiji (632–682), Wŏnch'ŭk (613–695)
Chan	"Meditation school" (Dhyāna)	Bodhidharma (5th–6th century), Shenxiu (*c.*606–706), Huineng (638–713), Shenhui (684–758), Mazu (709–788), Baizhang (749–814), Linji (d. 866), Dongshan (807–869), Caoshan (840–901), Yunmen (864–949), Chinul (1158–1210)
Jingtu	Pure Land	Tanluan (476–?), Daochuo (562–645), Shandao (?–805)
Zhenyan	"True word" (mantra)	Vajrabodhi (671–741), Śubhakarasiṃha (637–735), Amoghavajra (705–774)
Sanjie jiao	"Three Stages school" (a.k.a. "School of the Third Stage")	Xinxing (540–594)

Table 7.2 Mahāyāna Schools in China[40]

(1) Among the "exegetical lineages," mention may be made here of the so-called "Three Treatises" (Sanlun; Jpn., Sanron) school that devoted itself to the study and propagation of works by various Madhyamaka scholars; the "Abhidharmakośa school" (Jushe; Jpn., Kusha) focused on "The Treasury of Abhidharma" by the Indian Master Vasubandhu; and the "Vinaya" (Lü; Jpn., Ritsu) school, dedicated to elaborating the rules and rituals of the monastic order.

(2) Among the "systematic schools," some also gave pride of place to particular teachings and featured particular sūtras. Thus the Tiantai (Jpn., Tendai) school, named after its mountain headquarters on Mount Tiantai,

40 Further basic information about all these schools and figures may be found in Buswell and Lopez (2014).

privileged the *Lotus Sūtra* and developed its own philosophical views (see 9.4), while the Huayan (Jpn., Kegon) school was named after the "Flower Garland" (= Avataṃsaka) sūtra, and was famed for its doctrine of interpenetration (see 9.6.1). Both of these schools also developed schemas (called "division of the scriptures" ["panjiao"]) for classifying the whole of the Buddha's teachings in a progressive order culminating with their own featured sūtra, and both also evolved lines of patriarchs who traced their spiritual descent back to a recognized "founding father" (and ultimately through him back to the Buddha). A somewhat different kind of systematic school may be seen in the Chinese Yogācāra school, often known as Faxiang (Jpn., Hossō), which emphasizes the doctrine of Mind-Only (see 9.5).

(3) Among the "modal traditions," mention should be made of Chan (Jpn., Zen), Pure Land (Jingtu; Jpn., Jōdo), and esoteric Buddhism (Mijiao; Jpn., Mikkyō), which also emphasized lineages of patriarchs and master–disciple relationships, and were not without interest in specific texts, but were more focused on particular religious practices, such as meditation (see 10.6), and devotion to the Buddha Amitābha (see 8.4), and Tantric rituals (see 8.6).[41]

To some extent, and running the risk of being overly simplistic and too clear-cut, the "exegetical lineages" may be seen as extensions of the "vocation of books" described above in 7.3.1, and the "modal traditions" as new expressions of the "vocation of practice," with the "systematic schools" a sort of combination of the two. We should not forget, however, that this list of divisions of the Chinese saṃgha would not be complete without reference to the periodic appearance of what might be called "sects" or "cults." For instance, the "White Lotus Society" (Ch., Bailian she) was a name first given to a group of monks and laity gathered around the fourth-/fifth-century Master Huiyuan to venerate the Buddha Amitābha. The same name was later used by various lay Pure Land groups in the twelfth and fourteenth centuries and then by a revolutionary millenarian movement worshipping the future Buddha Maitreya in the fifteenth to seventeenth centuries. Mention might also be made here of the heretical "School of the Third Stage" (Sanjie jiao) (see 9.8.2), established by a charismatic monk named Xingxing (540–594) who propounded a radical notion of almsgiving suited, he claimed, for the period of the end of the Dharma.[42]

41 Ibid. See also Weinstein (1987).

42 On the White Lotus Society, see Overmyer (1976), and Haar (1999); on the School of the Third Stage, see Hubbard (2001).

7.5.3 Mahāyāna Schools in Japan

All of these Chinese schools, with the exception of the last two, are commonly said to have been "transmitted" to Japan. There are some problems with this notion if it implies a full and integral transplantation of particular Chinese schools into Japanese soil. In fact, though it is true that the "founders" of quite a few of the Japanese Buddhist schools, e.g. Kūkai, Saichō, Eisai, and Dōgen (see table 7.3), traveled to China, studied there, and in some ways thought of themselves as bringing back to Japan what they had learned there, the nature of Buddhist sectarianism in Japan came to be rather different from what it was on the mainland.

SCHOOL	ENGLISH/SANSKRIT	SOME MAJOR FIGURES
Sanron	"Three Treatises" (Madhyamaka)	Ekan (7th century)
Ritsu	"Vinaya"	Jianzhen (Ganjin) (688–763), Eison (1201–1290)
Tendai	Named after Mt. Tiantai in China	Saichō (767–822), Ennin (793–864), Enchin (814–891), Annen (b. 841), Genshin (942–1017), Jōjin (1011–1081), Ryōnin (1072–1132)
Kegon	"Flower Garland" (Avataṃsaka)	Li Tongxuan (635–730), Ryōben (689–773), Myōe (1173–1232), Gyōnen (1240–1321)
Hossō	"Dharma Characteristic" (a.k.a. "Consciousness-Only school"	Dōshō (629–700), Jōkei (1155–1213)
Zen (Rinzai, Sōtō, and Ōbaku schools)	"Meditation school" (Dhyāna)	Eisai (1141–1215), Dōgen (1200–1253), Daitō Kokushi (1282–1337), Ikkyū (1394–1481), Takuan (1573–1475), Yinyuan (Jpn., Ingen) (1592–1673), Hakuin (1685–1758), Ryōkan (1758–1831)
Jōdo, Jōdoshin, and Ji schools	Pure Land	Kūya (903–972), Ryōnin (1072–1132), Hōnen (1133–1212), Shinran (1173–1262), Kakunyo (1270–1351), Ippen (1239–1289), Rennyo (1415–1499)
Shingon	Esoteric teachings/"True word" (mantra)	Kūkai (774–835), Kakuban (1095–1143), Jiun (1718–1804)
Nichiren	Named after its founder (a.k.a. "Lotus school")	Nichiren (1222–1282)

Table 7.3 Mahāyāna Schools in Japan[43]

43 Further basic information about all these schools and most of these figures may be found in Buswell and Lopez (2014).

The integral transmission view, which is characteristic of much of the Japanese scholarship that first influenced Western buddhologists, owes a lot to the figure of Gyōnen (1240–1321), a Japanese monk who wrote several treatises on Buddhist schools, which he understood primarily as "lineage[s] of masters and disciples united by their study of particular texts and doctrines" (Dennis, 2005, p. 1236). For Gyōnen, Japanese schools were those that had antecedents in China and ultimately in India. He generally ignored other influences such as Korea and Central Asia, and imposed retroactively on China, and to some extent India, a basically thirteenth-century Japanese view of sectarianism.[44]

By then, in Japan, the fault-lines between the schools, which had never been very clear-cut in China, were becoming increasingly well defined. These sectarian divisions, moreover, were reinforced by internecine struggles in which the government sometimes became involved. Thus Kūkai, the founder of Shingon, did not always get along with Saichō, the founder of Tendai. Hōnen and other Pure Land teachers were exiled by the government at the instigation of other sects. Nichiren was also exiled, mostly for his vehemence both against the government and against all other sects. In time, differences were further accentuated by strong-armed tactics of the various sects. The Tendai monks of Mount Hiei, the Hossō monks of Kōfukuji in Nara, and the Shingon monks of Mount Kōya all developed troops of monastic warriors later called "sōhei" (monk-soldiers) to pressure various political factions in the government into supporting the causes of their separate monastic establishments. Sometimes these tactics involved armed conflicts. Sometimes the conflicts were between sects or sub-sects. Adolphson (2000, pp. 357–358) has counted over a hundred armed battles involving Mount Hiei and Kōfukuji monastic warriors between 1066 and 1390. Similarly, large groups of peasants, motivated by Pure Land teachers and ideology, organized religiously inspired uprisings and demonstrations known as ikkō ikki ("single-minded uprisings"), while Nichiren temples in Kyoto, who were allied with merchants, engaged in hokke ikki ("lotus uprisings").[45]

Another thing that reinforced Japanese Buddhist sectarianism and made it different from Chinese, was the affiliation of laypeople with particular schools. Shinran (1173–1262), the founder of the True Pure Land school (Jōdo shinshū), famously renounced monasticism and organized his followers

44 On Gyōnen's views of sectarianism, see Blum (2002), pp. 101–132. For an example of this view of Japanese schools, see Takakusu (1947).

45 On Saichō and Kūkai, see Groner (2000), and Abé (1999). On Hōnen and Nichiren, see Machida (1999), and Anesaki (1916). On monastic warfare, see Adolphson (2000; 2007), and Tamura (2000), pp. 124–125.

into parishes, thus giving them an exclusive identity that Pure Land devotees never really had in China. Similarly, Nichiren, because of the exclusivity of his message, demanded of his followers not only loyalty but renunciation of other traditions. Finally, during the Tokugawa period (1603–1867), the feudal government, in an effort to exert control over the population, demanded that all citizens affiliate with local Buddhist temples. Thus all Japanese Buddhist families came not only to self-identify but to be officially associated with particular temples that belonged to particular schools.

7.5.4 Mahāyāna Schools in Tibet

In 1.4, the four major schools of Tibetan Buddhism that exist today were introduced: the Nyingma, the Kagyü, the Sakya, and the Géluk (see table 7.4). In fact, divisions within the Tibetan Buddhist saṃgha are a bit more complicated than this.

SCHOOL	ENGLISH/SANSKRIT	SOME MAJOR FIGURES
Nyingma	"Old school"	Padmasambhava (8th century), Longchen Rabjam (Klong chen rab 'byams) (1308–1364), Jikmé Lingpa ('Jigs med gling pa) (1729–1798), Mipam (Mi pham) (1846–1912), Jamgon Kongtrül ('Jam mgon kong sprul) (1813–1899), Dudjom Rinpoche (bdud 'joms) (1904–1987)
Kagyü	"Oral Lineage school"	Tilopa (988–1069), Nāropa (1016–1100), Marpa (1012–97), Milarépa (Mi la ras pa) (1028–1111), Gampopa (Sgam po pa) (1079–1153), the 17 Karmapa Lamas (1111–present), Jamgon Kongtrül ('Jam mgon kong sprul) (1813–1899), Kalu Rinpoché (1905–1989), Chögyam Trungpa (Chos rgyam Drung pa) (1939–1987)
Sakya	"Grey Earth" school	Drogmi ('Brgo mi) (992–1072), Könchok Gyalpo (Dkon mchog rgyal po) (1034–1102), Sachen (Sa chen) (1092–1158), Sakya Paṇḍita (Sa skya Paṇḍiṭa) (1182–1251)
Géluk	"Virtuous school"	Tsongkhapa (Tsong kha pa) (1357–1419), the 14 Dalai Lamas (1419–present), the 11 Panchen (Paṇ chen) Lamas (1385–present)

Table 7.4 Mahāyāna Schools in Tibet[46]

46 Further basic information about all these schools and figures may be found in Buswell and Lopez (2014).

In a very helpful survey of Tibetan Buddhist schools, Kapstein (2005) distinguishes between:

(1) monastic "orders" that are institutionally distinct from one another and have their own hierarchies and own properties, and house an "identifiable membership." Among these Kapstein would include the four schools (and some of their subsects) mentioned above, as well as the Bon tradition (sometimes thought of as a different religion, but better counted, institutionally at least, as an additional Buddhist order);

(2) "lineages" consisting of successions of "spiritual teachers who have transmitted a given body of knowledge over a period of generations" (Kapstein, 2005, p. 1222). Sometimes such lineages have become associated with particular orders. Thus the succession of masters in the line of Marpa (Tilopa, Nāropa, Marpa, Milarépa, etc.) came to define the spiritual backbone of the Kagyü order. At other times, the lineage and its teaching have no specific institutional affiliation;

(3) and finally, "schools of thought" or "philosophical systems of tenets" (grub mtha'; Skt., siddhanta), which are studied in the Tibetan monastic curriculum, and mainly have relevance to scholars. These originated in India and are textually based. They include Mainstream systems of thought such as the Vaibhāṣika ("Followers of the *Vibhāṣa*") and Sautrāntika ("Followers of the Sūtras"), and Mahāyāna systems such as Yogācāra ("Practice of Yoga") and Madhyamaka ("Middle Way"). The Madhyamaka, in turn, is divided between Svātantrika "(Autonomists") and Prāsangika ("Consequentialists").[47]

Returning to the four main orders listed above, it has been observed that though there is a tendency to emphasize the differences between them, "more striking is how much they share in common" (Powers, 2007, p. 355). To be sure, the four orders emphasize different Tantric texts, different practices, different lineages of teachers, and different culminating teachings, and they may have different attitudes towards monastic celibacy. Thus the distinctions between them are more pronounced than the differences between Theravāda nikāyas. But the list of what the orders share in common is noteworthy as well: they all ordain monks according to the Mūlasarvāstivāda Vinaya; they all advocate Madhyamaka thought (see 9.2); they all practice the bodhisattva path (see 10.1) and Tantra (see 10.5); they all agree on the nature of the mind – as being that of clear light.[48]

---

47 On all of these philosophical traditions, see 9.2. For translations of Tibetan sources on the "system of tenets" (siddhanta), see Guenther (1971a), and Hopkins (1983), pp. 317–428.

48 For fuller discussion of the four orders, see Powers (2007), pp. 355–364.

Taken as a whole, there have been two different ways of categorizing the four orders. Sometimes, distinctions are made between the "Old Order," i.e. the Nyingma, and the other three orders, i.e. the Kagyü, Sakya, and Géluk. The Nyingma traces its roots back to the first dispensation of the Dharma into Tibet at the time of Padmasambhava and is based on "old translations" of Tantric texts, or on terma (gter ma) – treasure texts said to have been hidden away by the ancients for discovery at a later time by tertön (gter ston), "treasure-revealers." The Kagyü, Sakya, and Géluk claim to be based on so-called "new translations" of Tantric texts and originate with the second dispensation of the Dharma into Tibet in the eleventh century.

Starting in the nineteenth century, however, a more relevant distinction came to be made between the Géluk order, which was centered in Lhasa and politically dominant, and the "Non-Sectarian Movement" (Rimé [Ris med]) which began in Eastern Tibet and included monks of the Nyingma, Kagyü, and Sakya orders.

Another way of classifying Tibetan divisional traditions bypasses the notion of the four orders entirely. Thus the scheme of the "Eight Great Vehicle-Lineages of Achievement" (Drupgyü Shingta Chenpo Gye [sgrub brgyud shing rta chen po brgyad]) distinguishes between various paths and practices: (1) Nyingma traditions which, among other things, emphasize the practice of the "Great Perfection" (Dzokchen [Rdzogs chen]); (2) Kadam (bka' gdams) instructions said to have been first introduced to Tibet by Atiśa (982–1054); (3) "Path and Result" (lamdré [lam 'bras]) teachings, often associated with the Sakya school; (4) the Kagyü teachings associated with Marpa (1012–1097) and his lineage; (5) the "precepts of the Shang Valley" (Shangpa Kagyü [Shangs pa bka' brgyud]), which are similar to the Kagyü teachings of Marpa but are traced to the tenth-/eleventh-century teacher Kyungpo Naljor (Kyung po rnal 'byor); (6) "Pacification and Cutting Off" practices (shijé chö [zhi byued gcod]) which are traceable to the eleventh-century adept Padampa Sangyé (Pha dam pa sangs rgyas) and his female disciple Machik Labdrön (Ma gcig lab sgron); (7) Vajrayoga practices (dorje näljor [rdo rje rnal 'byor]) that are associated with the "Wheel of Time" (Kālacakra) Tantra; and (8) "Propitiation and Attainment of the Three Vajra States" (Dorje sumgyi nyyendrup [rdo rje gsum gyi bsnyen sgrub]), also associated with the Kālacakra Tantra.[49]

Finally, returning to the four orders discussed above, some mention

49 For cross-references to all of these traditions, see Buswell and Lopez (2014), p. 796.

should be made of splits within these four schools, mainly on the basis of lineages. Thus the Sakya have two major branches that trace their lineages to the fifteenth and sixteenth centuries. Kagyü are divided into "four major and eight minor" (Buswell and Lopez, 2014, p. 122) subsects, some of which developed considerable degrees of institutional independence. In this regard, as one scholar put it, "it is somewhat misleading to describe [Kagyü] as a single sect; there is, for example, no single head of the sect as in the case of [Sakya] or [Géluk]" (Buswell and Lopez, 2014, p. 121).

A division of a rather different type has emerged in recent times within the Géluk order between the Géluk establishment headed by the Dalai Lama, and a splinter movement (part of which calls itself the "New Kadampa tradition") that has set itself in opposition (sometimes rather vehement opposition) to the present Dalai Lama's ban on the veneration of the Dharma Protector Dorjé Shukden (Rdor rje shugs ldan). The origins of Dorjé Shukden date back to the seventeenth century. According to legend, a famous scholar, who was a rival candidate for the position of Dalai Lama, died in mysterious circumstances and was promptly reborn as an angry spirit seeking revenge in a variety of ways, against the fifth Dalai Lama who was the successful candidate (see 13.2.1). In order to appease him, the fifth Dalai Lama had him "converted" and made into a fierce Dharma protector, with the specific function of safeguarding the purity and supremacy of the Géluk sect, especially against perceived syncretisms with the Nying ma and, later, the Rimé ("non-sectarian") movements. As such, Dorjé Shukden was dutifully worshipped by Géluk teachers. In the twentieth century, however, the present fourteenth Dalai Lama banned his continued veneration within Géluk circles, in part out of fear that he was returning to his true original nature as a malignant force. This proscription upset a number of Géluk followers who saw Dorjé Shukden as a bulwark against a new Tibetan Buddhist ecumenism that they feared would encroach upon their Géluk tradition, and who claim to follow, in this view, the teachings of the late Junior Tutor of the Dalai Lama as well as those of an influential Géluk scholar, Phabongkha pa (1878–1943). The subsequent controversy and dispute (which at one point even turned violent with the murder of a prominent Géluk scholar who supported the Dalai Lama's ban) are too involved to trace here. For now, we need only note that the movement, which has started founding monasteries of its own (most notably the Shar Gaden monastery established in Southern India by practitioners asked by the Dalai Lama to leave their original monastery) is present world-wide on the web, but has physical centers in Switzerland and

Austria.[50] Thus, as mentioned in the introduction (1.4), one of the Tibetan temples in Lumbinī, the impressive Mother Temple of the Graduated Path to Enlightenment (Jangchup Lamrim Temple), belongs to this movement. When it was inaugurated, the ceremony was not attended by the Dalai Lama or any of his entourage, but by Gonsar Rimpoche, who has established several centers in Europe and elsewhere in memory of his teacher, Geshe Rabten, and is affiliated with this splinter movement.

7.6 SUMMARY

We have, in this chapter, examined ways in which the Buddhist saṃgha, once established, split up into groups of different kinds of identities. The early Buddhist councils were aimed, perhaps, at healing these rifts, but actually served to accentuate them. As a result, different Buddhist schools began to appear within Mainstream Buddhism. These schools emerged for a host of different reasons, some of them doctrinal, some of them not. As they grew, many of them developed their own Buddhist Canons and these differences are still reflected in the canonical collections extant today. In addition to these divisions, other fault-lines in the saṃgha appeared between monastics espousing different kinds of vocations and lifestyles, and different sorts of reactions to encounters with Western traditions. Another major division we looked at was that between Mainstream Buddhism and the Mahāyāna tradition. Once the latter came to be established in East Asian and Tibet, further divisions manifested themselves, taking on a variety of forms in China, Japan, and Tibet. Truly there were and are many Buddhisms.

50 On the Dorje Shugden controversy, see Buswell and Lopez (2014), p. 706, and Dreyfus (1998). On the murder of Lobsang Gyatso, see the "afterword" in Gyatso (1998), pp. 317–322. The Geden movement is affiliated somewhat with the New Kadampa tradition, founded by Geshe Kelsang Gyatso in England in 1991. On Kelsang Gyatso and the New Kadampa tradition, see Cozort (2003).

Part II

Further Elaborations of the Triple Gem

Chapter 8

Mahāyāna and Vajrayāna Ways of Meeting the Buddha/s

In chapters 2–7, we looked at views of the Buddha, Dharma, and Saṃgha within a basically (though not exclusively) Mainstream Buddhist framework. In the rest of this book (now that some of the schools of East Asia and Tibet have been introduced), I would like to circle back to look at those "three refuges" again, in a basically (though not exclusively) Mahāyāna framework. I shall start with the Buddha in this chapter, and move on to the Dharma in chapters 9–10, before finishing with the Saṃgha in chapters 11–13.

In Mainstream Buddhism, we were dealing with buddhas whose lives are all defined by time – whether that be the historical Śākyamuni with his eighty years on earth, or the longer-lived buddhas of the past, or those yet to come in the future such as Maitreya. According to the Pali tradition, the past Buddha Dipaṃkara lived for 100,000 years; Maitreya will live for 80,000. These are substantial lifespans but they are nothing compared to those posited for Śākyamuni by certain Mahāyāna sūtras. Indeed, as Buddhism developed, some radical changes occurred in the conceptions of who the Buddha was and how long he lived, and these very much influenced the question of his accessibility.

In what follows I will look at some Mahāyāna and Vajrayāna ways of meeting the buddha/s. First, however, it is important to look at two changes in buddhology: the new definition of the lifespan of Śākyamuni as found in the *Lotus Sūtra* (8.1), and the later development of the doctrine of the three bodies of the buddha/s (8.2). I shall then turn to look at the notion of pure lands, as places where one can meet the buddha/s either through visualization or rebirth (8.3), focusing in particular on the pure land of the Buddha

Amitābha (8.4). Then I shall look at ways of meeting the buddha/s in the figures of some of the great Mahāyāna bodhisattvas (8.5), and finally, I will examine ways of meeting the buddha/s in the Vajrayāna – in visualization, in maṇḍalas, and, in the Tibetan tradition, in the intermediate realm (bardo), and in this world in one's guru (8.6).

8.1 CHANGES IN THE VIEW OF THE BUDDHA: THE LOTUS SŪTRA AND ŚĀKYAMUNI'S LIFESPAN

A revolution in the conceptualization of the Buddha and indeed of the goals of Buddhists may be seen in the *Lotus Sūtra* (Skt., *Saddharma puṇḍarīka Sūtra*; Ch., *Miaofa lianhua jing*; Jpn., *Myōhōrengekyō*), a text that has been called "perhaps the most influential of all Mahāyāna sūtras" (Buswell and Lopez, 2014, p. 729). Composed in India perhaps in the first century CE, it was translated numerous times into Chinese, and it is in East Asia where it has had its greatest importance.[1]

One of its chapters addresses head-on the question of the lifespan of the Buddha. In it, Śākyamuni announces to his astonished disciples that even though people believe that he attained awakening under the Bodhi tree in Bodhgaya, in fact, "it has been incalculable, limitless hundreds of thousands of myriads of millions of [infinite numbers] of aeons" since he attained buddhahood (Hurvitz, 1976, p. 237). He then launches into a mind-boggling metaphor to drive the point home. This involves gathering up an infinite number of universes, reducing them all to dust, walking eastwards and, every time one passes through an infinite number of universes, depositing one mote of that gathered-up dust until it is all exhausted. Then one should gather all the universes thus traversed and reduce *them* all to dust, and then count *those* dust motes, imagining that each is an aeon: the number of aeons thus arrived at will still be shorter than the Buddha's lifespan. If this is not quite eternity, it is close to it.[2]

One of the immediate effects of this is to radically change our understanding of the whole of the Buddha's "historical" life. All the phases he went

1 For translations of the Chinese text of the *Lotus*, see Hurvitz (1976) and Watson (1993). For a translation of the Sanskrit, see Kern (1884). For a set of essays on it, see Teiser and Stone (2009).

2 See Hurvitz (1976), pp. 237–238 for the metaphor. The *Lotus* is not the only sūtra with a long-life chapter. See also Emmerick (1970), pp. 3–5. More generally on the life span of the Buddha, see Jaini (2001), pp. 191–200, and Lai (1981).

through – his life in the palace, his departure from home, his awakening at Bodhgaya, even his death and parinirvāṇa – are now revealed to have been expedient means (upāya) (see 9.3), not real events but pedagogical devices for teaching and converting others. The Buddha thus did not really attain enlightenment at Bodhgaya; he was already enlightened long before. And he will not really pass into extinction at Kuśinagarī, for he is still very much alive and will be for a long time to come. But he will announce that he will pass into extinction, and he will pretend to do so, so that others will make the most of this seemingly rare opportunity to encounter him.[3]

Hand in glove with this went another famous doctrine introduced and espoused by the *Lotus Sūtra*: the three different soteriological pathways that characterized earlier Buddhism – the practices leading to arhatship or pratyekabuddhahood, or full buddhahood – were now also shown to be makeshift distinctions, expedient means for encouraging persons of different capacities to embark on the path. In fact, instead of all of these pathways, according to the *Lotus Sūtra*, there is just the one vehicle to full buddhahood, the only actual goal. Whether they know it or not, therefore, all beings are, in the end, headed for buddhahood.

A second consequence of the Buddha's revelation of his lifespan in the *Lotus Sūtra* is to erase the separation between buddhas of the past and those of the present. The old view of the lineage of buddhas of the past was that no two of them could overlap in time; although several could exist in a single aeon, each had his own distinct buddha-age. Now, buddhas, with their quasi-eternal lifespans, can coexist in time. This point is driven home in a famous passage of the *Lotus Sūtra*, much depicted in East Asian Buddhist art, in which Śākyamuni sits on the same seat as Prabhūtaratna, a buddha from the far distant past.[4] There could hardly be a more graphic way to make the point that the old "rule" about the non-coexistence of buddhas of the past and present no longer applies. Another iconographic formulation of this same idea resulted in the popularization, in East Asia, of three buddhas of the past, present, and future (usually Dipaṃkara, Śākyamuni, and Maitreya), whose images were worshipped together on single altars.

A third important consequence of the quasi-eternal lifespan of the Buddha is the revelation that not only time, but also space is filled with countless buddhas. Indeed, in another famous scene from the *Lotus Sūtra*, Śākyamuni illuminates all the directions with a ray of light from his brow to reveal the

3 See Hurvitz (1976), p. 238.

4 Ibid., pp. 184–191.

presence there of as many buddhas as there are grains of sand in "five hundred myriads of millions of [infinite numbers] of Ganges rivers" (Hurvitz, 1976, p. 185). Each of these buddhas dwells in his own buddhafield or buddha land surrounded by "numberless thousands of myriads of millions of bodhisattvas" (Hurvitz, 1976, p. 185). This revelation of a "cosmos full of buddhas" was to radically change Mahāyāna buddhology. In the immediate context of the *Lotus Sūtra*, Śākyamuni invites them all to come to the opening of the ancient stūpa in which Prabhūtaratna sits. Buddhas can thus coexist not only in time but also in space.

8.2 THREE BODIES OF THE BUDDHA/S

These lines of thinking eventually gave rise in certain Mahāyāna schools to a new buddhology that came to replace or supplement the old two-body theory of the Buddha having a physical body and a doctrinal body (see 3.1). Rather, the Buddha was now said to have three bodies:

1. The makeshift body posited by the *Lotus Sūtra* as the form in which he appears on earth out of compassion for sentient beings came to be known as the nirmāṇakāya, or "magically fashioned body." Ontologically empty, it is created by the Buddha as an expedient means for teaching others. The human body in which the Buddha took birth as Śākyamuni at Lumbinī would be an example of a nirmāṇakāya.
2. The quasi-eternal glorified body in which the Buddha appears in the pure lands (see below) and preaches to the assemblies of bodhisattvas came to be known as the sambhogakāya, or shared body of enjoyment.
3. "Above" and "beyond" both of these bodies was the Dharma-body (Dharmakāya), which ceased referring simply to the corpus of the Buddha's teachings and came to stand for the absolute transcendent Truth-body of the Buddha – of all buddhas. Free from materiality, and beyond discursive or dualistic thought, it is to be realized by the mind of enlightenment as the only final reality of the cosmos.

8.3 MEETING THE BUDDHA/S IN THEIR PURE LANDS

The *Lotus Sūtra* does not name or feature any of these myriad sambhogakāyas and their attendant bodhisattvas in the "cosmos full of buddhas" revealed by Śākyamuni's ray of light. Nor does it describe their pure lands. However, other Mahāyāna traditions were to do so. In what follows, we will look briefly at traditions concerning the pure lands of the Buddhas Akṣobhya and Bhaiṣajyaguru, and then, in more detail, at the cult of the Buddha Amitābha (a.k.a. Amitāyus) and his "Land of Bliss."

8.3.1 Akṣobhya

The Buddha Akṣobhya was imagined to dwell in the pure land named "Utter Joy" (Abhirati), located far to the East. In some ways, his pure land in the East was but a counterpart to Amitābha's pure land in the West, but in other ways it differed significantly from it. Early references to Abhirati depicted it not so much as a pure land pre-established by Akṣobhya for his devotees, but as something that individual Buddhists might establish for themselves (through their good efforts) just as Akṣobhya did. Later, like Sukhāvatī (Amitābha's Land of Bliss), it came to be thought of more as a place of the Buddha one could be reborn in. One special note about Abhirati is the fact that women could be reborn there as women, and could even give birth there, without labor pains. This was not the case in the pure land of Amitābha where there was no birth-giving and where there were no distinctions of gender (which, in the culture of the times, meant, in effect, that women, in being reborn there, became men in the process). Some texts suggested that rebirth in Abhirati was to be had by observing the precepts and doing good, meritorious deeds, and in this too, as we shall see, it differs from traditions about Amitābha's pure land.[5]

8.3.2 Bhaiṣajyaguru

The Medicine Buddha, Bhaiṣajyaguru (Ch., Yaoshi; Jpn., Yakushi), was imagined to dwell in the Pure Land of Lapis Lazuli (called Vaiḍūryanirbhāsa), also far to the East. Its ground is made of lapis and its streets are paved

5 On Akṣobhya and his pure land, see Perera (1966), and Nattier (2000).

with precious stones and marked off with gold. His pure land, his own characteristics, and his twelve vows to help all sentient beings in various ways (the mere hearing of his name is said to bring on various boons) are described in the *Bhaiṣajyaguru Sūtra*, which was probably composed in North India in the second century CE, and was translated several times into Chinese.[6]

Bhaiṣajyaguru's forte or specialization, as his name implies, was to be a Buddha of Healing, as well as a guard against disease and other calamities, and it was in these capacities that he became (and continues to be) popular in China and Japan where his cult focused on making and venerating images of him, reciting his sutra, and repeating his name. In Japan, a number of temples were built for him very early on, e.g. the famous Yakushi-ji (Bhaiṣajyaguru temple) in Nara in 680. Moreover, the main image of the headquarters temple of the Tendai sect on Mount Hiei is of Bhaiṣajyaguru (Yakushi nyorai). His cult was also found, however, in South and Southeast Asia.

In Cambodia, for example, in the twelfth century, the "hospitals" established by the great Khmer king Jayavarman VII (twelfth–thirteenth century) all had main altars containing a triad of images: Bhaiṣajyaguru, who was said to "bring peace and health to those who so much as heard his name" and his two emanations, often thought of as acolyte bodhisattvas, Sūryaprabha ("Sunshine") and Candraprabha ("Moonshine") who together "kept beings out of the darkness of illness" (Coedès, 1959, p. 495).[7]

8.4 AMITĀBHA

The Buddha Amitābha ("Limitless Light," Ch., Amituo fo, Jpn., Amida butsu), a.k.a. Amitāyus ("Limitless Life," Ch., Wuliangshou fo; Jpn., Muryōju butsu), was imagined to dwell in the pure land known as the "Land of Bliss" (Sukhāvatī; Ch., jingtu; Jpn., jōdo), said to be "a hundred thousand billion buddha-fields to the west" and to feature trees and lotus blossoms made of different kinds of precious materials. Beings reborn there do not experience stress (duḥkha) of any kind, neither with their bodies nor with their minds. Throughout East Asia, the cult of Amitābha eventually came to outshine the cults of Akṣobhya and Bhaiṣajyaguru, not to mention that of Maitreya. Notions

6 For English translations and a discussion, see Birnbaum (1979), pp. 115–217.

7 On the Yakushiji in Nara, see McCallum (2009), pp. 201–236. On his cult in Japan, see Frédéric (1995), p. 110. More generally on Bhaiṣajyaguru, see Birnbaum (1979).

developed that there were basically two ways to meet the Buddha Amitābha. To use Nattier's language (see 3.7), one could meet Amitābha "there/now" by visualizing him in his pure land in one's own lifetime; or one could meet him "there/later" by taking steps to be reborn in his pure land in one's next life and to meet him after death.

8.4.1 Meeting Amitābha through Visualization

Let us start with the practice of visualization. One of the early sources in this regard is a proto-pure land sūtra called the *Pratyutpanna Samādhi*, one of the first Sanskrit texts to be translated into Chinese (in 179 CE). Its full title may be rendered as *The Discourse on the Meditation in which One is Brought Face to Face with the Buddhas of the Present* (Harrison, 1988, p. 2) but it uses, as its prime example, the buddha Amitābha and his western pure land of Sukhāvatī.[8]

A whole other text, the *Sūtra of the Meditation on the Buddha Amitāyus* (**Amitāyurdhyānasūtra*; Ch., *Guan wuliangshou jing*), is given over to describing the visualization of this pure land and its residents and how to get there. It starts simply by having the devotee sit facing the red ball of the sun setting in the west: one is to look at it, and keep one's mind on it until the image of it remains clear and fixed whether one's eyes are open or shut. Then one focuses on an image of pure and clear water, until it too can be kept in the mind's eye. Then one changes the water to ice, then to lapis lazuli. Then one visualizes a network of golden bejeweled ropes stretching across the lapis surface. Then the jewels emit rays of five hundred colors that rise up into the sky and form towers with different levels and galleries and banners flying. And when one can keep all this in mind whether one's eyes are open or shut, one is beginning dimly to see the land of Sukhāvatī. The visualization continues with the perception in the land of jewel trees, of lakes, and streams, and lotus blossoms. Then come instructions on how to see the throne on which the Buddha is sitting, and then, finally, the Buddha himself, and, to either side of him, the bodhisattvas Avalokiteśvara and Mahāsthāmaprapta, all of whose forms are described in detail. All these things should not be perceived vaguely but clearly and distinctly, with a fixed mind, just as one might see one's own face in a mirror.[9]

8 For a survey of notions of seeing the Buddha in the context of visualization, see Yamabe (1999), pp. 125–184. On the importance of the *Pratyutpanna Samādhi Sūtra* in combining emphasis on visualization and Amitābha in the context of perfection of wisdom doctrine, see also Harrison (1978).

9 For the visualization of Amitāyus and his pure land, see Takakusu (1894), pp. 169–177.

Visualization was an important practice in a number of different Buddhist traditions. As one early sūtra on the topic puts it, it meant being able to see the Buddha and hear him preach "right away while sitting here" (Harrison, 1998, p. 13), without having to die or be reborn elsewhere. It is important to realize that these "visions" were not considered to be dreams or hallucinations. Rather, in the context of Mahāyāna doctrine, they were just as valid a perception of reality as any other. Eventually, as we shall see below, such visualization techniques were also to be employed in Vajrayāna (Tantric) meditations.

8.4.2 Rebirth in the Pure Land

Within the Pure Land tradition, however, visualizations did not remain the only or even the primary way of getting to the Land of Bliss and of seeing Amitābha. As the Pure Land tradition developed, increasing emphasis was placed on being reborn "there/later," i.e. in one's next life.

Mahāyāna sūtras appear to know at least two related traditions about the Pure Land Sukhāvatī. One of these is that it was a "generalized religious goal" that one could attain through a variety of cultic and meritorious actions not necessarily related to the Amitābha at all. Thus, in some texts, devotional acts directed towards other buddhas (e.g. Bhaiṣajyaguru), or towards the maintenance of particular scriptures (by copying or repeating them), are said to result in rebirth in Sukhāvatī. The other, which we shall examine here, is that Sukhāvatī was a goal intimately bound up in the cult of Amitābha.[10]

In this regard, it should be said that in the *Large Sūtra Displaying the Land of Bliss* (*Sukhāvatīvyūha Sūtra*), the pure land as a whole and the salvation of beings there were thought to be the result of a series of vows taken by Amitābha, long ago when he was still a bodhisattva named Dharmākara, working his way towards buddhahood. Those vows, reflective of the Buddha's great compassion, specify not only the characteristics of the pure land, but who can get in them, and how. For example, Dharmākara vows that, once he becomes Amitābha, all other buddhas will praise his name everywhere; that he will appear in person at the moment of death to those devotees destined to be reborn in his pure land; that his land (now realized) will be a place where there will be no danger of falling into unfortunate realms of rebirth,

10 On the pure land as a generalized religious goal, see Schopen (2005), pp. 154–189.

where all beings will have golden skin, where they will be akin to the gods, where they will be endowed with magical powers, and where their lifespans will be immeasurable.[11]

As Pure Land thought developed, a number of Dharmākara's vows came to be of central importance. One of these was the eighteenth vow, which guarantees access to the pure land to any devotee who single-mindedly desires to be reborn there and who brings this aspiration to mind ten times.[12] In time, the primary way of doing this was interpreted as "calling on the name" of the Buddha with the formula "Praise to Amitābha Buddha" (Skt., Namo Amitābhāya; Ch., Namo Amituo fo; Jpn., Namu Amida Butsu), coupled with faith. This practice is called "recalling the Buddha" (Skt., Buddhānusmṛti; Ch., nianfo; Jpn., nembutsu). This went hand in glove with the development of the notion of the "grace" of the Buddha: one is saved – one is caused to be reborn in the pure land – solely by the power and compassion and merit of Amitābha, and not by one's own actions or visualizations or merits. In other words, one meets the Buddha in the pure land because he has vowed to meet us there.

It is clear from all this that anyone who makes it to the pure land is guaranteed at least two things: not being reborn again in one of the saṃsāric realms of rebirth; and eventually attaining enlightenment. This does not mean, however, that the tradition did not refrain from making distinctions between devotees. Although Japanese Pure Land schools founded in the eleventh/twelfth century appear to be fairly egalitarian and radical in their statements about who can get to the pure land, earlier traditions, such as those found in the final part of the sūtra on the meditation of Amitāyus, distinguish between several classes of devotees. There is much debate on the identity of the beings in these different divisions. One view is that the top class represents bodhisattvas, the middle class śravakas, and the bottom class ordinary laypersons including those who have much negative karma and are not even on the path. One thing that is clear is that it takes beings in the different classes and grades varying amounts of time to attain enlightenment, and varying amounts of time before they get to see Amitābha face to face. For the highest category of devotees, meeting Amitābha and reaching enlightenment are almost instantaneous upon their rebirth in the pure land. Others, however, may be reborn in the pure land inside the calyxes of giant lotus blossoms that shield their vision until those blossoms open up. Those

11 For a list of all the vows, see Strong (2008), pp. 198–199.
12 On the eighteenth vow, see Gómez (1996), pp. 167, 247–248 n17.

in the lowest subcategory of this division of devotees, for instance, have to remain enclosed in their lotus blossoms for twelve aeons prior to being able to see the Buddha, hear the Dharma, and become enlightened.[13]

8.5 MEETING THE BUDDHA IN THE GREAT BODHISATTVAS

Mention has been made several times of bodhisattvas associated with the various Mahāyāna buddhas. We have seen in chapter 2 that the word "bodhisattva," in the context of Mainstream Buddhism, refers either to Śākyamuni in one of his previous lifetimes while he was still working his way towards buddhahood, or to Maitreya (or one of the other future buddhas) who is doing the same in the present time. In the Mahāyāna, the applications of the term are greatly expanded. The word still means a "being set on buddhahood," but since buddhahood is now universalized as a soteriological goal, every sentient being can potentially embark on the path to it. Those that do are bodhisattvas, and we shall examine the bodhisattva path in 10.1.

Some beings, however, were thought to be more advanced on the bodhisattva path than others. These are the "great" bodhisattvas, beyond the possibility of retrogressing on the path and engaged by their vows in helping others onto it. Such "great bodhisattvas" are sometimes called "savior" or "celestial" bodhisattvas, and together with buddhas and other beings, they form what can appropriately be called a Mahāyāna pantheon. Like the Buddha, bodhisattvas are encounterable in a variety of ways – in their images, in places of pilgrimage associated with them, in visualizations, and in visions.[14]

Much ink has been spilled over the differences, in this context, between great bodhisattvas and buddhas. It is often stated, for instance, that the great bodhisattvas postpone their enlightenment indefinitely and choose to remain in this world for the sake of all sentient beings. As Williams (2009, pp. 58–62) has pointed out, however, this is basically nonsensical. Although the question is complex, from a popular point of view, great bodhisattvas can definitely be thought of as enlightened and enlightening beings. Like all bodhisattvas, they are "sentient beings set on buddhahood," but they might also be called "buddhas set on sentient beings." In this context, we should view bodhisattvas

13 On the theme of different categories of believers, see Gómez (1996), pp. 187–188, Frédéric (1995), pp. 140–144, Tanaka (1990), pp. 178–181, and Pas (1995), pp. 277–306.
14 For an iconographic description of the Mahāyāna pantheon, see Frédéric (1995).

and their cult perhaps not so much as ways in which we beings can meet the Buddha as ways in which the Buddha meets beings.[15]

8.5.1 Avalokiteśvara

Perhaps the best known of all the great bodhisattvas is Avalokiteśvara (Ch., Guanyin; Jap., Kannon; Tib., Chenrézik [Spyan ras gzigs]). The *Lotus Sūtra*, which we have cited already several times, contains a whole chapter devoted to him. There, the emphasis is not on his being a teacher of Dharma, but on his great compassion for the actual sufferings of beings in this world. If any devotee should get into trouble in any way – being about to drown, or being attacked, or imprisoned, or bitten by a snake – all he or she need do is to "recall" Avalokiteśvara in order to gain relief. As the sūtra puts it: "Seeing beings oppressed by hundreds of sorrows and afflicted by many sufferings, he looks down upon the world, including the gods, and protects it" (Strong, 2008, p. 192).

As mentioned in 1.4.1, Avalokiteśvara can be invoked with his famous mantra, "Oṃ Maṇi Padme Hūṃ," which not only calls on him for assistance for oneself, but also calls on him to relieve the sufferings of all beings. The six syllables of the mantra are each thought to correspond to one of the six realms of rebirth (see 1.4.1) and, when pronounced, to make the bodhisattva present in that realm. The mantra is particularly popular among Tibetans, many of whom intone it daily, or spin prayer wheels stuffed with copies of it, or inscribe it on stones placed by the side of circumambulation paths.[16]

In his compassion for the world, Avalokiteśvara can take on many different forms. Thus, he might be thought of as a chameleonic teacher: he can appear as a rich man to help rich men, as a brahmin to help brahmins, as a nun among nuns, as a monk among monks, as a young boy, or girl, or god, or nāga, or yakṣa, etc., among young boys, or girls, or gods, or nāgas, or yakṣas, etc. As a result, devotees can never be sure who might or might not be the bodhisattva. But Avalokiteśvara was also thought to have a number of standard iconic forms. In the *Lotus Sūtra*, it is specified that he can appear in any of thirty-three manners – whichever is most appropriate to the situation

15 For one discussion of the relationship of buddhas to bodhisattvas, see Holt (1991), pp. 39–46.
16 See Studholme (2002).

in which he finds himself. An alternate list of thirty-three iconographic forms of Avalokiteśvara became popular in East Asia, and remains today the basis of a pilgrimage circuit to thirty-three different temples in Western Japan. Among these forms, at least ten are female, a reflection of the fact that, in China, starting around the tenth century, Avalokiteśvara (Ch., Guanyin; Jpn., Kannon) took on a feminine guise and came to be venerated as a female bodhisattva – the so-called "goddess of mercy."[17]

Like the Buddha Amitābha, Avalokiteśvara has a "pure land" where he can welcome devotees. Called Mount Potalaka (Ch., Putuo; Jpn., Fudaraku), it is thought to be situated in the South Seas, but to be still part of this world of saṃsāra. Thus, for some, it was thought to be easier to get to than Amitābha's Sukhāvatī. In China, it was identified with the island called Putuo shan, off the southeastern coast, which has remained a major pilgrimage site for devotees of Guanyin to this day. In Tibet, the Potala palace, residence of the Dalai Lama (who is considered to be an incarnation of Avalokiteśvara), is named after the bodhisattva's pure land.[18]

8.5.2 Other Great Bodhisattvas

Avalokiteśvara was by no means the only bodhisattva to obtain great popularity in the Mahāyāna world. Sometimes paired with him (but also an important figure in her own right) is the female bodhisattva, Tārā (Ch., Duoluo; Jpn., Tara; Tib., Dölma [Sgrol ma]), whose cult remains prominent in Tibet, though it never fully developed in East Asia. Like Avalokiteśvara, Tārā is a savior figure who never fails to respond to persons in distress. She too can take on multiple forms (twenty-one are commonly listed). In her benign aspects, she is tireless in providing assistance to the oppressed and downtrodden. In her ferocious aspects, she saves sentient beings from their enemies by destroying those enemies. She also has a short mantra by which she can be invoked: "Oṃ Tāre Tuttāre Ture Svāhā."[19]

17 On Avalokiteśvara's chameleonic character, see Watson (1993), pp. 301–302. For a list of the thirty-three forms of the bodhisattva in Japan, see Frédéric (1995), pp. 156–162. On Guanyin, see Yü (2001). On his/her gender change, see ibid., pp. 293–351, and Reed (1992).

18 On Mount Potalaka being easier to reach than Sukhāvatī, see Ford (2006), pp. 111–112. On Mount Fudaraku, and the "suicide pilgrimages" there, see Moerman (2005), pp. 92–117. On Mount Putuo, see Yü (2001), pp. 353–406.

19 On Tārā, see Beyer (1973), M. Shaw (2006), pp. 306–354, and Wilson (1986).

Mañjuśrī (Ch., Wenshu; Jpn., Monju; Tib., Jampäl ['Jam-dpal]) is the bodhisattva most associated with the Buddha's quality of wisdom. Typically, he is depicted as carrying a sword that cuts through ignorance, and a book – a copy of the *Perfection of Wisdom Sūtra*. He is said to reside on Mount Wu-tai in the north of China (another of the four famous Buddhist mountains of China), where he can sometimes be glimpsed by pilgrims flying through the air on his great lion.[20]

Samantabhadra (Ch., Puxian; Jpn., Fugen; Tib., Kuntuzangpo [Kun-tu bzang-po]), whose name means "Universally good, " is an embodiment of the Buddha Dharma and compassion and has vowed especially to come to the aid of all those who recite and preserve the *Lotus Sūtra*. Typically, he is said to ride on a great white elephant. In China, he is said to reside on Mount Emei in the West.

Kṣitigarbha (Ch., Dizang; Jpn., Jizō; Tib., Sa yi snying po), whose name means "Earth-Womb," is associated with Mount Jiuhua in the south of China. It is said that, in a past life, Kṣitigarbha was so disturbed by the thought of beings undergoing infernal sufferings that he resolved to become a bodhisattva and liberate beings from hell. More generally, he came to be known as the guardian of all beings journeying on the pathways of rebirth into the six realms. In Japan, this became extended to being the protector of travelers in this world (such as children on their way to school), and of unborn or stillborn fetuses. In this way, in modern times, Jizō has become an important bodhisattva for women suffering from abortions or miscarriages (see 12.1.3).[21]

8.6 MEETING THE BUDDHA/S IN THE VAJRAYĀNA

All of the buddhas of the pure lands and all of these bodhisattvas, in addition to many others, are known in the Vajrayāna as well as in the Mahāyāna. In the Vajrayāna, however, the traditions about the buddhas tend to be more systematically organized. As an example of this, I would like to consider the set of five buddhas, known either as the five jinas (victors) or five tathāgatas, which is what I shall call them. Typically, these are depicted

20 For a brief introduction to Mañjuśrī, see Birnbaum (2005). See also Harrison (2000), and Tribe (1997). On visions of Mañjuśrī at Mount Wutai, see Cartelli (2004), and Stevenson (1996). On Wutai in general, see Lin (2014).

21 On Kṣitigarbha in general, see De Visser (1914); in Japan, see Glassman (2012).

in a maṇḍala where they are positioned in the four cardinal directions and the center, and where, through certain rituals and meditations they too may be "met."[22]

8.6.1 *Maṇḍalas and the Five Tathāgatas*

Maṇḍalas (literally, "circles") are of many types and have many strata of meaning. They are "sacred enclosures" (Snellgrove, 1987, p. 199) that can be relatively simple in structure or enrichingly complex. The more complex often consist of a series of concentric circles, set within squares, which recall the architecture of Indian four-sided temples, and/or royal palaces, and/or the cosmos itself. In these various "courtyards" are depicted the various buddhas, bodhisattvas, and other divinities of the pantheon. Some scholars have argued that the imagery of the maṇḍala is basically political – royal – in which the Buddha is seen as an overlord, who enters into relationships of different types with his vassals, other figures in the maṇḍala. Others have given basically psychological interpretations of the maṇḍala, often inspired by the work of Carl Jung. Within the maṇḍala, the innermost circle or "court" is the most sacred and significant, and typically contains the image of the principal "lord" of the maṇḍala – the Buddha, whose power and presence radiate outward and hold and define the structure as a whole.[23]

Some maṇḍalas may be very large indeed. For example, the great fifteenth-century Kumbum (Sku 'bum) stūpa at Gyantse in Central Tibet is a veritable three-dimensional maṇḍala in stone: it boasts seventy-five chapels containing hundreds of images, stacked over eight floors; at the very top (and center) is a chapel housing a statue of Vajradhara who, in the system being represented here, is the Ādibuddha – "the primordial and timeless Buddha from which all other buddhas and the whole universe emanate" (Ricca and Lo Bue, 1993, p. 51). Similarly, the ninth-century temple of Borobudur in Indonesia is a gigantic maṇḍala in stone containing over 2,500 sculpted reliefs and more than 500 buddha images.[24]

22 On the five tathāgatas, see Snellgrove (1987), pp. 189–213. Sometimes, the five tathāgatas are called the five celestial buddhas, or, wrongly, the five "dhyāni" (meditation) buddhas, a term that was coined by Brian Hodgson in the nineteenth century (see Conze, 1959, p. 189).
23 In general, on maṇḍalas in Tibet, see Brauen (1998). For a political interpretation of maṇḍalas, see Davidson (2002), pp. 131–144, 296–303, and Bjerken (2005). For a psychologically informed study, see Tucci (1961).
24 On Borobudur, see Gomez and Woodward (1981), and Miksic (1999).

The identity of the central Buddha (and of the other buddhas around him) can vary from one maṇḍala to another. Here, for simplicity's sake, I will focus on one common scheme, the one of the five tathāgatas, which eventually came to be of prime importance in Indian, Tibetan, and Japanese Vajrayāna, and which is classically expressed in the central court of the Vajradhātu maṇḍala (Jpn., Kongōkai), one of the two chief maṇḍalas of the Shingon (and Tendai) sects in Japan. Here the names and positions of the five buddhas are as follows: Vairocana, in the Center, Akṣobhya in the East, Ratnasambhava in the South, Amitābha in the West, and Amoghasiddhi in the North.[25]

These five buddhas "must be thought of ... as including all other Buddha- and bodhisattva-manifestations, who fill space in all directions" (Snellgrove, 1987, p. 208). In this sense, the maṇḍala is nothing more than a boiling down or epitomizing (in varying levels of detail) of the "cosmos full of buddhas" which we saw revealed by the ray of light issued by Śākyamuni in the *Lotus Sūtra*. Indeed, it can be argued that Vairocana (whose name means "Illuminator" or "Resplendent") is, in origin, none other than Śākyamuni renamed and now cosmicized.[26]

In Japan, Vairocana is, significantly, known as Dainichi (the "great sun") and, like the sun, he pervades everything, not only the other buddhas and bodhisattvas of the maṇḍala, but ultimately the whole of reality. From a doctrinal perspective, and simplifying somewhat, Vairocana is the Dharmakāya, and the four other tathāgatas may be thought of as his sambhogakāya manifestations (see 8.2). Further out from its center, the Vajradhātu maṇḍala also contains images of the thousand buddhas of the bhadrakalpa, i.e. the manifest bodies (nirmāṇakāya) or manuṣya (human) buddhas, as well as various bodhisattvas associated with the four tathāgatas. The maṇḍala can thus be thought of as a map of the manifestations of buddhahood. As a map, it has a dual function: it shows us the "lay of the land" – reality as it is; and it can guide us through that land. In the language of Geertz, it is both a "model of" buddhahood and a "model for" buddhahood (1979, p. 81). More simply, for our purposes, it may be thought of as an arena in which one can meet

25 Snellgrove (1987), p. 196, highlights the importance of the Vajradhātu maṇḍala scheme. On its Japanese Shingon expression, see Ten Grotenhuis (1999), and Kiyota (1978). The five tathāgatas are found in the central court of the Vajradhātu-maṇḍala, described in the *Sarvatathāgatatattvasaṃgraha*. Later the *Guhyasamāja Tantra* was to put Akṣobhya in the center and depict the buddhas in union with their consorts. See Snellgrove (1987), p. 211.

26 The equation of Vairocana and Śākyamuni in the maṇḍala is argued for by Snellgrove (1987), p. 196. For the Shingon take on this and its bypassing of Śākyamuni, see Abé (1999), p. 129.

the Buddha, with the understanding that such a meeting coincides with the realization of one's own buddhahood.

8.6.2 Ritual Consecration (Abhiṣeka)

In the Vajrayāna, such a meeting and realization involve "entering into the maṇḍala." Ceremonially, this is accomplished by a ritual of consecration called abhiṣeka (Jpn., kanjō), literally an "anointing" (with water) of a candidate for buddhahood. This not only replicates the coronation ceremony of kings, but it also ritually mimics the Mahāyāna myth whereby a bodhisattva, just prior to entering the final stage of the path and achieving buddhahood, is given an abhiṣeka (anointment) by the buddhas of the ten directions. In turn, this may be a distant echo of the myth of the bathing of the Buddha just after his birth. Either way, abhiṣeka may be seen as a precursor to buddhahood.[27]

In Japanese Vajrayāna (Shingon), there are actually several types of abhiṣeka corresponding to different stages of enlightenment: in the first, the initiand has his eyes opened to the world of the Buddha (equivalent to a first stage of enlightenment – the opening of the Dharma-eye). This is ritually enacted by introducing the initiand blindfolded into the room wherein the maṇḍala is laid out, and then removing the blindfold after he has thrown a flower onto the maṇḍala, thus establishing a bond – a personal relationship with the Buddha. In the second abhiṣeka, the initiand is said to receive instruction in the significance of the mantras and mūdras, ritually chanted formulae and hand gestures that imitate the speech and body of the buddhas. In the third, the initiand is thought to receive the direct transmission of the Dharma, akin to attaining awakening (or buddhahood) in this very body (sokushin jōbutsu).[28]

At a more general level, the "meeting" with the Buddha thus made possible may be said to amount to a merger – a ritual/meditational identification between the practitioner and the Buddha. The Dharmakāya of the Buddha (i.e. Vairocana) is commonly thought to manifest itself in this world in three modes defined as the Buddha's body, speech, and mind. These are the "three mysteries" (Skt., triguhya; Ch., san mi; Jpn., Sanmitsu) of the Dharmakāya which permeate the universe and so may also be found in the body, speech,

27 On abhiṣeka, see Davidson (2002), pp. 122–125. See also Shinohara (2014), pp. 73–78.
28 The information on the various abhiṣekas in Japan (Jpn., kanjō) is taken from Tajima (1959), pp. 270–273 [in French]. See also Abé (1999), pp. 123–141.

and mind of ordinary sentient beings. The three mysteries thus provide an opportunity for contact – a shared arena – in which sentient beings and buddhas can meet and merge. As the great Shingon Master Kūkai (774–835) put it, "the three mysteries of the Dharmakāya and sentient beings correspond, making it possible for sentient beings to be blessed and empowered by the Dharmakāya" (Abé, 1999, p. 129).[29]

Ritually and iconographically, these three mysteries are expressed in terms of mudrās (the hand gestures and bodily postures that characterize Vajrayāna rites), mantras (the sacred sounds uttered in rites which are different from ordinary speech), and meditation on the maṇḍalas. The significance of these is explained to the practitioner in the course of the abhiṣeka rites described above. Thus for an initiate, it is primarily Vajrayāna ritual, involving mūdras, mantras, and maṇḍalas, that sets up an arena – a middle ground in which the meeting and identification of the practitioner's body, speech, and mind with those of the Buddha is possible (see table 8.1).[30]

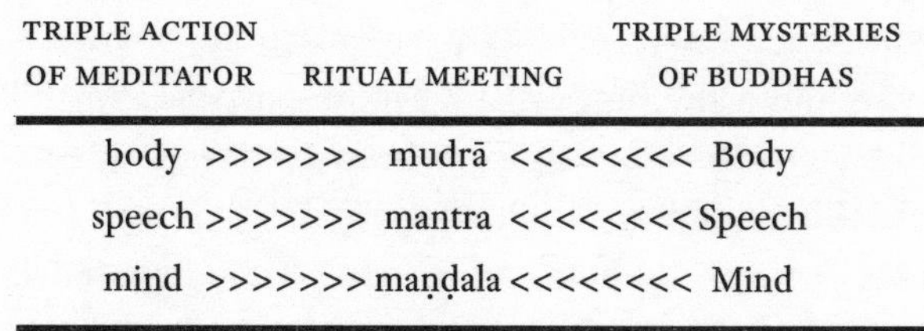

TRIPLE ACTION OF MEDITATOR	RITUAL MEETING	TRIPLE MYSTERIES OF BUDDHAS
body >>>>>>>	mudrā	<<<<<<<< Body
speech >>>>>>>	mantra	<<<<<<<< Speech
mind >>>>>>>	maṇḍala	<<<<<<<< Mind

Table 8.1 Meeting the Buddha in Vajrayāna Ritual[31]

8.6.3 Merging with the Buddha

Body, speech, and mind come together again in another Vajrayāna practice whereby union with the Buddha is made possible by visualizing the Buddha as oneself, or as entering into oneself. These methods, sometimes called Deity Yoga, originated in India and are still featured in Tibetan Vajrayāna practice. They are spelled out in instruction manuals called sādhanas (techniques for evocations).[32] The practice of visualization is often described in textbooks

29 On the three mysteries, see also Giebel (2004), p. 75.

30 On the importance of ritual and the use of mūdras, mantras, and maṇḍalas, see Kiyota (1978), p. 70.

31 Based on Kiyota (1978), p. 70.

32 For an introduction to sādhana, see Germano and Hillis (2005), p. 1287. Sharf and Sharf (2001), pp. 151–154, dispute that maṇḍalas were ever used as the bases for visualization.

as the meditative ability to create an image with one's mind and statically maintain its reality by dint of concentration. There is no doubt that such abilities are required, but, in fact, sādhanas generally describe visualizations that are not statically frozen but in constant motion, with images emerging and fading and transforming into one another. In this sense, the experience may be more like visualizing a videotape than a single snapshot.

A quick example may be given here, taken from a visualization of Vajrasattva (Tib., Dorje Sempa [Rdo rje sems dpa']) who is sometimes thought to be, like Vairocana, a personification of the Dharmakāya, and sometimes thought to be a sambhogakāya. After some preliminaries, the sādhana begins by instructing the meditator to visualize Vajrasattva as sitting on a moon disk on top of a lotus blossom directly above his or her head. His body is perfectly white and is adorned with many jewels symbolizing the Buddha-mind. He wears a five-pointed crown symbolizing the attainments of the five tathāgatas. In his heart is the syllable Hūṃ, around which are rotating the one hundred syllables of his mantra: "Oṃ vajrasattva samayam anupālaya / Vajrasattvatvenopatiṣṭha / dṛḍho me bhava / sutoṣyo me bhava / supoṣyo me bhava / anurakto me bhava / sarvasiddhiṃ me prayaccha / sarvakarmasu ca me cittaṃ śreyaḥ kuru / hūṃ / ha ha ha ha hoḥ / bhagavan sarvatathāgatavajra mā me muñca / vajrībhava mahāsamayasattva / āḥ."[33]

This is a famous mantra, much repeated by Tibetan practitioners today. Unlike most mantras, it actually has lexical meaning and can be translated as follows:

> Oṃ! Vajrasattva, preserve our coming together! Be present in your Vajrasattva-ness! Be firm for me! Be well pleased with me! Be fully nourishing for me! Be passionate for me! Grant me success in everything, and in all actions, make my mind lucid. Hūṃ! Ha ha ha ha hoḥ! O Blessed One, Vajra of all the tathāgatas, do not abandon me! Be a vajra-holder, O being of the great meeting! āḥ!

The meditator is to repeat as many times as possible the mantra, which, it should be noted, is not only an invocation of Vajrasattva but touches on themes and aspects of the union between him and the meditator. It also contains the three syllables Oṃ, āḥ, hūṃ, though not in their usual order. These three are thought to symbolize the body, speech, and heart/mind of the Buddha and are usually visualized at the forehead, throat, and heart. The "Ha ha ha

33 Skilton (1990).

ha hoḥ!" has been subjected to a variety of interpretations, one of which is that it is laughter; another is that these five syllables represent here the five tathāgatas, set next to (and encompassed by) the Hūṃ, which represents the mind of Vajrasattva.

As the sādhana continues, the Hūṃ (not the one in the hundred syllable mantra, but the one visualized as a seed syllable in Vajrasattva's heart) issues forth rays of light that radiate outwards and pervade the entire universe, and then return to Vajrasattva. Then, from that Hūṃ which is in Vajrasattva's heart/mind, those rays of light mixed with cleansing nectar, pour down like a waterfall onto the top of the meditator's head and down through his or her central channel (Tib., Sa u ma). We will deal with Tantric physiology in 10.5.2 below. Suffice it to say here that the central channel is the yoga channel that parallels the spine. The visualized nectar flows down through it, from the fontanel on the summit of the head, down to the meditator's own heart/mind, and then gradually spreads throughout the body. It cleanses everything and flushes out all negativities, all suffering, all traces of ego, bad karma, etc., until the body and mind are filled with nothing but nectar and light. Then, from the point above the head, Vajrasattva himself, as white light, sinks down through the central channel to the Hūṃ in the meditator's own heart/mind, where he is absorbed into the meditator, and "your body, speech, and mind become inseparable from Vajrasattva" (Willis, 1972, p. 86).[34]

8.6.4 Visions: Meeting the Buddha/s in Bardo

There is yet another visual way that one can meet buddhas and escape from saṃsāra in the Vajrayāna: according to Tibetan tradition, every time one dies, one passes through an intermediate state (Tib., bardo; Skt., antarābhava) prior to taking rebirth. Not all Buddhists schools accepted the theory of an intermediate state, but the Tibetan Vajrayāna did, and developed a scenario whereby this represents an opportunity for enlightenment that, with training, can be grabbed. The notion makes sense: the purpose of awakening is to escape from rebirth in one of the six realms. The bardo represents a time when one is precisely *not* in one of the six realms of rebirth, but "betwixt and between" them. The opportunity exists, therefore, to escape from saṃsāra in the interstices between death and rebirth.

34 More generally on the Vajrasattva mantra, see Skilton (1990), and Jayarava (2010).

This opportunity comes in the form of a series of visions which all persons are said to experience in the bardo. These visions are spelled out in the so-called *Tibetan Book of the Dead* (Tib., *Bardo Tödröl* [*Bar do thos grol*]), a ritual text of which there are many variant editions and translations. In Tibet, the moment of death is thought to come not with the stopping of the heart or the cessation of breath, but with the mind's experiencing the "clear light" of death, a state of consciousness that is free from duality, free from concepts, perfectly empty. In the *Tibetan Book of the Dead*, this is said to represent an opportunity for seeing the Dharmakāya which shares the qualities of this clear light.[35]

However, very few people recognize it as such. Instead they embark on the first week of bardo, during which they have a succession of visions of the five tathāgatas. Here the maṇḍala is spread out over time: on the first day of bardo, the Buddha Vairocana appears. He is white in color but emanates an intense, sharp, piercing, blinding blue light. This blue light is actually an invitation to enlightenment in the presence of the Buddha, but only those ready for it can recognize it as such. Most (because of karma) are attracted, instead, to a soft white light coming from the realm of the gods, and, failing to take refuge in Vairocana, they move on in the bardo. On the second day, the Buddha Akṣobhya appears in the east, and the same scenario repeats itself: he is blue in color, but most bardo-beings are scared away by the intense white light that emanates from him, and so do not grab the opportunity to meet him and gain enlightenment. Instead, they are attracted to a mild smoky-grey light coming from the realm of the hells. On the third day, Ratnasambhava appears in the south, but again, bardo-beings are attracted not to his unbearably blinding yellow light, but to the soft blue light of the realm of humans. On the fourth day, Amitābha appears in the west, but bardo-beings, shying away from his bright red light, move to the soft yellow light of the hungry ghosts. Finally, on the fifth day, Amoghasiddhi appears in the north, but most bardo-beings, afraid of his bright green light, are attracted to the soft red light of the realm of the asuras.

This same pattern continues in subsequent days during which all five tathāgatas appear together, and then, in the second week, they each appear individually in their wrathful forms as various manifestations of Heruka.

35 On the Tibetan Book(s) of the Dead and its/their various translations, see Lopez (2011). For a translation, see Freemantle and Trungpa (1975). Most Tibetan schools emphasize the experience of clear light as a marker of enlightenment, and the realization of emptiness. On the vision of the clear light at death, see Lati and Hopkins (1979), p. 18. On its equation with the Dharmakāya, see Freemantle and Trungpa (1975), p. 59.

Fearsome, demonic looking, adorned with garlands of skulls, blood drinking, in sexual union with their consorts, their buddhahood is even harder for bardo-beings to recognize, and most proceed on their way and enter what is known as the bardo of becoming which will lead them towards rebirth.[36]

According to the *Tibetan Book of the Dead*, the visions of the five tathāgatas, in both their benign and wrathful forms, are opportunities to have an experience of the sambhogakāya (following, at the moment of death, the opportunity to encounter the dharmakāya). In the final bardo of becoming, beings still have an opportunity to alter their karma so that they will be reborn in a place in which they will be able to meet a nirmānakāya, a magically fashioned body with which the Buddha appears in our world. But again, few take advantage of this opportunity.[37]

8.6.5 Buddha Embodiments in This World: Gurus and Tülkus

The hope to meet a buddha in one's next life brings us back again, full circle, to the early Buddhist desire to make merit, take action, so as to "catch" Maitreya or some other buddha-to-come in a future existence. The Mahāyāna/ Vajrayāna buddhology which we have just looked at, however, vastly increases the opportunities for such a meeting to take place.

When Tibetans take refuge in the Buddha, the Dharma, and the Saṃgha, they commonly add to the top of this list a "fourth" refuge: their teacher, their guru (lama [bla ma]). This is, of course, just a ritual, but it is in recognition of the fact that the teacher is "present and active," "there for them" – the embodiment of the Buddha's compassion in the here and now. In this sense, having a teacher who imparts the Dharma to one is another way of meeting the Buddha even though he is no more. Some Tibetans, in fact, affirm that the teacher is even more important than the Buddha precisely because he is not "absent." Such sentiments gave rise in Tibet to a great emphasis on guru devotion.[38]

Some Tibetan teachers, however, are more explicitly recognized as "embodiments" of the Buddha. The Tibetan word "tülku" (sprul sku) which is generally rendered into English as "incarnation" or "incarnate lama" is

36 On the wrathful form of buddhas in Tibetan iconography and ideology, see Linrothe (1999).
37 On this, see Freemantle and Trungpa (1975), p. 59.
38 See, for example, Sparham (1999).

actually a translation of the Sanskrit word "nirmāṇakāya" (see 8.2). Incarnate lamas are thus, philologically at least, magically fashioned bodies – manifestations – of the Buddha. They are also incarnations of the previous incarnation in their particular line, as though the Buddha magically fashioned not single bodies, but whole lineages of them. In this way, the present Panchen Lama, for instance, is thought to be a manifest embodiment of the Buddha Amitābha, but he is also a new manifestation in a lineage that included all the previous Panchen lamas. New incarnations, in any lineage of tülkus, are typically discovered when they are still very young (sometimes after the "testing" of a number of finalist candidates), and then trained in "the art of being buddhas," a parallel, perhaps, to the way that new buddha images need to be consecrated by being infused with buddha-qualities.

There are, in Tibet and in the Tibetan diaspora, hundreds of lineages of tülkus – manifest embodiments. The most famous one, of course, is the Dalai Lama, the spiritual head of Tibetans and also, until recently, their governmental leader. The Dalai Lama is sometimes called, in the popular press, a "living Buddha"; in fact, he is technically considered to be a manifestation not of the Buddha but of the bodhisattva Avalokiteśvara (Tib., Chenrézik). Avalokiteśvara, as we have seen, is the bodhisattva of compassion par excellence, and especially important to Tibetans as a kind of patron deity of that country.[39]

8.7 SUMMARY

In chapter 3, we examined a number of ways in which Buddhists have sought to overcome the "absence" of the Buddha after his parinirvāṇa by asserting his "presence" in the Dharma, in various pilgrimage sites, and in objects of devotion such as relics and images. We also saw how Buddhist legend provides another way of dealing with "our" Buddha's absence by anticipating the coming of the future Buddha Maitreya. In this chapter, we turned to the Mahāyāna tradition to discuss various other possibilities of meeting the Buddha/s in other "places" (such as the pure land, maṇḍalas, and the bardo), or in meditative visualizations in this life. All of these buddhological developments were informed by and influential on changes in Buddhist doctrine to which we must now turn.

39 On the selection of the Dalai Lama, see 13.2.1.

Chapter 9

Māhāyana Doctrinal Developments

In chapters 4 and 5, we examined some of the basic doctrinal configurations of early Buddhism – the Middle Way and the Four Truths. As the Buddhist tradition moved into East Asia and to Tibet, and as different Mahāyāna Buddhist schools of thought emerged, these basic configurations were not abandoned, but they were elaborated and added onto in a variety of ways. We have already looked, in the last chapter, at developments in buddhology by examining the question of where Mahāyānists and Vajrayānists thought they could "meet" the buddha/s. These developments are not unrelated to more general changes in Buddhist doctrines, which we shall explore in this chapter. We will start with the doctrine of emptiness (śūnyatā) (9.1), and its philosophical formulation by Nāgārjuna (9.2). We will then consider the notion of expedient means (upāya) (9.3), before looking at doctrines of the Chinese Tiantai school (9.4), of the Yogācāra school (9.5), and of the Flower Garland (Avataṃsaka) tradition (9.6). We will then finally explore the implications and ramifications of the Buddha Womb/Embryo (tathāgatagarbha) teaching (9.7), and the concomitant doctrine of the Buddha-nature (9.8). In each of these instances, we will also be moving from India to East Asia and/or Tibet.

9.1 EMPTINESS: THE SELFLESSNESS OF DHARMAS

The roots of the doctrine of "emptiness" may be found in Mainstream Buddhism, but it was in the Mahāyāna that it became a doctrine of fundamental importance. Around the start of the common era, there began to appear in India a new kind of Buddhist literature known as the Perfection of Wisdom (Prajñāpāramitā). The first text in this genre was probably that which came to be known as the *Perfection of Wisdom Sūtra in Eight Thousand Lines* (*Aṣṭasāhasrikā prajñāpāramitā*). Over the centuries, this basic work was both expanded into texts numbering 18,000, 25,000, and even 100,000 lines, and also condensed into shorter texts of 700, 500, and 300 lines (such as the *Diamond Sūtra* (*Vajracchedikā prajñāpāramitā*)), or even shorter works of just one page (such as the *Heart Sūtra* (*Prajñāpāramitā hṛdaya*), or even a single letter (the Letter "A"). The fact that, in this school of thought, the same basic message can be said to be contained in one letter, one page, or thousands of pages should warn us that we are entering a new world where language can operate in new ways and be both a trap and a liberation.[1]

One of the thrusts of the Perfection of Wisdom literature was to propound a doctrine known as "emptiness" (śūnyatā; Ch., kong; Jpn., kū; Tib., tongpa-nyi [stong pa nyid]), which one scholar has described as "refer[ring] to what dharmas (elements of reality) really are through what they are not" (Jackson, 2004, p. 809). What they *are not* is pretty clear: they are not what Mainstream Abhidharmists thought they were, i.e. real, independent, indivisible "atoms" with their own inherent unchanging existence (svabhāva – what philosophers call "quiddity" – see 4.3.2). What they *really are* is more difficult to explain.

As we have seen in 4.3.1, one of the hallmarks of early Mainstream Buddhism was to undermine the false notion of an unchanging eternal Self (Ātman) by means of an analysis of "persons" or "things," first into the different aggregates (skandhas) and then, more thoroughly, into various kinds of elements (dharmas). Even though these dharmas (or the vast majority of them that are conditioned) exist only for a split second, they are thought, in Mainstream Buddhism, to be ultimately "real" in that they have inherent self-existence ("svabhāva"). They form, so to speak, the building blocks of all that there is. The early Mahāyānists were critical of this atomistic assumption. Why stop, they asked, at the breakdown of the self of the person only to affirm the indivisibility of the dharmas, i.e. their svabhāva? If every person is selfless, shouldn't the dharmas that make up that person be selfless as well?

This move can easily be seen in the *Heart Sūtra* (*Prajñāpāramitāhṛdaya sūtra*), one of the shortest and best-known of the Perfection of Wisdom

1 On emptiness in Mainstream Buddhism, see Choong (1999), and Gómez (1977). For a survey of Perfection of Wisdom literature, see Conze (1960). For a translation of the sūtra in eight thousand lines, see Conze (1973). For translations of the shorter Perfection of Wisdom texts, including the *Heart* and *Diamond* sūtras (and the *Sūtra of the Blessed Perfection of Wisdom, the Mother of all the Tathāgatas, in One Letter*), see Conze (1974). For a translation of a longer one, see Conze (1975).

texts. Its brevity has made it the most frequently copied sūtra in the whole of Buddhist East Asia, and also one of the most popularly chanted texts in liturgical rituals in various Mahāyāna schools. In Japan, for instance, it remains today one of the few Buddhist sūtras that many lay devotees know by heart. It can be used in ritual, for meditation, for magical protection, in Tantric practices, for exorcism, etc., but here we shall look at it for its doctrinal content.[2]

It starts with a reference to an enlightened being, the bodhisattva Avalokiteśvara, contemplating the five aggregates (skandhas – see 4.3.1), and seeing that they are all empty of inherent self-existence. He then goes on to contemplate the dharmas (see 4.3.2), the elements of reality, and likewise realizes that they too are empty of any such svabhāva. They are without their own characteristics. This does not mean, however, that they do not exist. The *Heart Sūtra* goes on to make it clear that this only means that they do not exist in the way that the Mainstream Abhidharmists thought they existed, namely, they have no svabhāva. And in so far as unenlightened beings such as ourselves tend to think like Abhidharmists, they do not exist in any way we can easily conceptualize. All of this is summed up in a Sanskrit mantra at the very end of the *Heart Sūtra*: "gaté gaté pāragaté pārasaṃgaté bodhi svāhā." Roughly translated (the grammar of the mantra is disputed), this means: "Gone, gone, gone beyond, gone altogether beyond, Awakening!"[3]

The Mahāyāna doctrine of emptiness (like this mantra perhaps) seeks to force us to think in new ways about dharmas, and consequently in new ways about reality itself. And here we can see again the middle way character of Buddhism: emptiness represents a middle way between two binary opposites – the existence and non-existence of dharmas – poles which, in our present way of thinking, have no room for a middle way between them! Until we change our world view (by becoming enlightened), perhaps the best way to imagine these "empty dharmas" is by bouncing them off the two extremes of existence and non-existence (although this too may ultimately be said to be inadequate).[4]

2 On the many uses of the text, see Lopez (1996). Because of its condensed and abstruse nature, it has been the subject of numerous commentaries (see Lopez, 1988; McRae, 1988).

3 For a translation of the whole *Heart Sūtra*, see Conze (1958), pp. 77–107, and Strong (2008), pp. 154–155. It has been argued that the text was originally written in Chinese and then rendered into Sanskrit, in a reversal of the normal pattern (see Nattier, 1992).

4 A number of scholars have compared the change from a Mainstream Abhidharmist world view to the emptiness doctrine as akin to the move from Western classical physics to quantum theory. On this, see Ames (2003), and Zeilinger (2003).

By way of illustration, let me interject here a personal anecdote. Many years ago, in 1972, when my wife and I were living and studying among Tibetans in Dharamsala, in Northern India, we had an audience with the Dalai Lama. In those days, such things could be arranged rather readily, for His Holiness had a generous policy of agreeing to receive privately resident Western students who asked to see him. After a wide-ranging conversation on all sorts of things, our questions turned to the doctrine of emptiness. At this, His Holiness became quite animated, and, in order to illustrate for us the concept, he began pounding his right knee with his right hand exclaiming, in English, "Exists! Exists! Exists!" while gradually moving his left hand over. But then, just as his left hand was about to reach his right knee, he switched it back and began pounding his left knee: "Not exists! Not exists! Not exists!" Then back to his right: "Exists! Exists! Exists!" The message we got from this was clear: above all do not come to a halt at either of the extremes – do not think of emptiness as nothingness (nihilism), and do not think of it either as somethingness (eternalism). And if you cannot do this, as soon as you think of it as "nothing" make sure you correct that by thinking of it as "something."

The Dalai Lama's message may be found restated and expounded upon in the so-called *Treatise on the Great Perfection of Wisdom* (*Mahāprajñāpāramitā-śāstra*; Ch., *Dazhidu lun*), a truly monumental work that presents itself as a commentary on one of the large Perfection of Wisdom sūtras. The work, wrongly attributed to Nāgārjuna, is extant only in a Chinese translation by Kumārajīva done at the very beginning of the fifth century CE. The original was probably compiled in Northwest India or Central Asia towards the start of the fourth century CE and may be seen as a Mahāyānist reply to the Abhidharma teachings of the Sarvāstivādins.[5] In it, we can read:

> Everlasting – that is one extreme; passing away – that is another extreme; give up these two extremes to go on the Middle Way – that is the Perfection of Wisdom. Permanence is one extreme, impermanence is another; give up these two extremes to go on the Middle Way – that is the Perfection of Wisdom ... The existence of all dharmas is one extreme, the nonexistence of all dharmas is another; give up these two extremes to go on the Middle Way – that is the Perfection of Wisdom ... *That this is the Perfection of Wisdom – that is one extreme,*

5 On the authorship and date of the *Mahāprajñāpāramitā-śāstra*, see Lamotte (1949–1980), vol. 3, p. xiv [in French]. In the same work, Lamotte offers, in 2,500 pages, a still-only-partial but brilliantly annotated translation of the Chinese text.

that this is not the Perfection of Wisdom – that is another; give up these two extremes to go on the Middle Way – that is the Perfection of Wisdom.

(Strong, 2008, p. 156, emphasis added)

9.2 NĀGĀRJUNA AND THE MADHYAMAKA

One of the great systematizers and clarifiers of the Perfection of Wisdom's doctrine of emptiness was the philosopher Nāgārjuna (c. 150–250 CE) who, along with Āryadeva (c. 170–270 CE), founded the Madhyamaka (Middle Way) school of Buddhist thought. We know very little about Nāgārjuna's life, although legends about him abound. His major philosophical work was his *Root Verses on the Middle Way* (*Mūlamadhyamakakārikā*), whose terse and pregnant style made it and continues to make it the subject of much study and commentary. In addition, Nāgārjuna authored letters and hymns. For instance, his *Letter to a Friend* (*Suhṛlekkha*) advises an unnamed king how to cultivate insight but also how to do good and practice compassion in ruling his kingdom. In his *Hymn to the Inconceivable [Buddha]* (*Acintyastava*), he praises the Buddha, but as someone who has understood emptiness.[6]

In addition to the *Root Verses on the Middle Way*, two other philosophical treatises, one by Nāgārjuna and one by Āryadeva, became, in Chinese translation, the basis for the "Three Treatises school" (Ch., Sanlun; Jpn., Sanron), as Madhyamaka was known in East Asia (see 7.5.2). The school counts among its formative figures the translator Kumārajīva, and his disciple, Sengzhao (374–414), but the greatest of Sanlun teachers and the person who is often credited with its establishment as an institution was Jizang (549–623). One of Jizang's disciples was responsible for the transmission of Sanlun teachings to Japan, where the school survived for a bit as Sanron, one of the six Nāra schools. In both China and Japan, however, Sanlun/Sanron was pretty much eclipsed as an institution by the end of the eighth century.[7]

---

6 On Nāgārjuna's life and context, see Walser (2005; 2010). See also Ray (1997). For an introduction to and translation of the *Root Verses*, see Garfield (1995). For translations of other works by Nāgārjuna, see Lindtner (1986), and Westerhoff (2010a). On Madhyamaka literature in general, see Ruegg (1981). On Nāgārjuna's thought, see Westerhoff (2009). For a translation of *Letter to a Friend*, see Beyer (1974), pp. 10–18. For a translation of the *Hymn to the Inconceivable*, see Lindtner (1986), pp. 12–31.

7 On Madhyamaka in China, see Robinson (1976), and Liu (1994). On the six Nara schools, see Matsunaga and Matsunaga (1976), vol. 1, pp. 26–138.

In India and Tibet, the Madhyamaka became a major Buddhist school of thought that eventually came to be split into two branches – the Svātantrika ("Autonomists") and Prāsangika ("Consequentialists") – which differed primarily on their use of logic and the kind of argumentation they were willing to accept in propounding the view of emptiness. Retrospectively, the former came to be associated with the figure of Bhāvaviveka (*c.*500–570), and the latter with the views of Buddhapālita (*c.*470–540), and Candrakīrti (*c.*600–650), and, to some extent Śāntideva (*c.*680–760).[8]

To make matters more complicated, when Madhyamaka thought was first introduced into Tibet in the eighth century, it was established by Śantarakṣita (*c.*725–790) and his disciple Kamalaśīla (*c.*740–795), both of whom propounded, in addition to Bhāvaviveka's views, a kind of synthesis of Madhyamaka and Yogācāra. Later, after the second dissemination of Buddhism into Tibet, Candrakīrti's works came more to the fore, and the Prāsangika view remains dominant in Tibet up to the present, at least in Géluk circles. Candrakīrti, it might be added, was also a magician, who could demonstrate to his disciples the mind-made empty nature of things by walking through walls, and (going one step further) by giving the whole community "real" milk to drink, which he milked from the "picture" of a "cow" he drew on the "wall."[9]

Returning to Nāgārjuna, and using his work to generalize broadly about the whole of the Madhyamaka tradition, it is possible to enumerate a number of key points.

(1) Nāgārjuna occasionally claims that all he is doing is using argument to show that the philosophical assertions of others are ultimately not based on reason, but can be shown, through argument, to be self-contradictory and untenable. Most immediately, emptiness (śūnyatā) is a critique of the extremes of nihilism and eternalism, but it is extendable to all other "views," all other tenets. In this light, emptiness itself is not a philosophical position; if it were it would not be a method for realizing the middle way, but would itself be a "view" open to the same kind of criticism that Nāgārjuna directs towards all "views." This is part of what Nāgārjuna means when he declares

---

8 The translations "Autonomists" and "Consequentialists" are taken from Buswell and Lopez (2014), p. 883. On the Svātantrika, see Lopez (1987). On Bhāvaviveka, see Eckel (2009). On Candrakīrti, see Vose (2009). For an introduction to Śāntideva, and a translation of one of his major works, see Crosby and Skilton (1995).

9 For a helpful survey of the overall development of Madhyamaka, see Lang (2004). The story of Candrakīrti milking the picture of a cow is taken from Chimpa and Chattopadhyaya (1970), p. 199.

that emptiness is itself "empty." He claims to set up no tenets of his own, only to dismantle the tenets of others. Indeed, in the *Root Verses on the Middle Way* 13, verse 8, he declares that those who posit emptiness as a tenet are doomed to accomplish nothing.[10]

(2) Because of this, as we shall see, some have asserted that Nāgārjuna is nothing more than a nay-sayer, denying all realities. For Nāgārjuna, this would be a bad misunderstanding; it would be to fall into the trap of nihilism, which is precisely one of the extremes he wants to avoid. Nāgārjuna is such a thoroughgoing nay-sayer that he says "no" even to nihilism. At the same time, there is a difference between saying "no" to reality and saying "no" to descriptions of reality.

(3) In fact, Nāgārjuna argues that only with emptiness is reality as we know and experience it possible, in all of its constant changes and transformations. According to him, the (wrong) view that dharmas have inherent self-existence (svabhāva) would mean that they are each eternal, and so that they are static, unchangeable, not subject to causes or conditions. In such a frozen world, merit making involving karma, and meditation aiming at enlightenment would be impossible. Thus, in his *Root Verses on the Middle Way*, when a putative opponent objects that, "if everything is empty," there can be no arising or passing away of stress (i.e. no Four Truths, no nirvāṇa, no Buddha, no Buddhism), Nāgārjuna turns the tables on him and replies that it is *only* if we accept the emptiness of all these things that there can be arising and passing of stress, etc. In fact, for him, emptiness may be equated with the doctrine of interdependent origination (pratītyasamutpāda), which we examined in 5.2.

(4) Nāgārjuna, however, recognized that, ultimately, such assertions could be problematical. Perhaps for this reason, he accepted the premise (already found incipient in Mainstream Buddhism) that there are actually two truths, two legitimate ways of seeing things: worldly conventional (or provisional) truth (saṃvṛtisatya), and ultimate (or final object) truth (paramārthasatya). To speak of dharmas as interacting with one another, to speak of causes and consequences, is legitimate *conventionally*. In fact, as Nāgārjuna makes it clear in his *Root Verses on the Middle Way*, it is absolutely necessary, for without these concepts, without these words, there would be no way to speak validly or meaningfully about emptiness, about the ultimate. As he puts it: "The ultimate cannot be taught without resorting to conventions; and without

10 See on this Garfield (1995), pp. 212–215. On the emptiness of emptiness see Huntington (1989).

recourse to the ultimate, one cannot reach nirvāṇa" (Strong, 2008, p. 159). The notion of conventional truth is thus crucial for Nāgārjuna because he realizes that, without such a thing, words, concepts, teachings, his own philosophical arguments, etc., would have no validity, and the world would be a random, chaotic place. This does not mean, however, that all language and concepts were to be accepted as "truths." Those that led to a realization of ultimate truth could be, but notions such as "I have a Self," or "the world is eternal," etc., are just plain false.[11]

(5) In this light, it can be said that Nāgārjuna provides a new approach to the problem of cohesiveness and continuity of the self that we examined in 4.3. There, we saw that if our experience of the world and of ourselves is likened to a string of beads (dharmas), one of the problems is finding the glue or the thread that holds them together. Rather than look for some kind of pseudo-self that can act as a glue or thread, Nāgārjuna simply changes the whole premise of that world view: he deconstructs the notion that what we start with are "beads," by declaring that the dharmas are empty of "bead-like nature," i.e. of svabhāva. In the absence of "beads" (or of a string), the question of continuity becomes radically transformed. It thus becomes understandable why Nāgārjuna equates emptiness with the truth of interdependent origination, with the more radical understanding that, within this process, there are no "things" (i.e. intrinsic dharmas) originating or ceasing, but only origination and cessation. As one scholar put it, for Nāgārjuna, "existing is nothing more than an intersecting point of causal factors" (Williams, 2004, p. 581).

(6) At a less philosophical level it can be seen that Nāgārjuna effectively breaks down the barriers – *all* barriers – between people, things, concepts. By emptying out the dharmas of any self-existence, he makes them "selfless," and this means that there are no longer any divisions between beings, between objects, between conceptual oppositions or dichotomies. When black is defined as "black," i.e. as something having inherent self-existence as black, it will clearly be different than, separate from, "white." However, when inherent self-existence is done away with in emptiness, there can ultimately be no real difference, no barrier, between "black" and "white." More importantly, there can ultimately be no real difference, no real distinction or separation between existence and non-existence, between good and bad,

11 On the two truths in Mainstream Buddhism, see La Vallée Poussin (1988–1990), vol. 3, p. 910, and Hirakawa (1990), pp. 143–144. On the two truths in Tibetan Mādhyamika, see Newland (1992).

between purity and impurity, between subject and object, between male and female, between self and non-self, between Buddha and sentient being, etc. All these views were to have a lot of impact on subsequent Buddhist thought, and we will encounter them again in such things as Zen and Tantra (chapter 10). Perhaps the most significant extension of this line of reasoning, however, was Nāgārjuna's declaration that ultimately, "there is no distinction whatsoever between saṃsāra and nirvāṇa, *and* [just to make sure that the equation is clear and not lopsided] there is no distinction whatsoever between nirvāṇa and saṃsāra" (Strong, 2008, p. 162). Since both nirvāṇa and saṃsāra are empty of inherent self-existence, there are no borders between them. This, as we shall see, was to be a very significant insight, since it meant that this world of suffering, of stress, i.e. saṃsāra, was no longer to be seen as an arena to be abandoned in enlightenment for some other world or mindset, or even for some non-world – some negation of this world.[12]

(7) Nāgārjuna is clear, however, that such assertions about the absence of barriers between polar opposites, about the identity of black and white, of saṃsāra and nirvāṇa, do not mean that "all is one" – that we live in a monistic universe in which there is a single all-pervasive reality – emptiness. For one thing, that would make emptiness into "some-one-thing," and, as we have seen, Nāgārjuna was very clear that emptiness was itself empty. In fact, he was as suspicious of monism as he was of radical atomistic pluralism, and saw both as extremes to be avoided. The Tibetan poet/saint Milarépa put the point nicely. After proclaiming that, at the "stage of One-Taste," one realizes the identity of saṃsāra and nirvāṇa, he adds this caveat: "He who says that 'all is one' is still discriminating; in the Stage of One-Taste, there is no such blindness" (Chang, 1962, p. 31).

9.3 THE EXPANSION OF PROVISIONAL TRUTH: EXPEDIENT MEANS (UPĀYA)

It is fair to say that the Perfection of Wisdom and Madhyamaka thought were a sort of fillip for many other Mahāyāna doctrines. Some schools of thought developed particular aspects of it, others reacted against it, but all were influenced by it. It is not possible, in a work such as this, to trace the history of all these developments so, in what follows, I will limit myself to a few examples.

12 On the breakdown of difference between binary opposites, see Lang (2004).

The Madhyamaka's twin notions that saṃsāra = nirvāṇa, and that there can be provisional or conventional truths that are valid in that they are effective in leading to the ultimate truth, opened the way for the important Mahāyāna doctrine of upāya – expedient means (also called skillful means or skill-in-means). According to this, anything taught by the Buddha or by other enlightened teachers that leads one to a final realization of buddhahood is, in a sense, "true," or at least valid.

Precursors of the doctrine of upāya may be found in Mainstream Buddhism, but it was in Mahāyāna literature that it gained in importance. Here, I shall focus on an example from a text that we are already familiar with: the *Lotus Sūtra*. As mentioned, the oldest parts of the *Lotus Sūtra* were probably written around the beginning of the common era, in Sanskrit, in India, but it was in East Asia that the text achieved fame and prominence. It was translated a number of times into Chinese, but by far the most popular rendition was that of Kumārajīva, done in the year 406 CE. The sūtra was widely popular; it became a foundational text for the Tiantai (Jpn., Tendai) school systematized by Zhiyi (538–597) and later transmitted to Japan by Saichō (767–822). In time, it also became a salvational text for the Nichiren school of Japanese Buddhism and its various offshoots up to the present day.[13]

The doctrine of upāya (Ch., fangbian; Jpn., hōben; Tib., thabs) is often expressed in the *Lotus Sūtra* by means of parables. One of these is the story of the Phantom City, which may be briefly told as follows: a group of merchants hear that there is a land far away that contains unimaginable treasures. Under the guidance of a wise caravan leader, they set out across a vast empty wilderness in order to reach it. But the route is much longer and harder than they thought, and they soon become exhausted and discouraged. They tell their leader they want to give up and turn back. He encourages them to persevere, but they will not hear of it. So, being "a man of many expedients," and possessed of magical powers, he conjures up for them on the horizon the image of a great city, an oasis in the desert, and tells them that they will be able to rest there and then decide whether or not to go on. Accordingly, the caravan moves on and enters the city, and the merchants are able to rest and recover. The caravan leader then wipes out the phantom city and says to the group: "You must go now. The place where the treasure is close by. That great city of a while ago was a mere phantom that I conjured up so that you could rest"

13 On the *Lotus Sūtra* in different contexts, see Teiser and Stone (2009). Other sūtras famous for their presentation of upāya include the *Vimalakīrti nirdeśa* and the *Upāyakauśālya*. On Upāya, see also Pye (1978).

(Watson, 1993, p. 136). The text then explains that the caravan leader is the Buddha; the merchants are his disciples; the wilderness is saṃsāra, and the treasure they seek is buddhahood. The phantom city is the expedient means he devises to encourage his disciples on their way. It is illusory, but, importantly, it provides real rest. It corresponds to arhatship – the enlightenment of Mainstream Buddhists.

The same message is driven home in the more famous but more complex parable of the burning house that is found in the third chapter of the text. A rich man (= the Buddha) owns an old mansion (= saṃsāra) that catches on fire. He manages to get out but his little boys (= his disciples) are still inside. Unaware even that the place is burning (= their ignorance), they are happily playing and enjoying themselves. The father needs to find a way to lure them out. He realizes it will not do to run in and get them, since they will all run helter-skelter; he realizes that it will not do to shout "Fire!" since they are ignorant and, not knowing what to do, may panic. So he calls to them and tells them to come out and see the new toys he has gotten for them: a little deer cart (= the way to arhatship, the vehicle of the śrāvaka [disciples]); a little goat cart (= the vehicle of the pratyekabuddhas); and a little ox cart (= the vehicle of the bodhisattvas). In fact, he has none of these, but they do the trick. The boys come out; they are disappointed not to find the promised toy carts but comforted to all be given a single Great Ox Cart – the way of Buddhahood. From this, one of the major thrusts of the *Lotus Sūtra* becomes clear: the "three vehicles" (triyāna) of early Buddhism are shown to be provisional truths, expedient means for finding the "one vehicle" (ekayāna) of all to buddhahood. From this perspective, Mainstream Buddhist practices are not to be rejected; they are merely to be seen as way stations on what turns out to be the Mahāyāna path. This fact is reinforced in the sūtra by the Buddha's revelation to various of his disciples become arhats (e.g. Śāriputra) that they, in fact, though previously unbeknownst to them, are destined to become buddhas in the future.[14]

The *Lotus Sūtra*'s elaboration on the doctrine of upāya does not stop here, however. The Buddha also goes on to show how all the events of his own life – his birth, his striving for and attaining enlightenment, his First Sermon, his parinirvāṇa – can all be understood as not being final realities, but expedient means aimed at encouraging others to practice.

14 Watson (1993), pp. 57–73.

9.4 TIANTAI DOCTRINES

The *Lotus Sūtra*, as mentioned, was influential in the formation of a number of East Asian Mahāyāna schools. One of these was the Tiantai tradition, one of the so-called "systematic schools" (7.5.2) of Chinese Buddhism, whose de facto founder was the sixth-century monk, Zhiyi. The Tiantai school was, in fact, sometimes called "the Lotus school."[15] Here, I want to present a few of the ways in which upāya became incorporated into its principal doctrines.

In the *Lotus*, as we have just seen, upāya is a doctrine that allows for the incorporation of all Buddhist teachings into a single system whose singularity is only realized thanks to the teaching of the *Lotus Sūtra*. It assumes that, out of compassion, the Buddha addressed different beings according to their differing capacities for understanding. This view eventually came to define the Tiantai's classification of the Buddha's teaching (something that is known in Chinese as "panjiao" – "taxonomy of the teachings"), as well as its description of the Buddha's preaching career. According to the monk Zhiyi, the Buddha, immediately after his enlightenment, preached the *Avataṃsaka Sūtra* (see 9.6). This fully expressed what he wanted to say, but no one understood it. So, the Buddha resorted to expedient means. For the next twenty years, he preached the sūtras that became basic to Mainstream Buddhism; then he taught the Perfection of Wisdom and the emptiness doctrine; then he taught more advanced Mahāyāna texts such as the Vaipulya ("developed") sūtras. Finally, in his last days, he taught the *Lotus Sūtra* (as well as the *Nirvāṇa Sūtra* – see 9.8).[16]

But the Tiantai tradition was also to expand its understanding of the notion of expedient means in the development of its signature doctrine of the three truths: provisional, empty, and middle. Nāgārjuna, as we have seen, posited two truths: conventional (or provisional) and ultimate (= emptiness). Thus, for example, a chair can provisionally or conventionally be called a chair since it has arisen through various causes and conditions. It ultimately, however, is completely empty of any inherent self-existence, and so does not exist as a "chair." For Nāgārjuna, these two truths were stacked hierarchically, so to speak. The provisional truth led to but then was eclipsed by the ultimate truth. In this sense it was "merely" expedient means. Zhiyi and the Tiantai tradition, however, saw the provisional as "both a means to

15 For translations of Tiantai texts on the *Lotus Sūtra*, see Tsugunari et al. (2013).
16 Lusthaus (1998a).

and an expression of the ultimate truth. [In other words,] provisional and ultimate truth are nondual, even while maintaining their strict opposition" (Ziporyn, 2004, p. 846, emphasis added). This non-duality is embodied in the notion of the "middle" truth, in which there is no distinction between provisional and empty, no hierarchical relation between them.

Along with and as a consequence of this annulment of the hierarchy between provisional and ultimate truth, Zhiyi also expanded the notion of "provisional" to include all things and thoughts, even false and deluded ones. Armed with the notion of non-dualism, and inspired by Nāgārjuna's equation of saṃsāra and nirvāṇa, Zhiyi eliminated (or perhaps better, complexly recast) distinctions between defiled and non-defiled, good and evil. Now, any view (whether Buddhist or not), any thought (whether moral or not) could be both a stepping stone to realization and an expression of it. As one scholar put it: "Rather than attempt to eliminate deluded thinking to reach a purified mind, Zhiyi claimed each moment of deluded thinking was already identical to enlightenment. One merely has to see the mind and its operations as they are [i.e. as "middle"]. This idea was later taken over by the Chan (Zen) school which expressed it in sayings such as 'Zen mind is everyday mind'" (Lusthaus, 1998).[17] This, as we shall see, was to have important consequences, and was a view that got reflected in notions of the Buddha-nature and in Avataṃsaka (9.6) thought.

9.5 THE ONGOING DIALECTIC: THE YOGĀCĀRA SCHOOL

Despite the Madhyamaka's insistence that emptiness did not mean nihilism but rather that it kept active a middle way position, a number of Mahāyāna schools of thought did not see it that way. For them it was a doctrine that inclined too far towards the negativistic extreme, and was in need of correction, or at least of interpretation. In what follows, I want to look at one example of a teaching that, rightly or wrongly, sought to give more content, or, perhaps better, context, to the notion of emptiness.

The Yogācāra view can be introduced with the notion of the Three Turnings of the Wheel of Dharma, first presented in the *Sūtra on Explaining the Real Meaning* (*Saṃdhinirmocana Sūtra*), which dates from about the fourth century CE. According to this, the Buddha, in his First Sermon at the Deer Park in Sarnath, preached a view that denied the existence of an Ātman but

17 See also Ziporyn (2000) on this aspect of Zhiyi's thought.

affirmed the reality of the dharmas. This was the first turn of the Wheel of Dharma and can generally be equated with Mainstream Buddhism. Later, however, in the Perfection of Wisdom teachings, the Buddha proclaimed the emptiness of those dharmas and posited the Absolute in negative terms. This was the second turning of the Wheel of Dharma, and corresponds to the Madhyamaka and the emptiness doctrine, or at least a particular interpretation of it. Both the first and the second turnings were true, but not literally so; they were said to be neyārtha – doctrines that needed to be interpreted, to have their "meaning drawn out." The third turning of the Wheel of Dharma claims to state the Buddha's views directly in a way that is nītārtha – needing no interpretation. This is identified as the teachings of the Yogācāra (Yoga Practice) school.[18]

9.5.1 Asanga and Vasubandhu and the Development of the School

The Yogācāra school has been said to provide "perhaps the most sophisticated examination and description in all of Buddhism of how the mind works – in psychological, epistemological, logical, emotional, cognitive, meditative, developmental, and soteriological modes" (Lusthaus, 2004, p. 914). Because of this, the school is sometimes called the "Mind-Only" or "Consciousness-Only" teachings. The recognized founders of the school were the half-brothers Asanga and Vasubandhu (fourth to fifth century CE), who were originally Mainstream Buddhists before being converted to the Mahāyāna – Asanga supposedly by the bodhisattva Maitreya who is said to have dictated new texts to him, and Vasubandhu, somewhat later, by Asanga. Both scholars became prolific writers of treatises and commentaries, in which they systematized and developed teachings already found to some extent in the *Saṃdhinirmocana Sūtra*.[19]

In time, in India, the Yogācāra school divided into what one author has called "a logico-epistemic tradition" represented most notably by the scholars

---

18 For translations of the *Saṃdhinirmocana Sūtra* from the Chinese and from the Tibetan, see Keenan (2000), and Powers (1995). For a discussion of nītārtha and neyārtha, a concept traceable to Mainstream sources, see La Vallée Poussin (1988–1990), vol. 4, pp. 1363–1364, and Karunadasa (n.d.).

19 On Asanga and Vasubandhu and their conversion, see Davidson (1985), pp. 20–25, and Wayman (1997), pp. 89–148. See also Sakuma (2013). For references to translations of Asanga's works, see Lugli (2014). For translations of some of Vasubandhu's works, see Anacker (1984).

Dignāga (480–540) and Dharmakīrti (*c*.600–670), and "an abhidharma-style psychology" (Lusthaus, 2004, p. 915), represented by Sthiramati (510–570), and later by the Chinese pilgrim Xuanzang (600–664). Other divisions occurred when Yogācāra thought became established in China, first, between the Northern and Southern "Dilun" schools that disagreed on the interpretation of a commentary attributed to Vasubandhu ("Dilun" is the Chinese name of Vasubandhu's *Explanation of the Scripture of the Ten Stages* [*Daśabhūmikavyākhyāna*]). Later there was a divergence between the Dilun school and the "Shelun" school based on a text written by Asanga ("Shelun" is the Chinese name of Asanga's *Summary of the Great Vehicle* [*Mahāyānasaṃgraha*]). The Shelun school was more specifically associated with the great translator of philosophical texts, Paramārtha (499–569) who promulgated his own synthesis of Yogācāra and Womb of the Buddha (tathāgatagarbha) teaching, most notably by inventing an additional consciousness which he called the "immaculate consciousness" (amalavijñāna) and which he identified with the tathāgatagarbha. A few generations later, yet another Yogācāra school known as Weishi (Consciousness-Only) or Faxiang ("Dharma Characteristics") was established by Kuiji (632–82), one of the two chief disciples of the great scholar-traveler, Xuanzang, who had brought new Yogācāra texts back from India and on their basis sought to reconcile some of the factional disputes that had arisen in China. Instead, it itself became an object of controversy, in part because it rejected the notion of a tathāgatagarbha and, alone among all Chinese sects, it accepted (or seemed to accept) the existence of icchantikas.[20]

The Faxiang school was eventually transmitted to Japan where it was known as the Hossō school, and played a role of considerable philosophical importance from the Nāra period on. In Tibet, the Yogācāra never got established as an institutionalized school, but its teachings, imported from both India and China, and translated into Tibetan from both Sanskrit and Chinese, were studied assiduously by many masters, and remain influential as part of the monastic curriculum. Moreover, some of its assumptions about the power and place of the mind became incorporated into the practice of Vajrayāna.[21]

20 Lusthaus (2004). (On icchantikas, see 9.8.1.)

21 Information on the overall history of Yogācāra is from ibid., pp. 914–915. On Hossō, see Matsunaga and Matsunaga (1976), vol. 1, pp. 76–94, and Takakusu (1947), pp. 80–95.

9.5.2 *Yogācāra Doctrines*

Despite all of these divergences, it is possible to identify some key common Yogācāra doctrines, including: (1) the notion of "cognition-only" (vijñaptimātra), (2) the theory of the "three natures" (trisvabhāva) of reality, and (3) the theory of eight consciousnesses, including the so-called storehouse (or granary) consciousness (the ālayavijñāna).

(1) Cognition-Only: the primacy of the Mind in Yogācāra thought is reflected in some of the other names for this school: Cittamātra or Vijñaptimātra, meaning Mind- or Consciousness-Only. Sometimes, it is also called Vijñānavāda, although this designation is primarily used by non-Buddhist (Hindu and Jain) philosophers to describe the Buddhist school. The name Yogācāra, however, indicates that it was also a school of Yoga-practitioners, and it may be that their philosophical theories emerged originally from meditative visualization techniques in which the concentrated mind's creative capacity was obvious.[22]

It is sometimes said that the Yogācāra is, philosophically speaking, an "idealist" school, implying that it does not believe in the reality of the external world, that it sees the world and everything in it as being nothing but a projection of our consciousness. Such a view is potentially misleading. The Yogācāra does not focus on the notion that the "outside" world is unreal; rather it seeks to examine the whole ways in which we construct the idea of an "outside" and "inside" world to begin with. In particular, it seeks to break down the notion of subject–object dualism. In a sense, this is not that different from the Madhyamaka's effort to break down dharma–dharma dualism, except that the Yogācāra carries out its project in the context of the Mind. For it does affirm that everything we know – and the way in which we know it – is filtered through the mind, including the thought of the existence or non-existence of the "external" world. Moreover, the mind is a double-edged sword. On the one hand, it can cut through our ignorance and bring us to enlightenment. On the other hand, as long as we are unenlightened, it tricks us into thinking of things as existing "out there" in particular ways, and so sets up subject–object dualisms (or as the Yogācāra texts put it, "grasper–grasped" dualisms) which perpetuate desire. Lusthaus has explained all of this well: "Although the mind does not create the physical world, it generates the interpretative categories through which we know and classify the physical world, and it does this so seamlessly that we mistake our interpretations for

22 On the connection of Yogācāra doctrine to visualization, see Williams (2009), p. 89.

the world itself. Those interpretations, which are projections of our desires and anxieties, become obstructions ... preventing us from seeing what is actually the case" (2004, p. 917). The "trick" then, in Yogācāra, is not to be tricked by the mind, but to see what it is doing and how it operates, a knowledge that can lead us to a realization of "reality as it is."

(2) The three natures (trisvabhāva): as part of its analysis of the operations of the mind, the Yogācāra posited a doctrine it called the "three self-natures" (trisvabhāva) theory, although some have argued that this label is somewhat misleading because ultimately, all of these "natures" need to be understood as "non-self natures" (niḥsvabhāva) i.e. as lacking in inherent self-existence. The first "nature" is called "parikalpita" (imaginary or falsely-constructed). This is the world of subject–object dualism, or, put another way, the world as it was posited by Mainstream Abhidharmists, the state in which we commonly operate, attributing (through our ignorance) real inherent separate existence to things, to dharmas. The second "nature" is called "paratantra" ("other-dependent"). This is the view that realizes that the identity of things depends on causes and conditions outside themselves, on their interrelationships and interactions with other things, that nothing is independent or self-existent. This view of the world is akin to the Perfection of Wisdom's notion of emptiness. The third "nature" is called parinișpanna ("perfected," or "consummate"). This is the correct direct perception of reality as it is, in its "thusness."

These three natures were interpreted in different ways in Yogācāra circles, but one of the easiest to grasp is the one that Sponberg has called the "pivotal model." According to this, the primary nature of reality is the middle one, its "other-dependent nature." Either one misperceives this – one reifies it and chops it up into "things" and "dharmas," in which case, one sees reality in its falsely-constructed nature, i.e. saṃsāra; or one directly perceives it as it is, in which case one sees reality in its consummate nature, i.e. nirvāṇa. The move from ignorance to enlightenment thus does not involve changing worlds, but changing world views. As Sponberg (1982, p. 100) puts it, "the shift from the one perspective to the other represents the fundamental reorientation of the cognitive base of our knowledge, the *āśraya-parāvṛtti* [= "turning around in the seat of enlightenment"] that is the soteriological culmination of Yogācāra praxis."[23]

23 Sponberg further distinguishes the "pivotal model" (found in the *Mahāyānasaṃgraha*) from the "progressive model" which became more established in East Asia, and which envisaged the three natures as different stages in one's realization. For another presentation of the progressive model, see d'Amato (2005).

(3) The eight consciousnesses: I shall deal with the notion of this "fundamental transformation" more later, but first, it should be pointed out that, as another part of its programmatic analysis of the operations of the mind, the Yogācāra accepted a theory of eight different consciousnesses. (Actually, this is not completely accurate since, as we have seen above, Paramārtha posited a ninth consciousness, the amalavijñāna, but we shall not be concerned with that here.)

Early Buddhism, in its abhidharmic analysis of the elements of reality, distinguished six consciousnesses: five that corresponded to the five senses (eye, ear, nose, tongue, touch) and ensured contact between those organs and corresponding sense fields or objects (shapes, sounds, smells, tastes, touches); and the sixth, the mental consciousness that similarly arose when the mind (viewed as a sort of sixth sense organ) made contact with the field of mental objects (e.g. thoughts) (see table 4.3). Uniquely, among the six senses, the mind can think about what the other senses perceived, but the other five cannot cognize one another's fields (i.e. ordinarily, the nose cannot smell sounds, but the mind can think about both smells and sounds). The Yogācārins accepted these six consciousnesses, but felt that they failed to answer two important questions. Basically, these were the same two questions that had plagued Mainstream anātman theorists: why do we think we have a self if we do not have one? And, if we do not have one, what accounts for our personal, specifically karmic, continuity (especially since our mental continuums are periodically interrupted by things such as dreamless sleep, unconsciousness, or meditative trances of cessation)?[24]

Let me address the second question first. The Yogācāra answer to the question of karmic causal continuity comes with what was probably its most distinctive tenet: the notion that in addition to the six consciousnesses, we have a kind of mental reservoir called the storehouse or granary or "substratum" (Williams, 2009, p. 97) consciousness (ālayavijñāna). This is labeled as the eighth consciousness (on the seventh, see below).

The ālayavijñāna notion has its precursors in various Mainstream attempts to explain the continuity of self or selves and karma, such as the Theravādin doctrine of cittavibhanga or the Mahāsāṃghika notion of root-consciousness (mūlavijñāna) (see 4.3.4). In fact, the ālayavijñāna is sometimes called the mūlavijñāna, but it developed that notion considerably beyond what the Mahāsāṃghikas did with it.

24 On the eight consciousnesses, see Davidson (1985), pp. 199ff. On the problem of continuity and the trance of cessation, see Griffiths (1986).

Although it is called a consciousness, the ālayavijñāna has many features that might better characterize it as an "unconscious" or "subconscious" part of the mind. Various metaphors have traditionally been used to describe it, and they are often mixed together. The storehouse (ālaya) is said to be "perfumed" by our karmic acts; in other words, our intentional acts of body, speech, and mind (which involve the first six consciousnesses) leave a scent or an impression on our ālayavijñāna. Shifting to an agricultural metaphor, those scents are said to give rise to (or are simply likened to) "seeds" that are planted in the ground or stored in the granary. In keeping with the doctrine of impermanence, these seeds are said to be momentary but they instantly give rise to other seeds, and their perfume is contagious and lingers and defines a whole chain of seeds. Like real seeds, also, the seeds (or, more technically, the chains of seeds) in the ālayavijñāna can remain dormant (i.e. unconscious) for any amount of time, from a few moments to multiple lives, until a new conscious experience causes them to sprout, i.e. to ripen. This ripening is the fruit of the karmic deed that originally was "planted," and the metaphor can help explain how it is that karmic causes and effects can be separated by time yet still have continuity, and how it is that such causal chains can survive, even when the other consciousnesses stop operating (e.g. in moments of deep dreamless sleep, in unconsciousness, or during meditative trances of cessation).

Sometimes, a different image is used and the ālayavijñāna is likened to a river, or to a great ocean in which all of our karmic actions manifest themselves as waves – disturbances in the sea of consciousness, which ever move and change until they crash or peter out upon a shore. Either way, it can be seen that the ālayavijñāna receives, contains, and generates all of the events of karma and saṃsāra. Mainstream Buddhism sought to explain karmic personal continuity in terms of glue or threads that held chains of beads together; the ālayavijñāna is more like a constantly changing matrix or internet, into which and from which our karma is constantly being uploaded and downloaded.

For practical purposes, then (although this question is complex), it can be said that we each have our own storehouse consciousness, which, in the words of Williams, is "individual, continually changing, and yet serving to give a degree of personal identity and to explain why it is that certain karmic results pertain to this particular individual" (2009, p. 97). But how does this get mistaken for an unchanging, permanent Self?

Here we come to the other question mentioned above, the Yogācāra answer to which invokes the notion of yet another consciousness – the seventh – which is variously called the "defiled (or tainted) mind" ("kliṣṭa-manas") or the "grasping consciousness" (ādāna-vijñāna), or just plain "manas" (mind). According to the Yogācārins, it is this consciousness that tricks us into thinking that we, and indeed all things, have selves, into projecting them as separate and distinct from each other and from us, and so as being desirable objects that a subject can desire. More specifically our manas (the seventh consciousness) takes our ālaya (the eighth consciousness) as its object and freezes the continuity and contiguity it sees there into an unchanging Self.

To some extent, of course, this theory is tautological – declaring, in effect, that we construct things (and ourselves) as existing separately because we have a consciousness that does that – but it has the merit of locating the problem (and hence the solution) in a specific place. Once again, it is a matter of wrongly perceiving reality-as-it-is. If we return to the "pivotal model" of the three natures described above, it is possible to think of the ālayavijñāna (the internet) as the dependent nature (paratantra). What our manas (seventh consciousness) does is falsely construct it into the imaginary nature (parikalpita). What we need to do is to have a "fundamental transformation," to put an end to this process and view it as the consummate nature (pariniṣpanna).

The question for the Yogācāra then becomes: how do we do this? The practical answer given is pretty much a generic one. As Lusthaus, again, puts it: "bad seeds and perfumings need to be filtered out, while good seeds need to be watered and cultivated ... Mental disturbances ... such as greed, hatred, delusion, arrogance, wrong views, envy, shamelessness, and so on, are gradually eliminated, while karmically wholesome mental conditions, such as nonharming, serenity, carefulness, and equanimity, are strengthened" (Lusthaus, 2004, p. 919). All this is spelled out in different Yogācāra schemes of the path.

The doctrinal description of what happens once enlightenment is attained and an end is put to karma, however, is presented in a particular Yogācāra context that makes it noteworthy. The process described above as a "fundamental transformation" (aśrayaparivṛtti) of the whole way the Mind sees the world – a "metamorphosis of the model of reality at the time of enlightenment" (Davidson, 1985, p. 155) – is described more specifically in the context of the doctrine of the eight consciousnesses. Simply put, our mind, through meditational practice, ceases its discriminatory (vijñāna) activities, and comes to have direct cognitions (jñāna). The ālayavijñāna becomes a great mirror, or perfectly smooth ocean, no longer disturbed by new waves (or no longer receiving or engendering new seeds, depending on the metaphor), but perfectly reflecting thusness. The kliṣṭa-manas, ceasing to distinguish between self and other, no longer forms false projections of self. The mental consciousness and the other five sense consciousnesses no longer erect conceptual barriers between themselves and reality, but come to direct perception of it as it is.[25]

All in all, then, for the Yogācāra, enlightenment is marked by a radical change in the perception of the "world" from mediated to unmediated, from constructed to unconstructed. This may sound as though it were not too different from the Madhyamaka's ideal of "direct perception of emptiness (śūnyatā)," and, to be sure, there are parallels. But, in the Yogācāra context, the Mind is not to be denied; it sees the emptiness of things and persons but it itself (unlike śūnyatā) is not "empty." As Williams puts it, "there remains here a really existing, pure, nonconceptual, nondual flow of awareness" (2009, p. 96). And with such a mind, an enlightened person can do much in the world.

9.6 AVATAṂSAKA DOCTRINES

We have seen that the Madhyamaka, by emptying all dharmas of their ultimately unreal inherent self-existence (svabhāva), achieves a view of a world in which no distinctions between dharmas are made: saṃsāra = nirvāṇa, sentient beings = buddhas, black = white, etc. A helpful (though perhaps a rather simplistic) way of viewing the Avataṃsaka doctrine is that it tries to assert the same non-distinction, but through a positive metaphor; instead of emptying the dharmas, it fills them up, it shows how they totally interpenetrate one another, so that each dharma, in effect, contains within it all other dharmas, and is itself contained in all other dharmas.

The Avataṃsaka ("Flower Garland") school never existed in India; it was first established in China, where it was known as Huayan, and from there passed on to Korea (as Hwaŏm) and Japan (as Kegon). It gets its name and some of its teachings from a text called the *Flower Garland Discourse* (*Avataṃsaka Sūtra*; Ch., *Huayan jing*), which was first compiled probably somewhere in Central Asia in the fourth century CE, and first translated into Chinese by Buddhabhadra (359–429). The text is massive and obviously made up, in part, of separate sūtras which existed also as separate texts in their own right. The most famous of these (each of which runs to hundreds of pages)

25 This description of the transformation that happens at enlightenment is inspired by Lusthaus (2004), p. 919.

are the *Discourse on the Ten Stages* (*Daśabhūmika Sūtra*) which describes the ten stages of the bodhisattva path (see below), and the *Discourse on the Excellent Array* (*Gaṇḍavyūha Sūtra*), the last chapter of the text, which tells the story of the youth Sudhana who, on his quest for enlightenment, travels through the cosmos visiting no fewer than fifty-two teachers, each one of whom helps him and sends him on his way.[26]

Huayan traces its lineage through five great scholar-monks, who subsequently came to be known as the five patriarchs of the school. The most famous of them are probably Fazang and Zongmi, who was also recognized as a patriarch of the Chan (Zen) lineage. After Zongmi, the patriarchate came to an end, but the Huayan teachings continued to be important, not only in China, but also in Korea where it was introduced by Ŭisang (625–702) and eventually synthesized with Zen (Kor., Sŏn) by Chinul (1158–1210). In Japan, the school was established as Kegon, one of the six so-called Nara schools. Later major figures included Myōe (1173–1232), who restored the tradition in the Kamakura period, and Gyōnen (1240–1321), a famous Kegon scholar-monk at the Tōdaiji temple.[27]

The *Avataṃsaka Sūtra* as a whole opens with a revelation that the Buddha Śākyamuni, who has just attained enlightenment at Bodhgaya, is actually none other than the all-pervading Dharmakāya of the Cosmic Buddha Vairocana. Quite literally, his body, his speech, and his mind are said to pervade all lands throughout the universe which he also illuminates with his splendor. He is all buddhas, he is all beings, he is the whole of reality, which, at the same time, he transcends. Moreover, all worlds, all buddhas, all beings may be found in each hair on his body. Simply put, if everything can be found in the Buddha, the Buddha can be found in everything. What we have here is a Buddha-focused version of the doctrine of interpenetration. In time, it will not just be the Buddha who pervades and contains all beings, but all beings who mutually pervade and contain all beings, all dharmas that mutually pervade and contain

26 On the history of Huayan in China, Korea, and Japan, see Hamar (2007), pp. 169–335. Though the school did not exist in India, for its antecedents there, see Nattier (2007). On the history of the text, see Hamar (2007), pp. 87–167. For a translation of the *Daśabhūmika Sūtra*, see Honda (1968). For a translation of the *Gaṇḍavyūha*, see Cleary (1989a).

27 For short accounts of the five patriarchs, see Poceski (2004a). On Fazang, see Chen (2005; 2007). On Zongmi, see Gregory (1991), and Broughton (2009). On Chinul, see Buswell (1991). Also important for the Korean and Japanese schools was the Chinese Huayan lay recluse, Li Tongxuan (635–730), on whom see Gimello (1983), and Cleary (1989). On Japanese Kegon, see Matsunaga and Matsunaga (1976), vol. 1, pp. 94–108, and Takakusu (1947), pp. 108–125. On Myōe, see Tanabe (1992). On Gyōnen, see Blum (2002), pp. 51–68.

all dharmas, while, paradoxically, at the same time, remaining themselves. The universe seen in this way is called the dharmadhātu (dharma-realm).[28]

The image used in the sūtra to illustrate this is that of the "jewel net of Indra." The god Indra, it is said, has in his heaven a great net extending to infinity in every direction; at each knot of the net, there is a multifaceted jewel that reflects and is reflected in all the other jewels, all of which do not merely reflect one another, but reflect one another's reflections and re-reflections, etc. In this way, the whole of the net is reflected in each jewel, and each jewel is reflected in the whole of the net. The same lesson was driven home, in a more down-to-earth practical way, by the patriarch Fazang who, in order to graphically demonstrate the doctrine of interpenetration to the empress Wu Zedian (684–704), placed a candle in a room paneled by mirrors on every side. When he lit the candle for the empress, she could see it reflected and re-reflected and re-re-reflected ... in each and every mirror.[29]

9.6.1 Applications of Interpenetration

It is sometimes argued by scholars that the world of the *Avataṃsaka Sūtra* "is a world of vision, of magic, or miracle" (Williams, 2009, p. 133, quoting Tanabe, 1992, p. 11), that the views of the school were elaborated to make sense of the kind of coincidence of opposites made possible in meditative visualizations. This may be true but the philosophy of interpenetration was also something that had real-world applications. For instance, in recent years, the image of the jewel net of Indra described above has been commonly invoked by Buddhist environmentalists who see it as a graphic demonstration of the interconnectedness of the ecosystem. The poet Gary Snyder, for example, has sought to buddhaize ecology and ecologize Buddhism by the creative use of the metaphor of Indra's net, which allows him and others to see the entire world in a tree, or a fish, or a spotted owl.[30]

In traditional Asian societies, the same philosophy was put to use for political purposes. Some of the greatest East Asian supporters of the Avataṃsaka school and its doctrines were kings and emperors. Mention has already been made of Fazang's demonstration of the doctrine of mutual interpenetration

28 On the first chapter of the sūtra, see Cleary (1984), pp. 2–3, 55ff.
29 On Indra's net, see Cook (1977). Fazang's demonstration is recounted in Williams (2009), p. 140. For more on Wu Zedian, see Chen (2002a). Fazang also sought to explain the doctrine with his treatise on the golden lion, on which see Williams (2009), pp. 141–144.
30 Barnhill (1997). See also Ingram (1997), and Cook (1989).

for the empress Wu Zedian. She was not just a supporter of Fazang; she also sponsored the sculpting of a colossal image of the cosmic Buddha Vairocana in the caves at Longmen, near the capital. The same was done at Sokkuram near the Korean capital of Kyongju by King Kyŏngdŏk (r. 742–765) who erected a statue of Śākyamuni which, some say, represents him "at the moment he manifests as Vairocana in accordance with the opening chapter of the *Avataṃsaka*" (Sorensen, 2004, p. 339). And, in Japan, the emperor Shōmu (r. 724–749), probably in direct imitation of the empress Wu Zedian, had a sixteen-meter-high image of Vairocana (Jpn., Dainichi) cast in bronze at the Tōdaiji temple in the capital of Nara.[31] These colossal images (or their likenesses) still stand today not only as attractions to tourists and pilgrims alike, but as testimony to impressive royal/imperial sponsorship of the Avataṃsaka school.

The explanation for this sponsorship is twofold: first, the interpenetration of phenomena allowed for an identification between the ruler and the image and the Buddha. The empress Wu Zedian, for instance, identified herself both with the ideal figure of a world-ruling cakravartin king and with the future Buddha Maitreya. Second, the fact that Vairocana was the cosmic Buddha who pervaded the entire world was significant. For, as such, he extended not only his presence, but that of the ruler and the government throughout the kingdom. Huayan/Kegon, in other words, became a convenient ideology for ruling the nation.[32]

Largeness of size was not the only way artists sought to demonstrate the cosmic nature of Vairocana. Another way was to portray on his body (usually on his robes) miniature depictions of myriads of other Buddhas and beings. The same theme is found in the *Gaṇḍavyūha Sūtra*, the last chapter of the *Avataṃsaka Sūtra*, which tells the story of the young pilgrim Sudhana. In his quest for enlightenment and teachings, Sudhana finally came to see the bodhisattva Samantabhadra, who, in some ways, is a stand-in here for Vairocana. And in every single pore of the body of Samantabhadra, he saw "untold quadrillions of Buddha fields being entirely filled up with Buddhas." And then he "entered those world systems within the body of Samantabhadra" and, exploring each of them for an entire aeon, he "gradually came to equal the bodhisattva Samantabhadra in his quadrillions of vows and practices; he came to equal all the buddhas; he came to equal them in the pervasion of

31 On the construction of the great Buddha at the Tōdaiji, see Kidder (1972), pp. 115–117.

32 On Wu Zedian's self-identification with a cakravartin and Maitreya, see Forte (1976), pp. 125–170. For a survey of Huayan inspired art, see Sorensen (2004).

all fields ... He came to equal them in turning the Wheel of the Dharma; he came to equal them in the purity of knowledge; ... he came to equal them in great love, in great compassion, and in the inconceivable liberation of bodhisattvas" (Strong, 2008, p. 172).[33]

9.7 THE BUDDHA WOMB/EMBRYO (TATHĀGATAGARBHA) TEACHINGS

Nāgārjuna's assertion that "there is no distinction whatsoever between saṃsāra and nirvāṇa and no distinction whatsoever between nirvāṇa and saṃsāra" was bold, but also potentially problematical. If it was to be taken literally, as a *fait accompli*, it seemed to mean the end of religion, for if we in saṃsāra are already in nirvāṇa, there is no reason to search for the latter, to make merit, to quest for or attain enlightenment; the whole *raison d'être* of Buddhism more or less disappears. Needless to say, most Buddhists generally did not take it in that literal way (though some came close). Instead, they viewed it as a truth to be *realized*, and concluded that our fundamental *problem* is our failure to wake up to the truth of this equation, a failure that keeps us in saṃsāra. Still, the redefinition of saṃsāra as nirvāṇa was important. In a sense, the First Truth, stress (duḥkha), was now no longer seen as a *truth*, but more like a mistake. The truth is we are already enlightened ("in nirvāṇa"), but, paradoxically, we are not, because we have not yet realized that fact. Once we do, we will view this world of saṃsāra as it has always been – stressless and the same as nirvāṇa.

This shift in perspective opened the door for various explanations of just how it is that we are already enlightened while still in saṃsāra. One of these was the theory of the tathāgatagarbha, the womb or seed of the Buddha (tathāgata), a doctrine which one scholar has described as "an attempt to clarify the ontological basis upon which ordinary worldlings can realize Buddhahood" (Stone, 1999, p. 5). This became a crucial and very influential theory in Mahāyāna, especially in East Asia where it spawned many doctrinal developments.

The basic idea behind this notion, at least according to the *Sūtra on the Buddha Womb/Embryo* (*Tathāgatagarbha Sūtra*) that dates from the mid-third century CE, is that we all have latent within us the potentiality or the

33 Episodes from Sudhana's pilgrimage are depicted at the great stūpa of Borobudur in Indonesia. See Fontein (2012). For a more general survey, see Fontein (1967).

actuality of buddhahood.[34] The ambiguity reflected in the double use of the words "potentiality" and "actuality" plays off the dual thrust of the word "garbha," which can mean "embryo" or "seed" on the one hand, or "womb," or "matrix" or "storehouse" on the other. According to the first metaphor, the tathāgatagarbha represents the potentiality for buddhahood within us, something that we need to cultivate and develop. According to the second metaphor, it represents the actuality of buddhahood within us, something that is currently hidden by our defilements, such as greed, hatred, and delusion, but that we need to discover and make manifest. In this latter sense, the tathāgatagarbha is said to be eternal and unchanging. As one somewhat later sūtra, the *Lion's Roar of Queen Śrīmālā*, describes it, apart from the storehouse of defilements it is called the Dharma body of the Buddha; not apart from the storehouse of defilements, it is called the tathāgatagarbha.[35]

In this light, the tathāgatagarbha, which also came to be known as the "Buddha-nature" or "Buddha-element" (Buddhadhātu), seems, at times, to resemble an eternal and unchanging "Self," and is reminiscent, perhaps, of some of the things that were said about the Jain doctrine of the living soul (jīva) within us, or about the Ātman of the Vedānta. Indeed, in the *Mahāyāna Mahāparinirvāṇa Sūtra* (a.k.a. the *Nirvāṇa Sūtra*; Ch., *Niepan jing*) – which became, in East Asia, a Mahāyāna text of major importance – the uncreated and deathless Buddha-nature, the tathāgatagarbha that exists within all beings, is called the "true Self" (ātman). Ordinarily, we cannot see it due to our defilements, but once these are eliminated and seen to be fundamentally unreal, we can perceive our Buddha-nature, attain "great nirvāṇa," and realize our true selves.[36]

9.7.1 Resurgence of the True Self

This is striking language to find in a Buddhist sūtra where, generally speaking, the word "ātman" is anathema. And indeed, some other texts shy away from it. The *Scripture on the Descent to Lankā* (*Lankāvatāra Sūtra*), for example, makes no mention of "Self" in its discussion of the tathāgatagarbha, and instead

34 For an introduction to and translation of the *Tathāgatagarbha Sūtra*, see Grosnick (1995). See also the discussion in Williams (2009), pp. 103–28.

35 See Paul (2004), p. 44.

36 On the connections to Jain and Hindu notions of the Self, see Ruegg (1992), pp. 19–21. For translations of the *Nirvāṇa Sūtra*, see Yamamoto (1973), and Blum (2013). On the labeling of the tathāgatagarbha as the "true self," see Williams (2009), p. 108.

equates it with the "storehouse consciousness" (ālaya-vijñāna) (Suzuki, 1930, pp. 137–138). The *Analysis of the Jewel Lineage* (*Ratnagotravibhāga*), which became very popular in Tibet, simply states that "Self [here] is another name for not-Self" (see Williams, 2009, p. 112), and elsewhere identifies the tathāgatagarbha with emptiness. The same argument is developed in the *Buddha Nature Treatise* (*Foxing lun*), a sixth-century CE Chinese text, supposedly written by Vasubandhu, where it is spelled out as follows: "It is the true, essential eternal nature of things to lack a self. Therefore, the lack of self is real; it *is* the real nature of things. Therefore, it is called "self" or "perfection of self" (King, 1984, p. 260).[37]

Even within the *Nirvāṇa Sūtra* (which is a massive text), there are signs of ambiguity about the doctrine. At one point in the text, the Buddha indicates that he used the word "Ātman" strategically as a kind of expedient means (upāya) for teaching non-Buddhists. In a passage addressed to some brahmins who object to his anātman doctrine as too nihilistic, he assures them that he does not preach that sentient beings are without a self, for "what else can the Buddha nature be if not the self?" When they hear this, the brahmins immediately convert to Buddhism, become monks, and, resolving to attain buddhahood, practice the path. Even the birds and the beasts which happen to overhear the Buddha's words, we are told, resolve to attain enlightenment and soon abandon their animal forms. But then the Buddha adds, in an aside to his own disciples: "Good sons, the Buddha-nature is in fact not the self. For the sake of guiding sentient beings, I described it as the self" (Liu, 1982, p. 88).

The controversy did not end there, however. Especially in East Asia, the language of "true self" or "perfect self" or "supreme self" (even when it was explained as actually meaning "non-self") became quite prominent and significant. Chan (Jpn., Zen) Buddhism, for instance, is famous for its teaching that "the single most important thing in life is to discover the 'true self'" (King, 1984, p. 255). Thus, Ruegg may well be correct when he declares that, in Mahāyāna thought, we can find both a path in which reality is represented negatively and approached through negation, and a path in which it is represented positively and approached through affirmation.[38]

In the *Awakening of Faith in the Mahāyāna* (*Dashen qixinlun*), a text that, significantly, was composed in China in the sixth century CE and

37 Much the same point is made in other texts (see Ruegg, 1992, p. 25). For a study of the *Foxing lun*, see King (1991).
38 Ruegg (1992), pp. 42–43.

was very influential in the Chan/Zen school, we find the tathāgatagarbha approached through affirmation and promoted to the status of a metaphysical principle that denotes the absolute as it exists in the temporal, the transcendent in the phenomenal, the universal in the particular. It is the "One Mind" that we can discover within ourselves by introspection, by cutting down on our thoughts and activities, by eliminating unreal defilements, by returning to our original nature. As Williams has noted, this was a view that tallied nicely with both Confucian and Daoist notions. It also pointed to an aspect of Buddhist practice that was to be very influential in certain circles: the notion of sudden or spontaneous enlightenment. Since the defilements are fundamentally unreal, there is no need to eliminate them methodically; all one has to do is cut through them and "see" that one already is a buddha.[39]

9.8 BUDDHA-NATURE CONTROVERSIES

The claim that we are all originally enlightened, that that is our true nature, and that all we have to do is awaken to that fact (not necessarily an easy task!) gave rise, in East Asia especially, to various vigorous debates, some of which continue to this day.

In China, a succession of different views on the topic of the Buddha-nature may be found. The doctrine was especially influential on the development of Chan/Zen notions of one's true self, and of practices of sudden enlightenment (see 10.6); but it was also crucial in the notion of the "refuge of the Universal Buddha" developed by the Three Stages school (Ch., Sanjie jiao) founded by the controversial monk Xinxing (540–594 CE) whom some labeled as a heretic.[40]

In Japan, the issue of "original enlightenment" (Jpn., hongaku), that arose within the Tendai (Ch., Tiantai) school, became an important fault-line that separated different Japanese Buddhists sects. And the controversy continues to this day with the emergence in recent times of a Japanese movement known as Critical Buddhism (Jpn., hihan bukkyō) which criticizes original

39 For an introduction to and translation of the *Awakening of Faith*, see Hakeda (2005). For discussion, including parallels with Daoist and Confucian thought, see Williams (2009), pp. 117–119.

40 For one account of the notion of Buddha-nature in China, see Lai (1982). On the importance of tathāgatagarbha and Buddha-nature doctrine in Sanjie jiao, see Hubbard (2001), pp. 99–102.

enlightenment (and the tathāgatagarbha theory) as non-Buddhist and akin to the notion of a Self, and also as fraught with various political and societal implications.[41]

In Tibet, a major division arose and persisted, in some ways, until the present, between those who took the tathāgatagarbha teaching literally, and those who said it needed to be interpreted as simply an expedient means for teaching the truth of emptiness. In the latter group, which was known as the "empty of self (nature)" school (Tib., rangtong [rang stong]), were scholars such as Tsongkhapa (1357–1419), the founder of the Gélukpa school, who proclaimed that if the tathāgatagarbha theory were accepted literally, it would be the same as a non-Buddhist Ātman doctrine. For him, emptiness was empty and only to be described negatively as the absence of inherent self-existence. In the former, which was known as the "empty of other" school (Tib., shentong [gzhan stong]), were scholars such as Dolpopa (1292–1361) of the Jonangpa school, and thinkers from various other schools that became part of the so-called non-sectarian (rimé) movement (see 7.5.4). For them, the claim was that the self-empty view was appropriate for clearing away erroneous views, but that, at some point, one had to go beyond reasoning (e.g. in meditation), and then one realized that there is a real existing Absolute that is beyond conceptualization.[42]

It is not possible to follow here all these and various other debates that raged over the issue of the Buddha-nature. I shall limit myself therefore to just one: the ethical question of whether or not *all* sentient beings have the Buddha-nature. The issue was important because possession of the Buddha-nature was taken to indicate that a being would someday realize his or her or its true nature and attain buddhahood; it was, in other words, a sort of guarantee of enlightenment. But did *all* beings have the Buddha-nature? Did animals? Did plants? Did non-Buddhists?

9.8.1 Limitations to the Buddha-Nature: the Icchantika Debate

At the human level, the controversy was sparked by the development of the notion that some people – called icchantikas – did not, in fact, possess the

41 For a thorough and important study of "original enlightenment," see Stone (1999). On Critical Buddhism, see Hubbard and Swanson (1997). See also the comments of Williams (2009), pp. 122–125.

42 On shentong and rangtong stong, see the comments of Williams (2009), pp. 112–115. See also Hookham (1991), and Burchardi (2007).

Buddha-nature. The doctrine of icchantikas may have its roots in Mainstream canonical sources which assert the existence of beings whose "wholesome roots" (kuśalamūla) have been eradicated (samucchinna), although there is some debate there as well about whether or not this is to be taken as an irrevocable condition. Both sides of the debate can, in fact, be seen in various parts of the *Nirvāṇa Sūtra.* In the first part of the text (which may well have been an independent work), icchantikas (the word means something like "defined by desires") are described as vile, worthless, immoral, evil beings who are devoid of the Buddha-nature and can never – not in this or any future lifetime – realize buddhahood. As one scholar put it, "all in all, the account of the icchantika in the first five chapters [of the *Nirvāṇa Sūtra*] amounts to one of the most authoritative statements of eternal damnation in Buddhism" (Liu, 1984, p. 67). The second part of the sūtra initially continues the first part's condemnation of the worthlessness of the icchantika, even suggesting that no bad karma will come from killing an icchantika. There are hints, however, in this portion of the text, that buddhas and bodhisattvas may be able to redeem icchantikas by preaching to them. Finally, in the last portion of the sūtra, which was probably the latest to be written, we find an apparent reversal of position, and the declaration is made that the Buddha's compassion is such that "even the icchantikas possess the Buddha-nature."[43]

Some have argued that the Buddha never truly meant what he said in the first part of the sūtra about the irredeemable nature of the icchantikas, that it was an expedient means meant only to shake up evil-minded sinners to get them to reform their ways by putting the fear of eternal damnation into their heads. Nonetheless, the teaching was taken literally by some. Indeed, the monk Daosheng (*c.*360–434 CE) was famously ostracized and exiled when he disagreed with the view of the first part of the sūtra at a time when that was all that was available to Chinese Buddhists. The Buddha, he opined, would never have said such a thing. Daosheng was later exonerated when, some years afterwards, the last part of the sūtra affirming the universality of the Buddha-nature became available.[44]

43 On those whose wholesome roots are eradicated and their relationship to the icchantika, see Buswell (1992). The analysis of the *Nirvāṇa Sūtra*'s views is taken from Liu (1984).
44 On the life of Daosheng, see Kim (1990), pp. 13–21.

9.8.2 The End of the Dharma

The icchantika doctrine went hand in glove with the notion of the decline or end of the Dharma (Saddharma-vipralopa; Ch., mofa; Jpn., mappō). According to this, people's abilities to know the Buddha's teaching and to attain enlightenment have been progressively declining ever since the Buddha's parinirvāṇa. Different schemes outlined different stages of this gradual decline, but the notion that we have reached the worst period, the "end of the Dharma," when human capacities for making merit and achieving nirvāṇa are at their lowest, was a crucial ingredient in the Buddhist ideological mix in both China, where the period was thought by some to have started in the sixth century CE, and Japan, where it came to be dated to much later. It informed not only the notion that there could be such a thing as an icchantika, but other low estimates of humanity's dharmic capacity, such as the Three Stages school's classification of most humans in this day and age as "stupid." Such beings (who are explicitly likened to icchantikas) are incapable of observing the precepts or holding correct views.[45]

The notion of the decline of the Dharma and of human capacities for enlightenment also informed the views of various Chinese and Japanese Pure Land masters. In 8.4, we examined the notion of the pure land as a place where one can "meet the Buddha" either through visualization or through rebirth there as a result of one's faith and good works. Increasingly, as the Pure Land tradition developed, it came to be linked to the theory of the decline of the Dharma. Humans were seen as no longer capable of effectuating rebirth for themselves and needed to depend even more on the grace and power of the Buddha Amitābha. The Chinese Pure Land patriarch Daocho (562–645) was perhaps the first to make this link. It received its fullest expression, though, in the works of the Japanese Pure Land teachers, Hōnen (1133–1212) and Shinran (1173–1263), and Ippen (1234–1289) who developed the notion of "other power" (Jpn., tariki), i.e. complete dependence on Amida (= Amitābha), claiming that humans no longer had any "self-power" (Jpn., jiriki) to reach enlightenment on their own. Even chanting the name of the Buddha, which originally was seen as an *act* of faith, came to be seen as an expression of gratitude for Amida.[46]

45 On different schemes of the decline of the Dharma, see Nattier (1991). On the connection of the Three Stages school's views of stupid people to icchantikas, see Hubbard (2001), pp. 86–87.

46 Daocho's views on the other power are mentioned in Hubbard (2001), pp. 72–74. On Hōnen, see Machida (1999); on Shinran, see Dobbins (1989); on Ippen, see Hirota (1997).

9.8.3 Expansions of the Buddha-Nature Doctrine

The icchantika doctrine and the notion of the end of the Dharma are examples of a rather low estimate of the capacities of human beings for buddhahood. At the other end of the spectrum, however, we find a move to expand possession of the Buddha-nature not only to all humans but to non-human beings as well. In some texts, it is stressed that the Buddha-nature, the tathāgatagarbha, is present also in animals, a fact that, according to some, helped boost the ethic of vegetarianism among East Asian Buddhists, but that more generally proclaimed a kind of unity of sentient beings. In time, Chinese monks began expanding the notion to plants, a move that gave rise, in Japan, to a thousand-year debate over the "Buddhahood capacity of grasses and trees" (Jpn., sōmoku jōbutsu). This was best epitomized, perhaps, in a late eighteenth-century painting by the Japanese artist Itō Jakuchū, entitled "Vegetable Nirvāṇa" (Yasai Nehan). This depicts a classic scene of the Buddha at Kuśinagarī, lying on his right side beneath the two sal trees and surrounded by his grieving disciples; only, in place of the Buddha, the artist shows us a long Japanese white radish (daikon) stretched out on a farmer's basket and surrounded by a cluster of turnips, gourds, mushrooms, eggplants, etc., representing the disciples.[47]

Some were also willing to expand it to all of the natural world, whether alive or not. Thus, despite the *Nirvāṇa Sūtra*'s assertion that inanimate objects such as walls and stones are "devoid of the Buddha nature" (i.e. that they are, essentially, icchantikas), the monk Daosheng is said to have preached the Dharma to a field of rocks (who are said to have nodded in response). And the Chinese Zen Master Yunmen (862–949) could declare that "All sounds are the Buddha's voice, and all forms are the Buddha's shape" (App, 1994, p. 171). At a more doctrinal level, the great Japanese Zen Master and philosopher, Dōgen (1200–1253) reinterpreted the line in the latter part of the *Nirvāṇa Sūtra* that read "all *sentient* beings *have* the buddha-nature," as meaning "all *beings* (living and non-living) *are* the buddha-nature."[48]

Encapsulated into this single sentence are two important doctrinal shifts. On the one hand, Dōgen is extending the Buddha nature to all things – animate and inanimate – not only grass and trees, but mountains, sun, moon,

---

47 Harris (1997), pp. 390–393; Shimizu (1992), p. 202.

48 On the expansion of the Buddha-nature to animals, see Zimmermann (2002), p. 83. On its implications for vegetarianism, see Ruegg (1980), pp. 236–237. On the debate in Japan on the Buddha-nature of plants, see Rambelli (2001), and (2007), pp. 11–57. For a discussion of Dōgen's views, see Abe (1992), pp. 41–42.

and rivers, as well as fences, walls, tiles, and stones. On the other hand, he is declaring not just that these things, i.e. the entire phenomenal world, *have* the Buddha nature, that they somehow conceal it within themselves as an embryo to be nurtured or a treasure to be discovered, but that they *are* the Buddha-nature. As one author put it, for him, "the Buddha-nature is [not] a seed. It is already the flower: this very world of impermanence is the Buddha-nature" (Williams, 2009, p. 121). Perhaps more than any other Buddhist thinker, Dōgen comes closest to a literal assertion of Nāgārjuna's equation of saṃsāra and nirvāṇa, a move which, in effect, undermines traditional views of the Buddha-nature itself.[49]

9.9 SUMMARY

We have, in this chapter, followed through on a number of themes in Mahāyāna thought, stemming from Nāgārjuna's presentation of emptiness and of the doctrine of the two truths. This led us to explore the notion of expedient means (upāya), and to examine Tiantai, Yogācāra, and Avataṃsaka "adjustments" to earlier Madhyamaka views. We then explored various treatments of the notion of the Buddha Womb/Embryo teachings, and the related concept of Buddha-nature. With all of these doctrinal foundations in mind, it is now time to turn to look at some aspects of Mahāyāna practice.

---

49 The environmental implications of Dōgen's views are addressed in Parkes (1997), p. 123. Parkes goes on to wonder if Dōgen would have been willing to extend the Buddha-nature to all human-made goods, e.g. non-biodegradable plastics or radioactive waste. On Dōgen as a critic of original enlightenment ideas that were common in Japan at his time, see Stone (1999), pp. 72–76.

Chapter 10

The Bodhisattva Path, Tantra, and Zen

Mahāyāna doctrine is not all about philosophical metaphysical formulations; it is also about religious practices – ethics and the quest for buddhahood. Having looked, in the previous chapter, at what might be thought of as a Mahāyāna "vocation of books," I would like to turn, in this chapter, to its "vocation of practice." In what follows, I will start by looking at various portrayals of the bodhisattva path (10.1–4), before moving on to consider practices in Vajrayāna (10.5) and in Chan (Zen) (10.6).

10.1 THE BODHISATTVA PATH

In chapter 3, we considered various descriptions of the Mainstream Buddhist path, most of which focused on one and/or the other of the "three trainings" – practices concerning morality and meditation and the acquisition of wisdom. Mahāyānist descriptions of the path may be considered to be both (1) continuations of Mainstream views; and (2) departures from them. In some ways, the bodhisattva path in the Mahāyāna is not different from Śākyamuni's bodhisattva path in Mainstream Buddhism. Śākyamuni, long ago, as the brahmin Sumedha, inspired by the past Buddha Dīpaṃkara, rejected immediate enlightenment for himself and embarked on what can only be called his bodhisattva path to buddhahood (see 2.5). In doing so, he declared: "I would ... attain the highest Enlightenment, and, taking mankind aboard the ship of the Dharma, ford them across the ocean of saṃsāra" (Jayawickrama, 1990, pp. 17–18). He then proceeded to spend the next four incalculable ages as a bodhisattva (a "being-set-on-buddhahood"), working for the benefit of other sentient beings.

The difference in the Mahāyāna, of course, is that this determination and this goal – buddhahood – now come to be universalizable and potentially open to all. "Universalizable," it should be said, does not mean "universalized." Though the *Lotus Sūtra*, as we have seen, claims that buddhahood is the aim of everyone, even though some might not yet be aware of that, and though the *Nirvāṇa Sūtra* affirms that we all have within us the tathāgatagarbha, many other Mahāyāna texts accepted distinctions between the path of the bodhisattva and those of śravakas (disciples who are headed for arhatship) and of pratyekabuddhas (buddhas-for-themselves-alone), and of others not on any path at all. The Mahāyāna's bodhisattva path may be open to them, but they are not necessarily open to following it.[1]

10.2 SUDDEN AND GRADUAL

In presenting the Mahāyāna bodhisattva path, I want to start by mentioning a commonly made distinction, especially with regard to East Asian and Tibetan traditions, between those who conceived of the achievement of enlightenment as something "sudden" and those who viewed it as something "gradual," or, perhaps better, "graduated," i.e. divided into stages.[2]

I do this with some hesitation. In recent years, a number of scholars, especially of Chan/Zen Buddhism, have sought to problematize this sudden/gradual distinction, and have questioned its use as a yardstick by which to understand certain divergences within Chinese religions. McRae, for instance, has proposed that the term "sudden enlightenment" originated primarily as a slogan used by Shenhui (670–762), a master of the so-called Southern School of Chan in the Tang dynasty, eager to lambast the rival "Northern School" as "gradual" and to offer potential converts to his own lineage "a key to quick and easy achievement of the ultimate goal (in contrast to lifetimes of self-cultivation)" (McRae, 1987, p. 257). In this polemical context, it is noteworthy that the *Platform Sūtra of the*

1 For instance, Atiśa starts his *Lamp on the Path of Awakening* (*Bodhipathapradīpa*) with a declaration that there are three kinds of beings, lesser ones (aiming at better rebirth), middling ones, aiming selfishly at their own enlightenment, and superior ones, aiming at buddhahood. He is writing his book only for the latter (see Sonam, 1997). The *Inquiry of Ugra* (*Ugraparipṛcchā*) is similarly very clear that the bodhisattva path is not for everyone (see Nattier, 2003).

2 For a variety of essays on the topic, see Gregory (1987).

Sixth Patriarch (*Liuzu tan jing*), compiled somewhat later, seeks to explain away the issue by stating that the Dharma is neither sudden nor gradual; the two labels are simply due to the fact that some people are smart and quick to understand it (i.e. the Southern School), and others are stupid and slow (i.e. the Northern School)! Even so, the dichotomy was not always clear-cut and there was room for some who advocated gradual paths culminating in sudden enlightenment and others who theorized about sudden enlightenment followed by gradual cultivation.[3]

The divide between "subitists" (as the advocates of sudden enlightenment are sometimes called) and gradualists is thus a complex matter, but, keeping in mind the above caveats, it may be useful to unpack some of the issues at stake here. Whether artificial or not, the sudden/gradual distinction caught on at least ideologically and was not without its effect on subsequent practitioners and students of the tradition. Propaganda can, over time, come to define reality.

In my view, the sudden/gradual question may be seen in at least two contexts. First, the polarity can refer to a division of opinion over the nature of the bodhisattva path itself; and second, it can refer to a difference of opinion over the nature of the experience of enlightenment.

10.2.1 *Disagreements over the Nature of the Path: the Debate at Samyé*

In essence, the division of opinion over the nature of the path amounts to a disagreement over the role played by two of the three trainings of the traditional eightfold path – moral discipline and wisdom. Are merit making and good works, and intellectual study and comprehension of doctrine, a fundamental part of the path? Gradualists were inclined to say yes, and subitists were inclined to say no.

This can be seen in accounts of the royally sponsored debate (or debates – there may have been several) held between gradualists and subitists in Tibet at the end of the eighth century, and commonly called the Council of Lhasa, or the Debate at Samyé (bSam-yas). This featured a confrontation between the Indian Master Kamalaśīla (who, as we have seen in 9.2, propounded a kind of synthesis between Yogācāra and Madhyamaka) and a Chinese master

3 On the *Platform Sūtra*'s understanding of sudden and gradual, see McRae (2000), p. 91. On sudden enlightenment followed by gradual cultivation, see Gregory (1987a).

known as "Moheyan" (= Mahāyāna), who is said to have represented the Chan (or Zen) perspective.[4]

Kamalaśīla and his supporters represented the gradualist position and argued that much analytic wisdom and much effort in clearing away mental and moral defilements obstructing one's realization are needed to attain buddhahood. Moheyan, on the other hand (at least according to the Tibetan accounts), is presented as preaching the subitist way of "no-thinking," and also as claiming that karmic actions – whether meritorious or demeritorious – are hindrances to enlightenment; they are like white and black clouds which equally hide the sun, but what is needed is no clouds at all.[5] It becomes apparent then, in the context of the Debate at Samyé, that part of what the sudden approach meant was dispensing with thinking and with karmic action as part of the soteriological process.

Related to this, of course, was another issue concerning the length or, perhaps more accurately, the speed of the path. Simply put, is it something slow that may take countless rebirths, or is it something fast that can be accomplished in this very lifetime? In a seminal article on the topic, Stein suggested that the word for "sudden" (Ch., Dun; Tib., cig-char), especially in Tibetan texts, would better be translated as "simultaneous," or "all at once," with the implication that a "sudden" realization did not mean that enlightenment was reached "out of the blue" but as a result of traversing many stages simultaneously, in a single bound. In this context, sudden enlightenment might be called "direct enlightenment," and might be thought of as requiring more effort for quicker results.[6] The direct path may be viewed as a "shortcut" that rejects the long way up the mountain – the lifetimes of doing good work and improving one's karma, and/or the long practices of mental cultivation in which one gradually and systematically whittles away at defilements. As we shall see, both Zen and Tantra are commonly thought of as such shortcuts.

But it may also be that the path is viewed as so short, so quick, as to not really be a "path" at all. Thus some Tibetans, invoking the mountain metaphor, point out that sudden enlightenment "falls from above," while "practice" (i.e. gradual enlightenment) "climbs from below" (Stein, 1987, p. 44). In other

4 For a brief account of the Debate at Samyé, see Dalton (2004). For a more thorough study, see Ruegg (1992). For a presentation of sources on the debate, see Tucci (1986), pp. 313–434, and Houston (1980). For looks at both the Chinese and Tibetan sides of the question, see Roccasalvo (1980), and Gómez (1983; 1983a).

5 Obermiller (1931), vol. 2, pp. 193–194. Other sources present a rather different view of Moheyan's views and do not accuse him of being amoral (see Gómez, 1983).

6 Stein (1987).

words, it is not just that one *path* is faster than the other; the very nature of the enterprise is different. This takes us back to an age-old dilemma of Mahāyāna Buddhism: if we are already enlightened, if we have the Buddha-nature and so are already buddhas, any kind of practice – any notion of a path – will not get us to Buddhahood if it projects it as something we do not have. The disagreement between gradualists and subitists was thus not just a divide over the nature of the path; it also was a disagreement over the very possibility of enlightenment by one method or the other.

10.2.2 Disagreements over the Nature of Enlightenment

In addition to referring to the nature of the path, the sudden/gradual dichotomy can also be applied to a debate over the nature of the experience of enlightenment itself. Is the attainment of buddhahood akin to a gradual dawning, or is it more like a lightning flash? Is it like solving a mathematical equation step by step, or is it like intuiting the answer at first glance? The gradualists were inclined to the first view, the subitists to the second. More formally, sudden enlightenment has been defined as a "term [that] denotes nothing more than a nondualistic realization of religious truth achieved in a single moment of insight" (MacRae, 1987, p. 257).

Connected to this is the important question of whether buddhahood involves single or multiple experiences. Here, it seems to me, it is helpful to return to the notion of a tathāgatagarbha, and the aforementioned ambiguity embedded in the word "garbha." The word, as we have seen (9.7), can mean either a "container" or an "embryo," and so "tathāgatagarbha" can imply either that we have within us buddhahood itself or that we have within us the *potential* for buddhahood. In this context, we can see another dimension of the sudden/gradual question. Sudden enlightenment may refer to finding the treasure of our innate buddhahood, all at once, right away, i.e. realizing that we already *are* buddhas. Indeed, Chan/Zen texts that advocate subitist realization often present it as a direct pointing at one's Buddha Mind or Buddha-nature. Gradual enlightenment, on the other hand, may involve first discovering our innate *potential* for buddhahood, i.e. realizing that we are bodhisattvas, and then developing that potential. In the one instance, there is no more path to be traversed; in the other, there is. In this light, the discovery of one's potential for buddhahood can be likened to the awakening of one's bodhicitta – one's "mind set on enlightenment" – with the difference that bodhicitta is not something innate by nature, but something to which we must give rise.[7]

With all this in mind, I want to turn now to examine, first, some descriptions of the path that I will now label "graduated" (i.e. involving multiple steps). Then, I will present some examples of realizations that might be thought of as "sudden."

10.3 GRADUATED PATHS

The Mahāyāna literature on the various formulations of the graduated bodhisattva path is voluminous and was especially studied in Tibet. Mention here can only be made of the following: *The Stages of Meditation* (*Bhāvanākrama*) which consists of three treatises by none other than Kamalaśīla, the advocate of the gradual position at the Samyé debate; *Entering the Path of Enlightenment* (*Bodhicaryāvatāra*) by the Madhyamaka scholar-poet Śāntideva (*c.*650–750); *The Ornament of Realization* (*Abhisamayālaṃkara*), attributed to the bodhisattva Maitreya and important in the Tibetan Gélukpa curriculum; and *The Lamp on the Path of Awakening* (*Bodhipathapradīpa*) by Atiśa (*c.*980–1054) who was instrumental in the second dissemination of Buddhism in Tibet. Atiśa's work, in turn, became foundational for much of the subsequent Tibetan "Stages of the Path" (Tib., lam rim) literature, including *The Jewel Ornament of Liberation* (*Tarpa rinpoché gyen* [*Thar pa rin po che'i rgyan*]) by Milarepa's disciple Gampopa (1079–1153), and *The Great Exposition of the Stages of the Path* (*Lamrim Chenmo*), by the founder of the Géluk tradition, Tsongkhapa (1357–1419).[8] Taken together, their works cover such things as the development of bodhicitta (the mind set on enlightenment), the necessity of compassion, the practice of the perfections, the ten stages of the bodhisattva path, the five paths to Buddhahood, etc. Not all of these schemes can easily be correlated.

7 On bodhicitta, see 10.3.1. On the fundamental importance of the tathāgatagarbha theory in Mahāyāna soteriology and its relationship to the sudden/gradual dichotomy, see Ruegg (1992).

8 On the *Bhāvanākrama*, see Tucci (1986), pp. 467–492, Tucci (1971), and Gyatso (2001); for a translation of the *Bodhicaryāvatāra*, see Crosby and Skilton (1995); for translations of the *Abhisamayālaṃkara*, see Conze (1954), and Sparham (2006–2012); on its use in the Tibetan monastic curriculum, see Dreyfus (2003), p. 106. On the *Bodhipathapradīpa*, see Sonam (1997); for a translation, see http://www.berzinarchives.com; for *The Jewel Ornament of Liberation*, see Guenther (1971); on Tsongkhapa's *Lamrim*, see Lamrim Chenmo Translation Committee (2000–2004), and Wayman (1978; 1991).

10.3.1 Compassion and Bodhicitta

Kamalaśīla starts his *Stages of Meditation* with a declaration that "compassion alone is the first cause of all the qualities of buddhahood" (Beyer, 1974, p. 100). Most, though not all, presentations of the bodhisattva path similarly stress the importance of compassion, and of arousing the mind of enlightenment (bodhicitta), i.e. generating in oneself the desire and determination to attain buddhahood.[9] The two, in fact, are intimately bound together. Compassion for the suffering of others should be the motivating factor for the bodhisattva's desire to attain buddhahood. As Gampopa puts it: "The essence of the formation of an enlightened attitude (bodhicitta) is the desire for perfect enlightenment in order to be able to work for the benefit of others" (Guenther, 1971, p. 112). In this literature, this is commonly contrasted to the motivations of śravakas and pratyekabuddhas who are said to be interested only in enlightenment for themselves.

"Working for the benefit of others" means two things: relieving the suffering of others within saṃsāra through generosity, self-sacrifice, and assistance; and permanently relieving the suffering of others by showing them the way out of saṃsāra, i.e. the way to enlightenment. Both of these aims may be expressed in a bodhisattva's vow, which usually follows the awakening of bodhicitta, and which, depending on the text, can be more or less complex.

Śāntideva, for example, describes one rather elaborate vow, part of which reads: "May I be a protector of the unprotected, a guide for travelers on the way, a boat, a bridge, a means of crossing for those who seek the other shore" (Strong, 2008, p. 178). This, it might be noted, recalls the vow that, in the Pali tradition, the Buddha made aeons ago when, as the brahmin Sumedha, inspired by the past Buddha Dīpaṃkara, he likewise embarked on the path to Buddhahood. Rejecting immediate enlightenment for himself, Sumedha declared: "I would ... attain the highest Enlightenment, and taking mankind aboard the ship of the Dharma, ford them across the ocean of saṃsāra" (Jayawickrama, 1990, pp. 17–18).

In Śāntideva, however, the vow also spells out some specific determinations of how the bodhisattva will assist sentient beings while carrying out this great endeavor. Some of these recall some of the self-sacrificial schemes found in Mainstream jātakas, but others do not:

9 On the necessity of compassion, see, however, Nattier (2003), p. 145.

> May I ... become one who works for the complete alleviation of the suffering of all beings. May I be medicine for the sick; may I also be their physician and attend to them until their disease no longer recurs. With showers of food and water, may I eliminate their pain of hunger and thirst, and during ... periods of great famine, may I *be* their food and drink. May I be an inexhaustible storehouse for the poor, and may I always be first in being ready to serve them ... Nirvāṇa means to renounce everything. My mind is set on nirvāṇa, so because I am to renounce everything, it is best for me to give to others. I therefore dedicate this self of mine to the happiness of all beings. Let them smite me, mock me, or throw dirt at me ... Let them do whatever pleases them, but let no one suffer any [karmic] mishap on my account. Whether they direct toward me thoughts that are angry or kindly, may those very thoughts be a constant cause for their achieving all their aims ... Just as the buddhas of the past grasped the mind set on enlightenment and went on to follow the bodhisattva-training, so too do I give rise to the mind set on enlightenment for the well-being of the world, and so will I train in the stages of the bodhisattva path.
>
> (Strong, 2008, pp. 177–178)

If such thorough and universal compassion and determination mark the start of the bodhisattva path, how does one come to arouse those sentiments? Various techniques are advocated by various Mahāyāna authors, but in all cases they effectively constitute a sort of preliminary path to entering into the bodhisattva path. Some describe a series of meditations in which one contemplates the different kinds of suffering of beings in the different pathways of rebirth and then imagines that each of those beings has been one's beloved mother in some previous life. Therefore, one should feel intense filial compassion for their suffering. Others emphasize what is called the "exchange of self and other" – realizing that there is no difference between oneself and other living beings and so that one should act to alleviate their suffering as one would act to alleviate one's own. Still others add to this practical advice. For instance, Gampopa recommends that, if you become depressed at the thought of the length and difficulty of the path, remember that you possess the tathāgatagarbha, so your endeavors are guaranteed. He goes on to urge taking advantage of the opportunity of having been reborn as a human in order to practice, and then points to the need, from the start, of "spiritual friends," i.e. teachers who will instruct one in the nature of saṃsāra, in taking refuge and developing bodhicitta.[10]

10.3.2 The Stages of the Path, the Perfections, the Five Paths

Śāntideva declares that bodhicitta is really of two types, or has two phases. In addition to the mind resolved on enlightenment, there is also the mind proceeding towards enlightenment. It is this second mind that keeps motivating the practice of the bodhisattva path. The path is commonly described in terms of ten stages (the bodhisattva-bhūmis – see table 10.1), a scheme that is already found in a Mainstream text, the *Great Story* (*Mahāvastu*). The first level of attainment is called the "Joyous Stage" (pramuditā bhūmi) which is reached, at least according to one text, with the awakening of bodhicitta. The last, the tenth stage, the "Cloud of Dharma" (Dharmamegha bhūmi), is the stage of buddhahood. In between, a crucial marker is the seventh stage after which a bodhisattva can no longer retrogress on the path.[11]

The bodhisattva stages are sometimes correlated to the systematic elimination of defilements or afflictions (kleśa), mental states that cloud the mind. In this scheme, there are eighty-one defilements, and one starts by eliminating the nine grosser ones at stage two, and then progressively subtler and subtler ones in the following stages. The process is likened to beating the dirt out of one's clothes: it is relatively easy to get the "big dirt" out, but it takes great and repeated effort to eliminate the last vestiges of dirt – the very fine particles.[12]

The ten stages are also correlated with a focus on the practice of particular perfections (see table 10.1). In this scheme, to the usual Mahāyāna list of six perfections – the pāramitās of giving, moral behavior, meditation, patience, energy, and wisdom – are added four more: the perfections of expedient

10 For a discussion of the preliminaries to arousing bodhicitta, see Williams (2009), pp. 187–199, and Rabten (1984), pp. 305–366. For Gampopa's practical advice, see Guenther (1971), pp. 2–141.

11 On Śāntideva's distinction between two types of bodhicitta, see Williams (2009), p. 199. For the *Mahāvastu*'s list of the ten stages, see Jones (1949–1956), vol. 1, pp. 53–124. That the first level is reached right after bodhicitta is according to the *Scripture on the Ten Stages* (*Daśabhūmika Sūtra*). Other texts delay the start of the first stage until some time after the attainment of bodhicitta. See Williams (2009), pp. 200–208, for a survey of ten stages. Nattier (2003), pp. 151–152, points to the lack of reference to stages in the *Inquiry of Ugra*. For a description of different texts' various takes on the ten stages theory, see Hirakawa (1963), pp. 65–69.

12 On the elimination of defilements through various bodhisattva stages, see Hopkins (1983), pp. 104–108. Other systems count a total of 108 defilements.

means, of resolve or vow, of strength, and of knowledge. It is understood that all ten perfections are actually to be practiced at each stage, with emphasis placed, however, on the corresponding one. The inclusion of the ten pāramitās echoes the model of the bodhisattva path found in Mainstream Buddhism, where the various jātakas are said to be correlated with different perfections. Indeed, shortly after taking his vow for buddhahood, the future Śākyamuni is said to reflect on this question: "What are the contributory conditions to enlightenment?" And he realizes that they are the ten perfections, which "have to be fulfilled by bodhisattvas," and which, he adds, "are not in the sky above or on the earth below ... but are rooted within my heart" (Jayawickrama, 1990, p. 25). He then proceeds to spend the next four incalculable ages practicing them (exactly the same amount of time Tibetans claim is needed to practice the whole graduated path of the ten stages).[13]

BODHISATTVA STAGE (BHŪMI)	TEN PERFECTIONS (PĀRAMITĀ)
1. Joyful (pramudita) stage	Giving (dāna)
2. Free of defilements (vimala) stage	Ethical behavior (śīla)
3. Luminous (prabhākarī) stage	Meditation (dhyāna)
4. Radiant (arcīṣmatī) stage	Forbearance (kṣānti)
5. Difficult to conquer (sudurjayā) stage	Effort (vīrya)
6. Face to face (abhimukhī) stage	Wisdom (prajñā)
7. Going far (dūrāngamā) stage	Expedient means (upāya)
8. Immovable (acalā) stage	Resolve or vow (praṇidhāna)
9. Good thought (sadhumatī) stage	Strength (bala)
10. Cloud of Dharma (dharmameghā)	Knowledge (jñānā)

Table 10.1 The Ten Bodhisattva Stages and the Ten Perfections[14]

Finally, another scheme for describing the path which became very popular in Tibet is also one that originates from but is not found in Mainstream Buddhism (although the Tibetans claim it can be applied to Mainstream practice). This is the system of five paths:

13 On the Mahāyāna practice of perfections, see Meadows (1986), Dayal (1932), pp. 165–269, Matics (1970), pp. 47–140, and Skorupski (2002). There are various Pali lists of the ten perfections. The principal one (see Bodhi, 2005) specifies: generosity, morality, renunciation, wisdom, effort, patience, truthfulness, determination, loving-kindness, and equanimity. The four extra ones in Pali are different from the four extra ones in the Mahāyāna system.

14 Based in part on Kawamura (2004).

1. the path of the accumulation of merit (sambhāra-mārga; Tib., tsoklam [tshogs lam]), which one enters with the arising of bodhicitta. One then devotes oneself to observing moral precepts, venerating buddhas and teachers, and developing meditational abilities of concentration;
2. the path of application (prayoga-mārga'; Tib., jorlam [sbyor lam]). In English, this is also sometimes called the path of preparation; one continues to work on the practices in the first path and trains especially in the meditative practices of calmness (śamatha) and of insight (vipaśyanā);
3. the path of seeing (darśana mārga; Tib., tonglam [mthong lam]) during which one has a first direct unmediated perception of emptiness. This is sometimes said to correspond to entering the first of bodhisattva stages;
4. the path of cultivation or of meditation (bhāvanā mārga; Tib., gomlam [bsgom lam]). While deepening one's practice of insight and calmness, one gradually eliminates all mental defilements and all artificial or latent or resurgent notions of inherent existence. This comprises the remaining bodhisattva stages;
5. the path of no-more-learning (aśaikṣa mārga; Tib., miloblam [mi slob lam]) that corresponds to buddhahood.[15]

10.3.3 Routinization and Ritualization

The complexity and length of these various schematic depictions of the path have caused some scholars to wonder as to their function. Are these really guides for practice? And if so, are they at all practicable, and are they based on the experience of practitioners? Some have suggested that they were used as manuals, but the fact that they describe things to be done over countless aeons calls that into question. Sharf has criticized the fact that the "stages on the path" are often "interpreted as though they designated discrete 'states of consciousness' experienced by historical individuals in the course of their

15 For concise descriptions of the five paths, see Buswell and Lopez (2014), p. 615 (and the cross-references listed therein), and Guenther (1971), pp. 232–238. In the Huayan tradition, the path is depicted as having fifty-three stages – the ten faiths, the ten abodes, the ten practices of the perfections, the ten dedications, the ten bodhisattva bhūmis, virtual awakening, wondrous awakening, and buddhahood. For a description, see Cleary (1989), pp. 23–83.

meditative practice" (1995, p. 228). He does not deny that Buddhists have had and do have meditative experiences (although he thinks this has been overemphasized). However, he feels that "the elaborate Buddhist discourse pertaining to the 'path' ... [is] wielded more often than not in the interests of legitimation and institutional authority." These are not "reports of personal experiences" but "scholastic compendiums" by monks trying to push for or assert their own positions within the saṃgha (Sharf, 1995, p. 238). Dreyfus, who quotes Sharf, affirms much the same thing on the basis of his experience as a monk who went through the Tibetan Géluk monastic training for the géshé (dge bshes) degree. The assumption that those monks who study the path-texts intensively "must be interested in [them] for practical [meditative] reasons" is, he says, "unjustified"; simply put, they (or at least Gélukpas) do not practice this path. He goes on to ask why they spend so much time studying this material if they do not use it. His first answer is that these path-texts construct "a world view ... a meaningful universe" that affirms that "only sustained religious practices can effectively help humans ... overcome suffering." His second answer is that such study of the path is a form of making merit. This does not put it "at odds with so-called higher meditative practices but as continuous with them ... as part of the liberative ... dimension of the tradition" (Dreyfus, 1997, pp. 57–58).[16]

All this may serve to bring to the fore another dimension of the "practice" of the graduated Mahāyāna path: it, or at least the first part of it, is often ritualized and routinized and becomes, in a sense, a topic of contemplation in its own right. Atiśa, for instance, presents the arising of bodhicitta not as though it were something to be done once, at the moment of one's embarkation on the bodhisattva path, but something to be done repeatedly. He thus recommends developing bodhicitta – the mind set on enlightenment – again and again, at the end of a ritual called the seven-part offering. This, in itself, is a perfectly routine practice in the Tibetan tradition and consists of: facing (or imagining) a Buddha image or images, making (or imagining making) offerings to it, acknowledging all of one's own demerits, rejoicing in the meritorious deeds of all living beings, requesting the buddhas to teach the Dharma, asking them to remain in the world out of compassion, and dedicating the merit of all this to the cause of highest enlightenment. The ritual repetition of this not only makes merit, but creates a mindset in which the emphasis is on altruism and dedication.[17]

16 Dreyfus (2003), pp. 174–182. See also the overall discussion of this issue in Williams (2009), pp. 356–357 n27.

17 Sonam (1997), pp. 57–74, 149–150. For description of the seven-part practice which is often connected to guru yoga, see Gyatso (1988), pp. 92–116.

10.4 PATH SHORTCUTS

We have, thus far, looked at various expressions of the graduated path, and seen that, whether actually practiced or ritualized, they were thought to involve a long period (many lifetimes) of practice, as well as much merit making, and/or much doctrinal study, and/or much meditation and gradual elimination of defilements. It is time now to turn to those more direct paths which eschewed such things by emphasizing direct leaps or breakthroughs to enlightenment, shortcuts to it. In the remainder of this chapter, I will start with a discussion of Tantra and Vajrayāna practice (10.5), and go on to discuss the methods espoused by Chan/Zen (10.6).

10.5 TANTRA

Tantra in general is often said to be a quick path to enlightenment, making it possible to achieve buddhahood in a single lifetime. To a certain extent this is true, although practitioners warn that it is not to be engaged in without adequate preparation.[18] In this context, perhaps it would be better to think of Tantra as a shortcut at the end of a long path. The Tibetan Géluk school, for example, does not recommend the practice of Tantra until quite late in a monk's practice, after, for instance, the realizations of impermanence and emptiness, and the development of compassion and the mind set on enlightenment.

Part of the emphasis on a need for preparation comes from the thought that, without it (and even with it), Tantra may be dangerous. Geshe Ngawang Dhargyey, with whom I studied in Dharamsala long ago, used to liken Tantra to scaling the sheer face of a mountain in order to get to the top, rather than taking the long slow way around the back. It is faster but it is more dangerous, and it demands more skill and caution.

More specifically, Tantra is "dangerous" because it takes the non-duality of saṃsāra and nirvāṇa not as a goal to be realized but as a starting point for practice. Tantra is famous for using the things of this world to overcome attachment to this world. Rather than rejecting saṃsāric defilements (such as passion and sex), it affirms them as vehicles for realization. As one practitioner put it, "Just as water in the ear can be washed out with water, and

18 The Fourteenth Dalai Lama warns about the necessity of adequate preparation for the practice of Tantra in Gyatso (1977), p. 47.

a thorn removed by a thorn ... the wise can get rid of passion by means of passion itself."[19]

It should be said, however, that though Tantric practice is commonly thought of as a shortcut, it itself has been, to some extent, graduated. It is usual, for instance, to distinguish between four types of Tantric practice found in four types of Tantric texts: (1) Action (kriyā) Tantras emphasize ritual practices, and the chanting of dhāraṇī ("spells" – Sanskrit syllabic formulae that are thought to be powerful in themselves, to be evocative of buddhas, bodhisattvas, and gods, and to be merit making); (2) Performance (caryā) Tantras; (3) Yoga Tantras; and (4) Highest Yoga (anuttarayoga) Tantras. This last category is sometimes divided into two: the so-called Father Tantras and Mother Tantras (which Tribe more precisely calls Mahāyoga Tantras and Yoginī Tantras). For examples of each kind, see table 10.2.

Although all four (or five) of these types of Tantras involve the goal of buddhahood, and the combination of compassion and wisdom, and although all involve some forms of deity yoga, there are nonetheless distinctions between them. As the Dalai Lama has put it: "In Action Tantras external activities predominate. In Performance Tantras external activities and internal yoga are performed equally. In Yoga Tantras internal yoga is predominant. In Highest Yoga Tantras a path unequalled by any other is taught" (Gyatso, 1977, pp. 75–76).

The speed and directness of Tantric practice is made possible by several of its features. First, the use of visualization as a technique (especially in so-called Deity Yoga) enables one to "create" an ideal world of buddhas and bodhisattvas and to realize directly one's fundamental identity with them (see 8.6.3).

Second, one is not without help in doing this. The process is greatly speeded up by the help of a teacher, a guru (indispensable for Tantric practice) who is willing and able to initiate one into the practice of the short path. Such initiations (Skt., abhiṣeka – see 8.6.2) are called "empowerment" in Tibetan (wang [dbang]), and not only introduce the practitioner to the often secret methods of a particular practice but also establish for him or her a relationship with a tutelary deity (Skt., iṣṭadevatā; Tib., yidam) who will act as a divine guide the rest of the way. There are four basic types of initiation – vase, secret, knowledge, and word empowerments – with the highest yoga Tantra practices requiring all four.[20]

19 Quotation from the *Treatise on the Purification of Thought* (*Cittaviśuddhiprakaraṇa*) in Strong (2008), p. 208.

20 For a brief description of the four types of initiation, see Powers (2007), pp. 270–271.

CLASS OF TANTRA	EXAMPLE(S)	TRANSLATION (WHOLE OR PARTIAL) OR STUDY
Kriyā (Action) Tantras	Dhāraṇī texts	Strickmann (1990)
	Mañjuśrimūlakalpa (*Root Ritual Instruction of Mañjuśrī*)	Wallis (2002)
	Susiddhikara Sūtra (*Good at Accomplishment Discourse*)	Giebel (2001), pp. 109–324
Caryā (Performance) Tantras	*Vairocanābhisaṃbodhi Sūtra* (a.k.a. *Mahāvairocana Sūtra*) (*The Enlightenment of Vairocana*)	Giebel (2005); Hodge (2003); Wayman and Tajima (1992)
Yoga Tantras	*Sarvatathāgatatattvasaṃgraha* (a.k.a. *Tattvasaṃgraha Sūtra*) (*Compendium of Truth of All the Tathāgatas*)	Giebel (2001), pp. 17–107
	Nāmasaṃgīti (*Litany of Names (of Mañjuśrī)*)	Davidson (1995)
	Sarvadurgatipariśodhana Tantra (*Elimination of All Evil Destinies Tantra*)	Skorupski (1983)
Anuttara (Highest) Yoga (a) Mahāyoga Tantras	*Guhyasamāja Tantra* (*Secret Assembly Tantra*)	Wayman (1977); Wedemeyer (2008)
Anuttara (Highest) Yoga (b) Tantras	*Hevajra Tantra*	Snellgrove (1959); Willemen (1983)
	Saṃvarodaya Tantra (*Arising of the Supreme Pleasure*)	Tsuda (1974)
	Cakrasamvara Tantra (*Binding of the Wheels*)	Gray (2007)
	Kālacakra Tantra (*Wheel of Time*)	Arnold (2009)

Table 10.2 Tantras[21]

Third, Tantra emphasizes the simultaneous practice of wisdom (prajñā) and expedient means (upāya), the one leading to the understanding of emptiness (śūnyatā) and the other to the practice of compassion (karuṇā). These two things (wisdom and means) are, of course, fundamental parts of the bodhisattva path in general which, simply put, leads us to transcend this world of saṃsāra by coming to an understanding of its true nature, *and also*, at the same time, to be compassionately involved in this very same world in assisting other sentient beings by using effective means appropriate to their

21 Based in part on A. Tribe's chapter in P. Williams (2000), pp. 192–244.

situation. In the graduated path, however, at least from a Tantric perspective, the accumulation of wisdom and means is normally done as two separate enterprises, and each takes a long time.[22] In Tantra they are developed simultaneously, and on multiple levels, as we shall see shortly. Within the context of the doctrine of the Buddha's three bodies (see 8.2), it should be said, the Buddha himself can be thought of as embodying wisdom/emptiness in his truth body (his dharmakāya) and expedient means/compassion in his emanation body (his rūpakāya). Visualizers, therefore, unite wisdom and means when they "realize" the Buddha as a whole and see him in his enjoyment body (his sambhogakāya).

10.5.1 Uniting the Poles

There are many contexts or levels in which this union of wisdom and means can be expressed and achieved. One of the more noteworthy of these is in different symbolic manifestations of gender polarity. In Buddhist Tantra (unlike Hindu Tantra), expedient means is thought of as male, and wisdom is thought of as female, so that the joining of wisdom and means lends itself to being symbolized as sexual union. Such unions can be seen iconographically in what Tibetans call yab-yum (father-mother) images depicting a Buddha (= expedient means) in coitus with a consort (= wisdom) who embraces him, sitting on his lap. The same union can be actualized as part of a visualization in which the meditator identifies himself with the Buddha in union with "the Mother" who then form a single non-dual unit. Or, rarely and only by advanced practitioners, non-duality can be achieved by a ritual of controlled sexual union with a "real" partner who is referred to as a "seal" (mūdrā).[23]

At a ritual level, the union can be achieved by the simultaneous use of two symbolic ritual implements: a vajra (or thunderbolt; Tib., dorje [rdo rje]) which is held by the meditating ritualist in the right hand and symbolizes the masculine – compassion and means; and the bell (ghanta; Tib., dril bu) which is held in the left hand and symbolizes the feminine – emptiness and wisdom.

22 See Powers (2007), p. 274. Already in Mainstream Buddhism, it was asserted all buddhas, during the course of their previous lives as bodhisattvas, have "equally accumulated merit and knowledge" (La Vallée Poussin, 1988–1990, vol. 4, p. 1145).

23 For examples of visualized union, see the text translated in Beyer (1974), pp. 146–153, and also the translation entitled "The Ultimate Couple" in Gyatso (2004). On ritual partners, see Powers (2007), pp. 289–291; on the practice with them, see Davidson (2002), pp. 318–322.

10.5.2 Tantric Physiology

This union can also occur inside the meditator's body. Buddhist Tantra, it should be said, makes use of a subtle physiology according to which the human body contains within it 72,000 channels (Skt., nāḍī; Tib., tsa [rtsa]), a network which in its coverage is not unlike our neural or vascular systems, but differs from them in that it is invisible to Western science, and serves a distinct function. Sometimes it is compared to the system of channels in acupuncture. Along these channels flow "winds" or "breaths" (Skt., prāṇa; Tib., lung [rlung]), vital spirits perhaps not dissimilar to the Chinese notion of qi. The channels and winds are important not only in meditation but also in traditional Tibetan medicine. The winds can be directed to various parts of the body by consciousnesses which are said to travel mounted on the winds like a rider on a horse. The most important of the channels is the central one which runs parallel to the spine. It is surrounded by two other important channels – one on the left and one on the right, which intersect with it at various key points called "wheels" (Skt., cakra; Tib., tsakor [rtsa 'khor]). Cakras are also featured in Kuṇḍalinī Yoga and Hindu Tantra. In Buddhist practice, the number of cakras varies somewhat from source to source, but the most important of them are located at the crown of the head, the throat, the heart, the navel, the base of the spine, and the opening of the sexual organ.[24]

The central channel, called the avadhūti (Tib., tsa u ma [rtsa dbu ma]), and the heart cakra provide a locus within the body where non-duality can be realized, through a number of meditational visualizing techniques. One of these is for the meditator to use his/her concentration and inner powers of visualization to bring together in the central channel all of the winds (and the consciousnesses that they carry) that come from both sides of the body. This is a process that involves unblocking the openings between the right and left channels and the central channel, especially at the crown of the head cakra and the base of the spine cakra. In Tantra, the right hand symbolizes the male aspect of compassion and expedient means and the left hand the female aspect of emptiness and wisdom. The union of these two in the central channel is therefore equated with giving rise to bodhicitta – the compassionate mind set on the realization of emptiness.[25]

The practice, however, does not stop there. Once the winds have been gathered inside the central channel, a new expression of the basic duality

24 On channels and cakras, see the discussion in Cozort (1986), pp. 44–45.
25 On this meditation, see Powers (2007), p. 289.

(and new opportunities for overcoming it) are encountered. The polarity now becomes a vertical one, focusing on the winds in the upper end of the central channel on the one hand, and those at its lower end on the other. The endeavor of the meditator will be to bring them together in the heart cakra in the middle.

Here, an additional feature of Tantric subtle physiology needs to be introduced. Ideologically, Tantra may be thought of as stemming from both the Yogācāra school, with its emphasis on the primacy of Mind and its creative (or at least prismatic) powers, and the Madhyamaka school with its stress on emptiness. The mixture of these two pedigrees may be seen in the Vajrayāna's conceptualization of enlightenment as a realization or vision of "the clear light of the mind," something that is common, in one fashion or another, in all the Tibetan schools. In Tantric physiology, the Mind to be so realized resides not in one's head but in one's heart. More specifically, it is within an "indestructible drop" within the heart cakra.

Besides "channels" and "cakras," we also have within us red and white "drops" (Skt., bindu; Tib., tiglé [thig le]). These may be thought of as "cells" evolved from the white drop (= semen) and red drop (= blood, ovum) one has inherited from one's father and mother at the time of conception. The white drops are said to cluster in the cakra at the top of one's head, at least during one's lifetime. The red drops are said to cluster in the lower cakras. In the middle, at the heart cakra, is the original "indestructible" drop – the zygote inherited from one's parents, which is white on top and red at the bottom. This drop is said to last from the moment of one's conception to the time of one's death, and so assures continuity throughout a single lifetime. Inside it is an even subtler drop that lasts for the whole duration of one's existence in saṃsāra up until the moment of enlightenment; it is said to be made of very subtle consciousness and wind.[26]

The Tantric meditator who wishes to experience the clear light of the mind proceeds by using the winds gathered in the central channel above the heart cakra to move downwards towards it, and similarly uses the winds gathered in the central channel below the heart cakra to rise up to it. When the force of the winds causes the heart cakra to become "unblocked," union can occur: the red and white drops dissolve into the red and white parts of the indestructible zygote within the heart cakra. Usually, the movement and dissolution of these drops is said to be aided by the kindling of an inner heat, a great fire at the base of the central channel that is lit when the left

26 On the red and white drops, see Cozort (1986), pp. 72–73.

and right winds are first brought into it. This heat, identified with the fierce goddess Cāṇḍālī, and known in Tibetan as Tummo (gtum mo), causes the red and white drops to melt and detach from the walls of the channels to which they cling and to flow more easily where they are directed.[27] When the red and white drops have all dissolved into the indestructible zygote, the winds dissolve into the very subtle consciousness and wind at its center, and when all the winds have been dissolved, "the mind of clear light manifests" (Powers, 2007, p. 285).

This same process, it should be said, occurs naturally in the course of a person going through the experience of dying, but with different forces at work. Ordinarily, during one's lifetime, the white and red drops in one's body are kept separate from each other (in the upper and lower cakras) by the winds (our vital energies) that circulate through the body's channels. At death, these winds weaken and begin to dissipate. As they do, the white drops descend the central channel and gather in the heart cakra, and the red drops mount up and join them there as well. Then when all winds cease, consciousness leaves the body, and the person experiences what is known as "the clear light of death" (Powers, 2007, pp. 338–339). Unfortunately, people who lack training in Tantra are terrified by this experience and fail to recognize it for what it is – the clear light of the mind – and so follow their very subtle consciousness on to rebirth (see 8.6.4).

10.5.3 Mahāmūdra and Dzokchen (Rdzogs chen)

Tantric practices of the type just described may well be a short path to buddhahood, but they are obviously also highly structured. Before moving on to look at Chan/Zen, therefore, mention should be made of two Vajrayāna meditational practices that Harvey has dubbed "Tantric Techniques of Spontaneity" (2013, p. 357). Both consist primarily of methods of cutting down on and letting peter out thought processes that are said to occlude the naturally pure state of one's mind. In Mahāmūdra ("Great Symbol"; Tib., chyakgya chenpo [phyag rgya chen po]), mindfulness and śamatha (tranquility) meditations

27 On the practice of Tummo, one of the six yogas of Naropa, see Powers (2007), pp. 406–407. The meditation is said to have the effect of warming the body (to the point that adepts are able to dry wet cotton cloths wrapped around them on icy-cold nights – see the now classic account by David-Neel, 1971, pp. 216–229). Scientific data are consistent in showing the meditation is effective in raising body temperature by several degrees (see, for example, Benson, 1982).

are used to control and observe the processes of the mind in an effort to calm and silence it and get back to one's innate naturally enlightened state. This does not mean a trance: in Mahāmūdra, the steady mind is said to be no different than the flickering mind, and the ideal is to achieve a spontaneous way of being in the world. This teaching is associated with the Kagyü school and is often exemplified by such teachers as Milarépa and the siddhas ("accomplished ones") in Indian Tantra. Dzokchen ("Great Perfection") is an equivalent practice but associated with the Nyingma school. It aims at cutting through the ordinary operations of discursive thought to achieve a direct perception of the pure luminosity of the mind, so that "compassion and wisdom become spontaneous" (Powers, 2007, pp. 391–392).

10.6 DIRECT EXPERIENCES: CHAN/ZEN

Both Mahāmūdra and Dzokchen are occasionally likened to Chan/Zen. To some extent this is true, but the comparisons are somewhat facile and should not be pressed too far. It is often said (and Chan texts occasionally say it themselves) that Chan is a "separate transmission [of the Dharma] outside the teachings" that points directly at one's Buddha-nature (McRae, 2003, pp. 2–3). This is reflected in the tradition that the Chan/Zen lineage of the Dharma can be traced back through the Chinese patriarchs to Bodhidharma (who came from India) and prior to him all the way back to the Buddha, through the Masters of the Dharma (see 3.5). Chan is said to have originated when, in front of his disciples, the Buddha held up a flower; only Mahākāśyapa (the first Indian patriarch) understood, and smiled. As one scholar put it: "This story indicates the direct nature of much of Chan teaching, cutting straight through the trappings of discursive thought" (Williams, 2009, p. 119).

Significantly, unlike many of the other Chinese (and Japanese) Buddhist schools, Chan/Zen does not see itself as being associated with one particular sūtra or set of sūtras. Some early Chan monks may have been aficionados of the *Scripture on the Descent to Lankā* (*Lankāvatāra Sūtra*), but it was "more revered in the abstract than actually studied" (McRae, 2003, p. 62), and its place in the tradition was never akin to that of the *Lotus Sūtra* in Tiantai or the *Avataṃsaka Sūtra* in Huayan, for example. This does not mean that Chan/Zen monks were not scholarly inclined or prolific students of Buddhist texts. Chan/Zen literature is voluminous, and certain masters (e.g. Dōgen) figure among the most sophisticated philosophers Buddhism has ever produced. It is just that the soteriological place of textual learning on the path is different, and the tradition allows itself a certain iconoclastic questioning of scholarship, something that is emphasized, for instance, in the (completely apocryphal) legend of Huineng, the sixth Chinese patriarch, which proclaims him to be illiterate, a menial kitchen worker.[28]

The same thing can be said about merit making. A legend about Bodhidharma, the so-called first Chinese patriarch who is credited with bringing Chan from India, features an interview he is said to have had with the emperor Wu of the Liang dynasty (464–549), who was renowned as one of the greatest patrons of the Buddhist saṃgha in Chinese history. The emperor, wanting to get a measure of his own progress on the path, asked Bodhidharma how much merit he had made from building monasteries, endowing the community, funding Buddha images, distributing relics, sponsoring ordinations, sūtra-copying, etc. Bodhidharma is said to have replied: "No merit at all" (Broughton, 1999, p. 3). This does not mean that Chan practitioners are unconcerned with doing good deeds, moral discipline, or conducting or sponsoring rituals. They are. It is just that such things occupy a different place in the Chan path than they do in the graduated path.

The word "Chan" or "Zen" is derived from the Sanskrit "dhyāna" meaning meditative trance. Chan literature includes a number of formal meditation manuals giving advice as to how to practice. Chan meditation, however, is not "one thing." It gradually evolved over time, and as it moved from China to Korea and to Japan, it differed according to school, or even from master to master. Some of the earliest records of Chan meditation (end of the sixth century) feature something called "wall contemplation" (Ch., biguan), something that none other than Bodhidharma and his "disciple" Huike are said to have practiced, instead of "dabbling in scriptures" (Broughton, 1999, p. 5).[29]

In time, the notion of "wall contemplation" gave birth to a legend that Bodhidharma spent nine years in a cave, at the Shaolin Monastery, staring at an actual wall (to the point that his legs atrophied and fell off), and, indeed, monks in certain Zen sects, to this day, sit in meditation facing the wall. But "wall contemplation" probably originally meant some sort of śamatha

28 For more on the *Lankāvatāra Sūtra* in Chan, see McRae (1986), pp. 15–29. On the story of Huineng, see McRae (2000), and Yampolsky (1967).

29 Two Chan meditation manuals may be found in the *Platform Sūtra of the Sixth Patriarch* (*Liuzu tan jing*), and in Huangbo's *Essentials of the Transmission of Mind* (*Chuanxin fayao*), translated in McRae (2000), and McRae (2005a). More generally on meditation in China, see Kiyota (1978a), and Gregory (1986).

practice "that dispenses with all stages of progress and aims at pacifying the mind and achieving a state in which all things are one and the same" (Hudson, 2005, p. 1292). By this technique which "abides in brightness," and is "non-discriminative, quiescent and inactive" (Broughton, 1999, p. 67), one comes to realize one's own innate buddhahood.[30]

10.6.1 Kōans

Such seated meditation (Ch., zuochan; Jpn., zazen) was to remain a feature of Chan, but it also came to be criticized by the tradition, especially when it was thought that it risked becoming a mere activity, a means to an end. In this regard, a famous Zen story is instructive: it tells of a monk who was very earnest in practicing seated meditation in order to attain buddhahood. One day, he found his master busily rubbing a roof tile with a rock. He asked him what he was doing. "I'm grinding this tile to make it into a mirror," came the reply. "No amount of grinding will succeed in doing that!" objected the disciple. "Just so," replied the master, "no amount of seated meditation will bring you to enlightenment!"[31]

By the ninth century, emphasis (at least in certain Chan schools) began to shift to "encounter dialogues" and the use of kōans (Ch., gong'an; lit., "public case"), methods that came to be systematized during the Song dynasty (*c.*950–1300) – which in many ways was the Golden Age of Chan. McRae has stated that:

> the best way to understand such [encounters] is as a function of the fundamental mismatch of intention between the students and masters as depicted in these texts. The students are generally depicted as requesting assistance in ascending the path of Buddhist spiritual training toward enlightenment. The masters, for their part, are represented as refusing to accede to their students' naïve entreaties, instead deflecting their goal-seeking perspective and attempting to propel them into the realization of their own inherent perfection.
>
> (McRae, 2003, p. 78)

30 On the legend of Bodhidharma's cave meditation, see Shahar (2008), pp. 12–17. For a brief overview, see Hudson (1995). For various interpretations of wall-gazing, see McRae (1986), pp. 112–115.

31 For different tellings of this story, see McRae (2003), p. 80, and Faure (1997), p. 73.

Kōans "capture the dramatic and inscrutable encounters between masters and disciples" (Heine, 2002, p. 1). Generally, the masters are portrayed as instructing the disciples, but those instructions (if they can be called that) are "characterized by various types of logical disjunctions, inexplicable and iconoclastic pronouncements" (McRae, 2003, p. 78), "quixotic, paradoxical and often absurd utterances, reprimands, and gestures designed to twist and torment the ordinary rational mind and trigger a spiritual breakthrough to a realm beyond reason" (Heine, 2002, p. 1).

For example, here is a story about the ninth-century master, Juzhi (Jpn., Gutei):

> Whenever master Juzhi was asked a question, he would simply hold up one finger. One time a visitor to the temple asked Juzhi's attendant about his master's teachings. The boy also just held up one finger. When Juzhi heard about this, he cut off the boy's finger. The boy, screaming in pain, began to run away, but Juzhi called him back. When the boy turned around, Juzhi held up one finger. The boy experienced enlightenment.
>
> (Heine, 2002, p. 173)

There could hardly be a better example of "sudden awakening."

Such violence, of course, is not always featured, and, even when it is, it is not always on the teacher's side. For instance, consider the famous encounter between Bodhidharma and the person who was to succeed him as patriarch, Huike:

> As Bodhidharma sat in zazen meditation while facing a wall, Huike ... stood out in the snow. [Frustrated that Bodhidharma was paying no attention to him and not teaching him, Huike] cut off his arm [as a testimony of his sincerity and determination]. He then said: "Your disciple's mind is not yet at peace. I beg you, my teacher, please bring peace to my mind." Bodhidharma said, "Bring me your mind, and I will bring peace to it for you." Huike said, "I have looked for my mind, but it is not graspable." Bodhidharma said, "There, I have brought peace to your mind for you."
>
> (Heine, 2002, pp. 177–178)

When kōans first became known in the West, largely through the works of D. T. Suzuki, a great deal of emphasis was laid on the "enlightened," "non-rational," "spontaneous" character of some of their actions and responses. Kōans, it was maintained, could not be understood by the normal operations of the (Western) rational mind. The Zen experience, it was proclaimed, was inscrutable and went beyond thought, beyond rational discourse. In recent times, however, scholars have criticized Suzuki (and others) for their stress on mystical paradoxical impenetrability, and have emphasized the fact that kōans need to be viewed in the context – literary, cultural, and religious – in which they were first formulated. The two anecdotes just recounted, for instance, will be read differently when we realize that the sacrifices of fingers or arms were ritual devotional acts of dedication to the Buddha, which themselves were imitations of some of the sacrifices he is said to have made on his way to buddhahood.[32]

The case for the importance of context can be seen in various interpretations given to the following example: "A monk asked Dongshan (Jpn., Tōzan) 'What is "Buddha"?' Dongshan replied, 'Three pounds of hemp'" (McRae, 2003, p. 74). At first glance, this seems to make little sense. But perhaps that is the point. R. H. Blyth (who dedicated his 1966 translation of the *Gateless Gate* (Ch., *Wumen guan*; Jpn., *Mumonkan*) – one of the classic collections of kōans – to D. T. Suzuki) interprets it this way: "What is Buddha," he says, "is the most difficult question man can ask. [It is like] what is God? What is Truth? What is Life? ... Tōzan's answer comes then as a kind of anticlimax, too absurd to be serious, and if it does not make you laugh when you hear it, you are in a bad way indeed" (Blyth, 1966, p. 144). Alan Watts (who dedicated his book to his then three young children because they would "understand it all the better for not being able to read it") states, quoting Suzuki: "Various answers have been given by different masters to the question 'What is the Buddha?'... None, however, can excel Dongshan's 'three pounds of flax' [i.e. hemp]," and then he adds: "The masters are resolute in cutting short all theorizing and speculation about these answers. 'Direct pointing' entirely fails in its intention if it requires or stimulates any conceptual comment" (Watts, 1957, pp. 147–148). Both of these exegeses fit into the kind of scholarship that was common in Zen

32 Suzuki was an extremely prolific author. For some of his writings on Zen, see Suzuki (1958). For critiques of Suzuki, see Hu Shih (1953), and Sharf (1995a). One book which reflects a Suzuki approach to Zen and was quite influential in the West was Eugen Herrigel's *Zen in the Art of Archery* (1953). For a critique and contextualization of it, see Yamada (2009). On self-immolations in Chinese Buddhism, see Benn (2007).

Studies fifty years ago (and there were even further misunderstandings: when I first read this kōan in college, we associated hemp with marijuana and Dongshan's answer took on a whole new meaning!). The illogicality disappears, however, when it is realized, as McRae points out, that in the Tang dynasty, three pounds of hemp was "the standard allotment of cloth for a set of monks robes ... In other words, when asked the meaning of the word 'Buddha' [Dongshan] responded, more or less, 'A set of monk's robes is all it takes'" (McRae, 2003, p. 76).[33] This, in itself, of course, is not exactly a direct answer, and is demanding of further exploration and understanding, but it does mean that meditation on the answer to the question, "What is the Buddha?" would, in this case, proceed from a very different starting point. This example, of course, does not mean that all kōans "make sense," but at least it hints that they are not chaotic nonsense, and that they are rich and meaningful in their connotations.

10.6.2 Critical Phrases (Huatou)

Kōans as a whole were given to Zen students to be meditated upon and "resolved." In this way, they served to focus their thoughts. A further development in the practice came with a method which reduced the kōan to a single "critical phrase" or huatou (Jpn., watō; Kor., hwadu), often a single key word. For instance, one of the most common beginner-kōans given to Rinzai Zen monks today is the first case of the *Gateless Gate*: a monk asked Zhaozhou, "Does a dog have the Buddha-nature?" Zhaozhou answered "Wu!" (i.e. "No"). The "keyword" in this kōan would be "Wu!" (Jpn., "Mu!"). Doctrinally, of course, this answer flies in the face of the assertion that all beings have the Buddha-nature.[34] As a "critical phrase," however, it becomes a focus of concentration. The meditative process is well explained by Buswell:

> The [critical phrase] is the focus of a sustained investigation, via a more discursive examination of the question, "Why did Zhaozhou say a dog doesn't have the buddha-nature when the answer clearly should

33 McRae points out that this colloquial usage of the term was soon forgotten in China and so was not understood by Japanese masters such as Dōgen who took Dongshan to be referring to three pounds of sesame seeds, and struggled to understand what he meant.

34 For a contextual history of the emergence of the huatou, see Schlütter (2008), pp. 104–121.

> be that it does?," which is called "investigation of the meaning"; this investigation helps to generate questioning or "doubt," which is the force that drives this type of practice forward. As that investigation matures, it changes into a nondiscursive attention to just the word "no" itself, which is called "investigation of the word" because the meditator's attention is then thoroughly absorbed in this "sensation of doubt." This type of investigation is said to be nonconceptual and places the meditation at the "access to realization," viz. "sudden awakening."[35]

A fine example of this comes in the autobiographical account of the Japanese Master Hakuin (1686–1768), who struggled mightily with Zhaozhou's "Wu!" for over two years, experiencing great doubt and a period he called "Zen sickness," before finally achieving a breakthrough realization.[36]

Hakuin, in fact, was responsible for revivifying and systematizing kōan practice which was first introduced into Japan in the twelfth century. One of the features of the Japanese system is a hierarchization of kōans which are arranged in "degrees of difficulty" and given consecutively to Zen students, and also the use of "capping phrases" (jakugo), collections of approved possible "answers" or "responses" to kōans. Zen student practitioners will select a "capping phrase" that best exemplifies their understanding and try it out in one-on-one interviews (called dokusan) with the Zen master.[37]

Of the two main schools of Zen in Japan, Rinzai (Ch., Linji) and Sōtō (Ch., Caodong), the former stresses Hakuin's kōan practice more. Even though Dōgen, the founder of the Sōtō school, was himself a great kōan scholar, his emphasis was more on "just sitting" in zazen, which itself is reflective of the ideology behind sudden enlightenment. For him "just sitting" meant just that. Zazen meditation was not to be seen as a practice aiming at enlightenment but was itself enlightenment. Beings being buddhas already by nature do not need to become buddhas but merely to be what they already are, and this was best expressed through zazen. As one author put it: "This is a creative resolution to Chan/Zen's perennial problem of harmonizing the doctrine of sudden enlightenment with the real need for meditation practice" (Hudson, 1995, p. 1293).[38]

---

35 Buswell, in the online *Digital Dictionary of Buddhism* (s.v. "huatou"), http://www.buddhism-dict.net/ddb.

36 See Strong (2008), pp. 327–329.

37 On the use of capping phrases in kōan meditation, see Hori (2003).

38 On Dōgen's use of kōans, see Heine (1994).

10.7 SUMMARY

We have, in this chapter, looked at different conceptions of the Mahāyāna path to buddhahood. We began by examining the bodhisattva path and different opinions about its nature, as well as various characterizations of enlightenment. We then went on to consider several presentations of the graduated path to buddhahood, set out in East Asian and Tibetan traditions, as well as several examples of "shortcut" traditions exemplified in Tantra and in Zen.

Chapter 11

Saṃgha Situations: Places, Persons, and Practices in Thai Buddhism/s

In chapter 6, we examined some of the basic relationships and structures within the Buddhist order, and in chapter 7, we looked at some of the factionalism that developed within the community. In this chapter and chapters 12 and 13, I would like to approach matters in a slightly different fashion. I propose to look at historical as well as modern-day "saṃgha situations" by focusing on specific places, particular rites, and individual persons. Given the limitations of space, I have decided to restrict myself to traditions from just three countries. In what follows, I will use examples to illustrate Buddhism as it was and is lived in Thailand (in this chapter), in Japan (in chapter 12), and in Tibet (in chapter 13). I do so in the hopes that these several glimpses can help form some concrete concept of some aspects of Buddhist life in these regions and these traditions.

I have tried to make these examples as concrete and first hand as possible, so as to give a sense of the "realia" of Buddhism "on the ground," both in historic and contemporary times. Some instances are taken from the accounts of others, and some are based on my own experiences in these various settings. First, by way of introduction, I will start with a very brief account of the history of Buddhism in Thailand (11.1). Then, I will look at the phenomenon of temporary ordination in Thailand, focusing on a single contemporary individual's experience (11.2). Following that, we will become acquainted with the lives of two nineteenth-/twentieth-century Thai Buddhist saints (11.3), and then with the contemporary celebration of an annual festival in a northern Thai village (11.4). Finally, since Thai Buddhism is, today, found not only in Thailand but in other parts of the world, we will look at a Thai monastery in suburban London (11.5).

11.1 BUDDHISM IN THAILAND

Thai Buddhists, like their counterparts in Myanmar and Sri Lanka (see 1.2.2 and 1.2.4), often claim that Theravāda Buddhism was first introduced to their country by missionary monks sent by King Aśoka (third century BCE), even though there are also legends of mythic visits of the Buddha himself to the region. For them, Suvarṇabhūmi (the Golden Land) is located not in southern Myanmar as the Burmese claim, but in the region just south of Bangkok (and indeed, in line with this legend, the name chosen for the new Bangkok International Airport was "Suvarnabhumi").[1]

History, however, is more complex and nebulous than these traditions would have us believe. From early on (*c.* fourth century CE), and continuing thereafter, various kinds of Buddhism (Theravāda, other Mainstream schools, Mahāyāna, and Tantra), practiced in various regionally based and ethnically distinct cultures (Mon, Srivijayan, Khmer, Burmese), combined and competed in complex ways with Hindu Brahmanical elements as well as indigenous animistic beliefs, in the area that is now called Thailand. The Tai people themselves did not arrive in the region until the twelfth/thirteenth century CE, when they migrated south from southwestern China. Shortly thereafter, under the influence of Sinhalese lineages imported from Sri Lanka, a Theravāda orthodoxy was nominally adopted, and became dominant as the Tais established kingdoms centered on Chiangmai and Sukhothai. Subsequently, the capital moved to Ayudhya (in 1351) and then to Bangkok (in 1767, after Ayudhya was sacked by the Burmese). Despite the official ascendancy of Theravāda Buddhism, even today, "syncretism continues to define many Thai religious practices" (Swearer, 2004a, p. 831). Buddhism in Thailand, then, both has affinities with the Theravāda traditions of other South and Southeast Asian cultures, and also departs from them.[2]

1 For a discussion of the Aśokan Suvarṇabhūmi tradition, see Assavavirulhakarn (2010), pp. 59–65. For legends of the Buddha's visits to what is now Thailand, see Swearer, Sommai, and Phaitoon (2004).

2 On the early period, see Guy (2014). For a general history of Thailand, see Wyatt (1984).

11.2 THAI MONASTIC LIFE: TEMPORARY ORDINATION

One feature that distinguishes Thai Buddhist community life is the practice of temporary ordination. Students in my classes often have an idealized image of Buddhist monks as persons who have embarked on a lifelong quest for enlightenment and are committed to a regime of strict discipline and meditation. In fact, in Southeast Asia, individuals become monastics (either novices or fully ordained) for all sorts of reasons. Most Thai men (statistics vary from sixty to ninety percent) join the saṃgha for a limited amount of time (a few days or weeks, or typically for a rains-retreat of three months), in their teens (as novices) and/or early twenties (as full monks). For them, ordination is a way of making merit for themselves and for their families (especially their mothers). It is also a sort of cultural rite of passage, a coming-of-age experience prior to marriage and a career. It is commonly thought that men who have been monks (even for a short while) not only make better husbands once they resume their lay lives, but better businessmen, better merchants, better army officers, etc. Indeed, some companies will give their male employees paid leaves-of-absence to become ordained for a rainy season.

What follows is the account of the temporary monastic experiences of one man. Nattawud Daoruang (who later changed his name to Panrit Daoruang) started blogging at a young age about his life as a Thai teenager. He soon set up a web-based journal called "Thailand Life" which grew into a regular column for the *Bangkok Post*, in which he wrote daily accounts of his experiences as a child and young adult (he is now in his late twenties). Here, he chronicled his experiences with drugs, with gambling, with motorcycle racing, with prostitution, with teenage parenthood, with having to make it in a rough and tumble world. He also recalled his monastic experiences.

11.2.1 Life as a Novice

Nattawud initially became a novice when he was about eleven years old, at his parents' request when his grandfather was sick and passing away. This is a fairly common Thai practice: for a family member (often a young boy) to join the saṃgha temporarily, with the understanding that the merit from that will be transferred to an ill or dying relative. As Nattawud put it, "Thai people believe that when they die they will go to paradise by holding on to a monk's robe. So I became a monk to help my grandfather go to paradise." In such circumstances, most boys become monastics only for a few days, but Nattawud remained in the saṃgha for a month because it was the school holidays. He was ordained as a novice at the local wat (monastery/temple) next door to his grandparents' house. First, his hair and eyebrows were shaved off; next he was made to repeat some formulae in Pali which he did not understand, he was informed of the ten precepts, and then he was assisted in putting on a set of robes. The rest is best told in his own words:

"Afterwards, the monk took me with my parents to the place where I will sleep. In Thai it is called kuti. Mine was a little wooden building with three rooms. I shared it with two monks, Phra Noo and Phra Mongkhon. Upstairs were two bedrooms and the living room was downstairs. Phra Mongkhon slept downstairs. There was a t.v. (with cable t.v.), play station, radio, bookshelves, fridge, sink, kettle and clock. My bed was a thin mattress on the floor and a pillow. Outside was a bathroom and a toilet. I was very surprised when I saw the monks playing games on the Play Station. My parents didn't stay long and I was soon alone. I felt a little scared but the monks were kind to me. We played some games and then I went to bed at about 9 p.m....

"On the first day, the monks woke me up at 5.00 a.m. They told me to go and take a bath and put on my robes. We then had to meditate inside our kuti. I had never done this before, so they had to show me what to do. I sat down cross-legged and closed my eyes. I then repeated after the monk in Pali. I didn't understand the words at the time, but he told me the meaning later. Meditation helps you feel calm. We did this for about 30 minutes.

"At about 6 [a.m.] we left the temple for bintabat [almsround]. This is when monks go walking around the village for alms-giving. I went with Phra Noo and a dek wat, a temple boy who came to help carry the food. Phra Mongkhon went a different way. We walked down the same roads everyday. We were not allowed to wear shoes. My feet hurt and I had a lot of blisters. We stopped many times for people to give us food and drink. They waited outside their house for us and then called us to come over. When they gave the food to us we are not allowed to say 'thank you.' When people give to the monks it is called tam bun [making merit] ... We say a blessing to them and then go on walking down the road. We don't carry the food ourselves, we give it to the dek wat. After about one hour our black alms bowl and ... cloth bags were very full.

"Back at the temple, we chose which food we wanted to eat for breakfast and lunch. We then ate while the dek wat cleaned our kuti. After we had finished, the dek wat ate his share. Sometimes he gave some to the dogs and cats that lived in the temple. The dek wat also had to wash the dishes. I watched t.v., played video games and slept for a while. We had lunch at about 11.30 a.m. All monks have to finish eating before midday. We are not allowed to eat in the afternoon and evening, but we can drink milk.

"Most days were the same. I watched t.v., played video games, listened to the radio and read a cartoon book. Sometimes I went out to a local shop to buy more cartoon books. If I went out in the morning I sometimes bought a snack to eat. But I was not allowed to do that in the afternoon. Sometimes my parents came to visit me in the morning. They gave me food for breakfast and lunch. On those days I did not go out into the village. My parents had to wai me [bow to me], which is how we show respect in Thai. I felt shy because usually I wai my parents when I go to school and when I come back home. But this time they had to wai me because I was a novice monk. I was not allowed to wai them back. To wai, you put your hands together up to your chest and then bow your head down.

"In the evenings, I usually took a bath at about 8 p.m. Then I meditated with Phra Noo and Phra Mongkhon for about 30 minutes. I didn't like meditating because it was very boring and uncomfortable sitting still on the ground. I then went to bed straight away because we had to get up early in the morning.

"On the last day my parents came to pick me up. We had a special ceremony first called seauk. I had to repeat after the monk some words in Pali like before. I also had to change my robes and put on my shorts and t-shirt. I was happy to leave because I could now eat after lunch. I did not really enjoy myself but I was happy that I could help my grandfather."[3]

11.2.2 Experiences as a Monk

A few years later, in 2005 when he had turned twenty, Nattawud was ordained temporarily again, this time as a full monk, and this time for the sake of his mother, and "in order to make up for all the bad things [he had] done to [his] family" and friends. The ceremony itself lasted two days. On the first afternoon, he went to the temple with his mother and grandmother to light incense in honor of their dead ancestors, and to inform them that he would become a monk. He then proceeded to wash the feet of all his elder

3 http://www.thailandqa.com/forum/showthread.php?2795-Thai-men-becoming-monks.

relatives and pay his respects to them. Then it was time for his tonsure. His grandmother, followed by his other relatives, each cut off snippets of hair that were put on a lotus leaf that would later be floated on the river. Then his grandfather lathered his head and one of the monks shaved him. He then went back home and changed into the white robes of a candidate for ordination. Henceforth, he became known as a "naak" (Pali, nāga), the name given to all ordinands in honor of the snake divinity (nāga) who tried to become a monk despite not being a human. Before proceeding with the ceremony, however, he got in the back of a pickup truck and went in a festive procession around the neighborhood in order to pay his respects to the shrines of all the local divinities (phī), to announce to them his intention of becoming a monk, and to get their blessings. Then, along with his family and friends, he proceeded to the sala, or main assembly hall of the temple, where they listened to nine monks (an auspicious number) chanting, and then to a sermon by one of them on the importance of family. Token offerings were made to each of the monks, followed by a transfer of merit to dead relatives.[4]

The next day, the actual ordination ceremony was held not in the sala hall but in the smaller "bot," the monastery's chapel that has been consecrated by the placement around it of boundary stones (sīma) and that is reserved for all formal acts of the saṃgha. Nattawud, still dressed in white, walked to the temple in the midst of a great parade of relatives and acquaintances, accompanied by drummers and dancers and a band. After the whole party circumambulated the bot several times, they stopped in front of the building. There, he knelt on the ground, lit incense, and, in order to show his renunciation of worldly things, tossed coins over his shoulder into the crowd behind him who scrambled for these tokens of good luck. Inside the bot, all the monks of the wat, including the abbot, were waiting. Nattawud prostrated himself five times, then, holding his monk's robes over his forearms, his hands proffered in respect, he repeated, in Pali, the formulae requesting permission to wander forth. It should be said that, before becoming ordained as a full monk, he had once again (as he had nine years earlier) to go through the rite of becoming a novice (called wandering forth – pravrajya). This was then followed immediately by his full ordination proper (upasaṃpadā). The ritual itself has already been covered in chapter 4. Suffice it to say here that, once it was over, equipped with his robes and bowl, he then withdrew to his

4 On the story of the nāga who wanted to become a monk but could not, see Strong (2008), pp. 74–75. On the worship of phī in Thailand, see Tambiah (1970).

assigned lodgings in the monastery. He would remain a monk for the next three weeks.[5]

During this time, he was once again nominally expected to go on pindapatha (begging round) every morning, to behave decorously at all times, especially when outside the monastery, and to observe the 227 precepts of the Pali Vinaya. Basically, however, his daily routine was not that different from that which he had experienced as a novice (see above), except that this time, being older, he was more aware of some of the discrepancies between the ideals of monastic life and reality. As he explained to a foreign friend who asked him at the time about his going on alms rounds: "I have never walked so much in my life. I have to walk several kilometers every day. Wan Phra is the worst day. This is the Buddhist holy day like your Sundays [but falling on the phases of the moon in the lunar calendar]. A lot of people come out to make merit on those days. I had so much the other day that it filled up three or four bags. I had to come back by motorcycle taxi as it was too much to carry. We cannot refuse them because it would be very rude." He also discovered that, although, according to the rules of the Vinaya, Buddhist monks are not supposed to "handle gold and silver" (i.e. to touch and use money), in fact, lay persons commonly give them cash: "[Wan Phra] is also the day when we get a lot of money. They put it in envelopes for us as a way of making merit. Some monks can get 1000 baht [in 2005, about $25.00] or more. These monks have been here a long time so they know the good places to hang out. But I only got less than 200 baht. We keep the money ourselves because we have to pay for everything at the temple. We have to pay for electricity and water and things like that."

Asked what he found hardest about monastic life, Nattawud replied: "studying the yellow book. This is full of chants that we have to use during the day. Some chants we use everyday and they are the easiest to remember. However, sometimes we are invited to people's houses or funerals and there are different chants for us to remember. To help us, one of the monks is a senior and he leads the chanting and we follow. I cannot just pretend I am chanting by moving my lips. I really have to chant. I go outside the temple to do this about once or twice a week. We all take turns. The abbot is the person who chooses which monks can go. But he makes sure everyone has an equal chance. This is because we usually make money when we go and everyone

5 For descriptions and photos of each phase of the ceremony, see http://www.thailandlife.com/thai-monk/index.php. For a generalized account of Theravāda ordination, see Swearer (1995), pp. 46–52.

wants to do it. And the food is always very good. I sometimes get between 200 and 500 baht each time. But, one of my friends recently got 1000 baht for chanting at an ordination. It wasn't my turn that day."

Finally, asked which of the 227 precepts he found hardest to maintain, he admitted: "I don't really know them all. There are too many. I think you have to be here a long time before you can remember them all. But for me, the difficult ones are: not being allowed to be alone with a woman, not eating after lunch, not sleeping with a long pillow or on a soft mattress. But some monks do have a comfortable bed and pillows. They even have air-conditioning, cable TV and a computer in their room. There are different kinds of monks here. Some are serious about being a monk. Others are here because they cannot do anything else. If you stay in the right temple, it can be quite a comfortable life. Good food and good money. I think most monks make about 10,000 baht a month. There are of course some bad monks. I know that the ones in the kuti [monastic lodging] next door to mine take drugs. They order the drugs by mobile phone and it is delivered to their door by motorcycle taxi in the evening. Talking about delivery. Guess what I had for lunch today? My aunt ordered pizza for me!"[6]

Nattawud, of course, had no intention of remaining a monk the rest of his life. He was primarily doing this for his mother, and, a few weeks later, he in fact disrobed. It should be said that in Thailand, leaving the saṃgha has no stigma attached to it. The ceremony is, in fact, quite simple. Once an astrologically auspicious date and time for it have been determined, the disrobing monk goes to the abbot's quarters, where, after prostrating himself three times in front of the image of the Buddha, he is given one last chance to change his mind about his decision. If he decides not to, he then repeats three times the Pali formula stating, "I give up the training; let me be considered a householder." He then changes into lay clothing, returns to the abbot, and receives his blessings. The whole thing, it has been argued, should be seen not as a failure, but as a ritual rebirth of sorts. Having previously "died" to the world by becoming a monk, the ex-monk now re-enters the world, renewed by his monastic experience.[7]

---

6 http://www.thailandlife.com/thai-monk/life-in-a-thai-temple.html. For other real-life first-hand accounts of times in Thai Buddhist monasteries, see Pannapadipo (1997; 2001), and Terwiel (1994).

7 For an account of the ceremony of leaving the saṃgha, see Terwiel (1994), pp. 117–121.

11.3 THE LIVES OF TWO CHARISMATIC THAI MONKS

The prevalence of temporary ordination should not, of course, obscure the fact that numerous monks in Thailand (as elsewhere) opt for life-long careers in the saṃgha. In addition to all those who disrobe after a few months, there are venerable monks who, for personal, spiritual, or other reasons, remain in the order for many years. Some of these may rise through the ranks of the saṃgha hierarchy and hold important administrative posts. Others may eschew such posts and devote themselves to meditation or teaching. Prominent among these, in modern times, have been various "saints" – monastics who have achieved fame and leadership by virtue of their lifestyles and spiritual accomplishments. In what follows I want to look at two "saints" in particular, near contemporaries who, though now deceased, continue to inspire Thai Buddhists in the twenty-first century: Acharn ("teacher") Mun Bhūridatto (1871–1949), and Khruba ("holy man") Siwichai (1878–1939).

11.3.1 Acharn Mun

Acharn Mun grew up in a small village in northeastern Thailand not far from the Laotian border. When he was fifteen years old, he became a novice in his local wat where he remained for two years until he disrobed. At twenty-one, however, he opted to be ordained again, this time permanently as a full monk, at a wat in the provincial capital. There he devoted himself to the practice of Insight meditation (Vipassanā). One night he had a dream that convinced him that, if he exerted himself, he would be able to attain enlightenment in this very lifetime. Thereafter, he undertook to devote himself to the thirteen rigorous practices (dhutanga; Thai, thudong) which he observed for the rest of his life. These included such things as wearing robes made of discarded rags, owning only three robes, living only on what he obtained by begging, eating only one meal a day, living in the forest, staying in unsheltered places, and not lying down to sleep (see 7.3.4). This simple ascetic life of non-attachment was combined with a preference for intense meditation in solitude, in the open or in a forest hermitage. All told, Acharn Mun spent decades in the forests of the northeast, of Laos, and north of Chiang Mai near the Burmese border. Typically, according to his biographer, he would awaken at 3 A.M. and sit in meditation until it was time for him to go on his almsround to whatever village was nearby. On his return he would eat whatever was in his alms bowl, and then practice walking meditation, back and forth on a cleared path in the woods, until noon. He would then sit in meditation for an hour and a half, and follow that with two hours of walking meditation. He would then sweep the area he was staying in and do whatever chores were needed. This would be followed by a bath and more walking meditation until about 9 P.M., after which he would sit in meditation until 11 P.M., when he would go to sleep, only to wake up again at 3 A.M. the next day.[8]

In time, Acharn Mun's reputation for saintliness and wisdom grew. He began to attract disciples who came to learn from and be inspired by him, so that his forest hermitages became forest monastic centers in which a few dozen monks and novices would practice together – but in solitude – each in his own hut or on his own raised bamboo platform, spread out through the forest. Once a fortnight, they would gather for the recitation of the monastic code (Pāṭimokkha; Skt., prātimokṣa) and to listen to a sermon and receive instructions from the Master. In time, also, Acharn Mun's reputation for supernatural powers grew. He was rumored to have had all sorts of mystical experiences. He was thought to have overcome and converted demons; to have tamed wild tigers and snakes with his loving kindness; to have met direct disciples of the Buddha; to have had visions of and preached to various gods and nāgas and ghosts; to have healed others and himself by the power of the Dharma; and to have been able to levitate and read minds. He was widely considered by many to have accomplished his goal of becoming an arhat. After he died, surrounded by his disciples, his body was cremated, and his relics were collected and widely distributed to followers throughout Thailand, along with medallion-amulets struck with his image.[9]

11.3.2 *Khruba Siwichai*

Acharn Mun was a monk for meditators. He was, in fact, instrumental in reviving the tradition of forest monks in Thailand and the practice of the optional ascetic practices. He was not particularly interested in laypersons, although some may have been his devotees. He was not particularly interested in ordinary town-dwelling monks. But several of his disciples whom

8 Acharn Mun's name is also transliterated as "Man." Acharn Mun himself left no written works; his lifestory was written down by one of his disciples, Maha Bua Nyanasampanno, whose work has been translated into English several times (e.g. 1976). For a synopsis and discussion, see Tambiah (1984), pp. 81–110.

9 On Acharn Mun's death and funeral, see Keyes (1981), pp. 164–167.

he inspired and trained went on to become prominent meditation teachers in the forest monk tradition that he revived.[10]

Khruba Siwichai was a monk of a somewhat different character. Born in northern Thailand seven years after Acharn Mun, he also was inclined towards asceticism and also was thought to possess supernatural powers, but he became most renowned for inspiring communities to undertake great meritorious construction projects, and for his championing the cause of Northern Thai culture and tradition. Ordained as a novice in his local wat at the age of eighteen, he remained in the saṃgha and became a full monk at the age of twenty-one, when he immediately went off to practice meditation under a monk known for his asceticism. However, within a couple of months he returned home. Soon thereafter, when the abbot of his home monastery died, Siwichai and an equally young friend of his were left as the only monks in the monastery. Despite his youth, Siwichai took over a leadership role in the community. He organized the construction of a new wat, inspiring the villagers to give not only money but labor, and successfully celebrating the achievement as a potent act of communal merit-making. This was to be the first of many such projects. Over the next thirty years, he rallied communities in Northern Thailand to participate in the restoration of important religious monuments – the reliquary of Mount Doi Suthep, north of Chiang Mai city, the temple of Suan Dork in Chiang Mai itself, and the stūpa at Wat Camthewi in Lamphun. He also led them in more "worldly" enterprises such as the construction of bridges over rivers, and, most famously, the building of an eleven-kilometer access road up to the top of Mount Doi Suthep. All told, he is said to have been instrumental in carrying out over one hundred projects.[11]

At the same time, he became a figurehead in the resistance of Northern Thai Buddhists against the centralizing powers emanating from the capital of Bangkok. It should be said that in the late nineteenth century, the Siamese court started a movement to unify the nation politically, economically, and to some extent culturally and religiously. More specifically, this entailed undermining the religious autonomy of Northern Thailand (centered on the region of Chiang Mai) where the Buddhist traditions were sometimes quite different from those of Central Thailand. Part of this endeavor was a plan to establish

---

10 Among teachers in Acharn Mun's lineage may be counted such figures as Phra Acharn Lee Dhammadharo, Acharn Maha Boowa Ñāṇasampanno, and Acharn Fuan Jotiko. Many of their works have been translated and published by Thanissaro Bhikkhu, the abbot of Wat Metta Forest Monastery, near San Diego, CA.

11 Information on Khruba Siwichai is taken from Keyes (1981) and Cohen (2001). For information on a monk who emulated Siwichai, see Cohen (2010).

a centralized saṃgha authority in Bangkok that would control wats and the lives of monastics throughout the country, including the North. Thus, in the early twentieth century, a new law was passed, requiring all senior monks wishing to ordain new monks to obtain approval for doing so from their "district abbot," who in turn was controlled by a central government-appointed saṃgha official. When, however, Khruba Siwichai (who at this point was a well-respected elder and holy man) sought permission to ordain some of his followers, he was denied that right, for reasons that are unclear but may have been due to suspicions about his charismatic authority. Snubbed, Siwichai decided to ignore the central saṃgha's rule, and went ahead and performed the ordinations anyway. Such defiance could not be tolerated; in time, Siwichai was summoned to Bangkok to face charges of clerical insubordination. This, however, merely increased his popularity among the Northern Thai people, and eventually, the central saṃgha authorities relented, fearing that Siwichai's movement might develop into a full-blown millenarian uprising. Siwichai returned to Chiang Mai where he was received triumphantly by more than 8,000 followers at the railroad station. Today, Siwichai is still present – in his relics, in countless amulets, in lifelike wax images, in a large bronze statue/shrine at the base of the road to Doi Suthep, and in a museum built on the grounds of his home temple, Wat Ban Pang, in Lamphun province.[12]

11.4 THE END OF THE RAINS-RETREAT IN A NORTHERN THAI VILLAGE

The Thai Buddhist calendar is punctuated by a variety of festive occasions. One of the most important of these is Org Phansa marking the end of the rainy season (on the full moon day of the eleventh lunar month, usually October). At this time, monks gather for the pavāraṇā (Skt., pravāraṇa) ritual in which they confess or denounce (in closed assembly) any misdeeds they have committed or seen committed during the rains-retreat (see 6.6.2). More generally, community-wide celebrations are held to commemorate the Buddha's return to earth from Trayastriṃśa Heaven, where he had spent the rains preaching to his mother (see 2.7.9), and also to mark the end of the monks' rains-retreat when once again they are free to be "present" in this

12 On Siwichai and others during the national integration of Thailand, see Keyes (1971). On the ongoing popularity of Siwichai after his death, see the article by Sjon Hauser at http://www.sjonhauser.nl/khruba-si-wichai.html.

world. These Org Phansa festivities take on various forms in different parts of Thailand. In the Northeast, on the Mekong River, processions of decorated boats and boat races may be held. Elsewhere (e.g. in Central Thailand), an image of the Buddha may be brought down from the top of a hill in a grand procession of monks, symbolizing the descent of the Buddha from heaven. Everywhere, the end of the rains also ushers in the season for Bun Kathin, the especially meritorious presentation of robes (kaṭhina) and other gifts to the monks by the laity. This is one of the most important communal merit-making occasions of the year.[13]

In the fall of 1982, I was fortunate enough to spend Org Phansa at Wat Sirimongkol in a village north of Chiang Mai, not far from the town of Chiang Dao. In that community, they still practice the increasingly rare rite of inviting the arhat Upagupta (Pali, Upagutta; Thai, Phra Uppakhut) to come from his abode in the bottom of a nearby river to act as a protector of the festivities. More specifically, he is said to guard against the incursions of Māra who, in this context, is thought to manifest himself either as a drunk, or a thief, or a person who likes fighting, i.e. anyone who would disrupt the celebration. At the end of the festival, Upagupta is then ritually returned to the river.[14]

Such occasions, it should be said, are primarily organized not by the monks but by the laity, in particular by the village wat committee under the leadership of a dedicated elder layman known as an "acharn wat." The acharn wat is almost always a former monk who takes on ritual roles of prime importance in leading the people in merit-making activities, in calling on spirits (such as Upagupta in this case), in being an intermediary between ordinary lay villagers and members of the saṃgha. As Swearer (1976, p. 162) has put it, "[the acharn wat] mediates the spiritual power of the Sangha to the laity and the material gifts of the laity to the Sangha." His role is of special importance in Northern Thailand, where, in rural communities, there is often a shortage of "permanent" monks. At Wat Sirimongkol, for instance, when I visited there, there was only one monk – the abbot – and four or five young novices. The abbot, moreover, was only twenty-four years old and lived in a monastery in Chiang Mai while he pursued his education in the city. On

13 The boat races in Northeastern Thailand are connected to the mythology of the nāgas. At Nongkhai, the nāgas are thought to be responsible for shooting off mysterious fireballs that arise from the depths of the river each year at this time, and which have become a major tourist attraction. On Org Phansa and Bun Kathin in Central Thailand, see Wells (1960), pp. 103–111.

14 For full details, see Strong (1992), pp. 254–261.

Wan Phra (days of the new, quarter, half, and full moons), he would commute back to his village, and stay for the night before returning to the city the next day. When I knew him, he was desperately trying to find someone else to take his position as abbot so he could disrobe, although he had agreed not to do so until he could be replaced. In such a situation, it is understandable that the real religious "anchor" of the village was the acharn wat, a sixty-three-year-old layman of Shan ethnicity who had formerly been a monk for a number of years in nearby Myanmar.

None of this means that the abbot did not take his duties seriously. He did. Simply put, without him, there would have been no celebration of Org Phansa. He (or rather his presence) is what got things started. He played a crucial ritual role in, for instance, administering the three refuges and five precepts to the assembled laity, and in preaching a sermon. But most of all, as a member of the saṃgha, he (along with a fellow monk he had brought with him from Chiang Mai for the occasion) provided a field of merit for the villagers' offerings.

On Org Phansa, the monks do not go on their begging rounds for alms, but the villagers bring offerings to the wat. At Wat Sirimongkol, by daybreak, dāna was in full swing at three places: at the temporary shrine for Upagupta, where offerings of fruit, puffed rice, sweets, incense, and candles were made and the saint's blessing and protection were invoked; in front of the main hall of the wat where a row of large bowls had been set out to be filled with rice, and other foodstuffs; and in the abbot's kuti (residence), where group after group of villagers covered the floor in front of the abbot and his companion with bowls filled with special delicacies, nice sweets, and other specially prepared food offerings (see figure 11.1). Both at the main hall and in the abbot's quarters, laypersons often accompanied their offering by ritually pouring out water so as to transfer the merit of their act to deceased members of their family.

By 7:30 A.M., dāna had stopped, and the whole village assembled in the main hall of the wat, men towards the front, women towards the back. There, on behalf of all the laity, the acharn wat requested and the abbot administered the three refuges and the five precepts. This is the standard ritual beginning to virtually all Theravāda ceremonies, in which the people repeat after the monk Pali formulae well-known to them all. The three refuges are, of course, the Buddha, the Dharma, and the Saṃgha, while the five precepts are commitments to abstain (for how long is not specified) from taking life, from taking what is not given, from wrongful sensual pleasures, from false speech, and from intoxicants.[15]

15 For discussion of the three refuges and five precepts in a Thai ritual context, see Terwiel (1994), pp. 161–187.

The service that followed was highlighted by an address by the acharn wat and a sermon by the abbot. Both men reminded the villagers of the importance of Org Phansa and made special exhortations to them to contribute to the wat's current fund drive to raise money so as to be able to resume construction of a new kuti (residence for monks) (see figure 11.2). This turned out to be a pet project of the abbot, who sought to boost enthusiasm by arguing that the village needed a nice new building because, after all, foreigners (such as myself and Professor Louis Gabaude, a French scholar in Chiang Mai) came to visit it!

11.1 *Offerings at Org Phansa*

11.2 *Wat Sirimongkol: Fund Raising for the Future Kuti*

11.5 A THAI TEMPLE IN WIMBLEDON, ENGLAND

Not far from the All England Lawn Tennis and Croquet Club, in one of the posher neighborhoods of Wimbledon, England, on the grounds of what was formerly an estate, may be found an interesting Theravāda monastery, Wat Buddhapadipa. The temple actually predates its present location to which it was moved in the 1970s. It is set in a lovely landscaped park (complete with a small lake) and occupies the original older buildings of the estate, to which has been added a main chapel (Thai, bot) built in traditional Thai style. The wat houses a number of monks and attracts Thais and non-Thais alike, devotees and tourists, visitors of all sorts.[16]

Like many Buddhist establishments in the West, it serves many functions, religious and cultural. The establishment of the wat itself was sponsored by the Thai royal family as well as a committee of well-to-do, internationally minded, and influential Thai business people, politicians, and art patrons. To this day, it has significant links with the Thai embassy in London.

On festival days, it is a place where Thai people in the greater London area gather to celebrate together and to make meritorious donations to the monks, while non-Thais come to acquaint themselves with Thai culture and try out homecooked Thai foods. For instance, in 2011, the wat celebrated both bun kathin (the offering of robes to the monks) and loi krathong (the floating of candles on lotus-leaf rafts) together on the fullmoon day of November. The offering of robes to the monks was led by the Thai Ambassador to Great Britain in a solemn ceremony that continued with monastic chanting and a sermon. There then ensued, as part of the loi krathong celebration, a festive fair: food stalls sold delicious Thai dishes to all comers, as well as various kinds of souvenirs and cultural objects. In the afternoon, a welcoming address by a local Wimbledon official was followed by a cultural show featuring musical and dance performances from various parts of Thailand. There followed displays of Thai kick boxing, and a beauty contest for young women in which the winner was crowned as the new "Miss Noppamas." Such beauty pageants have become common in celebrations of loi krathong in some parts of Thailand. They are in honor of Nang Noppamas, a concubine of the thirteenth-century Sukhothai king Ramkhamhaeng. According to legend, she originated the practice of floating ("loi") lotus-leaf cups ("krathong"), with little oil lamps (today, mostly candles) burning in them, for which the celebration of loi

16 I would like to thank Benjamin Willatts for first taking me to Wat Buddhapadipa. On Wat Buddhapadipa in general, see Cate (2003).

krathong is now known. Up until then, according to one version of the story, the festival had featured paper lanterns that were lit and let go up into the air like so many balloons, but the king so admired the beauty of Nang Noppamas's myriad flickering lights moving downstream that from then on it focused on the release of small leaf-rafts on the water. Today there is much good-natured competition to see who can make the most beautiful krathong, and whose will float the longest before inevitably sinking into the water.[17]

Similar festivals of lights are held in many parts of Asia. In Thailand, various explanations are given as to its meaning. For some, it is a ritual in honor of the Mother of the Waters (Mae Khongkha), the Thai goddess of rivers, streams, and canals, who is thus asked for protection, and for forgiveness (for acts of pollution), and who is thanked for her beneficence (loi krathong happens soon after the end of the rainy season). For others, it is in honor of the Buddha's footprint, a relic that he left on the bank of the Nammadā River where it could be worshipped by the nāgas. For still others, it has a more symbolic significance and is thought to be a rite in which one can "float away" bad luck, disease, and misfortune. In Northern Thailand, it is sometimes said to be in honor of the saint Upagupta who is thought to reside underwater in a meditative trance, or in honor of a white female crow who, in a previous life, was the mother of the five buddhas of the present aeon. Whichever explanation is given, the ritual today, whether in Thailand or Wimbledon, where the krathong were floated on the small lake to end the day's festivities, is mainly appreciated for its beauty.[18]

Wat Buddhapadipa, however, is not just a place for communal festivals. Throughout the year, walking and sitting meditation sessions are held in the evenings four times a week. Once a month, on a Saturday, there is a weekend meditation retreat from 9 A.M. to 5 P.M., and three times a year there are week-long residential retreats. On most Sundays there are also Dharma classes in English, as well as a Dhamma-talk in Thai and a "Buddhist school" for Thai children that includes lessons in reading and writing Thai. Once a year, the wat also makes it possible for Thai boys in the London area to take temporary ordination, for two weeks.[19]

---

17 On loi krathong, see Rajadhon (2009), pp. 39–46, and Wells (1960), pp. 111–114.
18 On the Buddha's footprint in the Nammadā river, see Strong (2004), pp. 90–92. For different explanations of the meaning of the loi krathong rite, see Strong (1992), pp. 202–204. For more on the loi krathong and bun kathin ceremonies in Wimbledon, see http://www.buddhapadipa.org/event-write-up/kathina-and-loykratong-festival/.
19 For a schedule of the temple's activities, see http://www.buddhapadipa.org/activities/. The emphasis on meditation at Wat Buddhapadipa started early on its history. One of its first meditation teachers was Chao Khun Sobhana Dhammasudhi, who also helped run meditation workshops in many places (see Swearer, 1971, p. x).

In addition to all this, Wat Buddhapadipa is a place famous for its art. The wall paintings in its chapel, the only building done in traditional Thai style, are both strikingly original and rather controversial. The murals were executed over a period of eight years (from 1984 to 1992), by the Thai artists Chalermchai Kositpipap and Panya Vijinthanasam and their assistants.

One series of paintings is devoted to a very traditional theme – the life story of the Buddha – and yet, artistically, it is daring and filled with contemporary references. The scene of the Defeat of Māra, for instance, in typical Thai fashion, shows the Buddha on the seat of enlightenment in the earth touching gesture, which indicates his calling the earth to witness his merits and his right to occupy that throne. Beneath him may be seen another classical touch of Thai iconography: the figure of the Earth Goddess, Nang Thoranī, testifying to the Buddha's accomplishments by wringing out the long braid of her hair, from which comes the flood of his merits that sweep away the attacking armies of Māra, who sits atop a large elephant (see 2.7.6). To either side, Māra's hordes are depicted in disarray, and it is here that the artists have let fly their imaginations, and their wish to make this more than a traditional temple. For amid the jumble of Māra's army may be found various symbols of "Māra" from a host of times and cultures: an image of Ronald Reagan and Muammar Qadafi fighting together; of a Spanish conquistador representing colonial oppression; of a Japanese samurai; of the shark from the movie *Jaws*; of a nāga holding the NASA space shuttle in its grasp; of the horse from Picasso's painting *Guernica*; of Da Vinci's portrait of the Mona Lisa, etc. All this effectively serves to radically reinterpret and universalize the story of the Buddha's overcoming evil and temptation.[20]

Similarly, the extraordinary mural depicting the Buddha's descent from Trayastriṃśa Heaven is a mixture of the traditional and the unexpectedly contemporary. The Buddha is shown coming down from heaven, flanked by the gods Indra and Brahma and a host of other deities, but down below he is being welcomed by a mix of people of all sorts and from all over the world and various periods of history. Here, one can see Thai émigrés having a picnic and dancing amidst discarded cans of Heineken beer; Charlie Chaplin talking to a young man with a red Mohawk haircut; a group of elderly English pensioners; and, to one side, sitting on a chair, and benignly gazing down upon the crowd, sits the then British Prime Minister, Margaret Thatcher, with her dog at her feet.[21]

---

20 Cate (2003), pp. 79–82.

21 Ibid., pp. 31–32.

The shrine room at Wat Buddhapadipa contains three main Buddha images, gifted to the temple at various times in its history. In 1966, an unusual black bronze Buddha statue was given by the King of Thailand. The temple's committee of backers thought this aesthetically unappealing, however, and so raised funds and purchased a second, golden image of the Buddha that was dedicated in 1982. The black image was kept on the altar, however, because it was well liked by local devotees (and it had come from the king). Subsequently, a group of women lay supporters, from a Bangkok wat associated with one of Buddhapadipa's artists, gifted the temple an image which is a replica of the so-called Emerald Buddha, currently housed in the royal wat in Bangkok.

Emerald Buddha replicas are fairly common in Thai monasteries throughout the world. There is, for instance, one at the temple at Doi Suthep, a sacred mountain in Northern Thailand; there is another in Chiang Rai, also in the North. There is even one at the Thai Temple in Lumbinī (which was not part of our "tour" in chapter 1). For Thais, the original Emerald Buddha now in Bangkok is a Buddha statue fraught with significance, as it embodies multiple traditions. Legend has it that it has been enshrined and venerated as a holy object in most of the other centers of the Theravāda world. According to the saga of its various peregrinations, it is said to have spent time in India, in Sri Lanka, in the possession of the great Burmese king Aniruddha, in Angkor (Cambodia), in Chiang Mai (Northern Thailand), and in Luang Prabang and Vientiane (Laos) before being brought, at the end of the eighteenth century, to Bangkok, where it is now housed in its own special chapel in the Royal Monastery of the current Chakri dynasty. Its prestige as a palladium of Thai royalty devolves partly from this legendary pedigree, but the statue is also thought to have supernatural powers (especially for the purpose of rain-making). It is furthermore connected legendarily to two figures that are ideals of kingship: the god Indra (who is "king of the gods"), and the ideal ruler of the four quarters, the wheel turning monarch (cakravartin). The Emerald Buddha thus has many reverberations, at least for Thais, and its recall in an image in Wimbledon, in a wat sponsored by the Thai monarchy, is consequently loaded with significance.[22]

22 For more on the Emerald Buddha and its significance, see Reynolds (1978), Notton (1933a), and Narula (1994).

Chapter 12

Saṃgha Situations: Places, Persons, and Practices in Japanese Buddhism/s

Buddhism was first introduced to Japan from Korea in the sixth century, where, after a few false starts, it grew under the sponsorship of such legendary figures as Prince Shōtoku. During the Nara period (eighth century), it became further established as an instrument of governmental control, although it also grew in popularity. During this time, six official schools of Buddhism became established in the capital, and charismatic preachers such as Gyōki proselytized the countryside. The subsequent history of Japanese Buddhism is generally traced in terms of: (1) the establishment of various sects (e.g. Tendai, Shingon, Jōdo (Pure Land), Jōdo Shin (True Pure Land), Rinzai Zen, Sōtō Zen, Nichiren, Ji, Ōbaku Zen, etc.). Most of these sects (with the exception of Nichiren Buddhism) were imports of or heirs to various schools of Chinese Buddhism, even though sectarianism in Japan became differently defined than it was on the mainland (see 7.5.3); (2) the lives and teachings of major figures who were involved in the founding and development of these sects (e.g. Saichō, Kūkai, Ryōgen, Hōnen, Shinran, Eisai, Dōgen, Nichiren, Gyōnen, Ippen, etc.); (3) the politically defined periods during which these figures lived and these sects developed (e.g. Heian, Kamakura, Muromachi, Tokugawa, etc.).[1]

1 On the early period of Buddhism in Japan, see Deal (1995), Kidder (1972), and McCallum (2009). On the six Nara schools, see Matsunaga and Matsunaga (1976), vol. 1, pp. 26–138. On Gyōki, see Augustine (2005). For a sectarian approach to the history of Japanese Buddhism, see Matsunaga and Matsunaga (1976). For a biographical approach to the history of Japanese Buddhism, see Kashiwahara and Sonoda (1994). See appendix G for a general chronology of Buddhism in Japan with bibliographic suggestions.

In what follows, however, rather than focus on sectarian establishments and chronology, I am, once again, going to try to make things more concrete by looking at a few places and seeing how they are defined by various layers of tradition and practices. First, we shall look at three places in Kyoto, the ancient capital and cultural center of Japan: the so-called "Hexagonal Hall" (Rokkakudō) (12.1); a Tendai temple known as Shinnyodō (12.2); and the famous Zen rock garden at the Ryōanji Temple (12.3). Then, because practitioners of Japanese Buddhism are not found only in Japan (just as Thai Buddhists are found not only in Thailand), we shall visit a Zen center in Maine (U.S.A.) (12.4), and then, returning to Lumbinī, the so-called Japan-monastery (Nippondera) under construction there (12.5).

12.1 THE HEXAGONAL HALL (ROKKAKUDŌ)

Many cities have a spot that supposedly marks their center. In Kyoto, that spot is located in the courtyard of the Rokkakudō (Hexagonal Hall) temple. Located downtown, just southeast of the intersection of two of the city's major thoroughfares (Karasuma and Sanjō), it is today a small oasis in the hustle and bustle of urban life, squeezed in between much taller buildings. The Rokkakudō has a very long history, thoroughly intertwined with legend, and intersecting with the lives of several key figures in Japanese Buddhism.

12.1.1 Prince Shōtoku

The Hexagonal Hall was supposedly established in the late sixth century by none other than Prince Shōtoku, long before the city of Kyoto was actually founded and made into the new capital in 794 CE. Shōtoku's own story is thoroughly fictitious. His legend may have been initially formulated by the editors of the early eighth-century *Nihongi* (*Chronicles of Japan*) who were seeking, retrospectively, to develop the image of a great charismatic ruler, a father-of-our-country figure who would give historical precedence and legitimacy to the establishment of a Chinese-style imperial regime. Subsequent centuries saw the gradual accumulation of layers upon layers of legendary Shōtoku traditions. Generally speaking, Shōtoku and his aunt, the empress Suiko, are presented as being instrumental in importing Chinese culture to Japan in an effort to consolidate the nation, and Buddhism was seen as part of that culture. Thus, in the famous seventeen-article "Constitution" of Japan, with which Prince Shōtoku is credited, we can read, alongside the proposal to propagate a number of basically Confucian principles, the injunction to revere sincerely the Triple Gem of the Buddha, Dharma, and Saṃgha.[2]

In the popular tradition, Shōtoku's Buddhist affiliation was much emphasized, and he came to be seen pretty much as the establisher of that religion in Japan, although there is evidence that Buddhism was first introduced from Korea several generations before his time. He himself soon became the object of a cult and, in legend, he came to be thought of as a bodhisattva who had been miraculously conceived, had been remarkably precocious, and had become a great scholar (he is credited with commentaries on three important Buddhist sūtras). He is also said to have founded numerous early monasteries, among them Hōryūji (near Nara) and Shitennōji (in present-day Osaka).[3]

It is not surprising, therefore, to find him credited also with the founding of the Rokkakudō in Kyoto. According to one version of the popular tradition, the story is as follows: on an expedition to the area that is now downtown Kyoto but was then unsettled land, Shōtoku stopped to bathe in a pond. Entering the water, he left on the bank (and then forgot) a small talismanic image of the bodhisattva Kannon (Avalokiteśvara) which he was carrying. When he returned to get the image somewhat later, it had grown into a full-sized statue, and Shōtoku (unable to take it with him) decided to build for it a shrine which was little more than a roofed six-sided platform (probably symbolic of Kannon's compassion for beings in the six realms of rebirth). That supposedly was the origin of the "Hexagonal Hall," the Rokkakudō. Today, the pond has given way to a tank (with swans and koi carp) located just behind the still-hexagonal main hall of the temple which houses an important statue of Kannon.[4]

The early cult of this image (or rather of its predecessor, since no one is claiming that the present statue is the original one) is said to have been carried

---

2 For a convenient presentation of all the *Nihongi*'s entries on Shōtoku, see Deal (1999). On its editors creating Shōtoku's image, see Lee (2007), p. 48. For a translation of the seventeen-article constitution, see Aston (1972), vol. 2, pp. 128–133.

3 For versions and studies of the legend of Shōtoku, see Como (2008), Soper (1967), Kanaji (1985), and Nishimura (1985). For an art historical approach to these traditions, see Carr (2012).

4 On the story of the Rokkakudō's origins, see Lee (2007), p. 15, and Plutschow (1983), pp. 4–5.

out by Buddhist monks who lived in a small monastic hut (Jpn., bō) beside the pond (Jpn., ike), which accordingly was known as Ike-no-bō (the "hut at the pond"). The clerics there were in the habit of offering flowers to the image of Kannon. Much later, the display of such floral offerings developed into a sophisticated and refined art form, and, in the fifteenth century, a monk named Ikenobō Senno, who resided at the Rokkakudō, founded Ikenobō, the first school of flower arrangement (Jpn., ikebana) in Japan. Today, the sleek building that is the modern headquarters of the Ikenobō school towers over the old temple, but the abbot of the temple remains the current titular head of the flower arrangement school.

12.1.2 *Shinran*

The Rokkakudō, however, is known not just for its connections with Prince Shōtoku and flower arrangement; it is perhaps most famous for its association with Shinran (1173–1263), the great founder of the True Pure Land school (Jōdo Shinshū). Shinran was born in what is now the southern part of Kyoto. At an early age, after the death of his parents, he became a Tendai monk on Mount Hiei (to the northeast of the city), where he quickly gained a reputation as an ardent practitioner. He himself, however, was plagued by self-doubt, by his failure to repress sensual desires and his inability to attain enlightenment. So, in the year 1201, he resolved to undertake a hundred-day solitary meditation retreat at the Rokkakudō in Kyoto. There, after ninety-five days of strenuous practice, he is said to have had a religious experience. Subsequent traditions give various accounts of what happened. One has it that the bodhisattva Kannon appeared to Shinran at the Rokkakudō in the guise of Prince Shōtoku, and urged him to go and find the teacher Hōnen (1133–1212) who was then propagating Pure Land doctrines. Another version has it that Kannon appeared to Shinran as a young monk, dressed all in white, and told him that if he continued to suffer from sexual longings and wished to marry, he (Kannon) would take on the form of a beautiful woman and live conjugally with him and eventually lead him to the pure land in old age. There is a lot going on in these stories. The second version, for instance, is informed by the fact that, around this time, the bodhisattva Kannon (Ch., Guanyin; Skt., Avalokiteśvara) was undergoing an iconographic and ideological feminization in both China and Japan. At the same time, of course, one of the features of Shinran's career is that he did indeed eventually marry and proclaim himself to be "neither monk nor layman," so that this legend gives him (retrospectively) divine permission to abandon celibacy.[5]

12.1.3 Kannon, Jizō, and Fudō

In addition, the Rokkakudō is important for other reasons. It is, for instance, the eighteenth stop on the so-called Saikoku ("Western country") pilgrimage circuit that takes devotees to thirty-three temples in Western Japan, each housing a different famous image of Kannon. Indeed, large groups of pilgrims clad in white occasionally arrive at the temple to pay homage to the bodhisattva and the place, as part of their overall pilgrimage circuit. As a preliminary to their worship, they stop to purify themselves by rinsing their hands and mouths with water from the temple's fountain-fed basin, which they scoop up with long-handled ladles. This cleansing ritual called "temizu" ("hand-water") is routine and universal at all Shintō shrines but is also found at some Buddhist temples, as here at the Rokkakudō. Having thus purified themselves, the pilgrims will then, depending on how fast they are traveling, stop to light incense, make offerings, chant sūtras, listen to the story of the temple, and get their pilgrims' scrolls stamped at the temple office to certify their visit, before boarding their bus to head off to the next stop.[6]

Kannon is the main object of worship at the Rokkakudō, but is not the only Buddhist bodhisattva/divinity enshrined there. In fact, as one comes into the temple courtyard, one is greeted not only by banners that proclaim "Praise to the bodhisattva Kanzeon [= Kannon]," but also "Praise to the bodhisattva Jizō," and "Praise to Fudō Myō-ō."

As we saw in 8.5.2, Jizō (Skt., Kṣitigarbha; Ch., Dizang) is a bodhisattva

5 On the story of Shinran at Rokkakudō, see Dobbins (1989), pp. 22–24, and Matsunaga and Matsunaga (1976), vol. 2, pp. 86–89. On the feminization of Guanyin, see Yü (2001), pp. 293–352. The gender issues in this Shinran story are further complicated by the fact that, by the thirteenth century, Shōtoku was also popularly depicted as a young divine boy (see Guth, 1987, pp. 9–13). Indeed, that is the form in which he is currently portrayed in his image at the Rokkakudō. On the use of the Shinran story at Rokkakudō in the later traditions leading up to clerical marriage in Japan, see Jaffe (2001), pp. 50–52.

6 On the Saikoku Kannon pilgrimage, see Foard (1982), MacWilliams (1995), Hoshino (1997), Rugola (1986), and Gump (2005). The Saikoku Kannon pilgrimage is not the only thematic pilgrimage circuit in Japan. Even more famous are the eighty-eight sites on the island of Shikoku associated with the figure of the saint Kōbō Daishi (see Reader, 2005). On the island of Kyushu, there is also a circuit of twenty-eight temples on the Kunisaki peninsula associated with the twenty-eight chapters of the *Lotus Sūtra* (see Grapard, 1986, pp. 25–26).

with many salvific functions. At the Rokkakudō, what is featured is his role as Warabe Jizō – the protector of young children. Thus, one whole side of the temple courtyard is given over to red-bibbed and knit-capped images of Jizō as an infant. These have been sponsored by parishioner families wishing to memorialize and/or provide ongoing protection to the souls of children who died in infancy or childbirth, as well as to those who perished as miscarried or aborted fetuses. Indeed, in modern-day Japan, the figure of Warabe Jizō (protector of young children) tends to overlap with those of Jizō-as-ensurer-of-easy-childbirth (Koyasu Jizō) and Jizō who protects and memorializes miscarried and aborted fetuses (Mizuko Jizō).[7]

Fudō (Skt., Acala; Ch., Budong) is a representative of the class of "kings of magical knowledge" (Skt., vidyārāja; Jpn., myō-ō). He appears generally in wrathful form and is usually thought to be, in East Asia, an emanation of the Buddha Dainichi (Skt., Vairocana). He is portrayed as sitting on a rock, surrounded by a halo of flames, and holding in one hand a sword and in the other a noose, with which to bind and cut through passions and malignant forces. In Japan, images of him are often found at waterfalls, and in various temples inclined towards esotericism. At the Rokkakudō, a shrine for him may be found in one corner of the courtyard where there is a small spring and a moss-covered natural outcropping of rock, with, in front, a small image of Fudō, but as the signs nearby proclaim, the rock itself is thought to "be" Fudō. In front is a small trough of water with some scoops attached to long handles. These enable devotees to pour water over the rock and image, a common act of offering and purification with Fudō images.[8]

It should be apparent from all this that the Rokkakudō is not only a place steeped in history and legend; it is also a place that seeks to be alive to various needs of contemporary Buddhists.

12.2 THE RITUAL YEAR AT SHINNYODŌ

The same may be said about the second place I want to focus on in Kyoto. The Tendai sect temple Shinnyodō (official name, Shinsho-gokuraku-ji) is

7 On the growth of the cult of Jizō in Japan, see Glassman (2012). The bibliography on the cult of aborted and miscarried fetuses (mizuko) in Japan is immense. For two classic studies, see LaFleur (1992) and Hardacre (1999). See also Smith (1992; 2013). More generally on the bioethics of abortion in Buddhism, see Keown (1999).

8 On Fudō, see Frédéric (1995), pp. 203–208, Lane-Suzuki (1923), and Blacker (1975), pp. 174–175.

located in northern Kyoto, not far from Kyoto University, on the eastern side of Yoshida Hill, which itself is the site of a famous Shintō shrine. The temple's origins date back to the tenth century, when it was first established as a worship hall in the grounds of a villa belonging to the emperor's mother. It subsequently became a temple in its own right. Like most significant buildings in Kyoto, it was burnt down during the Ōnin wars (1467–1477) but rebuilt soon thereafter with Shogunal support. Its main hall (hondō) contains an important "hidden" image of Amida Buddha. Like other hidden images or "secret buddhas" (Jpn., hibutsu) in Japan, it is enshrined in a closed altar and so is normally not visible to worshippers except once a year in November when it is displayed.[9]

The temple grounds are famous for their maple trees, much admired by visitors in autumn. Subsidiary buildings include a shrine to Kannon, another to Jizō, a three-story pagoda, a bell tower, a hall for the performance of fire offerings (goma – see below). Nearby there is a small pond with an even smaller island featuring a shrine to the Shintō divinity, the goddess Benzaiten. Adjacent to the temple grounds is a vast cemetery, which merges into the graveyards of Kurodani, an important Pure Land sect temple just to the south, which is associated with Hōnen (1133–1212), the founder of the Jōdo school of Buddhism. The whole area is a kind of oasis within a busy cityscape.

Some years ago, when I was studying in Kyoto, I lived across the street from the Shinnyodō. I used to visit the temple regularly, go for walks in its grounds (this was before they started charging admission), and periodically attend rituals and ceremonies. In what follows, I want briefly to recount some of the latter, in order to give a sense of the cycle of rites performed at such a place. Most of these were organized and officiated by one young Tendai priest who, along with his elderly father, the abbot, was at that time the only resident in the temple (except for some university students who rented out rooms). It should be said that, since the nineteenth century, most Japanese Buddhist "monks" marry and the care of temples is passed on hereditarily; indeed, the young priest at the Shinnyodō was, when I knew him, under considerable pressure from his parents and from parishioners to get married and start a family.[10]

9 The most famous "secret Buddha" in Japan (also an image of Amida) is that found in the Zenkōji temple in Nagano, which is never exposed, although a replica of it is displayed every six years. See McCallum (1994).

10 On the situation of Tendai priests and temples in modern-day Japan, see Covell (2005). On the marriage of Japanese Buddhist clergy more generally, see Jaffe (2001).

12.2.1 *New Year's*

The ritual year at Shinnyodō begins with a very simple celebration: the marking of the New Year. As in many other Buddhist temples all over Japan, around midnight on December 31, interested parishioners and celebrating visitors gather at the temple bell tower to ring in the New Year. The ceremony at a few famous picturesque temples is broadcast live on television and watched throughout Japan, a more solemn (perhaps) version of the ball falling in New York's Times Square. At the Shinnyodō, things are more subdued and intimate. The priest has lit a small bonfire for neighborhood people to keep warm, and, one by one, old and young, men and women, adults and children, take a turn at sounding the bell. Japanese temple bells are large and clapperless. To ring them, one must swing a great log of wood that hangs horizontally from the ceiling of the bell tower, and "gong" them on their side. This is a gesture that requires a modicum of skill, and part of the fun of New Year's Eve is watching the different "swing-techniques" that people use when it comes their turn. The priest keeps careful track of the number of gongs; the bell is to be rung exactly 108 times. The number 108 is significant in many contexts in Buddhism; in this case it denotes the total number of defilements (Skt., kleśa; Jpn., bonnō) in humans. New Year is thus a purificatory process, a kind of exorcism in which people can cleanse themselves of their old negativities, and start the new year with a clean slate.

12.2.2 *Ḍākinī and the Recitation of the* Great Perfection of Wisdom Sūtra

The rest of the ritual year at the Shinnyodō tends to oscillate between rituals or celebrations that are held in the main hall (Jpn., hondō) and rites that take place in smaller detached auxiliary halls in the temple grounds. The former are often more oriented towards the community at large, while the latter tend to be more esoteric in nature, reflecting Tendai's association with the Japanese mikkyō (esoteric) tradition.

An example of the latter may be seen in a ritual that takes place in early spring: just off to the left of the entrance gate to the temple is a building that to all appearances looks like a small shrine to the Shinto god of rice and prosperity, Inari, whose emblem and messenger is the fox. In actuality, it is an Inari shrine that has been converted into a temple to Dakini-ten. In India

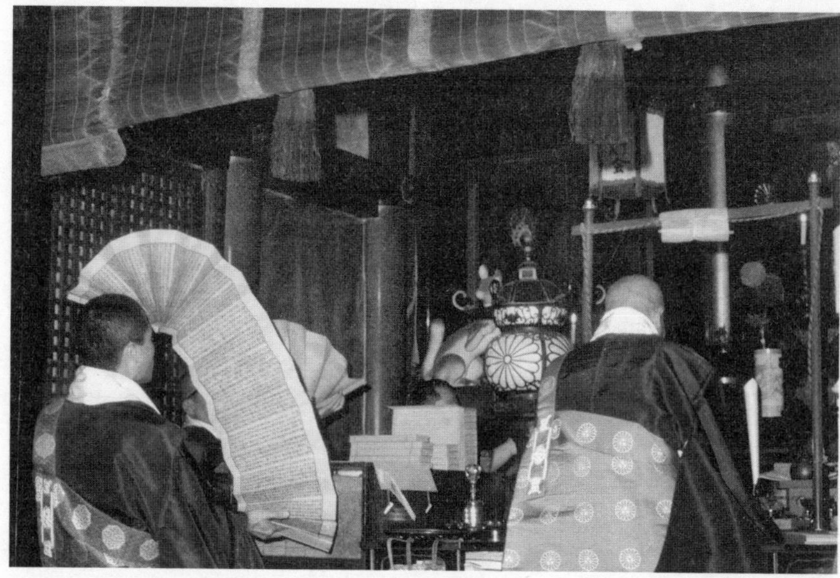

12.1 *Rapid "Tendoku" Method of Reciting the* Great Perfection of Wisdom Sūtra

and Tibet, Ḍākinī is a female quasi-demonic Tantric divinity associated with enlightenment and energy. In East Asia, where she is known as Dakini-ten (Ḍākinī-divinity), she has also come to be associated with foxes. Thus the overlap with Inari makes good sense. In Japan, she is typically depicted as riding on a white fox, on which she flies through the sky. The priest at Shinnyodō regularly venerates Dakini-ten in private. In mid-February, however, a public worship of her is held during which offerings are made and her image (which is usually hidden from view) is exhibited. On this occasion, other Tendai monks are invited to recite the *Great Perfection of Wisdom Sūtra* (Skt., *Mahāprajñāpāramitā-sūtra*; Jpn., *Dai Hannya haramita kyō*). The many volumes of this text, bound in accordion-like fashion, are stacked high on small tables in front of the altar, and the monks "read" them by the rapid method called "tendoku" ("turning-reading") which consists of letting the fan-like folded golden pages of the text cascade from one hand to another, while shouting out the title of the sūtra: "Dai Hannya Haramita Kyō ... !" (see figure 12.1). With five or six monks doing this simultaneously, the ritual-show is quite spectacular. The choice of this text, moreover, makes good sense, in light of Ḍākinī's association with Prajñāpāramitā and the emptiness doctrine. It also makes sense in that, in the Tendai tradition, the recitation of the *Great Perfection of Wisdom Sūtra* was associated with a ritual aimed at protecting the nation, as was, more generally, the veneration of Dakini-ten.[11]

The year in which I observed the ceremony, the recitation was then followed by a short talk by the Shinnyodō priest on the importance of Dakini-ten and of the *Great Perfection of Wisdom Sūtra*, and then by "counseling sessions" in which he met individually with parishioners and gave them advice but also mantras for protective or palliative care. One mantra given for a minor physical ailment was the common formula (to be repeated daily) known as the "Mantra of Light" (Jpn., kōmyō shingon), which was popularized by the monk Myōe (1173–1232), and, since then, has become important in the Kegon tradition as well as in Japanese esoteric sects. It runs as follows, in Sanskrit: "oṃ amogha vairocana mahāmudrā maṇipadma jvāla pravarttaya hūṃ." In sinicized Japanese pronunciation, this is rendered as: "On abokya beiroshanō makabodara mani handoma jimbara harabaritaya un," which can be translated as: "Praise be to the flawless, all-pervasive illumination of the great mudra [or seal of the Buddha]. Turn over to me the jewel, lotus, and radiant light."[12] Normally intended to help one attain enlightenment in this lifetime, or to ensure rebirth in Amida's pure land, it was here being used by the priest at Shinnyodō for curative, protective purposes.

12.2.3 *Main Hall Rituals*

Not long after the esoteric Dakini-ten ritual just described, a rather different festival is held in Shinnyodō's main hall. This is the celebration of the anniversary of the Buddha's final nirvāṇa, the *nehan-e*, which usually takes place in March. For a whole fortnight, one of the temple's major cultural treasures, a large (six by four meters) early eighteenth-century hanging scroll depicting the Buddha's parinirvāṇa (Jpn., nehan) is put on display. The scroll was originally commissioned and given to the Shinnyodō by members of the Mitsui family, founders of what eventually became one of the largest

11 On Ḍākinī in general, see Hermann-Pfandt (1992/1993). On her connection to foxes, see Strickmann (2002), pp. 261–263, and Smyers (1999), pp. 82–85. See also Simmer-Brown (2001). The practice of tendoku, specifically with regard to the "recitation" of the *Great Perfection of Wisdom Sūtra* dates back at least to the eighth century. See De Visser (2006), pp. 494–495. On Ḍākinī's association with Prajñāpāramitā, see Simmer-Brown (2001), p. 81. On the ritual recitation of the sūtra's association with protecting the nation, see Hur (2000), p. 39.

12 For this translation and transcription, and on the mantra more generally, see Unno (2004). On Myōe, see Tanabe (1992).

corporations and banks in the world (many early Mitsuis are buried in the Shinnyodō graveyard). It is famous for its profusion of details, showing not only the Buddha on his deathbed, surrounded by grieving disciples and divinities, and his mother descending from heaven to see him, but also, down below, well over a hundred animals (including an octopus and a cat and several species of fish), all come to mourn the Buddha's passing. The theme of the parinirvāṇa is echoed in another featured attraction of the Shinnyodō: a rock, sand, and moss garden, set against the backdrop of bushes and trees and the "borrowed landscape" of Kyoto's eastern hills, abstractly depicting the Buddha on his deathbed surrounded by his disciples.

Also in the main hall, in July, there is another celebration that focuses on the temple's artistic treasures. This is the so-called "mushi-harai" festival, an occasion on which all of the temple's art work and scrolls are taken out of storage and "given an airing," so as to get the "mushi" (vermin, bugs), i.e. bookworms and moisture and other things, out. On this day, the temple's hall takes on the appearance of a kind of art fair, with scrolls hanging from the rafters everywhere. Parishioners, art-appreciators, and other visitors flock to the hall for what is essentially an annual exhibit of the temple's treasures. It is also a celebration of the temple's history. Pride of place is given to its long illustrated scroll (emakimono), the *Shinnyodō engi*, which the priest explicates orally to all willing listeners, thereby recounting the story of the temple.

Finally, mention should be made here of another "main-hall-celebration" that takes place at the Shinnyodō in November, when the temple's maple leaves are at their most glorious color. This is the "jūya hōyō" (the "ten nights recitation") which focuses on the Buddha Amida, whose image, normally shuttered on the main altar, is exhibited on this day. On this occasion, the Pure Land connections of the Tendai sect come to the fore. Although the ritual is technically supposed to be conducted on ten consecutive nights, in the year in which I observed it, that was not possible. Instead, for the first nine nights, a recording of sūtra chanting was played from loudspeakers inside the main hall, the sliding doors of which were closed; no one was actually present, not even the priest. Only the cassette player was there blasting out hymns to Amida across the grounds and through the neighborhood! On the tenth, however, a full ceremonial celebration took place and lasted most of the afternoon and evening. On this day, a long cloth rope was attached to the image of Amida on the altar and run out of the front open door of the temple, suspended high like a telephone wire, and attached to a pole in the middle of the courtyard. At the base of this pole, a large tub of water had been set up, representing one of the ponds in Amida's pure land. In this, devotees could place memorial tablets of shaved wood on which they had written the names of deceased members of their families. The rite thus became a way for reasserting their relatives' rebirths in the pure land and connecting them to Amida. The actual ceremony began with a ritual circumambulation of the main hall by all who were present. The procession was led by the elderly abbot of Shinnyodō and a half-dozen Tendai monks from other temples who had been invited to help officiate. They were accompanied by a few yamabushi, mountain ascetics dressed in their distinctive colorful costumes and blowing on conch shells.

12.2.4 Goma

Not all rituals at the Shinnyodō are seasonal or annual; every month, the priest also performs a goma fire ritual, in one of the temple's small detached halls. Goma is most commonly associated with the Shingon sect, but it is also found in the Tendai tradition. As a ritual, it ultimately stems from the Vedic sacrificial fire ritual known as homa. Like its distant Indian antecedent, goma may basically be seen as a way of ritually meeting a divinity, in this case the king of magical knowledge, Fudō, who is a fiery and fierce emanation of the Buddha Dainichi (Skt., Vairocana). This is much the same sort of meeting that happens in rites associated with a Vajrayāna maṇḍala (see 8.6.1). In order to achieve it, the priest constructs a fire in a pit on an altar (the goma-dan), and, by means of mantras and mudrās (ritual hand gestures), invocations, offerings, and meditative visualizations, he calls the divinity down and meets him halfway, in the ritual arena. The result is both an empowerment and an opportunity for propitiation.[13]

Things are slightly more complicated, however, at the Shinnyodō's goma. For one thing, the goma-hall in which the rite is carried out by the priest is dedicated to Ganzan Daishi. Ganzan Daishi is the posthumous (and divinizing) name of the great Tendai patriarch Ryōgen (912–985). It means "great teacher of the third of the original [month]," and stems from the fact that Ryōgen died on the third day of the first month (of 985). Accordingly, at the Shinnyodō, goma is celebrated on the third day of each month. Over time,

13 For a discussion of goma (= homa) in East Asia, see Strickmann (1983). Strickmann bases most of his description on the *Susiddhikara Sūtra* (*Perfect Achievement Sūtra*) (translated in Giebel, 2001, pp. 123–310), but includes also some specific reference to its celebration at the Shinnyodō.

Ganzan Daishi came to be thought of as a very powerful protector/intercessor, considered to be not only the posthumous form of Ryōgen, but also, variously, a manifestation of Kannon (Skt., Avalokiteśvara), Fudō Myō-ō (Skt., Acalanātha), or even the demon king Maō (Skt., Māra).[14]

In the goma rite, it is his connection with Fudō that is featured, and, indeed, the goma-hall at the Shinnyodō has an image not only of Ganzan Daishi but also of Fudō Myō-ō on its altar. The part of the rite in which Ganzan Daishi is specifically invoked, however, is interesting because it reflects a different dimension of goma as a means of communicating the prayers of the faithful parishioners to the divinized Buddha. All month long, parishioners (and other visitors to the temple) can purchase from a box outside the goma-hall prayer-sticks on which they can write their names, ages, and a short request, such as success with exams, or a cure for an ailment. These are then deposited in another box whence they are collected by the priest. Then, on the third day of each month, during the goma rite, after invoking the presence of Ganzan Daishi in the fire on the altar, the priest reads each of the sticks out loud and tosses them one by one into the flames. In this way goma, which was originally an esoteric ritual performed by and for monastics, has become a means by which ordinary laypersons can use the powers of Tantric rites to convey their mundane wishes to the Buddha. This dimension of the rite is not commonly found in India or China.[15]

12.2.5 The Killing Stone

Finally, mention should also be made of another small subsidiary hall on the grounds of the Shinnyodō, one that houses a special image of the bodhisattva Jizō. The shrine is generally kept closed, but is opened on special occasions; either way, however, it can be venerated by individual devotees seeking particular boons. The image bears the unlikely name of the "Killing Stone" (Jpn., Sesshōseki), although it is also known as the "Kamakura Jizō." In brief, its story is as follows: long ago, the emperor Toba (1103–1156) was attracted to a beautiful woman in his court named Tamamo. She was actually a nine-tailed fox in disguise, with a history of seduction and destruction dating

14 On Ryōgen in general, see Groner (2002). On his demonic identity, see Wakabayashi (1999).

15 For a discussion of this with specific reference to the goma at Shinnyodō, see Strickmann (1996), pp. 367–368 [in French].

back to ancient times in China and even India. One day, the emperor became mysteriously ill; no one could determine why. In time, however, the yin-yang exorcist at court suspected Tamamo was the reason, and he denounced her as the fox that she was. Her true vulpine identity thus exposed, she fled the capital, going east to a place called Nasu, in a volcanically active hotsprings region in present-day Tochigi prefecture (north of Tokyo). There, in time, the fox spirit was hunted down by one of the emperor's retainers who shot it with a magical arrow. As it died, however, the shape-shifting fox took on the form of a large boulder which became known as the "life-killing stone" (sesshōseki), since, thereafter, any living beings that came close to it (birds, insects, animals, etc.) perished instantly. Several centuries later, a Sōtō Zen monk from Kamakura named Gennō (1324–1400) happened by the area and, knowing the troubles caused by the still malignant fox spirit/rock, he decided to subdue it definitively. Striking the stone with a hammer ("gennō" is still the word used for a particular kind of mason's hammer), he split it into pieces, and, confronting the liberated fox spirit, he converted it to Buddhism and brought it to enlightenment. The story became famous and was reworked into plays for the Noh, Kabuki, and Bunraku (puppet) theaters, as well as becoming the subject of woodblock prints in the Tokugawa period.

12.2 The "Killing Stone" Kamakura Jizō at Shinnyodō

More relevant for our purposes is the sequel which recounts that Gennō then took one of the pieces of rock and carved a statue of Jizō out of it. This image was soon moved to Kamakura where it was enshrined and worshiped in Gennō's temple.[16] Then, several centuries later (*c.*1600), an important

16 The story of the Killing Stone being brought to Kamakura is recounted in Mutsu (1930), pp. 175–180.

official named Munehirō had a dream in which the Jizō statue appeared to him and asked to be moved to the Shinnyodō in Kyoto where it could better pursue its function of saving sentient beings. Accordingly, the image was transported to the Shinnyodō, where it remains enshrined to this day (see figure 12.2). It is still known as the "Killing Stone," but, because it was formerly in Kamakura, it is also called the "Kamakura Jizō," which is perhaps more appropriate since, transformed into a bodhisattva, it has long abandoned its malignant ways; people today worship it generally for safety in the home, for happiness and long life, and more specifically for help in healing mental illness, and in getting cleared of false accusations.

The Kamakura/Shinnyodō Jizō, however, was made from only one part (or aspect) of the original Killing Stone; the other part remained in Nasu where, despite the story of Gennō converting the fox to Buddhism, its older bad reputation carried on. Most famously, the site was visited by the poet Matsuo Bashō (1644–1694). As he recounts in his *Narrow Road to the Deep North* (*Oku no hosomichi*): "The Killing Stone stands in the shadow of a mountain where a hot spring flows. The poisonous fumes continue unabated. There were so many dead insects – bees, butterflies – that we couldn't even tell the color of the sand" (Barnhill, 2005, p. 54). And the site inspired the following haiku verse: "The stench of the stone – / the summer grass red, / the scorching dew" (Barnhill, 2005, p. 158 n33). In part because of Bashō, and also because of the legend, the Killing Stone remains, to this day, a minor tourist attraction in Nasu, certainly far more famous than its benign and bodhisattva-ized "better half" in the Shinnyodō.

12.3 THE RYŌANJI ROCK GARDEN

The last site I want to "visit" in Kyoto is much more famous (at least today) than the previous two. Located to the north of the city, the Ryōanji ("Dragon Peace Monastery") was, like many other Kyoto temples, originally the villa/property of a Heian aristocrat. Nestled at the foot of the hills, it featured a large artificial pond, popularly called the Mandarin Duck pond, still today a great attraction. In the mid-fifteenth century, the estate was acquired by a shogunal lord, Hosokawa Katsumoto, and it was he who first built a Zen monastery on the land. This was the Ryōanji, a Rinzai temple belonging to the Myōshinji school. The building was almost immediately destroyed during the Ōnin Civil Wars that ravaged the capital from 1467 to 1477. It was rebuilt shortly thereafter, only to be burnt to the ground in a fire in 1797, after which it was reconstructed again.

What makes it famous today, and what earned it designation as a UNESCO World Heritage Site (in 1994), and a spot on the "must-see" list for every tour of Kyoto, is the "dry landscape" garden in front of the abbot's quarters. This garden, which probably dates from the sixteenth century, has come to be thought of as a classic expression of a "Zen" rock garden, and is visited every year by hundreds of thousands of tourists from all over the world. It consists of fifteen rocks or boulders, some of them surrounded by a bit of moss, arranged in five groups (of five, three, three, two, and two rocks respectively), all set in a "sea" of raked white pebbles, twenty-two meters wide and nine meters deep. The pebbles are raked into lines suggesting ripples on the surface of water. On one side (the north) is the open veranda of the abbot's quarters, from which the garden is viewed. Enclosing the garden on the southern and western sides is a low orangeish earthen wall (itself a national treasure) topped by a heavy tile roof, and, on the eastern side, a taller whitewashed wall. There is no vegetation in the garden at all (apart from the moss), but over the top of the wall can be seen a screen of trees, among which stands an old weeping cherry that slightly overhangs the wall (see figure 12.3).[17]

This is said to be the descendant of a cherry tree that was seen by the shogun Toyotomi Hideyoshi (1537–1598) when he visited Ryōanji in 1588. Hideyoshi and six companions all wrote poems about the cherry tree, which at that time appears to have been in or right next to the garden, by the abbot's veranda. What is striking, however, is that none of their poems makes any mention of the rock garden per se. Because of this, some have suggested that the rock garden did not even exist then and was added only in the seventeenth century, but it seems more likely that it was there but was viewed as something incidental and ordinary, and certainly not as the epitome of "Zen."[18]

Today, no one would think of setting foot in the garden, on the surface of the sea of pebbles dutifully raked daily by monk/gardeners (and anyone who did so would be promptly escorted out by security). Yet a 1799 drawing of the garden in *Illustrated Guide to Notable Gardens and Sites in the Capital*

17 For a description, discussion, and aesthetic appreciation of the Ryōanji garden, see Kuitert (2002), pp. 98–107, and Berthier (2000), pp. 30–58. A tour of the whole garden may be found on maps.google.com (search for Ryoanji).

18 See Yamada (2009), pp. 139–141. A cherry tree can be seen in an old line drawing of the garden in Kuitert (2002), p. 103. Yamada (2009), p. 143, quotes the account of a gardener who worked at Ryōanji and recalls that his master told him that the ground under the garden was full of old tree stumps.

12.3 *The Ryōanji Rock Garden*

(*Miyako Rinsen Meishō Zue*) by Akisato Ritō (who was himself a well-known garden designer) clearly shows a group of visitors standing in the garden among the rocks where a monk is apparently explaining their significance.[19]

The earliest written records of the garden, *c.*1680, describe it as smaller than today (consisting of only nine large stones), and call it the "Tigers-crossing-the-river garden." This is an allusion to a famous Chinese riddle-story, which is found in many versions in world folklore, describing a mother tigress's dilemma in how to get her three cubs (one of which was antagonistic towards the other two and would kill them in her absence) across a stream safely (given that she could only carry one of them at a time). I will leave it to the reader to figure out the answer. Sometime before the 1797 fire, the garden was expanded in size and six rocks were added to make a total of fifteen, but still it continued to be thought of as representing a mother tiger and her cubs crossing a river.[20] The point here is that the garden was then seen as allegorical rather than symbolic, and "playful" rather than deeply meaningful of some Zen truths. It also remained relatively little known as

19 Reproduced in Kuitert (2002), p. 105, Yamada (2009), p. 109, and Plutschow (1983), p. 139.
20 Kuitert (2002), pp. 98–107.

a place and not always well maintained. As one scholar put it: "During the seventeenth and through the nineteenth centuries ... [and] up until around 1950, [Ryōanji] was a poor, deserted temple standing in a bamboo grove, rarely visited by anyone" (Yamada, 2009, p. 110).

It is not altogether clear how it got propelled, after the Second World War, from relative obscurity to world-wide fame, how it went from being "the garden of the tiger cubs crossing the river" to *the* Zen Garden par excellence. Some say that its popularity as a place of beauty mushroomed after it appeared in the 1949 hit film, *Banshun* (*Late Spring*). That may be true but, as Yamada points out, its (brief) appearance in that melodrama makes no mention of "Zen" whatsoever (2009, pp. 162–163). Yet the very next decade all kinds of references start appearing in popular guides to Kyoto gardens about the Ryōanji being the garden most expressive of Zen enlightenment, transcending, in its simplicity, sensual splendors and embodying "what is called the beauty of the Void" (Jpn., mu no bi) (Yamada, 2009, pp. 164–165).

The word "Mu" (Ch., "Wu") that is used here literally means "No" or "Nothingness" and is, as we have seen, featured in Zhaozhou's (Jpn., Joshu's) kōan about the dog having the Buddha-nature (see 10.6.2). Simply put, a Zen meditator who understands the meaning of "Mu" has experienced satori (awakening). From this we can see that somehow, in the 1950s and early 1960s, the rock garden at Ryōanji came to be thought of as a sort of Zen kōan – something to be "solved" or "understood" by going beyond words, beyond even discursive thought. This view was endorsed and promoted also by the chief priests of Ryōanji who, after the war, were given to lecturing about the garden to visitors to the temple. As one of them put it, "When I sit here [in an interior room] and listen to the footsteps of the visitors on the wooden floor as they leave, I can tell who has really understood the garden well and who is leaving without understanding it at all" (Yamada, 2009, p. 166). This is a direct reference to the "interviews" that occur in Zen training in which disciples daily approach the master to present to him their "solution" to the kōan they are working on. It is said that accomplished Zen masters can tell which disciples have reached a significant insight merely from the sounds of their footsteps as they approach.[21]

In any case, the notion that Ryōanji was something whose deep meaning was to be "understood" was certainly what I had in mind when I first visited the garden, as a college student, in the summer of 1968. I had just arrived in Japan from Europe via the Trans-Siberian railroad and Ryōanji was the first

21 Yamada (2009), p. 166.

place I went to in Kyoto. It was early in the morning and, mercifully, there were only a few other persons there (normally the place is mobbed with tour groups). I remember sitting there cross-legged on the veranda trying to just look. Then suddenly, for reasons I do not fully understand, after about twenty minutes, I could not take it any more: I jumped up and literally fled out of the temple, rushed down the hillside, back to the city. Four years later, I visited Ryōanji again, with some trepidation. But this time, the crowds were there en masse and I could not even get a "first-row" seat on the veranda. By then the temple had installed loudspeakers overhead that, every five minutes or so, blared out looped tape recordings giving, in Japanese and English, explanations of the history and meaning of the garden. I remember being quite upset by this until a companion pointed out to me that "this too is Zen."

12.4 THE BUDDHA'S BIRTHDAY AT THE MORGAN BAY ZENDŌ

At about the same time that the Ryōanji was becoming identified as a "Zen" garden, Walter Nowick, an American musician, arrived in Japan. This was the same time that a variety of young Americans arrived there, e.g. Gary Snyder, Robert Aitken, Philip Kapleau – each in his own way an important figure in the early phases of Zen in America in the 1950s and 1960s.[22]

Nowick had become interested in Zen in New York at the Buddhist Society of America, later called the First Zen Institute of America, founded by Sasaki Sokei-an, a grand-disciple of Shaku Soyen, the first notable Zen master to visit the United States at the Chicago World's Fair in 1893. After Sokei-an's death in 1945, the First Zen Institute was run by his widow, Ruth Fuller Sasaki. Since there was no roshi ("teacher") in New York at that time, Mrs. Sasaki told Nowick to go to Kyoto to seek out her own former teacher, Zuigan Goto Roshi, then the abbot of Daitokuji, one of the great Rinzai Zen training centers. He did so and remained there about fifteen years, never becoming a monk, but ardently practicing zazen while teaching music and English on the side.[23]

Eventually Goto Roshi told him to go back to the United States and to teach Zen there, but to wait a while before doing so. So, in 1965, his master having

22 Fields (1992), p. 209.

23 On the First Zen Institute of America see http://www.firstzen.org/history.php, and, on Shaku Soyen, see Tweed (1992), pp. 31–33. On Sasaki Sokei-an and Ruth Fuller Sasaki, see Fields (1992), pp. 175–192. More generally on Zen in America, see Hori (1998), and Seager (1999), pp. 90–112. On Walter Nowick's story, see LeVine and Morgan Bay Zendo (2008).

passed away, he returned to America and settled in an old farmhouse in Surry, Maine, where he had summered as a child. True to his master's intentions, he at first refrained from teaching (though not from practicing) Zen, but gathered around him an eclectic and international group of music students, whom he tutored, while working the farm on the side. But people learned that one of Goto Roshi's "Dharma heirs" was living in Maine, and began to ask him to teach. Eventually he agreed, and established the Moonspring Hermitage on the property in Surry. There, in the late sixties and seventies, he attracted a group of students who varied widely in education, age, and background. Some were men, some were women, some were married with children, some were single:

> some were teachers, artists, musicians, and writers. One was an architect, another was a lawyer, a couple were doctors, and one was a college professor. Most had had experience with meditation though not always with Zen practice per se. All were attracted by the prospect of working closely with a teacher ... and of combining meditation practice with day-to-day living in a challenging environment that just happened to be extraordinarily beautiful as well. To some, it was also important that, unlike most other Buddhist teachers in the U.S. who wore robes, Walter [Nowick] wore boots and ordinary work clothes except when he was in the Sanzen House [for master-disciple "interviews"] or the Zendo [for meditation].
>
> (LeVine and Morgan Bay Zendō, 2008, p. 26)

Together they built, literally and figuratively, a community that worked, living off the land and practicing together.

In the mid-1980s, Nowick began to give more time to his love of music and to his concern about the threat of nuclear war and his desire for world peace. He himself agreed to perform all thirty-two Beethoven and thirty-two Haydn piano sonatas in Ellsworth, Maine, to benefit the non-profit Ground Zero campaign. Then he founded the Surry Opera Company, a motley group of local people and Zen students, only some of whom had any musical training. They put on Verdi's *Aida* locally, and then began to tour, first in Maine and the States, and then internationally, with Nowick leading them to perform in Kyoto, and then to the Soviet Union where they staged *Boris Godunov* and *Porgy and Bess.*[24]

---

24 See LeVine and Morgan Bay Zendō (2008), pp. 40–41, and Mrozicki (n.d.).

In 1985, Nowick, realizing his commitment to music was increasingly dominating his time, announced his retirement from formal Zen teaching and resigned his post at the Moonspring Hermitage. Eventually, he also relinquished ownership of the Hermitage and adjacent property, which passed to a board of trustees consisting of several of Nowick's former students. Under their guidance, Moonspring Hermitage became the Morgan Bay Zendō, and, as a center, it broadened its orientation to other spiritual paths, hosting retreats for "Tibetan, Chan, Native American, Qi Gong, and other traditions ... while continuing to maintain a long-established protocol within the Zendo" (LeVine and Morgan Bay Zendo, 2008, p. 43). Walter Nowick passed away in 2013 at the age of eighty-seven.

In the Spring of 2014, I visited the Morgan Bay Zendo for a celebration of the Buddha's birthday. About twenty people had gathered for the occasion from different parts of Downeast Maine. The actual celebration was preceded by two twenty-minute sessions of zazen (seated meditation) in the zendō, the meditation hall that was built by members of the community in 1971. The building is a marriage of Japanese and Western architecture. Outside, it looks somewhat like a chalet, but inside it resembles a traditional Japanese-style zendō, with its black slate floor and two-foot-high platforms (Jpn., tan) covered with tatami mats for the meditators to sit on, its shoji window screens, and image of the bodhisattva Mañjuśrī. From April to November, zazen meditation is regularly held at Morgan Bay on Sunday mornings, and twice a week during the summer. In addition, there are periodic, more intensive and lengthier retreats led by various invited teachers.

After zazen, on the day of my visit, the group moved from the zendō over to the Assembly Hall for a brief celebration of the Buddha's birthday, led by Hugh Curran, who practiced under Walter Nowick and is one of the current leaders of Morgan Bay. A small image of the baby Buddha, just emerged from his mother's side, and standing upright, one arm raised (see 2.7.1), was set in a shallow basin. One by one, individuals approached and ladled some sweet tea over the image, thus repeating the acts of ablution that were performed by the gods Indra and Brahma after the Buddha's actual birth. While they did so, the rest of the group stood around in a circle and chanted repeatedly (in English) the verse for the ritual: "Today the Tathagata is bathed by us all. / Deep wisdom and clarity bring such happiness. / May living beings everywhere / who are overwhelmed by suffering / see the Dharmakaya in this very world." This is the gist of what is usually a somewhat longer ceremony in more traditional settings. Following the bathing of the Buddha image, all members of the group shared in conversation and a potluck lunch.[25]

12.5 THE JAPAN TEMPLE IN LUMBINĪ

Following this account of the Buddha's birthday, it seems appropriate to return to the Buddha's birthplace, Lumbinī, and to look at one more place illustrative of Japanese Buddhism. As mentioned in 1.3.3, the Japan Temple (Nippondera) is located in a central spot in Lumbinī's Mahāyāna zone. Plans for it started in 1993, but to date it remains unfinished and is not yet open due to construction delays and sponsorship difficulties. The temple, whose main hall is of impressive dimensions, is a project of the Sōkyō ("Whole Teaching") Foundation, which was founded by Umehara Sōzan (b. 1961) and recognized as a "religious corporation" in Japan in 1986. This is a legal status granted by the government to both major religious groups (Buddhist, Christian, etc.) and to multiple "New Religions."

The phenomenon of "New Religions" (Jpn., shin shūkyō), which appeared in Japan starting in the nineteenth century, continued in the first half of the twentieth, and mushroomed after the Second World War and in the late twentieth century, has been much studied by historians of religions and sociologists. Some of these movements are rooted in Buddhist traditions, some in Shintō, and some in an eclectic mixture of religiosity and new age beliefs. In any case, dozens of such movements have arisen over the past 150 years, some quite small, and some (e.g. Sōka Gakkai, Risshō kōsei-kai, Reiyū-kai, Tenri-kyō) with memberships in the millions.[26]

In all the lists of New Religions that I have come across, I have never seen mention of Umehara's Sōkyō Foundation, which, in any case, is hard to categorize. Umehara's primary interest lies in what he calls (in English) "tomb-logy" (Jpn., bōsōgaku) – the study of aspects of tombs and the importance of their design and location. This, of course, is a preoccupation that has ancient roots not only in Japan but in China as well, where the correct siting of graves according to geomantic (fengshui) principles was and remains of great importance. But "tomb-logy" goes beyond mere geomancy to include the symbolic and spiritual significance of the layout of graves and

25 On the ritual bathing of infant images of the Buddha, see Rhi (2010).

26 For a list of forty New Religions (with statistics) originating in different periods, see Mullins, Shimazono, and Swanson (1993), pp. 227–228. The literature on New Religions is immense. For a bibliographic essay and discussion, see Astley (2006).

their monuments for the living as well as for the dead. This preoccupation may help explain the stoppage of construction of the Nippondera: at the time of this writing, the organization had put the Lumbinī project on hold and turned all of its resources towards helping persons devastated by the 2011 earthquake, tsunami, and nuclear disaster in Fuskushima, Japan, many of whom had seen family graves wiped out.[27]

It may, at first, seem strange for a foundation dedicated to the "science of tombs" to undertake to build a Japanese Buddhist temple at the Buddha's birthplace. It makes more sense, however, when it is remembered that one of the chief unifying features of Japanese Buddhism throughout much of its history has been its preoccupation with and specialization in funerary rites and death-related practices and beliefs. In modern times, one of the chief ritual functions of Buddhist priests is to perform mortuary rites, and temples are often the sites of extensive cemeteries, as we saw in the case of the Shinnyodō. Indeed, it has become a truism to point out that many Japanese today personally have nothing to do with Buddhist priests or a temple until someone in their family dies (just as some in the West might have nothing to do with a Christian minister or church until they get married or have a funeral). As a consequence, contemporary popular Buddhism has sometimes been criticized as nothing but "funerary Buddhism" (Jpn., sōshiki bukkyō), i.e. something largely devoid of other spiritual significance.[28]

This focus is usually traced to the feudal Tokugawa period (1603–1868), during which all citizens were ordered to register at local Buddhist temples, in part to combat lingering Christian missionary influence, and in part to better control the population. This directive was enforced by the rule that only official Buddhist priests connected to these temples could bury the dead and hold memorial services for them. Thus families that did not register as Buddhists (or were refused registry) at local temples might soon find themselves with their ancestors uncared for, or, perhaps worse, with an undisposed corpse on their hands.[29]

---

27 On Umehara and the Sōkyō foundation, see http:www5b.biglobe.ne.jp/~bosou/men/men.htm. For a video tour of the unfinished temple, see http://www.youtube.com/watch?v=VpxDhoi_-lk.

28 The term sōshiki bukkyō originated with Tamamuro Taijō's book of the same title, published in 1963. His criticism of contemporary Buddhism was, however, perhaps not altogether fair (see Stone and Walter, 2008, p. 1). On the business of funerals by temples in modern Japan, see Covell (2005), pp. 165–190.

29 On the connections of Tokugawa Buddhism to mortuary rites, see Williams (2005), pp. 13–58, and Hur (2007). On funeral rituals in medieval Japan, see Gerhart (2009).

In fact, this Buddhist "monopoly on death" in Japan has its roots much earlier than the Tokugawa period. Almost from the start of its introduction to Japan in the sixth century CE, Buddhism took over caring for the dead, moving into a vacuum readily left open by early indigenous ("Shintō") beliefs which, preoccupied with notions of purity and pollution and laying great stress on life and vitality, were happy to have as little to do with the dead as possible. This was a pattern that continued for much of the rest of Japanese history.[30]

The Sōkyō Foundation, however, in its establishment of the Japan Temple at Lumbinī, was not concerned only with gravesites and funerary Buddhism; according to its literature, somewhat like the Nipponzan Myōhōji (see 1.3.3), it was also interested in enshrining relics of the Buddha in memorial pagodas, not only in Nepal but at sacred spots throughout the world. The connection between this and tomb-logy is spelled out as follows: "Desiring the prosperity of the family and the perpetuity of descendants, we venerate family graves; and desiring the prosperity of the company and the happiness of employees, we venerate company pagodas. These are noble acts, but even more important is to venerate and make offerings to Buddha-relic pagodas that are built with prayers for world peace and human happiness."[31] So far, the Sōkyō foundation appears to have built three peace relic pagodas, in Sirubari (Nepal), in Chiang Mai (Thailand), and in Tsukuba (Japan).[32]

12.6 CONCLUSION

We have, in this chapter, looked at a variety of sites in order to get a better grasp of Japanese "saṃgha situations." Starting with the Hexagonal Temple in Kyoto, we moved on to the Shinnyōdō and Ryōanji in the same city, before looking at a Zen center in Maine and a "New Religion" center in Lumbinī. There are, of course, an almost infinite number of other places that we might have "visited"; these can only serve to give an introductory glimpse of the some of the complex and multifarious situations that help characterize the Buddhism/s of Japan.

---

30 On the ancient roots of Japanese Buddhist preoccupation with death rites, see Stone and Walter (2008), p. 2. For a study of early, largely pre-Buddhist mortuary rituals in Japan, see Ebersole (1989).

31 http://www5b.biglobe.ne.jp/~bosou/well/well5.htm.

32 On the Sirubari peace pagoda, see http://commonholysanctuary.org/PhotoGallery NP.php?ID=0.

Chapter 13

Saṃgha Situations: Places, Persons, and Practices in Tibetan Buddhism/s

From Japan, we now turn to Tibet for some examples of saṃgha situations in a largely Vajrayāna context. Once again, I will begin by focusing on places, and some of the personalities and practices and layers of tradition attached to them. I want to start in Lhasa, presently capital of Tibet and a sacred site of ancient standing (13.1) and the traditional residence of the Dalai Lamas (13.2). Then I want to look at various types of Tibetan monastics, including ordinary scholar-monks, and extraordinary "mad monks" (13.3). Following that, I want to consider the monastery of Samding (bsam sding) in Central Tibet, seat of one of the only female lines of reincarnations (13.4). Finally, as in the last two chapters, I will look at an example of a Tibetan Buddhism in the West, in this case, a center in Barnet, Vermont (U.S.A.) (13.5).

13.1 LHASA JOKHANG

Spiritually speaking, the most important place in Lhasa, the present capital of Tibet, is the Jokhang temple (a.k.a. the Tsug-lha-khang [gtsug lha khang]). Situated at the heart of the old town, it dates back to the very foundation of the city, if not before. Its sacrality is defined by the fact that it houses a most important object of devotion: the Jowo (Jo bo) Rinpoché – a sacred image representing the Buddha as a young prince, prior to his great departure. Traditionally, the Jokhang is said to have been built by one of the first great kings of Tibet, Songtsen Gampo (Srong btsan sgam po), sometime around the year 640 CE. Historically speaking, Songtsen Gampo may or may not have been a Buddhist, but he was clearly depicted as such by later tradition which looked back to him as one of the "three great religious kings" of the ancient Yarlung dynasty, and held him to be an incarnation of Avalokiteśvara.[33]

Architecturally, the Jokhang reflects Newar influences, and legend associates it with the king's Nepalese wife, the princess Bhṛkutī. In recognition of this, its main entrance faces the west, towards Nepal. The Jowo image, however, is said to have been brought to Tibet from China by the king's Chinese wife, the Princess Wencheng. It was initially housed in another famous ancient temple, the Ramoché (Ra mo che), which faces east towards China and is popularly known as the "Chinese Tiger" (Gya thak [rgya stag]). At some point, not too long thereafter, the Jowo image was moved to the Jokhang, and the Nepalese image there was moved to the Ramoché. The reasons and the date for this switch are much disputed, but the end result was to give primacy to the Jokhang. At the same time, implicit in this story is the recognition of a double influence on Tibetan Buddhism: from China, and from Nepal/India. We shall see other iterations of this tension in what follows.[34]

When Tibetans go on pilgrimage to Lhasa, then, it is primarily to the Jokhang and the Jowo Rinpoché image (the "Precious Jowo") that they are headed, sometimes from hundreds of kilometers away. In Lhasa itself, many of these devotees may be seen circumambulating the Jokhang on any of three different concentric routes: an inner circuit (nangkor [nang bskor]) which is a corridor within the Jokhang itself; a kilometer-long middle circuit (barkor [bar bskor]) which encircles the whole of the Jokhang complex of buildings through the streets of the old town; and a much longer outer circuit (lingkor [gling bskor]) which encompasses much of the city of Lhasa including the Potala palace.[35]

13.1.1 Pinning Down the Demoness

Geomantically, the Jokhang is said to stand at the very center not only of Lhasa but of the whole of Tibet, which is conceived of as a kind of maṇḍala.

33 On the three religious kings, see Powers (2007), pp. 144–155. On origins of Lhasa as a town, see Blondeau and Gyatso (2003).

34 For an account of the legends and history of the Jokhang, see Blondeau and Gyatso (2003), Alexander (2005), pp. 27–72, and Vitali (1990), pp. 69–88. On the Ramoché, see Alexander (2005), pp. 75–89. As a Nepalese temple with a Chinese image, the Jokhang can be seen as reflecting the confrontation and syncretism in Tibet of two Buddhist traditions: the Chinese to the east and the Indian and Nepalese to the west and south. For a slightly later iteration of this polar tension, see Kapstein (2000), pp. 23–37.

35 Dowman (1988), pp. 40–41. See also Buswell and Lopez (2014), p. 472.

This is reflected in several other building schemes. In Lhasa itself, eight protector shrines (known as the Rigsum gonpo lhakhang [Rigs gsum mgon po lha khang]) were erected at equal distances all around the Jokhang, facing outwards in the four cardinal and four intermediate directions. These are traditionally attributed to King Songtsen Gampo, but early records of them are unclear. Each shrine featured images of three bodhisattvas – Avalokiteśvara, Mañjuśrī, and Vajrapāṇi – who together served to guard against malignant forces from whatever direction. Very little of the original buildings remains today, although efforts were made to restore some of them after their desecration during the cultural revolution.[36]

More broadly, another mandalaic tradition puts the Jokhang at the center of twelve other temples which were built in ancient times to pin down the body of a giant demoness, thought to lie supine and spread-eagled over the entire territory of Tibet. The Jokhang was intended to anchor the demoness's heart, while the other twelve temples were located, in three concentric squares, at her two shoulders and two hips, her two elbows and two knees, and her two hands and two feet. Together, these temples not only marked out a maṇḍala centered on the Jokhang in Lhasa but also reflected a pattern of imperial rule and subjugation. The first square of temples, pinning down the demoness's shoulders and hips, were located in areas from which the king recruited the four wings of his army; the second square of temples that pinned down the demoness's elbows and knees also controlled the provinces of Tibet; and the third, outermost square, that pinned down the demoness's hands and feet subjugated the outlying border regions.[37]

13.1.2 Flood Control

In addition to being located at the very center of the Tibetan cosmos, the Jokhang temple is said to have been built originally on the site of an ancient lake which King Songtsen Gampo had filled in with dirt and stones transported by goats (hence the original name of the town as "Rasa" – the place of goats – rather than its subsequent designation as "Lhasa" – the place of gods). In fact, the plain in which Lhasa is situated was historically a rather

36 On the rigsum gonpo shrines, see Alexander (2005), pp. 91–100.

37 For a list of the temples and their locations, see Dowman (1988), pp. 284–287. On the myth of the demoness, see Gyatso (1987), and Bellezza (1997), pp. 159–230. On the use of the maṇḍala pattern in various dimensions of ideology and administration, see French (1995), pp. 85–87, 178–179.

marshy area, periodically subject to the flooding of the Kyichu river. Almost from the start, floodwater appears to have been a perennial problem, and legend has it that Songtsen Gampo not only filled in the area of the Jokhang, but undertook to contain the Kyichu in its bed by the construction of dikes. He is also said to have backed up those efforts through a series of magical meditations designed to keep the waters at bay. The place where he did this, known as Songtsen Gampo's Meditation Hollow, is presently located inside the Ani Tsham-khung convent (the "Recluse-pit nunnery"), not far from the Jokhang, and currently the residence of some eighty nuns (see figure 13.1).

Water control remained important, so much so that, up until modern times, at the end of the Great Prayer Festival (Mönlam chenmo [smon lam chen mo]) held every New Year at the Jokhang (see 13.1.4), the assembled crowds of monks from the Drepung (Bras spungs) and Séra (Se ra) monasteries would go down to the Kyichu river and add rocks to its embankments. They thereby protected the city and the temple. Indeed, a popular belief had it that if Lhasa were ever to be overrun by flood waters, the Jowo statue would be taken away by water deities (Tib., klu; Skt., nāgas) into their subterranean abodes.[38]

All told, then, the Jokhang is in several ways an important center and symbol, signifying Buddhist order in its many dimensions, and keeping at bay chaotic forces – whether those be thought of as demonic or as natural calamities. The Jokhang is also the site of many rituals and devotional activities. Here I shall look at two in particular: first, the general practice of making grand prostrations, done as a common everyday devotion primarily by laypersons but by monastics as well (this is not specific to the Jokhang but is found everywhere in Tibet); and second, the just mentioned Great Prayer Festival, celebrated annually in Lhasa over a two-week period by monks, shortly after New Year.

13.1.3 Grand Prostrations

The practice of grand or "outstretched" prostrations is a common expression of devotion and dedication by Tibetan Buddhists everywhere. Those embarking on the bodhisattva path (see 10.1) may undertake to do vast numbers of these (typically 100,000), but, more routinely, ordinary devotees will

38 Blondeau and Gyatso (2003), p. 29. For more on the importance of flood control, see Sorensen (2003), and Akester (2001).

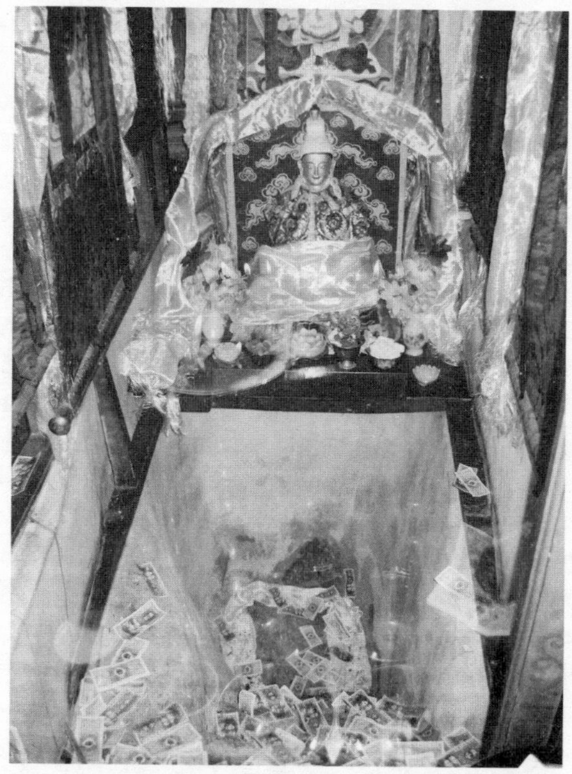

13.1 *Cash Offerings in Songtsen Gampo's "Hollow" at Ani Tsham-khung Convent in Lhasa*

prostrate (typically three times) whenever they come into the presence of a Buddha image or a high lama or their guru or some other object or person of devotion.

The grand prostration itself consists of joining the palms of one's hands together, holding them up on top of one's head, and then, in a slow but flowing motion, bringing them down, and pausing at one's forehead, one's throat, and one's heart, and then bending down to stretch them out on the ground, until one is lying face down, flat on the ground, arms and hands extended towards the object of devotion. Then one gets back up to a standing position, before starting on another prostration. Sometimes, devotees will use cloth pads to cover their hands so as to protect them from repeated sliding along the ground. Others may employ special, smooth, prostration boards.[39]

39 On grand prostrations, see Dhargye (1982), pp. 53–54.

At virtually any time of day, crowds of people can be seen doing grand prostrations in the outer courtyard of the Jokhang, directing their devotion to the image of the Jowo Buddha inside. Others may do repeated grand prostrations (instead of walking) along any of the circumambulation routes (typically the Barkor or the Lingkor) that encircle the holy site. In this method, devotees do one grand prostration and then get up and do another one from the spot where their outstretched hands touched the ground. Thus they gradually inch forward, marking their whole circumambulation with their bodies. More extremely, some pilgrims may undertake to use this method to proceed all the way to Lhasa from their home places, sometimes hundreds of kilometers away, taking months to accomplish the journey. I once encountered on a highway northeast of Lhasa two monks who were thus making their way to the Jokhang. They had about seventy-five kilometers to go (see figure 13.2).

Grand prostrations are not only ritual expressions of devotion and dedication; when done correctly, they are also meditative practices ultimately aimed at achieving buddhahood. According to Géshé Ngawang Dhargye, in the practice of prostrations may be found the practice of all six perfections (pāramitā) of the bodhisattva path (see 10.1) : (1) to make prostrations is to give an example that will inspire others – this is to practice the perfection of

13.2 Two Monks on the Highway Northeast of Lhasa Doing Grand Prostrations

generosity (dāna); (2) to make sure you do prostrations in the proper way – this is to practice discipline (śīlā); (3) to endure the hardship of making repeated prostrations – this is to practice forbearance (kṣantī); (4) to do prostrations enthusiastically in order to help all sentient beings – this is to practice energy (vīrya); (5) to fix your attention on the object to which you are paying homage – this is to practice concentration (dhyāna); and (6) to understand the emptiness of the object of homage and of yourself as the person making the prostration – this is to practice wisdom (prajñā). At the same time, prostrations are seen as helping the devotee build what will eventually be a Buddha body. To place your two hands on top of your head – this is to plant the seeds for developing a "cranial protuberance" (uṣṇīṣa), one of the Buddha's thirty-two physiognomic signs (see 2.7.1). To touch your forehead with your hands – this marks the spot of your future urṇā as a Buddha. To touch your throat and your heart helps you develop the Buddha's speech, and his wisdom. When you are lying on the ground, you should think that, by your action, you will gain as much merit as there are atoms in the area that you are covering with your body, and that you will use this merit to attain enlightenment for the sake of all sentient beings. Finally, you should not rest on the ground but rise up as soon as possible; this is a sign of your determination to free yourself from saṃsāra.[40]

Finally, it should be said that prostrations are by no means the only expression of Tibetan faith and devotion. Years ago, the anthropologist and Tibetanist Robert Ekvall listed prostrations as only one of "six Tibetan universals of religious observance" which variously characterized actions of body, speech, and mind. The other five (which cannot be gone into here but which equally mark the practice of pilgrims at the Jokhang) were the attitude of faith (Tib., dépa [dad pa]); the recitation of mantras (and other formulae) such as "Oṃ Maṇi Padme Hūṃ"; the making of offerings, symbolic or substantive, to the object of devotion; the performance of circumambulation; and the practice of divination.[41]

13.1.4 The Great Prayer Festival

In addition to being a year-round magnet for devotees and pilgrims, the Jokhang was also, in traditional Tibet, the hub of an important annual event:

40 Géshé Ngawang Dhargye, oral teachings, Dharamsala, 18 April 1972.

41 On all of these, see Ekvall (1964).

the celebration of the "Great Prayer Festival" (Tib., Mönlam Chenmo). Many of the Tibetan Buddhist sects had and still have their own prayer festivals, but the great one in Lhasa was the affair of the Géluk school. It was first established in 1409 by Tsongkhapa, the founder of the Géluk, to celebrate the fifteen days of miracles performed by the Buddha in his lifetime in order to defeat the heretic teachers (see 2.7.9). Held over a two-week period, in conjunction with the celebration of the Tibetan new year (Tib., losar; lo gsar), it served as an annual reassertion of the supremacy of Buddhism over malignant and non-Buddhist forces. It also aimed at stemming the tide of the decline of the Dharma and ushering in the arrival of the future Buddha Maitreya. During the festival period, "monks ruled" in Lhasa – not only because thousands of them came into town for the celebration from the great Géluk monasteries of Sera, Drepung, and Ganden (Dga' ldan) near Lhasa and from other places all over Tibet, but also because during this time the city government itself was formally handed over to a Géluk hierarch from Drepung who retained all religious and secular authority for the duration of the celebration. That authority was enforced, sometimes none too gently, by so-called "warrior" or "athlete" monks (dob-dob [ldob ldob]), who patrolled the streets and imposed fines on anyone considered to be improperly dressed or disorderly.[42]

Daily, in the Jokhang, multitudes of monks would assemble to recite prayers intended to benefit the Dharma as well as all sentient beings, including the crowds of laypersons who came to watch and listen. At the same time, in Lhasa itself, various traditional New Year's celebrations took place, which similarly had the purpose of expelling the old and the evil, and ushering in the new and the good. For instance, in the Potala, on the second day, various members of the nobility dressed up in ancient costumes from the time of the Tibetan kings and paid homage and made great offerings to the Dalai Lama and watched dances that invoked the victory of divinities over demons. They then went to watch, at the base of the Potala, the so-called "sky-dancing rope game," in which some acrobats would form balancing feats at the top of an extremely tall pole before descending a diagonally stretched rope to the ground. The acrobats were traditionally from the province of Tsang, and their feats (which, historically, apparently occasionally led to their falling to their deaths) were viewed as a kind of tribute and ritual resubmission of the whole people of Tsang, payment for their opposition,

---

42 On the dob-dob at New Year's, see Richardson (1993), p. 22. More generally, see Goldstein (1964), and Richardson (1986).

in the seventeenth century, to the Fifth Dalai Lama (who defeated them in his bid for political power).[43]

Another New Year's ritual reaffirmation of the "powers of good" (as defined by Tibetan Buddhist "orthodoxy") is made on the twenty-fourth day of the first month, towards the end of the Great Prayer festival. On that occasion several large butter sculptures (torma [gtor ma]) are brought out of the Jokhang by two lines of laymen. These are said to contain all the accumulated evil influences of the past year. They are taken in procession to an open field south of the city where they are set in the midst of a brushwood pyre. A parade of high monastic dignitaries as well as the Néchung (Gnas chung) state oracle follow the procession there. The oracle then shoots an arrow into the pyre, and the torma butter sculptures are set alight, thus burning up all the evil they have stored. At the same time, some old cannons are fired towards a mountainside south of the Kyichu river, at a hillside which is deemed to be inauspicious as it is said to be the burial place of Lang Darma, the "evil" king who persecuted Buddhism in the ninth century.[44]

13.2 THE POTALA AND THE DALAI LAMAS

The Jokhang, of course, is not the only famous focal point in Lhasa. Ever since the seventeenth century, the city's most monumental and well-known building has been the Potala Palace, built during the reign of the Great Fifth Dalai Lama (1617–1682). Named after Potalaka, the mythic pure land of the bodhisattva Avalokiteśvara, it served as the personal residence of all subsequent Dalai Lamas. In addition, it contained myriad offices, assembly halls, and monastic buildings. Today, with the Fourteenth Dalai Lama in exile in India (since 1959), it is officially a museum, and has been recognized as a UNESCO World Heritage site (see figure 13.3).[45]

Each Dalai Lama is thought to be the reincarnation of his predecessor and, at the same time, a manifestation of Avalokiteśvara. This system of succession by reincarnation was first employed by the Karmapa lamas in the Kagyü school in the twelfth century, and later adopted by the Gélukpa, sometime

43 Richardson (1993), pp. 14–20.

44 Richardson (1993), pp. 39–49. On the Great Prayer Festival, in general, see also Tucci (1980), pp. 151–153. On the Néchung oracle, see Nebesky-Wojkowitz (1993), pp. 444–454.

45 On the Potala, see Chayet (2003), and Larsen and Sinding-Larsen (2001), pp. 103–112.

13.3 Potala Palace, Lhasa

after their foundation by Tsongkhapa (1357–1419). It rapidly became complementary to the other chief system of monastic succession from teacher to disciple. Today, there are hundreds of reincarnation lineages in Tibet (many of which have continued in exile), as well as many teaching lineages, with which they coexist. Incarnates are generally known as "tülkus" (sprul sku), literally meaning the "manifest body [of a Buddha]" (Skt., nirmāṇakāya).[46]

The Dalai Lama line of reincarnations actually originated with a prominent hierarch of the Géluk school, Sönam Gyatso (Bsod nams rgya mtsho) (1543–1588). He established a close relationship with Altan Khan, the most powerful Mongol chieftain at the time, serving as his primary spiritual advisor. Together, they revived the so-called "patron–priest" relationship between Mongol secular overlords and Tibetan religious leaders that had first been established some centuries earlier by Sakya Pandita and a descendant of Chinggis Khan.[47] It was Altan Khan who bestowed upon Sönam Gyatso the Mongolian title "Ta lé" (i.e. Dalai) meaning "ocean [of wisdom]." Sönam Gyatso then gave the same title, out of respect, to two of his forerunners in the Géluk hierarchy who posthumously came to be seen as the First and Second Dalai Lamas, while he himself was thought of as the third reincarnation in the line.

46 For a listing and brief account of all the Dalai Lamas, see Buswell and Lopez (2014), pp. 209–210. On the lineage of Karmapas, see Quintman (2004).

47 On the succession of teachers in the Sakya school, see Stearns (2003).

The Géluk alliance with the Mongols was further solidified with the Fourth Dalai Lama, who was actually a grandson of Altan Khan, and then with the Fifth Dalai Lama, who formed a coalition not only with the Mongols but with Central Tibetan aristocrats and Nyingma hierarchs to establish a new government, centered in Lhasa, with himself as both its political and religious head, ruling from the newly built Potala. When the Kagyü sect and forces in the province of Tsang resisted his power move, he ordered them smashed militarily in no uncertain terms.[48] In order to further consolidate his power, and to thank him for his support, he then named his teacher, Losang Chökyi Gyaltsen (Blo bzang chos kyi rgyal mtshan), who was abbot of the Tashi Lunpo (Bkra shis lhun po) monastery in Tsang, as the first Panchen Lama (pan chen bla ma). From then on, the figure of the Dalai Lama ceased being just the head of the Drepung Monastery and the Géluk school, and came to be recognized as the spiritual *and political* leader of the whole of Tibet.

The degree to which the Dalai Lamas have actually exercised political power, however, has varied greatly over the years. The nature of the system was such that, until a new Dalai Lama reached adulthood, effective power was exercised by a regent, who was sometime loath to give it up. Some Dalai Lamas (e.g. the Sixth, Seventh, and Eighth) were not inclined to or allowed to rule politically; others (e.g. the Ninth, Tenth, Eleventh, and Twelfth) died young, sometimes under mysterious circumstances. The Thirteenth Dalai Lama (1876–1933), however, ruled effectively and attempted to institute reforms at a time when great changes were beginning to impinge upon Tibet; while the present, Fourteenth Dalai Lama, Tenzin Gyatso (Bstan 'dzin Rgya mtsho), born in 1935, has seen some of the consequences of those changes. Ever since 1959, he has lived in exile in India, having fled Lhasa as a result of the Chinese occupation of his country.[49]

13.2.1 Finding a New Dalai Lama

When a Dalai Lama dies, immediate steps are taken to locate the child in whom he has been reborn. A regent is appointed and a search committee is

48 See Sperling (2001).

49 For a succinct discussion of all the Dalai Lamas, see Sparham (2003). On the Sixth Dalai Lama, who was a poet and somewhat of a libertine, see Aris (1989), pp. 107–214, and Barks (1992); on the Seventh Dalai Lama, see Mullin (1999). On the Thirteenth Dalai Lama, see Bell (1946). On the Fourteenth and his exile, see Avedon (1984), and Hicks and Chogyam (1990).

formed. Hints that the previous Dalai Lama may have given as to the locale of his next birth are considered. Oracles are consulted. Meditative visions are sought on the shores of a remote alpine lake sacred to Palden Lhamo (dpal ldan lha mo; Skt., Śrīdevī), the protective goddess of Tibet, and especially of the Dalai Lamas. Eventually, search parties are set out, incognito, to look for and investigate the claims of various possible candidates. Through this process, the field is narrowed down to a few finalists, who are observed and tested, sometimes repeatedly, in various ways.[50]

Two of the most commonly mentioned ways for finally determining the identity of the new Dalai Lama are the test where candidates are asked to recognize objects that had formerly belonged to the previous Dalai Lama, and the so-called "golden urn method." Use of the "golden urn" was first advocated by the Chinese in the early eighteenth century, following the death of the Sixth Dalai Lama. It consisted of placing the names of finalist candidates in a golden bowl and picking from them the name of the winner, supposedly at random. Something similar had previously been done for the initial selection of the Fifth Dalai Lama, who was chosen over two other finalists. Those were turbulent times, however, and the identity of the boy who was the winner (the Fifth Dalai Lama) was kept secret for six years, during which he lived with his mother in south-central Tibet. When things settled down, and the Géluk powers-that-be wished to have the now six-year-old candidate officially recognized as the Fifth Dalai Lama, there were some who insisted that his selection be reconfirmed by asking him to differentiate between objects, some of which had previously belonged to the Fourth Dalai Lama. This was the second method of verification. Interestingly, in his autobiography, the Fifth Dalai Lama later recalled the occasion with disarming frankness: "The monastic official ... showed me statues and rosaries (that belonged to the Fourth Dalai Lama and other people), but I was unable to distinguish between them! When he left the room I heard him tell the people outside that I had successfully passed the tests. Later, when he became my tutor, he would often admonish me and say: 'You must work hard, since you were unable to recognize the objects!'" (Karmay, 2003, p. 69).

In the case of the present Fourteenth Dalai Lama, all accounts suggest that the object-recognition test was more honestly carried out. One of the most down-to-earth and straightforward recollections of the occasion may be found in a memoir by the Dalai Lama's mother, Diki Tsering. She recalls three separate visits in 1938 to her house in Amdo, in far northeastern Tibet/

50 On Palden Lhamo, see Heller (2003), pp. 82–87.

northwestern China, by some strangers from Lhasa, and her two-and-a-half-year-old son's rather remarkable behavior and statements at the time. On the last of these occasions, the boy was presented with various ritual objects – two rosaries, two ritual drums, etc. – and told he could have one. In all instances, he chose without hesitation the object that had belonged to the previous Thirteenth Dalai Lama, claiming that it was his own. After some more testing and the paying of a sizable bribe to the local Chinese Muslim warlord in order to gain his consent to "release" the finalist candidate, the search party and the whole family set out on the long journey to Lhasa, where he was welcomed as the new Dalai Lama.[51] Even at this point, however, there was still talk of using the "golden urn" as one final test, but apparently that did not happen although, according to his mother, years later, when the Dalai Lama was fourteen, at a time of intense political infighting in Lhasa, lots were drawn to confirm his selection and quiet those who questioned his identity, even then. Needless to say, the Dalai Lama successfully passed that test, which took place in the Jokhang, in front of the image of the Jowo Buddha.[52]

13.3 SCHOLARS AND MAD SAINTS

Besides the Dalai Lamas, the history of Tibetan Buddhism is filled with stories of all kinds of religious figures – erudite scholars, other incarnate lamas, eccentric hermits, venerated teachers, powerful abbots, wandering holy men and women, charismatic monks and nuns, etc. – who have succeeded one another over the generations. In what follows, I would like to highlight two lifestyles in particular that are sometimes presented as epitomizing a polarity said to characterize the Tibetan saṃgha, a Vajrayāna version, perhaps, of the South Asian polarity between the "vocation of books" and the "vocation of meditation." On the one hand, there are those Tibetan monastics who are engaged in scholarly studies, pursued generally within a community setting, and aimed at achieving high academic degrees; on the other hand, there are those who opt for semi-solitary wandering lives and whose reputations are built on their being accomplished practitioners whose transcendent understandings are thought to be reflected in their eccentric, antinomian behavior.[53]

51 Tsering (2000), pp. 75–85. For the Dalai Lama's own account of this, see Gyatso (2010), pp. 42–46. See also Hicks and Chogyam (1990), pp. 17–23.

52 Tsering (2000), p. 124.

53 For one presentation of this polarity, see Samuel (1993).

13.3.1 Drepung Monastery and Monastic Studies

As an example of the first, it is worth taking a brief look at one of the large monastic universities of Tibet. Along with Séra and Ganden, Drepung has stood as one of the great centers of Géluk learning in the Lhasa area. Located about eight kilometers outside town, it was founded in the early fifteenth century, and housed about 10,000 monks at the time of the Chinese invasion in 1950. Somewhat like Cambridge or Oxford University, Drepung was actually organized into a number of different more or less independent "colleges," each with its own abbot. Each college, in turn, comprised a number of "houses" or residence halls. Since monks came to Drepung from all over the Tibetan cultural area and even beyond, the houses tended to be places for monks from a particular region who spoke the same dialect and faced the same challenges of adjusting to central Tibetan language and ways. For instance, when Lobsang Gyatso (who was a monk at Drepung until he fled to India in 1959) first arrived at the monastery, he joined Phukhang house in Loséling (Blo gsal gling) College, which accepted monks from the region of Kham in Eastern Tibet where he was from. There he was quickly put under the tutelage of the house guru, and began his course of study.[54]

The full curriculum for a "book monk" (pechawa [dpe cha ba]) normally took fifteen to twenty years and involved graduated courses of study centered around particular topics and particular texts. After mastering basic principles of debate and epistemology, monks would go on to study (for a period of many years) the doctrines of the Perfection of Wisdom and the bodhisattva path, and Madhyamaka philosophy. Then, towards the end of their student careers, they would turn to the Abhidharma and the Vinaya, before finally (if they went that far) sitting for their géshé (lit., "spiritual friend" [Skt., kalyāṇamitra]) degree.[55]

Throughout, the emphasis was on memorization and debate, and the intensive study and exegesis of the text and meaning of certain key doctrinal works. For the first several years, students tended to focus mainly on manuals, textbook summaries of doctrines and traditions generally composed by past great scholars of the Géluk school. Then, however, they would tackle a number of erudite Indian Mahāyāna philosophical treatises (in Tibetan translation) and various Tibetan commentaries on them. In the Géluk tradition, for

54 On the structure of Drepung, see Goldstein (1998), p. 20. On Lobsang Gyatso's arrival there, see L. Gyatso (1998), p. 55.

55 Dreyfus (2003), pp. 112–114; Newland (1996), p. 207.

instance, great attention was paid to three works: the *Ornament of Realization* (*Abhisamayālaṃkara*) by Maitrenatha, which serves as a guide to Perfection of Wisdom doctrines; the *Commentary on Valid Cognition* (*Pramāṇavārttika*), by Dharmakīrti, which is a key treatise on Buddhist logic and epistemology; and the *Introduction to the Middle Way* (*Madhyamakāvatāra*), by Candrakīrti, a major commentary on Nāgārjuna's most important work.[56]

The annual schedule at Drepung began with New Year's celebrations that were immediately followed by the Great Prayer Festival in Lhasa which many monks from Drepung attended. Then, for most of the rest of the year, there alternated periods of debate with shorter "break" periods, punctuated half way through by the six-week "summer retreat" during which many monks would move into hermitage-like caves on the mountains above Drepung. This, although not quite as long, was a period equivalent to the South Asian Buddhist rains-retreat. The final debate period of the year, the Winter Debate, lasted a month and was judged by senior scholars from all three Géluk monasteries.

During debate periods, scholar-monks' daily schedules were quite rigorous, involving getting up at 5:30 A.M., attending several daily monastic assemblies (for chanting and prayers), and engaging in periods of study/memorization of texts, lessons with one's teacher, and two debate sessions in the debate courtyard – from 1:00 to 4:00 P.M., and again from 7:00 P.M on, sometimes until midnight.[57]

Debates were actually of two types. First, there were the daily debates with a partner, in which "monks pair with each other, one standing and playing the role of the questioner, and the other sitting down and playing the role of the defender" (Dreyfus, 2003, p. 250). The standing monk will pose his questions, generally on recognized topics, with certain stylized ritual gestures involving a back and forth movement and a clapping of the hands. Depending on the sitting monk's answer, he will then fire off another question. This sounds somewhat staid but is far from it. The use of sarcasm, clever language, jokes, shouts, and general roughhousing to ruffle one's opponent is rather common. In time, the two monks may switch roles and, if the debate heats up and goes on a long time, other monks may gather round to listen and sometimes intervene with comments of their own. All of this is a way

56 For translations or partial translations of these texts, see Sparham (2006–2012), Tillemans (2000), and Huntington (1989).

57 Gyatso (1998), pp. 70–72. For the traditional schedule at Sera monastery, and the modern one in exile in India, see Dreyfus (2003), pp. 246, 250.

13.4 Monastic Exam-Debate at Tashilhumpo Monastery, Shigatse

for monks to rehearse what they have learned, to hone their analytical and deductive skills and progress to a deeper than mere surface understanding. Monks who are good only at rote memorization and can cite texts at length in their questions or responses are respected but not admired as much as those who can truly illuminate the gist of the material.[58]

Second, much less frequently, there were formal debates, i.e. examinations. In these a single student sits as the candidate-to-be-examined, with the whole class arrayed in rows in front of him. Anyone in the audience can get up and question the candidate or intervene and refine the points being made by another questioner. These sessions too can be quite lively and heated, especially when they take place between different monastic colleges (see figure 13.4).[59]

Throughout his career, a scholar-monk may undergo several such testings, more or less as rites of passage, but the only one that results in a degree is the final géshé exam. There were actually several types of géshé: those who pass exams in front of their whole monastic college; those who pass exams in

58 Gyatso (1998), pp. 86–87.
59 Dreyfus (2003), pp. 250–251.

front of their whole monastery (e.g. Drepung); and those who pass exams in front of an assembly of all three monasteries (Drepung, Sera, and Ganden). Successful candidates in the latter exams, which were usually held in the Jokhang in Lhasa during the Great Prayer Festival, became known as "divine scholars" (hlaram [lha.rams]).[60]

Very few scholar-monks, however, ever reached the point of becoming a géshé (of whatever type). This was not so much a matter of failure as a matter of deciding not to persist through two decades of arduous academics, or of embarking on other paths. At Drepung, for instance, many monks would opt to go back to their home territories after a few years of study, either out of concern for their families, or lack of funds to pursue their studies, or to take up local monastic posts. Alternatively, they might opt to stay at Drepung, and become ordinary monks, not in the scholarly track.[61]

It should be remembered that, in traditional Tibet, the book-monks (pechawa) whom we have been talking about constituted only a small portion of the entire monastic community. At a place like Drepung, it has been estimated that they made up no more than ten percent of the monastic population. The others were mostly "common monks" (tramang [grwa dmangs]) who "had some monastic work obligations" but "had to spend a considerable amount of time in income-producing activities. Some ... practiced trades like tailoring and medicine, some worked as servants for other monks, some engaged in trade, and still others left the monastery at peak agricultural times to work for farmers." This was because "Drepung did not provide its monks with either meals via a community kitchen or payments in kind and money sufficient to satisfy their needs" (Goldstein, 1998, p. 21), although they often received offerings of tea and other foodstuffs at ritual assemblies.

13.3.2 Mad Monks: the Case of Tangtong Gyalpo

Quite different from "the mainstream exegetical traditions" that we have been considering, and "that held canonical Indian Buddhism as the primary referent," was what has been called "the visionary movement ... [that] drew on meditative and revelatory realizations to produce new materials ... and new doctrines" (Gyatso, 1981, p. iii). Among the representatives of this

60 Ibid., p. 255. See also Mills (2003), pp. 237–240.
61 Lobsang Gyatso (1998) is quite frank about his inclinations to go home, especially in the first years of his time at Drepung.

visionary movement are those individuals who have become known as "saintly madmen" (lama nyönpa [blama smyon pa]) because of their antinomian behavior and their apparent disdain for conventions and regular monasticism.

The most famous and well-loved of the Tibetan "saintly madmen" is probably Milarépa (1040–1123) who eventually, after undergoing many trials, received the teachings from Marpa (1012–1097). His popularity was assured 350 years after his death when his lifestory – emphasizing his early suffering in life, his magical powers, his persistence under Marpa's tutelage, and his subsequent antinomian behavior – and his teachings in the form of semi-ecstatic "songs" were written down by Tsangnyön Heruka (Gtsang smyon heruka) (the "Mad Man of Tsang") (1452–1507), himself another famous eccentric and antinomian figure.[62] Other famous "mad lamas" include Ü-nyön (dbus smyon) (1458–1532),"the saintly madman of [the province of] Ü," and Drug-nyön ('brug smyom) (1455–1529), "the saintly madman of Bhutan,"[63] but the one I want to focus on here is Tangtong Gyalpo (Thang stong rgyal po) (1361?–1485), variously known as the "Madman of the Empty Valley" (Lungtong Nyönpa), the "father of Tibetan drama," and the "iron-bridge man."[64]

Antinomian behavior has a long history within the Tantric tradition, as a reflection of a yogin's realization of the non-duality of saṃsāra and nirvāṇa, as well as the emptiness of all phenomena, including such categories as good and evil, pure and impure, meritorious and demeritorious. The Tibetan mad saints are thus heirs to a tradition that goes back to India and was expressed especially in the lifestories of the Tantric "great accomplished ones" (mahāsiddhas).[65] Many Tibetan mad yogins are associated with the Kagyü school; Tangtong Gyalpo is usually affiliated with the Nyingma school, but his popularity was really non-sectarian. Early in life, he is said to have been an ordinary monk, but one day he had a vision of Padmasambhava engaging in Tantric sexual union with the goddess Vajravārāhī and pointing out to him yogins engaged in eating human flesh and yoginīs drinking chang (barley beer) from skull-cups. He took this as a sign that he too should engage in

62 For traditional stories about all of these figures, see Gyaltsen (1990). For a biography of Naropa, see Guenther (1963); for Marpa, see Trungpa and the Nalanda Translation Committee (1982); for Tsangnyön's biography of Milarépa, see Quintman (2010). For a translation of Milarépa's songs, see Chang (1962).

63 On Ünyön, see Erhardt (2010). On Drug-nyön, see Dowman and Paljor (1980).

64 On Tangtong Gyalpo, see J. Gyatso (1980) and Stearns (2007).

65 See Dowman (1985).

such activities. He went into a meditative retreat for three years, at the end of which Padmasambhava appeared to him again and instructed him to give up the life and robe of a monk and become a wandering Tantric adept, dressed in a single cloak.

There followed a whole series of unconventional behaviors: he once taught the Dharma to a donkey; he once danced in a crowded street, "holding a lump of brown sugar in his right hand and a piece of shit in his left, taking a bite from one and then the other" (Stearns, 2007, p. 73); he once circumambulated a stūpa in the nude for three days straight, announcing that he was planning to build such a stūpa himself; he once interrupted the teachings of another guru by riding his horse into the assembly hall, and then distributing tea to all the monks from a single cup. He was also famous for his longevity (achieved through meditative powers) and is said to have lived for 125 years. Images of him in Tibet show him as having very long white hair and beard.[66]

Tangtong Gyalpo, however, is famous for more than just being an eccentric holy man, and the founder of a line of inspired teachings. He was also a man in touch with the common people. He sought to communicate his teachings not just through philosophical treatises but through the public performance of plays – the genre of Tibetan drama – which he is credited with founding. Moreover, throughout Tibet and Bhutan, he is best known as the designer and builder of dozens of iron-chain suspension bridges, some of which are still in use today. These enabled local people and long-distance pilgrims to cross otherwise impassable rivers. He was also an architect who designed and supervised the construction of temples and stūpas, one of which, the Riwoche (Ri bo che), is still extant and widely considered to be a masterpiece of fifteenth-century Central Tibetan architecture.[67]

13.4 SAMDING: FEMALE INCARNATIONS AND A CONTEMPORARY BUDDHIST

About one hundred kilometers southwest of Lhasa, one comes to one of the great sacred lakes of Tibet, Yamdrok-tsho. Over 600 square kilometers in

66 Stearns (2007), pp. 66–68.

67 On his being "father of Tibetan opera," see Gyatso (1986). On his role as bridge-builder, see Stearns (2007), pp. 33–58. For a listing and description of the bridges attributed to him, see Gerner (2007). On Riwoche, see Vitali (1990), pp. 123–136.

surface area, it lies at an altitude of about 4,400 meters, and is surrounded by high peaks. On a map, its various bends and bays make it vaguely resemble the shape of a scorpion. In the middle of a peninsula, jutting out in between what would be the two "claws" of the scorpion, there is a smaller separate lake, known as the lake of the demoness. Overlooking that lake stands the monastery of Samding (Bsam sding). When I visited it in 2005, the last twelve kilometers of dirt track from the nearest town of Nakartse had not yet been paved.

All this makes it sound like a rather isolated spot in the middle of nowhere, and yet it is not. Mythologically, Samding is a "power-place" of central importance, it being said that, if ever the monastery were to be destroyed, the demoness lake would overflow and inundate the whole of Tibet which would be destroyed. More realistically, Samding stands just off one of the main routes from Lhasa to Gyantse (a large and historically important city), and, since the fifteenth century, it has been the seat of a line of female incarnate lamas, all successive manifestations of the Tantric goddess Dorje Phagmo (Rdo rje phag mo; Skt., Vajravārāhī – "Thunderbolt Sow"), herself a form of Vajrayoginī, whom one scholar has called "the original and prototypical female Buddha of the Tantric Pantheon" (M. Shaw, 2006, p. 359). There are exceedingly few female lines of incarnation in Tibet, and of these, the Samding Dorje Phagmo is by far the most famous and prominent. The lineage itself started with Chokyi Dronma (Chos kyi sgron ma) (1422–1456), a female disciple of a famous prolific teacher belonging to the Bodongpa (Bo dong pa) sect, and herself, for a while, the Tantric consort of Tangtong Gyalpo, whom we have just considered.[68]

The present Dorje Phagmo is the twelfth incarnation in the lineage. Her story is worth recounting as it well illustrates some of the dilemmas faced by prominent Tibetan monastics in modern times, under Chinese rule. Unlike the Dalai Lama (and many other high incarnate lamas), Dorje Phagmo chose to remain in Tibet after the communist takeover in 1950, and again after the Dalai Lama's exile in 1959, and to ride the rollercoaster of Chinese state–saṃgha relations that has gone on since then. Today, she remains both the lama of Samding and a Communist party official residing in Lhasa.

Shortly after the birth of the Twelfth Dorje Phagmo in 1938, various

68 On the legend of the lake overflowing, see Diemberger (2007), p. 269. The story is also reported by Das (2001), p. 149. Stearns (2007), p. 6, notes the relationship of Chokyi Dronma and Tangtong Gyalpo. For a study of Chokyi Dronma, see Diemberger (2007), pp. 25–238. For a study of one aspect of Chogle Namgyal's work, see Smith (2001), pp. 179–208.

auspicious signs, mostly remembered retrospectively, hinted that she was an extraordinary child. Had she been a boy, her parents would probably have read these signs as hinting that she might have been an incarnate lama, but she was a girl so, in their minds, that was not a possibility. At that time, the family was living west of Lhasa and did not even know that the previous (Eleventh) Dorje Phagmo had passed away and that a search was on for her reincarnation. They first found out when one of the monastery's search parties arrived in their community. The young (Twelfth) Dorje Phagmo was then three years old; the group from Samding happened to meet her, and were astonished when she called out by name and greeted as an old friend a young woman in their party who had been the late Eleventh Dorje Phagmo's assistant. No one in the family had any idea who this person was, but apparently their three-year-old daughter knew her! Eventually, after more tests, she was affirmed as the new Dorje Phagmo in Lhasa by both the then regent of Tibet and the young Fourteenth (present) Dalai Lama, who would have been about eight years old at the time.[69] The family promptly moved to Samding, where the young Dorje Phagmo was given over to the care of tutors who trained her thoroughly in the practices and doctrines of her tradition.

Soon, however, all of their lives were to change radically; in 1950, the People's Liberation Army arrived. At first, the Chinese followed a policy of respecting and trying to win over local elites, including monastics. As a high-ranking lama, Dorje Phagmo, then a girl in her teens but also a prominent figure, was pandered to by the Chinese. In 1955 and again in 1957, she was invited to go to Beijing (as had the Dalai Lama before her), where she met Chairman Mao Zedong and Premier Zhou Enlai, and was named one of the vice-presidents of the Chinese Buddhist Association and appointed to the Chinese People's Political Consultative Conference. Then, however, she returned to Samding and pursued her religious training, culminating in 1958, when she went to Lhasa where she met the Dalai Lama and received various meditative initiations from his tutors. The next year, in March, the Dalai Lama fled into exile, and soon afterwards, Dorje Phagmo and her older sister followed after him, escaping first to Bhutan and then to India. At the time, she would have been twenty-one.

Her parents, however, remained behind in Tibet, and shortly they sent a

69 See Diemberger (2007), pp. 299–301. Her selection was not uncontroversial at the time (there being several other candidates), and it was subsequently contested by various Tibetans in exile, once she began cooperating with the Chinese government.

message to the two girls, telling them that things had settled down, and that they should return. Chinese agents in India similarly encouraged them to do so, and, once they decided to go back home, arranged for their travel by plane on a circuitous route that took them first to Afghanistan, and then to Moscow, before returning to Beijing, where they arrived just in time for the tenth anniversary celebration of the People's Republic (October 1, 1959). Dorje Phagmo was welcomed back by Chairman Mao himself as a "female living Buddha," and honored by many high officials as a returning patriot who had made the right decision.[70]

It was not long, however, before she probably wondered if she had. In 1964, the Panchen Lama, who had been similarly pandered to by the Chinese, was condemned by Mao as a reactionary. In 1965, Dorje Phagmo's father (who, like some other elite Tibetans, had tried to work with the Chinese) was jailed. Then, at the outset of the Cultural Revolution, in 1966, Samding monastery was completely ransacked by Red guards and left in ruins. The monks scattered, and Dorje Phagmo herself was arrested. But the Cultural Revolution eventually ran its course, the political pendulum swung back, and Dorje Phagmo was rehabilitated, and reappointed to a position of influence as vice-chair of Tibet's Political Consultative Conference. As such, she began to work for the restoration of Samding. With the help of the head monk, Thubten Namgyal, Samding's monastics were reassembled, the buildings were reconstructed, and old rituals and festivals were revived. Today, at Samding, rites are performed, teachings are taught, community life continues, and a new syncretism seems to have emerged. Like many Buddhist temples in Tibet, it exists at a crossroads between tolerance and control, between sponsorship and oppression, between religion and tourism. As Diemberger has put it:

> When the grand seasonal celebrations take place [at Samding today], local people gather at the monastery to receive a blessing, monks and nuns from branch monasteries come to pay their respects and join in the religious activities, officials come from the county seat and from Lhasa, and even a few tourists might turn up. Everyone makes a different sense of the Buddhist and communist rituality blending in a continuum that seems much less paradoxical than it sounds when described. Is the event genuine or staged? Is it a strategic use of religion for political purposes or a strategic use of politics for religious

70 Ibid., pp. 301–308.

> purposes? The answer lies with each of the participants, mirrored in their personal view of the occasion and in the different "interpretative communities" that they create.
>
> (Diemberger, 2007, pp. 313–14)

13.5 A TIBETAN DHARMA CENTER IN VERMONT, U.S.A.

At about the same time that Dorje Phagmo was returning to Tibet (1959), many other incarnate lamas and high-ranking teachers were fleeing into exile, following in the footsteps of the Dalai Lama. One of these was Chögyam Trungpa, who has been called "one of the most influential Tibetan teachers of the twentieth century in introducing Tibetan Buddhism to the West" (Buswell and Lopez, 2014, p. 927).

Born in Kham in Eastern Tibet in 1939, he was, early in life, recognized as the eleventh incarnation in the Drungpa line of tülkus affiliated with the Kagyü school. Ordained as a novice and then as a monk, he was trained by both Kagyü and Nyingma teachers. After escaping to India in 1959, he moved to Great Britain where he attended Oxford University in 1963, and, four years later, started a meditation center he named Samyé Ling in an old hunting lodge at Eskdalemuir in the lowlands of Scotland. At about the same time, he abandoned his monastic vows of celibacy, got married, and embarked on a career as a lay teacher. Shortly thereafter (1969), he moved to the United States and established a monastic center in an old dairy farm of several hundred acres in Barnet, Vermont, that had been gifted to him by his American disciples. He called the place Tail of the Tiger, a name he got out of the *Yijing*. A few years later (1974), after he moved to Colorado (where he founded the Naropa Institute, now Naropa University), Tail of the Tiger was renamed Karmê Chöling ("Dharma Place of the Karma (Kagyü Lineage)"), a name given to it by His Holiness, the Sixteenth Karmapa Lama, one of the titular heads of the Kagyü school.[71]

---

71 Chögyam Trungpa's early life is recounted in his autobiography (Trungpa, 1971). See also Midal (2004), pp. 29–60. I shall not go into here the second part of his career in Colorado and Nova Scotia. For a fascinating account of the whole of his life by his British wife, see Mukpo (2006). Mukpo does not seek to hide Trungpa's more antinomian (?) behaviors (extramarital sex, alcohol, drugs, impulsiveness, and, late in life, aspirations to grandeur), which she associates with teachers in the "mad monk" tradition. Nor does she gloss over the tragic scandal that broke after Trungpa's death concerning the comportment of his chosen successor, Ösel Tendzin (Thomas Rich) who eventually died of AIDS in 1991. For another account, see Fields (1992), pp. 365–367.

Today, after more than forty years, Karmê Chöling is a thriving community, with over thirty-five persons in residence who work and practice and live together there. It also has an extensive calendar of programs.[72] The place has evolved and expanded since its foundation; the original farmhouse has been added on to so as to allow for dormitory-style rooms for residents and program participants and a large shrine room for meditation and rituals. An old barn has been refurbished into another worship/assembly hall. An extensive organic flower and vegetable garden has been developed. There are plans (and a site chosen) for the construction of a stūpa. But physically, Karmê Chöling still remains unpretentious, eschewing the opulence that some other Western Buddhist centers have taken on.

A walk in the woods behind the main building leads up to the purkhang (pur khang) or "crematorium stūpa" where, in May 1987, Chögyam Trungpa was cremated. Often purkhang are destroyed after use, but this one has been kept as a memorial of sorts. It stands in the midst of an open meadow, where at the time of the cremation many hundreds of devotees gathered, along with high-ranking lamas from the Kagyü and Nyingma traditions. On this occasion, the poet Allen Ginsberg, who had also become a disciple of Trungpa, wrote a poem in which he listed all the things that he "noticed" at the ceremony – a testimony not only to the departed teacher but also to the practice of mindfulness.[73]

The path up to the purkhang leads through the woods. To one side are a couple of clusters of sturdy tents, set up to house volunteers who come to work and reside at Karmê Chöling for parts of the summer. To the other are several "retreat areas" to which access is restricted. There, spread out through the woods, eight secluded cabins have been built for meditators interested in and ready for solitary meditation retreats of a minimum of seven days on up to several weeks or months. Such solitary retreats are a Kagyü tradition going back to before the time of Milarépa.[74]

Karmê Chöling bills itself as a Shambhala Meditation Retreat Center. As such it is one of over 150 meditation centers world-wide now led by Sakyong Mipham Rinpoché, Chögyam Trungpa's son and Dharma successor. In

---

72 See http://www.karmecholing.org/programs.php.

73 For an account of Trungpa's funeral, see Mukpo (2006), pp. 380–394. For Allen Ginsberg's poem, see: http://www.tricycle.com/special-section/cremation-chogyam-trungpa-vidyadhara. On his somewhat turbulent relationship with Trungpa, see Triglio (2014).

74 On the solitary retreat cabins, see http://www.karmecholing.org/cabin_retreats.php.

Tibetan tradition, Shambhala (Skt., Śambhala; Tib., Dejung [Bde 'byung]) is a mythic, hard-to-get-to, utopic land said to be located in the north beyond the Himalayas. It is much featured in the *Kālacakratantra* and associated texts. According to these, sometime in the future, when Buddhism has been wiped out of our world, there will occur a great apocalyptic battle: the king of Shambhala will lead his armies out of his realm, and thoroughly defeat all the forces of evil. He will then establish a new golden age, in which life expectancy will be long, work will be effortless, and all people will be devoted to the Dharma.[75]

Like many myths, this one can be taken literally, but can also be viewed metaphorically. Thus, some see the victory of Shambhala warriors as an outward expression for an inner journey of awakening, resulting in a victory of mind over ego (Bernbaum, 1980, p. 252). "Shambhala training," which was formulated by Chögyam Trungpa and is taught at Karmê Chöling, is a "series of contemplative workshops ... [involving] the study and practice of Shambhala warriorship ... [a] path [which] shows how to take the challenges of daily life in our modern society as opportunities for both contemplative practice and social action."[76] The full training program involves many stages to be gradually accomplished by serious practitioners. Levels I to V, which can be done in five weekend workshops, "provide a strong foundation in mindfulness-awareness meditation practice, emphasizing the development of genuineness, confidence, humor, and dignity within the complexity of daily life."[77] This is then followed by a series of eight other trainings called the Sacred Path and culminating in the "Warrior Assembly."[78]

In addition, Karmê Chöling also offers month-long group meditation retreats, called "dathün," involving "sitting and walking meditation, Buddhist chants, talks, and a short work session."[79] As in some forms of mindfulness practice (see 5.4.2), awareness of things and thoughts and feelings is developed. Also, at Karmê Chöling, certain Zen practices have been incorporated into dathün. For instance, in an innovation that was started by Chögyam Trungpa himself, participants usually eat their meals in the ōryōki style, a meditative ritualized way of eating stemming from Japanese Zen monasteries. In ōryōki great attention is paid to detail and to the way of manipulating

75 For a brief synopsis of information on Shambhala, see Buswell and Lopez (2014), pp. 748–749. For accounts of the mythic kingdom, see Bernbaum (1980).
76 http://www.shambhala.org/shambhala-training.php.
77 Ibid.
78 See Trungpa (1984) for more on his views of Shambhala training.
79 http://www.karmecholing.org/dathun.php.

the set of nested bowls that are used for different foodstuffs in the meal. Meditators accept only what they can eat and are expected to finish all that they have taken. At the end of the meal, the eater cleans his or her own bowls, again in a prescribed ritualized manner.

In addition to dathün, Karmê Chöling offers an array of other programs throughout the year, including kyūdō (the way of the bow) – a Japanese form of archery – and qigong – a Chinese Daoist inspired form of meditative movement. Of special note is a six-month-long (from April to October) apprenticeship program in organic gardening(-cum-meditation) under the guidance of a Dutch master gardener. All of these programs, of course, cost money, and registrants are expected to submit fees to cover room and board and instruction.

13.6 CONCLUSION

We have, in this chapter, looked at a series of Tibetan "saṃgha situations," from the Lhasa Jokhang to Karmê Chöling. It is likely that forty years ago none of these places would have been mentioned in a book of this sort. The Tibetan diaspora, which brought Chögyam Trungpa (and so many other teachers) to India, Europe, and then America, has served to put Tibetan Buddhism on the map not only of Western practitioners, but of Western scholars as well.

I sometimes say, flippantly, that "when I was in college there were five books in English on Tibetan Buddhism, and four of them were 'written' by W. Y. Evans-Wentz." While not quite accurate, this nonetheless reflects the tremendous change that has occurred in the interim; not only have the works (both translations and secondary studies) on Tibetan Buddhism become innumerable, but the practice of the Dharma has been spread throughout the world. The same, as we have seen in chapters 11 and 12, may be said for the Theravāda and Mahāyāna traditions. Truly Buddhism/s, which began in Northern India with the preaching of the Middle Way and then expanded to the rest of Asia, have become, in this century, world religion/s.

Appendices

APPENDIX A. A SHORT CHRONOLOGY OF BUDDHISM IN INDIA

DATE	FIGURES/EVENTS	FURTHER READING OR CROSS-REFERENCES
6th–4th century BCE	Possible period within which the Buddha lived	Bechert (2004) + see chapter 1
4th–3rd century BCE	Possible period within which the Council of Vaiśālī took place	See 7.1.2
3rd century BCE	Reign of King Aśoka who becomes patron of Buddhism	Thapar (1961) + see 6.1.5
2nd–1st century BCE	Great Stūpa at Sāñcī built	Dehejia (1996)
1st–2nd century CE	Nāgārjuna establishes the Madhyamaka School	Walser (2005) + see 9.2
2nd century CE	Late Sātavāhana and Andhra Ikṣvāku kingdoms in the South; coexistence of Buddhism and Hinduism; Buddhist stūpas established at Amarāvatī and Nāgārjunakoṇḍā	Knox (1992)
4th century	Asanga and Vasubandhu found the Yogācāra tradition	Anacker (1984), pp. 7–28 + see 9.5.1
4th– 6th century	Gupta Empire during which Buddhism and art flourish	Smith (1983), pp. 129–153; Williams (1982)
399–414	Chinese monk Faxian in India	Legge (1886)
*c.*500	Nālanda Buddhist University is founded and flourishes until the 12th century	Dutt (1962), pp. 328–348
629–645	Chinese monk Xuanzang in India	Li (1995)
671–695	Chinese monk Yijing in India	Takakusu (1896)
8th–12th century	The Pāla period. Patrons of Mahāyāna; spread of Vajrayāna. Odantapurī and Vikramaśīla monastic universities established	Davidson (2002); Dutt (1962), pp. 349–353
13th century	Demise of Buddhism in North India. Destruction of Nālanda University and Bodhgaya	Roerich (1959)
1891	Founding of the Mahābodhi Society; gradual "rebuddhification of Bodhgaya"	See 1.2.1 + Doyle (1997)
1891–1956	Life of B.R. Ambedkar who helps reestablish Buddhism in India	Zelliot (1996) + see 1.2.1
1959	Arrival of the Dalai Lama from Tibet who takes up exile in India	Hicks and Chogyam (1990), pp. 120–175

APPENDIX B.
A SHORT CHRONOLOGY OF BUDDHISM IN SRI LANKA

DATE	FIGURES/EVENTS	FURTHER READING
5th century BCE	Mythic visits of the Buddha to the island	Oldenberg (1982), pp. 117–129
3rd century BCE	Forest monks settle in cave monasteries	Coningham (1995)
	Aśoka's son Mahinda reputedly converts King Devānampiya Tissa	Geiger (1912), pp. 88–96
3rd century BCE–10th century CE	Capital at Anurādhapura. Differing fortunes there of Mahāvihāra, Abhayagiri, and Jetavana sects	Rahula (1956)
	Reign of King Duṭṭhagāmaṇī (161–37 BCE); builds great stūpa over the Buddha's relics	Berkwitz (2007), pp. 159–252; Greenwald (1978)
	King Vaṭṭagāmiṇī sponsors writing down of the Pali Canon (1st century BCE)	
	Visit of Chinese pilgrim Faxian (5th century CE); sees the tooth relic and Bodhi tree in Anurādhapura; describes saṃgha as rich and prosperous	Legge (1886), pp. 101–107
	Buddhaghosa (5th century) compiles commentaries on Pali Canon; systematizes Theravāda teachings	Law (1923)
11th–13th century	Capital at Polonnaruwa	
	King Vijayabāhu asks Burmese for help in restoring ordination lineage on the island (1070 CE)	Gunawardana (1979); Panditha (1954/1955)
	King Parākramabāhu I (1153–86) ushers in exclusive turn to Theravāda	
14th–15th century	Hinduization of Buddhist culture; evolving pantheon of Buddhist, Hindu, and local deities	Holt (2004a)
	Monk-poet Vīdāgama Maitreya leads forest monk protest against Hinduization of Buddhist culture (*c.*1435)	Reynolds (1970), pp. 269–277; Rajakaruna (1972)
1590s–1815	Capital at Kandy; successive encroachment of Portuguese, Dutch, and British colonial powers	Strathern (2007); Harris (2006)
	Reign of King Kīrti Śrī (1751–1815) who has a complex relationship to many faiths	Holt (1996)
	Monk Saranaṃkara founds the Siyam sect, introduced from Thailand (18th century)	Blackburn (2001)
	Monk Hikaduve Sumangala (1827–1911) helps define Buddhism over, under, and in the colonial experience	Blackburn (2010)
20th century	Nationalism, revival, and politicization of Buddhism	Bond (1988); Gombrich and Obeyesekere (1988); Tambiah (1992)

APPENDIX C.
A SHORT CHRONOLOGY OF BUDDHISM IN MYANMAR (BURMA)

DATES	FIGURES/EVENTS	FURTHER READING
5th century BCE	Mythic visits of the Buddha to the region; arrival of relics	Tatelman (2000), pp. 180–186; Shorto (1970)
3rd century BCE	Legendary arrival of Aśokan missionaries	Aung-Thwin (2005)
4th–9th century CE	Buddhist Pyu kingdoms centered in Śrī Kṣetra. Southeast Indian (Andhra) influences on the court and on Pali-based Theravāda Buddhism	Stargardt (1990)
11th–13th century	First Burmese kingdom centered in Bagan (Pagan). Mahāyāna and Vajrayāna influences from Bengal; prominence of the Ari sect. Growth of Theravāda, which, later legends claim, was established as the official religion during this period. Reigns of Aniruddha (1044–78) and Kyanzittha (1084–78). Mongol invasion (1287) is sometimes credited with fall of Pagan	Luce (1969–1970); Than Tun (1959); Aung-Thwin (1998)
1312	New capital in Upper Burma is established in Ava	
1472–1492	Reign and reforms of Dhammazedi, a former monk. Proclaims new orientation to Theravāda Sri Lankan Mahāvihāra lineage	Taw Sein Ko (1892)
17th century	Dynamic growth of Theravāda; many translations of Pali texts into Burmese; flourishing of Abhidharma study	
18th century	Great robes controversy between two monastic factions	Mendelson (1975), pp. 31–75
18th–19th century	Reigns of King Bodawpaya (1781–1819) and Thibaw (1876–1885), in Mandalay, ending with the British conquest of all of Burma	Mendelson (1975), pp. 66–118; Sarkisyanz (1965)
19th century–1947	British colonial influence	Mendelson (1975), pp. 173–235
1948–1962	Buddhism in newly independent Burma. Sixth Theravāda Buddhist Council held under the auspices of Prime Minister U Nu	Mendelson (1975), pp. 236–355
1962–present	Buddhism and military rule	Schober (2011)

APPENDIX D.
A SHORT CHRONOLOGY OF BUDDHISM IN CAMBODIA

DATES	FIGURES/EVENTS	FURTHER READING
1st–6th century CE	Chinese reports on kingdom of "Funan" in Cambodia and South Vietnam; Sanskrit inscriptions, Hindu court culture	Harris (2005), pp. 3–8; Vickery (2003)
7th–8th century	Kingdom of Zhenla: presence of Hinduism and gradual increase of Mahāyāna	Harris (2005), pp. 8–11; Vickery (1998)
9th century–1431	Angkor Period: early kings. Śaivite court culture; gradual spread of Mahāyāna and Tantra; reign of Suryavarman II (1113–1150); expansion of Khmer empire; construction of Angkor Wat, dedicated to Viṣṇu; reign of Jayavarman VII (1181–1219): Mahāyāna Buddhism ascendant; construction of Bayon temple; Chinese diplomat Zhou Daguan visits Angkor (1296–97); gradual rise and eventual ascendancy of Theravāda Buddhism (13th–14th century)	Harris (2005), pp. 11–25; Harris (2007); Woodward (2001)
15th–16th century	Thai incursions into Cambodia; continued prevalence of Theravāda	Harris (2005), pp. 30–34
16th–19th century	Theravāda dominance with some interludes	Harris (2005), pp. 35–48
19th–20th century	Buddhism, colonialism, and modernity	Hansen (2007); Harris (2005), pp. 105–130
20th–21st century	Buddhism and Cambodian nationalism; persecution by the Khmer Rouge, and recovery afterwards	Harris (2005), pp. 131–224; Marston and Guthrie (2004), pp. 133–226; Kent and Chandler (2008)

APPENDIX E.
A SHORT CHRONOLOGY OF BUDDHISM IN THAILAND

DATE	FIGURES/EVENTS	FURTHER READING
5th century BCE	Mythic visits of the Buddha to the region	Swearer, Sommai, and Phaitoon (2004)
3rd century BCE	Legendary arrival of Aśokan missionaries	
6th–10th century CE	Mon Kingdom of Dvaravati occupies most of what is present-day Thailand; form of Pali Buddhism, mixed with Hinduism and Mahāyāna	Brown (1996)
*c.*8th century – 1292	Buddhist Mon kingdom of Haripuñjaya established in the north	Swearer (1998)
10th–14th century	Thai kingdom of Lan Na in the far north adopts Theravāda; in 1292, Mangrai captures Haripuñjaya and founds city of Chiang Mai; propagates Theravāda	Wyatt and Wichienkeeo (1998)
11th–13th century	Khmers occupy much of Dvaravati; mixture of Hinduism, Mahāyāna, and Theravāda	
13th–14th century	Capital at Sukhothai. Tai kingdom established after freeing itself from Mon and Khmer dominance. Theravāda preponderant	Griswold (1967)
1279–1298	Reign of Sukhothai King Ramkhamhaeng. In a possibly spurious inscription, the king presents himself as a benevolent ruler over a pious and prosperous Buddhist land	
1351–1767	Capital at Ayudhya; repeated Burmese invasions of Tai and Lan Na territory; first encounters with Western colonial powers (e.g. France); capital sacked by Burmese in 1767	Wyatt (1984), pp. 61–138
1767–present	Capital at Bangkok; Buddhist reforms under reign of King Mongkut (r. 1851–1868), and social changes under King Chulalongkorn (r. 1868–1910)	Ishii (1986)

APPENDIX F. A SHORT CHRONOLOGY OF BUDDHISM IN CHINA

DATES	FIGURES/EVENTS	FURTHER READING
1st century CE	First evidence of Buddhism in China; supposed arrival of missionary monks during the reign of the emperor Ming (58–75 CE)	Ch'en (1964), pp. 21–55; Zürcher (1959), pp. 18–42; Tsukamoto (1985), pp. 39–112
2nd century	An Shigao arrives from Central Asia and translates many Mainstream Buddhist texts into Chinese	
2nd century	Lokakṣema arrives from Central Asia and translates many Mahāyāna Buddhist texts into Chinese	
*c.*3rd century	Mouzi writes apologetic in defense of Buddhism	Keenan (1994)
334–416	Huiyuan establishes center at Mount Lu; starts a group devoted to the Buddha Amitābha and his western pure land; writes tract on why monks should not bow down to the emperor	Tsukamoto (1985), pp. 757–898
355–434	Daosheng propagates *Nirvāṇa Sūtra* and argues for belief in potential buddhahood of all beings	Kim (1990), pp. 13–21; Ch'en (1964), pp. 112–120
399–414	Faxian travels to India; returns to translate texts	Legge (1886)
433	Sri Lankan nuns arrive and re-establish nuns' ordination lineage in China	Heirman (2001)
Early 6th century	Bodhidharma, legendary establisher of Chan Buddhism, arrives in China from India	Broughton (1999)
538–597	Zhiyi establishes the Tiantai school	Hurvitz (1962); Donner and Stevenson (1993)
596–667	Life of Daoxuan, who establishes the Vinaya school in China	Kieschnick in Buswell (2004), p. 202
601–604	Emperor of Sui dynasty distributes Buddha relics as part of campaign to use Buddhism to help reunite empire	Chen (2002)
629–645	Xuanzang travels to India; returns to translate texts and help establish Mind-Only school of Buddhism	Li (1995)
638–713	Life of Huineng, supposed sixth patriarch of Chan Buddhism, whose sudden enlightenment teachings are later propagated by Shenhui (684–758)	McRae (2000)
643–712	Fazang helps establish Huayan school during reign of empress Wu	Chen (2007)
8th century	Vajrabodhi and Amoghavajra help establish the Mijiao (Esoteric) school of Buddhism	Chou (1945); Orzech (1998)

DATES	FIGURES/EVENTS	FURTHER READING
845	Great persecution of Buddhism by the emperor Wuzong	Ch'en (1964), pp. 226–233
9th–13th century	Song dynasty: efflorescence and definition of Buddhism, especially Chan and Tiantai schools and Pure Land tradition	Gregory and Getz (1999); Halperin (2006); Schlütter (2008)
13th–14th century	Tibetan Buddhism made state religion during the Mongol Yuan dynasty	Jerryson (2007)
16th–17th century	Zhuhong and other monastic leaders synthesize Chan and Pure Land traditions; debates within Chan	Yü (1981); Wu (2011)
1644–1911	Tibetan-style Buddhism under the Manchus; 19th-century intellectual exploration of Buddhism for moral and political reform	Berger (2003); Chan (1985); Elverskog (2006)
1900–1950	Reforms of Buddhism led by Taixu and others	Welch (1967; 1968); Pittman (2001)
1950–present	Rollercoaster relationship of Buddhism and Communism	Welch (1972); Fisher (2012); Birnbaum (2003)

APPENDIX G.
A SHORT CHRONOLOGY OF BUDDHISM IN JAPAN

DATES	FIGURES/EVENTS	FURTHER READING
6th century CE	Buddhism officially introduced to Japan from Korea	Deal (1995)
7th century	Initial flowering of Buddhism; Prince Shōtoku, according to legend, becomes major patron and sponsor of Buddhism	McCallum (2009); Como (2008); Deal (1999); see also 12.1.1
8th century	Nāra period; six official schools of Buddhism established in the capital; charismatic preachers such as Gyōki proselytize the countryside	Matsunaga and Matsunaga (1976), vol. 1, pp. 26–138; Augustine (2005)
794–1333	Heian and Kamakura periods; establishment of Tendai and Shingon schools; development of Pure Land, Zen, and Nichiren traditions	Matsunaga and Matsunaga (1976), vol. 1, pp. 139–258, and vol. 2, pp. 1–310; Stone (1999); Goodwin (1994); Payne (1998)
	Saichō (767–822) establishes the Tendai school on Mount Hiei	Groner (2000)
	Kūkai (774–835) establishes the Shingon school on Mount Koya	Abé (1999); Hakeda (1972)
	Kūya (903–972), "the holy man of the marketplace," popularizes chanting the name of Amida Buddha	Chilson (2007); Matsunaga and Matsunaga (1976), vol. 1, pp. 217–218
	Life of Ryōgen (912–985); growth and transformation of the Tendai tradition	Groner (2002)
	Hōnen (1133–1212) establishes the Jōdo (Pure Land) school	Machida (1999)
	Eisai (1141–1215) establishes the Rinzai Zen school	Dumoulin (1988–1990), vol. 2, pp. 14–50; Matsunaga and Matsunaga (1976), vol. 2, pp. 183–192
	Life of Jōkei (1155–1213), Hossō sect critic of Pure Land movement in the Kamakura period	Ford (2006)
	Life of Myōe (1173–1232), Shingon-Kegon monk involved in revivifying traditional Buddhism in Kamakura period	Tanabe (1992); Morrell (1987)
	Shinran (1173–1263) establishes the True Pure Land school (Jōdo shinshū)	Dobbins (1989), pp. 21–47

DATES	FIGURES/EVENTS	FURTHER READING
794–1333	Dōgen (1200–1253) establishes the Sōtō Zen school	Heine (2006); Kodera (1980); Bodiford (1993), pp. 21–37; Kim (1980); Faure (1987)
	Nichiren (1222–1282) establishes the Nichiren school	Anesaki (1916); Rodd (1980), 3–46; Stone (1999), 242–299
	Gyōnen (1230–1331) furthers the Pure Land tradition in Kamakura period	Blum (2002)
	Ippen (1239–1289) establishes the Jishū school of Pure Land Buddhism	Hirota (1997)
1337–1573	Muromachi period	Tsang (2007); McMullin (1984)
	Life of Ikkyū (1394–1481), iconoclastic Zen monk	Sanford (1981)
	Life of Rennyo (1415–1499), "second founder" of Jōdo shinshū; ascendancy of the Honganji branch of Pure Land	Rogers and Rogers (1991); Blum and Yasutomi (2006)
1600–1867	Tokugawa period. Buddhism promoted and used as state religion	Williams (2005); Hur (2000; 2007)
	Life of Suzuki Shōsan (1579–1655), Zen master and warrior	King (1986)
	Establishment of the Obaku Zen sect by Chinese monk Yinyuan Longqi and two others (1681)	Baroni (2000; 2006)
	Life of Ishida Baigan (1685–1784), founder of Shingaku combining Confucianism, Buddhism, and Shintō	Sawada (1993)
	Life of Hakuin (1686–1768), reformer of Rinzai Zen tradition and of kōan study	Yampolsky (1971); Waddell (1999)
	Life of Ryōkan (1758–1831), Zen master, poet, and hermit	Haskel and Abé (1996)
1868–present	Meiji, Taishō, Shōwa, and Heisei eras	
	Separation of Buddhism and Shintō in Meiji	Ketelaar (1990)
	Marriage of monastics	Jaffe (2001)
	Temple life	Covell (2005); Arai (1999)
	Buddhism and abortion	LaFleur (1992)
	New Religions	Hardacre (1984); Machacek and Wilson (2000)

APPENDIX H.
A SHORT CHRONOLOGY OF BUDDHISM IN VIETNAM

DATES	EVENTS/FIGURES	FURTHER READING
2nd century CE	Legend of first four temples built to enshrine four "Lady Buddhas"; influence from India and Chinese traditions	Taylor (1983), pp. 81–82; C. Nguyen (1997), pp. 70, 332–334; T. Nguyen, (1997), pp. 9–74
10th century	Independence gained from China	For a short presentation of all the historical periods below, see Nguyen (2004)
968–1400	Đinh, Lý, and Trần dynasties: all supported and enjoyed the support of Buddhism	T. Nguyen (1997), pp. 75–164
1428–1802	Later Lý dynasty; neo-Confucianism outrivals Buddhism	T. Nguyen (1997), pp. 165–222
1802–1945	Nguyễn dynasty; government inclined towards Confucianism, but Buddhism influential among people and intelligentsia. French rule from 1883 to 1945	T. Nguyen (1997), pp. 223–260
1883–1945	French rule; also time of Buddhist revival	De Vido (2007)
1945–1975	Government inclination towards Catholicism under Diêm regime; Buddhist resistance in the 1960s	Hanh (1967)
1975–present	Government inclination towards Communism	

APPENDIX I. A SHORT CHRONOLOGY OF BUDDHISM IN TIBET

DATES	FIGURES/EVENTS	FURTHER READING
7th–9th century CE	Rise of Tibetan Empire under Yarlung Kings	Kapstein (2006), pp. 51–83; Yeshe De Project (1986a), pp. 200–318
	Introduction of Buddhism with support of the Dharmic kings (e.g. Khri Srong lde bstan (r. 755–98))	Kapstein (2000)
	Arrival of Padmasambhava (8th century)	Kunsang (1993)
	Great debate between Chinese and Indian Buddhists at Samye (*c.*797)	Dalton (2004); Houston (1980)
	Supposed "persecution" of Buddhism under King gLang Darma (840s) and disintegration of Tibetan empire	Yamaguchi (1996)
10th–12th century	Buddhist renaissance	Davidson (2005); Kapstein (2006), pp. 95–109
	Life of Atīśa (982–1054)	Chattopadhyaya (1967)
	Life of Marpa (1012–1097)	Trungpa and Nalanda Translation Committee (1982)
	Life of Milarépa (1040–1123)	Quintman (2010)
13th–14th century	Mongol power and Sakya ascendancy	
	Life of Sakya Pandita (1182–1251)	Stearns (2001), pp. 159–169
	Life of Bu sTon (1290–1364); editing of Tibetan canon	Ruegg (1966)
14th–20th century	Gelug ascendancy	Brauen (2005)
	Life of Tsongkhapa (1357–1419)	Thurman (1982)
	Life of the Fifth Dalai Lama (1617–1682)	Powers (2007), pp. 165–168
	Life of the Thirteenth Dalai Lama (1876–1933)	Tada (1965)
	Life of the Fourteenth Dalai Lama (b. 1935)	Hicks and Chogyam (1990); Avedon (1984)
1959–present	Tibet in China and in exile	Goldstein (1997); Goldstein and Kapstein (1998); Hilton (2000)

Bibliography of Works Cited

Abe, M. 1992. *A Study of Dōgen: His Philosophy and Religion*, ed. S. Heine. Albany, State University of New York Press

Abé, R. 1999. *The Weaving of Mantra: Kūkai and the Construction of Esoteric Buddhist Discourse.* New York, Columbia University Press

Adolphson, M. S. 2000. *The Gates of Power: Monks, Courtiers, and Warriors in Premodern Japan.* Honolulu, University of Hawai'i Press

——2007. *The Teeth and Claws of the Buddha: Monastic Warriors and Sōhei in Japanese History.* Honolulu, University of Hawai'i Press

Agostini, G. 2004. "Buddhist Sources on Feticide as Distinct from Homicide." *Journal of the International Association of Buddhist Studies*, 27, pp. 63–96

——2008. "Partial Upāsakas." In: Gombrich and Scherer-Schaub, 2008, pp. 1–34

Akester, M. 2001. "The 'Vajra Temple' of gTer ston Zhig po gling pa and the Politics of Flood Control in 16th Century lHa sa." *Tibet Journal*, 26, pp. 3–24

Alexander, A. 2005. *The Temples of Lhasa: Tibetan Buddhist Architecture from the 7th to the 21st Centuries.* Singapore, Times Editions

Allen, C. 2002. *The Search for the Buddha: The Men who Discovered India's Lost Religion.* New York, Carroll & Graf

Almond, P. C. 1988. *The British Discovery of Buddhism.* Cambridge, Cambridge University Press

Ames, M. M. 1964. "Magical-animism and Buddhism: A Structural Analysis of the Sinhalese Religious System." In: *Religion in South Asia*, ed. E. B. Harper. Seattle, University of Washington Press, pp. 21–52

Ames, W. L. 2003. "Emptiness and Quantum Theory." In: Wallace, 2003, pp. 285–304

An Yang-Gyu. 2003. *The Buddha's Last Days: Buddhaghosa's Commentary on the Mahāparinibbāna Sutta.* Oxford, Pali Text Society

Anacker, S. 1984. *Seven Works of Vasubandhu: The Buddhist Psychological Doctor.* Delhi, Motilal Banarsidass

Anālayo (Bhikkhu). 2006. "The Ekottarika-āgama Parallel to the Saccavibhanga-sutta and the Four (Noble) Truths." *Buddhist Studies Review*, 23, pp. 145–153

——2007. "The Arahant Ideal in Early Buddhism, the Case of Bakkula." *Indian International Journal of Buddhist Studies*, 8, pp. 1–21

——2010. "Once Again on Bakkula." *Indian International Journal of Buddhist Studies*, 11, pp. 1–28

——2010a. "Attitudes Towards Nuns: A Case Study of the *Nandakovāda* in the Light of its Parallels." *Journal of Buddhist Ethics*, 17, pp. 331–400

——2011. "Mahāpajāpatī's Going Forth in the Madhyama-āgama." *Journal of Buddhist Ethics*, 18, pp. 268–318

——2011a. *A Comparative Study of the Majjhima-nikāya*. Taipei, Dharma Drum Publishing, 2 vols

——2012. "Teaching the Abhidharma in the Heaven of the Thirty-Three: The Buddha and His Mother." *Journal of the Oxford Centre for Buddhist Studies*, 2, pp. 9–35

——2012/2013. "The Chinese Parallels to the *Dhammacakkappavattana sutta*." *Journal of the Oxford Centre for Buddhist Studies*, 3, pp. 12–46

Anderson, C. S. 1999. *Pain and its Ending: The Four Noble Truths in the Theravāda Buddhist Canon*. Delhi, Motilal Banarsidass

Anesaki, M. 1916. *Nichiren the Buddhist Prophet*. Cambridge, Harvard University Press

App, U. 1994. *Master Yunmen*. New York, Kodansha

Appleton, N. 2010. *Jātaka Stories in Theravāda Buddhism: Narrating the Bodhisatta Path*. Farnham, Ashgate

Arai, P. K. R. 1999. *Women Living Zen: Japanese Sōtō Buddhist Nuns*. New York, Oxford University Press

Aris, M. 1989. *Hidden Treasures and Secret Lives*. London, Kegan Paul

Arnold, E. A., ed. 2009. *As Long as Space Endures: Essays on the Kālacakra Tantra in Honor of H.H. the Dalai Lama*. Ithaca, Snow Lion

Aronson, H. B. 1980. *Love and Sympathy in Theravāda Buddhism*. Delhi, Motilal Banarsidass

Assavavirulhakarn, P. 2010. *The Ascendency of Theravāda Buddhism in Southeast Asia*. Chiang Mai, Silkworm Books

Astley, T. 2006. "New Religions." In: Swanson and Chilson, 2006, pp. 91–114

Aston, W. G. 1972. *Nihongi: Chronicles of Japan from the Earliest Times to A.D. 697*. Tokyo, Charles E. Tuttle Co., 2 vols

Augustine, J. M. 2005. *Buddhist Hagiography in Early Japan: Images of Compassion in the Gyōki Tradition*. London, RoutledgeCurzon

Aung, S. Z. and C. A. F. Rhys Davids. 1915. *Points of Controversy or Subjects of Discourse*. London, Pali Text Society

Aung-Thwin, M. A. 1998. *Myth and History in the Historiography of Early Burma*. Athens, OH, Ohio University Center for International Studies.

——2005. *The Mists of Rāmañña: The Legend that was Lower Burma*. Honolulu, University of Hawai'i Press

Avedon, J. 1984. *In Exile from the Land of Snows*. New York, Knopf

Aviv, E. 2011. "Ambitions and Negotiations: The Growing Role of Laity in Twentieth-century Chinese Buddhism." *Journal of the Oxford Centre for Buddhist Studies*, 1, pp. 39–59

Bailey, G. and I. Mabbett. 2003. *The Sociology of Early Buddhism*. Cambridge, Cambridge University Press

Banerjee, A.C. 1957. *Sarvāstivāda Literature*. Calcutta, The World Press

Bareau, A. 1955. *Les premiers conciles bouddhiques*. Paris, Annales du Musée Guimet

——1963. *Recherches sur la biographie du Buddha dans les sūtrapiṭaka et les vinayapiṭaka anciens: de la quête de l'éveil à la conversion de Śāriputra et de Maudgalyāyana*. Paris, Ecole Française d'Extrême-Orient

——1970–1971. *Recherches sur la biographie du Buddha dans les sūtrapiṭaka et les vinayapiṭaka anciens: II. Les derniers mois, le parinirvāṇa et les funérailles*. Paris, Ecole Française d'Extrême-Orient, 2 vols

——1974. "La jeunesse du Buddha dans les sūtrapiṭaka et les vinayapiṭaka anciens." *Bulletin de l'Ecole Française d'Extrême-Orient*, 61, pp. 199–274

——2013. *The Buddhist Schools of the Small Vehicle*, trans. S. Boin-Webb. Honolulu, University of Hawai'i Press

Barks, C. 1992. *Stallion on a Frozen Lake: Love Songs of the Sixth Dalai Lama*. Athens, GA, Maypop Books

Barnhill, D. L. 1997. "Great Earth Sangha: Gary Snyder's View of Nature as Community." In: Tucker and Williams, 1997, pp. 187–217

——2005. *Bashō's Journey: The Literary Prose of Matsuo Bashō*. Albany, State University of New York Press

Baroni, H. J. 2000. *Obaku Zen: The Emergence of the Third Sect of Zen in Tokugawa Japan*. Honolulu, University of Hawai'i Press

——2006. *Iron Eyes: The Life and Teachings of the Obaku Zen Master Tetsugen Dōko*. Albany, State University of New York Press

Barth, A. 1918. *Oeuvres de Auguste Barth. Tome quatrième: comptes rendus et notices (1887–1898)*. Paris, Ernest Leroux

Bartholomeusz, T. J. 1994. *Women under the Bō Tree: Buddhist Nuns in Sri Lanka*. Cambridge, Cambridge University Press

Basham, A. L. 1951. *History and Doctrines of the Ājīvikas: A Vanished Indian Religion*. Delhi, Motilal Banarsidass

Batchelor, M. 2006. *Women in Korean Zen: Lives and Practices*. Syracuse, Syracuse University Press

Bautze-Picron, C. 2008. "The Emaciated Buddha in Southeast Bangladesh and Myanmar (Pagan)." In: *Miscellanies about the Buddha Image*, ed. C. Bautze-Picron. Oxford, BAR International Series, pp. 77–96

Bays, G. 1983. *The Voice of the Buddha: the Beauty of Compassion*. Berkeley, Dharma Publishing, 2 vols

Beal, S. 1871. *A Catena of Buddhist Scriptures from the Chinese*. London, Trübner and Co.

——1875. *The Romantic Legend of Śākya Buddha: A Translation of the Chinese Version of the Abhiniṣkramaṇasūtra*. London, Trübner and Co.

Bechert, H. 1973. "Notes on the Formation of Buddhist Sects and the Origins of Mahayana." In: *German Scholars on India*, vol. 1. Varanasi, Cultural Department of the Embassy of the Federal Republic of Germany

——1982. "The Importance of Aśoka's So-called Schism Edict." In: *Indological and Buddhist Studies Volume in Honour of Professor J. W. de Jong on his Sixtieth Birthday*, ed. L. A. Hercus, F. B. J. Kuiper, T. Rajapatirana and E. R. Skrzypczak. Delhi, Sri Satguru Publications, pp. 61–68

——1992. "Buddha-field and Transfer of Merit in a Theravāda Source." *Indo-Iranian Journal*, 35, pp. 95–108

——ed. 1995. *When Did the Buddha Live? The Controversy on the Dating of the Historical Buddha*. Delhi, Sri Satguru Publications

——2004. "Buddha, Life of." In: Buswell, 2004, pp. 82–88

Bechert, H. and R. F. Gombrich, eds. 1984. *The World of Buddhism: Buddhist Monks and Nuns in Society and Culture*. London, Thames and Hudson

Bell, C. 1946. *Portrait of a Dalai Lama*. London, Collins

Bellezza, J. V. 1997. *Divine Dyads: Ancient Civilization in Tibet*. Dharamsala, Library of Tibetan Works and Archives

Beltz, J. 2005. *Mahar, Buddhist and Dalit: Religious Conversion and Socio-Political Emancipation*. New Delhi, Manohar

Benn, J. A. 2007. *Burning for the Buddha: Self-Immolation in Chinese Buddhism*. Honolulu, University of Hawai'i Press

Benn, J. A., L. Meeks and J. Robson, eds. 2010. *Buddhist Monasticism in East Asia: Places of Practice*. London, Routledge

Benson, H. 1982. "Body Temperature Changes during the Practice of gTummo Yoga." *Nature*, 195, pp. 234–235

Berger, P. A. 2003. *Empire of Emptiness: Buddhist Art and Political Authority in Qing China*. Honolulu, University of Hawai'i Press

Berkwitz, S. C. 2007. *The History of the Buddha's Relic Shrine: A Translation of the Sinhala Thūpavaṃsa*. Oxford, Oxford University Press

——2010. *South Asian Buddhism: A Survey*. London, Routledge

Bernbaum, E. 1980. *The Way to Shambhala: A Search for the Mythical Kingdom beyond the Himalayas*. New York, Anchor Books

Berthier, F. 2000. *Reading Zen in the Rocks*, trans. G. Parkes. Chicago, University of Chicago Press

Beyer, S. 1973. *The Cult of Tārā*. Berkeley, University of California Press

——1974. *The Buddhist Experience: Sources and Interpretations*. Encino, Dickenson

Bidari, B. 2009. *Lumbini Beckons*. Kathmandu, Hillside Press

Bingenheimer, M., B. Anālayo and R. S. Bucknell. 2013. *The Madhyama Āgama (Middle Length Discourses), Volume 1*. Berkeley, Bukkyo Dendo Kyokai America

Birnbaum, R. 1979. *The Healing Buddha*. Boulder, Shambhala

——2003. "Buddhist China at the Century's Turn." *China Quarterly*, 174, pp. 428–450

——2005. "Mañjuśrī." In: *Encyclopedia of Religion*, vol. 8, ed. L. Jones. Farmington Hills, Macmillan Reference U.S.A., p. 5675

Bischoff, R. 1995. *Buddhism in Myanmar: A Short History*. Kandy, Buddhist Publication Society

Bjerken, Z. 2005. "On Maṇḍalas, Monarchs, and Mortuary Magic." *Journal of the American Academy of Religion*, 73, pp. 813–841

Blackburn, A. M. 1999. "Looking for the *Vinaya*: Monastic Discipline in the Practical Canons of the Theravāda." *Journal of the International Association of Buddhist Studies*, 22, pp. 281–310

——2001. *Buddhist Learning and Textual Practice in Eighteenth-Century Lankan Monastic Culture*. Princeton, Princeton University Press

——2010. *Locations of Buddhism: Colonialism and Modernity in Sri Lanka*. Chicago, University of Chicago Press

——2012. "Lineage, Inheritance, and Belonging: Expressions of Monastic Affiliation from Laṅkā." In: Skilling, Carbine, Cicuzza and Pakdeekham, 2012, pp. 275–296

Blacker, C. 1975. *The Catalpa Bow: A Study of Shamanistic Practices in Japan*. London, Allen and Unwin

Blondeau, A.-M. and Y. Gyatso. 2003. "Lhasa, Legend and History." In: Pommaret, 2003, pp. 15–38

Blum, M. L. 2002. *The Origins and Development of Pure Land Buddhism*. Oxford, Oxford University Press

——2013. *The Nirvana Sutra (Mahāparinirvāṇa Sūtra), Volume 1*. Berkeley, Bukkyo Dendo Kyokai America

Blum, M. L. and S. Yasutomi, eds. 2006. *Rennyo and the Roots of Modern Japanese Buddhism*. Oxford, Oxford University Press

Blyth, R. H. 1966. *Zen and Zen Classics: Mumonkan*. Tokyo, Hokuseido Press

Bode, M. 1893. "Women Leaders of the Buddhist Reformation." *Journal of the Royal Asiatic Society*, pp. 517–566, 763–798

Bodhi (Bhikkhu). 1978. *The Discourse on the All-Embracing Net of Views: The Brahmajāla Sutta and its Commentaries.* Kandy, Buddhist Publication Society

——1995. *The Great Discourse on Causation: The Mahānidāna Sutta and its Commentaries.* Kandy, Buddhist Publication Society

——2000. *The Connected Discourses of the Buddha: A Translation of the Saṃyutta Nikāya.* Boston, Wisdom Publications

——2005. *A Treatise on the Paramis: From the Commentary to the Cariyapitaka by Acariya Dhammapala* (The Wheel, No. 409/411). Kandy, Buddhist Publication Society

——2009. *The Revival of the Bhikkhuni Ordination in the Theravada Tradition.* Penang, Inward Path

——2012. *The Numerical Discourses of the Buddha: A Translation of the Anguttara Nikāya.* Boston, Wisdom Publications

Bodiford, W. M. 1993. *Sōtō Zen in Medieval Japan.* Honolulu, University of Hawai'i Press

Boisvert, M. 1996. "Death as Meditation Subject in the Theravāda Tradition." *Buddhist Studies Review*, 13, pp. 37–54

Bond, G. D. 1988. *The Buddhist Revival in Sri Lanka: Religious Tradition, Reinterpretation and Response.* Columbia, University of South Carolina Press

Boucher, D. 1993. "The *Prātityasamutpādagāthā* and Its Role in the Medieval Cult of the Relics." *Journal of the International Association of Buddhist Studies*, 14, pp. 1–27

——2008. *Bodhisattvas of the Forest and the Formation of the Mahāyāna: A Study and Translation of the Rāṣṭrapālaparipṛcchā-sūtra.* Honolulu, University of Hawai'i Press

Brauen, M. 1998. *The Maṇḍala: Sacred Circle in Tibetan Buddhism*, trans. M. Wilson. Boston, Shambhala

——ed. 2005. *The Dalai Lamas: A Visual History.* Chicago, Serindia

Brekke, T. 1998. "Contradiction and the Merit of Giving in Indian Religions." *Numen*, 45, pp. 287–320

Brinker, H., H. Kanazawa and A. Leisinger. 1996. *Zen Masters of Meditation in Images and Writings.* Ascona, Artibus Asiae Supplements (no. 40)

Bronkhorst, J. 1985. "Dharma and Abhidharma." *Bulletin of the School of Oriental and African Studies*, 48, pp. 305–320

——1995. "The Buddha and the Jainas Reconsidered." *Asiatische Studien/Etudes Asiatiques*, 49, pp. 330–350

——1998. "Did the Buddha Believe in Karma and Rebirth?" *Journal of the International Association of Buddhist Studies*, 21, pp. 1–19

——2000. *The Two Traditions of Meditation in Ancient India.* 2nd edition. Delhi, Motilal Banarsidass

——2004. "Karma (Action.)" In: Buswell, 2004, pp. 214–217

——2005. "Les reliques dans les religions de l'Inde." In: *Indische Kultur im Kontext: Rituale, Texte und Ideen aus Indien und der Welt: Festschrift für Klaus Mylius*, ed. L. Göhler. Wiesbaden, Harrassowitz Verlag, pp. 49–85

——2007. *Greater Magadha: Studies in the Culture of Early India.* Leiden, E.J. Brill

——2011. *Buddhism in the Shadow of Brahmanism.* Leiden, E.J. Brill

Broughton, J. L. 1999. *The Bodhidharma Anthology: The Earliest Records of Zen.* Berkeley, University of California Press

——2009. *Zongmi on Chan.* New York, Columbia University Press

Brown, R. L. 1984. "The Śrāvastī Miracles in the Art of India and Dvāravatī." *Archives of Asian Art*, 37, pp. 79–95

——1996. *The Dvāravati Wheels of the Law and the Indianization of South East Asia.* Leiden, E.J. Brill

Burchardi, A. 2007. "A Look at the Diversity of the Gzhan stong Tradition." *Journal of the International Association of Tibetan Studies*, 3, pp. 1–24
Burlingame, E. W. 1921. *Buddhist Legends*. Cambridge, Harvard University Press, 3 vols
Burnouf, E. 1852. *Le Lotus de la Bonne Loi*. Paris, Imprimerie Nationale
Buswell, R. E. 1991. *Tracing Back the Radiance: Chinul's Korean Way of Zen*. Honolulu, University of Hawai'i Press
——1992. "The Path to Perdition: The Wholesome Roots and Their Eradication." In: Buswell and Gimello, 1992, pp. 107–134
——ed. 2004. *The Encyclopedia of Buddhism*. New York, MacMillan Reference
Buswell, R. E. and R. M. Gimello, eds. 1992. *Paths to Liberation: The Mārga and its Transformations in Buddhist Thought*. Honolulu, University of Hawai'i Press
Buswell, R. E. and D. S. Lopez, eds. 2014. *The Princeton Dictionary of Buddhism*. Princeton, Princeton University Press
Cabezón, J., ed. 1992. *Buddhism, Sexuality and Gender*. Albany, State University of New York Press
Cabezón, J. I. 2004. "Scripture." In: Buswell, 2004, pp. 755–758
Cabezón, J. I. and R. R. Jackson, eds. 1996. *Tibetan Literature: Studies in Genre*. Ithaca, Snow Lion
Cantwell, C. 2010. *Buddhism: The Basics*. London, Routledge
Carr, K. G. 2012. *Plotting the Prince: Shōtoku Cults and the Mapping of Medieval Japanese Buddhism*. Honolulu, University of Hawai'i Press
Carrithers, M. 1983. *The Forest Monks of Sri Lanka: An Anthropological and Historical Study*. Delhi, Oxford University Press
——1983a. *The Buddha*. Oxford, Oxford University Press
Cartelli, M. A. 2004. "On a Five-Colored Cloud: The Songs of Mount Wutai." *Journal of the American Oriental Society*, 124, pp. 735–757
Carter, M. L. 1990. *The Mystery of the Udayana Buddha*. Naples, Istituto Universitario Orientale
Cate, S. 2003. *Making Merit, Making Art: A Thai Temple in Wimbledon*. Honolulu, University of Hawai'i Press
Chakravarti, U. 1987. *The Social Dimensions of Early Buddhism*. Delhi, Oxford University Press
Chan, S. 1985. *Buddhism in Late Ch'ing Political Thought*. Hong Kong, Chinese University Press
Chang, G. C. C. 1962. *The Hundred Thousand Songs of Milarepa*. New York, Harper and Row
Chapin, H. 1933. "The Ch'an Master Pu-tai." *Journal of the American Oriental Society*, 53, pp. 49–52
Charney, M. W. 2006. *Powerful Learning: Buddhist Literati and the Throne in Burma's Last Dynasty, 1752–1885*. Ann Arbor, University of Michigan Centers for South and Southeast Asian Studies
Chattopadhyaya, A. 1967. *Atiśa and Tibet*. Delhi, Motilal Banarsidass
Chayet, A. 2003. "The Potala, Symbol of the Power of the Dalai Lamas." In: Pommaret, 2003, pp. 40–52
Cheetham, E. 1994. *Fundamentals of Mainstream Buddhism*. Boston, Charles E. Tuttle Co.
Chen, J. 2002. *Monks and Monarchs, Kinship and Kingship: Tanqian in Sui Buddhism and Politics*. Kyoto, Scuola Italiana di Studi sull'Asia Orientale
——2002a. "*Śarīra* and Scepter: Empress Wu's Political Use of Buddhist Relics." *Journal of the International Association of Buddhist Studies*, 25, pp. 33–140
——2005. "Fazang (643–712): The Holy Man." *Journal of the International Association of Buddhist Studies*, 28, pp. 11–84

——2007. *Philosopher, Practitioner, Politician: The Many Lives of Fazang (643–712).* Leiden, E.J. Brill

Ch'en, K. K. S. 1964. *Buddhism in China: A Historical Survey.* Princeton, Princeton University Press

——1973. *The Chinese Transformation of Buddhism.* Princeton, Princeton University Press

Childers, R. C. 1909. *A Dictionary of the Pali Language.* London, Kegan Paul, Trench, Trübner

Chilson, C. 2007. "Eulogizing Kūya as More than a Nenbutsu Practitioner: A Study and Translation of the *Kūyarui.*" *Japanese Journal of Religious Studies,* 34, pp. 305–327

Chimpa (Lama) and A. Chattopadhyaya. 1970. *Tāranātha's History of Buddhism in India.* Calcutta, K.B. Bagchi and Co.

Choong, M.-K. 1999. *The Notion of Emptiness in Early Buddhism.* Delhi, Motilal Banarsidass

Chou, I-L. 1945. "Tantrism in China." *Harvard Journal of Asiatic Studies,* 8, pp. 241–332

Chung, I. 1999. "A Buddhist View of Women: A Comparative Study of the Rules for *Bhiksus* and *Bhiksunis* based on the Chinese *Pratimoksa.*" *Journal of Buddhist Ethics,* 6, pp. 29–105

Clarke, S. 2000. "The Existence of the Supposedly Non-existent *Śikṣādattā-śrāmaṇerī*: A New Perspective on Pārājika Penance." *Bukkyō Kenkyū,* 29, pp. 149–176

——2009. "Monks who Have Sex: Pārājika Penance in Indian Buddhist Monasticisms." *Journal of Indian Philosophy,* 37, pp. 1–43

——2010. "Creating Nuns Out of Thin Air: Problems and Possible Solution Concerning the Ordination of Nuns According to the Tibetan Monastic Code." In: *Dignity and Discipline: Reviving Full Ordination for Buddhist Nuns,* ed. T. Mohr and J. Tsedroen. Boston, Wisdom Publications, pp. 227–238

——2014. *Family Matters in Indian Buddhist Monasticisms.* Honolulu, University of Hawai'i Press

Cleary, T. 1984. *The Flower Ornament Scripture: A Translation of the Avatamsaka Sutra.* Boulder, Shambhala

——1989. *Entry into the Realm of Reality: The Text.* Boston, Shambhala

——1989a. *Entry into the Realm of Reality: The Guide [by] Li Tongxuan.* Boston, Shambhala

Coedès, G. 1959. "L'assistance médicale au Cambodge au XIIe siècle." In: *Présence du Bouddhisme,* ed. R. de Berval. Saigon, France-Asie, pp. 493–496

Cohen, P. T. 2001. "Buddhism Unshackled: The Yuan 'Holy Man' Tradition and the Nation-State in the Tai World." *Journal of Southeast Asian Studies,* 32, pp. 227–247

——2010. "A Buddha Kingdom in the Golden Triangle: Buddhist Revivalism and the Charismatic Monk Khruba Bunchum." *Australian Journal of Anthropology,* 11, pp. 141–154.

Cole, A. 1998. *Mothers and Sons in Chinese Buddhism.* Stanford, Stanford University Press

Collins, S. 1982. *Selfless Persons: Imagery and Thought in Theravāda Buddhism.* Cambridge, Cambridge University Press

——1990. "On the Very Idea of the Pali Canon." *Journal of the Pali Text Society,* 15, pp. 89–126

——1998. *Nirvana and Other Buddhist Felicities.* Cambridge, Cambridge University Press

——2014. "Reflections on the Dichotomy Rūpakāya/Dhammakāya." *Contemporary Buddhism: An Interdisciplinary Journal.* http://dx.doi.org/10.1080/14639947.2014.932481

——ed. (forthcoming). *The Vessantara Jātaka.* Columbia, Columbia University Press

Como, M. I. 2008. *Shōtoku: Ethnicity, Ritual and Violence in the Japanese Buddhist Tradition.* Oxford, Oxford University Press

Cone, M. and R. F. Gombrich. 1977. *The Perfect Generosity of Prince Vessantara*. Oxford, Clarendon Press

Coningham, R. A. E. 1995. "Monks, Caves and Kings: A Reassessment of the Nature of Early Buddhism in Sri Lanka." *World Archaeology*, 27, pp. 222–242

Coningham, R. A. E., et al. 2013. "The Earliest Buddhist Shrine: Excavating the Birthplace of the Buddha, Lumbini (Nepal)." *Antiquity*, 87, pp. 1104–1123

Conze, E. 1954. *Abhisamayālaṃkara*. Rome, Istituto Italiano per il med-ed Estremo Oriente

——1956. *Buddhist Meditation*. New York, Harper Torchbooks

——1958. *Buddhist Wisdom Books, Containing the Diamond Sutra and the Heart Sutra*. London, George Allen & Unwin

——1959. *Buddhism: Its Essence and Development*. New York, Harper Torchbooks

——1960. *The Prajñāpāramitā Literature*. The Hague, Mouton

——1967. *Buddhist Thought in India*. Ann Arbor, University of Michigan Press

——1973. *The Perfection of Wisdom in Eight Thousand Lines and Its Verse Summary*. Bolinas, Four Seasons Foundation

——1974. *The Short Prajñāpāramitā Texts*. London, Luzac

——1975. *The Large Sutra on Perfect Wisdom, with the Divisions of the Abhisamayālankāra*. Berkeley, University of California Press

Cook, F. H. 1977. *Hua-yen Buddhism: The Jewel Net of Indra*. University Park, Pennsylvania State University Press

——1989. "The Jewel Net of Indra." In: *Nature in Asian Traditions of Thought*, ed. J. Baird Callicott and R. T. Ames. Albany, State University of New York Press, pp. 213–229

Coomaraswamy, A. K. 1926–1927. "The Origin of the Buddha Image." *Art Bulletin*, 9, pp. 287–329

Cousins, L. S. 1973. "Buddhist Jhāna: Its Nature and Attainment According to the Pali Sources." *Religion*, 3, pp. 115–131

——1996. "Good or Skilful? Kusala in Canon and Commentary." *Journal of Buddhist Ethics*, 3, pp. 136–164

——2012. "The Teachings of the Abhayagiri School." In: Skilling, Carbine, Cicuzza and Pakdeekham, 2012, pp. 67–128

Covell, S. G. 2005. *Japanese Temple Buddhism: Worldliness in a Religion of Renunciation*. Honolulu, University of Hawai'i Press

Cowell, E. B. 1894. "The Buddha-carita of Aśvaghosha." In: Cowell, 1894a, part I

——(ed). 1894a. *Buddhist Mahāyāna Texts*. Oxford, Clarendon Press

——. 1895–1907. *The Jātaka or Stories of the Buddha's Former Births*. Cambridge, Cambridge University Press, 6 vols

Cox, C. 1992. "Attainment through Abandonment: The Sarvāstivādin Path of Removing Defilements." In: Buswell and Gimello, 1992, pp. 63–106

——1995. *Disputed Dharmas: Early Buddhist Theories on Existence*. Tokyo, International Institute for Buddhist Studies

——2004. "Abhidharma." In: Buswell, 2004, pp. 1–7

——2004a. "Mainstream Buddhist Schools." In: Buswell, 2004, pp. 501–507

Cozort, D. 1986. *Highest Yoga Tantra*. Ithaca, Snow Lion

——2003. "The Making of the Western Lama." In: Heine and Prebish, 2003, pp. 221–248

Crosby, K. 2000. "Tantric Theravāda: A Bibliographic Essay on the Writings of François Bizot and Others on the Yogāvacāra Tradition." *Contemporary Buddhism*, 1, pp. 141–198.

——2004. "Theravāda." In: Buswell, 2004, pp. 836–841

——2013. "The Inheritance of Rāhula: Abandoned Child, Boy Monk, Ideal Son and Trainee." In: Sasson, 2013a, pp. 97–123

——2014. *Theravada Buddhism: Continuity, Diversity, and Identity.* Chichester, Wiley Blackwell

Crosby, K. and A. Skilton. 1995. *Śāntideva: The Bodhicaryāvatāra.* Oxford, Oxford University Press

Crosby, K. and J. Khur-Yearn. 2010. "Poetic *Dhamma* and the *Zare*: Traditional Styles of Teaching Theravāda amongst the Shan of Northern Thailand." *Contemporary Buddhism*, 11, pp. 1–26

Cueppers, C., M. Deeg and H. Durt, eds. 2010. *The Birth of the Buddha: Proceedings of the Seminar Held in Lumbini, Nepal, October 2001.* Lumbini, Lumbini International Research Institute

Cutler, S. M. 1997. "Still Suffering After All These Aeons: The Continuing Effects of the Buddha's Bad Karma." In: *Indian Insights: Buddhism, Brahmanism and Bhakti*, ed. P. Connolly and S. Hamilton. London, Luzac Oriental, pp. 63–82

D'Amato, M. 2005. "Three Natures, Three Stages: An Interpretation of the Yogācāra *Trisvabhāva*-Theory." *Journal of Indian Philosophy*, 33, pp. 185–207

Dalton, J. 2004. "Bsam Yas Debate." In: Buswell, 2004, pp. 69–71

Das, S. C. 2001 [1899]. *Journey to Lhasa and Central Tibet.* New Delhi, Paljor Publications

David-Neel, A. 1971. *Magic and Mystery in Tibet.* New York, Dover Publications

Davids, C. A. F. R. 1900. *A Buddhist Manual of Psychological Ethics.* London, Pali Text Society

Davids, C. A. F. R. and F. L. Woodward. 1917–1930. *The Book of Kindred Sayings.* London, Pali Text Society, 5 vols

Davids, T. W. R. 1880. *Buddhist Birth Stories.* London, Trübner & Co.

——1890–1894. *The Questions of King Milinda.* Reprint edn., 1963. New York, Dover, 2 vols

——1899–1924. *Dialogues of the Buddha.* London, Pali Text Society, 3 vols

Davids, T. W. R. and H. Oldenberg. 1882. *Vinaya Texts.* Oxford, Oxford University Press, 3 vols

Davids, T. W. R. and W. Stede. 1921–1925. *Pali-English Dictionary.* London, Pali Text Society

Davidson, R. M. 1985. "Buddhist Systems of Transformation: Aśraya-parivṛtti/parāvṛtti among the Yogācāra." Ph.D. dissertation, University of California, Berkeley

——1995. "The Litany of Names of Mañjuśrī." In: Lopez, 1995a, pp. 104–125

——2002. *Indian Esoteric Buddhism: A Social History of the Tantric Movement.* New York, Columbia University Press

——2004. "Vajrayāna." In: Buswell, 2004, pp. 875–877

——2005. *Tibetan Renaissance: Tantric Buddhism in the Rebirth of Tibetan Culture.* New York, Columbia University Press

Davis, E. L. 2001. *Society and the Supernatural in Song China.* Honolulu, University of Hawai'i Press

Dayal, H. 1932. *The Bodhisattva Doctrine in Buddhist Sanskrit Literature.* London, Kegan Paul

De Casparis, J. G. and I. W. Mabbett. 1999. "Religion and Popular Beliefs of Southeast Asia Before c. 1500." In: *The Cambridge History of Southeast Asia, Volume One, Part One*, ed. N. Tarling. Cambridge, Cambridge University Press, pp. 276–339

De Jong, J. W. 1997. *A Brief History of Buddhist Studies in Europe and America.* Tokyo, Kōsei Publishing

De Silva, L. 1981. *Paritta: The Buddhist Ceremony for Peace and Prosperity in Sri Lanka.* Colombo, Government Printing House

De Silva, R. 2004. "Reclaiming the Robe: Reviving the Bhikkhunī Order in Sri Lanka." In: *Buddhist Women and Social Justice: Ideals, Challenges, and Achievements*, ed. K. L. Tsomo. Albany, State University of New York Press, pp. 119–136

De Vido, E. A. 2007. "Buddhism for This World: The Buddhist Revival in Vietnam, 1920 to 1951, and Its Legacy." In: *Modernity and Re-enchantment: Religion in Post-revolutionary Vietnam*, ed. P. Taylor. Singapore, Institute of Southeast Asian Studies, pp. 250–296

De Visser, M. W. 1914. *The Bodhisattva Ti-tsang (Jizō) in China and Japan*. Berlin, Oesterheld

——1923. *The Arhats in China and Japan*. Berlin, Oesterheld

——2006 [1935]. *Ancient Buddhism in Japan*. Mansfield Centre, Martino Publishing

Deal, W. E. 1995. "Buddhism and the State in Early Japan." In: Lopez, 1995, pp. 216–227

——1999. "Hagiography and History: The Image of Prince Shōtoku." In: Tanabe, 1999, pp. 316–333

Deeg, M. 1995/1997. "Origins and Development of the Buddhist Pañcavārṣika." *Nagoya Studies in Indian Culture and Buddhism – Saṃbhāṣā*, 16, pp. 67–90 (part I), and 18, pp. 63–96 (part II)

——1999. "The Sangha of Devadatta: Fiction and History of a Heresy in the Buddhist Tradition." *Journal of the International College for Advanced Buddhist Studies*, 2, pp. 183–218

——2003. *The Places Where Siddhārtha Trod: Lumbinī and Kapilavastu*. Lumbini, Lumbini International Research Institute

——2010. "Why is the Buddha Riding on an Elephant? The Bodhisattva's Conception and the Change of Motive." In: Cueppers, Deeg and Durt, 2010, pp. 93–128

Dehejia, V. 1991. "Aniconism and the Multivalence of Emblems." *Ars orientalis*, 21, pp. 45–66

——ed. 1996. *Unseen Presence: The Buddha and Sanchi*. Mumbai, Marg Publications

Demiéville, P. 1954. "La Yogācārabhūmi de Saṅgharakṣa." *Bulletin de l'Ecole Française d'Extrême-Orient*, 44, pp. 339–346

——1987. "The Mirror of the Mind." In: Gregory, 1987, pp. 13–40

Dennis, M. 2005. "Buddhism, Schools of: East Asian Buddhism." In: Jones, 2005, pp. 1246–1251

Dessein, B. 2007. "The First Turning of the Wheel of Doctrine – Sarvāstivāda and Mahāsaṃghika Controversy." In: *The Spread of Buddhism*, ed. A. Heirman and S. P. Bumbacher. Leiden, E. J. Brill, pp. 15–48

Dhargye, N. (Geshe). 1982. *An Anthology of Well-Spoken Advice on the Graded Path of the Mind*, trans. S. Tulku, ed. A. Berzin. Dharamsala, Library of Tibetan Works and Archives

Diemberger, H. 2007. *When a Woman Becomes a Religious Dynasty: The Samding Dorje Phagmo of Tibet*. New York, Columbia University Press

Dilgo Khyentse. 2008. *Brilliant Moon: The Autobiography of Dilgo Khyentse*, trans. A. J. Palmo. Boston, Shambala

——2010. *The Collected Works of Dilgo Khyentse*, ed. M. Ricard and V. Kurz. Boston, Shambhala

Dobbins, J. C. 1989. *Jōdo Shinshū: Shin Buddhism in Medieval Japan*. Bloomington, University of Indiana Press

Donner, N. and D. B. Stevenson. 1993. *The Great Calming and Contemplation*. Honolulu, University of Hawai'i Press

Dowman, K. 1985. *Masters of Mahāmūdra: Songs and Histories of the Eighty-Four Buddhist Siddhas*. Albany, State University of New York Press

——1988. *The Power-Places of Central Tibet*. London, Routledge and Kegan Paul

Dowman, K. and S. Paljor. 1980. *The Divine Madman: The Sublime Life and Songs of Drukpa Kunley*. Clearlake, Dawnhorse Press

Doyle, T. N. 1997. "Bodh Gayā: Journeys to the Diamond Throne and the Feet of Gayāsur." Ph.D. dissertation, Harvard University

Drewes, D. 2010. "Early Indian Mahāyāna Buddhism I: Recent Scholarship." *Religion Compass*, 4, pp. 55–65

——2010a. "Early Indian Mahāyāna Buddhism II: New Perspectives." *Religion Compass*, 4, pp. 66–74

Dreyfus, G. 1997. "Tibetan Scholastic Education and the Role of Soteriology." *Journal of the International Association of Buddhist Studies*, 20, pp. 31–62

——1998. "The Shuk-den Affair: History and Nature of a Quarrel." *Journal of the International Association of Buddhist Studies*, 21, pp. 227–270

——2003. *The Sound of Two Hands Clapping: The Education of a Tibetan Buddhist Monk.* Berkeley, University of California Press

——2004. "Dge lugs (Geluk)." In: Buswell, 2004, pp. 215–216

Dudjom (Rinpoche). 1991. *The Nyingma School of Tibetan Buddhism: Its Fundamentals and History.* Somerville, Wisdom Publications

Dumoulin, H. 1988–1990. *Zen Buddhism: A History*, trans. J. W. Heisig and P. Knitter. New York, MacMillan, 2 vols

Dundas, P. 1992. *The Jains.* London, Routledge

Duroiselle, C. 1920–1921. "The Talaing Plaques on the Ananda Temple." *Epigraphia Birmanica*, 2, parts 1–2

Durt, H. 1982. "La 'visite aux laboureurs' et la 'méditation sous l'arbre *jambu*' dans les biographies sanskrites et chinoises du Buddha." In: *Indological and Buddhist Studies: Volume in Honour of Professor J. W. de Jong on his Sixtieth Birthday*, ed. L. A. Hercus. Delhi, Satguru Publications, pp. 95–120

——1991. "Bodhisattva and Layman in the Early Mahayana." *Japanese Religions*, 16, pp. 1–16

——2001. "The Vicissitudes of Vāsiṭṭhī/Vāsiṣṭhā who Became Insane due to the Loss of her Child." *Journal of the International College for Advanced Buddhist Studies*, 2, pp. 147–182

Dutt, S. 1924. *Early Buddhist Monachism.* London, Kegan Paul, Trench and Trübner

——1962. *Buddhist Monks and Monasteries of India.* London, George Allen and Unwin

Ebersole, G. L. 1989. *Ritual Poetry and the Politics of Death in Early Japan.* Princeton, Princeton University Press

Ebrey, P. B. and P. N. Gregory, eds. 1993. *Religion and Society in T'ang and Sung China.* Honolulu, University of Hawai'i Press

Eck, D. L. 1981. *Darśan: Seeing the Divine Image in India.* Chambersburg, Anima

Eckel, M. D. 1992. *To See the Buddha: A Philosopher's Quest for the Meaning of Emptiness.* Princeton, Princeton University Press

——2009. *Bhavaviveka and His Buddhist Opponents.* Cambridge, Harvard University Press

Egge, J. 2002. *Religious Giving and the Invention of Karma in Theravāda Buddhism.* Richmond, Curzon

Ehrhardt, F.-K. 2010. "The Holy Madman of dBus and His Relationships with Tibetan Rulers in the 15th and 16th Centuries." In: *Geschichten und Geschichte: Historiographie und Hagiographie in der asiatischen Religionsgeschichte* (= Historia religionum 30). Uppsala, pp. 219–246

Ekvall, R. B. 1964. *Religious Observances in Tibet: Patterns and Function.* Chicago, University of Chicago Press

Elverskog, J. 2006. *Our Great Qing: The Mongols, Buddhism and the State in Late Imperial China.* Honolulu, University of Hawai'i Press

Emmerick, R. E. 1970. *The Sūtra of Golden Light.* London, Luzac & Co.

Ensink, J. 1952. *The Questions of Rāṣṭrapāla.* Zwolle, De Erven J. J. Tijl

Falk, M. L. 2007. *Making Fields of Merit: Buddhist Female Ascetics and Gendered Orders in Thailand.* Seattle, University of Washington Press

Falk, N. 1979. "The Case of the Vanishing Nuns: The Fruits of Ambivalence in Ancient Indian Buddhism." In: *Unspoken Worlds: Women's Religious Lives in Non-Western Cultures*, ed. N. Falk and R. Gross. San Francisco, Harper, pp. 207–224

——1990. "Exemplary Donors of the Pāli Tradition." In: *Ethics, Wealth, and Salvation: A Study in Buddhist Social Ethics*, ed. R. F. Sizemore and D. K. Swearer. Columbia, University of South Carolina Press, pp. 124–144

Faure, B. 1987. "The Daruma-shū, Dōgen and Sōtō Zen." *Monumenta Nipponica*, 42, pp. 25–55

——1995. "Quand l'habit fait le moine: The Symbolism of the Kāṣāya in Sōtō Zen." *Cahiers d'Extrême-Asie*, 8, pp. 335–369

——1997. *The Will to Orthodoxy: A Critical Genealogy of Northern Chan Buddhism*, trans. P. Brooks. Stanford, Stanford University Press

——1998. *The Red Thread: Buddhist Approaches to Sexuality*. Princeton, Princeton University Press

——2009. *Unmasking Buddhism*. Oxford, Wiley Blackwell

Feer, L. 1891. *Avadāna-çataka: cent légendes (bouddhiques)*. Paris, Ernest Leroux.

Fields, R. 1992. *How the Swans Came to the Lake: A Narrative History of Buddhism in America*. Boston, Shambhala Publications

Findly, E. B. 2003. *Dāna: Giving and Getting in Pali Buddhism*. Delhi, Motilal Banarsidass

Fiordalis, D. 2008. "Miracles and Superhuman Powers in South Asian Buddhist Literature." Ph.D. dissertation, University of Michigan

Fiordalis, D. 2013. "Abhijñā/Ṛddhi (Extraordinary Powers)." In: *Oxford Bibliographies Online Buddhism* (http://www.oxfordbibliographies.com)

Fisher, G. 2012. "Buddhism in China and Taiwan." In: McMahan, 2012, pp. 69–88

Flügel, P. 2010. "The Jaina Cult of Relic Stūpas." *Numen*, 57, pp. 389–504

Foard, J. H. 1982. "The Boundaries of Compassion: Buddhism and National Tradition in Japanese Pilgrimage." *Journal of Asian Studies*, 41, pp. 231–252

Fontein, J. 1967. *The Pilgrimage of Sudhana: A Study of Gaṇḍavyūha Illustrations in China, Japan and Java*. The Hague, Mouton

——2012. *Entering the Dharmadhatu: a Study of the Gaṇḍavyūha Reliefs of Borobudur*. Leiden, E.J. Brill

Ford, J. L. 2006. *Jōkei and Buddhist Devotion in Early Medieval Japan*. Oxford, Oxford University Press

Forte, A. 1976. *Political Propaganda and Ideology in China at the End of the Seventh Century*. Naples, Istituto Universitario Orientale

Foucher, A. 1917. "The Greek Origin of the Image of Buddha." In: *The Beginnings of Buddhist Art*, trans. L. A. Thomas and F. W. Thomas. Paris, Paul Geuthner, pp. 111–138

——1917a. "The Great Miracle at Śrāvastī." In: *The Beginnings of Buddhist Art*, trans. L. A. Thomas and F. W. Thomas. Paris, Paul Geuthner, pp. 147–184

——1963. *The Life of the Buddha According to the Ancient Texts and Monuments of India*, trans. S. B. Boas. Westport, Greenwood Press

Foulk, T. G. 2004. "*Chanyuan qingui* and Other 'Rules of Purity' in Chinese Buddhism." In: *The Zen Canon. Understanding the Classic Texts*, ed. S. Heine and D. S. Wright. Oxford, Oxford University Press, pp. 275–312

——2006. "Rules of Purity in Japanese Zen." In: *Zen Classics: Formative Texts in the History of Zen Buddhism*, ed. S. Heine and D. S. Wright. Oxford, Oxford University Press, pp. 137–169

——2008. "Ritual in Japanese Zen Buddhism." In: Heine and Wright, 2008, pp. 21–82

Frasch, T. 2012. "The Theravāda Buddhist Ecumene in the 15th Century: Intellectual Foundations and Material Representations." In *Buddhism across Asia: Networks of*

Material, Intellectual and Cultural Exchange, ed. T. Sen et al., Singapore, Institute of Southeast Asian Studies, 1, pp. 347–70

Frauwallner, E. 1956. *The Earliest Vinaya and the Beginnings of Buddhist Literature.* Rome, ISMEO

Frédéric, L. 1995. *Buddhism.* Paris, Flammarion

Freemantle, F. and C. Trungpa. 1975. *The Tibetan Book of the Dead: The Great Liberation through Hearing in the Bardo.* Berkeley, Shambhala

Freiberger, O., ed. 2006. *Asceticism and Its Critics: Historical Accounts and Comparative Perspectives.* Oxford, Oxford University Press

French, R. R. 1995. *The Golden Yoke: The Legal Cosmology of Buddhist Tibet.* Ithaca, Cornell University Press

Frye, S. 1981. *The Sūtra of the Wise and the Foolish (mdo bdsans blun) or the Ocean of Narratives (üliger-ün dalai).* Dharamsala, Library of Tibetan Works and Archives

Ganguly, S. 1994. *Treatise on Groups of Elements.* Delhi, Eastern Book Linkers

Garfield, J. L. 1995. *The Fundamental Wisdom of the Middle Way.* New York, Oxford University Press

Geertz, C. 1979. "Religion as a Cultural System." In: *Reader in Comparative Religion.* 4th edn, ed. W. A. Lessa and E. Z. Vogt. New York, Harper & Row, pp. 78–89

Geiger, W. 1912. *The Mahāvaṃsa or the Great Chronicle of Ceylon.* London, Pali Text Society

Gerhart, K. M. 2009. *The Material Culture of Death in Medieval Japan.* Honolulu, University of Hawai'i Press

Germano, D. and G. A. Hillis. 2005. "Buddhist Meditation: Tibetan Buddhist Meditation." In: Jones, 2005, pp. 1284–1290.

Germano, D. and K. Trainor, eds. 2004. *Embodying the Dharma: Buddhist Relic Veneration in Asia.* Albany, State University of New York Press

Gerner, M. 2007. *Chakzampa Thangton Gyalpo: Architect, Philosopher, and Iron Chain Bridge Builder*, trans. G. Verhufen. Thimpu, Center for Bhutan Studies

Gernet, J. 1995. *Buddhism in Chinese Society: An Economic History from the Fifth to the Tenth Centuries*, trans. F. Verellen. New York, Columbia University Press

Gethin, R. 1992. *The Buddhist Path to Awakening, A Study of the Bodhi-Pakkhiyā Dhammā.* Leiden, E.J. Brill

——1994. "Bhavanga and Rebirth According to the Abhidhamma." In: *The Buddhist Forum*, vol. 3, ed. T. Skorupski and U. Pagel. London, School of Oriental and African Studies, pp. 11–35

——1998. *The Foundations of Buddhism.* New York, Oxford University Press

——2008. *Sayings of the Buddha.* Oxford, Oxford University Press

Giebel, R. W. 2001. *Two Esoteric Sutras: The Adamantine Pinnacle Sutra. The Susiddhikara Sutra.* Berkeley, Numata Center

——2004. *Shingon Texts.* Berkeley, Numata Center

——2005. *The Vairocanābhisaṃbodhi Sutra.* Berkeley, Numata Center

Gimello, R. 1983. "Li T'ung-hsüan and the Practical Dimensions of Hua-yen." In: Gimello and Gregory, 1983, pp. 321–389

Gimello, R. M. and P. N. Gregory, eds. 1983. *Studies in Ch'an and Hua-yen.* Honolulu, University of Hawai'i Press

Glassman, H. 1999. "The Tale of Mokuren: A Translation of Mokuren-no-sōshi." *Buddhist Literature*, 1, pp. 120–161

——2012. *The Face of Jizō: Image and Cult in Medieval Japanese Buddhism.* Honolulu, University of Hawai'i Press

Goldstein, M. C. 1964. "Study of the ldab ldob." *Central Asiatic Journal*, 9, pp. 123–141

——1997. *The Snow Lion and the Dragon: China, Tibet, and the Dalai Lama*. Berkeley, University of California Press

——1998. "The Revival of Monastic Life in Drepung Monastery." In: Goldstein and Kapstein, 1998, pp. 15–52

Goldstein, M. C. and M. T. Kapstein, eds. 1998. *Buddhism in Contemporary Tibet: Cultural Survival on the Sino-Tibetan Frontier*. Berkeley, University of California Press

Gombrich, R. F. 1966. "The Consecration of a Buddha Image." *Journal of Asian Studies*, 26, pp. 23–36

——1971. *Precept and Practice: Traditional Buddhism in the Rural Highlands of Ceylon*. Oxford, Clarendon Press

——1971a. "Merit Transfer in Sinhalese Buddhism: A Case Study in the Interaction between Doctrine and Practice." *History of Religions*, 11, pp. 203–219

——1980. "The Significance of the Former Buddhas in the Theravādin Tradition." In: *Buddhist Studies in Honour of Walpola Rahula*, ed. S. Balasooriya et al. London, Gordon Fraser, pp. 62–72

——1988. *Theravada Buddhism: A Social History from Ancient Benares to Modern Colombo*. London, Routledge and Kegan Paul

——1992. "Dating the Buddha: A Red Herring Revealed." In: *The Dating of the Historical Buddha/Die Datierung des Historischen Buddha, Part 2*, ed. H. Bechert. Göttingen, Vandenhoeck & Ruprecht, pp. 237–262

——1994. "The Buddha and the Jains." *Asiatische Studien/Etudes Asiatiques*, 48, pp. 1069–1096

——1996. *How Buddhism Began: The Conditioned Genesis of the Early Teachings*. London, Athlone Press

——2009. *What the Buddha Thought*. London, Equinox

Gombrich, R. and G. Obeyesekere. 1988. *Buddhism Transformed: Religious Change in Sri Lanka*. Princeton, Princeton University Press

Gombrich, R. and C. Scherer-Schaub, eds. 2008. *Buddhist Studies: Papers of the 12th World Sanskrit Conference*. Delhi, Motilal Banarsidass

Gómez, L. O. 1977. "Proto-Mādhyamika in the Pāli Canon." *Philosophy East and West*, 26, pp. 137–165

——1983. "The Direct and Gradual Approaches of Zen Master Mahāyāna." In: Gimello and Gregory, 1983, pp. 69–167

——1983a. "Indian Materials on the Doctrine of Sudden Enlightenment." In: Lai and Lancaster, 1983, pp. 393–434

——1996. *The Land of Bliss: The Paradise of the Buddha of Measureless Light*. Honolulu, University of Hawai'i Press

Gómez, L. O. and H. Woodward, eds. 1981. *Barabudur: History and Significance of a Buddhist Monument*. Berkeley, Asian Humanities Press

Goodrich, L. C. 1942. "The Revolving Bookcase in China." *Harvard Journal of Asiatic Studies*, 7, pp. 130–161

Goodwin, J. R. 1994. *Alms and Vagabonds: Buddhist Temples and Popular Patronage in Medieval Japan*. Honolulu, University of Hawai'i Press

Grapard, A. G. 1986. "Lotus in the Mountain, Mountain in the Lotus." *Monumenta Nipponica*, 41, pp. 21–50

Gray, D. B. 2007. *The Cakrasamvara Tantra (The Discourse of Śrī Heruka)*. New York, American Institute of Buddhist Studies at Columbia University

Green, P. 2000. "Walking for Peace: Nipponzan Myohoji." In: Queen, 2000, pp. 128–156

Greenwald, A. 1978. "The Relic on the Spear: Historiography and the Saga of Duṭṭhagāmaṇī." In: Smith, 1978, pp. 13–35

Gregory, P. N., ed. 1986. *Traditions of Meditation in Chinese Buddhism.* Honolulu, University of Hawai'i Press

——ed. 1987. *Sudden and Gradual: Approaches to Enlightenment in Chinese Thought.* Honolulu, University of Hawai'i Press

——1987a. "Sudden Enlightenment Followed by Gradual Cultivation: Tsung-mi's Analysis of Mind." In: Gregory, 1987, pp. 279–320

——1991. *Tsung-mi and the Sinification of Buddhism.* Princeton, Princeton University Press

Gregory, P. N. and D. A. Getz, eds. 1999. *Buddhism in the Sung.* Honolulu, University of Hawai'i Press

Griffiths, P. J. 1986. *On Being Mindless: Buddhist Meditation and the Mind-Body Problem.* La Salle, Open Court

Griswold, A. B. 1957. *Dated Buddha Images of Northern Siam.* Ascona, Artibus Asiae, Supplementum (no. 16)

——1967. *Towards a History of Sukhodaya Art.* Bangkok, National Museum

Groner, P. 2000. *Saichō: The Establishment of the Japanese Tendai School.* Honolulu, University of Hawai'i Press

——2002. *Ryōgen and Mount Hiei: Japanese Tendai in the Tenth Century.* Honolulu, University of Hawai'i Press

Grosnick, W. H. 1995. "The Tathāgatagarbha Sūtra." In: Lopez, 1995, pp. 92–106

Gross, R. M. 1993. *Buddhism after Patriarchy: A Feminist History, Analysis, and Reconstruction of Buddhism.* Albany, State University of New York Press

Guenther, H. V. 1963. *The Life and Teaching of Nāropa.* London, Oxford University Press

——1971. *The Jewel Ornament of Liberation by sGam.po.pa.* Berkeley, Shambhala

——1971a. *Buddhist Philosophy in Theory and Practice.* Harmondsworth, Penguin Books

Gummer, N. 2005. "Buddhist Books and Texts: Ritual Uses of Books." In: Jones, 2005, pp. 1261–1265

Gump, S. E. 2005. "Mythologies and Miracles: The Saikoku Kannon and Peregrinogenesis." *Southeast Review of Asian Studies*, 27 [http://www.uky.edu/Centers/Asia/SECAAS/Seras/2005/2005TOC.html]

Gunawardana, R. A. L. H. 1979. *Robe and Plough: Monasticism and Economic Interest in Early Medieval Sri Lanka.* Tucson, University of Arizona Press

Guth, C. M. 1987. "The Divine Boy in Japanese Art." *Monumenta Nipponica*, 42, pp. 1–23

Guthrie, E. 2004. "A Study of the History and Cult of the Buddhist Earth Deity in Mainland Southeast Asia." Ph.D. dissertation, University of Canterbury, New Zealand

Gutschow, K. 2004. *Being a Buddhist Nun: The Struggle for Enlightenment in the Himalayas.* Cambridge, Harvard University Press

Guy, J. 2014. *Lost Kingdoms: Hindu-Buddhist Sculpture of Early Southeast Asia.* New York, Metropolitan Museum of Art

Gyaltsen, K. K., 1990. *The Great Kagyu Masters.* Ithaca, Snow Lion Publications

Gyatso, J. 1980. "The Teachings of Thang-stong rgyal-po." In: *Tibetan Studies in Honour of Hugh Richardson*, ed. M. Aris and Aung San Suu Kyi. New Delhi, Vikas Publishing House, pp. 111–119

——1981. "The Literary Transmission of the Traditions of Thang-stong rgyal-po: A Study of Visionary Buddhism in Tibet." Ph.D. dissertation, University of California at Berkeley

——1986. "Thang-stong rgyal-po, Father of the Tibetan Drama: The Bodhisattva as Artist." In: *Zlos-gar: The Tibetan Performing Arts*, ed. J. Norbu. Dharamsala, Library of Tibetan Works and Archives, pp. 91–104

——1987. "Down with the Demoness: Reflections on the Feminine Ground in Tibet." *Tibet Journal*, 12, pp. 38–53

——2004. "The Ultimate Couple." In: *Buddhist Scriptures*, ed. D. S. Lopez, Jr. London, Penguin Books, pp. 488–494

——2005. "Sex." In: Lopez, 2005, pp. 271–290

Gyatso, L. 1998. *Memoirs of a Tibetan Lama*, trans. G. Sparham. Ithaca, Snow Lion Publications.

Gyatso, T. (H.H. Dalai Lama XIV). 1977. "Essence of Tantra." In: *Tantra in Tibet*, trans. and ed. J. Hopkins. Ithaca, Snow Lion Publications, pp. 13–79

——1988. *The Union of Bliss and Emptiness*, trans. T. Jinpa. Ithaca, Snow Lion Publications

——2001. *Stages of Meditation*, trans. L. Jordhen, L. C. Ganchenpa and J. Russell. Ithaca, Snow Lion Publications

——2010. *My Spiritual Journey: Personal Reflections, Teachings, and Talks*, collected by S. Stril-Rever, trans. C. Mandell. New York, HarperOne

Haar, B. J. ter. 1999. *The White Lotus Teachings in Chinese Religious History.* Honolulu, University of Hawai'i Press

Hakeda, Y. S. 1972. *Kūkai: Major Works Translated, with an Account of his Life and a Study of his Thought.* New York, Columbia University Press

——2005. *The Awakening of Faith Attributed to Aśvaghoṣa.* Berkeley, Numata Center

Halperin, M. 2006. *Out of the Cloister: Literati Perspectives on Buddhism in Sung China, 960–1279.* Cambridge, Harvard University Press

Hamar, I., ed. 2007. *Reflecting Mirrors: Perspectives on Huayan Buddhism.* Wiesbaden, Otto Harrassowitz

Hamilton, S. 1996. *Identity and Experience. The Constitution of the Human Being According to Early Buddhism.* London, Luzac Oriental

——2000. *Early Buddhism: A New Approach. The I of the Beholder.* Richmond, Curzon Press

Hanh, Thich Nhat. 1967. *Vietnam: Lotus in a Sea of Fire.* New York, Hill and Wang

Hansen, A. R. 2004. "Cambodia." In: Buswell, 2004, pp. 105–110

——2007. *How to Behave: Buddhism and Modernity in Colonial Cambodia, 1860–1930.* Honolulu, University of Hawai'i Press

Hansen, V. 1990. *Changing Gods in Medieval China, 1127–1276.* Princeton, Princeton University Press

Hara, M. 1980. "A Note on the Buddha's Birth Story." In: *Indianisme et bouddhisme.* Louvain, Institut Orientaliste, pp. 142–157

——1989/1994. "Birth of Extraordinary Persons: The Buddha's Case." In: *The Yogi and the Mystic: Studies in Indian and Comparative Mysticism*, ed. K. Werner. 1. Richmond, Taylor and Francis, pp. 69–81

Hardacre, H. 1984. *Lay Buddhism in Contemporary Japan: Reiyūkai Kyōdan.* Princeton, Princeton University Press

——1999. *Marketing the Menacing Fetus in Japan.* Berkeley, University of California Press

Harris, E. J. 2006. *Theravāda Buddhism and the British Encounter: Religious, Missionary and Colonial Experience in Nineteeth Century Sri Lanka.* London, Routledge

Harris, I. 1997. "Buddhism and the Discourse of Environmental Concern: Some Methodological Problems Considered." In: Tucker and Williams, 1997, pp. 377–402

——2005. *Cambodian Buddhism: History and Practice.* Honolulu, University of Hawai'i Press

Harris, P. 2007. *Zhou Daguan, A Record of Cambodia, the Land and its People.* Bangkok, Silkworm

Harrison, P. M. 1978. "Buddhānusmṛti in the Pratyutpanna-Buddha-Saṃmukhāvasthita-Samādhi-Sūtra." *Journal of Indian Philosophy*, 6, pp. 35–57

——1987. "Who Gets to Ride in the Great Vehicle? Self-image and Identity among the Followers of the Early Mahayana." *Journal of the International Association of Buddhist Studies*, 10, pp. 67–89

——1995. "Searching for the Origins of the Mahayana: What Are We Looking For?" *Eastern Buddhist*, n.s., 28, pp. 48–69

——1998. *The Pratyutpanna Samādhi Sutra*. Berkeley, Numata Center

——2000. "Mañjuśrī and the Cult of the Celestial Bodhisattvas." *Chung-Hwa Buddhist Journal*, 13, pp. 157–193

——2003. "Mediums and Messages: Reflections on the Production of Mahayana Sutras." *Eastern Buddhist*, n.s., 35, pp. 115–151

——2004. "Canon." In: Buswell, 2004, pp. 111–115

Harvey, P. 1995. *The Selfless Mind: Personality, Consciousness and Nirvana in Early Buddhism*. Richmond, Curzon Press

——2000. *An Introduction to Buddhist Ethics*. Cambridge, Cambridge University Press

——2007. "'Freedom of the Will' in the Light of Theravāda Buddhist Teachings." *Journal of Buddhist Ethics*, 14, pp. 35–98

——2009. "The Four Ariya-saccas as 'True Realities for the Spiritually Ennobled' – the Painful, its Origin, its Cessation, and the Way Going to This – Rather than 'Noble Truths' Concerning These." *Buddhist Studies Review*, 26, pp. 197–222

——2010. "An Analysis of Factors Related to the *Kusala/akusala* Quality of Actions in the Pāli Tradition." *Journal of the International Association of Buddhist Studies*, 33, pp. 175–209

——2013. *An Introduction to Buddhism: Teachings, History and Practices*. 2nd edition. Cambridge, Cambridge University Press

Haskel, P. and R. Abé. 1996. *Zen Master Ryōkan: Poems, Letters and Other Writings*. Honolulu, University of Hawai'i Press

Hayashi, Y. 2003. *Practical Buddhism among the Thai-Lao*. Kyoto, Kyoto University Press

Hayes, R. P. 2000. "A Buddha and his Cousin." In: *The Psychology of Mature Spirituality, Integrity, Wisdom, Transcendence*, ed. P. Young-Eisendrath and M. Millar. London, Routledge, pp. 17–26

Heim, M. 2004. *Theories of the Gift in South Asia: Hindu, Buddhist, and Jain Reflections on Dāna*. New York, Routledge

Heine, S. 1994. *Dōgen and the Kōan Tradition*. Albany, State University of New York Press

——2002. *Opening a Mountain: Kōans of the Zen Masters*. Oxford, Oxford University Press

——2006. *Did Dōgen go to China: What He Wrote and When He Wrote It*. Oxford, Oxford University Press

Heine, S. and C. S. Prebish, eds. 2003. *Buddhism in the Modern World: Adaptations of an Ancient Tradition*. New York, Oxford University Press

Heine, S. and D. S. Wright. 2008. *Zen Ritual: Studies of Zen Buddhist Theory in Practice*. Oxford, Oxford University Press

Heirman, A. 2001. "Chinese Nuns and their Ordination in Fifth Century China." *Journal of the International Association of Buddhist Studies*, 24, pp. 275–304

——2002. *Rules for Nuns According to the Dharmaguptakavinaya: the Discipline in Four Parts*. Delhi, Motilal Banarsidass

Heller, A. 2003. "The Great Protector Deities of the Dalai Lamas." In: Pommaret, 2003, pp. 81–98

Henderson, G. and L. Hurvitz. 1956. "The Buddha of Seiryōji." *Artibus Asiae*, 19, pp. 5–55

Herath, D. 1994. *The Tooth Relic and the Crown*. Colombo, n.p.

Hermann-Pfandt, A. 1992/1993. "Ḍākinīs in Indo-Tibetan Tantric Buddhism: Some Results of Recent Research." *Studies in Central and East Asian Religions*, 5/6, pp. 45–63

Herrigel, E. 1953. *Zen in the Art of Archery*. New York, Pantheon Books

Hicks, R. and Ngakpa Chogyam. 1990. *Great Ocean: An Authorized Biography of the Monk Tenzin Gyatso, His Holiness the Fourteenth Dalai Lama*. London, Penguin Books

Hilton, I. 2000. *The Search for the Panchen Lama.* New York, Norton

Hirakawa, A. 1963. "The Rise of Mahāyāna Buddhism and its Relationship to the Worship of Stupas." *Memoirs of the Research Department of the Toyo Bunko*, 22, pp. 57–106

——1982. *Monastic Discipline for the Buddhist Nuns.* Patna, Jayaswal Research Institute

——1990. *A History of Indian Buddhism: From Śākyamuni to Early Mahāyāna*, trans. P. Groner. Honolulu, University of Hawai'i Press

Hirota, D. 1997. *No Abode: The Record of Ippen.* Honolulu, University of Hawai'i Press

Hocart, A. M. 1923. "Buddha and Devadatta." *Indian Antiquary*, 52, pp. 267–272

Hodge, S. 2003. *The Mahā-Vairocana-Abhisaṃbodhi Tantra with Buddhaguhya's Commentary.* London, RoutledgeCurzon

Holt, J. C. 1981. *Discipline: The Canonical Buddhism of the Vinayapiṭaka.* Delhi, Motilal Banarsidass

——1981a. "Assisting the Dead by Venerating the Living: Merit Transfer in the Early Buddhist Tradition." *Numen*, 28, pp. 1–28

——1991. "Protestant Buddhism?" *Religious Studies Review*, 17, pp. 1–6

——1991a. *Buddha in the Crown: Avalokiteśvara in the Buddhist Traditions of Sri Lanka.* New York, Oxford University Press

——1996. *The Religious World of Kīrti Śrī: Buddhism, Art, and Politics in Late Medieval Sri Lanka.* New York, Oxford Unniversity Press

——2004. "Sri Lanka." In: Buswell, 2004, pp. 795–799

——2004a. *The Buddhist Viṣṇu: Religious Transformation, Politics and Culture.* New York, Columbia University Press

——2009. *Spirits of the Place: Buddhism and Lao Religious Culture.* Honolulu, University of Hawai'i Press

Honda, M. 1968. "Annotated Translation of the Daśabhūmikasūtra." In: *Studies in South, East, and Central Asia*, ed. D. Sinor. New Delhi, International Academy of Indian Culture, pp. 116–276

Hookham, S. K. 1991. *The Buddha Within: Tathāgatagarbha Doctrine According to the Shentong Interpretation of the Ratnagotravibhāga.* Albany, State University of New York Press

Hopkins, J. 1983. *Meditation on Emptiness.* London, Wisdom Publications

Hori, V. S. 1998. "Japanese Zen in America: Americanizing the Face in the Mirror." In: Prebish and Tanaka, 1998, pp. 49–78

——2003. *Zen Sand: The Book of Capping Phrases for Kōan Practice.* Honolulu, University of Hawai'i Press

Horner, I. B. 1936. *The Early Buddhist Theory of Man Perfected.* London, Williams and Norgate

——1938–1952. *The Book of the Discipline.* London, Pali Text Society, 6 vols

——1954–1959. *The Collection of the Middle Length Sayings.* London, Pali Text Society, 3 vols

——1978. *The Clarifier of the Sweet Meaning.* London, Pali Text Society

Horton, S. J. 2007. *Living Buddhist Statues in Early Medieval and Modern Japan.* New York, Palgrave MacMillan

Hosaka, G. 1966. "Āśrava." In: Malalasekera, 1966, vol. 2, pp. 202–214

Hoshino, E. 1997. "Pilgrimage and Peregrination: Contextualizing the Saikoku Junrei and Shikoku Henro." *Japanese Journal of Religious Studies*, 24, pp. 271–299

Houston, G. W. 1980. *Sources for a History of the bSam yas Debate.* Sankt Augustin, V.G.H. Wissenschaftsverlag

Hu Shih. 1953. "Ch'an (Zen) Buddhism in China: Its History and Method." *Philosophy East and West*, 3, pp. 3–24

Hubbard, J. 2001. *Absolute Delusion, Perfect Buddhahood. The Rise and Fall of a Chinese Heresy.* Honolulu, University of Hawai'i Press

Hubbard, J. and P. L. Swanson, eds. 1997. *Pruning the Bodhi Tree: The Storm over Critical Buddhism.* Honolulu, University of Hawai'i Press

Hudson, C. 2005. "Buddhist Meditation: East Asian Buddhist Meditation." In: Jones, 2005, vol. 2, pp. 1290–1295

Huntington, C. W. 1989. *The Emptiness of Emptiness: An Introduction to Early Indian Mādhyamika.* Honolulu, University of Hawai'i Press

Huntington, S. L. 1990. "Early Buddhist Art and the Theory of Aniconism." *Art Journal*, 49, pp. 401–408

——1992. "Aniconism and the Multivalence of Emblems: Another Look." *Ars Orientalis*, 22, pp. 111–156

——2012. *Lay Ritual in the Early Buddhist Art of India: More Evidence against the Aniconic Theory – the J. Gonda Lecture.* Amsterdam, Royal Netherlands Academy of Arts and Sciences

Hur, N. 2000. *Prayer and Play in Late Tokugawa Japan: Asakusa Sensōji and Edo Society.* Cambridge, Harvard University Press

——2007. *Death and Social Order in Tokugawa Japan: Buddhism, Anti-Christianity, and the Danka System.* Cambridge, Harvard University Press

Hurvitz, L. 1962. *Chih-i: An Introduction to the Life and Ideas of a Chinese Buddhist Monk.* Brussels, Mélanges chinois et bouddhiques

——1976. *Scripture of the Lotus Blossom of the Fine Dharma.* New York, Columbia University Press

Hüsken, U. 2000. "Rules, Buddhist (Vinaya): Historical." In: Johnston, 2000, pp. 1088–1091

——2000a. "The Legend of the Establishment of the Buddhist Order of Nuns in the Theravāda Vinaya-Pitaka." *Journal of the Pali Text Society*, 26, pp. 43–69

Idema, W. L. 2008. *Personal Salvation and Filial Piety: Two Precious Scroll Narratives of Guanyin and Her Acolytes.* Honolulu, University of Hawai'i Press

Ingram, P. O. 1997. "The Jewelled Net of Nature." In: Tucker and Williams, 1997, pp. 71–88

Ishii, Y. 1986. *Sangha, State, and Society: Thai Buddhism in History*, trans. P. Hawkes. Honolulu, University of Hawai'i Press

Jackson, R. 2004. "Śūnyatā (Emptiness)." In: Buswell, 2004, pp. 809–810

Jaffe, R. M. 2001. *Neither Monk nor Layman: Clerical Marriage in Modern Japanese Buddhism.* Princeton, Princeton University Press

Jaini, P. S. 2001. *Collected Papers on Buddhist Studies.* Delhi, Motilal Banarsidass

Jayarava (Dharmacārī). 2010. "The Hundred Syllable Vajrasattva Mantra." *Western Buddhist Review*, 5, see: http://www.westernbuddhistreview.com/vol5/index.html

Jayatilleke, K. N. 1963. *Early Buddhist Theories of Knowledge.* London, George Allen and Unwin

Jayawickrama, N. A. 1990. *The Story of Gotama Buddha: The Nidāna-kathā of the Jātakaṭṭhakathā.* Oxford, Pali Text Society

Jerryson, M. K. 2007. *Mongolian Buddhism: The Rise and Fall of the Sangha.* Bangkok, Silkworm

Johnston, E. H. 1936. *The Buddhacarita or Acts of the Buddha.* Calcutta, Baptist Mission Press

——1937. "The Buddha's Mission and Last Journey (Buddhacarita xv to xxviii)." *Acta Orientalia*, 15, pp. 26–62, 85–111, 231–292

Johnston, W. M. ed. 2000. *Encyclopedia of Monasticism.* Chicago, Fitzroy Dearborn Publishers

Jones, J. J. 1949–1956. *The Mahāvastu.* London, Pali Text Society, 3 vols

Joshi, L. 1977. *Studies in the Buddhistic Culture of India*. Delhi, Motilal Banarsidass

Juo-Hsüeh (Bhikkhunī). 2008. "Who is Afraid of Gold and Silver? A Study of the Rule against Monetary Gifts in the Various Vinayas." In: Gombrich and Scherer-Schaub, 2008, pp. 35–95

Kabilsingh, C. 1984. *A Comparative Study of Bhikkhuni Patimokkha*. Varanasi, Chakhambha Orientalia

——1991. *Thai Women in Buddhism*. Berkeley, Parallax Press

Kanaji, I. 1985. "Three Stages in Shōtoku Taishi's Acceptance of Buddhism." *Acta Asiatica*, 47, pp. 31–47

Kapstein, M. T. 2000. *The Tibetan Assimilation of Buddhism: Conversion, Contestation, and Memory*. Oxford, Oxford University Press

——2005. "Buddhism, Schools of: Tibetan and Mongolian Buddhism." In: Jones, 2005, pp. 1022–1029

——2006. *The Tibetans*. Malden, Blackwell

Karlsson, K. 1999. *Face to Face with the Absent Buddha: The Formation of Buddhist Aniconic Art*. Uppsala, Uppsala University

Karmay, S. G. 2003. "The Fifth Dalai Lama and His Reunification of Tibet." In: Pommaret, 2003, pp. 65–80

Karunadasa, Y. n.d. "Theravada Version of the Two Truths." See www.skb.or.kr/down/papers/094.pdf.

Kashiwahara Y. and K. Sonoda, eds. 1994. *Shapers of Japanese Buddhism*. Tokyo, Kosei Publishing

Katz, N. 1982. *Buddhist Images of Human Perfection*. Delhi, Motilal Banarsidass

Kawamura, L. S. 2004. "Bodhisattva(s)." In: Buswell, 2004, pp. 58–60

Kawanami, H. 2010. "The Politics of Gender Identity amongst Buddhist Nuns in Myanmar." In: *Contested Spaces: Citizenship and Belonging in Contemporary Times*, ed. M. Thapan. Hyderabad, Orient Blackswan, pp. 212–229

Keenan, J. P. 1994. *How Master Mou Removes our Doubts*. Albany, State University of New York Press

——2000. *The Scripture on the Explication of Underlying Meaning*. Berkeley, Numata Center

Kemper, S. E. G. 2015. *Rescued from the Nation: Anagarika Dharmapala and the Buddhist World*. Chicago, University of Chicago Press

Kent, A. and D. Chandler, eds. 2008. *People of Virtue: Reconfiguring Religion, Power and Moral Order in Cambodia Today*. Copenhagen, Nordic Institute of Asian Studies

Kent, R. K. 1994. "Depictions of the Guardians of the Law: Lohan Painting in China." In: *Latter Days of the Law: Images of Chinese Buddhism 850–1850*, ed. M. Weidner. Lawrence, Spencer Museum of Art, pp. 183–213

Keown, D., ed. 1999. *Buddhism and Abortion*. Honolulu, University of Hawai'i Press

Kern, H. 1884. *Saddharma-Puṇḍarīka or the Lotus of the True Law*. Oxford, Clarendon Press

——1901. *Histoire du bouddhisme dans l'Inde*, trans. G. Huet. Paris, Ernest Leroux

Ketelaar, J. E. 1990. *Of Heretics and Martyrs in Meiji Japan: Buddhism and its Persecution*. Princeton, Princeton University Press

Keyes, C. F. 1971. "Buddhism and National Integration in Thailand." *Journal of Asian Studies*, 30, pp. 551–567

——1981. "Death of Two Buddhist Saints in Thailand." *Journal of the American Academy of Religion, Thematic Studies*, 48, pp. 151–180

——1983. "Merit-Transference in the Kammic Theory of Popular Theravāda Buddhism." In: *Karma: An Anthropological Inquiry*, ed. C. F. Keyes and E. V. Daniel. Berkeley, University of California Press, pp. 261–286

Khoroche, P. 1989. *Once the Buddha was a Monkey: Ārya Śūra's Jātakamālā*. Chicago, University of Chicago Press

Kidder, J. E. 1972. *Early Buddhist Japan*. New York, Praeger

Kim, H. 1980. *Dōgen Kigen – Mystical Realist*. Tucson, University of Arizona Press

Kim, Y. 1990. *Tao-sheng's Commentary on the Lotus Sūtra*. Albany, State University of New York Press

King, S. B. 1984. "The Buddha Nature: True Self as Action." *Religious Studies*, 20, pp. 255–267

——1991. *Buddha Nature*. Albany, State University of New York Press

King, W. 1986. *Death was his Kōan: The Samurai Zen of Suzuki Shōsan*. Berkeley, Asian Humanities Press

Kiyota, M. 1978. *Shingon Buddhism: Theory and Practice*. Honolulu, University of Hawai'i Press

——ed. 1978a. *Mahāyāna Buddhist Meditation: Theory and Practice*. Honolulu, University of Hawai'I Press

Kloetzli, R. 1983. *Buddhist Cosmology*. Delhi, Motilal Banarsidass

Kloppenborg, R. 1973. *The Sūtra on the Foundation of the Buddhist Order (Catuṣpariṣatsūtra)*. Leiden, E.J. Brill

——1974. *The Paccekabuddha: A Buddhist Ascetic*. Leiden, E.J. Brill

Knox, R. 1992. *Amaravati: Buddhist Sculpture from the Great Stūpa*. London, British Museum

Kodera, T. J. 1980. *Dōgen's Formative Years in China*. London, Routledge and Kegan Paul

Kornfield, J. 1977. *Living Buddhist Masters*. Santa Cruz, Unity Press

Koros, A. C. de. 1982 [1836–1839]. *Analysis of the Kanjur*. Delhi, Sri Satguru Publications

Kuan, T. 2009. "Rethinking Non-Self: A New Perspective from the *Ekottarika-āgama*." *Buddhist Studies Review*, 26, pp. 155–175

Kuitert, W. 2002. *Themes in the History of Japanese Garden Art*. Honolulu, University of Hawai'i Press

Kunsang, E. P. 1993. *The Lotus-Born: The Life of Padmasambhava*. Boston, Shambhala

Kusuma (Bhikkhunī). 2000. "Inaccuracies in Buddhist Women's History." In: *Innovative Buddhist Women: Swimming against the Stream*, ed. K. L. Tsomo. Surrey, Curzon Press, pp. 5–12

Kyaw, P. P. and K. Crosby. 2013. "The Buddha and his Brothers: Expressions of Power, Place and Community by the Network of Mahāmuni Images of Arakan, Bangladesh and Burma." In *Proceedings of the Buddhist Art Forum*, ed. D. Park and K. Wangmo. London, Archetype Publications, pp. 263–274

La Vallée Poussin, L. de. 1908. "Pratyekabuddha." In: *Encyclopaedia of Religion and Ethics*, ed. J. Hastings. New York, Charles Scribner's, vol. 10, pp. 152–154

——1928. "Les neuf kalpas qu'a franchis Śākyamuni pour devancer Maitreya." *T'oung pao*, 26, pp. 17–24

——1936–1937. "Musīla et Nārada: le chemin du Nirvāṇa." *Mélanges chinois et bouddhiquies*, 5, pp. 189–222

——1988–1990. *Abhidharmakośabhāṣyam*, trans. L. M. Pruden. Berkeley, Asian Humanities Press, 4 vols

LaFleur, W. R. 1992. *Liquid Life: Abortion and Buddhism in Japan*. Princeton, Princeton University Press

Lai, W. 1982. "Sinitic Speculations on Buddha-Nature: The Nirvāṇa School." *Philosophy East and West*, 32, pp. 135–149

Lai, W. and L. Lancaster, eds. 1983. *Early Ch'an in China and Tibet*. Berkeley, Asian Humanities Press

Lai, W. W. 1981. "The Predocetic 'Finite Buddhakāya' in the Lotus Sutra." *Journal of the American Academy of Religion*, 49, pp. 447–469

Lamotte, E. 1935–1936. "Le traité de l'acte de Vasubandhu: Karmasiddhiprakaraṇa." *Mélanges chinois et bouddhiques*, 4, pp. 151–288

——1949–1980. *Le traité de la grande vertu de sagesse.* Louvain, Institut Orientaliste, 5 vols

——1954. "Sur la formation du Mahāyāna." In: *Asiatica: Festschrift Friedrich Weller*, ed. J. Schubert and U. Schneider. Leipzig, Otto Harrassowitz, pp. 48–69

——1988. *History of Indian Buddhism*, trans. S. Webb-Boin. Louvain-la-neuve, Institut Orientaliste

Lamrim Chenmo Translation Committee. 2000–2004. *The Great Treatise on the Stages of the Path.* Ithaca, Snow Lion Publications

Lancaster, L. R. 1974. "An Early Mahāyāna Sermon about the Body of the Buddha and the Making of Images." *Artibus Asiae*, 36, pp. 287–291

——2005. "Buddhist Books and Texts: Canon and Canonization." In: Jones, 2005, pp. 1251–1258

Lane-Suzuki, B. 1923. "Fudō the Immovable." *Eastern Buddhist*, 2, pp. 126–153

Lang, K. 2004. "Madhyamaka School." In: Buswell, 2004, pp. 479–485

Larsen, K. and A. Sinding-Larsen. 2001. *The Lhasa Atlas: Traditional Tibetan Architecture and Townscape.* Boston, Shambhala

Lati Rinbochay and J. Hopkins. 1979. *Death, Intermediate State and Rebirth in Tibetan Buddhism.* London, Rider

Law, B. C. 1923. *The Life and Work of Buddhaghosa.* Calcutta, Thacker, Spink and Co.

——1924. *Designation of Human Types.* London, Pali Text Society

——1952. *The History of the Buddha's Religion (Sāsanavaṃsa).* Delhi, Sri Satguru Publications

Ledderose, L. 2004. "Carving Sutras into Stone before the Catastrophe: The Inscription of 1118 at Cloud Dwelling Monastery near Beijing." *Proceedings of the British Academy*, 125, pp. 381–454

Lee, K. D. Y. 2007. *The Prince and the Monk: Shōtoku Worship in Shinran's Buddhism.* Albany, State University of New York Press

Lefferts, L., S. Cate and W. Tossa. 2013. *Buddhist Storytelling in Thailand and Laos: The Vessantara Jataka Scroll at the Asian Civilisations Museum.* Singapore, Asian Civilisations Museum

Legge, J. 1886. *A Record of Buddhistic Kingdoms.* Reprint edition. New York, Paragon Books

Legittimo, E. I. 2009. "The Case of Bakkula According to the Chinese Ekottarikāgama." *Indian International Journal of Buddhist Studies*, 10, pp. 91–103

Lenz, T. 2003. *A New Version of the Gāndhārī Dharmapada and a Collection of Previous-Birth Stories.* Seattle, University of Washington Press

Leoshko, J. ed. 1988. *Bodhgaya, the Site of Enlightenment.* Bombay, Marg Publications

Lessing, F. D. and A. Wayman. 1978. *Introduction to the Buddhist Tantrica Systems.* Delhi, Motilal Banarsidass

Lévi, S. and E. Chavannes. 1916. "Les seize arhat protecteurs de la loi." *Journal asiatique*, 8, pp. 5–48, 189–304

LeVine, S. 2001. "The Finances of a Twentieth Century Buddhist Mission: Building Support for the Theravāda Nuns' Order of Nepal." *Journal of the International Association of Buddhist Studies*, 24, pp. 217–240

LeVine, S. and D. N. Gellner. 2005. *Rebuilding Buddhism: The Theravada Movement in Twentieth-Century Nepal.* Cambridge, Harvard University Press

LeVine, S. and Morgan Bay Zendō. 2008. *A Brief History of Moonspring Hermitage*, ed. H. Curran and S. Guilford. Surry, ME, Morgan Bay Zendo

Lévy, P. 1968. *Buddhism: A "Mystery Religion"?* New York, Schocken Books

Lewis, T. T. ed. 2014. *Buddhists: Understanding Buddhism through the Lives of Practitioners.* Chichester, Wiley Blackwell

——2014a. "Two Noted Householders of the Buddha's Time: Upasika Vishakha and Upasak Anathapindika." In: Lewis, 2014, pp. 29–38

Lewis, T. T. and S. M. Tuladhar. 2010. *Sugata Saurabha: An Epic Poem from Nepal on the Life of the Buddha, by Chittadhar Hṛdaya.* Oxford, Oxford University Press

Li, R. 1961. *The Sixteen Arhats and the Eighteen Arhats.* Beijing, Buddhist Association of China

——1993. *The Biographical Scripture of King Aśoka.* Berkeley, Numata Center

——1995. *A Biography of the Tripiṭaka Master of the Great Ci'en Monastery of the Great Tang Dynasty.* Berkeley, Numata Center

——1996. *The Great Tang Dynasty Record of the Western Regions.* Berkeley, Numata Center

Likhitpreechakul, P. 2011. "The Legend of the Earth Goddess and the Buddha." *Journal of the Oxford Centre for Buddhist Studies,* 1, pp. 108–113

Lin, W.-C. 2014. *Building a Sacred Mountain: The Buddhist Architecture of China's Mount Wutai.* Seattle, University of Washington Press

Lindtner, C. 1986. *Master of Wisdom: Writings of the Buddhist Master Nāgārjuna.* Oakland, Dharma Publishing

Ling, T. 1980. *Buddhist Revival in India: Aspects of the Sociology of Buddhism.* London, MacMillan

Linrothe, R. 1999. *Ruthless Compassion: Wrathful Deities in Early Indo-Tibetan Esoteric Buddhist Art.* Boston, Shambhala

Liu, M.-W. 1982. "The Doctrine of the Buddha-Nature in the Mahāyāna *Mahāparinirvāṇa Sūtra.*" *Journal of the International Association of Buddhist Studies,* 5, pp. 63–94

——1984. "The Problem of the *Icchantika* in the Mahāyāna *Mahāparinirvāṇa Sūtra.*" *Journal of the International Association of Buddhist Studies,* 7, pp. 57–82

——1994. *Madhyamaka Thought in China.* Leiden, E.J. Brill

Lopez, D. S. 1987. *A Study of Svātantrika.* Ithaca, Snow Lion Publications

——1988. *The Heart Sūtra Explained: Indian and Tibetan Commentaries.* Albany, State University of New York Press

——ed. 1995. *Buddhism in Practice.* Princeton, Princeton University Press

——ed. 1995a. *Religions of India in Practice.* Princeton, Princeton University Press

——ed. 1995b. *Curators of the Buddha.* Chicago, University of Chicago Press

——1996. *Elaborations on Emptiness: Uses of the Heart Sūtra.* Princeton, Princeton University Press

——ed. 1996a. *Religions of China in Practice.* Princeton, Princeton University Press

——1998. *Prisoners of Shangri-La: Tibetan Buddhism and the West.* Chicago, University of Chicago Press

——ed. 2005. *Critical Terms for the Study of Buddhism.* Chicago, University of Chicago Press

——2011. *The Tibetan Book of the Dead: A Biography.* Princeton, Princeton University Press

Luce, G. H. 1969–1970. *Old Burma – Early Pagan.* Ascona, Artibus Asiae (Supplementum 25), 3 vols

Luczanits, C. 2010. "Prior to Birth: The Tuṣita Episodes in Indian Buddhist Literature and Art." In: Cueppers, Deeg and Durt, 2010, pp. 41–92

Lugli, L. 2014. "Asanga," In: *Oxford Bibliographies On Line – Buddhism.* http://www.oxfordbibliographies.com

Lusthaus, D. 1998. "The Chinese Buddhist Schools: Tiantai." *Routledge Encyclopedia of Philosophy.* London, Routledge, see http://www.rep.Routledgecom/article/G002SECT7

——1998a. "Buddhist Philosophy – Chinese." *Routledge Encyclopedia of Philosophy.* London, Routledge, see http://www.rep.Routledgecom/article/G002SECT7
——2004. "Yogācāra School." In: Buswell, 2004, pp. 914–921
Machacek, D. and B. Wilson, eds. 2000. *Global Citizens: The Sokagakkai Buddhist Movement in the World.* Oxford, Oxford University Press
Machida, S. 1999. *Renegade Monk: Hōnen and Japanese Pure Land Tradition.* Berkeley, University of California Press
MacQueen, G. 1981. "Inspired Speech in Early Mahāyāna I." *Religion*, 11, pp. 309–319
MacWilliams, M. 1995. "Buddhist Pilgrim/Buddhist Exile: Old and New Images of Retired Emperor Kazan in the Saigoku Kannon Temple Guidebooks." *History of Religions*, 34, pp. 303–328
Mair, V. H. 1983. *Tun-huang Popular Narratives.* Cambridge, Cambridge University Press
Malalasekera, G. P. 1960. *Dictionary of Pali Proper Names.* London, Pali Text Society, 2 vols
——ed. 1966. *Encyclopaedia of Buddhism.* Colombo, Government Press
Marston, J. and E. Guthrie. 2004. *History, Buddhism, and New Religious Movements in Cambodia.* Honolulu, University of Hawai'i Press
Matics, M. L. 1970. *Entering the Path of Enlightenment.* New York, MacMillan
Matsunaga, D. and A. Matsunaga. 1976. *Foundations of Japanese Buddhism.* Los Angeles, Buddhist Books International, 2 vols
McCallum, D. F. 1994. *Zenkōji and its Icon: A Study in Medieval Japanese Religious Art.* Princeton, Princeton University Press
——1998. "The Replication of Miraculous Images: The Zenkoji Amida and the Seiryoji Shaka." In: *Images, Miracles and Authority in Asian Religious Traditions*, ed. R. H. Davis. Boulder, Westview Press, pp. 207–226
——2009. *The Four Great Temples: Buddhist Archaeology, Architecture, and Icons of Seventh-Century Japan.* Honolulu, University of Hawai'i Press
McCullough, H. C. 1988. *The Tale of the Heike.* Stanford, Stanford University Press
McDaniel, J. T. 2011. *The Lovelorn Ghost and the Magical Monk: Practicing Buddhism in Modern Thailand.* New York, Columbia University Press
McDermott, J. P. 1984. *Development of the Early Buddhist Concept of Kamma/Karma.* Delhi, Motilal Banarsidass
——1984a. "Scripture as the Word of the Buddha." *Numen*, 31, pp. 22–39
McGovern, W. M. 1923. *A Manual of Buddhist Philosophy: Cosmology.* London, Kegan Paul
McMahan, D. L., ed. 2012. *Buddhism in the Modern World.* London, Routledge
——2013. "Meditation." *Oxford Bibliographies on Line – Buddhism.* (http://www.oxfordbibliographies.com)
McMullin, N. 1984. *Buddhism and the State in Sixteenth Century Japan.* Princeton, Princeton University Press
McRae, J. R. 1986. *The Northern School and the Formation of Early Ch'an Buddhism.* Honolulu, University of Hawai'i Press
——1987. "Shen-hui and the Teaching of Sudden Enlightenment in Early Ch'an Buddhism." In: Gregory, 1987, pp. 225–278
——1988. "Ch'an Commentaries on the Heart Sūtra." *Journal of the International Association of Buddhist Studies*, 11, pp. 87–115
——2000. *The Platform Sutra of the Sixth Patriarch.* Berkeley, Numata Center
——2003. *Seeing through Zen.* Berkeley, University of California Press
——2005. "Daoxuan's Vision of Jetavana: The Ordination Platform Movement in Medieval Chinese Buddhism." In: *Going Forth: Visions of Buddhist Vinaya*, ed. W. M. Bodiford. Honolulu, University of Hawai'i Press, pp. 68–100

——2005a. "Essentials of the Transmission of Mind." In: *Zen Texts*, ed. J. R. McRae. Berkeley, Numata Center, pp. 1–42

——2005b. "Buddhism: Schools of Chinese Buddhism." In: Jones, 2005, pp. 1235–1241

Meadows, C. 1986. *Āryaśūra's Compendium of the Perfections*. Bonn, Indica et Tibetica Verlag

Mendelson, E. M. 1961. "A Messianic Buddhist Association in Upper Burma." *Bulletin of the School of Oriental and African Studies*, 24, pp. 560–580

——1975. *Sangha and State in Burma: A Study of Monastic Sectarianism and Leadership*. Ithaca, Cornell University Press

Mettanando (Bhikkhu) and O. Von Hinüber. 2000 "The Cause of the Buddha's Death." *Journal of the Pali Text Society*, 26, pp. 105–117

Midal, F. 2004. *Chögyam Trungpa: His Life and Vision*, trans. I. Monk. Boston, Shambhala

Miksic, J. 1999. *The Mysteries of Borobudur*. Hongkong, Periplus

Mills, M. A. 2003. *Identity, Ritual and State in Tibetan Buddhism: The Foundations of Authority in Gelukpa Monasticism*. London, RoutledgeCurzon

Mitra, K. 1924. "Cross-Cousin Relation between Buddha and Devadatta." *Indian Antiquary*, 53, pp. 125–128

Moerman, D. M. 2005. *Localizing Paradise: Kumano Pilgrimage and the Religious Landscape of Premodern Japan*. Cambridge, Harvard University Press

——2010. "The Death of the Dharma: Sutra Burials in Early Medieval Japan." In: *The Death of Sacred Texts: Ritual Disposal and Renovation of Texts in the World Religions*, ed. K. Myrvold. Aldershot, Ashgate, pp. 71–90

Molesworth, K. and U. Müller-Böker. 2005. "The Local Impact of Under-Realisation of the Lumbinī Master Plan: A Field Report." *Contributions to Nepalese Studies*, 32, pp. 183–211

Mollier, C. 2008. *Buddhism and Taoism Face to Face: Scripture, Ritual, and Iconographic Exchange in Medieval China*. Honolulu, University of Hawai'i Press

Morrell, R. E. 1987. *Early Kamakura Buddhism: A Minority Report*. Berkeley, Asian Humanities Press

Mrozicki, K. n.d. "Surry Opera Company." http://surry.mainememory.net/page/3427/display.html

Mukpo, D. J. 2006. *Dragon Thunder: My Life with Chögyam Trungpa*. Boston, Shambhala

Mullin, G. H. 1999. *Gems of Wisdom from the Seventh Dalai Lama*. Ithaca, Snow Lion Publications

Mullins, M. R., S. Susumu and P. L. Swanson, eds. 1993. *Religion and Society in Modern Japan*. Berkeley, Asian Humanities Press

Murcott, S. 1991. *The First Buddhist Women*. Berkeley, Parallax Press

Mus, P. 1998. *Barabuḍur: Sketch of a History of Buddhism Based on Archaeological Criticsm of the Texts*, trans. A. W. Macdonald. New Delhi, Indira Gandhi National Centre for the Arts

Mutsu, I. 1930. *Kamakura, Fact and Legend*. Tokyo, Times Publishing Co.

Nakamura, H. 1977. *Gotama Buddha*. Los Angeles, Buddhist Books International

Ñāṇamoli (Bhikkhu). 1960. *The Minor Readings (Khuddakapāṭha)*. Oxford, Pali Text Society

——1976. *The Path of Purification*. Boulder, Shambhala, 2 vols

Ñāṇamoli (Bhikkhu) and Bodhi (Bhikkhu). 1995. *The Middle Length Discourses of the Buddha: A Translation of the Majjhima Nikāya*. Boston, Wisdom Publications

Narada (Thera). 1962. *Discourse on the Elements*. London, Pali Text Society

——1969–1981. *Conditional Relations*. London, Pali Text Society, 2 vols

Narula, K. S. 1994. *Voyage of the Emerald Buddha*. Kuala Lumpur, Oxford Unversity Press

Nattier, J. 1991. *Once Upon a Future Time: Studies in a Buddhist Prophecy of Decline*. Berkeley, Asian Humanities Press

——1992. "The Heart Sūtra: A Chinese Apocryphal Text." *Journal of the International Association of Buddhist Studies*, 15, pp. 153–223

——2000. "The Realm of Akṣobhya: A Missing Piece in the History of Pure Land Buddhism." *Journal of the International Association of Buddhist Studies*, 23, pp. 71–102

——2003. *A Few Good Men: The Bodhisattva Path According to the Inquiry of Ugra (Ugraparipṛcchā)*. Honolulu, University of Hawai'i Press

——2004. "Buddha(s)." In: Buswell, 2004, pp. 71–74

——2007. "Indian Antecedents of Huayan Thought: New Light from Chinese Sources." In: Hamar, 2007, pp. 109–138

Nattier, J. and C. Prebish. 1977. "Mahāsāṃghika Origins: The Beginnings of Buddhist Sectarianism." *History of Religions*, 16, pp. 237–272

Nebesky-Wojkowitz, R. 1993. *Oracles and Demons of Tibet*. Kathmandu, Tiwari's Pilgrims Book House

Newland, G. 1992. *The Two Truths in the Mādhyamika Philosophy of the Ge-luk-ba Order of Tibetan Buddhism*. Ithaca, Snow Lion Publications

——1996. "Debate Manuals (Yig Cha) in dGe lugs Monastic Colleges." In: Cabezón and Jackson, 1996, pp. 202–216

Nguyen, C. T. 1997. *Zen in Medieval Vietnam*. Honolulu, University of Hawai'i Press

——2004. "Vietnam." In: Buswell, 2004, pp. 879–883

Nguyen, T. T., ed. 1997. *History of Buddhism in Vietnam*. Washington, Council for Research in Values and Philosophy

Nietupski, P. K. 2009. "Guṇaprabha's *Vinayasūtra* Corpus: Texts and Contexts." *Journal of the International Association of Tibetan Studies*, 5 (http://www.thlib.org/collections/texts/jiats/#!jiats=/05/nietupski/)

Nikam, N. A. and R. McKeon. 1959. *The Edicts of Aśoka*. Chicago, University of Chicago Press

Nishimura, S. 1985. "The Prince and the Pauper: The Dynamics of a Shōtoku Legend." *Monumenta Nipponica*, 40, pp. 299–310

Norman, K. R. 1969. *The Elders' Verses I: Theragāthā*. London, Pali Text Society

——1983. "The Pratyeka-Buddha in Buddhism and Jainism." In: *Buddhist Studies, Ancient and Modern*, ed. P. Denwood. London, Curzon, pp. 92–106

——1995. *The Elders' Verses II: Therīgāthā*. Oxford, Pali Text Society

——1996. *The Rhinoceros Horn and Other Early Buddhist Poems*. Oxford, Pali Text Society

Notton, C. 1933. *P'ra Buddha Sihinga*. Bangkok, Bangkok Times Press

——1933a. *The Chronicle of the Emerald Buddha*. Bangkok, Bangkok Times Press

Nyanaponika, T. and H. Hecker. 1997. *Great Disciples of the Buddha*. Boston, Wisdom Publications

Nyanasampanno, M. B. 1976. *The Venerable Phra Acharn Mun Bhuridatta Thera, Meditation Master*, trans. S. Buddhasukh. Bangkok, Mahamakut Press

Nyaupane, G. P. 2009. "Heritage, Complexity and Tourism: The Case of Lumbinī Nepal." *Journal of Heritage Tourism*, 4, pp. 157–172

Obermiller, E. 1931. *History of Buddhism (Chos-hbyung) by Bu-ston*. Heidelberg, Otto Harrassowitz

Obeyesekere, R. 2009. *Yasodharā, the Wife of the Bōdhisattva*. Albany, State University of New York Press

Ohnuma, R. 2006. "Debt to the Mother: A Neglected Aspect of the Founding of the Buddhist Nuns' Order." *Journal of the American Academy of Religion*, 74, pp. 861–891

——2007. *Head, Eyes, Flesh, and Blood: Giving Away the Body in Indian Buddhist Literature.* New York, Columbia University Press

——2012. *Ties that Bind: Maternal Imagery and Discourse in Indian Buddhism.* Oxford, Oxford University Press

Oldenberg, H. 1982 [1879]. *The Dīpavaṃsa: An Ancient Buddhist Historical Record.* Reprint edition. New Delhi, Asian Educational Services

Olivelle, P. 1996. *The Upaniṣads.* Oxford, Oxford University Press

Omvedt, G. 2003. *Buddhism in India: Challenging Brahmanism and Caste.* New Delhi, Sage Publications

Orzech, C. D. 1998. *Politics and Transcendent Wisdom: The Scripture for Humane Kings in the Creation of Chinese Buddhism.* Albany, State University of New York Press

Overmyer, D. L. 1976. *Folk Buddhist Religion: Dissenting Sects in Late Traditional China.* Cambridge, Harvard University Press

——1988. "Messenger, Savior, and Revolutionary: Maitreya in Chinese Popular Religious Literature of the Sixteenth and Seventeenth Centuries." In: Sponberg and Hardacre, 1988, pp. 110–134

Panditha, V. 1954/1955. "Buddhism in the Polonnaruva Period." *Ceylon Historical Journal* [Special Issue on the Polonnaruva Period] 4, pp. 113–129

Pannapadipo, P. (Phra). 1997. *Phra Farang: An English Monk in Thailand.* London, Arrow Books

——2001. *Little Angels: Life as a Novice Monk in Thailand.* London, Arrow Books

Pannasiri (Bhikkhu). 1950. "Sigālovāda-sutta." *Visva-Bharati Annals*, 3, pp. 150–228

Parkes, G. 1997. "Voices of Mountains, Trees, and Rivers: Kūkai, Dōgen, and a Deeper Ecology." In: Tucker and Williams, 1997, pp. 111–125

Pas, J. 1995. *Visions of Sukhāvatī.* Albany, State University of New York Press

Paul, D. 1979. *Women in Buddhism.* Berkeley, Asian Humanities Press

——2004. "The Sutra of Queen Śrīmālā of the Lion's Roar." In: *The Sutra of Queen Śrīmālā of the Lion's Roar [and] The Vimalakīrti Sutra.* Berkeley, Numata Center, pp. 1–61

Payne, R. K., ed. 1998. *Re-Visioning "Kamakura" Buddhism.* Honolulu, University of Hawai'i Press

Penner, H. H. 2009. *Rediscovering the Buddha: Legends of the Buddha and their Interpretation.* Oxford, Oxford University Press

Perera, H. 1966. "Akṣobhya." In: Malalasekera, 1966, vol. 1, pp. 363–366

Pittman, D. A. 2001. *Towards a Modern Buddhism: Taixu's Reforms.* Honolulu, University of Hawai'i Press

Plutschow, H. E. 1983. *Historical Kyoto.* Tokyo, Japan Times

Poceski, M. 2004. "China." In: Buswell, 2004, pp. 139–145

——2004a. "Huayan School." In: Buswell, 2004, pp. 341–347

Pommaret, F., ed. 2003. *Lhasa in the Seventeenth Century: The Capital of the Dalai Lamas*, trans. H. Solverson. Leiden, E.J. Brill

Powers, J. 1995. *Wisdom of Buddha: The Saṃdhinirmocana-sūtra.* Berkeley, Dharma Publishing

——2007. *Introduction to Tibetan Buddhism.* Ithaca, Snow Lion Publications

——2009. *A Bull of a Man: Images of Masculinity, Sex, and the Body in Indian Buddhism.* Cambridge, Harvard University Press

Pranke, P. 2004. "Myanmar." In: Buswell, 2004, pp. 574–578

Prasad, H. S., ed. 1991. *Essays on Time in Buddhism.* Delhi, Sri Satguru Publications

Pratt, J. B. 1928. *The Pilgrimage of Buddhism and a Buddhist Pilgrimage.* New York, MacMillan

Prebish, C. S. 1994. *A Survey of Vinaya Literature.* Taipei, Jin Luen Publishing

——1996. *Buddhist Monastic Discipline: The Sanskrit Prātimokṣa Sūtras of the Mahāsāṃghikas and Mūlasarvāstivādins.* Delhi, Motilal Banarsidass
——2004. "Councils, Buddhist." In: Buswell, 2004, pp. 187–189
Prebish, C. S. and D. Keown. 2006. *Introducing Buddhism.* New York, Routledge
Prebish, C. S. and K. K. Tanaka, eds. 1998. *The Faces of Buddhism in America.* Berkeley, University of California Press
Priestley, L. C. D. C. 1999. *Pudgalavāda Buddhism: The Reality of the Indeterminate Self.* Toronto, Centre for South Asian Studies
Prip-Moller, J. 1967. *Chinese Buddhist Monasteries: Their Plan and its Function as a Setting for Buddhist Monastic Life.* 2nd edition. Hongkong, Hongkong University Press
Pruitt, W. 1998. *The Commentary on the Verses of the Therīs.* Oxford, Pali Text Society
Przyluski, J. 1926. *Le concile de Rājagṛha.* Paris, Paul Geuthner, 2 vols
Pye, M. 1978. *Skilful Means: A Concept in Mahayana Buddhism.* London, Duckworth
Queen, C. 1996. "Dr. Ambedkar and the Hermeneutics of Buddhist Liberation." In: Queen and King, 1996, pp. 45–72
——ed. 2000. *Engaged Buddhism in the West.* Boston, Wisdom Publications
Queen, C. S. and S. B. King, eds. 1996. *Engaged Buddhism: Buddhist Liberation Movements in Asia.* Albany, State University of New York Press
Quintman, A. 2004. "Karma pa." In: Buswell, 2004, pp. 417–419
——2010. *The Life of Milarepa [by] Tsangnyön Heruka.* New York, Penguin Books
Rabten (Geshe). 1984. *Essential Nectar: Meditations on the Buddhist Path,* trans. M. Willson. London, Wisdom Publications
Radich, M. 2007. "The Somatics of Liberation: Ideas about Embodiment in Buddhism from Its Origins to the Fifth Century C.E." Ph.D. dissertation, Harvard University
——2010. "Embodiments of the Buddha in Sarvāstivāda Doctrine: With Special Reference to the *Mahāvibhāṣā.*" *Annual Report of the International Research Institute for Advanced Buddhology at Soka University,* 13, pp. 121–172
Rahula, W. 1956. *History of Buddhism in Ceylon: The Anurādhapura Period.* Colombo, M.D. Gunasena
——1959. *What the Buddha Taught.* New York, Grove Press
Rajadhon, P. A. 2009. *Essays on Thai Folklore.* 3rd edition. Bangkok, Institute of Thai Studies, Chulalongkorn University
Rajakaruna, F. M. 1972. *The World's True Welfare: The Lōväḍa Sangarāva – A Didactic Poem of the 15th Century from Sri Lanka by the Venerable Vīdāgama Maitreya.* Kandy, Buddhist Publication Society
Rambelli, F. 2001. *Vegetal Buddhas: Ideological Effects of Japanese Buddhist Doctrines on the Salvation of Inanimate Beings.* Kyoto, Scuola Italiana di Studi sull'Asia Orientale
——2007. *Buddhist Materiality: A Cultural History of Objects in Japanese Buddhism.* Stanford, Stanford University Press
Ray, N.-R. 1936. *Sanskrit Buddhism in Burma.* Amsterdam, H.J. Paris
Ray, R. A. 1994. *Buddhist Saints in India: A Study in Buddhist Values and Orientation.* New York, Oxford University Press
——1997. "Nāgārjuna's Longevity." In: Schober, 1997, pp. 129–159
Reader, I. 2005. *Making Pilgrimages: Meaning and Practice in Shikoku.* Honolulu, University of Hawai'i Press
Reed, B. E. 1992. "The Gender Symbolism of Kuan-yin Bodhisattva." In: Cabezón, 1992, pp. 159–180
Reynolds, C. 1970. *An Anthology of Sinhalese Literature up to 1815.* London, Allen and Unwin
Reynolds, F. E. 1972. "The Two Wheels of Dhamma: A Study of Early Buddhism." In:

The Two Wheels of Dhamma: Essays on the Theravada Tradition in India and Ceylon, ed. B. L. Smith. Chambersburg, American Academy of Religion, pp. 6–30

——1978. "The Holy Emerald Jewel: Some Aspects of Buddhist Symbolism and Political Legitimation in Thailand and Laos." In: Smith, 1978a, pp. 175–193

——1997. "Rebirth Traditions and the Lineages of Gotama: A Study in Theravāda Buddhology." In: Schober, 1997, pp. 17–39

Rhi, J. 1991. "Gandhāran Images of the 'Śrāvastī Miracle': An Iconographic Reassessment." Ph.D. dissertation, University of California at Berkeley

——2010. "The Birth of the Buddha in Korean Buddhism: Infant Buddha Images and the Ritual Bathing." In: Cueppers, Deeg and Durt, 2010, pp. 321–344

Ricca, F. and E. L. Bue. 1993. *The Great Stupa of Gyantse: A Complete Tibetan Pantheon of the Fifteenth Century*. London, Serindia Publications

Richardson, H. 1986. *Adventures of a Tibetan Fighting Monk*, ed. T. Skorupski. Bangkok, Tamarind Press

——1993. *Ceremonies of the Lhasa Year*. London, Serindia Publications

Ritzinger, J. and M. Bingenheimer. 2006. "Whole Body Relics and Chinese Buddhism – Previous Research and Historical Overview." *Indian International Journal of Buddhist Studies*, 7, pp. 37–94

Robinson, R. H. 1976. *Early Mādhyamika in India and China*. Delhi, Motilal Banarsidass

Robinson, R. H., W. L. Johnson and Thanissaro (Bhikkhu). 2005. *Buddhist Religions: A Historical Introduction*. 5th edition. Belmont, CA, Thomson Wadsworth

Robson, J. 2009. *Power of Place: The Religious Landscape of the Southern Sacred Peak (Nanyue 南嶽) in Medieval China*. Cambridge, Harvard University Press

Roccasalvo, J. F. 1980. "The Debate at bSam yas: A Study in Religious Contrast and Correspondence." *Philosophy East and West*, 30, pp. 505–520

Rockhill, W. W. 1907. *The Life of the Buddha*. London, Kegan Paul, Trench, Trübner

Rodd, L. R. 1980. *Nichiren: Selected Writings*. Honolulu, University of Hawai'i Press

Roerich, G. 1959. *Biography of Dharmasvāmin, a Tibetan Monk Pilgrim*. Patna, K.P. Jayaswal Research Institute

Rogers, M. L. and A. T. Rogers. 1991. *Rennyo: The Second Founder of Shin Buddhism*. Berkeley, Asian Humanities Press

Rotman, A. 2008. *Divine Stories: Divyāvadāna, Part I*. Boston, Wisdom Publications

——2009. *Thus Have I Seen: Visualizing Faith in Early Indian Buddhism*. Oxford, Oxford University Press

Ruegg, D. S. 1966. *The Life of Bu ston Rinpoche*. Rome, Istituto Italiano per il Medio ed Estreme Oriente

——1980. "Ahiṃsā and Vegetarianism in the History of Buddhism." In: *Buddhist Studies in Honour of Walpola Rahula*, ed. S. Balasooriya et al. London, Gordon Fraser, pp. 234–241

——1981. *The Literature of the Madhyamaka School of Philosophy in India*. Wiesbaden, Otto Harrassowitz

——1992. *Buddha-nature, Mind and the Problem of Gradualism in a Comparative Perspective*. New Delhi, Heritage Publishers

Rugola, P. F. 1986. "Japanese Buddhist Art in Context: The Saikoku Kannon Pilgrimage Route." Ph.D. dissertation, Ohio State University

Ruppert, B. D. 2000. *Jewel in the Ashes: Buddha Relics and Power in Early Medieval Japan*. Cambridge, Harvard University Press

Sadakata, A. 1997. *Buddhist Cosmology: Philosophy and Origins*. Tokyo, Kōsei Publishing

Saddhatissa, H. 1975. *The Birth-Stories of the Ten Bodhisattas and the Dasabodhisattuppattikathā*. London, Pali Text Society

Sakuma, H. 2013. "Remarks on the Lineage of the Indian Masters of the Yogācāra school: Maitreya, Asaṅga, and Vasubandhu." In: *The Foundation for Yoga Practitioners: The Buddhist Yogācārabhūmi Treatise and its Adaptations in India, East Asia and Tibet*, ed. U. T. Kragh. Cambridge, Harvard University Press, pp. 330–366
Samuel, G. 1993. *Civilized Shamans: Buddhism in Tibetan Societies*. Washington, Smithsonian Institution
Sanford, J. H. 1981. *Zen-Man Ikkyū*. Chico, Scholars' Press
Sangharakshita. 1986. *Ambedkar and Buddhism*. Glasgow, Windhorse Publications
Sarao, K. T. S. 2010. *Urban Centres and Urbanisation as Reflected in the Pāli Vinaya and Sutta Piṭakas*. New Delhi, Munshiram Manoharlal
Sarkisyanz, E. 1965. *Buddhist Backgrounds of the Burmese Revolution*. The Hague, M. Nijhoff
Sasaki, S. 1992. "Buddhist Sects of the Aśoka Period (2) – Saṃghabheda (1)." *Bukkyō Kenkyū/ Buddhist Studies* (Hamamatsu) 21, pp. 157–176
Sasson, V. R. 2007. *The Birth of Moses and the Buddha: A Paradigm for the Comparative Study of Religions*. Sheffield, Sheffield Phoenix Press
——2009. "A Womb with a View: The Buddha's Final Fetal Experience." In: *Imagining the Fetus*, ed. V. R. Sasson and J. M. Law. Oxford, Oxford University Press, pp. 55–72
——2013. "The Buddha's 'Childhood'." In: Sasson, 2013a, pp. 75–96
——ed. 2013a. *Little Buddhas: Children and Childhood in Buddhist Texts and Traditions*. Oxford, Oxford University Press
Sawada, J. A. 1993. *Confucian Values and Popular Zen: Sekimon Shingaku in Eighteenth-Century Japan*. Honolulu, University of Hawai'i Press
Schlütter, M. 2008. *How Zen became Zen: The Dispute over Enlightenment and the Formation of Chan Buddhism in Song Dynasty China*. Honolulu, University of Hawai'i Press
Schober, J., ed. 1997. *Sacred Biography in the Buddhist Traditions of South and Southeast Asia*. Honolulu, University of Hawai'i Press
——1997a. "Buddhist Just Rule and Burmese National Culture: State Patronage of the Chinese Tooth Relic in Myanma." *History of Religions*, 36, pp. 218–243
——1997b. "In the Presence of the Buddha: Ritual Veneration of the Burmese Mahāmuni Image." In: Schober, 1997, pp. 259–288
——2011. *Modern Buddhist Conjunctures in Myanmar*. Honolulu, University of Hawai'i Press
Schoening, J. D. 1996. "Sūtra Commentaries in Tibetan Translation." In: Cabezón and Jackson, 1996, pp. 111–124
Schopen, G. 1975. "The Phrase 'sa pṛthivīpradeśaś caityabhūto bhavet' in the Vajracchedikā: Notes on the Cult of the Book in Mahāyāna." *Indo-Iranian Journal*, 17, pp. 147–181
——1997. *Bones, Stones and Buddhist Monks*. Honolulu, University of Hawai'i Press
——2000. "Hierarchy and Housing in a Buddhist Monastic Code: A Translation of the Sanskrit Text of the *Śayanāsanavastu* of the *Mūlasarvāstivāda-vinaya* – Part One." *Buddhist Literature*, 2, pp. 92–196
——2004. "Mahāyāna." In: Buswell, 2004, pp. 492–499
——2004a. "Mūlasarvāstivāda-Vinaya." In: Buswell, 2004, pp. 572–573
——2004b. *Buddhist Monks and Business Matters: Still More Papers on Monastic Buddhism in India*. Honolulu, University of Hawai'i Press
——2005. *Figments and Fragments of Mahāyāna Buddhism in India: More Collected Papers*. Honolulu, University of Hawai'i Press
Seager, R. H. 1999. *Buddhism in America*. New York, Columbia University Press
Scheible, K. 2014. "The Female Householder Mallika." In: Lewis, 2014, pp. 13–20
Senart, E. 1882. *Essai sur la légende du Buddha*. Paris, E. Leroux
Seneviratne, H. L. 1978. *Rituals of the Kandyan State*. London, Cambridge University Press

Shahar, M. 2008. *The Shaolin Monastery: History, Religion, and the Chinese Martial Arts.* Honolulu, University of Hawai'i Press

Sharf, R. H. 1995. "Buddhist Modernism and the Rhetoric of Meditative Experience." *Numen*, 42, pp. 228–283

——1995a. "The Zen of Japanese Nationalism." In: Lopez, 1995b, pp. 107–160

——1999. "On the Allure of Buddhist Relics." *Representations*, 66, pp. 75–99

——2002. *Coming to Terms with Chinese Buddhism: A Reading of the Treasure Store Treatise.* Honolulu, University of Hawai'i Press.

Sharf, R. H. and E. H. Sharf. 2001. *Living Images: Japanese Buddhist Icons in Context.* Stanford, Stanford University Press

Shaw, M. 2006. *Buddhist Goddesses of India.* Princeton, Princeton University Press

Shaw, S. 2006. *The Jātakas: Birth Stories of the Bodhisatta.* London, Penguin Books

——2006a. *Buddhist Meditation: An Anthology of Texts from the Pali Canon.* New York and London, Routledge

Shimizu, Y. 1992. "Multiple Commemorations: The Vegetable Nehan of Itō Jakuchū." In: *Flowing Traces: Buddhism in the Literary and Visual Arts of Japan*, ed. J. H. Sanford, W. R. LaFleur and M. Nagatomi. Princeton, Princeton University Press, pp. 201–233

Shinohara, K. 2014. *Spells, Images, and Maṇḍalas: Tracing the Evolution of Esoteric Buddhist Rituals.* New York, Columbia University Press

Shorto, H. L. 1970. "The Gavampati Tradition in Burma." In: *R.C. Majumdar Felicitation Volume*, ed. H. B. Sarkar. Calcutta, K.L. Mukhopadhyay, pp. 15–30

Silburn, L. 1955. *Instant et Cause: le discontinu dans la pensée philosophique de l'Inde.* Paris, J. Vrin

Silk, J. A. 2002. "What, if Anything, is Mahāyāna Buddhism? Problems of Definitions and Classifications." *Numen*, 49, pp. 355–405

——2003. "Dressed for Success: The Monk Kāśyapa and Strategies of Legitimation in Earlier Mahāyāna Scriptures." *Journal asiatique*, 291, pp. 173–219

——2004. "Slavery." In: Buswell, 2004, pp. 780–781

——2009. *Riven by Lust: Incest and Schism in Indian Buddhist Legend and Historiography.* Honolulu, University of Hawai'i Press

Simmer-Brown, J. 2001. *Dakini's Warm Breath: The Feminine Principle in Tibetan Buddhism.* Boston, Shambhala

Skilling, P. 1992. "The Rakṣā Literature of the Śrāvakayāna." *Journal of the Pali Text Society*, 16, pp. 109–182

——1993–1994. "A Note on the History of the Bhikkhuni-Sangha (II): The Order of Nuns after the Parinirvana." *WFB Review*, 31, pp. 29–49

——2005. "Cutting Across Categories: The Ideology of Relics in Buddhism." *Sōka Daigaku Kokusai Bukkyōgaku Kōto Kenkyū-jo Nenpō/Annual Report of the International Institute for Advanced Buddhology at Soka University*, 8, pp. 269–322

——2008. "Dharma, Dhāraṇī, Abhidharma, Avadāna: What was taught in Trayastriṃśa?" *Sōka Daigaku Kokusai Bukkyōgaku Kōto Kenkyū-jo Nenpō/Annual Report of the International Research Institute for Advanced Buddhology at Soka University*, 11, pp. 37–60

Skilling, P., J. A. Carbine, C. Cicuzza and S. Pakdeekham, eds. 2012. *How Theravāda is Theravāda? Exploring Buddhist Identities.* Chiang Mai, Silkworm Books

Skilton, A. 1990. "The Vajrasattva Mantra: Notes on a Corrected Sanskrit Text." *The FWBO [Friends of the Western Buddhist Order] Puja Book*, 5th edition. Glasgow, Windhorse Publications

Skorupski, T. 1983. *The Sarvadurgatipariśodhana Tantra: Elimination of All Evil Destinies.* Delhi, Motilal Banarsidass

——2002. *The Six Perfections: An Abridged Version of E. Lamotte's French Translation of Nāgārjuna's Mahāprajñāpāramitāśāstra, Chapters xvi–xxx.* Tring, Institute of Buddhist Studies

Smith, B. L., ed. 1978. *Religion and Legitimation of Power in Sri Lanka.* Chambersburg, PA, Anima Books

——ed. 1978a. *Religion and Legitimation of Power in Thailand, Laos, and Burma.* Chambersburg, PA, Anima Books

——ed. 1983. *Essays on Gupta Culture.* Delhi, Motilal Banarsidass

——1992. "Buddhism and Abortion in Contemporary Japan: Mizuko Kuyō and the Confrontation with Death." In: Cabezón, 1992, pp. 65–90

——2013. *Narratives of Sorrow and Dignity: Japanese Women, Pregnancy Loss and Modern Rituals of Grieving.* New York, Oxford University Press

Smith, E. G. 2001. *Among Tibetan Texts: History and Literature of the Himalayan Plateau.* Boston, Wisdom Publications

Smyers, K. A. 1999. *The Fox and the Jewel: Shared and Private Meanings in Contemporary Japanese Inari Worship.* Honolulu, University of Hawai'i Press

Snellgrove, D. L. 1973. "Śākyamuni's Final Nirvāṇa." *Bulletin of the School of Oriental and African Studies*, 36, pp. 399–411

Snellgrove, D. 1959. *The Hevajra Tantra.* Oxford, Oxford University Press, 2 vols

——1987. *Indo-Tibetan Buddhism: Indian Buddhists and their Tibetan Successors.* Boston, Shambhala

Sonam Rinchen (Geshe). 1997. *Atisha's Lamp for the Path to Enlightenment*, trans. and ed. R. Sonam. Ithaca, Snow Lion Publications

Soothill, W. E. and L. Hodous. 1937. *A Dictionary of Chinese Buddhist Terms.* London, Kegan Paul, Trench and Trübner

Soper, A. C. 1959. *Literary Evidence for Early Buddhist Art in China.* Ascona, Artibus Asiae

——1967. "A Pictorial Biography of Prince Shotoku." *Metropolitan Museum of Art Bulletin*, 25, pp. 197–215

Sorensen, H. H. 2004. "Huayan Art." In: Buswell, 2004, pp. 337–340

Sorensen, P. K. 2003. "Lhasa Diluvium: Sacred Environment at Stake: The Birth of Flood Control Politics, the Question of Natural Disaster Management and Their Importance for the Hegemony over a National Monument in Tibet." *Lungta*, 16, pp. 84–134

Sparham, G. 1999. *The Fulfillment of All Hopes: Guru Devotion in Tibetan Buddhism, by Tsongkhapa.* Somerville, Wisdom Publications

——2003. "Dalai Lama." In: Buswell, 2004, pp. 192–196

——2006–2012. *Abhisamayālaṃkara with Vṛtti and Aloka.* Fremont, Jain Publishing Company

Sperling, E. 2001. "'Orientalism' and Aspects of Violence in the Tibetan Tradition." In: *Imagining Tibet*, ed. T. Dodin and H. Räther. Boston, Wisdom Publications, pp. 317–329

Spiro, M. E. 1967. *Burmese Supernaturalism.* 2nd edition. Englewood Cliffs, Prentice Hall

——1982. *Buddhism and Society: A Great Tradition and its Burmese Vicissitudes.* 2nd edition. Berkeley, University of California Press

Sponberg, A. 1982. "The Trisvabhāva Doctrine in India and China." *Ryūkoku daigaku bukkyō bunka kenkyūjo kiyō/Bulletin of Institute of Buddhist Cultural Studies Ryukoku University*, 21, pp. 97–119

Sponberg, A. and H. Hardacre, eds. 1988. *Maitreya, the Future Buddha.* Cambridge, Cambridge University Press

Stadtner, D. M. 2005. *Ancient Pagan: Buddhist Plain of Merit.* Bangkok, River Books

——2011. *Sacred Sites of Burma: Myth and Folklore in an Evolving Spiritual Realm.* Bangkok, River Books

Stargardt, J. 1990. *The Ancient Pyu of Burma*, vol. 1. Cambridge, Publications on Ancient Civilizations in Southeast Asia

Stcherbatsky, T. 1970 [1923]. *The Central Conception of Buddhism and the Meaning of the Word 'Dharma'.*" Delhi, Motilal Banarsidass

Stearns, C. 2001. *Luminous Lives: The Story of the Early Masters of the Lam 'Bras Tradition in Tibet.* Boston, Wisdom Publications

——2004. "Sa sKya (Sakya)." In: Buswell, 2004, pp. 751–752

——2007. *King of the Empty Plain: The Tibetan Bridge Builder, Tangtong Gyalpo.* Ithaca, Snow Lion Publications

Stein, R. A. 1987. "Sudden Illumination or Simultaneous Comprehension: Remarks on Chinese and Tibetan Terminology." In: Gregory, 1987, pp. 41–65

Stevenson, D. B. 1996. "Visions of Mañjuśrī on Mt. Wutai." In: Lopez, 1996a, pp. 203–222

Stone, J. I. 1999. *Original Enlightenment and the Transformation of Medieval Japanese Buddhism.* Honolulu, University of Hawai'i Press

Stone, J. I. and M. N. Walter, eds. 2008. *Death and the Afterlife in Japanese Buddhism.* Honolulu, University of Hawai'i Press

Strachan, P. 2004. *Ananda Temple.* In: Buswell, 2004, p. 17

Strathern, A. 2007. *Kingship and Conversion in Sixteenth-Century Sri Lanka: Portuguese Imperialism in a Buddhist Land.* Cambridge, Cambridge University Press

Strickmann, M. 1983. "Homa in East Asia." In: *Agni: the Vedic Ritual of the Fire Altar*, ed. F. Staal. Delhi, Motilal Banarsidass, vol. 2, pp. 418–455

——1990. "The Consecration Sūtra: A Buddhist Book of Spells." In: *Chinese Buddhist Apocrypha*, ed. R. E. Buswell. Honolulu, University of Hawai'i Press, pp. 75–118

——1996. *Mantras et mandarins: le bouddhisme tantrique en Chine.* Paris, Gallimard

——2002. *Chinese Magical Medicine*, ed. B. Faure. Stanford, Stanford University Press

Strong, J. S. 1979/1980. "The Legend of the Lion-Roarer: A Study of the Buddhist Arhat Piṇḍola Bharadvaja." *Numen*, 26, pp. 50–88

——1983. *The Legend of King Aśoka.* Princeton, Princeton University Press

——1985. "The Buddhist Avadānists and the Elder Upagupta." In: *Tantric and Taoist Studies in Honour of R. A. Stein*, vol. 3, ed. M. Strickmann. Mélanges chinois et bouddhiques, vol. 22. Bruxelles, Institut Belge des Hautes Etudes Chinoises, pp. 862–881

——1990. "Rich Man, Poor Man, Bhikkhu, King." In: *Ethics, Wealth and Salvation: A Study in Buddhist Social Ethics*, ed. R. F. Sizemore and D. K. Swearer. Columbia, University of South Carolina Press, pp. 107–123

——1992. *The Legend and Cult of Upagupta.* Princeton, Princeton University Press

——1995. *The Experience of Buddhism: Sources and Interpretations.* 1st edition. Belmont, Thomson Wadsworth

——1997. "A Family Quest: Rāhula, Yaśodharā and the Bodhisattva in the *Mūlasarvāstivāda Vinaya* and Related Traditions." In: Schober, 1997, pp. 113–128

——2001. *The Buddha: A Beginner's Guide.* Oxford, Oneworld

——2004. *Relics of the Buddha.* Princeton, Princeton University Press

——2005. "Merit: Buddhist Concepts." In: Jones, 2005, vol. 9, pp. 5872–5875

——2005a. "Māra." In: Jones, 2005, vol. 8, pp. 5690–5691

——2007. "The Buddha's Funeral." In: *The Buddhist Dead*, ed. B. J. Cuevas and J. I. Stone. Honolulu, University of Hawai'i Press, pp. 32–59

——2008. *The Experience of Buddhism: Sources and Interpretations.* 3rd edition. Belmont, Thomson Wadsworth

——2010. "The Triple Ladder at Saṃkāśya: Traditions about the Buddha's Descent from Trayastriṃśa Heaven." In: *From Turfan to Ajanta: Festschrift for Dieter Schlingloff on the Occasion of his Eightieth Birthday*, ed. E. Franco and M. Zin. Lumbini, LIRI, pp. 967–978

——2011. "The Buddha as Ender and Transformer of Lineages." *Religions of South Asia*, 5, pp. 171–188
——2012. "Explicating the Buddha's Final Illness in the Context of his Other Ailments: The Making and Unmaking of Some Jātaka Tales." *Buddhist Studies Review*, 29, pp. 17–33
——2012a. "The Commingling of Gods and Humans, the Unveiling of the World, and the Descent from Trayastriṃśa Heaven: An Exegetical Exploration of Minor Rock Edict I." In: *Reimagining Aśoka: Memory and History*, ed. P. Olivelle, J. Leoshko and H. P. Ray. New Delhi, Oxford University Press, pp. 348–361
——2013. "When Are Miracles Okay? The Story of Piṇḍola and the *Kevaddha Sutta* Revisited." In: *Studies on Buddhist Myths: Texts, Pictures, Traditions and History*, ed. B. Wang, J. Chen, and M. Chen. Shanghai, Zhongxi shuju, pp. 13–44
——forthcoming. "The Beginnings of Buddhist Pilgrimage: The Four Famous Sites in India."
——forthcoming a. "The *Sigālovada sutta* or: How to be a Good Rich Man (Gṛhapati)."
——forthcoming b. "The Buddha, Fact and Fiction: A Kaleidoscopic History of Western Views of the Buddha" In: *History as a Challenge to Buddhism and Christianity*, ed. E. Harris and A. Kirk. St. Ottilien, EOS Verlag
Strong, J. S. and S. M. Strong. 1973. "A Post-Cultural Revolution Look at Buddhism." *China Quarterly*, 54, pp. 321–330
Studholme, A. 2002. *The Origins of Oṃ Maṇipadme Hūṃ: A Study of the Kāraṇḍavyūha Sūtra*. Albany, State University of New York Press
Suzuki, D. T. 1930. *Studies in the Lankavatara Sutra*. London, Routledge and Kegan Paul
——1958. *Essays in Zen Buddhism*. London, Rider, 3 vols
Swanson, P. L. and C. Chilson, eds. 2006. *Nanzan Guide to Japanese Religions*. Honolulu, University of Hawai'i Press
Swearer, D. K. 1971. *Secrets of the Lotus*. New York, MacMillan
——1976. "The Role of the Layman Extraordinaire in Northern Thai Buddhism." *Journal of the Siam Society*, 64, pp. 161–167
——1995. *The Buddhist World of Southeast Asia*. Albany, State University of New York Press
——1998. *The Legend of Queen Cāma*. Albany, State University of New York Press
——2004. *Becoming the Buddha: The Ritual of Image Consecration in Northern Thailand: Sources and Interpretation*. Princeton, Princeton University Press
——2004a. "Thailand." In: Buswell, 2004, pp. 830–836
Swearer, D. K., P. Sommai and D. Phaitoon. 2004. *Sacred Mountains of Northern Thailand and their Legends*. Bangkok, Silkworm
Tada, T. 1965. *The Thirteenth Dalai Lama*. Tokyo, Toyo Bunko
Tajima, R. 1959. *Les deux grands maṇḍalas et la doctrine de l'ésotérisme Shingon*. Tokyo, Maison Franco-Japonaise
Takakusu, J. 1894. "Amitâyur-Dhyâna-Sûtra, The Sûtra of the Meditation on Amitâyus." In: Cowell 1894a, part 2, pp. 161–201
——1896. *A Record of the Buddhist Religion as Practiced in India and the Malay Archipelago by I-Tsing*. London, Clarendon Press
——1947. *The Essentials of Buddhist Philosophy*, ed. W. T. Chan and C. A. Moore. Honolulu, University of Hawai'i
Takei, J. and M. P. Keane. 2001. *Sakuteiki: Visions of the Japanese Garden*. Boston, Tuttle Publishing
Tambiah, S. J. 1970. *Buddhism and the Spirit Cults in North-East Thailand*. Cambridge, Cambridge University Press
——1976. *World Conqueror and World Renouncer*. Cambridge, Cambridge University Press

——1984. *The Buddhist Saints of the Forest and the Cult of Amulets.* Cambridge, Cambridge University Press

——1992. *Buddhism Betrayed? Religion, Politics, and Violence in Sri Lanka.* Chicago, University of Chicago Press

Tamura, Y. 2000. *Japanese Buddhism: A Cultural History.* Tokyo, Kosei Publishing

Tan, Z. 2002. "Daoxuan's Vision of Jetavana: Imagining a Utopian Monastery in Early Tang." Ph.D. dissertation, University of Arizona

Tanabe, G. G. 1992. *Myōe the Dreamkeeper: Fantasy and Knowledge in Early Kamakura Buddhism.* Cambridge, Harvard University Press

Tanabe, G. J., ed. 1999. *Religions of Japan in Practice.* Princeton, Princeton University Press

Tanaka, K. K. 1990. *The Dawn of Chinese Pure Land Buddhist Doctrine.* Albany, State University of New York Press

Tange, K. (and Urtec). 1978. *Master Plan for the Development of Lumbini, Phase II. Final Report.* n.p., n.p.

Tannenbaum, N. 1995. *Who Can Compete Against the World? Power-Protection and Buddhism in Shan Worldview.* Ann Arbor, Association for Asian Studies

Tatelman, J. 2000. *The Glorious Deeds of Pūrṇa.* Delhi, Motilal Banarsidass

Taw Sein Ko. 1892. *The Kālyāni Inscriptions Erected by King Dhammaceti at Pegu in 1476 A.D.* Rangoon, Government Printing Press

Taylor, J. L. 1993. *Forest Monks and the Nation-State: An Anthropological and Historical Study in Northeastern Thailand.* Singapore, Institute of Southeast Asian Studies

Taylor, K. W. 1983. *The Birth of Vietnam.* Berkeley, University of California Press

Teiser, S. F. 1988. *The Ghost Festival in Medieval China.* Princeton, Princeton University Press

——2006. *Reinventing the Wheel: Paintings of Rebirth in Medieval Buddhist Temples.* Seattle, University of Washington Press

Teiser, S. F. and J. I. Stone, eds. 2009. *Readings of the Lotus Sūtra.* New York, Columbia University Press

Ten Grotenhuis, E. 1999. *Japanese Maṇḍalas: Representations of Sacred Geography.* Honolulu, University of Hawai'i Press

Terwiel, B. J. 1994. *Monks and Magic: An Analysis of Religious Ceremonies in Central Thailand.* Bangkok, White Lotus

Than Tun. 1959. "Mahākassapa and His Tradition." *Journal of the Burma Research Society,* 42, pp. 99–118

Thanissaro (Bhikkhu). 1993. *The Mind Like Fire Unbound.* Barre, MA, Dharma Dana Publications

——1996. *The Wings to Awakening.* Barre, MA, Dhamma Dana Publications

——2004. "Wilderness Monks." In: Buswell, 2004, pp. 897–898.

——2007. *The Buddhist Monastic Code I: The Pāṭimokkha Rules Translated and Explained.* Valley Center, Metta Forest Monastery

——2007a. *The Buddhist Monastic Code II: The Khandhaka Rules Translated and Explained.* Valley Center, Metta Forest Monastery

——2007–2012. "Bhikkhunī Pāṭimokkha: The Bhikkhunīs' Code of Discipline." http://www.accesstoinsight.org/tipitaka/vin/sv/bhikkhuni-pati.html

Thapar, R. 1961. *Aśoka and the Decline of the Mauryas.* Oxford, Oxford University Presss.

Thiên Châu (Thich). 1999. *The Literature of the Personalists of Early Buddhism,* trans. S. Boin-Webb. Delhi, Motilal Banarsidass

Thittila, U. 1969. *The Book of Analysis.* London, Pali Text Society

Thomas, E. J. 1927. *The Life of Buddha as Legend and History.* London, Routledge and Kegan Paul

Thurman, R. 1982. *Life and Teachings of Tsong Khapa.* Dharamsala, Library of Tibetan Works and Archives

Tieken, H. 2000. "Aśoka and the Buddhist 'Saṃgha': A Study of Aśoka's Schism Edict and Minor Rock Edict I." *Bulletin of the School of Oriental and African Studies,* 63, pp. 1–30

Tillemans, T. J. F. 2000. *Dharmakīrti's Pramāṇavārttika. An Annotated Translation of the Fourth Chapter (Parārthānumāna). Volume 1 (k. 1–148).* Sitzungsberichte der philosophisch-historischen Klasse der Österreichischen Akademie der Wissenschaften 675. Band. Vienna, Verlag der Österreichischen Akademie der Wissenschaften

Tiyavanich, K. 1997. *Forest Recollections: Wandering Monks in Twentieth-Century Thailand.* Honolulu, University of Hawai'i Press

Trafford, P. 2010. "Textual Origins of the Ten Good Deeds." http://paultrafford.blogspot.com/2010/06/textual-origins-of-ten-good-deeds.html

Trainor, K. 1997. *Relics, Ritual, and Representation in Buddhism: Rematerializing the Sri Lankan Theravāda Tradition.* Cambridge, Cambridge University Press

Trevithick, A. 2006. *The Revival of Buddhist Pilgrimage at Bodh Gaya (1811–1949): Anagarika Dharmapala and the Mahabodhi Temple.* Delhi, Motilal Banarsidass

Tribe, A. 1997. "Manjusri: Origins, Role and Significance. Parts I and II." *Western Buddhist Review,* 2. http://www.westernbuddhistreview.com/vol2/index.html

Triglio, T. 2014. "Legendary Beat Poet: Allen Ginsberg." In: Lewis, 2014, pp. 115–123

Trungpa, C. 1971. *Born in Tibet.* Harmondsworth, Penguin Books

——1984. *Shambhala: The Sacred Path of the Warrior.* Boston, Shambhala

Trungpa, C. and the Nalanda Translation Committee. 1982. *The Life of Marpa the Translator.* Boston, Shambhala

Tsai, K. A. 1994. *Lives of the Nuns: Biographies of Chinese Buddhist Nuns from the Fourth to Sixth Centuries.* Honolulu, University of Hawai'i Press

Tsang, C. R. 2007. *War and Faith: Ikkō Ikki in Late Muromachi Japan.* Cambridge, Harvard University Press

Tsering, D. 2000. *Dalai Lama, My Son: A Mother's Story,* ed. K. Thondup. London, Virgin Publishing

Tsiang, K. R. 2005. "Embodiments of Buddhist Texts in Early Medieval Chinese Visual Culture." In: *Body and Face in Chinese Visual Culture,* ed. H. Wu and K. R. Tsiang. Cambridge, Harvard University Press, pp. 49–78

Tsomo, K. L., ed. 1988. *Sakyadhītā: Daughters of the Buddha.* Ithaca, Snow Lion Publications

——1996. *Sisters in Solitude.* Albany, State University of New York Press

——2004. "Prātimokṣa." In: Buswell, 2004, pp. 667–669

Tsuda, S. 1974. *The Saṃvarodaya-Tantra: Selected Chapters.* Tokyo, Hokuseido Press

Tsugunari, K., J. M. Logan, T. Abbott, M. Ichishima and David W. Chappell. 2013. *Tiantai Lotus Texts.* Berkeley, Bukkyo Dendo Kyokai America

Tsukamoto, Z. 1985. *A History of Early Chinese Buddhism,* trans. L. Hurvitz. Tokyo, Kodansha, 2 vols

Tucci, G. 1961. *The Theory and Practice of the Maṇḍala,* trans. A. Brodick. London, Rider

——1971. *Minor Buddhist Texts Part III.* Rome, Istituto Italiano per il med-ed Estremo Oriente

——1980. *The Religions of Tibet,* trans. G. Samuel. Berkeley, University of California Press

——1986. *Minor Buddhist Texts, Parts I and II.* Delhi, Motilal Banarsidass

Tucker, M. E. and D. R. Williams, eds. 1997. *Buddhism and Ecology.* Cambridge, Harvard University Press

Tweed, T. A. 1992. *The American Encounter with Buddhism 1844–1912.* Chapel Hill, University of North Carolina Press

Uesaka, S. 2001. *Archaeological Research at Maya Devi Temple, Lumbini.* Tokyo, Japan Buddhist Federation

United Trungram Buddhist Foundation. 2013. *World Center for Peace and Unity: Lumbini Udyana Mahachaitya.* Taipei, n.p.

Unno, M. 2004. *Shingon Refractions: Myōe and the Mantra of Light.* Somerville, Wisdom Press

Upasak, C. S. 1975. *Dictionary of Early Buddhist Monastic Terms Based on Pali Literature.* Varanasi, Bharati Prakashan

Vajirañāṇavarorasa (Prince). 1973. *Ordination Procedure.* Bangkok: Mahamakut Educational Council.

Van Zeyst, H. G. A. 1966. "Bimbisāra." In: Malalasekera, 1966, vol. 3, pp. 115–118

Velez de Cea, A. 2004. "The Criteria of Goodness in the Pāli Nikāyas and the Nature of Buddhist Ethics." *Journal of the Buddhist Ethics,* 11, pp. 123–142

Verardi, G. 2010. "Buddha's Birth and Reassessment of the Archaeological Evidence." In: Cueppers, Deeg and Durt, 2010, pp. 19–39

Vetter, T. 1994. "On the Origin of Mahayana Buddhism and the Subsequent Introduction of Prajñāpāramitā." *Asiatische Studien/Etudes asiatiques,* 48, pp. 1241–1281

——1998. "Explanations of Dukkha." *Journal of the International Association of Buddhist Studies,* 21, pp. 383–387

Vickery, M. 1998. *Society, Economics, and Politics in pre-Angkor Cambodia: the 7th and 8th Centuries.* Tokyo, Toyo Bunko

——2003. "Funan Reviewed: Deconstructing the Ancients." *Bulletin de l'Ecole Française d'Extrême-Orient,* 90, pp. 101–143

Vitali, R. 1990. *Early Temples of Central Tibet.* London, Serindia Publications

Vose, K. 2009. *Resurrecting Candrakīrti: Disputes in the Tibetan Creation of Prāsangika.* Boston, Wisdom Publications

Waddell, N. A. 1999. *Wild Ivy: The Spiritual Autobiography of Zen Master Hakuin.* Boston, Shambhala

Wakabayashi, H. 1999. "From Conqueror of Evil to Devil King: Ryōgen and Notions of *Ma* in Medieval Japan Buddhism." *Monumenta Nipponica,* 54, pp. 481–507

Waldschmidt, E. 1953–1956. *Das Mahāvadānasūtra: ein kanonischer Text über die sieben letzten Buddhas.* Berlin, Akademie Verlag

Waley, A. 1931–1932. "Did Buddha Die of Eating Pork?" *Mélanges chinois et bouddhiques,* 1, pp. 343–354

Wallace, B. A., ed. 2003. *Buddhism and Science: Breaking New Ground.* New York, Columbia University Press

Wallis, G. 2002. *Mediating the Power of Buddha: Ritual in the Mañjuśrīmūlakalpa.* Albany, State University of New York Press

Walser, J. 2005. *Nāgārjuna in Context: Mahāyāna Buddhism and Early Indian Culture.* New York, Columbia University Press

Walshe, M. 1987. *Thus Have I Heard: The Long Discourses of the Buddha.* London, Wisdom Publications

Walters, J. S. 1990. "The Buddha's Bad Karma: A Problem in the History of Theravāda Buddhism." *Numen,* 37, pp. 70–95

——1994. "A Voice from the Silence: the Buddha's Mother's Story." *History of Religions,* 33, pp. 358–379

——1995. "Gotamī's Story." In: Lopez, 1995, pp. 113–138

——2000. "Buddhist History: The Sri Lanka Pāli Vaṃsas and their Commentary." In: *Querying the Medieval: Texts and the History of Practices in South Asia,* ed. R. Inden, J. Walters and D. Ali. New York, Oxford University Press, pp. 99–164

Warren, H. C. 1896. *Buddhism in Translations.* Cambridge, Harvard University Press
Wasson, R. G. 1982. "The Last Meal of the Buddha." *Journal of the American Oriental Society,* 102, pp. 591–603
Watson, B. 1993. *The Lotus Sutra.* New York, Columbia University Press
Watts, A. W. 1957. *The Way of Zen.* Harmondsworth, Penguin Books
Wayman, A. 1977. *The Yoga of the Guhyasamājatantra.* Delhi, Motilal Banarsidass
——1978. *Calming the Mind and Discerning the Real.* New York, Columbia University Press
——1991. *Ethics of Tibet: Bodhisattva Section of Tsong-Kha-Pa's Lam Rim Chen Mo.* Albany, State University of New York Press
——1997. *Untying the Knots in Buddhism: Selected Essays.* Delhi, Motilal Banarsidass
Wayman, A. and R. Tajima. 1992. *The Enlightenment of Vairocana.* Delhi, Motilal Banarsidass.
Wedemeyer, C. 2008. *Āryadeva's Lamp that Integrates the Practices: The Gradual Path of Vajrayāna Buddhism According to the Esoteric Community Noble Tradition.* New York, American Institute of Buddhist Studies
Weinstein, S. 1987. "Buddhism: Chinese Buddhist Schools." *Encyclopedia of Religion.* 1st edition, ed. Mircea Eliade. New York, MacMillan, vol. 2, pp. 482–487
Weise, K. 2013. *The Sacred Garden of Lumbini: Perceptions of the Buddha's Birthplace.* Paris, UNESCO Publications
Welbon, G. R. 1968. *The Buddhist Nirvāṇa and its Western Interpreters.* Chicago, University of Chicago Press
Welch, H. 1967. *The Practice of Chinese Buddhism.* Cambridge, Harvard University Press
——1968. *The Buddhist Revival in China.* Cambridge, Harvard University Press
——1972. *Buddhism under Mao.* Cambridge, Harvard University Press
Wells, K. E. 1960. *Thai Buddhism: Its Rites and Activities.* Bangkok, n.p.
Westerhoff, J. 2009. *Nāgārjuna's Madhyamaka: A Philosophical Introduction.* New York, Oxford University Press
——2010. "Nāgārjuna." In: *Stanford Encyclopedia of Philosophy,* ed. E. N. Zalta. http://plato.stanford.edu/archives/fall2010/entries/nagarjuna/
——2010a. *The Dispeller of Disputes: Nāgārjuna's Vigrahavyāvartani.* New York, Oxford University Press
Wijayaratna, M. 1990. *Buddhist Monastic Life According to the Texts of the Theravāda Tradition,* trans. C. Grangier and S. Collins. Cambridge, Cambridge University Press
——1991. *Les moniales bouddhistes: naissance et développement du monachisme feminine.* Paris, Editions du Cerf
Willemen, C., B. Dessein and C. Cox. 1998. *Sarvāstivāda Buddhist Scholasticism.* Leiden, E.J. Brill
Willemen, C. 1983. *The Chinese Hevajratantra.* Leuven, Peeters
——1994. *The Storehouse of Sundry Values.* Berkeley, Numata Center
——2004. "Dharma and Dharmas." In: Buswell, 2004, pp. 216–224
——2009. *Buddhacarita: In Praise of Buddha's Acts.* Berkeley, Numata Center
Williams, D. R. 2005. *The Other Side of Zen: A Social History of Sōtō Zen Buddhism in Tokugawa Japan.* Princeton, Princeton University Press
Williams, J. G. 1982. *The Art of Gupta India: Empire and Province.* Princeton, Princeton University Press
Williams, L. 2000. "A Whisper in the Silence: Nuns before Mahāpajāpatī?" *Buddhist Studies Review,* 17, pp. 167–173
——2002. "Red Rust, Robbers and Rice Fields: Women's Part in the Precipitation of the Decline of the Dhamma." *Buddhist Studies Review,* 19, pp. 41–47
Williams, P. (with A. Tribe). 2000. *Buddhist Thought: A Complete Introduction to the Indian Tradition.* London, Routledge

——2004. "Nāgārjuna." In: Buswell, 2004, pp. 581–582

——2009. *Mahāyāna Buddhism: The Doctrinal Foundations.* 2nd edition. London, Routledge

Willis, J. D. 1972. *The Diamond Light of the Eastern Dawn: A Collection of Tibetan Buddhist Meditations.* New York, Simon and Schuster

Wilson, J. B. 1996. "Tibetan Commentaries on Indian Śāstras." In: Cabezón and Jackson, 1996, pp. 125–137

Wilson, L. 1996. *Charming Cadavers: Horrific Figurations of the Feminine in Indian Buddhist Hagiographic Literature.* Chicago, University of Chicago Press

——2003. "Human Torches of Enlightenment: Autocremation and Spontaneous Combustion as Marks of Sanctity in South Asian Buddhism." In: *The Living and the Dead: Social Dimensions of Death in South Asian Religions*, ed. L. Wilson. Albany, State University of New York Press, pp. 29–50

Wilson, M. 1986. *In Praise of Tārā: Songs to the Saviouress.* London, Wisdom Publications

Wiltshire, M. G. 1990. *Ascetic Figures Before and in Early Buddhism.* Berlin, Mouton de Gruyter

Witanachchi, C. 1966. "Ānanda." In: Malalasekera, 1966, vol. 1, pp. 529–536

Woodward, F. L. and E. M. Hare. 1932–1936. *The Book of the Gradual Sayings.* London, Pali Text Society, 5 vols

Woodward, H. W. 2001. "Practice and Belief in Ancient Cambodia: Claude Jacques' *Angkor* and the *Devarāja* Question." *Journal of Southeast Asian Studies*, 32, pp. 249–261

Wray, E., C. Rosenfeld and D. Bailey. 1972. *Ten Lives of the Buddha: Siamese Temple Painting and Jātaka Tales.* Tokyo, Weatherhill

Wu, J. 2011. *Enlightenment in Dispute: The Reinvention of Chan Buddhism in Seventeenth Century China.* Oxford, Oxford University Press

Wyatt, D. K. 1984. *Thailand: A Short History.* New Haven, Yale University Press

Wyatt, D. K. and A. Wichienkeeo. 1998. *The Chiang Mai Chronicle*, 2nd edition. Bangkok, Silkworm

Wynne, A. 2007. *The Origin of Buddhist Meditation.* London, Routledge

Yakai, K. n.d. *Soto Zen Texts for Daily Services: A Study Guide.* See http://www.scribd.com/doc/79055740/Texts-for-Daily-Services-A-Study-Guide-Kokyo

Yalman, N. 1962. "The Ascetic Buddhist Monks of Ceylon." *Ethnology*, 1, pp. 315–328

Yamabe, N. 1999. "The Sūtra on the Ocean-Like Samādhi of the Visualization of the Buddha: The Interfusion of the Chinese and Indian Cultures in Central Asia as Reflected in a Fifth Century Apocryphal Sūtra." Ph.D. dissertation, Yale University

Yamada, I. 1980. "Premise and Implications of 'Interdependence' (Pratityasamutpada)." In: *Studies in History of Buddhism*, ed. A. K. Narain. Delhi, B.R. Publishing, pp. 373–399

Yamada, S. 2009. *Shots in the Dark: Japan, Zen and the West*, trans. E. Hartman. Chicago, University of Chicago Press

Yamaguchi, Z. 1996 "The Fiction of King Dar-Ma's Persecution of Buddhism." In: *De Dunhuang au Japon: études chinoises et bouddhiques offertes à Michel Soymié*, ed. J.-P. Drège. Geneva, Librairie Droz, pp. 231–258

Yamamoto, K. 1973. *The Mahāyāna Mahāparinirvāṇa-sūtra: A Complete Translation from the Chinese Classical Language.* Oyama, Karinbunko, 3 vols

Yampolsky, P. B. 1967. *The Platform Sutra of the Sixth Patriarch.* New York, Columbia University Press

——1971. *The Zen Master Hakuin: Selected Writings.* New York, Columbia University Press

Yeshe De Project. 1986. *The Fortunate Aeon: How the Thousand Buddhas Become Enlightened.* Berkeley, Dharma Publishing, 4 vols

——1986a. *Ancient Tibet: Research Materials.* Berkeley, Dharma Publishing.

Yü, C. 1981. *The Renewal of Buddhism in China: Chu-hung and the Late Ming Synthesis.* New York, Columbia University Press

——2001. *Kuan-yin: The Chinese Transformation of Avalokiteśvara.* New York, Columbia University Press

Yu, A. C. 2005. *State and Religion in China.* Chicago, Open Court

Zafiropulo, G. 1993. *L'illumination du Buddha. De la quête à l'annonce de l'éveil. Essais de chronologie relative et de stratigraphie textuelle.* Innsbruck, Verlag des Instituts für Sprachwissenschaft der Universität Innsbruch

Zeilinger, A. 2003. "Encounters Between Buddhist and Quantum Epistemologies." In: Wallace, 2003, pp. 387–398

Zelliot, E. 1996. *From Untouchable to Dalit: Essays on the Ambedkar Movement.* New Delhi, Manohar Publishers

Zhiru. 2007. *The Making of a Savior Bodhisattva: Dizang in Medieval China.* Honolulu, University of Hawai'i Press

Zimmermann, M. 2002. *A Buddha Within: The Tathāgatagarbha Sūtra – The Earliest Exposition of the Buddha-Nature Teaching in India.* Tokyo, International Research Institute for Advanced Buddhology

Zin, M. 2006. "About Two Rocks in the Buddha's Life Story." *East and West*, 56, pp. 329–358

Ziporyn, B. 2000. *Evil and/or/as the Good: Omnicentrism, Intersubjectivity, and Value Paradox in Tiantai Buddhist Thought.* Cambridge, Harvard University Press

——2004. "Tiantai School." In: Buswell, 2004, pp. 845–851

Zürcher, E. 1959. *The Buddhist Conquest of China: The Spread and Adaptation of Buddhism in Early Medieval China.* Leiden, E.J. Brill, 2 vols

——1982. "Prince Moonlight: Messianism and Eschatology in Early Medieval Chinese Buddhism." *T'oung pao*, 68, pp. 1–75

——1984. "'Beyond the Jade Gate': Buddhism in China, Vietnam and Korea." In: Bechert and Gombrich, 1984, pp. 193–211

Index

References to images are in italics; references to footnotes are indicated by n.